THE BURDEN OF THE PAST

THE BURDEN OF THE PAST

History, Memory, and Identity in Contemporary Ukraine

Edited by Anna Wylegała and Małgorzata Głowacka-Grajper

INDIANA UNIVERSITY PRESS

Editorial work for this book was supported by the Institute of Philosophy and Sociology,
Polish Academy of Sciences, and Institute of Sociology, University of Warsaw.

This book is a publication of

Indiana University Press
Office of Scholarly Publishing
Herman B Wells Library 350
1320 East 10th Street
Bloomington, Indiana 47405 USA

iupress.indiana.edu

© 2020 by Indiana University Press

All rights reserved
No part of this book may be reproduced or utilized in any form or by any means, electronic or mechanical, including photocopying and recording, or by any information storage and retrieval system, without permission in writing from the publisher. The paper used in this publication meets the minimum requirements of the American National Standard for Information Sciences—Permanence of Paper for Printed Library Materials, ANSI Z39.48-1992.

Manufactured in the United States of America

Cataloging information is available from the Library of Congress.

ISBN 978-0-253-04670-3 (hdbk.)
ISBN 978-0-253-04671-0 (pbk.)
ISBN 978-0-253-04673-4 (web PDF)

1 2 3 4 5   25 24 23 22 21 20

CONTENTS

Note on Transliteration   vii

List of Abbreviations   ix

Introduction / Anna Wylegała and Małgorzata Głowacka-Grajper   1

Part I   The Memory of Holodomor

1. Idle, Drunk, and Good for Nothing: Cultural Memory of the Rank-and-File Perpetrators of the 1932–33 Famine in Ukraine / Daria Mattingly   19

2. The *Lieux de Mémoire* of the Holodomor in the Cultural Landscape of Modern Ukraine / Wiktoria Kudela-Świątek   49

Part II   World War II in the Ukrainian Memory

3. The War of Memory in Times of War: May 9 Celebrations in Kyiv in 2014–15 / Tetiana Pastushenko   77

4. (In)different Memory: World War II in the Memory of the Last War's Generation in Ukraine / Mykola Borovyk   91

Part III   Heroes or Traitors: Creating a Heroic Canon

5. Symon Petliura, the Ukrainian People's Republic, and National Commemoration in Contemporary Ukraine / Matthew D. Pauly   117

6. Glory to the Heroes? Gender, Nationalism, and Memory / Olesya Khromeychuk   140

Part IV   Traces of the Lost Multiethnicity and Memory of the Ethnic Cleansing

7. Memory, Monuments, and the Project of Nationalization in Ukraine: The Case of Chernivtsi / Karolina Koziura   167

8. Collective Memory of the Holocaust in Post-Soviet Ukraine / Anna Chebotarova   183

9 Extermination of the Roma in Transnistria during World War II: Construction of the Roma Collective Memory / Anna Abakunova   206

10 Poland and Poles in the Collective Memory of Galician Ukrainians / Anna Wylegała   229

Part V History and Politics in a Post-Soviet State: Ukraine, Russia, and Independence

11 Ukraine between the European Union and Russia since 1991: Does It Have to Be a Battlefield of Memories? / Tomasz Stryjek   253

12 A Desired but Unexpected State: The 1990s in the Memory and Perception of Ukrainians in the 21st Century / Joanna Konieczna-Sałamatin   277

Index   299

NOTE ON TRANSLITERATION

The transliteration system used in the book follows the Library of Congress rules for transliteration from Ukrainian and Russian, but we decided to simplify it (e.g., leaving out ligatures) for ease of reading. Names, including place names, are transliterated according to the source language, which means that the capital of Ukraine is usually transcribed as Kyiv, not Kiev, but when quoted from Russian-language sources becomes Kiev.

ABBREVIATIONS

AK—Armia Krajowa (Home Army)
CC CP(b)U—Central Committee of the Communist Party (Bolshevik) of Ukraine
GPU—Gosudarstvennoe Politicheskoe Upravlenie (State Political Directorate)
ITF—Task Force for International Cooperation
KNS—Komitety nezamozhnykh selian (Committees of Nonwealthy Peasants)
KPU—Komunistychna Partiia Ukrainy (Communist Party of Ukraine)
NEP—Novaia Ekonomicheskaia Politika (New Economic Policy)
NKVD—Narodnyi Komissariat Vnutrennikh Del (People's Commissariat for Internal Affairs)
OSOAviaKhim—Obshchestvo Sodeistvia Oborone i Aviatsionno-Khimicheskomu Stroitel'stvu (Society of Assistance to Defense and Aviation-Chemical Construction)
OUN—Orhanizatsiia Ukrains'kykh Natsionalistiv (Organization of Ukrainian Nationalists)
RSChA—Robitnycho-Seliansk'a Chervona Armiia (Workers' and Peasants' Red Army)
SVU—Spilka Vyzvolennia Ukrainy (Union for the Liberation of Ukraine)
SZR—Sluzhba Zovnioshnioi Rozvidky (Foreign Intelligence Service of Ukraine)
TsK KP(b)U—Tsentralnyi Komitet Komunistychnoi Partii (Bolshevykiv) Ukrainy (Central Committee of the Communist Party [Bolshevik] of Ukraine)
TsDAHOU—Tsentralnyi Derzhavnyi Arkhiv Hromads'kykh Orhanizatsii Ukrainy (Central State Archive of the Civic Organizations of Ukraine)
UAOC—Ukrainian Autocephalous Orthodox Church
UIPN—Ukrains'kyi Instytut Natsional'noi Pam'iati (Ukrainian Institute of National Memory)
UNR—Ukrains'ka Narodna Respublika (Ukrainian People's Republic)
UPA—Ukrains'ka Povstans'ka Armiia (Ukrainian Insurgent Army)
USSR—Union of Soviet Socialist Republics
WKP(b)—Vsesoiuznaia Komunisticheskaia Partiia (Bol'shevikov) (All-Union Communist Party [Bolshevik])
ZUNR—Zakhidnioukrains'ka Narodna Respublika (West Ukrainian People's Republic)

THE BURDEN OF THE PAST

INTRODUCTION

Anna Wylegała and Małgorzata Głowacka-Grajper

This book was written at an exceptional moment in Ukrainian geopolitics. The idea to relate in various voices the significance and function of the past in contemporary Ukraine appeared in 2014, during a seminar dedicated to new memory studies. At that time, shortly after the Euromaidan, we came to the conclusion that Ukrainian history, memory, and identity are now intertwined more than ever and they are also strongly connected to domestic and foreign policies. The texts contained in this volume were written in 2015–16, already after Ukraine's loss of Crimea and the country's entanglement in the ongoing devastating conflict with Russia in Donbas, as well as the West's habituation to this state of affairs. In a country engaged in war, it suddenly became clear that history was of tremendous importance. First, because both sides of the conflict have used it to legitimize, explain, and strengthen (in ways that are sometimes fair and sometimes not) their own positions and arguments. On numerous occasions, the Russian media have referred to the participants of the Euromaidan as fascists and *banderovtsy* (followers of Stepan Bandera, a leader of Ukrainian nationalism from the interwar period). In turn, several battalions of volunteer Ukrainian troops who fight Russian separatist forces in Donbas use symbols and slogans borrowed from the Organization of Ukrainian Nationalists and the Ukrainian Insurgent Army. Second, the state of war became a catalyst for internal discussions about history and its influence on contemporary Ukrainian national and state identity, though often these debates indirectly refer to and engage Russia. At the time when our authors were writing their texts, Ukraine was swept by the so-called *leninopad* (a mass tearing down of Soviet monuments); the head of the Ukrainian National Institute of Remembrance, Volodymyr Viatrovych—a historian with a traditional approach to the role of history in the shaping of national identity—had already been in tenure for over a year; and a Polish film about the Ukrainian genocide of Poles in Volhynia sparked the first truly significant debate on the subject since Ukraine regained independence. History also became the subject of legislation—in April 2015, the Ukrainian parliament voted for a bill defining which historical groups deserved to be called "a force fighting for Ukrainian independence."[1] The bill also threatened to pursue those who would insult the organizations and formations mentioned in it. In addition, the parliament voted to desovietize the public space, which led to the renaming of several thousand villages and cities, including the capitals of two *oblasts*.

Under such conditions, together with the authors of the texts included in this volume, we asked ourselves questions about the mutual ties between history, identity, politics, and memory. We wondered about the degree to which the situation of posttransformational and wartime "memory fever" was unique to Ukraine and, more generally, to Central and

Eastern Europe. Of course, we are not the first to reflect on this subject—the specificity of identity and memory in this area of Europe has fascinated researchers for years, and the apex of this fascination coincided with the political transformation after the fall of communism. One of the elements of the transformation were the changes in collective approaches toward the past. In this context, it seems important to regard Ukraine as a part of a larger whole—Central and Eastern Europe.

History and Memory: Ukraine in Central and Eastern Europe

The communist era, when Europe was divided by an "iron curtain," strengthened thinking about the continent as divided into two parts: the Western and Eastern (or Central Eastern) part. The diversified dynamics of postcommunist transformations in particular countries and the vision of the Soviet Union as having a huge impact on societies that were included in its borders led to another division—some began to distinguish between two Eastern Europes: Central Europe and post-Soviet (Eastern) Europe.[2] The past and its impact on the contemporary situation were of fundamental importance. It is a history that has marked various areas of Europe, and hence the question of memory began to play a key role in discussions on European identity.

The differences in the memory of events of the 20th century in Europe can be divided into two categories. First, the differences arise from history—the courses of both World War II and the postwar period looked different in the East and the West. The greatest tragedies of World War II occurred in the East. Most of the millions of victims in Central-Eastern Europe, about whom Timothy Snyder writes in his book *Bloodlands*, died in mass killings and ethnic cleansings, with the Holocaust being the primary culprit, in prisoner-of-war camps, from hunger during numerous resettlements and escapes. Others survived, but suffered because of being expelled from their homelands.[3] The war brought about repressions by the occupiers, but it also became a catalyst for a rapid intensification of preexisting conflicts between ethnic and social groups. After the war, the memory of some of these atrocities became hidden or even forbidden during the communist era, which itself has also generated a new set of tragic memories.

The second group of differences results from the way memory is used by individual countries in the region. The memory of events from recent history undoubtedly has a dimension pertaining to identity—it enables the identification of members of a group and assigns them specific characteristics. It is also, however, an important factor influencing power—both in domestic policy and in international relations. The different interpretations of the past can be used to build a certain position in the public sphere but also to exclude specific groups and individuals. Further, the past is of great importance in relations between countries—it can become the basis for forging alliances or igniting conflicts. Many countries in Central and Eastern Europe have faced the problems arising from this. With a change in the interpretation of the past and the revealing of events that had hitherto remained hidden came a need to revise relations with other countries. During the communist period, such problematic events were marginalized or even removed from collective memory (not always successfully). After the fall of communism, some of the countries of the region fell into a memory trap; on the one hand, the processes of social recollection revealed old conflicts (sometimes bloody and dramatic ones), but, on the other hand, cooperation between the countries of the former communist bloc proved to be an important part of building their geopolitical security (which can be seen on the example of relations between Poland and Ukraine).

It is difficult to overestimate the impact that World War II had on shaping the memory of European societies.[4] But because memory of this war is a memory of the harms that some Europeans did to others, after several decades it became necessary to establish a common framework for a moral narrative about the war.[5] Initially, only Germany, as the initiator of the Holocaust, had to build a memory around their responsibility for war crimes. But later, other countries were also included in the common narrative about the war, and the memory of the Holocaust has become what Tony Judt and Jeffrey Olick called an "enter-ticket" into the European community.[6] In the countries of Central and Eastern Europe, however, the central role of the Shoah aroused controversy because these communities wanted to extend the framework of European memory to also commemorate the horrors of communism.[7] It immediately turned out that building a common European memory poses many problems, and the memory of communism, which is an important element of the collective memory and identity in Central and Eastern Europe, has no such significance for Western European societies and often remains incomprehensible to them.[8]

But the nations of Central and Eastern Europe suffered under two totalitarian regimes—Nazism and communism. This is a strong point of difference from the experience of Western Europeans, who experienced only the former. The result is that debates comparing the two totalitarianisms have no social significance in Western Europe, whereas on the eastern part of the continent they remain an important part of memory discourse. To an observer from the outside, the double experience of totalitarianism seems to be a common ground among inhabitants of Eastern Europe, but it in turn is interpreted differently in various countries of the region. In addition, the interpretation changes with time with the emergence of subsequent memory markers (to borrow a term proposed by Wulf Kansteiner) and new events (e.g., postcommunist nostalgia).[9]

The postcommunist transformation brought a fundamental change to Central and Eastern Europe—it was in fact a "reordering of meaningful worlds," as Katherine Verdery writes.[10] Events and characters from the past had begun to be rediscovered and taken out of the realm of social oblivion. New interpretations of already known events have appeared in public discourse, alongside phenomena that were previously unthinkable in the public sphere—the pluralization of memory and the conflicts related to it.[11] All these processes and social phenomena were connected and influenced by the memory boom in Europe as a whole: "Whereas in 1945 there was much that was in need of being forgotten, 1989 required a lot to be remembered. Thus, the 1990s witnessed the undertaking of several revisions of the postwar memory culture, both officially due to state interventions and demands from the European Union, and locally through initiatives by individual action and minority groups."[12] The memory boom also raised questions of what should be remembered, how memory conflicts should be resolved, and who had the right to be perceived as a victim.[13] Researchers studying memory in Central and Eastern Europe point out that the categories used to describe the events of the 20th century in this area are inconsistent. The complex ethnic, national, religious, political, and ideological situations in these countries create obstacles not only to finding a uniform interpretative framework for individual national and local communities, but also for the history of the entire region. Such obstacles further compound the difficulty of presenting narratives about the region's past to audiences in other European countries. As Tea Sindbæk Andersen and Barbara Törnquist-Plewa note, "Categories such as victims, perpetrators, collaborators and bystanders, often used in the Western discourse about World War II, are very difficult to apply in discussing the memories of those from Central, Eastern and South-Eastern Europe. Both individuals and national and ethnic groups in this region often shifted their roles with the many, often violent, turns in the history of the 'century of extremes.'"[14] This equivocalness of categories relating to the past makes memory a living element of social life, at both the national and the local level. In addition, it causes strong emotions and often becomes a primary indicator of the identity of individuals and entire communities.

Events caused social memory in Central and Eastern Europe to become significant also in the western part of the continent. They led to a shift in the perception of memory in the east among Western scholars. As Pakier and Wawrzyniak note, researchers and activists in the public sphere are gradually abandoning the ideas that have thus far marginalized the memory of Eastern Europe: "While previously the East Europeans found it difficult to draw the attention of their Western counterparts with regard to questions of their history and memory, the official commemorations and public controversies of the last few years show that Eastern Europe has become an important trigger for discussions about the content and form of a European narrative."[15]

Struggles with the past in post-Soviet countries, especially in Ukraine, sparked new discussions and led to a reinterpretation of established concepts of social memory in Europe. In that context, a reflection on the collective memory in Ukraine seems particularly challenging.

Ukraine's Exceptionalism; or, Why Ukraine?

Ukraine shares all the features of Eastern European problematic relationships with its past, but at the same time it is exceptional enough to deserve special attention. It is not only the largest country in the region but probably one of the most internally diverse, and its internal diversity has its roots in history. "Difficult history" is an overused phrase, but if one wanted to have an exemplary case, Ukraine would certainly qualify. In the context of managing a difficult past, and especially the memory of it, 20th-century history provides the majority of controversial issues and attracts a large part of the attention of academics, as well as the wider public.[16] In the past century Ukraine was a central part of what Snyder calls the bloodlands and a venue of the most tragic, brutal, and dramatic historical and political events.[17] It would make little sense to summarize this history here even if we had the space, but, in our opinion, certain peculiarities of the period should be emphasized for a better understanding of this book's sources and aims. In the 20th century, Ukraine experienced a few wars and uprisings, several changes of political regimes, border shifts, and radical mass population movements, and, last but not least, the Holocaust and other ethnic purges. All this alone was not unique and concerned most countries in the region. What matters more is the fact that in the case of Ukraine, all these events were the result of, or were accompanied by, exceptional—even for Central-Eastern Europe—violence on a massive scale, which involved ordinary people as victims, bystanders, and perpetrators. In his book about the material legacy of Jews in postwar Germany and Poland, Michael Meng accurately notes that in Central and Eastern Europe, the Holocaust was an experience so total and yet so tangible that the classic category of the passive bystander loses its descriptive usefulness.[18] Employing a different theoretical framework and using German biographical sociology propagated by Fritz Schütze, one might say that in the 20th century almost every average Ukrainian was dragged into a life trajectory that he or she could not control.[19] It appears that the totality, inevitability, and tangibility of the period characterize the Ukrainian experience of history and at the same time explain why the traumatic past remains so significant and continues to influence the present. Historical violence, whether it concerned one as a victim, witness, or perpetrator, is too heavy a burden in Ukraine for subsequent generations to forget about it. Our book is largely built on examining the historical experience of massive violence and the ways in which it is remembered, used, and abused in the present—along with its sometimes considerably long-term consequences (such as the shape of current-day urban space or the relations with a neighbor who was and continues to be an aggressor). The majority of our authors reference the most difficult events and processes from Ukraine's 20th-century history, and nearly all of them—apart from the political transformation of 1991—brought violence upon the common man. The repressions of a totalitarian state against its citizens in the 1930s (the Great Famine), World War II, postwar underground fights for independence (of the Ukrainian Insurgent Army) with the Red Army, the Holocaust and other ethnic purges, especially against Poles (but also the deportations of Tatars and Germans, which are not included in our selection of texts), the fight against dissidents in the 1960s through the 1980s, are the key events in this category.

One could state that many other Eastern European countries are similarly burdened by their own difficult past. Nevertheless, a few issues make Ukraine exceptional and explain why, apart from the extraordinary brutality of 20th-century events just mentioned, history still matters so much in this country now, almost thirty years after the collapse of the Soviet Union and the creation of an independent Ukrainian state. The first reason brings back the question of Ukrainian internal diversity. What modern Ukraine inherited from the states that once ruled the various parts of its territory were not only different political and cultural traditions but also different experiences and assessments of crucial historical events, and, stemming from that, different—sometimes quite contradictory—definitions of national community, national heroes and villains, "ours" and "others."[20] Even when we exclude the ethnic minorities whose experiences are obviously different from those of the majority group (e.g., the experience of Jews, Poles, Germans, or Tatars during the war), the meaning of World War II to ethnic Ukrainians from western and eastern Ukraine will be absolutely different. For example, only Galicians and Volhynians will remember the Soviet occupation of 1939–41. The Polish-Ukrainian conflict of the 1940s will be of importance only in the western part of the country,[21] while the Soviet repressions of the 1930s will be a part of family memories in the center and east only, and in the west it will remain an element of socially constructed memory, or, to use and transform LaCapra's term, secondary memory.[22]

Much has been written about the symbolic division of Ukraine into west and east: one must mention the famous and influential polemic between two Ukrainian intellectuals, Yaroslav Hrytsak and Mykola Riabchuk, who argued for two or, metaphorically, twenty-two Ukraines, and shaped all further discussion on this topic.[23] Also, sociologists and other scholars in the social sciences researched issues of the internal diversification of Ukraine, paying attention not only to attitudes towards history, but also norms, values, political orientations and other markers of social identity.[24] It is obvious that no simple line based on any criterion can be drawn on the map, but undoubtedly the division exists and is palpably felt in Ukrainian society. What are changing over time are the diversifying factors that are perceived as most important by Ukrainian society. Whereas in the past language (Ukrainian or Russian as the mother tongue and language of communication) and creed (Greek Orthodox and three separate and largely competing patriarchates of the Orthodox Church) played crucial roles, it seems that after the conflict with Russia began in 2014, political orientations and loyalties became more significant.[25] Whether or not it is surprising, history tends to be used and misused in defining political loyalties in this conflict rather often: the process of desovietization means not only condemning Soviet rule and a severance from the communist past, but also a demonstrative distancing from contemporary Russia, which acts and is perceived as the successor of the Soviet Union. We claim that different historical experiences in themselves do not constitute a problem—it is the lack of integration of various experiences into one more or less coherent national narrative or lack of approval for the presence of contradictory narratives in one society that is at fault. Used together with other markers, the contradictory and competing historical narratives within Ukrainian society might serve as *pars pro toto*, symbolizing, representing, or even replacing a much more complex social phenomenon—and they often do.

This leads us to the second issue—Ukraine is not left alone to deal with most of its problems with the past. There is another player in the field—Russia. In theory, Russia takes care of the interests of the very distinct imperial minority, that is, Russians and Russophones in Ukraine who still constitute a considerable percentage of the Ukrainian population. But, in reality, Russia instrumentally uses Ukraine's complex situation to strengthen its own domination in the region and to keep Ukraine in its sphere of influence.[26] It is not surprising that the difficult past connected with interethnic conflicts involves negotiating memory with the communities or states in question—decade-lasting Polish-Ukrainian discussions about the Volhynian genocide or the Volhynian tragedy are the best example of this.[27] Russian involvement in Ukrainian internal debates on history, however, goes far beyond willing neighborly cooperation. As many authors have claimed, Russia under Putin is attempting to reestablish its imperial status by all available means.[28] Until very recently, its activities in Ukraine involved mostly soft power, with a defense of the "correct" version of history (especially that of World War II) among the most visible examples. Russia considers Ukraine an inevitable part of its imperial past and struggles to force Ukraine to remain a part of its imperial future. In this situation, any Ukrainian attempt to follow an alternative to Russia's interpretation of the two nations' and states' relationship and common past is perceived by the Russian state as jeopardizing its world-power status. The Russian reaction to the Ukrainian internal crisis of 2013–14, accusing the Ukrainian opposition of promoting a "new fascism," showed precisely that historical rhetoric can be successfully employed in international politics, while the subsequent annexation of Crimea proved how realistic Russian dreams of power are.

The third factor explaining Ukrainian uniqueness in terms of the significance of memory and history is connected with the broader condition of the Ukrainian state and society. Ukraine belongs to a group of post-Soviet countries that did not manage to conduct a successful economic and political transformation and where the (political) nation-building process is still a work in progress, one that is mutually interconnected with a search for national and historical identities.[29] When one looks at Ukrainian debates on history and identity in the last two decades, it becomes clear that although in theory they aimed to create a new, common historical narrative, they actually focused on issues with great potential for internal conflict. The most obvious and meaningful example of this were President Yushchenko's unsuccessful attempts to reconcile UPA (Ukrainian Insurgent Army) veterans and Red Army veterans. At the same time, some important discussions did not take place at all or were conducted on a scale that did not go beyond narrow academic or intellectual circles. Ukraine is still waiting for its Jan T. Gross,[30] to cite the Polish case, who would start a real nationwide discussion on Ukrainian involvement in the Holocaust; the same holds true for the role of the UPA in the Volhynian massacre of Poles in 1943.[31]

While debates on the dark sides of Ukraine's past are taking place, mostly among scholars outside the country, emotional discussions on the domestic heroic canon (with Russia in the background) have often served as substitutes for debates on economy and politics, although objectively the latter would have made more of an impact on the quality of life of the ordinary Ukrainian.[32] Thus, instead of solving social problems, these debates have polarized society and have made other problems less visible. What is more, after the Revolution of Dignity, a clear tendency toward putting heroic history first can be observed. It is not surprising that at a time of military and political conflict with Russia, Ukraine has attempted to build its strong state and national identity in opposition to the aggressor state. This strategy includes stressing those elements of Ukrainian history that have proved to be politically "useful," such as the centuries-long fight for Ukrainian independence, its distinction from Russia and later from the Soviet Union in its culture and civilization, and, finally, the political identity of Ukraine during various historical periods, including World War II.[33] All this is fully understandable, but it seems that certain discussions of its difficult past (including Ukrainian involvement in the Holocaust, the ethnic cleansing of Poles, or the military actions of the UPA against Ukrainian civilians) have been postponed to an undefined future because they would demand a critical assessment of this part of Ukrainian history, which is now being promoted as one of its most glorious moments. Also, a settling of accounts would be necessary to amend the history of Ukrainians as heroes and victims with the occasional role of perpetrators. Of course, none of this means that such discussions did not happen at all.[34] But tendencies to deny and ignore the dark moments in Ukrainian history prevail. One might want to mention the hysterical reaction of Ukrainian media to the Israeli president's speech in Ukrainian parliament in September 2016, when he mentioned the Ukrainian collaboration in the Holocaust, or the cancelation of the screening of Wojciech Smarzowski's movie *Wołyń* (Volhynia) in Kyiv the same fall.

All these issues are interconnected and make contemporary Ukraine not only a military but also a symbolic battleground where differences in historical experience, the memory of a difficult past, identity problems, and international politics are intertwined. History is a part of Ukrainian everyday life and influences it to a greater extent than in most other Central and East European countries. One of the goals of this book is to show the internal anatomy of these complex relationships.

Goals and Structure of the Book

Much has been written on the uneasy marriage of history, politics, and identity in Ukraine. Especially in the first decade after the collapse of the Soviet Union, scholars were attracted by the *in statu nascendi* processes of the nation building in the country, which were immersed in and influenced by history: starting with Catherine Wanner's ground-breaking "Burden of Dreams," political scientists' articles on Ukrainian nation building's relationship with history, or the collection of essays on the broadly understood historical memory and contemporary meaning of history by many prominent Ukrainian and foreign historians, such as Yaroslav Hrytsak, Andrii Portnov, and Zenon Kohut; these are only the most striking examples.[35] Some important areas of research where state memory politics manifest themselves are commemorations and the school curriculum, intellectual discourse on historical topics, and historiography.[36] Our book aims to add to this discussion by focusing on a very specific element of the Ukrainian puzzle discussed in the previous section—namely, memory. Choosing memory and its manifestations—biographical, familial, group, and collective memory, the politics of memory, commemorations, and memory in art and discourse(s)—was a significant decision grounded in our conviction that it is still an underresearched topic in Ukrainian studies. Of course, memory studies on and in Ukraine are no longer a blank spot, especially since memory studies in general have gained more attention from Western scholars in the last decade. The vast majority of works on memory in Ukraine have been dedicated to the connections between commemoration and politics, and when they do touch on collective memory, they are of a theoretical, rather than an empirical, character and are written mostly by historians.[37] Although empirical studies on vernacular collective memory do exist, they usually focus on certain regions or present only specific case studies.[38] What is decidedly missing in Ukrainian memory studies are large systematic reviews (both qualitative and quantitative) that would also illustrate the scale of the examined phenomena, as well as solid empirical studies dedicated to specific issues in Ukrainian collective memory, such as the memory of the UPA and the Holocaust. Our collection cannot substitute for a monograph with a detailed approach to various aspects of Ukrainian historical memory, but it is an attempt at a broad overview of this area from the perspective of multiple authors and various methodologies. Although several edited volumes on European and Central-Eastern European memory have been published recently, none of them focuses specifically on Ukraine.[39]

Our idea for the book was to present issues of the largest importance from the point of view of the Ukrainian people and state. For this reason, we combine the analysis of the social memory and the politics of memory on both the state and the local level. When we speak about social memory, we mean the collective practices of remembrance and the set of narrations of the past that can be found in the various groups in the Ukrainian society. Some of these practices and narratives are rather local, while others are widespread and present in the way of thinking of many Ukrainians. We considered these issues to be primarily subjects that are for some reason difficult, and in the end, it was the problematic nature of the past that became the common thread linking the studies in this volume. A difficult past is one that divides and creates obstacles for the construction of a cohesive national or state identity because it precludes the negotiation of norms and values that can be considered common. Such elements of history, still sparking heated debates in Ukraine, include World War II, with a special mention of the perception of the UPA, and, in a wider context—the issue of creating a new canon of heroes and traitors, as well as an evaluation of the legacy of the Soviet Union. In our book, this subject is tackled by Tetiana Pastushenko and Mykola Borovyk (World War II), Matthew D. Pauly (Petliura as an element of the new canon), Olesya Khromeychuk (UPA), and, indirectly, Joanna Konieczna-Sałamatin (political transformation and the fall of the USSR). Another category of difficulty is history as it relates to guilt and responsibility, with a reckoning that is painful to national pride, and finally the history of minority groups and the history of marginalization and silence. These issues can be found in chapters authored by Daria Mattingly (the perpetrators of the Great Famine), Karolina Koziura (negation of multiethnicity), Anna Chebotarova (Holocaust), Anna Abakunova (the Holocaust of the Roma), and Anna Wylegała (deportation and ethnic purge of Galician Poles). A difficult past also prevents, or cannot allow for, creating normal, proper relations with neighboring countries, especially when cooperation with them is important from a cultural and economic perspective and from the point of view of national security—this is discussed by Tomasz Stryjek, but indirectly also by Anna Wylegała. A problematic history is also one which is connected to a traumatic experience of change, violence, and a total "involvement" of the individual in history, or trajectory—which was discussed as a feature characterizing the Ukrainian historical experience in the 20th century. Directly or indirectly, all texts in this volume relate to a difficult past.

We wanted to collect texts from authors working with different methodologies and presenting various disciplines and research perspectives, which is an undeniable advantage of a collection in general. Authors from the social sciences base their conclusions on qualitative (ethnographic—Anna Abakunova, Karolina Koziura; sociological—Anna Wylegała, Anna Chebotarova, Tetiana Pastushenko; and oral history—Mykola Borovyk, Daria Mattingly) and qualitative research (Joanna Konieczna-Sałamatin, Anna Chebotarova). Our authors analyze public discourse, commemorative practices, and social participation in them (Wiktoria Kudela-Świątek, Matthew D. Pauly, Tetiana Pastushenko, Karolina Koziura), art and media (Olesya Khromeychuk and Matthew D. Pauly), new archival sources (Daria Mattingly), and finally the debates of historians and state historical policy (Tomasz Stryjek). Vernacular memory—the memory of "common people"—is analyzed on several levels since the presented studies concern memory that is individual and biographical (Mykola Borovyk), collective (Anna Abakunova, Anna Chebotarova), and familial (Anna Wylegała); belongs to a local community (Anna Chebotarova, Daria Mattingly, Anna Wylegała), a minority group (Anna Abakunova), one generation (Mykola Borovyk), or several generations; and the process of intergenerational transmission between them (Anna Wylegała).

The five parts of our book are organized around the factual scope of the texts. In general, the chapters follow chronological sequence, although some departures from the rule were necessary to preserve factual coherence. In the first part, two scholars present the contemporary memory and commemoration of the Great Famine (Holodomor). Daria Mattingly analyzes the images of rank-and-file perpetrators of the famine in the social memory of contemporary Ukraine. She combines the memories of village activists and party plenipotentiaries in two villages in different regions and archival data to show, at a microhistorical level, the little-known story of petty officials. The second side of the memory of the Holodomor is presented in the next chapter, by Wiktoria Kudela-Świątek. She shows the memory as a highly political one. By analyzing the various initiatives aimed at commemorating the Great Famine, she tries to investigate the possible political motivations of creating a *lieux de mémoire* of the Holodomor in Ukraine.

The second part of the book concerns World War II. Tetiana Pastushenko describes the commemorative practices of the Day of Victory over Nazi Germany and how they have changed after the revolutionary events at Maidan in the winter of 2013–14, the Russian annexation of Crimea, and the commencement of war in Donbas. She points out that the commemorative practices are now concentrated not on the heroic narrative with its military aspects but on the figures of the "victims." Mykola Borovyk analyses the impact of the experience and memory of World War II on the shaping of collective identities in Ukraine. Based on the autobiographical narratives of the oldest generation of Ukrainians, the text attempts to measure the influence of Soviet and post-Soviet memory politics on the level of the individual.

The third part of the book deals with controversies over the creation of the Ukrainian heroic canon of the 20th century. Matthew D. Pauly investigates the contemporary discussion of Symon Petliura, the military and political leader of the directory of the Ukrainian People's Republic (UNR). He argues that attempts to build a non-Soviet alternative history of Ukrainian statehood have been complicated by the Soviet-sponsored memory of Petliura and other UNR figures and claims that contemporary conflict in Ukraine can be traced partially back to this lack of consensus on the precedence for Ukrainian statehood and political leadership. Olesya Khromeychuk's chapter examines the role of gender in remembering the nationalist movement of the 1930s–50s in contemporary Ukraine. It traces the developments in memory politics in post-Maidan Ukraine, paying particular attention to the work of the Ukrainian Institute of National Memory, at the same time examining representations of nationalist women in historiography, cinema, and literature.

The fourth part concerns events connected with ethnic purges and Ukraine's lost multiethnicity. Karolina Koziura describes the cityscape of Chernivtsi as a symbolic battlefield through which various exclusive and inclusive myths are created and negotiated. Through the in-depth analyses of local politics of memory, she highlights the forms of urban nostalgia that conceal the nationalizing project of the Ukrainian state on the one hand and the search for Chernivtsi's new urban identity on the other. Anna Chebotarova deals with the problem of the status of the Holocaust in Ukrainian collective memory. Based on the results of a statistical survey and in-depth interviews with the inhabitants of three Ukrainian towns that became mass-killing sites of the Shoah during World War II (Balta, Vyzhnytsia, and Zolochiv), the chapter shows the perception of the Holocaust at the national and local levels.

Anna Abakunova examines the collective memory of the Roma on their deportation and annihilation in Transnistria Governorate, which was controlled by Romanian authorities during World War II. The chapter analyzes how the fact of deportation and survivors' experience among the Roma affect their individual memory, but it also discusses Roma collective memory and the basis for its construction on the social, political, and historical levels. Anna Wylegała provides us with a microsociological study of the memory of Poles in contemporary Galicia, where they used to be an important and numerous ethnic group before World War II. Based on almost one hundred interviews, it focuses not only on how Poles and the Polish state of various periods are remembered today, but also on what is being silenced and excluded from the local collective narrative. The author analyses the influence of family memory transfer, education, social stratification, and local and Ukrainian politics of memory.

The final part of the volume deals with the complicated entanglement of history and politics in post-Soviet Ukraine. Tomasz Stryjek characterizes the public construction of images of the past and their use during the period between 2004 and 2014 through the prism of the activities of the last three presidents of Ukraine and Ukraine's relationship with the European Union. He claims that the absence of desovietization after 1991 and the lack of a policy aimed at overcoming the memory of Ukrainian nationalism in the 20th century constitute the main problems in this field. Joanna Konieczna-Sałamatin presents a reconstruction of Ukrainians' memory of the early processes of transformation: changes to the political and economic system together with state- and nation-building. She explains why the persistent positive attitude toward the proclamation of Ukrainian independence in 1991 is accompanied by a negative evaluation of the dissolution of the Soviet Union and how these attitudes have changed over time.

* * *

In her brilliant article on Ukrainian memory and memory politics published in 2013, Oxana Shevel, using a term developed by Jan Kubik and Michael Bernhard, stated that it is mainly the Ukrainian elites that function in the "fractured" regimes of memory of most important historical events.[40] The ordinary people in turn are not as divided and manage to coexist with each other without engaging in exhausting memory wars in their daily lives. At the same time, Shevel claims that Ukraine still has a chance to develop "pillarized regimes of memory," that is, in short, a society with pluralistic visions of the past that do not compete and do not fight with each other.[41] The studies gathered in our volume decisively confirm the thesis that political elites are involved in "fractured memory regimes" and the same concerns most of the intellectual and local elites. To this group of people actively participating in the field of memory we would add individuals of specific and strong biographical experience who are targeted by one of the memory regimes: such people as UPA and Red Army veterans. Because of the biographical experience these people—and sometimes also their children and grandchildren, or other people who adopt their perspective and become attached to their kind of experience—might be easily mobilized by relevant memory regimes and thus enter the memory war(s) of the elites. As has been seen in Ukraine and outside its borders, this mobilization can be instrumentally and successfully provoked by external powers. If scholars are allowed to take the liberty of formulating wishes and prognoses, we believe that a "pillarized" memory field instead of a "fractured" or superficially homogeneous one would be of the best use and advantage for contemporary Ukrainian society. In the current political situation, however, the construction of the Ukrainian memory field is not entirely in the hands of Ukrainian society and its elites. Other participants in this process include Russia, the European Union (to a lesser extent), and Ukraine's other neighbors, especially Poland. Since the difficult past can be easily misused, we sincerely hope that Ukraine will have the opportunity to engage in a democratic discussion on its history and identity.

Notes

1. See Himka, "Legislating Historical Truth."
2. See Herrschel, *Borders*.
3. Snyder, *Bloodlands*. See also Ther and Siljak, *Redrawing Nations*.
4. See, for example, Lebow, Kansteiner, and Fogu, *Politics of Memory*.
5. Mithander, Sundholm, and Velicu, *European Cultural Memory*.
6. Judt, *Postwar*; Olick, *Politics of Regret*.
7. See Mithander et al., *European Cultural Memory*.
8. See, for example, Pakier, *European Holocaust Memory*.
9. Kansteiner, "Finding Meaning." See also Todorova and Gille, *Post-communist Nostalgia*.
10. Verdery, *Political Lives*.
11. See Sindbæk and Törnquist-Plewa, *Disputed Memory*; Mink and Neumayer, *History, Memory and Politics*.
12. Mithander et al., *European Cultural Memory*, 14.
13. See, for example, Ash, "Trials, Purges and History."
14. Sindbæk Andersen and Törnquist-Plewa, *Disputed Memory*, 2.
15. Pakier and Wawrzyniak, *Memory and Change*, 1.
16. This does not mean that earlier periods of Ukrainian history do not provoke any controversies—to mention only the various opinions on the most notable Ukrainian hetmans, Bohdan Khmelnytskyi or Ivan Mazepa. The independent Ukrainian research organization Rating regularly conducts opinion polls on a set of the best-known historical figures, usually including Yaroslav the Wise, Princess Olga of Kyiv, the above-mentioned hetmans, and a few others. For concise overviews of Ukrainian history in general, see Yakovenko, *Narysy istorii Ukrainy*; Hrytsak, *Narysy istorii Ukrainy*; Plokhy, *Gates of Europe*.
17. Snyder, *Bloodlands*.
18. Meng, *Shattered Spaces*, 23.
19. Schütze and Rieman, "Trajectory."
20. On differences in historical culture and identity in Ukraine, see Himka, "Basic Historical Identity Formations." Specifically, on the various aspects of the formation of the new heroic canon based, among others, on different historical experiences, see, for example, Marples, *Heroes and Villains*; and Yurchuk, *Reordering*. For a useful overview of the recent Ukrainian debates on one of the more eagerly discussed issues in this field, namely, the figure of Stepan Bandera, see Amar, Balyns'kyi, and Hrytsak, *Strasti za banderoiu*.
21. The importance is shown by quantitative studies conducted in the first decade of the 21st century. The situation has changed only slightly after the public discussion about the Polish movie *Wołyń* by Wojciech Smarzowski (devoted to the Volhynian massacre of the 1943 and officially prohibited in Ukraine) that took place in Ukrainian media in fall 2016. Unfortunately, at the moment of writing this book only very preliminary results of the new opinion polls were available. For the aforementioned quantitative studies, see Berdychowska, "Ukraińcy wobec Wołynia." For the results of the new opinion poll, see http://hvylya.net/analytics/politics/kak-ukraintsyi-smotryat-na-otnosheniya-mezhdu-ukrainoy-i-polshey.html, accessed February 3, 2017.
22. See LaCapra, *History and Memory*.
23. See Hrytsak, "Dvadtsiat' dvi Ukrainy," and Riabchuk, *Dvi Ukrainy*; an example of further references to this discussion: Chernysh, "Odna, dvi chy dvadtsiat' dvi Ukrainy."
24. See the special issue of the journal *Ukraina Moderna* from 2007, "L'viv-Donetsk: social'ni identychnosti w suchasnii Ukraini," presenting what is thus far the largest comprehensive quantitative study on the internal

diversity in Ukraine. A current project on these issues is in progress, but with only preliminary results available: https://media.wix.com/ugd/ff1dca_bbdc8040f8ca449b87a32e82d6cba52b.pdf.

25. For an overview of the language situation in Ukraine in the first decade of independence, see Bilaniuk, *Contested Tongues*, and Masenko, "Movna sytuatsiia Ukrainy."

26. According to a Ukrainian nationwide census conducted in 2001, 17.3 percent of the citizens of Ukraine claimed Russian as their nationality. See http://2001.ukrcensus.gov.ua/results/general/nationality/, last accessed March 1, 2016. The next census is planned for the year 2020. For a general definition of the "imperial minority," see Brubaker, *Nationalism Reframed*. Specifically, for an analysis of the situation of Russians in post-1991 Ukraine, see, for example, Solchanyk, "Russians in Ukraine." For a recent qualitative analysis of the phenomena in western Ukraine, see Demel, "Gdzie są ojczyzny zachodnioukraińskich Rosjan?"

27. For an overview of these discussions, see Kasianov, "Burden of the Past."

28. Van Herpen, *Putin's Wars*; Bugajski, *Cold Peace*; Lucas, *New Cold War*.

29. There is a vast literature on Ukrainian transition, as well as on nation- and state-building. For a few examples, see Wilson, *The Ukrainians*; Kuzio, *Ukraine: State and Nation Building*; Kasianov, *Ukraina 1991–2007*. For the most up-to-date monograph broadly covering the field, see Kuzio, *Ukraine: Democratization*.

30. Gross, *Neighbors*.

31. For an overview of Ukrainian public debates on the Holocaust, see Himka, "Reception of the Holocaust"; Podol's'kyi, "Ukrains'ke suspil'stvo"; Rossoliński-Liebe, "Debating." The most recent development of the discussion happened after Polish film director Wojciech Smarzowski shot a movie on the Volhynian massacre in fall 2016. For a short overview of the discussion that followed in Ukraine, see Konończuk, "Ukraińcy patrzą."

32. Most significant texts on the topic were written by foreign academics. See Carynnyk, "Zolochiv movchyt"; Himka, "The Lviv Pogrom"; Rossoliński-Liebe, "Ukraińska policja"; Rudling, "The OUN, the UPA and the Holocaust." Also, the book that was supposed to start a Ukrainian debate on the nation's involvement in the Holocaust among the wider public (but failed) was written by a foreign scholar: Bartov, *Erased*. For an overview of the academic discussion on Bartov's book, see http://uamoderna.com/arkhiv/11-pamiat152009, accessed May 14, 2019.

33. See Himka, "Legislating Historical Truth."

34. In October 2015, a new committee of historians accredited by the Polish and Ukrainian Institutes of National Remembrance was created.

35. Wanner, *Burden of Dreams*. See, for example, Kuzio, "History, Memory and Nation Building"; Hrytsak, *Strasti za natsionalizmom*; Portnov, *Istorii dla domashnioho vzhytku*; Kohut, *Korinnia identychnosti*.

36. See, for example, Zashkilniak, "Istoriia 'svoia' i istoriia 'chuzha'"; Popson, "Ukrainian History Textbook"; Narvselius, "Tragic Past"; Hnatiuk, *Pożegnanie*; Stryjek, *Jakiej przeszłości potrzebuje przyszłość?*.

37. For one of the most interesting research articles on commemoration, see Zhurzhenko, "Memory Wars." For theoretical works of historians on collective memory, see Hrynevych, "Gespaltene Erinnerung," and Hrytsak, "Istoriia i pam'iat."

38. For a selection of the most interesting studies of this kind, see Ivanova, "Regionalnyie osobiennosti kolektivnoi"; Jilge, "Competing Victimhoods; Grinchenko, "Ostarbeiter of Nazi Germany"; Richardson, "Disciplining the Past"; Bodnar, "Tam bulo dobre."

39. For the most interesting titles, see the section "History and Memory: Ukraine in Central and Eastern Europe" of this Introduction. Others are Kubik and M. Bernhard, eds., *Twenty Years after Communism*; Blacker, Etkind, and Fedor, *Memory and Theory*.

40. Shevel, "Politics of Memory"; Kubik and Bernhard, *Twenty Years after Communism*.

41. It is necessary to note that so far the term *pillarization* has been used mainly in relation to the political systems in Holland and Belgium and by political science scholars. In this text, we refer to the transformed term used by Kubik and Bernhard and Shevel, not to its original meaning linked to the description of the political system.

Bibliography

Amar, Tarik. C., Ihor Balyns'kyi, and Yaroslav Hrytsak, eds. *Strasti za banderoiu*. Kyiv: Hrani–T, 2006.

Ash, Timothy Garton. "Trials, Purges and History Lessons: Treating a Difficult Past in Post-communist Europe." In *Memory and Power in Post-War Europe*, edited by Jan-Werner Müller, 265–82. Cambridge: Cambridge University Press, 2002.

Bartov, Omer. *Erased: Vanishing Traces of Jewish Galicia in Present-Day Ukraine.* Princeton, NJ: Princeton University Press, 2007.
Berdychowska, Bogumiła. "Ukraińcy wobec Wołynia." *Zeszyty Historyczne* 146 (2003): 65–104.
Bilaniuk, Laada. *Contested Tongues: Language Politics and Cultural Correction in Ukraine.* Ithaca, NY: Cornell University Press, 2005.
Blacker, Uilleam, Alexander Etkind, and Julie Fedor, eds. *Memory and Theory in Eastern Europe.* Palgrave Studies in Cultural and Intellectual History. New York: Palgrave Macmillan, 2013.
Bodnar, Halyna. "'Tam bulo dobre i tut ie nepohano zhyty': osoblyvosti istorychnoi pamiati ukraiintsiv, pereselenykh iz Polshchi." In *Ukraina-Polshcha: istorychna spadshchyna i suspil'na svidomist'*. Vol. 2, *Deportatsii 1944–1951*, 20–36. L'viv: Instytut Ukrainoznavstva im. Kryp'iakevycha, 2007.
Brubaker, Rogers. *Nationalism Reframed: Nationhood and the National Question in the New Europe.* Cambridge: Cambridge University Press, 2006.
Bugajski, Janusz. *Cold Peace: Russia's New Imperialism.* Westport: Praeger, 2004.
Carynnyk, Marko. "Zolochiv movchyt." *Krytyka* 10 (2005): 14–17.
Chernysh, Nataliia, "Odna, dvi chy dvadtsiat' dvi Ukrainy: 'Sotsiolohichnyi analiz sotsialnykh identychnostei predstavnykiv triokh pokolin' meshakntsiv L'vova i Donetska.'" *Dukh i Litera* 11–12 (2003): 6–21.
Demel, Grzegorz. "Gdzie są ojczyzny zachodnioukraińskich Rosjan?" *Kultura i Społeczeństwo* 2 (2015): 183–98.
Forrester, Sibelan, Magdalena J. Zaborowska, and Elena Gapova, eds. *Over the Wall/After the Fall: Post-communist Cultures through an East-West Gaze.* Bloomington: Indiana University Press, 2004.
Grinchenko, Gelinada. "The Ostarbeiter of Nazi Germany in Soviet and Post-Soviet Ukrainian Historical Memory." *Canadian Slavonic Papers / Revue canadienne des slavistes* LIV, nos. 3–4 (September–December 2012): 401–26.
Gross, Jan T. *Neighbors: The Destruction of the Jewish Community in Jedwabne, Poland.* Princeton: Princeton University Press, 2001.
Herpen, Marcel H. van. *Putin's Wars: The Rise of Russia's New Imperialism.* Lanham: Rowman and Littlefield, 2014.
Herrschel, Tassilo. *Borders in Post-socialist Europe: Territory, Scale, Society.* Farnham, UK: Ashgate, 2011.
Himka, John-Paul. "The Basic Historical Identity Formations in Ukraine: A Typology." *Harvard Ukrainian Studies* 28, nos. 1–4 (2006): 483–500.
———. "The Lviv Pogrom of 1941: The Germans, Ukrainian Nationalists, and the Carnival Crowd." *Canadian Slavonic Papers / Revue canadienne des slavistes* 53, 2–4 (2011): 209–43.
———. "Legislating Historical Truth: Ukraine's Laws of 9 April 2015." *Ab Imperio*, April 21, 2015. Accessed July 25, 2019. https://www.academia.edu/12056628/Legislating_Historical_Truth_Ukraines_Laws_of_9_April_2015.
———. "The Reception of the Holocaust in Postcommunist Ukraine." In *Bringing the Dark Past to Light: The Reception of the Holocaust in Postcommunist Europe*, edited by J. Michlic and J.-P. Himka, 627–61. Lincoln: University of Nebraska Press, 2013.
Hnatiuk, Ola. *Pożegnanie z imperium: Ukraińskie dyskusje o tożsamości.* Lublin, Poland: Wydawnictwo UMCS, 2003.
Hrynevych, Vladyslav. "Gespaltene Erinnerung: Der zweite Weltkrieg im ukrainischen Gedenken." *Osteuropa* 4–5 (2005): 88–102.
Hrytsak, Yaroslav. "Dvadtsiat' dvi Ukrainy". *Krytyka* 4, no. 54 (2003): 3–6.
———. "'Istoriia i pam'iat': Amneziia, Ambivalentsiia, Aktyvizatsiia." In *Ukraina: Protsesy natsiotvorennia*, edited by Andreas Kappeler, 365–80. Kyiv: K.I.S, 2011.
———. *Narysy istorii Ukrainy: formuvannia modernoi ukrains'koi natsii XIX–XX st.* Kyiv: Heneza, 1996.
———. *Strasti za natsionalizmom.* Kyiv: Krytyka, 2002.
Ivanova, Yelena. "Regionalnyie osobiennosti kolektivnoi pamiati studentov o holokoste w sovremennoi Ukrainie." *Holokost i suchasnist': Studii v Ukraini i Sviti* 2 (2008): 9–28.
Jilge, Wilfried. "Competing Victimhoods—Ukrainian Narratives on World War II." In *Shared History–Divided Memory: Jews and Others in Soviet-Occupied Poland, 1939–1941*, edited by Elazar Barkan, Elizabeth A. Cole, and Kai Struve, 103–31. Leipzig: Leipziger Universitätsverlag, 2007.
Judt, Tony. *Postwar: A History of Europe since 1945.* London: Penguin, 2006.
Kansteiner, Wulf. "Finding Meaning in Memory: A Methodological Critique of Collective Memory Studies." *History and Theory* 41 (2002): 179–97.

Kasianov, Georgiy. "The Burden of the Past: The Ukrainian-Polish Conflict of 1943–44 in Contemporary Public, Academic and Political Debates in Ukraine and Poland." *Innovations* 3–4 (2006): 247–59.

———.*Ukraina 1991-2007: Narysy novitnioi istorii*. Kyiv: Nash Chas, 2007.

Kohut, Zenon. *Korinnia identychnosti: Studii z ranniomodernoii ta modernoii istorii Ukrainy*. Kyiv: Krytyka, 2004.

Konończuk, Wojciech. "Ukraińcy patrzą na 'Wołyń.'" *Tygodnik Powszechny* 47 (2016).

Kubik, Jan, and Michael H. Bernhard, eds. *Twenty Years after Communism: The Politics of Memory and Commemoration*. Oxford: Oxford University Press, 2015.

Kuzio, Taras. "History, Memory and Nation Building in the Post-Soviet Colonial Space." *Nationalities Papers* 30, no. 2 (2002): 241–64.

———. *Ukraine: Democratization, Corruption, and the New Russian Imperialism*. Routledge Studies of Societies in Transition No. 9. Santa Barbara, CA: Praeger, 2015.

———. *Ukraine: State and Nation Building*. Routledge Studies of Societies in Transition 9. London: Routledge, 1998.

LaCapra, Dominik. *History and Memory after Auschwitz*. Ithaca, NY: Cornell University Press, 1998.

Lebow, Richard N, Wulf Kansteiner, and Claudio Fogu. *The Politics of Memory in Postwar Europe*. Durham, NC: Duke University Press, 2006.

Lucas, Edward. *The New Cold War: Putin's Russia and the Threat to the West*. New York: St. Martin's Griffin, 2014.

Marples, David. *Heroes and Villains: Creating National History in Contemporary Ukraine*. Budapest: Central European University Press, 2008.

Masenko, Larysa. "Movna sytuatsiia Ukrainy": *Nezalezhnyi kulturolohichnyi chasopys Ji* 35 (2004): 8–19.

Meng, Michael. *Shattered Spaces: Encountering Jewish Ruins in Postwar Germany and Poland*. Cambridge, MA: Harvard University Press, 2011.

Mink, Georges, and Laure Neumayer, eds. *History, Memory and Politics in Central and Eastern Europe: Memory Game*. New York: Palgrave, 2013.

Mithander, Conny, John Sundholm, and Adrian Velicu, eds. *European Cultural Memory Post-89*. Amsterdam: Rodopi, 2013.

Narvselius, Eleonora. "Tragic Past, Agreeable Heritage: Post-Soviet Intellectual Discussions on the Polish Legacy in Western Ukraine." *The Carl Beck Papers in Russian and East European Studies* 2401 (2015): 1–75.

Olick, Jeffrey K. *The Politics of Regret: On Collective Memory and Historical Responsibility*. New York: Routledge, 2007.

Pakier, Małgorzata. *The Construction of European Holocaust Memory: German and Polish Cinema after 1989*. Frankfurt am Main: PL Academic Research, 2013.

Pakier, Małgorzata, and Wawrzyniak Joanna, eds. *Memory and Change in Europe: Eastern Perspectives*. New York: Berghahn, 2016.

Plokhy, Serhii. *The Gates of Europe: A History of Ukraine*. New York: Basic Books, 2015.

Podol's'kyi, Anatolii. "Ukrains'ke suspil'stvo i pam'iat' pro holokost: sproba analizu deiakykh aspektiv." *Holokost i Suchasnist': Studii v Ukraini i Sviti* 1 (2009): 47–59.

Popson, Nancy. "The Ukrainian History Textbook: Introducing Children to the 'Ukrainian Nation.'" *Nationalities Papers* 29, no. 2 (2001): 325–50.

Portnov, Andrij. *Istorii dla domashnioho vzhytku: esei pro pol's'ko-rostjs'ko-ukrains'kyi trykutnyk pam'iati*. Kyiv: Krytyka, 2013.

Riabchuk, Mykola. *Dvi Ukrainy: real'ni mezhi, virtual'ni ihry*. Kyiv: Krytyka, 2003.

Richardson, Tanya. "Disciplining the Past in Post-Soviet Ukraine: Memory and History in Schools and Families." In *Politics, Religion and Memory: The Past Meets the Present in Contemporary Europe*, edited by Frances Pine, Deema Kaneff, and Haldis Haukanes, 109–35. Munster, Ger.: Lit, 2004.

Rossoliński-Liebe, Grzegorz. "Debating, Obfuscating and Disciplining the Holocaust: Post-Soviet Historical Discourses on the OUN–UPA and Other Nationalist Movements." *East European Jewish Affairs* 42, no. 3 (2012): 199–241.

———. "Ukraińska policja, nacjonalizm i zagłada Żydów w Galicji Wschodniej i na Wołyniu." *Zagłada Żydów: Studia i materiały* 13 (2017): 57–79.

Rudling, Peter A. "The OUN, the UPA and the Holocaust: A Study in the Manufacturing of Historical Myths." *The Carl Beck Papers in Russian and East European Studies* 2107 (2011): 1–72.

Schütze, Fritz., and Gerhard Riemann. "'Trajectory' as Basic Theoretical Concept for Analyzing Suffering and Disorderly Social Processes." In *Social Organization and Social Process: Essays in Honor of Anselm Strauss*, edited by David R. Maines, 333–58. New York: Transaction, 1991.

Shevel, Oksana. "The Politics of Memory in a Divided Society: A Comparison of Post-Franco Spain and Post-Soviet Ukraine." *Slavic Review* 70, no. 1 (2011): 137–64.
Sindbæk Andersen, Tea., and Barbara Törnquist-Plewa, eds. *Disputed Memory: Emotions and Memory Politics in Central, Eastern and South-eastern Europe*. Berlin: De Gruyter, 2016.
Snyder, Timothy. *Bloodlands: Europe between Hitler and Stalin*. New York: Basic Books, 2010.
Solchanyk, Roman. "Russians in Ukraine: Problems and Prospects." In *Cultures and Nations of Central and Eastern Europe: Essays in Honor of Roman Szporluk*, edited by Zvi Gitelman, Lubomyr Hajda, John-Paul Himka, and Roman Solchanyk, 539–54. Cambridge, MA: Harvard University Press, 2001.
Stryjek, Tomasz. *Jakiej przeszłości potrzebuje przyszłość? interpretacje dziejów narodowych w historiografii i debacie publicznej na Ukrainie 1991–2004*. Warsaw: ISP PAN, 2007.
Ther, Philipp, and Ana Siljak, eds. *Redrawing Nations: Ethnic Cleansing in East-Central Europe 1944–1948*. New York: Rowman and Littlefield, 2001.
Todorova, Maria, and Zsuzsa Gille, eds. *Post-Communist Nostalgia*, New York: Berghahn, 2010.
Ukraina Moderna. "L'viv-Donetsk: social'ni identychnosti w suchasnii Ukraini." Special issue edited by Yaroslav Hrytsak, Andrii Portnov, and Victor Susak. Kyiv, L'viv: Krytyka, 2007.
Wanner, Catherine. *Burden of Dreams: History and Identity in Post-Soviet Ukraine*. State College, PA: Penn State University Press, 1998.
Wilson, Andrew. *The Ukrainians: Unexpected Nation*. 4th ed. New Haven, CT: Yale University Press, 2015.
Verdery, Katherine. *The Political Lives of Dead Bodies*. New York: Columbia University Press, 1999.
Yakovenko, Nataliia. *Narysy istorii Ukrainy z naidavnishykh chasiv do kintsia XVII stolittia*. Kyiv: Heneza, 1997.
Yurchuk, Yuliya. *Reordering of Meaningful Worlds: Memory of the Organization of Ukrainian Nationalists and the Ukrainian Insurgent Army in Post-Soviet Ukraine*. Stockholm Studies in History No. 103. Stockholm: Stockholm University, 2014.
Zashkilniak, Leonid. "Istoriia 'svoia' i istoriia 'chuzha.'" *Krytyka* 9–10 (2009): 24–26.
Zhurzhenko, Tatiana. "Memory Wars and Reconciliation in the Ukrainian-Polish Borderlands: Geopolitics of Memory from a Local Perspective." In *Memory and Politics in Central and Eastern Europe: Memory Games*, edited by Georges Mink and Laure Neumayer, 173–92. New York: Palgrave Macmillan, 2013.

ANNA WYLEGAŁA is Assistant Professor at the Institute of Philosophy and Sociology, Polish Academy of Sciences. She is author of *Displaced Memories: Remembering and Forgetting in Post-War Poland and Ukraine* and *Przesiedlenia a pamięć: studium (nie) pamięci społecznej na przykładzie ukraińskiej Galicji i polskich 'ziem odzyskanych'* (Resettlement and memory: study of social memory on the example of Ukrainian Galicia and Polish "recovered lands").

MAŁGORZATA GŁOWACKA-GRAJPER is Associate Professor at the Institute of Sociology, University of Warsaw. She is author of *Transmisja pamięci. Działacze sfery pamięci i przekaz o Kresach Wschodnich we współczesnej Polsce* (The transmission of memory: memory activists and narratives of former Eastern Borderlands in contemporary Poland).

PART I
THE MEMORY OF HOLODOMOR

1

IDLE, DRUNK, AND GOOD FOR NOTHING

Cultural Memory of the Rank-and-File Perpetrators of the 1932–33 Famine in Ukraine

Daria Mattingly

THIS CHAPTER FOCUSES ON IDENTICAL TRACES OF THE rank-and-file perpetrators of the 1932–33 famine in Ukraine and their portrayal in cultural memory. Although the role of the party leaders and security service in the famine has been studied in detail by Viola, Vasyl'iev, Doroshko, and Shapoval, the scholarship on the men and women who facilitated the mass famine on the ground is still at its initial stages.[1] Who were these people and how are they remembered? Transferring overarching typology of the perpetrators of mass violence suggested by Smeulers to the Holodomor yields some possible answers and reveals previously understudied groups of such participants as female perpetrators.[2] This typology splits perpetrators on the basis of their motivation into six groups: professionals, profiteers and careerists, fanatics, sadists and criminals, followers, and compromised perpetrators.[3] This nuanced approach to addressing the famine facilitators also could be found in cultural memory—namely in *samvydav* and *tamvydav* Ukrainian novels. Post-Soviet Ukrainian and diaspora prose, on the other hand, is still being dominated by dichotomy of the sadist profiteering Other, quisling sons, and repentant communists, which mirrors their portrayal in the Soviet Ukrainian novels as "unflinching" Bolsheviks and weak or counter-revolutionary officials.

Thus this chapter will be developed by looking into (a) *methodology, typology, and sources* used to establish the mechanism of the famine on the ground; (b) *the search brigades* and their (c) *various groups of perpetrators* on the village level. Then depiction of the perpetrators in (d) *Ukrainian novels* will be explored. In conclusion, similarities and differences between the portrayals of the perpetrators will be discussed.

Methodology and Sources

The 1932–33 famine was a crime against humanity that claimed millions of lives.[4] People who organized and executed the crime were the perpetrators. Since the line between the perpetrators and the victims in the famine was sometimes blurred (perpetrators could become victims and vice versa) the term *participants* or *actors* will be used where applicable. Some scholars consider the following legislative provisions helped bring on the famine and made men and women engaged in their enforcement complicit in mass violence:

1. Collective and individual farmers had to surrender grain and renounce their right to retain any for their own consumption or seed reserve. The state also collected shares of meat, milk, eggs, and other produce from collective and individual farmers.[5]
2. The homes of all peasants could be searched arbitrarily; if grain was found, the peasants could be prosecuted for theft.
3. Collective farms, villages, and entire districts were blacklisted or actually turned into ghettos—supply of any goods, including salt, kerosene, and matches, was stopped, all available foodstuffs confiscated and removed, and commerce and communications banned.
4. From November 20, 1932, meat procurements were demanded fifteen months in advance from the collective farms and farmers who failed to meet grain procurement targets. Thus the peasants had to either slaughter their cattle or buy meat at the market. This punitive measure contributed to the fact during the famine almost half the rural population was left without any livestock;[6] all grain previously distributed to collective farmers for use on the farms was ordered to be returned; all existing grain reserves in the villages were confiscated and credited toward procurement.[7]
5. Any produce found in the fields resulted in prosecution under the law of August 7, 1932, against "pilfering."
6. Commerce in food was banned until the procurement quotas were met (decreased several times over 1932–33, they were never met).[8]
7. Restricted rail travel for peasants.

The mechanism of the famine included cooperation between many institutions of the modern state in their efforts to remove all foodstuffs from the victims and ensure the starving did not have access to the storehouses or the fields and could not escape the villages. House searches, looming large in oral memory, were conducted by the search brigades that were organized and overseen by the local officials or party plenipotentiaries. Local officials, in their turn, received their orders from district officials and formed liaisons with security services who helped to enforce policies in cases of failure of local officials or insurgency. Detailed study of all participants of the legislative provisions would be beyond the scope of this chapter, and therefore people involved in enforcing the first five points will be assessed: searches, removal of foodstuffs and valuables, and refusal of available resources to the starving.

A plethora of many nonlethal functions that all together contributed to mass murder but made it possible for the actors not to perceive themselves as perpetrators. Empowered or instructed to carry out a task, an official or a village activist did not necessarily intentionally cause harm to the victims. Perpetration was diffused behind the screen of collectivization, grain procurement, and the so-called class war. Each perpetrator could feel that his or her part did not change anything and there was little point in objecting. Or their involvement was part of a great transformation of the country. Or they could not feel anything at all. Thus, few of them later reflected on their actions as acts of perpetration. They were activists, officials, conductors, guards, teachers, field guards involved in collectivization and grain procurement. In most cases, a participant had a specific function to fulfill for his or her job. The mundane job of being a watch at a granary in a village during the famine contributed to the organized starvation by denying emaciated villagers grain. Although some supporting roles fall short of criminal responsibility, their importance should not be minimized.

In identifying participants of the famine, it is important to consider the timeframe, which was not limited to 1932–33. The Holodomor would not have been possible without a wider context of collectivization and a habituation to violence. Participants referred to removal of land and other property from private ownership, displacement and deportation, and various repressions and executions as "the third front." But this war was fought not in a distant trench war but in the villages of largely agrarian country since the Soviet rule was established and *prodrazverstka* (confiscation of food and other agricultural products) in 1921. It was a mixture of state-sanctioned violence and gross violations of human rights that unfolded gradually and progressively. After years of hands-on involvement during collectivization it became more difficult for participants to escape the cycle of violence they were part of. As in the circumstance of the subjects in Milgram's experiment on obedience who would not have given the victim the highest shock without earlier small shocks, the perpetrators of the Holodomor had previous experience of collective violence.[9]

Nevertheless, the rank-and-file perpetrators were not entirely mere cogs in the machine or being forced into perpetration. Although most people are naturally influenced by authority or groups, some choose not to progress on a continuum of destructiveness.[10] Indeed, during the Holodomor, some local officials and activists refused to accept unrealistic procurement targets or search houses of their neighbors. As nineteen-year-old activist Olena Dun from Kamiani Potoky in Kremenchuk district recalled, "Once the village council sent me to an old woman. There I found a hungry woman crying. I was like her myself, why would I look for whatever she had? You can put me on trial tomorrow but I won't go and I didn't go."[11] It is the agency of the perpetrators—that is, the reasons behind their choice for participation, that many scholars of collective violence and international crimes—including Hilberg, Fromm, Gupta, and Mann—base their typologies on. Perhaps the most detailed, inclusive, and overarching typology is the one by Smeulers.[12] How this typology could be applied to the Holodomor is illustrated in table 1.1. One perpetrator can belong to a few groups simultaneously.

The sources for this chapter include documents from republican, provincial, and district archives in Ukraine, village museums, and private collections. Major corpuses of oral memory, memoirs, and diaries were also consulted. Using witness testimonies on the identities and activities of perpetrators presents several challenges.[13] Although some scholars reflect on the impossibility of bearing witness to a traumatic event, Schmidt argues that "the interruptions, the silence, and even the flaws within Holocaust survivor testimonies are symptomatic expressions of the internal truth."[14] In perpetrator testimonies this nonwitnessing, lack of internal truth, and political agenda is "a constitutive element of genocide" or crime against humanity.[15] Indeed, many perpetrators keep silent or conceal their perspective by speaking in Bolshevik jargon—impersonal and distanced. Such accounts also present a hermeneutic problem. Their authors, as former perpetrators, consciously attempt to represent themselves in a positive light and bear ambivalence to witnessing as a political act, for most of the memoirs were published in the West during the Cold War.

According to Christian Gerlach, in order to ensure some certainty, one has to use the testimonies as supportive evidence together with many sources and testimonies of the same

Table 1.1. Typology of the perpetrators of Holodomor.

Group	Definition	Participation in the Holodomor
Professionals	Trained to enforce policies, which at times include violence.	Security services (GPU), militia, and—in some cases—the army.
Profiteers and careerists	Benefit from participation.	Use their position of power to benefit financially, to settle scores with neighbors, or to advance their party career through deployment in the village.
Fanatics (5%)	Driven by ideology or greater good.	Plenipotentiaries from the cities and local communists who "firmly believed that the ends justified the means. Our great goal was the universal triumph of Communism, and for the sake of the goal everything was permissible—to lie, to steal, to destroy hundreds of thousands and even millions of people."
Sadists and criminals (5%)	Take advantage of situation to fulfill sadistic or other criminal deviations.	Tortured, raped, and murdered the victims.
Followers (65%)	Majority of participants that simply follow orders or comply with authority.	Collective farmers, officials, plenipotentiaries, communists, young people. When confronted by the victims about his actions leading to the deaths of children, one activist replied, "Well, and what else . . . that's it, we are sent and we are doing it."
Compromised ordinary people	Usually vulnerable people coerced into participation by threats or by force.	"They faced a choice to collect a certain amount . . . or to be thrown out. Everybody wanted to live. . . . The ones who searched were ordinary people like us."

Source: Prepared by the author. Data from Bilousko et al., *Natsional'na knyha*. Poltavska, 980; Haman et al., *Natsional'na knyha*: Cherkas'ka, 918; L. Kopelev, *I sotvoril sebe kumira*, 285.

events.[16] Christopher Browning develops this method of recovering factuality by conducting four tests: self-interest, vividness, possibility, and probability.[17] In other words, of prime interest are statements in the testimony that are contrary to the self-interest of the perpetrator, the degree of detail in the events described, the lack of direct contradiction by other sources, and indirect confirmation in other documents.

To illustrate how this methodology works in case of the Holodomor perpetrators, we can use one of Browning's examples. Eichmann in his testimonies describes himself in his early career as an idealist,[18] as Kopelev did in portraying himself as a true believer in 1932–33 in his memoir *I sotvoril sebe kumira* [The education of a true believer]. Kopelev claimed he genuinely believed that the peasants hoarded grain needed for international revolution or, more specifically, that a young peasant woman he helped to detain could have been a spy. None of these claims, in fact, could be reliably verified for two reasons. First, the claims relate to someone's *beliefs* and serve self-interest in representing oneself in a positive light. Second, most people in the village of Popivka, where Kopelev was "working," were already starving in 1932–33 and more than two thousand out of six thousand inhabitants died.[19] It was not possible that these men, women, and children chose to die while hoarding grain. Neither was the girl Kopelev detained a spy. She was an individual farmer who returned from the hospital after having an abortion and could provide little information of interest to foreign intelligence services, whom she could not contact, since Popivka was far away from the border and all means of communication were controlled by the authorities. Kopelev's misrepresentation of these points is as improbable and impossible as the falsities in Eichmann's self-representation.

Search Brigades

The mechanism of man-made famine starts with withholding of food from the victims. Soviet historiography defines the members of the brigades as "the best, leading collective farmers. In Ukraine and Northern Caucasus village councils created commissions out of best collective farmers that revealed facts of theft and hiding bread."[20] Although there is no dedicated research or known archival documents with statistical data on activist brigades who confiscated foodstuffs, some details can be found in the reports by GPU (*Gosudarstvennoye Politicheskoye Upravlenie*; State Political Directorate) service personnel and local party officials, complaints from the victims, and personal files. The documents, however, cover only the brigade members who either refused to follow orders (questioned procurement plans, distributed foodstuffs) or were accused of excesses on the ground (profiteers, drunks, sadists, and murderers). That is not to say that profiteering was not widespread: indeed, requisition of foodstuffs and dispossession was accompanied with violence and profiteering.

Oral memory can help reconstruct a broader picture of activist brigades. Individual memory of traumatic experience is deeply personal and fluid, but the more than two hundred survivor testimonies from the voluminous *National Book of Memory of the Holodomor Victims* (2008) can supplement oral memory to ensure the greater accuracy required for quantitative analysis. The book is the first analysis of perpetrators of the famine based on the questionnaire by Valentyna Borysenko.[21] Although the testimonies were not collected for a statistical survey, the pool of subjects was fairly balanced by geography within Poltava province and age at the time of the famine. The answers elaborate on demographics and the brigade size; identities and the actual perpetration and institutional composition.

The brigades were predominantly male, but all-female teams are also known. Some of the members were poor, some not. Almost all survivors comment on knowing the perpetrators before and after the famine through a variety of social roles—as neighbors, distant relations or relations-to-be, coworkers, and so on. 80 percent of survivors commented that search brigades consisted of local, or *svoi*, people, including collective farmers and village officials—usually the head of the village council or the chairman of the collective farm or brigade leader. The size of the group varied, with an average brigade consisting of four or five members. In general, perpetrators felt more comfortable in numbers, but brigades with one to three members were not rare—31 percent. A number of survivors explained that collective farmers' participation in searches or watching the fields was part of their mundane job, like working in the field: "the brigade was put together, whoever wanted to could sign up. They used to collect all food. They said: 'According to the law.' And what can you do about it?"[22] For many, the reality of the searches, and particularly long-term impact of their actions, had perhaps not sunk in, which makes participation in the searches altogether banal.

When survivors were asked to name the members of the brigades, only 54 percent of survivors did. Almost all identified men and women were residents of the villages they operated in or came from a village nearby. The teams that included plenipotentiaries from the cities were recalled by 17 percent of survivors, with only 3 percent of the testimonies describing searches or *trusy* (quakes) being conducted by people from outside the village, or *chuzhi*. The question remains, however, why 46 percent of survivors did not provide any names. They offered various reasons: they forgot, were too young to remember or had reservations, especially if perpetrators' families still lived in the village at the time of the interview. Another possible explanation is that survivors did not regard the members of the brigades as perpetrators. A rather telling instance was the survivor who did not consider her father a perpetrator although he was in the brigade. Her family house was searched ten times a month and her father eventually died of hunger. "I remember an incident, my father was [in the brigade] there, so they got inside the house and found a big barrel with water. My father looked inside and went away, but the other [member] dipped his arm all the way down. At that second, the owner stabbed him from behind. The owner was murdered of course; such incidents took place."[23]

The number of brigades in a village depended on its size. Usually one brigade would operate in an allocated part of the village known as *kutok* or *sotnia* (corner or hundred). In some cases, however, brigades would be relocated to work in the neighboring villages or other districts so that perpetrators were not connected to the victims personally and thus be more effective. In survivor testimonies, the brigades are often mentioned by such descriptive names as *aktyv/isty* (activists), *buksyry* (tugboats), *vlada* (authorities), *bryhady* (brigades), *shtyrkhachi* (poachers), *krasna mitla* (red broomstick), *komizany* (from *Komnezam*—Committee of Poor Peasants), and *komsomolts'* (Komsomol).

From November 1932, activist brigades could requisition other agricultural produce in lieu of grain. These actions devastated peasant households. The brigades were supposed to procure grain from the peasants who did not meet targets, but only one out of 210 survivors said perpetrators confiscated only bread. A total of 52 percent of survivors tell of activists confiscating everything: foodstuffs, livestock, personal items, valuables, clothes, and so on. Later, some of the confiscated goods were sold by the village council, whereas other items were kept by the activists or their relatives: "I remember one [man] wearing my father's suede jacket for a long time."[24] During the searches, every possible hiding place was checked manually or with steel rods to pierce soil and walls or soft areas in the gardens in winter. The beds, cots, chests, ovens, and even chimneys were often damaged. The searches mostly took place during the day, though the activists could also come at night to catch the victims by surprise. A quarter of survivors felt the brigade would stop only when there was nothing left to take.

Upon arrival, the brigade would usually demand the grain or other foodstuffs. According to 98 percent of the testimonies, they did not present any documents authorizing them to do the searches, and neither did the victims expect it. Nor did they have to be armed: only 29 percent of survivors remember one member of the brigade having a rifle or a shotgun. The survivors denied any resistance was possible, for the brigades members "could do anything" or the victims were "too scared even to say a word."[25] Many survivors described babies being thrown out of cradles in search of food hidden under their pillows. There were instances of perpetrators locking children inside houses and stopping up the chimney to threaten to suffocate them while demanding that parents join the collective farm.[26] The evidence of violence during the searches is abundant in all corpuses of oral memory. Indeed, 83 percent of survivors in Poltava province remembered members of their families or people they knew being either deported, dekulakized, or imprisoned and physically and verbally abused during the famine.

The number of resources differed from province to province, and so did local officials' approaches to managing supplies, but in some villages nobody was spared from hunger. 21 percent of survivors asserted that everyone in their village, including the perpetrators, starved. In fact, 2 percent recalled local activists and their families dying from malnourishment too.[27] But more than a half of survivors (54%) remembered brigades, activist leaders, and their families spared of starving during the famine. No quantitative data exist on the numbers of those defecting from the brigades, but some activists helped the victims to hide food in their allotments because they were not subjected to searches.[28] In many instances, brigade members did not search as meticulously as others. In other words, perpetration, as survival, was individual experience and depended on circumstances. As in the case study by Browning, when two officers had opposite reactions to the policemen asking to be spared the duty of shooting the victims, various officials at district and village levels had different approaches to evasion of duty by their subordinates.[29]

Finding "the righteous ones" in the brigades is problematic. The existing collection of testimonies on 140 people helping others during the Holodomor includes unverified accounts. For example, a son of a chairman of a collective farm describes his father as the savior of Uzdytsia in Hlukhiv district, Sumy province, and reports that not a single person there died during the Holodomor.[30] The list of the victims in the same village in the *National Book of Memory of the Holodomor Victims*, however, contains 65 names, more than 60 percent of whom were children. Survivors almost unanimously (95%) consider "authorities" responsible for organizing the famine.[31] The "authorities" include the whole vertical structure of government—from Stalin to the village activists. Only 2 percent suggested that it was "people like us" who made this devastating famine possible.

The Various Groups of Perpetrators

The vast majority of the survivors name the village council and to a lesser degree the board of the collective farm as the chief organizer of the searches. A total of 30 percent of survivors also mention the district officials as involved and name the members of the following groups in the brigades: KNS, *peredovyky* (shock workers), teachers, Komsomol, field guards—and that is the order this overview will follow.

KNS

Komitety Nezamozhnykh Selian (*Komnezamy*, committees of nonwealthy peasants) were state-sponsored organizations in the Ukrainian countryside between 1920 and 1933 that supported and enforced various state policies on the ground. Some historians, including James

Mace, argue that the famine of 1933 is a measure of their success in grain procurement, for key village perpetrators indeed were KNS members and KNS was instrumental during collectivization in Ukraine.[32] Other researchers argue that KNS failed to be an effective force during the famine because of its poor management and neglect by the state. Ukrainian officials commented at the time that "KNS works so poorly that if there had been no lists of members one would think KNS does not exist" or "village KNS does not exist in real life, only on paper."[33] Levandovs'ka concludes that the involvement of tens of thousands of plenipotentiaries from the city proves KNS could not facilitate the famine, which is further supported by oral memory. Upon arrival to the village, party plenipotentiaries sought support of KNS members for any activity, and more often than not they dominated collectivization committee, helped to compile lists for dekulakization, and provided intelligence.

In the 1920s, KNS members were granted favorable conditions for loans and industrial goods distribution in the village. According to Mace, such conditions attracted to this organization both marginal and "parasite" elements of the village that embraced violence and theft and built KNS its infamous reputation.[34] When KNS was subordinated to village councils and lost some of its privileges in 1925, as the state took a break from confiscations and radical policies during the New Economic Policy, 54 percent of its activists left the organization.[35] During collectivization, however, the government again allowed them arbitrariness and illegality for which its elements were granted immunity, and KNS members "threw themselves into a decisive offensive against the kulaks, showing heroic initiative during important economic and political campaigns in the village."[36] Nevertheless, some KNS members refused to search houses.[37] Moreover, only 20 percent of KNS members joined collectives by the end of 1929.[38]

Indeed, only 3 percent of 212 survivors name those who searched their houses as primarily KNS. One survivor describes KNS as idle, whereas the rest call them activists, profiteers, or peasants who joined collective farms with nothing.[39] Several accounts mention *komnezamivky* (female members of KNS). Nadiia Shulika from Hrynky in Hlobynskyi district recalls that search brigades in their village had many KNS women: "Some 'seasoned' girls gathered there, used to put red scarves on and search the huts."[40] These women clearly challenged gender expectations at the time: they wore modern clothes, had short haircuts, and did not leave food for children, as other witness remember. Crucially, they were engaged in perpetrating behavior that was reserved for men. While Soviet historians regarded female members of KNS as evidence of women political participation, the number of women in KNS increased only in winter 1922–23 and during the collectivization—that is, when membership gave access to distribution of resources, especially for socially vulnerable women such as widows. (See fig. 1.1.)[41]

Female participation in KNS, however, was never higher than 25 percent.[42] For example, the report on KNS in Volyn *okrug* (administrative unit smaller than province) records 5,136 women in KNS (or 14.2% of all members) in 1925. The report also comments on many peasants calling KNS members "drunks, good-for-nothings, and bastards."[43] The industrious nonwealthy peasants who used the benefits of KNS membership to become self-sufficient by the end of the decade no longer qualified as KNS and were purged from its ranks regularly, with waves of expulsions as high as 840,316 at a time.[44] According to Voloshenko and

Fig. 1.1 Joint plenum of Volyn and Korosten district KNS in 1930. *Source*: Courtesy of Tsentral'nyi Derzhavnyi Kinofotofono Arkhiv Ukrainy imeni Hordiia Semenovycha Pshenychnoho.

Bilokon, the remaining members used the loans and tax credits from the state to buy food, luxury items, and alcohol rather than investing in farm equipment, acquisition of land, or increasing their profits.[45]

Peredovyky

Peredovyky (shock collective farmers), on the other hand, were peasants known for their hard work. By the time the Stakhanovite movement gained momentum in 1935, Maria Demchenko, Nadiia Zahlada, Pasha Angelina, and other shock workers in the countryside had been part of this socialist movement for years. They also had another detail in common: participation in the famine, even if tangentially. A careful analysis by the author of more than thirty biographies of the stakhanovite women of the countryside reveals that almost all of them participated in the famine. They all came from poor families and worked as laborers from childhood. They actively supported collectivization, if not the founding mothers of the local collective farms. Being village activists entailed participation in dekulakization, thus joining the continuum of destruction that fed into the famine.

This can be better illustrated with two examples. Demchenko (1912–95), from Starosillia in Cherkasy province, a celebrated sugar-beet grower who met Stalin, returned to her native village after the New Economic Program to join the newly organized collective farm in 1928. In March 1933, when the death rate in Starosillia was soaring, Demchenko was awarded

Komsomol membership for "diligent work at the farm." Witnesses recall how the starving peasants hoped to find some sugar beets left behind in the field after the harvest, but Demchenko and her brigadier Davyd Burda made "every effort not to leave a single beet in the field or by the road."[46] Demchenko and her circle of friends worked closely with local officials, in particular the secretaries of the village Komsomol and the district party committee. She described their work together succinctly: "We destroyed the kulaks and took everything in our hands. Now everything is in our power, and they are crazy with jealousy."[47] Demchenko experienced hostility to her in the village and left several years later.

Unlike Demchenko, Nadiia Zahlada (1894–1977) in Vysoke, Zhytomyr province, stayed in her native village until death. A collectivization activist herself, she even chaired the collective farm in 1944 when they "could not find a man for the job."[48] A poor, illiterate widow with six children, she supported collectivization. During the famine, she adopted an infant orphan left by her neighbors and organized an orphanage in the village where most victims were children under the age of one. Recollecting the past thirty years later, Zahlada rather carefully commented, "When thinking about conscience I remember how unreasonably we managed the farms under Stalin. All we cared were the targets, not the right things. . . . How much damage was inflicted on so many farms. . . . So many people were forced to go against their own conscience!"[49]

Teachers

"There is not a single village where teachers are not part of grain procurement or collectivization brigade."[50] Their functions included agitation, assisting the activists in house searches, transporting grain, dekulakization, storing confiscated goods, scrutinizing private mail, informing security services, and other activities. Village teachers reported on their students' parents hiding grain or even searched the very houses. Out of 74,046 teachers in Ukraine, almost two-thirds worked in the countryside, and therefore almost 50,000 of them participated in the famine.[51]

This cooperation was not always smooth: teachers complained of poor food provisions, inadequate accommodation and school premises, delays in pay, and illegal practices of local officials (demand to work in the fields, taxation, sexual harassment of female teachers, for a few examples). Being outsiders, teachers also faced conflicts with local activists during the famine. For example, in the village of Tarasivka, the teacher was the only person who voted for dekulakization in the meeting.[52] By supporting the unpopular state policies, they also faced hostility from the victims: there was only one village in Annopil district where the peasants did not physically assault a teacher.[53] Though some fled the countryside, most stayed and proceeded with grain procurement. There were cases of remorse, too. The teacher Savinska in Velyka Obukhivka, Myrhorod district, returned to their owners the children's clothes that she had confiscated earlier that day.[54]

One of the challenges teachers faced in their work was cognitive dissonance. After all, they were not trained to enforce the policies with violence and had to rationalize their participation beyond the cliché phrases of class struggle and a better future. This can be illustrated with a letter one female teacher from Uzyn (Kyiv) wrote to Stalin after he accused people on the ground, like her, of the excesses that occurred during collectivization and called for a halt in the campaign. In the small town, where 1,563 out of 6,000 died, there were ample examples of such excesses that perpetrators like her were forced into committing. In the letter, the teacher accused Stalin of knowing about the whole process and its repercussions and blaming the rank-and-file unfairly.[55] More important, she feared that Stalin's article undermined her authority and made her gruesome work futile: "How many times was I begged, cursed, and sworn at when taking away grain and other goods. A dirty hut, a bunch of pale ragged people. You come to collect all 'extra' bread, potatoes and tell them their cow, chickens, and pigs are not theirs anymore. You also demand money for tractors and all their savings (I've heard of others being sued for not procuring enough). And once a peasant attacked us with an axe!"[56]

Party Plenipotentiaries and District Officials

The other outsiders among village perpetrators were party plenipotentiaries and district officials, special brigades of activists from other villages or districts or organizations, less often security service personnel. Party plenipotentiaries, in their turn, were drawn from various institutions to work in the countryside. Some came as the 25-thousanders (named after the all-Soviet mobilization campaign during which some twenty-five thousand men and women were sent to the countryside to enforce collectivization) or during other drives to "strengthen" the existing farms. Viola describes plenipotentiaries like 25-thousanders as predominantly male, of working-class origin, more than half of them party members or party candidates.[57]

Throughout 1932, thousands of "proven comrades," most of them with a good record of work in the village during collectivization, were deployed to procure grain.

District officials had similar demographics. Personal files of 125 communists working at the party committees on the district level in twelve *okrugs* in 1930 reveal them as predominantly male (only 3.5% were women), with only primary education and of working-class background. With an average party membership of nine years, some of them were Red Army veterans.[58] Ethnic composition of the officials reflected the ethnic makeup of the urban population in Ukraine at the time. Very few of them spoke Ukrainian.[59]

In 1928, party member officials in Dnipropetrovsk district were assessed on their level of knowledge of Ukrainian culture and language: 65.5 percent did not speak the language and never read Ukrainian literature, only 3.5 percent could write and read in Ukrainian and spoke fluently, and another 31 percent had some knowledge of both the language and the literature.[60] The latter figure on the knowledge of Ukrainian language and literature should be assessed carefully. Indeed, Kopelev's claim that he spoke Ukrainian fluently, which helped him to win some peasants' trust during collectivization, appears to be exaggerated when juxtaposed with the testimony of the survivor who recollected Kopelev and his colleagues speaking in "a strange, alien language" while they took the last food from his family.[61]

Speaking Russian alienated them from the peasants, forging the image of the Other and resulting in antisemitism not forgotten after the events of ten years earlier. Perhaps that prompted students at Tul'chyn pedagogical college to protest against Jewish students being sent to the countryside in 1928: "How could you send the Jews to the village? How would they converse with our women there? Only Ukrainians could be sent to the village."[62]

Nevertheless, the Kremlin did prefer to send cadre from the Russian Federation to procure grain in Ukraine. In December 1932, Kaganovich telegraphed Stalin commenting on Ukrainian plenipotentiaries being unreliable despite being delegated by the CC CP(b)U (Central Committee of the Communist Party [Bolshevik] of Ukraine) and the warnings they received. Kaganovich suggested sending workers from the Russian Federation to Odessa and Dnipropetrivs'k provinces as well as plenipotentiaries from the military.[63] This suggestion was approved and executed in January 1933.

Individual experiences of party plenipotentiaries and district officials vary greatly. Upon arrival, they held various positions at the village level—chairmen of collective farms, teachers, secretaries of the party cells, and so on. They also had to organize (or help) and report on grain procurement. Some deserted, some avoided taking any actions, and others embraced violence or profited or simply followed the orders. The leadership in Kharkiv received many reports on plenipotentiaries deserting their positions in droves, getting drunk with local activists, or criticizing the very policies they were expected to enforce. Some plenipotentiaries committed suicide after being "ridden with guilt and full of sympathy for the starving" when they were powerless to change anything.[64]

At the same time, there voluminous accounts of plunder, rape, and murder by plenipotentiaries as early as in 1929 that were regularly reported by party officials and security services in 1932–33.[65]

Like local activists, party plenipotentiaries and district officials risked being attacked or killed by the peasants as well as being purged by their superiors. The head of the DPU in Ukraine, Balyts'kyi, reported that eleven thousand were arrested in relation to procurement within the first four months of the grain requisition campaign. Over the course of the following month (between November 15 and December 15, 1932), a further sixteen thousand were arrested. This figure included 2,260 from collective farm management, including 409 collective farm heads. A total of 108, or 0.6 percent, were sentenced to death.[66] The total number of arrests in connection to grain procurement in 1932 was twenty-seven thousand.[67] Those who retained their positions received regular telegrams from *oblast* committees demanding the fulfillment of quotas within five or ten days. In some *oblasts*, the DPU servicemen in their full uniform would visit collective farms and insist that management fulfill the quotas.[68]

Was everyone who failed to fulfill procurement quotas purged or put on trial? While there is no quantitative analysis on the subject, the highly publicized show trials of district officials offer insight into what one could potentially expect for not reaching grain procurement quotas set for a district. In the case of Orikhiv, for instance, sixteen district officials were tried in late 1932 for failing to meet the grain procurement target, which they argued was unrealistic. Some of them reportedly pressured the management of local communes and collective farms to leave some grain behind for forage, seeds, and other funds. None of them pleaded guilty, despite the pressure put on them by Skrypnyk, the commissioner of education at the time, who demanded that they all be sentenced to execution by firing squad.[69] Only one official was sentenced to death; two were pardoned, and the rest received various terms in camps. Shortly after the sentences were announced publicly, the death sentence was changed to imprisonment, and all of them were released by 1935.[70] Most continued to work for the government and later retired.

Fig. 1.2 Village activists in the field; Stepan S. is far left. *Source*: Private archive of Stepan S.

Nevertheless news of lower-level perpetrators being punished was repeated at many meetings on all levels. For instance, Raiev, Rabidzhanovych, and Freed, who worked with Kopelev in the villages of Kharkiv province, were sentenced to short terms in labor camps and exile for anti-Soviet agitation. After returning to Kharkiv in 1933, they started collecting emaciated children from the train stations and providing them with shelter and their own rations.[71]

Most plenipotentiaries avoided immediate repressions, like Kravchenko, Goychenko, Hrygorenko, and Kopelev, who later wrote memoirs. Some stayed in the village, like Stepan S. He was sent to the village during collectivization in 1929,[72] and by the beginning of the famine he worked as a teacher in the village of Toporyshche in Zhytomyr province, where he helped to close down a local church.[73] Coming from a working-class Ukrainian family in a town in south Ukraine, Stepan received secondary education and later joined Komsomol. After the famine, Stepan married a local girl whose father died in the Holodomor.[74] Stepan continued to teach in the school and during World War II he enlisted in the infantry, where he served from 1941 to 1945. His comrades in arms commented on his bravery at the frontline, which brought him three decorations.[75] After the war, he taught at the same school, raised a family, and died in the late 1970s. Local oral memory collected in the village as part of a broader research project suggests that Stepan led an ordinary life after the famine and did not display any abnormal behavior. (See fig. 1.2.)

Archival materials add to the list of plenipotentiaries college students who were deployed to assist collectivization and grain procurement along with university teaching fellows. "In Adriivka in Sanzharskyi district, there was a college, and dozens of those boys with guns, split into smaller groups with 1–3 village council members, went to Svatunivka, Bazarivka, Nekhvoroshcha."[76] Their young age could be regarded as a vulnerability the state used to coerce them into participation, though some of them had no illusions. One such student, sent to procure grain in late 1932, commented on the man-made nature of the famine, the incompetence of people like him in agriculture, and local officials profiteering.[77] The students were joined by personnel from the army. According to the political office of RSChA (*Robitnycho-Seliansk'a Chervona Armiia*, Workers' and Peasants' Red Army), in spring 1933, 186 brigades of soldiers and officers worked in the countryside searching for grain hidden by the peasants. They discovered 374 pits where peasants had stored grain.[78]

Buksyry

There were other outsiders that carved themselves deep in oral memory. So-called *buksyry* (tugboat) brigades. While they are often conflated with the village activists, they were drawn from party members and collective farmers from outside—other villages, workers from the factories nearby, or civil servants. They were organized by decisions of district, provincial party committees, or the CC CP(b)U to help procurement in administrative units that were underperforming. *Buksyry* brigades were generally larger than teams of local activists and sometimes numbered as much as eight hundred. Appearance of such large numbers of strangers intimidated the peasants and minimized their chances to hide any food. Composition of a brigade depended on the organization within which it was set up.

One such *buksyr* brigade of more than two hundred men and women from Zinoviev *okrug* started its work in autumn 1930 and included mostly party members who had experience in procuring grain in 1928–29. In the districts this brigade was sent to, its members met with hostility from local officials and peasants alike. Some farmers refused to house newcomers and called them "foreigners" and "red broomsticks," so they had to sleep outside. After a few days and expulsions from the party, most local officials cooperated. One of them, however, pleaded with the district committee to lower the grain target, saying, "If you don't, I'm afraid the head of the village council and the chairman of the farm will take their lives." The official was transferred to another village, and the tugboat brigade ensured that the original target was met. In fact, in five days, this brigade confiscated more grain than local perpetrators had had in months.[79]

Field Guards

As the 1933 harvest approached, many victims turned their hopes to the fields. So did the party leaders in Kharkiv, but for a different reason—they did not want the starving to "pilfer" and instructed district officials to protect the fields with party members guarding the fields. Many nonparty farmers also volunteered to guard the fields, usually armed with a rifle or a whip, on horseback or on the newly erected wooden towers. Pavlo Ivashko from Kobeliaky in Poltava explained becoming a guard and having to follow orders: "Local people, collective farmers. . . . You got a job allocated to you and you will do it. . . . They were at work, these people did their work."[80] Very often, it was the children who helped to guard the

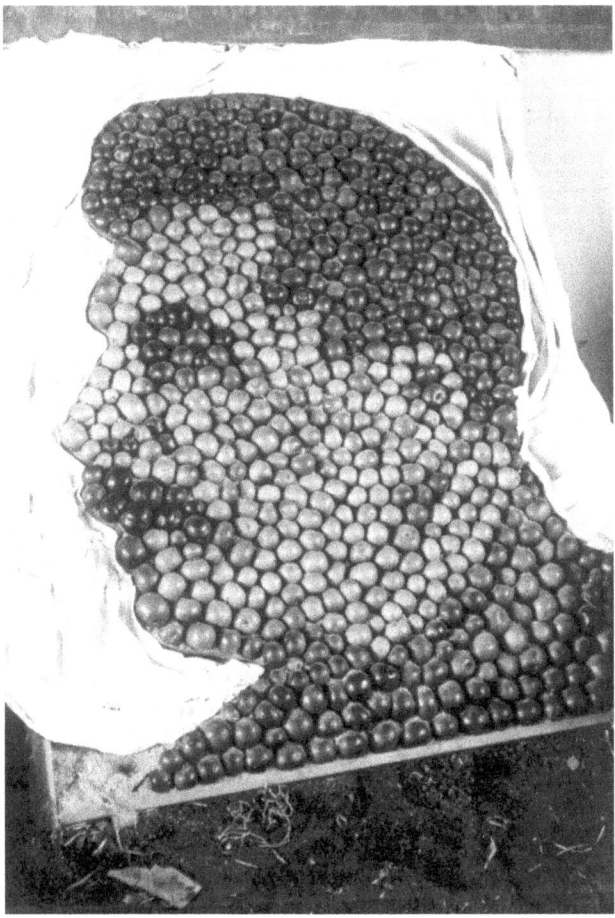

Fig. 1.3 This portrait of Stalin was put together from apples by collective farmers in Donetsk province in 1934. *Source*: Courtesy of Tsentral'nyi Derzhavnyi Kinofotofono Arkhiv Ukrainy imeni Hordiia Semenovycha Pshenychnoho.

fields: during summer in 1933, more than 540,000 school-age children helped to collect ears of wheat after the harvest and to guard the fields.[81]

Some survivors recall that the fields were guarded by nonlocal people. Indeed, sometimes the responsibility to watch the fields was delegated to the members of OSOAviaKhim or the army.[82] In 1933, thousands of activists from the city cells of OSOAviaKhim were deployed in the countryside "to guard the new harvest." In the first days of August 1933, Bohdanov, the chairman of the central council of Ukrainian OSOAviaKhim, reported to the Politburo of CC of CP(b)U in reference to their earlier request for 2,200 OSOAviaKhim volunteers to watch the fields in *sovkhozy*. He stated that 2,420 its men and women were deployed at 141 farms, which was just "a part of the great effort" by OSOAviaKhim in the village. For example, Kharkiv province council sent seven hundred of its military-educated activists from the city to the collective farms, apart from providing additional members to protect the harvest at the state farms. Overall, there were over 21,000 OSOAviaKhim members protecting the 1933 harvest in Ukraine.[83]

Some were strict and punished anyone who dared to cut ears of wheat in the fields. Others turned a blind eye to the children swollen with hunger walking in the fields. Apart from physical punishment, the guards could also bring the offenders to the village council, where they will be dealt with by police. Security service also reported numerous cases of offenders being lynched by mobs of collective farmers, activists, and local officials when caught in the fields. In June 1933, associate head of Ukrainian GPU Karl Karlson reported to the first secretary of CC CP(b)U Stanislav Kosior on the number of lynching cases rising rapidly. In 51 districts, there were 111 such cases in June 1933. The mobs of one to two hundred peasants instigated by village councils, activists, and party members savaged offenders to death. In fact, local officials and activists took part in or initiated 66 of 111 reported cases in which 145 people died and 247 were wounded.[84] Thus the role of the guards in the famine should not underestimated: already by the beginning 1933, tens of thousands of people were caught in the fields, breaking into storehouses or granaries; 54,645 of them were convicted under the law of August 7, 1932, and two thousand of them executed.[85]

Representation in Ukrainian Novels

Although any public mention of the famine was a criminal offense in the Soviet Union, many Soviet writers did mention starvation in published works, explaining it as poor harvest or kulak sabotage.[86] Considering the long history of Ukrainian literature serving both as a public forum and as a repository of cultural memory in absence of civil institutions, some writers used Aesopian language to avoid censorship, published abroad, or disseminated their works illegally via *samvydav* or *samizdat*, "self-published" literature. A large number of literary works on the famine were written in the Ukrainian diaspora, and a growing number of novels on the Holodomor are now being produced and older works have been republished.

This part of the chapter is a chronological explorative overview of the novels that reached the mass readership in Ukraine and therefore are part of the cultural memory.[87] The selected Soviet novels were distributed via public libraries from the 1930s onward; the novels by the writers in diaspora were circulated as *samvydav* and, after 1991, were included in school curricula or used as film scripts; the post-Soviet works overviewed here received literary awards and are being republished. Therefore, they can be regarded as part of cultural memory of the Holodomor. These novels can form three groups chronologically and by the political context they were produced within by their interpretation of the agency of local perpetrators. Soviet perpetrators have *embraced* modality, dissident writers portray *dispersed* agency, while post-Soviet Ukrainian writers and those in diaspora use *displaced* modality in their take on local facilitators of the famine. The aim of this overview is to establish these major patterns in depiction of the rank-and-file perpetrators in Ukrainian prose and thus demonstrate discrepancy between identities and memorial traces of the perpetrators. Ukrainian Soviet literature of the early 1930s was subjected to censorship, but it nevertheless offers an elaborate picture of the rank-and-file perpetrators and even occasionally mentions the famine. Indeed, many writers themselves were, if not the participants, then at least witnesses of the famine and therefore offer vivid accounts of the events. For instance, Arkadii Liubchenko based his short novel *Kostryha* (1933) on his visits to the countryside at the time.[88] The perpetrators are nameless and they are everywhere: "All teachers in the district were organized, together with pupils, to pull (a quote from the protocol) peasants out of the debt to the state."[89] Likewise, Ivan Kyrylenko, the author of the novel on collectivization *Avanposty* (The outposts, 1933), had a good knowledge of the perpetrators on the ground through his position as a personal secretary to the chairman of the Central Executive Committee of Ukraine, Hryhorii Petrovskyi. During the Holodomor, Petrovskyi received thousands of letters from the peasants and perpetrators alike, which provided Kyrylenko with ample material.

In Kyrylenko's novel, the key perpetrators in the village of Petrivka are unflinching communists: a village Komsomol leader, Motora, and a worker from Kharkiv, Obushnyi. They both are determined to find class enemies, believe procurement targets realistic even if they have "to sizzle" any peasants resisting them. This is not a first assignment for Obushnyi, and he immediately gathers local Red veterans, all members of the village council and collective farm board, KNS, and shock collective farmers—twenty-five people in total. He notes to himself that only a few activists understand Soviet policies and most are indifferent. He explains the lack of local support with the fact that many peasants did not side with the Soviets during the civil war: "at that time every fifth [person] here was fighting for Petliura or in gangs. We can count on few."[90]

His comments echo the words of the perpetrators in the memoir of Lev Kopelev. In 1932, Kopelev was sent to work in a grain procurement brigade in the village of Petrivtsi in Poltava province. A local GPU plenipotentiary explained the lack of support to Kopelev: "There are counter-revolutionary elements in all villages here. In Petrivtsi there are about twenty of those . . . who took arms against us and spilt our blood. . . . There were as many gangs in civil war here as there are fleas on a dog."[91] Thus Obushnyi, like Kopelev's colleagues in real life, deems ideological education of such activists futile and threatens them into obedience with repression. To ensure control, he splits the activists into small brigades with a trusted comrade in each. Each brigade is judged on achieving its target. After a few weeks, all brigades merge into one in which all members are bound by trust and shared experience. The combined brigade, according to them, brings "true devastation" to the peasants and finds hidden bread. They work by the words "No hesitation at the front. Got an order—follow it!" though some complain that daily house searches resemble abuse rather than a battle.[92]

Another episode in *Avanposty* that reads like a documentary is the speech of the secretary of the central committee at the orientation meeting for the party plenipotentiaries in Kharkiv. The secretary stresses the importance of the class war and the role of the plenipotentiaries in that battle: "three hundred Bolsheviks heard the words and dressed [them] in familiar pictures of class struggle in the village."[93] Most of them, like Obushnyi, worked at the factories or mines where their life was very similar to those of the characters in Émile Zola's *Germinal* (1885): a struggle for a better life. The wording of the secretary's speech in *Avanposty* is strikingly similar to the speech of the republican official at a similar event in 1932.[94] According to Kravchenko, after that speech, he preferred to think that the peasants were somehow responsible for the famine. This train of thought was what some communists might have believed in or *wanted* to believe, as it made their life *safer*.[95] Thus not all party plenipotentiaries were, like Obushnyi, ideological participants.

Finally, Kyrylenko discusses the generational divide between perpetrators and victims. The young people are ambitious and enthusiastic and follow party plenipotentiaries. They destroy the icons their mothers worship and play accordion instead of the traditional *kobza* or fiddle. This divide is also discussed by other writers. In *History of Happiness* (1934) by Ivan Le, a pioneer denounces his father for hiding grain and has a mental breakdown; another activist dekulakizes his parents in order to become a chairman of the collective farm. A Komsomol named Kyrylo in *Voseny* (*In Autumn*, 1933) by Mykola Dukyn, reminds his mother that he might shoot her if she steals even a handful of grain from the collective farm again. He is a guard at the barn and days earlier had shot a peasant in the back. In Kyrylenko's novel, the youth is joined by a handful of female activists who complain local officials are not involving women in the campaigns. The peasants spread rumors that these women are promiscuous and lynch them. Indeed, the female activists defy gender expectations: "Varvara fights the neighborhood, *dosvitky*, perennial peasant passivity"[96] and does not sleep at night in hopes of catching other peasants milling grain.

Anatoliy Dimarov's novel *The Hungry Thirties* (A parable about bread, 1989), on the famine perpetrators, was cut by censor Mul'tykh from a larger epic *I budut liudy* (There will be people, 1964). The censor's conclusion epitomizes official guidance on writing about the Holodomor perpetrators: "completely re-evaluate the events in the village in late 1929–early 1930 according to the documents and existing historiography; show the most important, positive side of collectivization; illuminate the key role of village activists and party cells in socialistic transformation of the village."[97] Instead, the novel provides a nuanced picture of the perpetrators based on Dimarov's own past. His father was dekulakized while his mother participated in dekulakization in a different village, where she relocated with her children in order to escape. Dimarov remembers her crying when a peasant she dekulakized committed suicide. That man was a father of his school friend.[98]

In his novel, Dimarov explores the vertical hierarchy of perpetrators—from village activists and district officials to the province leaders and Stalin. The events start in Khorol, where Hryhoriy Ginzburg, the secretary of the district party committee, finds himself under pressure from the province committee to speed up collectivization. Confused with the discrepancy between Stalin's views on collectivization and his own experience, he writes a letter to Stalin explaining how devastating collectivization is and that many officials like him share this view.[99] Then Ginzburg is summoned to the provincial party committee and expelled from the party. In defiance, he shoots himself dead. Maksudov comments on higher rates of suicide among party officials as the result of their being "ridden with guilt and full of sympathy for the starving" and their inability to change anything.[100]

Career-driven colleagues of the deceased Ginzburg take his place. One of them, Put'ko, travels to the village of Tarasivka to meet local activists. The head of the village council, Hanzha, a Red veteran, refuses to use repressions and is sentenced to three years in prison. His nephew, Volod'ka Tverdokhlib, now the chairman of the newly created collective farm, complies with using repressive measures. Feeling empowered by district backing, "Volod'ka suddenly felt that he wielded frightening power: he could run whoever he liked out of the village."[101] He gradually changes: first, he compiles a list of innocent people to deport to Siberia, then he facilitates the famine, and then starves his father-in-law to death. Hanzha's partner, Ol'ha, follows the orders as well. Although she laments her husband's fate, she testifies against him. However, Ol'ha and Tverdokhlib face different futures mainly because of gender. Put'ko condemns her initially active public position as outrageous and intends to punish Ol'ha: "This woman had raised her hand herself! Besides, she had been Hanzha's mistress. We won't let you forget that until the day you die, dearie! You'll remain forever under suspicion."[102]

Dimarov also explores the character of the compromised perpetrator, which he knew too well from his mother's experience, in the character of Tania, a village teacher. She disapproves of the policies, but she remains silent because she fears for herself and her children. Defined through her relation to men—her father was a priest, her husband and brother sent to Siberia—she is grateful not to be included in the brigade to dekulakize the peasants she rents a room from. She starves too. When a school warden makes a comment on children starving needlessly, Tania is silent with fear and will stay so for the rest of her life.

Through the character of Tania, Dimarov raises the question of the role of the modern state in the famine. First, it is the culture of fear in the vertical structure of the totalitarian state. When Ginzburg is waiting for the meeting with the district party secretary, he finds himself in the company of other district officials waiting in front of big black-leather doors. The material of these doors reminds Ginzburg of the black leather in the Chekist uniform, which add the authority to the higher Soviet officials. It was the bureaucracy of the state that made people like Tverdokhlib dangerous. He is similar to Eichmann in claims of his own ignorance: "Had he wanted people to die like this? Had he thought about this as he swept the grain out of the village? Sweeping it out to the last granule, just to fulfil that forthcoming plan."[103] He has neither killed anyone personally nor ordered anyone to be killed. He is not a psychopath, nor are his subordinates who confiscate grain from the families in order to save it from "being fed to your children," which makes them "terribly and terrifyingly normal."[104]

Another novel on the famine that was published abroad was Vasilii Grossman's *Forever Flowing* (1970).[105] The writer explores four types of perpetrator of Stalinist policies, including sadists, compromised ordinary people, followers, and ideological participants. Grossman includes a confession of the party plenipotentiary, Anna Stepanovna Mikhaliova, who was deployed in Ukraine to procure grain. Her confession provides a panoply of village perpetrators. She recalls how propaganda dehumanized peasants in her eyes, and how most participants were ordinary people—a fact that later terrifies her, which echoes the point made by Dimarov. Twenty-two years old at the time of the famine, she worked as a cleaner at the district party committee in Russia before she was sent to Ukraine, where "private property ruled the khokhol's head."[106] She reflects that most actors were "honest people," whereas profiteers or the people settling personal scores were few, yet their part in the famine is essentially the same. While other district officials use their participation to advance their career, Anna chooses to become a cook because she no longer can be part of the state machine implicit in mass murder. Now looking at her participation with disgust, she sees people she assisted in murdering. Like Jean-Paul Sartre's protagonist from *The Wall* (1939), she cannot live the life the way she did previously; her past haunts her like "shrapnel in the heart." Shortly after her confession, she dies of cancer.

Grossman did not take part in collectivization himself, but his depiction of the perpetrator is profoundly detailed and nuanced. In my interview with the author's daughter, Ekaterina Grossman revealed that the writer based the character of Anna Stepanovna on a real person, Pelageia Semenova. Originally from Likhoslavsk in Russia, Pelageia indeed was sent to Ukraine. It remains unknown whether Pelageia regretted her participation or what her motivations were. According to the family of the Soviet poet Nikolai Zabolotskii, for whom Pelageia worked as a maid after the famine, she was strongly suspected of informing secret services on Soviet writers and, at some point, Zabolotskii asked her to leave. Pelageia later received an apartment in central Moscow as a gift from the state and lived there till her death.

Ukrainian novels written in diaspora present a completely different take on perpetrators. *Maria: The Chronicle of One Life* (1934) by Ulas Samchuk and *The Yellow Prince* (1962) by Vasyl' Barka are recommended for reading in school curricula and thus contribute to the cultural memory of generations of Ukrainians who were educated after 1991. One of the few fictional films on the Holodomor, *Holod-33* (1991), was based on the novel *The Yellow Prince*. Perpetrators in these novels are depicted as the Other, in line with the vision of Ukrainian nationalist ideology on Russian aggression on Ukraine.[107]

The novel by Samchuk is a brief chronicle of a life of a Ukrainian peasant woman, Maria, which starts with her birth in the last quarter of 19th century and ends with her death in 1933. Her story points to the destructive influence of the outside world on Ukrainian peasantry that leads to the famine. Militarism and imperial power "transform a civilized peasant into an uncouth military man" who destroys the village, which is "a golden country" and "a country of labor and bread."[108]

Yevhen Onatskyi, in his foreword to the 1952 edition of *Maria*, speaks of local perpetrators who "drown in the waves of evil and corruption of Moscow flooding."[109] Thus, perpetration is associated with the Other, as one of the tortured characters exclaims: "Our country has not known such a Tatar-like plundering."[110] Even the guards in the fields are not locals but "the soldiers of great and bright future that came here from the distant north" or "the creatures with high cheekbones."[111] Samchuk's point of view springs from his long advocacy for the independence of Ukraine and his blame of Moscow for the famine, as seen in his publications in OUN periodicals.[112]

But the very life of the protagonist Maria belies the reality of an idyllic village prior to collectivization and the famine. Orphaned at the age of six and neglected by her relatives, Maria works from an extremely young age. She is illiterate, and, despite her hard work, she is in the lowest social stratum. Her first three children die of infectious diseases that regularly ravage the countryside. Maria's son Maksym displayed sadistic traits of torturing animals long before the famine. Thus, the village was a place of "labor and bread" and was as well habituated to violence, cruelty, and premature death.

Maksym, the quisling son of Maria, becomes the main perpetrator figure in the novel. His farming skills are poor and during the war he serves at the rear. He denounces his brother, disowns and evicts his own parents, and watches his sister and her infant starve to death. Some critics regard him as a fanatic because he defends the advantages of collective farming, advocates sexual emancipation, and shoots at icons. In the same time, Maksym shows clear traits of a profiteer: party work frees him from the manual work he detests and allows him to send his children to the city. But Maksym is brutally murdered by his father. To summarize, Maksym combines many features of the Holodomor perpetrator: a quisling, communist, profiteer, sadist, atheist, and Russian-speaking. Yet this character brings the agency back to the village precisely because he had displayed negative qualities prior to the famine and embraces the violence. Such a perpetrator challenges the writer's thesis that locals were "unconscious" accomplices that with "demagogical slogans push the village to its moral and physical ruin"—Maksym was fully aware of his actions.[113]

Ultimately, Samchuk points to the role of the modern state as the machinery of the famine. Millions of perpetrators follow the orders from the top: Komsomol members who are "strange, very strange young people" but also "monsters," "hyenas," and "children that sold their souls" who search houses, close down the church, and torture victims. These policies are supported in media with its poets, epics, and academics and are enforced by the party, the army, and the security service. His novel depicts village reporters who provided intelligence to the GPU, propaganda brigades, and "clever-eyed" shock workers and their brigade leaders.

Barka's novel *The Yellow Prince* (1962) also places the agency with the Other. In the foreword, the author names the perpetrators: the army, the security service, the police, and workers from Russia. Those who executed the orders on the ground had nothing humane left in them—they were "devilish thugs": they shoot children gleaning in the fields and take away the last porridge from a baby. In presenting the famine as a struggle between evil and good, the novel offers a nuanced approach in depicting the perpetrators. Otrokhodin, a party plenipotentiary, combines three types: a careerist, a sadist, and the Other (Russian). He also controls local perpetrators. He despises the peasantry and dreams of the benefits of a life in the capital. He imitates Stalin in his looks as well as in his methods of dealing with people in order to succeed and interprets ideology as it suits him. A fanatic type of perpetrator is touched upon briefly when protagonists hear about an activist suddenly dying, which the characters interpret as poetic justice.

When local Komsomol members close the church, they feel uneasy facing a congregation that they know well. The young men hide their eyes and reply with impatience. During one house search, an old woman approaches a fellow peasant guarding the discoveries in the cart. She pleads with him to leave food for her grandchildren. At first the man ignores the woman but then recalls the orders of superiors and knocks her down. She later dies. Likewise, collective farmworkers search the clothes of fellow farmers for grain after a day at work. The protagonist concludes that fellow villagers voting in favor of Soviet policies are no better than the officials confiscating grain. Barksa also describes city bureaucrats who enjoy their rations, make "speeches on building happiness," and blame the victims for the famine. The narrator voices his dismay: "not a single being has ever bathed in lies, like the Red party. . . . Whoever dared to disagree or appeal to conscience is savaged at once."[114] Barka sees many participants as compromised perpetrators coerced into violence by fear.

Barka also depicts perpetrators who try to help the victims. One head of the collective farm advises artisans to flee the village and fears a tragic end for himself. Like Dimarov, Barka includes the suicide of a secretary of the district party committee after receiving the orders from Moscow to procure more grain. The victims comment on this person being honest in his own way when others conform to party expectations. Despite various types of perpetrators and their motives, Moscow reappears throughout the novel as the major perpetrator—the Yellow Prince.

The post-Soviet novels, written by postmemory writers, present an amalgamation of archival research and witness accounts in a format established by the writer in diaspora. For instance, *Chorna doshka* (The black board, 2014) is the story of a perpetrator-turned-victim Oles' Ternovyi in a small village of Veselivka. His diary is rediscovered by his great-grandson Sashko, who suffers from nightmares about the Holodomor. The shared name (Sashko and Oles' are nicknames for Olexander) stresses the transgenerational connection between the famine and today. The narrator explains that, from 1932 on, expropriations were done by people sent to the village from all parts of the Soviet Union, but the victims in the novel comment on their being local: "People are ours, yet something changed them in such a way."[115] All perpetrators in the novel face poetic justice: insanity, repressions, violent death, or suicide.

Doliak starts with ideological participants: Oles' and other reporters of the district newspaper and Palamarchuk, head of the local village council. They both participate in grain procurement but soon become disillusioned and are repressed: Palamarchuk is murdered during the interrogation and Oles' is denied his food rations. There is a group of compromised perpetrators: the young local people who perform the searches and inform on and disown their families: "scooped children up and stuffed their brains with tales. . . . When you take each of them separately, there is nothing wrong with them, boys like boys."[116] The second type of perpetrator is the sadistic GPU agent Kaliuzhnyi. He hates peasants and tortures them. He is joined by other agents (a Jew, Mark Milman, and a Russian, Vesna) and local officials: a chairman of the collective farm, the KNS head, and a Russian plenipotentiary. One of Doliak's characters is a drunk sociopath Hrishka—another Russian, stressing the non-Ukrainian ethnicity of most perpetrators through language. Most of them wear black leather jackets and the victims referred to them as "black-skins." Perpetrators wearing black leather jackets is an additional tool to make the violence "psychologically palatable to perpetrators and observers alike."[117]

Although in the Soviet prose on collectivization Jews are participants like any others, post-Soviet prose is abundant with Jews as chief perpetrators on the ground. Doliak's Mark Milman has "Asian cheek bones" and murders children in front of their parents. On one occasion, he accuses one peasant of antisemitism and tortures him to death; on another occasion, he throws two women into an enclosure with a bull. This reading of the Chekist is not new. In 1923, Vynnychenko described a typical Chekist as a Jew coming from a traditional milieu of a small town. Jewish petty bourgeoisie and intelligentsia joined the party ranks or the army in their struggle to survive during the postrevolutionary period. He traced the fury of the unflinching Jewish Chekist to his experience of suffering. Participation in grain requisition in the early 1920s contributed to establishing the link between Jews and communists in popular perception in the village.[118] The proportion of Jews within the party and the Cheka and its successors was indeed disproportionate to their proportion in the general population in the 1920s, but the number of Ukrainians in Soviet state machine increased consistently from the late 1920s.[119] Constituting about a third of the Communist Party (Bolshevik) of Ukraine and being involved in less-than-popular enforcement policies might explain the impression that Jews were behind collectivization and the famine.

Finally, Leonid Kononovych gives a look at the perpetrators after the famine in his novel *Tema dlia medytatsii* (A theme for meditation, 2004).[120] Because the survivors and the perpetrators continued to live in the same village, the past events shaped their lives. In the novel, Yur investigates the murder of his grandfather by the activists during the famine. Yur learns of their identities gradually as his grandmother constructs his post-memory of the Holodomor: she calls the activists not good people and parasites who destroyed their family. He tracks down the surviving activists and realizes that the underlying problem is the communist regime itself, as activists all were born in the same small thatched huts as the victims but chose to become perpetrators. Again, much as in Doliak's work, most perpetrators in Kononovych's novel die prematurely, commit suicide, become ill, or are avenged.

First, there is a group of sadists, all of them women—Dziakunka, Bovkunykha, Chykyldykha, and Stepa. They enjoy conducting house searches, and torturing and killing. Stepa burned victims' heels, gouged eyes out, and stabbed people. Yur explains their participation as poor mental health and concludes that aberrant behavior became the new norm. He further explains that young, beautiful women were the cruelest of all because they "refused to fulfil traditional female role of housekeeping and childbirth and became the activists instead." This explanation is not new—violent women are often portrayed in the media and literature as abnormal, insane maniacs who are often more cruel than their male counterparts. Their image in popular culture is reduced to "mothers, monsters or whores."[121] They either deny their womanhood or abuse their sexuality. Female participation in mass violence during the famine did not fit the worldview of the traditional rural community, which celebrated nurturing, virtuous, and restrained women. Yet ordinary women commit horrendous crimes and physically abuse and kill their victims for the same reasons as men.[122]

Second, perpetrators include the existing village establishment—teachers, officials, various collective farmworkers. One of them, Bahriy, who was in charge of local brigades, became the headmaster of the village school after the famine. He sees no sense in establishing higher moral ground. Bahriy killed at least three people on his own initiative in 1933, but he justifies it by the general violence at the time. One of the activists, Stoian, is a profiteer whose family benefited from loyal service to the regime for generations. Yur sees the culture of perpetration entrenched in the state machine, and with a silent acceptance of many, his country remains the hostage of its gruesome past.

Concluding Remarks

The typology of the Holodomor perpetrators on the ground could be developed further, but even its initial application reveals how significant an inclusive approach is for understanding the famine's mechanism. With the availability of archival material and corpuses of oral memories, more analysis of the rank-and-file perpetrators has become possible. Which, in turn, invites approaches developed in the study of collective violence and genocides. Cultural memory, as an explorative overview of the Ukrainian prose demonstrates, provides only a glimpse into perpetrators' experience. In most cases, the novels skim over hundreds of thousands collective farmers, informers, field guards, and teachers or leave them as voiceless and nameless participants. Seeing them as trained professionals, profiteers, careerists, fanatics, sadists or criminals, followers, and compromised perpetrators helps to explain and go beyond the cliché of "activist," "Other," or abnormal type. A nuanced typology also allows us to avoid the moralistic approach that many Ukrainian writers employ, which results in a dichotomous depiction whose poles change sides after the collapse of the Soviet Union.

The militant Bolshevik writing of 1928–33 focuses on a war in the countryside that, like most wars, demands action, results in victims, and proceeds from soldiers following orders. War is the dominant metaphor, and the village is a backward place. Traditionalist ways need to be upturned like the soil in the boundaries between the fields of individual farmers. The perpetrator is gendered, and the female perpetrators show qualities previously reserved for men: bravery, strength, and emotional detachment. The writing identifies the perpetrators on the village and district level and describes the conditions of the villagers' work. Most perpetrators are locals, though the crucial role of outsiders also has a hand. The masses are characterized as indifferent, though they eventually followed orders.

In contrast to Bolshevist writers, the *samvydav* and *tamvydav* novels offer a nuanced picture of men and women on the ground. Writers like Grossman provide detailed portraits of the perpetrators as part of the tragedy that enveloped Ukrainian villages at the time. Likewise, Dimarov reaches beyond the Other in his analysis of the perpetrators: both he and Grossman describe how participants make their choice and later realize the impact of their experience. The writers also touch on the role of the modern state in the Holodomor—countless perpetrators physically removed from their victims at their office desks or undertaking detailed tasks unrelated to the actual murder. Nonetheless, they all are links in the same chain that leads to the famine. To sum up, the rank-and-file perpetrators are ordinary people in extraordinary circumstances and, as these writers assert, this fact makes the events even more tragic.

Similarly, the writers who worked in the Ukrainian diaspora emphasized the Other among the perpetrators on the ground. Even if they were locals, they were men and women known for their deviant behavior: sadists, profiteers, criminals, the idle, and the drunks. The outsiders speak Russian or look Asian or come from the city. The scenes of house searches echo the survivor testimonies when the last food left for the children is destroyed and infants are thrown out of their cradles. The ideological participants soon are disillusioned and vanish, and local collaborators receive poetic justice. Most likely, this emphasis on the Other results from the dedication of the authors like Samchuk to the cause of Ukrainian nationalism and the narrative of victimhood.

Placing the agency with the Other and even resurrecting the literary figure of the Jewish commissar can be found in many post-Soviet Ukrainian novels. Oral memory describes brigades as drawn from locals with district officials only coordinating their searches, but writers like Doliak emphasize the presence of Russian-speaking officials and servicemen during the searches and tortures. Along a similar vein, female perpetrators are portrayed in post-Soviet prose as the women who abuse their sexuality, defy their biological role of mother, and engage in unnatural activities. Although Soviet writers point to the fact that the victims and the perpetrators were habituated to the violence stemming from the postrevolutionary years, postmemory writers stress that the victims are impressed by the cruelty of the local perpetrators. Finally, post-Soviet writers insist on poetic justice for the perpetrators, which is not attested beyond anecdotal evidence. Consistent with the genre, the novel on historical events is an interpretation of the author. Some writers offer prosopographical readings of the perpetrators, while others provide vignettes of groups such as profiteers, compromised ordinary people, professionals, followers, fanatics, and sadists. It is generally accepted that most perpetrators of mass violence are ordinary people with rather banal motives but, in most post-Soviet literature, the rank-and-file perpetrators of the Holodomor remain marginal elements in the village community. Most Ukrainian writers continue to grapple with the traumatic past and the sensitive issue of local perpetration, which suggests that cultural memory of the perpetrators might change in time should scholarship on the subject develop further.

Notes

1. Vasyl'iev et al., *Partiino-radians'ke kerivnytstvo Ukrains'koi SSR*; Vasyl'iev and Viola, *Kolektyvizatsiia i selianskyi opir*; Drovozyuk, "Sotsialno-psychologichny portret"; "Povedinka sil's'lykh aktyvistiv"; Lysenko, "Typologiia povedinky"; "Informatsiyno-analitychni dokumenty"; Demchenko, "Svidchennia pro Holodomor."
2. Smeulers, "Female Perpetrators," 207–53.
3. Smeulers, "Perpetrators of International Crimes," 233–65.
4. Council of Europe, Resolution 1723, 2010, accessed March 1, 2015, http://assembly.coe.int/main.asp?Link=/documents/adoptedtext/ta10/eres1723.htm.
5. S. Maksudov, "Victory over the Peasantry," *Harvard Ukrainian Studies*, vol. 25, no. 3/4 (2001): 188–189. This view on legislative framework of the famine is also shared by Yurii Shapoval, H. Papakin, S. Kulchytskyi, A. Graziosi, G. Yefimenko, L. Hrynevych, and others.
6. In 1932–1933, around 50 percent of the peasants in Ukraine did not have any livestock, compared to 12 percent in 1931. See *Narodne hospodarstvo USRR*, 252.
7. Rudych and Pyrih, *Holod 1932–1933 rokiv na Ukraini*, 250–54, 278–79, 296–99.
8. Moshkov, *Zernovaia problema v gody sploshnoi kollektivizatsii sel'skogo khoziaistva SSSR (1929–932 gg.)*.
9. Milgram, *Obedience to Authority*.
10. Milgram, *Obedience to Authority*.
11. Bilousko et al., *Natsional'na knyha*, 1036.
12. Smeulers, "Perpetrators of International Crimes," 233–65.
13. US Congressional-Presidential Commission on the Ukraine Famine, 1990; *Holod-33*; Oral History Program at Prairie Centre for the Study of Ukrainian Heritage (1992–1993); *Ukrainskyi Holocaust 1932–1933*; *Natsional'na knyha*; *Share the Story*.
14. Felman and Laub, *Testimony*; Schmidt, "Perpetrators' Knowledge," 97.
15. Schmidt, "Perpetrators' Knowledge," 98.
16. Gerlach, "Eichmann Interrogations," 429, 434, 442.
17. Browning, "Perpetrator Testimony," 11–12.
18. Browning, "Perpetrator Testimony," 9.
19. Shupyk, Bilan, and Osheka, *Doroha do domu*, 46.
20. Trifonov, *Ocherki istorii klassovoi bor'by*, 255.

21. Bilousko et al., *Natsional'na knyha*, 916–1088.
22. Bilousko et al., *Natsional'na knyha*, 1060.
23. Bilousko et al., *Natsional'na knyha*, 1082.
24. Bilousko et al., *Natsional'na knyha*, 922.
25. Interview with Nina Chervatiuk in Toporyshche, May, 8, 2014.
26. Bilousko et al., *Natsional'na knyha*, 963.
27. Bilousko et al., *Natsional'na knyha*, 1044, 1188.
28. Bilousko et al., *Natsional'na knyha*, 1091.
29. Browning, *Ordinary Men*, 62.
30. Tylishchak and Yaremenko, *Liudianist' u neliudianyi chas*, 111.
31. Lavryk et al., *Natsional'na knyha*, 176.
32. Mace, "The Komitety Nezamozhnykh Selian," 487–503.
33. Levandovs'ka, "Role of Committees," 122.
34. Mace, "The Komitety Nezamozhnykh Selian."
35. Levandovs'ka, "Role of Committees," 414.
36. O. Fesenko in *Visti VUTsVK* on May 9, 1930, p. 5, as quoted in Mace, *Komitety nezamozhnykh selyan*, 497.
37. Zahorskyi and Stoyan, *Komitety nezalezhnykh selyan Ukrainy*, 393.
38. Zahorskyi and Stoyan, *Narysy istorii komitetiv nezamozhnykh selian*, 130.
39. Bilousko et al., *Natsional'na knyha*, 935, 940, 1011, 1019, 1087, 1174.
40. Bilousko et al., *Natsional'na knyha*, 940.
41. Berezovchuk, *Komnezamy Ukraiiny*.
42. Voloshenko and Bilokon, "Zhinky u lavakh KNS," 63–67.
43. TsDAHOU, fond 1, opys 20, sprava 2126, 128–29.
44. Levandovs'ka, "Role of Committees," 120; Zahorskyi and Stoyan, *Komitety nezalezhnykh selyan Ukrainy*, 26.
45. Voloshenko and Bilokon, "Zhinky u lavakh KNS," 63–67.
46. Shmerling, *Maria Demchenko*.
47. Shmerling, *Maria Demchenko*, 48.
48. Prykordonnyi, "Chelovek bogatii sovest'iu," 16.
49. Zahlada, "Dorozhite chestiu khleboroba," 1.
50. TsDAHOU, fond 1, opys 20, sprava 3099, 5.
51. Efimenko, *Sotsial'ne oblychchia vchytel'stva USRR*.
52. TsDAHOU, fond 1, opys 20, sprava 3099, ark. 2–3.
53. TsDAHOU, fond 1, opys 20, sprava 3099, ark. 9.
54. Bilousko et al., *Natsional'na knyha*, 1081.
55. Hai, *Natsional'na knyha pam'iati*, 115.
56. TsDAHOU, fond 1, opys 20, sprava 3107, ark. 27.
57. Viola and Vasil'ev, *Kollektivizatsia i krest'ianskoe soprotivlenie na Ukraine*, 229.
58. The data is drawn from the okruhy of Volyn', Lubny, Luhans'k, Mariulop', Melitopol', Mykolaiiv', Nizhyn, Pervomais'k, Pryluky, Poltava, Proskuriv, Odessa. TsDAHOU, f. 1, op. 20, spr. 3470, ark. 26 and TsDAHOU, f. 1, op. 20, spr. 3493, ark. 1-132.
59. TsDAHOU, f. 1, op. 20, spr. 3470, ark. 26 and TsDAHOU, f. 1, op. 20, spr. 3493, ark. 1-132.
60. TsDAHOU, f. 1, op. 20, spr. 3470, ark. 26 and TsDAHOU, f. 1, op. 20, spr. 3493, ark. 1-132.
61. UCRDC, Katalog Spogaviv, no. 99, Oleksii Konoval, p. 3.
62. Hrynevych, *Chronicle of Collectivization*, vol. 1, bk. 1, June 1928, 329.
63. Russian State Archive of Social and Political History, Moscow (hereafter cited as RGASPI), fond 81, opis 3, delo. 232, list 53.
64. Maksudov and Olynyk, "'Dehumanization,'" 144.
65. Snyder, *Bloodlands*, 47. A large amount of materials on abuse of peasants and collective farmworkers by officials, plenipotentiaries, and activists during collectivization, grain procurement, and other campaigns in 1931–33 is available at TsDAHOU. Most examples are in fond 1, opys 20 (spravy 2829, 3145, 3219, 3684, 4618, 4657, 4825, 5256, 5384, 5489, 5819, among many others).
66. RGASPI, f. 81, op. 3, delo. 215, list 11.
67. Borysenko, ed., *Rozsekrechena pam'iat*, 428–29.
68. RGASPI, f. 81, op. 3, delo. 215, list. 11.

69. HDA SBU, f. 16, op. 25 (1951), spr. 3, ark. 198.
70. HDA SBU, f. 16, op. 25 (1951), spr. 3, ark. 200.
71. Kopelev, *I sotvoril sebe kumira*, 245.
72. Stepan S. *Autobiography*, from Stepan S.'s family archive, unpublished manuscript (1953).
73. 1932–1933—Volodars'kyi raion. Storinkamy holodu (Novohrad-Volyns'kyi: NOVOhrad, 2008), 48.
74. Kopiichenko et al., *Natsional'na Knyga Pam'iati*, 352.
75. Khamidov, *Odnopolchane*, 61–124.
76. Bilousko'ko et al., *Natsional'na knyha*, 1075.
77. Haman et al., *Natsional'na nyha*, 798.
78. Bem, "Politychni nastroi ukrains'koho selianstva v umovakh kolektyvizatsii sil's'koho hospodarstva (Istoriohrafichnyi ohliad)."
79. TsDAHOU, fond 1, opys 20, sprava 3144, ark. 123–29.
80. Bilousko et al., *Natsional'na knyha*, 984.
81. P. Postyshev, *Itogi 1933 sel'skokhoziaistvennogo goda i ocherednyie zadazhi KP(b)U. Rech na ob'iedinennom plenume TsK i TsKK KP(b)U 19 noiabria 1933 goda* (Khar'kov: Partizdat TsK KP(b)U, 1933), 17.
82. OSOAviaKhim [Society of Assistance to Defense and Aviation-Chemical Construction] was a militarized organization founded in 1927 by an amalgamation of several volunteer societies that sought to develop defense knowledge and skills in Soviet society. Its members were as young as fourteen. Among its alumni were cosmonauts Valentina Tereshkova and Yuri Gagarin, rocket engineer Sergei Korolev, and partisan heroine Zoia Kosmodemianskaia.
83. TsDAHOU, fond 1, opys 20, sprava 6333, ark. 162.
84. TsDAHOU, fond 1, opys 20, sprava 6395, ark. 96–98.
85. Shapoval, "Povelitelnaia neobkhodimost."
86. Liubchebko, "Kostryha"; Kyrylenko, *Avanposty*; Stel'mach, *Chotyry Brody*.
87. Assmann and Czaplicka, "Collective Memory."
88. Liubchenko, *Yoho tayemnytsia*.
89. Liubchenko, *Zbirka ukrains'kykh novel*, 151.
90. Kyrylenko, *Avanposty*, 42.
91. Kopelev, *I sotvoril sebe kumira*, 248.
92. Kyrylenko, *Avanposty*, 57.
93. Kyrylenko, *Avanposty*, 11.
94. Kravchenko, *I Chose Freedom*, 131.
95. Grigorenko, *Memoirs*, 109.
96. Kyrylenko, "Avanposty," 6.
97. Dimarov, *Prozhyty i rozpovisty*, 181.
98. Dimarov, *Prozhyty i rozpovisty*, 37.
99. Dimarov, *In Stalin's Shadows*, 132.
100. Maksudov and Olynyk, "Dehumanization," 144.
101. Dimarov, *In Stalin's Shadows*, 132.
102. Dimarov, *In Stalin's Shadows*, 137.
103. Dimarov, *In Stalin's Shadows*, 157.
104. Arendt, *Eichmann in Jerusalem*, 276.
105. Grossman, *Forever Flowing*.
106. Grossman, *Forever Flowing*, 149.
107. Shkandrij, *Ukrainian Nationalism*, 232.
108. Samchuk, *Maria*, 73.
109. Samchuk, *Maria*, 12.
110. Samchuk, *Maria*, 147.
111. Samchuk, *Maria*, 187.
112. Shkandrij, *Ukrainian Nationalism*, 227.
113. Samchuk, *Maria*, 15.
114. Barka, *Zhovtyi kniaz*, 163.
115. Doliak, *Chorna doshka*, 136.
116. Doliak, *Chorna doshka*, 145.

117. Shkandrij, *Jews in Ukrainian literature*, 149.
118. Vynnychenko, "Do ievreis'koho pytannia na Ukraini."
119. Schapiro, *Russian Studies*, 286; Shkandrij, *Jews in Ukrainian literature*, 141.
120. Kononovych, *Tema*.
121. Sjoberg and Gentry, *Mothers*, 98.
122. Smeulers, "'Female Perpetrators," 207.

Bibliography

Arendt, Hannah. *Eichmann in Jerusalem: A Report on the Banality of Evil*. New York: Penguin Books, 1964.
Assmann, Jan, and John Czaplicka. "Collective Memory and Cultural Identity." *New German Critique* 65 (1995): 125–33.
Barka, Vasyl. *Zhovtyi kniaz*. Kyiv: Naukova Dumka, 2008.
Bem, Natalia. *Politychni nastroi ukrains'koho selianstva v umovakh sutsilnoii kolektyvizatsii sil'skoho hospodarstva (kinets' 1920-kh–1933 rr.)*. Dis. kand. ist. nauk/N. Bem PhD diss., National Academy of Sciences, Kyiv, 2004.
Berezovchuk, Mykola. *Komnezamy Ukraiiny v borot'bi za sotsialism*. Kyiv, 1965.
Bilousko, Oleksandr, Yu. Varchenko, V. Mokliak, and T. Pustovit, eds. *Natsionalna Knyha pam"iati zhertv Holodomoru 1932–1933 rr. v Ukraini. Poltavska oblast* (Poltava, Ukraine: Oriiana, 2008).
Browning, Christopher. R. *Ordinary Men: Reserve Police Battalion 101 and the Final Solution in Poland*. New York: Aaron Asher Books, 1992.
———. "Perpetrator Testimony: Another Look on Adolph Eichmann." In *Collected Memories: Holocaust History and Postwar Testimony*. Madison: University of Wisconsin Press, 2004.
Demchenko, Tamara. "Svidchennia pro Holodomor iak dzherelo vyvchennia fenomenu stalins'kykh aktyvistiv." *Problemy istorii Ukrainy* 2, no. 19 (2010).
Dimarov, Anatolii, *In Stalin's Shadows*. Melbourne: Bayda Books, 1989.
———. *Prozhyty i rozpovisty: Povist pro simdesiat lit*. Kyiv: Dnipro, 1997–1998.
Doliak, Natalia. *Chorna Ddoshka*. Kharkiv, Ukraine: Klub simeinoho dozvillia, 2014.
Drovozyuk, Stepan. "Sotsialno-psykholohichnyi portret sil's'koho 'aktyvista' 20–30 rr v Ukrains'kii historiohrafii." *Problemy istorii Ukrainy* 9 (2003): 360–72.
Dukyn, Mykola. *Voseny* [In autumn]. Kharkiv, 1933.
Efimenko, Hennadiy, *Sotsialne oblychchia vchytel'stva USRR v konteksti transformatsii suspilstva (1920-ti roky)*. Kyiv, 2007.
Felman, Shoshana, and Dori Laub, *Testimony: Crises of Witnessing in Literature, Psychoanalysis and History*. New York: Routledge, 1992.
Gerlach, Christian. "The Eichmann Interrogations in Holocaust Historiography." *Holocaust and Genocide Studies* 15, no. 3 (Winter 2001): 428–52.
Goychenko, Dmytro. *Krasniy aApokalipsis*. Kyiv: Ababagalamaga, 2014.
Graziosi, Andrea, ed. *After the Holodomor. : The Enduring Impact of the Great Famine on Ukraine*. Cambridge, MA: Harvard University Press, 2013.
Grigorenko, Petro. *Memoirs*. London: Harvill Press, 1983.
Grossman, Vasiliy. *Forever Flowing*. New York: Harper and Row, 1972.
Hai, Anatoliy, ed. *Natsional'na knyha pam"iati zhertv Holodomoru 1932–1933 rr. v Ukraini: Kyivs'ka oblast*. Kyiv, 2008.
Haman, Petro, et al. *Natsional'na knyha pam"iati zhertv Holodomoru 1932–1933 rr. v Ukraini.: Cherkas'ka oblast*. Cherkasy, Ukraine: Vydavnytstvo Yu. Chabanenko, 2008.
Hilberg, Raul. *Perpetrators, Victims, Bystanders: The Jewish Catastrophe*. New York: Harper Perennial, 1992.
Holod 1932–1933 rokiv na Ukraini: Ochyma istorykiv, movoiu dokumentiv. Kyiv, 1990.
Holodomor 1932–1933 rokiv v Ukraini. Dokumenty i materialy. Kyiv, 2002.
Holod-33: Narodna knyha-memorial [Hunger-33: Peoples Book Memorial]. 1991.
Hrynevych, Liudmyla, ed. *Chronicle of Collectivization and the Holodomor in Ukraine*, vol. 1, bks. 1–3. Kyiv: Krytyka, 2012.

"Informatsiyno-analitychni dokumenty organiv DPU USRR iak dzherelo vyvchennia dial'nosti sil's'kykh aktyvistiv v umovakh sutsil'noii kolektyvizatsii (kinets' 1920-kh–pochatok 1930-kh rr)." *Z arkhiviv VUChK-GPU-NKVD-KGB* 1, no. 34 (2010): 336–57.

Khamidov, Kh. *Odnopolchane* (Tashkent, Uzbekistan, 1981).

Kononovych, Leonid. *Tema dlia medytatsii*. L'viv: Kalvaria, 2004.

Kopelev, Lev. *I sotvoril sebe kumira*. Ann Arbor, MI: Ardis, 1978.

Kravchenko, Victor. *I Chose Freedom: The Personal and Political Life of a Soviet Official*. London: Robert Hale Limited, 1947, 91–131.

Kul'chyts'ky, Stanislav. *Holodomor 1932–1933 yak gGenotsyd: Trudnoshchi usvidomlennia*. Kyiv: Nash Chas, 2008.

Kyrylenko, Ivan. *Avanposty*. Kharkiv, Ukraine: Khudozhnia Literatura, 1935.

———. "Avanposty," *Molodniak: Molodyi Bil'shovyk* no. 3 (1933): 6.

Lavryk, Oleksandr et al. *Natsional'na knyha pam"iati zhertv Holodomoru 1932–1933 rr. v Ukraini: Sums'ka oblast*. Sumy, Ukraine: Sobor, 2008.

Le, Ivan. *Istoriia Radosti* [History of happiness] Kharkiv, 1934.

Levandovs'ka, Elina. "The Role of Committees of Poor Peasants in Realization of the Soviet Policy in Ukrainian Village." Zaporizhia, Ukraine: Naukovi pratsi istorychnnoho fakul'tetu Zaporiz'koho natsional'noho universytetu, 2013, no. 37.

Liubchenko, Arkadiy. *Yoho Tayemnytsia* [His secret]. Paris: Vil'na Dumka, 1966.

———. "Kostryha" *Zbirka ukrains'kykh novel*. New York: Taras Shevchenko Scientific Society in America, 1955.

Lysenko, Olena. "Typologiia povedynky sil's'kykh aktyvistiv u konteksti zdiysnennia sutsil'noii kolektyvizatsii sil's'koho hospodarstva v Ukraini (pochatok 1930-kh rr)." *Istoriia Ukrainy* 36 (2010): 189–203.

Mace, James. "The Komitety Nezamozhnykh Selian and the Structure of Soviet Rule in the Ukrainian Countryside, 1920–1933," *Soviet Studies* 35, no. 4 (October 1983), 487–503.

Mahryts'ka, Iryna, ed. *Vriatovana pam"iat. : Holodomor 1932–1933 rr. na Luhanshchyni. Svidchennia ochevydtsiv*. Luhans'k, Ukraine: Promdruk, 2008.

Maksudov, Sergey. "Victory over the Peasantry." *Harvard Ukrainian Studies* 25, nos. 3–4 (2001): 188–89.

Maksudov, Sergey, and Marta. D. Olynyk., "Dehumanization: The Change in the Moral and Ethical Consciousness of Soviet Citizens as a Result of Collectivization and Famine." *Harvard Ukrainian Studies* 30, nos. 1–4 (2008).

Milgram, Stanley. *Obedience to Authority*. London: Pinter and Martin, 2010.

Moshkov, Yuriy. *Zernovaia problema v gody sploshnoi kollektivizatsii sel'skogo khoziaistva SSSR (1929–1932 gg.)*. Moscow, 1966.

Narodne hospodarstvo USRR. Kyiv, 1935.

Natsional'na knyha pam"iati zhertv Holodomoru 1932–1933 rokiv v Ukraini. Zhytomyrs'ka oblast. Zhytomyr, Ukraine: Polissya, 2008, 350–52.

1932–1933—Volodars'kyi raion: storinkamy holodu. Novohrad-Volynskyi, Ukraine: NOVOhrad, 2008.

Noll, William. *Transformatsiia hromadians'koho suspil'stva. Usna istoria ukrains'koi selianskoi kultury 1920–1930 rokiv*. Kyiv: Rodovid, 1999.

Postyshev, Pavel. *Itogi 1933 selskokhoziaistvennogo goda i ocherednie zadazhi KP(b)U: Rech na obiedinennom plenume TsK I TsKK KP(b)U 19 niabria 1933 goda*. Kharkov, Ukraine: Partizdat TsK KP(b)U, 1933.

"Povedinka sil's'lykh aktyvistiv pid chas sutsil'noii kolektyvizatsii ta holodomoru ukrains'koho narodu (1932–1933 rr)." *Istoriia Ukrainy* 34 (2007): 67–79.

Prykordonnyi, D. "Chelovek bogatii sovest'iu," *Ogoniok* no. 44 (1962): 16.

Rudych, Feliks, and Ruslan Pyrih, eds. *Holod 1932–1933 rokiv na Ukraiini: Ochyma istorykiv, movoiu dokumentiv*. Kyiv: Vyd-vo politychnoii literatury Ukraiiny, 1990.

Samchuk, Ulas. *Maria: khronika odnoho zhyttia*. Kyiv: Radianskyi Pysmennyk, 2008.

Schapiro, Leonard. *Russian Studies*. New York: Viking, 1988.

Schmidt, Sibylle. "Perpetrators' Knowledge: What and How Can We Learn from Perpetrator Testimony?" *Journal of Perpetrator Research* 1, no. 1 (2017): 85–104.

Shapoval, Yurii, ed. *The Famine-Genocide of 1932–1933 in Ukraine*. Toronto: Kashtan Press for the Ukrainian Canadian Civil Liberties Association, 2005.

———. "Povelitelnaia neobkhodimost: god 1932." *Den*, November 23, 2002. https://day.kyiv.ua/ru/article/panorama-dnya/povelitelnaya-neobhodimost-god-1933-y.

———. *Ukraina 20-50-kh rokiv: storinky nenapysanoi istorii*. Kyiv: Naukova Dumka, 1993.
Shkandrij, Myroslav. *Jews in Ukrainian literature: representation and identity*. New Haven, CT: Yale University Press, 2009.
———. *Ukrainian Nationalism: Politics, Ideology, and Literature, 1929–1956*. London: Yale University Press, 2015.
Shmerling, Vladimir. *Maria Demchenko*. Moscow: Molodaia Gvardiia, 1936.
Shupyk, Dmytro, Stepan Bilan, and Vasyl Osheka. *Doroha do domu (Isoria sela Popivky Myrhorods'koho raionu Poltavs'koii oblasti)*. Poltava, Ukraine: 2013.
Sjoberg, Laura, and Caron Gentry. *Mothers, Monsters, Whores—Women's Violence in Global Politics*. London: Zed Books, 2007.
Smeulers, Alette, "Female Perpetrators—Ordinary and Extra-ordinary Women." *International Criminal Law Review* no. 2 (2015): 207–53.
———. "Perpetrators of International Crimes: Towards a Typology." In *Supranational Criminology: Towards a Typology of International Crimes*, edited by Alette Smeulers and Roelof Haveman, 233–65. Antwerpen: Intersentia, 2008.
Snyder, Timothy. *Bloodlands: Europe between Hitler and Stalin*. London: Bodley Head, 2010.
Stel'makh, Mychailo. *Chotyry Brody* [Four fords]. Kyiv: Ukraiins'kyi Pys'mennyk, 2003.
Stepan S. *Autobiography*, 1953. Toporyshche, Ukraine: unpublished manuscript, 1953. Shared with the author by Stepan S.'s family along with the photographs from the family archive in 2015. In possession of the author.
Tragediia sovetskoy derevni. Kollektivizatsiia i raskulachivanie. Dokumenty i materialy 1927–1939: v 5 t. Vol. 2. Moscow, 2000, vol. 2, 791.
Trifonov, Ivan. *Ocherki istorii klassovoi bor'by v SSSR, 1921–1937*. Moscow, 1960.
TsDAHOU [Tsentralnyi Derzhavnyi Arkhiv Hromadskykh Orhanizatsii; Central National Archive of Public Organizations]. fond 1, opys 20, sprava 2126.
Tylishchak, Volodymyr, and Victoria Yaremenko, eds. *Liudianist' u neliudianyi chas*. L'viv: Chasopys, 2013.
Ukrainian Canadian Congress and Ukrainian World Congress. *Share the Story* (online collection). Ukrainian Canadian Congress and Ukrainian World Congress, 2008.
Ukrainskyi Holocaust 1932–1933: Svidchennia tykh khto vyzhyv [Ukrainian holocaust 1932–1933: testimonies of those who survived], 2005–14.
Vasyl'iev, Valeriy, Nicolas Werth, and Serhii Kokin. *Partiino-radians'ke kerivnytstvo Ukrains'koi SSR pid chas Holodomoru 1932–1933: Vozhdi: Pratsivnyky: Aktyvisty: Zbirnyk dokumentiv ta materialiv, uporiad*. Kyiv: Instytut istorii Ukraiiny, 2013.
Vasyl'iev, Valeriy, and Lynne Viola. *Kolektyvizatsiia i selians'kyi opir na Ukraini (lystopad 1929–mart 1930)*. Vinnytsia, Ukraine: Logos, 1997.
Viola, Lynne. *The Best Sons of the Fatherland: Workers in the Vanguard of Soviet Collectivization*. New York–Oxford: Oxford University Press, 1987, 120.
———. *Kolektyvizatsiia i selianskyi opir na Ukraiini (lystopad 1929–mart 1930)*. Vinnytsia, Ukraine: Logos, 1997.
Viola, Lynne, Victor Danilov, Nikolai Ivnitskii, and Denis Kozlov, eds. *The War against the Peasantry, 1927–1930: The Tragedy of the Soviet Countryside*. New Haven, CT: Yale University Press, 2005.
Viola, Lynne, and V. Vasil'ev, eds., *Kollektyvizatsia i krest'ianskoe soprotivlenie na Ukraine* (Vinnytsia, 1997).
Voloshenko, V., and G. Bilokon, "Zhinky u lavakh KNS: shtrykhy do sotsial'noho portretu," *Materiały VII Międzynarodowej naukowipraktycznej konferecji „Naukowa myśl informacyjnej powieki-2011."* Vol. 9, 63–67. Prawo. Historia: Przemyśl. Nauka i studia.
Vynnychenko, V. "Do ievrcis'koho pytannia na Ukraini." *Khronika* no. 21–22 (2000): 159.
Zahlada, Nadiia. "Dorozhite chestiu khleboroba! Govorit Nadezhda Grigorievna Zaglada," *Pravda*, no. 237, August 25, 1962.
Zahorskyi, Pavlo, and Pylyp Stoyan. *Komitety nezalezhnykh selyan Ukrainy (1920–1930): Zbirnyk dokumentiv i materialiv*. Kyiv, 1968.
———. *Narysy istorii komitetiv nezamozhnykh selian*. Kharkiv, Ukraine: Vydavnytsvo AN URSR, 1960.

DARIA MATTINGLY is a Leverhulme Early Career Fellow at University of Cambridge where she also teaches on Soviet history. Her current book project focuses on Jews in the Holodomor.

2

THE *LIEUX DE MÉMOIRE* OF THE HOLODOMOR IN THE CULTURAL LANDSCAPE OF MODERN UKRAINE

Wiktoria Kudela-Świątek

IN THE LAST FEW DECADES, WE HAVE BEEN witness to the creation of a memory event, the Great Famine of 1932–33, in Ukrainian historiography and the public sphere. It has evolved from a marginal event against the backdrop of collectivization of agriculture in the Soviet Union to an event that was crucial to the formation of the contemporary Ukrainian nation.

The Great Famine (Holodomor, Great Famine of 1932–33) refers to a famine in the years 1932–33 in the Soviet Union, which had particularly intense effects on the territory of the former Ukrainian Soviet Republic (now Eastern and Central Ukraine).[1] The Holodomor was the consequence of the collectivization of agriculture, which had been forced upon the people by the management of the Communist Party and the Soviet Union's government, and the strict enforcement of obligatory levies of produce that were imposed on the peasants by the authorities in amounts that exceeded village production capabilities.[2]

In Soviet times, the Great Famine was under one of the greatest taboos, one that was neglected in both historiography and public discourse. Despite the silence of Soviet governance, the communities of the Ukrainian diaspora in the United States and Canada have undertaken a series of initiatives to commemorate and shed light on this event. As soon as Ukraine gained independence, the subject of the famine started to appear in public. At first it aroused the interest of right-wing intellectuals and then it became an element of politics aiming at Ukrainization of society, to eventually be a crucial formational event for the contemporary Ukrainian nation.[3]

In fact, the Ukrainian politics of historical memory in commemorating the Holodomor was neither uniform nor unequivocal. Successive presidents (Viktor Yushchenko in particular) tried to use the Holodomor to create an image of Ukraine as a victim nation of the Soviet system.[4] Both the activities connected with commemorating the Holodomor and the public debate on the subject, which revealed internal divisions within Ukrainian society, have become the object of an academic debate, which culminated in the publication of a book by Georgii Kasianov, *Danse macabre*.[5] And yet in this work the author avoids the intriguing subject of the visual culture of the Holodomor, particularly within—for me at least—the ideological context.

But one cannot ignore the fact that already from the early 1990s memorials commemorating the Great Famine had become a noticeable element of modern Ukraine's cultural landscape. They affect the way contemporary Ukrainians feel about and experience the historical expanse. For a memorial is one of the simplest signs of identity, the artistic synthesis of national memory. It reminds one of those who created history and who were instrumental in ensuring that the world that surrounds us today is as it is and not as different in some way. And above all, it addresses the need for the collective memory that brought it to life, it tells of the artists who designed it, of their experience of history, and constitutes an example of their interpretation of such events.

Previously, memorials of the Great Famine have been an object of studies by Alexandra Veselova, Tatiana Zhurzhenko, and Vitalii Ohiienko.[6] But these researchers focused on only one selected aspect of monumental representations (either metaphoric or architectural). Veselova thought about the way the Holodomor is commemorated, and the other two researchers mostly focused on the discourse practices that had arisen from specific historical politics in Ukraine.

To date, analysis of the places of memory of the Ukrainian Holodomor did not apply Pierre Nora's concept of *lieux de mémoire*. Moreover, the subject of cemetery memorials or places that are referred to as burial places, which serve as an important form of commemorating the Holodomor, have not yet been taken up for academic discussion.

I conducted my first analysis of the Holodomor memorials in Ukraine in 2008.[7] What seemed to be of much more interest to me was a reflection on a vision of the Holodomor as a historic event that was preserved in the memory sites by the communities creating such sites.[8]

But in this chapter I discuss issues of location and the various formal and aesthetic approaches. Against this backdrop, a smaller selection of examples is analyzed in detail, drawing out the particulars of their construction and design. And the subject of my research is the culture of memory about the Holodomor in Ukraine in its institutional aspect as imposed from above, as well as the artistic visions of these forms of imagination created by artists in the various places of memory for the event. I have set myself the task of analysizing the process wherein the significance of the experience of the Great Famine has been given a political meaning for the national identity of Ukrainians. In memory studies, it is the memorial that is regarded as the catalyst for such social processes.[9] This is why the scope of my analyis encompasses memorials and burial places commemorating the Holodomor in Ukraine.

From 2006 to 2008 I analyzed the register of momuments I had received from the Ukrainian Ministry of Culture. From 2012 to 2014 I worked with a catalogue compiled by an employee of the Ukrainian Institute of National Memory, Vitalii Ogiienko.[10] In addition, during the last ten years, I have personally visited the majority of the analyzed memorials in the large cities of Ukraine and have followed the ongoing events accompanying their unveiling. That said, only in the case of a small group of memorials has it been possible to reach sources containing all the information necessary for a thorough and satisfactory analysis of the symbolic layer. I will, therefore, want to illustrate my theoretical deliberations with a detailed analysis of the memorial called the Candle of Memory in Kyiv.

My fundamental source materials were administrative documents defining the principles for the commemoration of the Holodomor within the public domain (the directives and rulings of the Verkhovna Rada of Ukraine as well as those of subsequent Ukrainian presidents), the annual speeches of the presidents of Ukraine, the articles published in the national and regional press accompanying the unveiling of particular memorials, and artistic literature, including the contributions of well-known architects designs at particular sites of memory (such as Kyiv). In the case of the Candle of Memory memorial in Kyiv, also the internet page with entries in the national competition for memorial designs. I would like to emphasize that only in relation to a small group of memorials was one able to reach sources that contained all the necessary information, which impeded conduction of a full analysis of the symbolic layer in a satisfying way.

I do not divide Ukraine into parts in my deliberations, for example, into west and east. For I am of the position that the culture of commemorating the Holodomor exists beyond political divisions. It is, however, worth remembering that only a part of present-day Ukraine experienced the Great Famine (the part that belonged to Poland before the war), although memorials to the Holodomor are erected all over the country. I treat this state of affairs as an element of the complex process of the unification of memory.

The methodology in the analyses follows that of Alon Confino, with the assumption that first and foremost we will undertake in any researching of collective memory as a reflection on the shape and essence of the group identity shared by the members of a community, the identity that bonds a group despite various interests and motivations. I have dwelt less on the way that the past can manifest itself now than on why one vision and not other visions of the past has gained recognition or was ultimately rejected. Therefore, equally in my considerations, I have attempted to combine reflection both on memory as such and the politics of memory, as well as the politics of countermemories. For only in taking the phenomenon as a whole and not distinguishing individual questions—not placing them into, for example, chronological order—can one fully convey the essence of the complexity of memory, in the form of the representation of memory as in its adoption or rejection.

As Stuart Hall, the creator of the theory of coding and decoding, has noted, there is a difference between coded knowledge and uncoded knowledge. The content that the recipient is going to ascribe to a work will depend on the recipient's experiences and the environment. These factors also explain why one recipient fully accepts the symbolism concluded by the author, while another rejects it or does not understand it. I consequently also am of the view that the meaning of a monument lies somewhere between the premises of the creator and the interpretation of the recipient. The recipient will not be able to fully read the meanings the artist intended; each one of those who view the work will decode the symbolic menaing of the monument in an individual and unique way.

In this context, it is crucial to take a look at the so-called *lieux de mémoire* of the Great Famine in Ukraine. I undertake this research that way because the *lieux de mémoire* embody different forms of the memory of Holodomor inside Ukraine. The different ways in which these forms of Holodomor memory resonate and the various expressive strategies they employ allow for the study of trends in the history of politics of the period in which the *lieux de mémoire* were constructed.

Within the thinking of such demarcated theoretical frames, the recipient of a work of art, such as in my case a memorial to the victims of the Holodomor in Ukraine, does not accept it passively; they are constantly negotiating its significance. The presented semiotic analysis of the symbolic layer of Holodomor memorials was based on knowledge about the presence of particular symbols as well the meanings ascribed to them in Ukrainian culture, the folk and funerary art of this nation, something supported by the relevant subject literature. Where it was possible, references have been made to the general European context for the symbols that constitute the symbolic canon of the visual cuture of Holodomor memory.

What is more, I want to reflect on the public visibility of the Holodomor and the future of this particular form of shaping the Holodomor past by actors in the present. In my opinion, Ukraine has its own tradition of Holodomor victims and survivals commemoration. Thus, the Ukrainian model of the memory of the Great Famine is analyzed as a formative event for the modern Ukrainian nation.

First, I wonder whether that memory merely copies the postcommunist aesthetics of recovering from harm and filling in the "white spots," and whether the visual culture of the Great Famine is still being purposely limited to communicating the national content of treating the famine as genocide perpetrated on the Ukrainian nation by the Soviet regime. Therefore, in order to find an answer to that question, I will define two key terms, *places of memory* and *nonplaces of memory*. Next I will analyze the visual representations of the Holodomor both in the form of memorials (understood as places of memory) and as burial places (understood as nonplaces of memory).

What is worth adding is that in the first case we are talking about sites of memory created in different times and in different locations, and thus representing different images of the Holodomor. The places of the second group should be referred to as burial places because of their location. What turns out to be crucial here is a differentiation of memorials erected at cemeteries and what we are calling burial places as *nonplaces of memory*, rediscovered by local communities in the process of revising the image of the Soviet past in Ukraine. I will mostly be interested in finding answers to questions about the character and diversity of the monumental images of Ukrainian culture in Holodomor memory.

The Holodomor and the Concept of *Lieux de Mémoire*

Research on places of memory has gained more attention thanks to Pierre Nora's multivolume work *Les lieux de mémoire*, which was published from 1984–93.[11] The idea of the work quickly found its supporters in several European countries. But the inconsistent assumptions of Nora's concept at that time demonstrated that the assumptions formulated required further elaboration or precision. Nora did not define the term directly, leaving readers free to add to or clarify the phenomenon of what constituted a *lieu de mémoire*. Paradoxically, this amorphousness made his concept extremely attractive to potential followers. Yet the expectations of supporters have been met in the numerous papers that either referred to his concept or were based on it.

In the treatment the French places of memory in his work, Nora used the term *lieux de mémoire* to refer to "places with memory."[12] The basic function of a *lieu de mémoire* is to protect the memory of a group of people. It is created for society so that it can form a society's image and the image of its history.

My standpoint is that the place of memory should be understood both as a material place (place of memory) and as an imaginary place (realm of memory). In fact, the Great Famine in itself, treated as a breakthrough in the history of Ukraine and at the same time an object of cult for Ukrainian circles abroad or disputes (mainly in the country), is already a *lieu de mémoire*, understood as a realm of memory. But memories of famine, cultivated in places of symbolic meaning with the purpose of fostering ties with other generations and strengthening the spirit of unity, will be places of memory of the Great Famine, in other words, places understood as the real spaces of memory of a particullar event.

In Nora's original concept, "places of memory" replace the real and authentic live memory that used to accompany us for thousands of years but now exists no more.[13] Nora juxtaposes these places with the so-called *milieux* or environments of memory: *milieux de mémoire*. Moreover, *lieux* for Nora, functioning as a representation of memory, guarantee that the memory will be preserved in them and will be open for anyone who wants to come closer. In other words, places of memory are always present wherever cultural memory exists.[14] Nora emphasizes that such places are artificial and deliberately or consciously created to help us remember the past, which is necessary to give meaning to our lives.

Applying the term "places of memory" to the Great Famine suggests that, on the one hand, in Ukraine it has become a symbolic element of the commemorative heritage of the Ukrainian nation and, on the other, that it will be considered according to Nora's classic understanding of a "place of memory." At the beginning, we should point to a significant difference between the French and the Ukrainian experience. In the case of commemorating the Great Famine in Ukraine, we cannot say that the *milieux de mémoire* have changed into *lieux de mémoire* (to be in agreement with Nora's concept) in order to preserve the memory of the event. The memory of it has not faded with time—to make this fading a stimulus for its preservation for future generations in the "places of memory." This kind of memory was absent in the social awareness of a generation that was later called the generation of the Holodomor victims and, in fact, even more at the level of the Soviet Union's politics of memory. Not earlier than in the 1990s was the Great Famine recovered from a general amnesia and acquired a specific meaning. Moreover, it has even become a key element in the process of creating a new Ukrainian code of memory. We should be aware that there were no *mileux de mémoire* of the Great Famine in Soviet times in Nora's understanding of spaces or circles of memory preserving a live memory about the Great Famine. The fact of the Holodomor was ignored in historical narration about the past of Soviet Ukraine, making it completely forgotten. Places of memory connected with that event are thus supposed to revive the Holodomor (or its present vision) in the cultural landscape. This does not arise from the wish to block the forgetting process but rather from the need to learn the historical facts that were concealed during the Soviet regime in this country.

The Great Famine also generally referred to the degradation of funeral habits, as burials were conducted in a dehumanized and mass way. Bodies were carried to cemeteries or simply moved away from residential areas and dropped into prepared ditches. The bodies were wrapped in blankets or were dropped uncovered into the ditches. The places of such mass graves were never marked. The witnesses of the events often recalled that the ground would move for a long time because the dead were sometimes put into shallow graves with those who were barely alive, as it was pointless to wait another day until they did die.[15] Similar images were retrieved from witness reports. During the Perestroika, crosses commemorating these events began to be put up at some cemeteries.[16] At the beginning of the 1990s, such memorials could be created only thanks to the memory, involvement, and enthusiasm of private sponsors or organizations.[17] The ditches were commemorated no earlier than on the sixtieth anniversary of the Holodomor—in 1993. The symbolic graves were created mainly in places that the local community considered authentic places of mass burials. The newly created sites of memory were supposed to morally compensate for the lack of graves of all the anonymous victims of the Great Famine.

The fact that no cases of cultivating the Holodomor memory in these places during Soviet times were noted in any memoirs or in documentation is also of interest for my considerations. Therefore, when speaking about these sites, I do not refer to the term *milieux de mémoire*, although I do use Nora's concept in my analysis. When describing these sites, I call them nonplaces of memory.

Although it originates from Nora, the term mainly refers to the concept of nonplaces as formulated by Marc Auge. These spaces remain in opposition to places understood as a humanized space allowing an individual to define his or her own identity. The author of the term states that it should refer to places involving space in general (airports, motorways, supermarkets, etc.). Such places will not provide answers to questions about one's identity or history, for they are products of modernization.[18] Claude Lanzmann proposed the term "non-places of memory" to define the so-called deformed places, that is, places of the mass extermination of Jews.[19] In this understanding, the term would be a complete contradiction of the term "place of memory" as used by Nora. We are speaking here about a special situation in which the local community has no need to cultivate a memory about the place and, to be more precise, about the event connected with that place.

Roma Sendyka expanded the definition of nonplaces to a series of places functioning as localizations of various acts of mass violence.[20] These are dispersed places connected with forms of institutionalized violence, lacking any form of marking or commemorating of the event or are provided with improper documentation of the commemoration act. A common feature of such places, as specified by Sendyka, is the presence of human remnants. Nonplaces of memory do not, however, have any common topographic features or physical properties. They can be located in urban areas and in the countryside; they can be small and can have a wide territorial range.

These sites have become places of memory at the same time and in parallel with the initiation of an enthusiastic movement for erecting Holodomor memorials in larger cities (district capitals) on the sixtieth anniversary of the tragedy. At the same time, in smaller towns, the construction of memorials was initiated at cemeteries, on sites that were either not connected with places of mass graves of the famine victims or had so far functioned as unmarked mass graves.

If in the context of the debate on Holodomor monumental culture we were to divide the places of memory after Krzysztof Pomian into "dominant" and "dominated" ones,[21] the cemetery sites would certainly belong to the latter group, for they have mostly been constructed by representatives of the local community, even if the initiative resulted from an imposed execution of the plan of commemorating the Great Famine's victims.[22] We could state grandiloquently, however, that they still have been created out of a deeper need and mostly as a wish to make a symbolic grave for people who were not buried with proper respect during the time of the famine. In this way, the local community wants to symbolically restore the dignity of its deceased compatriots, and therefore the erection of a memorial is accompanied by consulting the oldest inhabitants of the village and by asking about the location of the burial sites during the famine in order to put a memorial there. The official unveiling of such memorials would also involve a celebration of religious services for the tragically deceased. Cemeteries seem to be the most appropriate places for situating memorials to honor national mourning.

The common feature of places where the victims of the Holodomor are buried is that such a memorial is to commemorate what continues to hurt, to commemorate what the local society or community is unable to put distance from. Holodomor Therefore memorials do not aspire to provide meaning, a positive interpretation of the event, but are merely to symbolize the wound that is still unable to heal; the suffering that does not cease to plague and that is passed on from generation to generation. This illustrates the belief of certain memory communities that the crimes that constituted the Holodomor are to remain present forever within social memory, that it cannot be forgotten in the ethical meaning of the word, and consequently no historical distance can be adopted in relation to it.[23]

The dominating memorials in the case of the Holodomor are those in which the act of remembrance is unparalleled suffering; though the recollection about it is here designed to convey a positive mission for the descendants. History is in such a place commemorated in the place of memorial, which tells of it and the reverse—such places make the historical narrative realistic. Those Holodomor memorials that have been constructed beyond the mass burial graves of the victims have been ascribed an identity function within the public expanse. They are meant in a lofty and paradoxically praiseworthy way to present those inhabitants of Ukraine who died as a result of the Great Famine so as to reveal the sacrifice endured by the Ukrainian nation on its way to independence. In order to explain how this happened I would like to examine more exactly the genesis of the Holodomor's visual culture.

About the Emergence of Visual Culture of the Holodomor in Ukraine

A symbolic figure of the Great Famine, built by the Ukrainian diaspora in times when the subject of Stalin's genocide was one of the greatest taboos of the Soviet collective memory, has become a part of the heritage restored by contemporary people with the aim of looking for the historical truth and of understanding their national identity. Members of the US and Canadian diaspora created the memorial spontaneously. In Ukraine, the official ritual of commemoration has developed gradually, balancing between separation from the Soviet commemorative tradition and the replication of patterns used by immigrant artists.[24]

The memorials that were created in Ukraine (if we are talking about the first decade of independence) were supposed to meet the requirements of the authorities at the time. They were a kind of contract for public procurement at successive anniversaries of the Holodomor, starting with the sixtieth anniversary of the event. They generally lack any features that would make them unique—they are similar, almost as if formed of the same matrix. Angels, crosses, and women with children, differing very little from one another, are found in hundreds of Ukrainian villages, also in areas that were not affected by the 1930s famine (within the borders of the Ukrainian SSR) or in lands that used to belong to Poland in the interwar period.

Since 1993, the year of the sixtieth anniversary of the tragedy, the nation's memory about the victims of the Great Famine, expressed up to then in spontaneous commemorative acts, started to be put in defined, institutionalized frames, which enabled it to be realized through the operation of government agencies and with state money. From that very moment, each anniversary of the Great Famine was an excuse for erecting memorials, but each commemoration also brought new trends and forms of presentation. Now the monuments to the victims of the Great Famine of 1932–33 can be found in each larger town in Ukraine. Another point of this mass erection of memorials was the issuing of the official regulation by the authorities at that time honoring the memory of famine victims by putting up crosses or other signs and organizing masses for the deceased in Orthodox churches.[25]

At the beginning, the visual culture of the Holodomor was closely connected with forms of commemorating the Great Patriotic War in the entire Soviet Union (see fig. 2.1). This was an unconsciously chosen standard, for with time it turned out that both kinds of memory and the related communities started to compete about the form of the emerging Ukrainian national identity. Since the Great Famine has been placed in the center of ideas that created the nation after 1991 in post-Soviet Ukraine, the places of memory that were connected with it became an effective way of fighting the Soviet symbolic domain in Ukraine, understood after Lech Nijakowski as a territory of the symbolic ruling of a group.[26] Therefore, places of memory related to milestones in the Soviet culture of memory (monuments to the struggle and martyrdom of the Soviet nation during the Great Patriotic War) were removed wherever possible, and where it was not possible to remove them, monuments and museums to the victims of the Great Famine of 1932–33 were built.

Memorials of the Great Patriotic War were one of the most appropriate means of Soviet propaganda, forming the myth of the vanquishing of fascism. From the 1940s until the dissolution of the Soviet Union, thousands of memorials to the victims of the war were unveiled on the territories of all Soviet republics. At least one memorial stands in each village from which soldiers marched to the front, not to mention towns and larger cities, where there are more. In this way, the Great Patriotic War became the omnipresent memory of the Soviet nation.[27]

In my view, during the first decade of an independent Ukraine, it was possible to see significant similarities in the two memory cultures. In that time, the form of the Great Famine memorials of the 1990s reflected, to a large extent, the visual culture of the Great Patriotic War that had begun in the 1960s. In truth, the intentions of those who created Holodomor memorials were disparate, yet this did not change the fact that the commemoration of the anniversary of the Great Famine rather recalled the celebrations for Victory Day, just as the monuments erected for this occasion were characterized by a didacticism and moralizing drawn from Soviet art.

Fig. 2.1 Three monuments: the Memorial to the Soldiers of the Great Patriotic War (on the left), National Museum "Holodomor Victims Memorial" (in the center), and a bell tower of Kyiv Pechersk Lavra (on the right). *Source*: Photo by the author.

This competition between the two kinds of memory is also visible in the localization of the memorials. Both the memorials of the Great Patriotic War and those of the Holodomor were localized in places that were important to the local community or were distinguished in the town's landscape. In Soviet times, these were generally the centers of squares or places that stood out from the surroundings (e.g., a hill or a bend of the river), which strictly limited both the size and the composition of the memorial. Therefore, memorials of the Holodomor started to be analogically located in places that were particularly important to the local communities (squares, city centers).

As a matter of fact, with the course of time a new individual canon for the memory of the Holodomor has been created, one that significantly differs from the forms commemorating the Great Patriotic War; yet one equally significant and fundamental for the Ukrainian policy of memory. What is more, at the same time, the cultural memory of the Great Patriotic War has witnessed a number of key changes including the redefinition of celebrations of Victory Day, the introduction of poppy symbols based on British Poppy Day.[28]

Irrespective of their aesthetic form, Holodomor memorials in fact serve a community function: they unite and gather the "community of memory" in mourning the deceased victims of the Great Famine, just as the Great Patriotic War memorials were supposed to convince people of the Soviet Union's sacrifice in that war, offered for the sake of victory. I would like to state, after Mourad Djebabla, that a memorial commemorating the deceased represents the memory of the community, but it also refers to the very personal mourning of an individual that brings understanding and acceptance.[29] The memorial thus becomes a starting point for the common memory, a place of memory assembling a community in the same recollection.

The Great Famine memorials affect how people feel and how they live in the historical space, mainly by influencing the reflection and emotional sphere; they form a vision of the Great Famine and trigger reflections about the nation's past.[30]

Their main aim was to stimulate empathy and to enliven the belated national mourning. It just so happened that since the 1980s, as one result of the policy of glasnost in the entire Soviet Union, architecture has been dominated by a unique, nonstandard approach to the concept of monumental architecture.[31] What was built at the time were mostly architectural complexes that combined original means of expression, typical of various arts. The created compositions were spatial and, to be understood, had to be analysed gradually, starting with separate parts or cycles. Only through such learning about the memorial could we create the entire, that is, the compact image, of the composition from separate impressions.

This general trend in Soviet monumental architecture affected the emerging post-Soviet monumental art in Ukraine and, in effect, the developing visual culture of the Holodomor memorial. One point was to commemorate the event in Ukraine's history that had a rank similar to the Great Patriotic War's, and therefore the memorials were similar in their form to those presenting the civil victims of World War II. Another point was that the genesis of the events was different, and thus the aesthetics of the Holodomor memorials were completely different from the models used by Soviet architects. Instead of bronze or marble sculptures of heroes, the most frequent were a starving orphan in shabby clothes or a mother weeping over her dead child or killing it herself to free it from starvation. These memorials are mainly monumental architectural complexes, with a multilevel and eclectic (religious, state, and folk) symbolic. On the one hand, such solutions could indicate the continuation of certain aesthetic models as accepted by the authorities of independent Ukraine (since architects educated according to Soviet monumental aesthetics in Soviet times were still active) and, on the other, aesthetic inspiration among the Ukrainian diaspora, especially because the symbolic image of the Holodomor stood in this regard in complete contradiction to the Soviet monumental culture. This was an ideal opposition to a secular, transnational symbolic devoid of any individual characteristics and associated with commemoration of the Great Patriotic War.

Models adapted directly or as inspirations for artists have become the basis for the new Ukrainian culture of Holodomor memory. This is evidenced in the copying of certain symbols or images from some urban memorials (especially those found in the capital or abroad) in other cities of Ukraine. For instance, the memorial in Smile, Sumy Oblast (by Alexy Fed'ko), resembles in its composition the memorial in Windsor, Ontario, Canada. The memorial in Vyshhorod (by Boris Kirilov and Oles Sidoruk) is certainly based on one in Canadian Edmonton, whereas the one at the cemetery in Lypky, Kyiv district, seems to be an exact duplicate of the memorial at St. Michael Church in the center of Kyiv. A true copy of the "Bitter Memory of Childhood" memorial, forming a part of the architectural complex at the memorial in Kyiv, was constructed in Khoruzhivka (Sumy Oblast), the hometown of the former Ukrainian president, Viktor Yushchenko. Another copy of that statue was used as a central element of the installation devoted to Holodomor victims at the Canadian Museum for Human Rights in Winnipeg.

What we are getting here, in my opinion, is a relatively new but recognizable memorial thesaurus. We can even speak of "ready-to-use" visual representations that come with the Holodomor subject matter, as the developed visual image of the Holodomor has been attributed exclusively to memorials commemorating that very event and cannot be compared to any other forms of commemorating famines or mass exterminations.

The visual culture of the Holodomor, which originated from both Soviet and emigration models, reflects the need for understanding the sacrifice and giving it some meaning, of reworking the trauma by commemoration. It is not, however, only about the act of commemorating the victims and creating a material, tangible testimony of remembering them. Therefore, it may be interesting to look at the most common symbols in order to find the features that would be typical of the Ukrainian aesthetics of the Holodomor culture of memory.

The Symbols of Martyr at the Holodomor Visual Culture

Memorials of the Holodomor in Ukraine are clearly characterized by aesthetics of martyrdom and mourning and, in effect, by referring to religious symbols: a dome, a bell, a cross, the number 33 (the age of Christ and the year of hunger in Ukraine), or the memorial's location near an Orthodox church or chapel. Symbols of Eastern Orthodox Christianity are predominant here, although the victims represent various nationalities and faiths. What is significant is that this predominance refers to memorials built in Ukraine and abroad, as for example the only two memorials to the victims of the Holodomor in Poland, which are located in places connected with either the Eastern Orthodox or Greek Catholic Church. In Warsaw, a memorial in the shape of a cross is located at the Orthodox cemetery, whereas the one in Kraków is on the wall of the Uniate Church. At the cemetery in Dniprovska (Dnipropetrovsk Oblast), the local architect, Alexei Blocha, used a cross that had decorated the dome of the local Orthodox church and that was desecrated by the Bolsheviks during the Stalin era. In Znizhky, Kharkiv Oblast, a symbolic grave for the victims of the Great Famine was built in the place of the cemetery chapel that had been demolished by the Bolsheviks in the 1930s.

Te religious references can also be explained as an expression of the wish to compensate the victims for years of non-memory and for lack of religious burial as a result of the forced secularization of Soviet society. The connection to the Orthodox Church gives society a chance to take part in commemorating those who starved and to live the unlived national mourning.

The close vicinity of a local Uniate or Orthodox church can sometimes be explained by the fact that the commemorating is initiated by clerics or active parishioners; this is usually the case among émigrés. In Ukraine, a return to national history coincided with a religious rebirth. The use of a religious symbolic was to implicate the dehumanized, non-Christian, barbaric character of the driving force, the Soviet authority.

An angel is a religious symbol that often appears on memorials to victims of the famine. Images of angels, especially in funeral aesthetics, have become the object of numerous analyses. Why these supernatural creatures are so interesting may be explained in various ways. I believe that this trend reflects the return to a fascination with religious matters and with the spiritual world, and it shows an opposition to limiting our lives to what is visible and material.[32] The motif of an angel, justified from the theological point of view, can thus be expressed in a secular way. Angels are supposed to take the dead who have suffered on earth directly to heaven and to mourn them in a human way. The figure of an angel can be found on one of the Holodomor memorials in Kyiv and on another one in the center of Zhytomyr. In both cases, angels are presented as silhouettes mourning the victims of the famine.

A bell is yet another symbol used by artists designing the Holodomor memorials. When put on memorials to the victims of the famine, it represents a live historical memory of the nation, constantly reminding us of the past. We can see this clearly in the Memory Mound in Lubny (Poltava Oblast), which was constructed in September 1993 according to the design of Anatoly Ignashechenko. The mound was given the form of a bell with a cross. Inside the bell are small bells, in a number corresponding to the historic regions of Ukraine. A similar mound was later built in Mykolaiv. These two memorials differ according to the regional varieties of the folk motifs that decorate them.

The most common symbol that is used in the Great Famine memorials is the cross, a symbol of Christianity or, more precisely, the passion, death, and resurrection of Jesus Christ. In this sense, it is used to commemorate the victims of the Holodomor and gives it a Christian meaning. The cross ascribes Christian values to the victims and, at the same time, puts them in opposition to the oppression of the atheist country during Stalinist times.[33] The symbol of the cross, which takes on different forms, can be seen on any memorial. It can be a small cross on a map that is an element of the memorial, or the memorial alone can be made in the shape of a cross. In Ukraine they were built on the sites of demolished churches or chapels or in former cemeteries. In the last decade, these churches have started to be rebuilt, and the memorials, because they are close to the new churches, acquired a new meaning. In Kyiv, at St. Michael Church in the heart of the Ukrainian capital, the victims of the Great Famine are commemorated with a memorial showing a woman hanging on a cross with a dead child in her womb.

Cemeteries are another symbolic place for the localization of Holodomor memorials. As sacral sites, they constitute an important element of social memory. Memorials located at cemeteries gain more symbolic power from their surroundings. They are mostly dedicated to the victims of totalitarianism, are often symbolic, and are supposed to serve as graves for the deceased who, for various reasons, do not have graves.[34]

What is interesting with respect to Holodomor memory is that the cemetery sites have also been created at cemeteries in towns that were not a part of Soviet Ukraine during the Great Famine and were thus not affected by the famine. This is certainly a result of the emerging Ukrainian symbolic domain in these areas, with the Holodomor memorial as a distinguishing sign, although it results not from the need of discovering the real place of burial of the Great Famine's victims (as is the case in towns that suffered from hunger in the 1930s), but more from the need to respect common victims and from a sense of community and solidarity with Ukrainian citizens whose forebeasrs fell victim to the famine. In such a case, we are rather speaking of a memorial at the cemetery and not at the "cemetery site." The location therefore becomes an element of the symbolic background and not the historic context for the memorial. The reason is that funeral aesthetics is considered in Ukraine to be the most appropriate form of cultivating the memory of Holodomor victims, and so memorials in Western Ukraine are deliberately located at cemeteries, thus creating an invisible bond of understanding with the rest of the country.

The mass construction of Great Famine memorials has led to the development of a specific code represented in the symbolic of the cemetery memorials, which combines the symbolic of Holodomor memorials with sepulchral culture to a much greater extent than the symbolic of memorials in other places. These memorials, however, are most often very simple and unsophisticated. One of the interesting aspects is the architectural form of the tombstones, which are mostly designed as either wooden, stone, or iron crosses. They are made of various materials and come in different forms that have their artistic and regional justification. Rural stone crosses, designed by anonymous authors, exemplify naive art, although they clearly show the stylistic characteristics of the workshop.[35] Cemetery memorials are usually made as steles, crosses, or obelisks. Sometimes the cross is decorated with an ear of wheat or put on a symbolic mound. In my opinion, these memorials are an aesthetic reference to the landscape in which they are located rather than to (e.g., urban) memorials as such. They sometimes look like the remnants of graves, and only the inscription can tell us why they were erected at the local cemetery.

The funeral aesthetics of Great Famine memorials turns into a celebration of death. What I mean is that a great number of memorials show death by presenting people mourning the dead or struggling to survive. Special attention should be paid to the symbol of a "weeping mother of sorrow," which is supposed to emphasize great tragedy, pain, and suffering or to show Ukraine as a living creature fighting for survival.[36]

Ears of grain and bread are other motifs used on the memorials. In the Christian world, they can be unmistakably associated with the substance that is transformed into the body of Christ, and in effect they symbolize the spiritual transformation of man.[37] In the Holodomor memorials, however, they acquire a different meaning than that in European art: they do not carry any sacral load.[38] In the memorials to the victims of the Great Famine, they represent bread that is brought to the starving by contemporary people. The use of this motif is thus an artistic symbol of the effect of the rule of five ears of grain.[39] These symbols were used in the same way in memorials in Kharkiv and in the Kapustyanka village (Kyiv Oblast, Iahotyn region).

The manipulation of both Christian and funeral symbolic is undoubtedly supposed to maintain permanent national mourning in these memorials. The memorials are to communicate the genocidal character of the Great Famine in a metaphysical sense, not to justify the thesis in a legal sense. They aim to convince the viewer about the scale and size of suffering and cruelty. The Holodomor is mass extermination that strikes at the very heart of the Ukrainian culture because of its agricultural character and because deprives Ukraine of its future. Therefore, the suffering of the family: of women and even more of children is one of the most common elements (apart from the strictly national and religious symbols).

A very interesting memorial using this theme is the one in Cherkas'ka Lozova near Kharkiv, designed by Alexandr Ridnyi. A family: a father, mother, and two children, are in the center of the composition. The design of the memorial has raised some controversy, for the father is looking towards the east, toward Russia. His hands crossed over his chest have also gained many interpretations, including a threatening approach toward the Kremlin authorities. At this point, I would like to focus on the figures of the woman and the children. Overwhelmed by the suffering and misery of her close ones, the woman is raising her hands in prayer. The children are horrified and cling to their parents. We get the impression that they are not standing on a hill but on the edge of a precipice. All this confirms the immense human suffering and despair arising from the Holodomor experience.

The figures of the deceased or of starving children in the memorials to victims of the Holodomor symbolize the dramatic consequences of the Great Famine for Ukraine, which are often emphasized in the historiography. The artists of these compositions evoke our compassion and empathy for the defenseless children who were sometimes left behind. Their aim is to shock the viewer, who does not need to acquire any knowledge about the Holodomor or to live experience it personally.

The Holodomor memorials are characterized by a certain eclecticism from a combination of funeral (religious) symbolic and Ukrainian national and folk symbolic. Undoubtedly, the religious and sacral character of the visual culture of the Holodomor results, on the one hand, from the need to negate the Soviet visual culture, especially in its aspect of commemorating suffering in monumental art, and, on the other, from the wish to emphasize the ruthless character of the atheist Soviet country that caused the tragedy. The suffering of millions of Ukrainians during the Great Famine becomes in this way a key element of Ukrainian national martyrdom, a way of coming to terms with the Soviet past, because in case of the Great Famine, as in the case of other Soviet repressions, it is difficult to tell the perpetrators from the victims.[40]

The Candle of Memory Memorial in Kyiv

The Memorial in Commemoration of Famines' Victims in Kyiv, a museum built during the presidency of Viktor Yushchenko and crowning his historical politics, is the epitome of the Ukrainian commemorative policy toward the Holodomor and, at the same time, the new Ukrainian monumental aesthetics. In my opinion, the memorial represents a long-term commemorative policy of the Holodomor.

In its original form, the design of this memorial, executed by a team under the supervision of a Kyivan architect, Anatolii Haydamaka, resembled a belfry, or a chapel of memory. Such a design might have resulted from the closeness of the Kyiv Pechersk Lavra, the greatest pilgrimage area in Orthodox Ukraine. The decorative elements referred exclusively to the Christian symbolic; pagan symbols, typical of Ukrainian folk culture, were absent. In modifications made during construction works, one can see the urge to create a specific image of the past, a specific vision of the Great Famine as promoted by the media of the time in Ukraine. Today the memorial consists of several smaller compositions: angels of sorrow, millstones of destiny, a girl with an ear of wheat, the Candle of Memory, the Hall of Memory (underground), and the blackboards behind the statue and the Viburnum Grove. In general, these elements constitute very individual architectural compositions that can commonly be called a Memorial to the Holodomor.[41]

One can enter the museum from different sides. One can enter the complex from the Arsenalna metro station and can pass the memorial to the soldiers of the Great Patriotic War. One can also start from the Kyiv Pechersk Lavra. Guides begin their tours from Lavr'ska street, where two statues of kneeling angels with their hands crossed over their chests stand. The memorials are decorated with small crosses.

A stone pavement leading from the angels to the Candle of Memory, which is referred to by the guides as the soil of memory, symbolizes Ukraine's highly fertile black soils. About halfway down the entrance to the underground memorial is a square surrounded by round, flat millstonelike stones, which are scattered aound in a seemingly careless manner. The Ukrainian researcher Vitalii Ohiienko points to the possible double interpretation of this symbol.[42] On the one hand, the shape of the entire composition resembles a clock, perhaps a clock of history, and, on the other, it represents the number of famine victims who died daily in Ukraine (twenty-four thousand human lives). Such an interpretation is justified by the fact that the number of stones is twenty-four. Moreover, millstones are agricultural tools that were confiscated in the times of the famine. By considering the author's original Christian idea and the close vicinity of the Kyiv Pechersk Lavra, we can compare the stones to a prosphoron, a small loaf of leavened bread used in Orthodox Christian liturgy. Each stone has a cross engraved inside it that is decorated with ears of grain.

In this symbolic stone circle, in the very center of it, stands the statue of a girl with a handful of wheat. The composition is officially called Bitter Memory of Childhood (see fig. 2.2). The girl is holding five ears of wheat as a symbol of the rule of five ears of grain. She is standing on a stone pedestal whose shape resembles one of the stones in the stone composition around the memorial. The thesis this part of the memorial makes Christian references is even more difficult to reject in that locating the girl in the center of a square might be seen as a wish to show the death of a child as the sacrifice of the Ukrainian people made on the altar of history (see fig. 2.3). As we know, babies and children were the largest group of starvation victims. The authors decided to decorate the pedestal with a fragment of a poem by Taras Shevchenko, inscribed in gold: "To the Dead, the Living, and to Those Yet Unborn" ("*I mertvym, i zhyvym, i nenarodzhenym*"). In a wider context, the fragment should be understood as "in warning and in memory." What is also important is that visitors leave sweets underneath the statue, but they rarely leave flowers. According to a custom in the Orthodox tradition, people take food to the cemetery and leave it on the graves of their relatives. Does this mean that the visitors see cemetery symbolism in this place and use practices known from other spheres of life? Or is this symbolism more appropriate for them as a form of commemorating the Great Famine? We cannot answer these questions accurately and exhaustively, for we are still moving within the space of the intentions of the author and as a visitor who is trying to guess them or even give them his or her own interpretation.

Fig. 2.2 National Museum's Holodomor Victims Memorial. In the foreground is a statue known as the Bitter Memory of Childhood. *Source*: Photo by the author.

Fig. 2.3 Altar of history in the center of the museum's exhibition. *Source*: Photo by the author.

Fig. 2.4 Black crosses surrounding the monument and a figure of a crucified gold stork. *Source*: Photo by the author.

In the background, just behind the girl, is a huge white monument resembling a candle, hence its name: the Candle of Memory. The monument is thirty meters high and its texture is similar to that of a Ukrainian traditional fabric, *rushnyk*. The monument resembles a ritual cloth, since we can see white-thread embroidery on a white background (similar fabrics were used in traditional wedding ceremonies). The cross-stitch motif provided is a very enchanting symbol of Ukrainian culture. The guides often comment that the crosses decorating the monument are of different sizes: the small ones symbolize little children and the large ones symbolize the adults. Their shape resembles bees, which symbolize traditional Ukrainian culture. All this gives a typical image of the Ukrainian rural landscape. Four black crosses, arranged at equal intervals, surround the monument. The way they are made looks like barbed wire. Figures of golden storks are enclosed or hang on the crosses (see fig. 2.4). A stork has much significance in Ukrainian folk culture: it symbolizes the cosy peace of home. Storks are clearly associated with the landscape, with the peace and wealth of the area in which they live. The golden color symbolizes the wealth of a Ukrainian village (which is very often exposed in order to obtain an appropriate contrast with elements that are to present the situation in Ukraine after the Holodomor). The crucifixion of storks is to indicate the doom of the old world that has irreversibly been lost. Individual figures of birds are freed or taken down from the cross, and then they symbolize hope and a rebirth of Ukraine after decades of oppression by Soviet governance.

The composition shows a mixture of folk and Christian symbols. We get the impression that the Christian symbols are used more in an artistic and symbolic way and not as symbols that are to be associated with the Orthodox Church, the faith of the famine's victims. The symbolic is sublime and devoid of religious meaning—the authors used it just as they used many other folk or pagan symbols, that is, only to convey specific meanings with composition elements understandable to a wide group of recipients.

Most guides finish the tour by proposing a moment of silence as a way of showing respect to the deceased of the Holodomor. The observance of a minute of silence is also proposed to foreign visitors, including official delegations from other countries. Personally, when I visited the memorial for the first time, I did not see in it the greatest place of memory of the Great Famine, as it is usually considered. I was interested in people who, like me, tried to find themselves in that space affected by the memory of the Holodomor and to recover from the celebration of suffering as a national asset. I thought that the Ukrainians, being a victim nation that wants to convince itself of the importance of such events as the Great Famine, need places of memory that can become a kind of temple. Such places as exist aim only at arousing an emotional attitude toward the national history, and from the visitor they require contemplation only of the image of the past as presented in the given exhibition, sculpture, or artistic installation. The viewer is not the coauthor of the exhibition providing his or her subjective interpretation of what the author has to present but is rather a common consumer who is expected to provide nothing more than his or her presence and contact with such a vision of the past as he or she is offered in the given place. Only with time, did I realize that it is not a place of cultivating suffering but rather a temple that is supposed to eventually bring about an inner transformation of contemporary Ukrainians who are both lost in the excess of past symbols that are not always precise, understandable, and clear and have been forced

68 | *The Burden of the Past*

Fig. 2.5 On the left, the entrance to the museum (to the depth of the earth) and on the right the exit from the museum (into the light). *Source*: Photo by the author.

to remain in a place devoted to an event they know very little about. It is noticeable that the stairs leading to the main entrance are directed downward, to the depth of the earth, to the land of the dead, whereas the way to the blackboards at the end of the exposition features other stairs that lead the visitor out into the light (see fig. 2.5). Such a metaphor of transition, cleansing by immersion in the suffering of predecessors, learning the truth about the past of a nation, has been planned as a procedure to help Ukrainians properly understand the significance of the Holodomor in the Ukrainian national identity.

Conclusions

Two decades of Ukraine's independence have affected the final development of the visual culture of the Holodomor. This was possible because of cultural diffusion between the Western diaspora and the independent Ukrainian country, for example, and the copying of aesthetic models that were typical of the Soviet monumental culture and related to a gradual separation from the Soviet heritage. At present, Christian, martyrdom, and funeral aesthetics are all predominant, on the background of folk and national symbols.

The memory of the Holodomor, present in the aesthetics of memorials or would-be burial places, does not seem to be reconciled with the nightmare of the past. Its aim is to cultivate national mourning. It is difficult to state whether this is a question of the times or the condition of the Ukrainian society. In this regard, it is important to understand that the Great Famine sites of memory also have their history.

A discussion on the symbolic in the context of visual representations of the Holodomor inevitably leads to one's moving within the unpresentability of such experiences as the Great Famine. The fact is very often indicated by the improper choice of symbols, their excessive number, or the use of different symbols (sometimes contradictory ones, e.g., Christian and pagan symbols on one object) to communicate one's idea. The helplessness of artists who learned about the Holodomor from the reports of other people or from literature emphasizes the close connection between the memorials and the state-enforced vision of the collective memory of the event.

What is also symptomatic is that in the case of different forms of commemorating the Holodomor we still speak of the so-called antimemorials. Sculptures that would not be monumental and would not refer directly to the past (like the Memorial against Fascism, War, and Violence in Hamburg, which sinks into the ground) and that would operate with an abstract or negative form have not yet been created, which means that the Ukrainians do not want to forget about the memory of the Great Famine, for the need to rework it by using traditional commemorating forms is still active. As places of memory, memorials to the victims of the Great Famine not only commemorate them by the information and symbols they contain, but they also preserve, restore, and process the history. Ukraine has developed its own individual style of architecture by which artists can tell of the tragic events of the Holodomor. The memorials have abandoned the typical symbolism of traditional Soviet architecture by rejecting its inauthentic character. The only difficulty is the choice of composition that would be appropriate for martyrdom. Whether it is the religious discourse that has been used so far, based on a Christian symbolic, or commercial discourse presented in the form of parks and gardens, is not important. But important is how the Ukrainians seem not to be in want of abandoning the postcommunist need of recalling the forgotten victims of the previous systems. The subject of separation from the Soviet legacy, in which the memory about the victims of the Holodomor plays a significant role, is therefore still valid.

In analyzing the visual historiography of the Great Famine in Ukraine, I perceive its definite correctness and its exceptional nature. I am of the view that the visual culture remembering the Holodomor once taken from Soviet and émigré models and patterns reflects at present the need to understand the sacrifice suffered, the conveying of meaning onto it, the reworking of trauma through commemoration. And this is a feature independent of where the memorial is located. To a large degree, the matter does not concern the act of commemorating the victims and the creation of a material, tangible memory of them. Without doubt, the religious, sacral character of the Holodomor visual culture results, on the one hand, from the need to negate Soviet visual culture particularly in the question of the commemoration of suffering in monumental art and, on the other, from a desire to emphasize the ruthless nature of the aetheist Soviet state that was the perpetrator of the tragedy itself. The suffering of millions of Ukrainians during the Great Famine becomes in this way a key element in Ukrainian national martyrology, a means of settling accounts with the nation's communist past; for in the case of the Great Famine, as with other cases of Soviet repression, there is no means of differentiating the perpetrators from the victims.

Notes

This research was supported in part by a research grant to the project Places of Memory of the Holodomor, 1932–1933 from the Holodomor Research and Educational Consortium in 2017, http://holodomor.ca/hrec-grants-2017/.

1. The terms "Holodomor" and "Great Famine of 1932–33" are sometimes used interchangeably, although each of the terms carries a specific interpretation of the event of famine in the Soviet Ukraine of 1932–33. The Great Famine is the more neutral of the two terms, in that it names the event as a historical fact. The term "Holodomor" indicates the artificial, deliberate, and genocidal character of the (manmade) famine. At the same time, being an exoticism, and a Ukrainian word (*holod + mor* = dying from hunger), it emphasizes the national and exclusive character of the event.
2. Conquest, *Harvest of Sorrow*.
3. The Holodomor as the *lieu de mémoire* was analyzed by the following authors: Öhman, "From Famine to Forgotten Holocaust"; Kasianov, "Open Grave"; and Jilge, "Holodomor."
4. Jilge, "Competing Victimhoods," 121.
5. Kasianov attempted to analyze the development of Ukrainian public and academic discourse on the Great Famine of 1932–33. Pointing to the political character of the Holodomor memory, Kasianov in 2010 differentiated the Holodomor understood as a historiographic or even political concept (and proposed writing Holodomor with quotation marks, that is, as "Holodomor" in this context) from the famine as a historic event of the 1930s (Kasianov, *Danse macabre*). In the same year, Kasianov published a paper in English in which he presented the main assumptions of the monograph: "Holodomor."
6. Veselova, "Memorial'ni"; Zhurzhenko, "Capital of Despair"; Zhurzhenko, "Commemorating"; Ohiienko, "Vizualna kul'tura"; Ohiienko, "Memorial'na."
7. Kudela-Świątek, "Pamięć," 114–15.
8. Kudela-Świątek, *Miejsca (nie)pamięci*.
9. Yurchuk, *Reordering*, 8–10.
10. The database of the Holodomor monuments was collected in the regions of Ukraine at the request of the Ukrainian Institute of National Memory. See more at http://www.holodomor-monuments.org/, accessed May 15, 2019.
11. Nora, *Lieux de mémoire*.
12. Nora, "Between Memory and History."
13. Maier, "Surfeit of Memory?"
14. Nora, "Between Memory and History," 12.
15. Veselova, "Uvichnennia," 50.
16. Veselova, "Uvikopomnennia," 232.
17. Veselova, "Uvikopomnennia," 229.
18. Auge, *Non-places*, 75–115.
19. Lanzmann, "Non-lieux."
20. Sendyka, "Pryzma."
21. Pomian, "Divided Memory."
22. Veselova, "Uvikopomnennia"; Veselova, "Uvichnennia"; Veseleva, "Pam"iatni znaky."
23. More about that: Kudela-Świątek, *Miejsca (nie)pamięci*.
24. Memorials built by émigré artists, detached from the historical and social context (or more precisely from the place of the event), are significantly different from the accepted ways of commemorating the Great Famine in Ukraine. It is not surprising that their authors decided to speak about the untold past. In the case of memorials of the Holodomor erected in the West, we usually see many symbols that are sometimes contradictory. They overpower with their size and excess of hidden meanings. The memorial in the shape of a circle in Edmonton or the personification of Ukraine as a woman enclosed in a rectangle in the memorial in Winnipeg (in the time of the Holodomor Ukraine was cut off from any outside aid as a result of the Soviet Union's conspiracy of silence) both indicate diversities in aesthetics and means of expression between the Ukrainian and emigrant culture of memory. Symbols chosen by émigré artists in the United States and Canada were supposed to make passersby aware that the Great Famine had taken place in the history of mankind and of its scale. Western societies with Ukrainian minorities have knowledge about the Holocaust, about the tragedy of the Jewish nation, but they know

nothing about the Holodomor. By erecting memorials, artists belonging to the diaspora in the West wanted to draw the attention of their fellow citizens to the tragedy of the Ukrainian people in the Soviet Union—hence the use of eclectic national, religious, and folk symbols. To fulfill this aim, the artists put up national symbols, such as emblems and flags, at the erected monuments. For the same purpose, the author of the memorial in Windsor, Canada, used a map of Ukraine to illustrate the scale of the tragedy. The Ukrainian nature of the Great Famine was also rendered by Ukrainian folk symbols, for example, mounds. The memorial in Calgary (Alberta, Canada) by Ihor Novosilec, unveiled in 1999 thanks to the Ukrainian community in Canada, belongs to this category. A small emblem of Ukraine is located on the southern wall of the stele. A trident can also be found at the memorials in London (England), Edmonton, and Windsor.

25. Ukaz prezydenta Ukrainy 38/93: Pro zakhody u zv'iazku z 60-my rokovynamy holodomoru v Ukraini vid 19 February 1993, accessed May 15, 2015, http://zakon4.rada.gov.ua/laws/show/38/93.

26. Nijakowski, *Domeny symboliczne*, 69–70.

27. Yekelchyk, "Memory Wars."

28. Kudela-Świątek, "Kultura pamięci II."

29. Djebabla, "Pamięć zaklęta," 261.

30. Determining the final number of memorials, irrespective of their form (mass graves, symbolic cemeteries, cenotaphs, etc.), is an extremely difficult task. The difficulty basically results from the fact that, for various reasons, the district authorities in smaller towns decided to construct memorials that would be common to the victims of the Great Famine and to those of the Great Terror. This would confirm the efficiency of the government's historical politics, listing the Great Famine as an element of the Great Terror against the Ukrainian people as a nation. For a researcher of places of memory related to the famine of the 1930s in Ukraine, the joint memorials make estimates even more complicated.

31. Veligotskaia, Zhyzdrinskaia, and Kolomiiets, *Monumental'no-dekorativnoie*, 9.

32. Hall, *Leksykon symboli*, 178; Carr-Gorum, *Słownik symboli*, 21; Battistini, *Symbole i alegorie*, 150.

33. Hall, *Leksykon symboli*, 15–16; Carr-Gorum, *Słownik symboli*, 135; Mozdyr, *Ukrains'ka narodna memorial'na skul'ptura*, 11.

34. Nijakowski, *Domeny symboliczne*, 69–70.

35. Kolbuszewski, *Cmentarze*, 90–91.

36. Skoryk, "Znaity symvol," 8.

37. Hall, *Leksykon symboli*, 221; Carr-Gorum, *Słownik symboli*, 49.

38. Kolbuszewski, *Cmentarze*, 105; Hall, *Leksykon symboli*, 221; Carr-Gorum, *Słownik symboli*, 105.

39. In 1932–33 the rule of five ears of grain was imposed, by which anyone who picked more than five ears of grain faced the death penalty; see more at Stark, "Holodomor."

40. Kudela-Świątek, *Miejsca (nie)pamięci*.

41. The term *Holodomor* was reserved for the Great Famine of 1932–33 only up to some point in time. Since the mid-1990s, the term has also been used in historical papers to refer to other periods of famine in Soviet Ukraine in the times of the Great Terror. What is interesting is that the name of the last Saturday of November in the Ukrainian language, which used to be considered as the Great Famine Commemoration Day, unequivocally indicates that it should be devoted to commemorating the victims of all Soviet famines in Ukraine (*den pam'iati zhertv Holodomoriv*). *Holodomory v Ukraini*.

42. Ohiienko, "Vizual'na kul'tura," 114–19.

Bibliography

Augé, Marc. *Non-places: Introduction to an Anthology of Supermodernity*. Translated by John Howe. London: Verso, 1995.

Battistini, Matilde. *Symbole i alegorie*. Translated by Karolina Dyjas. Warsaw: Arkady, 2005.

Carr-Gomm, Sarah. *Słownik symboli w sztuce: motywy, mity, legendy w malarstwie i rzeźbie*. Translated by Bożenna Stokłosa. Warsaw: RM, 2001.

Conquest, Robert. *The Harvest of Sorrow: Soviet Collectivization and the Terror-Famine*. New York: Oxford University Press, 1986.

Djebabla, Mourad. "Pamięć zaklęta w kamieniu: Czytanie pomników ofiar Wielkiej Wojny w Québecu (1919–1939) jako miejsc pamięci." Translated by Kamilla Kuźmicka. In *Inscenizacje pamięci*, edited by Izabela Skórzyńska, Christine Lavrence, and Carl Pépin, 259–68. Poznań, Pol.: Wydawnictwo Poznańskie, 2007.

Hall, James. *Leksykon symboli sztuki Wschodu i Zachodu*. Translated by Jan Stanisław Zaus and Bohdan Baran. Kraków, Pol.: Baran i Suszczyński, 1997.

Hirsch, Marianne. "The Generation of Postmemory." *Poetics Today* 29, no. 1 (2008): 103–28.

Holodomory v Ukraini 1921–1923, 1932–1933, 1946–1947: Materialy do bibliohrafii dokumental'nykh publikatsii. Compiled by L. Odynoka, L. Prykhod'ko, and R. Romanovs'kyi. Kyiv: Derzhavnyi komitet arkhiviv Ukrainy, Ukrains'kyi naukovo-doslidnyi instytut arkhivnoi spravy ta dokumentoznavstva, 2005.

Jilge, Wilfried. "Competing Victimhoods—Post-Soviet Ukrainian Narratives on World War II." In *Shared History–Divided Memory: Jews and Others in Soviet-Occupied Poland, 1939–1941*, edited by Elazar Barkan, Elizabeth A. Cole, and Kai Struve, 103–31. Leipzig: Leipziger Universitätsverlag, 2008.

———. "Holodomor und Nation: Der Hunger im ukrainischen Geschichtsbild." *Osteuropa* 54, no. 12 (2004): 147–63.

Kasianov, Georgii. *Danse macabre: Holod 1932–1933 rokiv u politytsi, masovii svidomosti ta istoriohrafii (1980-ti–pochatok 2000-kh)*. Kyiv: Nash Chas, 2010.

———. "Razrytaja mogila: golod 1932–1933 godov v ukrainskoj istoriografii, politike i massovom soznanii." *Ab Imperio* no. 3 (2004): 237–69.

———. "The Holodomor and the Building of a Nation." *Russian Politics and Law* 48, no. 5 (2010): 25–47.

Kolbuszewski, Jacek. *Cmentarze*. Wrocław, Pol.: Wydawnictwo Dolnośląskie, 1996.

Koval'chuk, Olena, and Tamara Marusyk. *Holodomor 1932–1933 rr. v URSR i ukrains'ka diaspora pivnichnoi Ameryky*. Chernivtsi, Ukraine: Nashi, 2010.

Kudela-Świątek, Wiktoria. "Kultura pamięci II wojny światowej na Ukrainie." *Rocznik Instytutu Europy Środkowo-Wschodniej* 13, no. 2 (2015): 67–102.

———. *Miejsca (nie)pamięci: o upamiętnianiu ukraińskiego Wielkiego Głodu z lat 1932–1933*. Kraków, Pol.: Akademicka, 2014.

———. "Pamięć i 'miejsca pamięci' Hołodomoru: krajobraz po bitwie." *Nowa Ukraina* 1–2, nos. 5–6 (2008): 102–18.

Lanzmann, Claude. "Les non-lieux de la mémoire." In *Au sujet de Shoah: Le film de Claude Lanzmann*, edited by Michel Deguy, 280–92. Paris: Belin, 1990.

Maier, Charles. "A Surfeit of Memory? Reflections on History, Melancholy and Denial." *History and Memory* 5, no. 2 (1993): 136–51.

Mozdyr, Mykola. *Ukrains'ka narodna memorial'na skulptura*. Kyiv: Naukova Dumka, 1996.

Nijakowski, Lech. *Domeny symboliczne: konflikty narodowe i etniczne w wymiarze symbolicznym*. Warsaw: Scholar, 2008.

Nora, Pierre. "Between Memory and History: Les Lieux de Mémoire." Translated by Marc Roudebush. *Representations* no. 26 (1989): 7–24.

———. *Les lieux de mémoire*. Vols. 1–7. Paris: Gallimard, 1984–93.

Ohiienko, Vitalij. "Memorial'na polityka vshanuvannia pam'iati zhertv Holodomoru 1932–1933 rr. v Ukraini." *Hileia* 61, no. 6 (2012): 72–77.

———. "Vizual'na kul'tura pam'iatnykiv zhertvam holodomoru v Ukraini." *Hileia* 65, no. 10 (2012): 114–19.

Öhman, Johan. "From Famine to Forgotten Holocaust: The 1932–1933 Famine in Ukrainian History." In *Echoes of the Holocaust: Historical Cultures in Contemporary Europe*, edited by Klas-Goran Karlsson, and Ulf Zander, 223–53. Lund, Sweden: Nordic Academic Press, 2003.

Pomian, Krzysztof. "Divided Memory: European Sites of Memory as Political and Cultural Phenomenon" (2011). Accessed May 15, 2015, http://www.enrs.eu/articles/219:divided-memory.

Sendyka, Roma. "Pryzma—zrozumieć nie-miejsce pamięci (non-lieux de mémoire)." *Teksty Drugie* 1–2 (2013): 323–44.

Serbyn, Roman. "Letter to the Editor." *Nationalities Papers* 40, no. 2 (2012): 291–93.

Skoryk, Larysa. "Znaity symvol." *Obrazotvorche mystetstvo* 3 (1990): 7–9.

Stark, Renate. "Holodomor, Famine in Ukraine 1932–1933: A Crime against Humanity or Genocide?" *Irish Journal of Applied Social Studies* 10, no. 1 (1998): 20–30.

Ukaz prezydenta Ukrainy 38/93: Pro zakhody u zv'iazku z 60-my rokovynamy holodomoru v Ukraini vid 19 February 1993. Accessed May 15, 2015, http://zakon4.rada.gov.ua/laws/show/38/93.

Veligotskaia, N., A. Zhyzdrinskaia, and N. Kolomiiets. *Monumental'no-diekorativnoie iskusstvo v arckhitekturie Ukrainy*. Kyiv: Budivelnyk, 1989.
Veselova, Oleksandra. "Memorialni znaky i pam'iatnyky zhertvam holodu-henotsydu 1932–1922 rr. v Ukraini." *Kraieznavstvo* no. 1–2 (2009): 169–79.
———. "Pam'iatni znaky i pam'iatnyky zhertvam Holodu-henotsydu 1932–1933 rr. v Ukraini." *Problemy istorii Ukrainy* 13 (2005): 434–41. Accessed August 10, 2019, http://history.org.ua/JournALL/pro/13/21.pdf.
———. "Uvikopomnennia zahyblykh vid holodnoho moru." In *Holod—henotsyd 1933 roku v Ukraini:istoryko-politilohichnyi analiz sotsialno-demohrafichnykh ta moralno-psykholohichnykh naslidkiv*. Materialy mizhnarodnoi naukovo-teoretychnoi konferentsii na vidznachennia 65-richchia trahedii ukrains'koho narodu, Kyiv, November 28, 1998. Compiled by S. Kulchytskyi, O. Veselova, L. Luk'ianenko, and V. Marochko, 218–42. Kyiv: M. P. Kots, 2000.
———. "Uvichnennia pam'iati zhertv holodomoru-henotsydu 1932–1944 rokiv v Ukraini." *Ukrains'kyi istorychnyi zhurnal* no. 2 (2004), 50–67.
Yekelchyk, Serhy. "Memory Wars on the Silver Screen: Ukraine and Russia Look Back at the Second World War." *Australian and New Zealand Journal of European Studies* 5, no. 2 (2013): 4–13.
Yurchuk, Yuliya. *Reordering of Meaningful Worlds: Memory of the Organization of Ukrainian Nationalists and the Ukrainian Insurgent Army in Post-Soviet Ukraine*. Stockholm: Stockholm University, 2014.
Zhurzhenko, Tatiana. "'Capital of Despair': Holodomor Memory and Political Conflicts in Kharkiv after the Orange Revolution." *East European Politics and Societies* 25, no. 3 (2011): 597–639.
———. "Commemorating the Famine as Genocide: The Contested Meanings of Holodomor Memorials in Ukraine." In *Memorials in Times of Transition*, edited by Susanne Buckley-Zistel and Stefanie Schäfer, 221–41. Cambridge: Intersentia, 2014.

WIKTORIA KUDELA-ŚWIĄTEK is Assistant Professor at the Institute of History and Archival Studies, Pedagogical University of Cracow, Poland. She is the author of *Unremembered . . . an Oral History; Example Narrations of Poles from Kazakhstan about the Repressions over Nationality and Religion* and *Eternal Memory: Monuments and Memorials of the Holodomor, 1932–1933*.

PART II
WORLD WAR II IN THE UKRAINIAN MEMORY

3

THE WAR OF MEMORY IN TIMES OF WAR

May 9 Celebrations in Kyiv in 2014–15

Tetiana Pastushenko

May 9 is one of the few Soviet holidays that is still actively celebrated, both officially and privately, in Ukraine and in other countries of the former Soviet Union. A possible reason might be the powerful individual component of the event itself. Still living are witnesses of those years, the direct participants of military actions and victims of Nazism. Most every Ukrainian family has its own account of the suffering and memory about the war.[1] Numerous groups of participants of the war include the multiethnic victims of Stalin, the Nazi and Romanian regimes, and those who collaborated with these regimes or simply survived in wartime circumstances by taking the least risk possible. Included also would be the experiences of the Red Army soldiers, the captives of Germans, servicemen of the Wehrmacht, and fighters of the Organization of Ukrainian Nationalists and the Ukrainian Insurgent Army. Such a cornucopia of Ukrainian experiences during the war determines the variety of memories about that war. Modern society is witnessing a certain competition among the categories of the victims, as well as among the heroes who fought in the Allied Forces, Nazi German units, and the Red Army or positioned themselves as "fighters for the independent Ukrainian state." The situation has allowed some politicians to claim that memory about the war became the reason for the societal split in modern Ukraine, the reason for the new "war for the war."[2]

Conflicting interpretations of memory about the war have found their reflection in the traditions of marking the Day of Victory over Nazi Germany in post-Soviet Ukraine. The most dramatic changes in commemoration practices took place after the revolutionary events in Maidan Nezalezhnosti in the winter of 2013–14, the Russian annexation of the Crimea, and the outbreak of war in Donbas. This chapter aims to present some results of two projects dealing with research on May 9 celebrations in Ukraine. In 2014, a German historian, Jochen Hellbeck, initiated a project titled "History and Dialogue in Ukraine: The May 9 Documentary Project." The project brought together six Ukrainian historians, six photographers, and a French photographic artist, Eric Gourlan, to work in Kyiv, Odesa, Kharkiv, L'viv, and Donetsk to monitor and film short interviews with the participants in the celebrations. In 2015 the same group of Ukrainian historians joined an international project called "Victory—Liberation—Occupation: War Memorials and Commemoration Marking the 70th Anniversary of WWII Ending in Post-socialist Europe" (headed by Mischa Gabowitsch), which covered twenty East European and Russian cities.[3] The two projects had a similar mission: to observe closely and to do short interviews with the attendees, discovering their attitudes toward the holiday and the memorial site. In total, thirty interviews were done in Kyiv in 2014 and thirty again in 2015. Since the bulk of information is still being processed, in this chapter I will concentrate on the events in Kyiv that I witnessed personally. The research focuses on the following two questions: How have public Victory Day celebration practices changed? What are the attitudes to the new traditions among the actual participants?

A Historical Outline: "The Traditional May 9 Military Parade"

Before commencing an analysis of the events marking Victory Day celebrations in 2014–15 in Kyiv, it is necessary to provide a short outline on how this day was marked previously, what ceremonies, and which scenarios of festive acts had been most widespread in the capital city (in our case). The history of May 9 celebrations in the Soviet Union and in post-Soviet countries has only recently become a subject of scholarly research.[4] Most studies dealing with the politics of memory about World War II have concentrated either on representation of the war in the public space or on studying the holidays (both Soviet and post-Soviet) in general.[5] The few works on Victory Day rituals do not provide a systematic overview of the peculiarities of the holiday in Ukraine.[6] The Ukrainian authors somehow prefer researching local celebration dynamics, let us say in Kharkiv, or choose a limited chronological period, omitting descriptions of the holiday in the whole diachronic retrospective of 1946–2015.[7]

Victory Day celebrations in Ukraine are connected with Soviet festive traditions,[8] which occurred during three periods. The first started on May 8, 1945, when a decree by the Presidium of the Supreme Council of the Soviet Union ordered the ninth day of May as the "Day of an All-National Holiday—Victory Day."[9] Even though this state holiday lost its status as a day off in December 1947, it is during this period that the tradition of laying flowers at the monument of the unknown soldier took its roots. The eternal fire is lit by certain monuments, and gatherings of schoolchildren and workers with participants of the war are organized. A second period, starting in April 1965, when Victory Day regained its day-off status, was marked by an extreme boom in the cult of the Great Patriotic War as the greatest accomplishment of Soviet society. The third period continues until today and is characterized by transformations of the holiday ceremonies of May 8–9 in post-Soviet and postsocialist countries.

The general scenario of marking May 9 that emerged in 1946–91 in the Soviet Union consisted of paying a military tribute to the deceased and to honoring the living veterans. Kyiv, for example, has preserved from 1965 until today the official mournful ritual of laying flowers at the Glory Obelisk on the grave of the unknown soldier and at other monuments linked to the war. On May 9 or the previous day, solemn assemblies of state officials and war veterans would be organized and there would be outdoor collective servings of "soldier porridge," concerts by both amateur and professional musicians, and fireworks in the evening. Only on exceptional occasions, however, was the Day of Victory over Nazism marked by a military parade. In Moscow military parades took place on the anniversaries in 1965, 1985, and 1990.[10] Kyiv held such parades only in 1965 and 1990. Sometimes the anniversary years were specially celebrated with veteran demonstrations on Khreshchatyk Street and an assembly or a military-and-sport performance at the Central Stadium (1975, 1985). The core of the Soviet festive system firmly remained within the anniversary of the October Revolution on November 7 and the International Workers' Solidarity Day on May 1; traditionally, these dates were marked with military parades and mass demonstrations.[11] That said, Victory Day to some extent competed with or challenged the "old" festive occasions and, therefore, had no universal meaning in the Soviet festive calendar.[12]

The fall of the Soviet Union caused a gradual change in the cultural landscape in the former republics and a rethinking of the festive dates and ceremonies. Russia has incorporated May 9 into the national festive calendar. Beginning in 1995, Moscow's Red Square has hosted annual military parades exceptionally on May 9 (and not July 12, which is Russia Day);[13] since 2008 the parades have demonstrated modern implements of warfare. Victory Day has transformed into one of the central celebrations to demonstrate the power and the state's global geopolitical ambition, as well as to appeal to the victory of the Soviet Union over National Socialism.[14] Post-Soviet Ukraine held only two May 9 parades involving modern military units—in 1995 and in 2010.[15] Generally, one could say that the universal elements of the celebration have been preserved, meaning the ritual commemoration of the fallen and honoring the veterans. The traditional Soviet aesthetics and music accompanying the event too have remained, with the national yellow-and-blue flag becoming an essential symbolic element of the festivities. Since 2000, under the influence of the growing importance of the event in Russia, Kyiv's official marking schedule has included a solemn veteran walk down Khreshchatyk and Maidan Nezalezhnosti.[16] In 2010 Viktor Yanukovych marked his coming into office with the first May 9 military parade in fifteen years.[17] The years 2011–13 were a time of historical military performances in the city center, which were organized with the participation of civic activists and war veterans. In fact, we can see a gradual shift away from the Soviet standards of Victory Day celebrations. In the recent decade, marking the May 9 has in fact turned into a loyalty test for Ukrainian presidents, whereas the geopolitical struggle over hegemony in the post-Soviet space has metamorphosed into a conflict of historical narratives about the war and has been described much in the terminology of war.

The War of Narratives and Symbols

Revolutionary events in the autumn of 2013 and winter of 2014, the annexation of the Crimea, and the war in Donbas, which had taken thousands of lives by spring of 2015 pushed Ukrainian politicians toward taking more radical steps in the public presentation of World War II.[18] President Petro Poroshenko's decree of March 24, 2015, on marking May 8 as the Day of Memory and Reconciliation has, for the first time since Ukraine gained its independence, called the war with Nazi Germany World War II and not the Great Patriotic War.[19] It also outlined the main forms of marking the victory over Nazism and commemorating the victims of World War II and canceled a number of festive events for the seventieth anniversary of Victory Day planned in 2013, among them a military parade down Khreshchatyk.

The four laws on the decommunization of Ukraine passed by the Ukrainian Parliament (*Verkhovna Rada*) on April 9, 2015, should also be considered in the context of the counter-propaganda on the times of war. All four laws directly influence commemorative practices linked to World War II and aim to deconstruct the communist ideology and to legitimize new sociocultural practices.[20] The law "Perpetuation of the Victory over Nazism in the World War II 1939–45" confirmed annual state-level celebration on May 9 of the Day of Victory over Nazism in World War II and on May 8 as the Day of Memory and Reconciliation. The law on the fighters for Ukrainian independence included the participants of the Ukrainian liberation movement, members of the Organization of Ukrainian Nationalists, and combatants of the Ukrainian Insurgent Army into the general narrative of national history.[21] In addition, another law prohibited the use of both Nazi and communist symbols in political actions. Thus, Ukraine became the second country among the fifteen post-Soviet republics, after Lithuania, to pass such stringent restrictions on Soviet and Nazi symbols.

The adopted laws caused a downpour of criticism from people holding liberal and legal positions and from professional historians. One group of the academics said decommunization laws contradict many existing laws and international obligations to freedom of speech. They also lack a clear mechanism for implementing them. This scientist had thought it was a populist move by the government.[22] Support for the laws proceeded from the assumption that since communism and Nazism were equally evil ideologies, condemnation of one necessarily entails, both logically and morally, condemnation of the other. If denazification is crucial, so too is decommunization. Moreover, confronting and overcoming Ukraine's brush with totalitarianism is indispensable to the country's pro-Western trajectory. As is often the case, the laws make tradeoffs between freedom and justice.

Historical symbols from World War II times became a clear marker for both European integration supporters and the bearers of pro-Russian sentiments. During the revolution in the winter of 2013–14, protesters used the national symbols of Ukraine, the Ukrainian flag, and the combat red-and-black flag of the Organization of Ukrainian Nationalists. The so-called Anti-Maidan protesters chose as their symbols the flags of the Russian Federation and the Communist Party and the St. George Ribbon that had previously been used on Victory Day.[23] After the flight of President Viktor Yanukovych to Russia and the revolutionaries' coming to power, the supporters of Russian policies on Ukraine used the St. George ribbon to show their approval of Russia and their opposition to the new Kyiv authorities. Moreover, during the occupation of the Crimea and the unfolding of Russian aggression in the east of Ukraine, pro-Russian militant separatist formations also wore St. George Ribbons. Therefore, in the spring of 2014, this symbol acquired unambiguous negative connotations and since then has been associated with the supporters of anti-Ukrainian movements. It is noteworthy, however, that the original idea behind the introduction of the St. George Ribbon had been to balance the ritual and emotional aspects of the celebration to give people "the possibility to 'show' their attitude to the holiday of the Great Victory and to express their respect for and gratitude to the front-line veterans."[24]

The history of mass use of the St. George Ribbon on May 9 festivities began in 2005 with the sixtieth anniversary of the victory. On its eve, in autumn of 2004, the Orange Revolution took place in Ukraine; it got its name from the mass use of the symbol of the presidential campaign of Viktor Yushchenko—an orange ribbon—by the protesters in order to identify themselves.[25] It might have been the success of the revolution and the simplicity and popularity of such a symbol as a ribbon that inspired some journalists from the RIA Novosti information agency to suggest a festive campaign called the "St. George Ribbon." The point was to wear or to stick on one's possessions a two-colored black-and-orange ribbon. The idea became unexpectedly popular, with the tradition of wearing the ribbon quickly spreading beyond Moscow. In 2005 the St. George Ribbon appeared at official celebrations in Kyiv and simply on the clothes or accessories of the attendees. The new symbols encouraged the creation of new rituals and traditions, as in Sevastopol in 2010 during the May 9 celebration, when a three-hundred-meter-long and 1-meter-wide black-and-orange cloth set the record for the largest St. George Ribbon in Ukraine.[26] Noting the obvious success of the symbol, Serguei Oushakine points out that any clear historic differentiation is absent from it.[27] The ribbon reproduces the colors of a whole group of military decorations of the Russian Empire, the White Movement, Russian nationalist émigré organizations, the Red Army, and the Russian Federation. It has turned into one of the most recognizable post-Soviet symbols, quite a material subject of import of new memorial practices and a certain element of the "symbolic commemorative presence" of the empire in post-Soviet states.[28]

On the eve of May 9, Ukrainian television channels adopted a new symbol as their thematic screen logo—the poppy. The design was created by a Kharkiv designer, Serhii Mishakin, who used the world-famous Remembrance Poppy—a symbol commemorating people killed in the war—and reworked it into a graphic stylization of a flower resembling a wound.[29] "The point was not just to develop a new accessory but to suggest a re-evaluation of the 'holiday' in the public Ukrainian conscience, shifting the accent from the emotion of victory to the realization of the terror of war and commemoration of the perished. That is why the revolutionary 'Glory to the Heroes!' was replaced by a new motto, 'Never Again!,' the traditional '1941–1945' turned into '1939–1945.'"[30]

During the festive days of 2014, the new logo was largely present on television screens and at official celebrations, but one could also notice it as street graffiti, homemade poppy pins on the clothes of people in public transport and on passersby far from the memorial places. The St. George Ribbon was also widely present in the visual space of the celebration. In Kyiv it was worn by representatives of organized communist groups, handed out by volunteers to the usual participants in the festive events.

The year 2015 brought a more vivid change, as the new symbol received state support.[31] Its dissemination was also commercialized—Kyiv souvenir shops offered a large variety of poppy metal badges, stickers, pins, jewelry, and so on. On May 9, several dozen volunteers handed out free poppy symbols to everyone who was willing to take them. A poppy flower anniversary coin appeared with the name "70 years of Victory 1945–2015," as did an artistic stamp and an envelope called "Eternal Memory to the Heroes: 1941–1945."[32] City advertisement banners and intercity highway billboards also showed the new symbol. Even the Motherland Monument—a central ninety-two-meter sculpture of the "Memorial Complex: National Museum of the History of the Great Patriotic War"—was dressed in a poppy diadem.

The visual perception of the 2015 festive crowd was reminiscent of a carnival. People wore ethnic clothes, wore military uniform from various times, or decorated themselves (sometimes even their pets) with various ethnic or national symbols; one could see all possible kinds of poppies. People wearing the St. George Ribbon in Kyiv were few. It was possible to see how inventive the participants of the holiday demonstrated holding ribbons with authentic military decorations (the Order of Glory or the medal For Victory over Germany) or guard ribbons. Some respondents acknowledged in the interviews that they would have liked to wear the ribbon but were afraid of possible conflicts with other participants since it had begun to be associated with the Russian aggression and the death of thousands of people.

The Topography of the Holiday and the Commemoration Ceremony

The spatial arrangement of May 9 celebrations in Kyiv had been formed in Soviet times. Official Victory Day events have been centered on monuments erected in various parts of the city, set on mass graves, or devoted to various categories of participants of the war. High-level official commemoration ceremonies have traditionally taken place near two monuments—the Obelisk of Eternal Glory on the Grave of the Unknown Soldier and on the grounds of the Memorial Complex: National Museum of the History of the Great Patriotic War 1941–1945. Kyiv festive events have been arranged in Khreshchatyk Street and in the square that bore the name of Kalinin after the October Revolution (*Zhovtneva*) and is presently called Independence Square (Maidan Nezalezhnosti). In Soviet times, this area hosted annual parades and demonstrations. In post-Soviet Ukraine, Khreshchatyk and Maidan Nezalezhnosti have transformed into a space for political activities of the citizens, official state events, and various entertainment shows. Since 2000, the city's main street has been the place for an annual veteran walk. In the general script of May 9 festive events, the festive parade, the memorial laying of flowers at the Glory Obelisk, and the assembly at the Museum of War have been combined. Thus, in post-Soviet Ukraine the holiday atmosphere shifted from the commemoration and glorification of participants of the war to festivities. It was moved from peripheral memorial places to the central street of the city.

After the tragic events of February 18–21, 2014, Maidan and Khreshchatyk gained not only symbolic but also memorial importance. Honoring those murdered, who are known as the Heavenly Hundred (*Nebesna Sotnia*), organizing any entertaining events at Maidan was prohibited.[33] Consequently, it was decided in 2015 not to hold there the traditional May 9 veteran walk. To hinder any self-organized demonstrations, the road on the central street of Kyiv was occupied with empty paper boxes laid to form a giant motto reading "Remembering* 1939–1945 * Winning."[34] The authors of the performance explained that their main objective was to attract public attention and to use the boxes to gather gifts for Ukrainian soldiers.

The Kyiv festive activities were being organized against the background of an international discussion on marking the seventieth anniversary of the end of the war in Europe and in insisting on the "right to celebrate according to one's own script."[35] It was for the first time that on May 8, devoted to Victory Day, a special session of the Parliament took place with the participation of UN Secretary-General Ban Ki-moon, representatives of diplomatic missions, and foreign parliaments and members of the Ukrainian government. The seats of the members of Parliament were taken by World War II veterans and soldiers of the Ukrainian

Army and Volunteer Battalions who had been fighting in Donbas. The evening was marked by two all-Ukrainian actions: "The First Minute of Peace" and a literature and art performance called "The Voice of Heroes," which presented the new holiday—the Day of Memory and Reconciliation.

May 9, 2015, saw the official memorial ceremony of laying flowers at the Obelisk of Eternal Glory on the Grave of the Unknown Soldier.[36] The same day, on the square in front of the National Museum of the History of the Great Patriotic War, Ukrainian Army recruits took their military oath. Among the entertainment events, we should mention the parade of military orchestras from Ukraine, Poland, Jordan, Serbia, Lithuania, and Estonia. The traditional May 9 fireworks were canceled in 2015 (just as in 2014) for security reasons.

The above-mentioned official festive ceremonies in Kyiv have been characterized by the involvement of new actors. Besides state officials and Red Army veterans, Ukrainian Insurgent Army (UPA) veterans, former prisoners of Nazi concentration camps, and Ukrainian Army soldiers who had been fighting in Donbas participate. Symbolic pictures showing a former Red Army soldier and a UPA combatant sitting next to each other during a parliamentary session or the president and prime minister with their families joining the festive concert and seated among the veterans were to send a powerful message for the unity of a modern society traumatized by war. The literature and art performance "The Voice of Heroes" was directed at involving the younger generation in the festive events. It consisted of pieces of modern poetry, a performance by well-known theater actors and Ukrainian rock and pop singers, many of whom had taken an active part in the protests at Maidan. The traditional musical repertoire of the 2015 celebrations was expanded with folksongs, songs of Ukrainian Sich Riflemen (*Sichovi Stril'tsi*) and the UPA, and songs by modern Ukrainian musicians. The festive script sought to be, citing one of the organizers, actor and director Yevhen Nishchuk, "personal, not artificial, without too much pathos."[37]

There were also a number of alternative events in Kyiv on that day. In the city center, near the "Arch of Friendship of Nations" (*Arka Druzhby Narodiv*), a solemn meeting of opposition bloc (*Opozytsiiny Blok*) political party supporters took place.[38] On the grounds of the Museum of the War was a performance called "Immortal Regiment," organized by the Kyiv City Organization of Veterans and the Inter television channel.[39] The performance can be traced back to May 9, 2012, when in Tomsk (Russia) the participants of such a demonstration brought along portraits of their relatives who were war veterans. In three years, the demonstration has spread to fifteen countries of the world. In Kyiv it gathered about a hundred participants, who walked the Walk of Memory around the grounds of the Museum of the War.

Another important festive element of Victory Day has always been the common consumption of alcohol.[40] It stems from a folk commemorative tradition—"to drink to those resting in peace of the soul." Unlike previous years, in 2015 these informal celebration practices could not be seen. Even in 2014, when all mass events were canceled because of threats of a terrorist act, one could still see young Afghanistan war veterans treating World War II veterans to some vodka. The modern military action in Donbas and the daily news of the deaths of young soldiers on contemporary front lines have deprived the holiday of its former casualness and, so to say, "festivity." As a young woman mentioned in her interview, "There is no feeling of real victory, because there is war again." The absence of the aforementioned "folk" celebration practices points to some extent to the political motivation of participation in the events.

"I Came to State My Opinion as a Citizen"

One of the main aims of our research on May 9 celebration traditions was to find out why people came to a memorial on that very day. Almost all the interviewees answered this question by reminiscing about their relatives who had taken part in the war and claimed they came to commemorate them. After a few minutes of communication, however, it became clear that the main motive to attend was to state their political opinions. Only one woman said it was her birthday that day and that she "rests and is happy to see so many people around." The respondents' narratives can be roughly broken up into three groups: opponents of the new authorities, supporters of the new authorities, and neutral respondents, such as one woman, a surgeon, who openly stated, "I too haven't been attending this very place, the Park of Glory, for many years. But today I am here because I am protesting against the shameful Ukrainian government. . . . I came to state my opinion as a citizen."[41] Another woman, whom we met near the subway station, was holding her great-grandfather's portrait and protesting the newly introduced Day of Memory and Reconciliation: "We should not reconcile, we must celebrate the Victory!"[42] Worries about the fate of Russians in Ukrainian society, about the fate of this nation in the world at large prompted a forty-year-old researcher to come to the celebration for the first time in many years. His narrative represents the third, neutral, group: "Well, to some extent this is already a tradition, to some—an attempt to understand if reconciliation is possible, an attempt to have a look at our society and its ways. What is really a pity is that the whole world is against Russia. This is really scary for me, a Russian person."[43]

The representatives of the other party, who supported the new symbols and memorial practices, came to the holiday so as not to "give it away" to their opponents. An aged woman, a doctor, holding a portrait of her mother in military uniform, said, "And especially this year. You know, how offensive I find that Moscow, you see, is understating the contribution of our Ukrainian people to this patriotic or World War II. . . . To humiliate us this way, to shout out to the whole world that the Ukrainians, as they claim, were not at all important there. That is why I mark the holiday every year and this year *especially*!"[44] In total, about half the respondents in Kyiv said that they visit the memorial Park of Glory and the Museum of the War every year on May 9. Three confessed that they had not been attending the festivities "since school."

Having posed the question "What is this day [May 9] to you?" we also received three categories of replies. To six informants, it meant celebrating Victory Day: "Victory Day is the day of the victory. The day of memory or the day of grief—this is something I do not understand, frankly speaking."[45] Twelve of the thirty interviewees attended to honor the memory of the dead, the memory of their relatives and participants of the war. A young Ukrainian soldier, who was under medical treatment in a Kyiv hospital, however, stated, "The day of grief; it is surely a victory, a victory over evil, but not a holiday."[46] Others called May 9 both a day of memory and a day of victory. A young woman, walking with her grandfather's portrait in the Immortal Regiment walk, stressed that on this day it is important "to honor the memory of the deceased and to encourage those who are still alive, to congratulate the people who brought us the victory, the veterans."[47]

Discourse on the holiday presents two oppositions that can be roughly called a neo-Soviet (Russian) one and a national identity (Ukrainian) one. The neo-Soviet perspective consists of three most widespread rhetorical figures: "our grandfathers fought," "a duty to remember," and "the victory is one for all" or a "unity" figure. It is noteworthy that the neo-Soviet narrative is often also used by respondents who are neutral to the new authorities and the new festive rituals. Citing Judy Brown, such a rhetoric represents a local and supernational post-Soviet solidarity.[48] The national identity discourse has a reflexive nature, as if responding to a predictable opposition. It consists of figures, one of which can be labeled "our grandfathers fought too." It is, nonetheless, complemented by the figure of the victims, but not the "victims in the name of the victory" but that of the unjustified losses and suffering that overshadow the value of the victory as such: "Soviets jammed the enemy with corpses and that is only how they won."[49] Russian involvement in the military action in Donbas made the "duty to remember" figure vulnerable, especially when it is combined with the word *peace*: "people died so that today we can have peace." Here is one example of such a deconstruction in wording of a young woman who came to the celebration with her ninety-year-old grandfather and her son of school age: "It is 2015. We have no peace; we have undergone aggression from our brother country. It is very depressing. Now veterans again speak of peace that is nonexistent. This is most terrible."[50] The typical figures, such as "it is our common holiday" or "we are one great Slavic nation," have also been criticized or rethought. In the neo-Soviet discourse they are supplemented with a reference to "the one" who seems to hinder the unity: "and they try to separate us," or with rhetorical questions such as "Who needed to separate us?" There is also an easy answer: "authority is authority and people are people."

The main expectation of the holiday attendees is to experience a sense of elation from common participation in the collective ritual. To feel that, a young woman economist only had to walk through the festive crowd: "It is so nice to see how people have this understanding. They are not sitting somewhere in their homes, you know, but are all out in such a difficult time, hard time for Ukraine. I am also glad that our people, well, when it is a disaster then they unite, become as one. And, of course, everyone wants peace, that there is love, that this war is finally ending."[51] Veterans interviewed by the project's participants evaluated the holiday by applying the standard of notable events celebrated by everyone.[52] "Before, it used to be an absolute holiday. Everyone was walking down Khreshchatyk and we were in the very first rows."[53] A parade on Khreshchatyk is the ideal of a festive Victory Day event for one-third of the respondents. Next to feeling nostalgic about one's youth—"I took part in parades when I was younger"—the veterans remember all Soviet demonstrations as one single blend in the parade on Victory Day. "So, on May 9 and May 1, I opened the parade on Khreshchatyk on a motorcycle. Well, we opened with the red, the flag of labor—the sickle and hammer one. And what is now—everything totally messed up!"[54] or "We had Khreshchatyk traditionally left for Victory Day: there used to be demonstrations, parades."[55] Bygone festive ceremonies are associated with strongly positive feelings—"they used to respect us more then"; though the phrase of a forty-year-old scholar—"I haven't attended parades since school"—points to the element of coercion in Soviet times.

Older-generation memories of Victory Day dissolve in the wider narrative of the Soviet past, which points to one more reason for the popularity of this holiday—it gives a chance to go back in time to the Soviet past. This was most clearly worded by a man in a sailor shirt and a peakless cap with his grandfather's and father's medals on his chest. Even though his grandfather, who was in the infantry throughout the war, had never celebrated this day, the sailor-clad man saw it first and foremost as a great holiday, a great joy. "We were brought up this way," he explained, "say, myself, I lived in the Soviet Union and celebrated these holidays in the Soviet Union."[56] For him, Victory Day brought back memories of his youth, his service in the Soviet army, his employment in the construction of military factories, and respect for his profession. "How can I say that we lived wrongly," he summed up. Thus, in this case, the May 9 holiday is associated not with the war but with memories of Soviet holidays, reminiscences about celebrating this "memory about the war" in the Soviet Union.

Conclusions

The preparation and implementation of festive events in Kyiv marking the last day of World War II in Europe in 2014 and 2015 took place under conditions of an ideological and open military conflict between Ukraine and the Russian Federation. This influenced both the form of the holiday and the attitudes of its attendees. The main innovation of the events lies in the dismissal of the Victory Day narrative that divides people into winners and losers, thus leaving no place for discussion of the tragic experiences of the war. The official legal introduction of the May 8 celebration of the Day of Memory and Reconciliation, the May 9 celebration of the Day of Victory over Nazism in World War II, and official use of the term "World War II" instead of "the Great Patriotic War" allow for expansion of the historical and chronological context of the festive dates and the involvement of new participants. Having adopted the alternative poppy symbol and having refused the military parade on Khreshchatyk, Ukraine has taken the first steps in restoring the memorial character of this special day, depriving it of military trappings. In July 2015, the Memorial Complex "National Museum of History of the Great Patriotic War 1941–1945" was renamed the "National Museum of the History of Ukraine in the Second World War: Memorial Complex," thus testifying to the systematic exclusion of this Soviet ideological cliché from the official Ukrainian discourse.

The festive presentations of both May 8 and May 9 have also unveiled changes in the social structure of Ukrainian society. Soldiers of the Ukrainian Army have been important participants of the festive events. Their presence during the holiday was encouraged not only by the general growth of respect for the military in a society in a state of war or by the desire to demonstrate the symbolic continuity of generations, but rather by a compensatory dimension—the need and wish to publicly honor soldiers killed in the war in Donbas.

At the same time, the newly adopted practices do not reflect all aspects of memory about World War II in Ukraine. Memory about the Holocaust is left in a blind zone. In fact, the new commemoration practices seem to be aligned with the frames of the same Soviet discourse about the Great Victory, where the May 9 is associated with warfare and military losses but not with the liberation of concentration camps and the extermination of millions of Jews. Having faced such criticism, one of the directors of the Day of Memory and Reconciliation performance, Yevhen Nishchuk, replied, "We somehow left these aspects out. I do not think it was done on purpose."⁵⁷ Therefore, one of the perspectives for the script of events would be a further shift of accents in commemoration of the war and the inclusion of the voices of victims next to the heroic narrative.

The need for such a shift is also reflected in the results of the survey conducted by the project's participants. It showed that the visitors of the May 9 festive commemoration also used rhetorical figures about the victims. For about a third of the informants, the day is about grief and commemoration of the perished. The same interviews, however, showed that remembering the war as such is secondary to the main motives, namely the need to state one's own point of view, to confirm one's social or group identity, to cope with nostalgia or the need for positive emotions, such as feelings of unity or solidarity.

Notes

1. Public opinion polls conducted in Ukraine in 2013 showed that 68 percent of residents had lost at least one of their relatives in the war and, for 82 percent of respondents, May 9 remains a great holiday (http://rb.com.ua/blog/9-maja-prazdnik-so-slezami-na-glazah/). In 2016 the question was worded differently: "What is the most popular holiday for you?" "May 9," answered 35 percent of respondents (http://kiis.com.ua/?lang=ukr&cat=reports&id=619&page=1).

2. Wylegała, "Podzielona czy zróżnicowana?"; Hrynevič, "Vijna za Vijnu"; Hrynevič, "Gespaltene Erinnerung"; Jilge, "Politics of History"; Scherrer, "Konkurrierende"; Scherrer, "Siegesmythos."

3. Gabowitsch, Gdaniec, and Makhotina, *Kriegsgedenken*; Gabowitsch, "Tag des Sieges"; Hellbeck, "Zerklüftete Gedenken"; Hellbeck, "Wie der Krieg"; Makhotina, "9. Mai"; Pastushenko, "9. Mai."

4. Gabowitsch, "Pamiatnik."

5. Tumarkin, *Living and Dead*; Rolf, *Sowjetische Massenfest*.

6. Svet, "Staging."

7. Brown, "Walking Memory"; Sklokina, "Ofitsiina radians'ka polityka pam'iati"; Zhurzhenko, "Chuzha viina"; Yekelchyk, "Leader."

8. Ukraine was a part of the Soviet Union as the Ukrainian Soviet Socialist Republic.

9. See the text of the decree by the Presidium of the Supreme Council of the Soviet Union at the Garant database, http://base.garant.ru/198106/#friends#ixzz3wMQduQJ7.

10. *Radians'ka Ukraina* (Soviet Ukraine), May 10, 1965, 1985, 1990.

11. Rolf, *Sowjetische Massenfeste*, 141.

12. Yekelchyk, "Leader"; Tumarkin, *Living and Dead*; Weiner, *Making Sense*.

13. On Russia Day, a military parade was held only once in 2003.

14. Rolf, *Sowjetische Massenfeste*, 352.

15. *Uryadovyi kurier* [Governmental courier], May 11, 1995, and May 12, 2010. It is important to note that in 1994 the tradition of military parades in Kyiv on August 24, Independence Day, was introduced. To date, twelve parades have been held. Most of them (eight) were held during the presidency of Leonid Kuchma (1994–2005) and two during the office of Viktor Yushchenko (2005–10). President Viktor Yanukovych (2010–14) did not hold the festive parade on Independence Day; instead, he ordered military parades in Kyiv, Odesa, Sevastopol, and Kerch on the occasion of the sixty-fifth anniversary of the victory in the Great Patriotic War in 2010. After the annexation of the Crimea and during the war with Russia in Donbas, Kyiv resumed the tradition of devoting the military parades on Khreshchatyk to Independence Day.

16. *Khreshchatyk*, May 11, 2000, *Khreshchatyk*, April 30, 2002, http://www.kreschatic.kiev.ua/ua/2213/art/5247.html.

17. "Parade in Kyiv," https://www.youtube.com/watch?v=_IEhaTFLQXQ, last modified May 9, 2013.

18. From May 2014 to February 2015, Ukraine suffered almost uninterrupted heavy fighting. During that time, the country had already lost at least 1,675 soldiers of the Armed Forces of Ukraine and volunteer battalions and more than six thousand civilians. Thousands of civilians were missing or captured; nearly one million people from the Crimea, Donetsk, and Luhansk regions became internally displaced persons. (For the text of the speech

by president of Ukraine Petro Poroshenko, see his speech to the Ukrainian parliament on May 8, 2015, http://tsn.ua/politika/emociyna-promova-poroshenka-v-radi-do-richnici-peremogi-povniy-tekst-426136.html.

19. Poroshenko, "About the Celebration."

20. Motyl, "Kiev's Purge."

21. This chapter uses the term "Ukrainian liberation movement" for a long list of movements, governments, and organizations that fought for an independent Ukraine throughout 20th-century Soviet rule.

22. More on the debate is on the *Krytyka* webpage: http://krytyka.com/ua/solutions/opinions, retrieved May 7, 2018. See also Marples, "Open Letter"; European Commission for Democracy through Law, "Law on the Condemnation of the Communist and National Socialist (Nazi) Regimes."

23. See more about the St. George Ribbon in Oushakine, "Remembering," 284–87.

24. Oushakine, "Remembering," 286.

25. Solod'ko, "Liudy'."

26. "V Sevastopole razvernuta rekordnaia georgievskaia lenta," Agentstvo Stratehichnykh Doslidzhen, retrieved May 8, 2010, http://sd.net.ua/2010/05/08/v_sevastopole_razvernuta_rekordnaja_georgievskaja_lenta.html.

27. Oushakine, "Remembering," 286–87.

28. Brown, "Performativnaia pamiat'." On May 16, 2017, the St. George Ribbon was officially banned in Ukraine, with those who produce or promote the symbol subject to fine or temporary arrest. According to former president Petro Poroshenko, the symbol had become a symbol of "of the aggression against Ukraine of 2014–2017." Censor.net, retrieved July 31, 2019, https://censor.net.ua/en/n443697.

29. From the website of Serhii Mishakin "3Z. Work. Who. Things," retrieved May 7, 2018, http://3z.com.ua/work/never-again/.

30. Mishakin, "Kvitka maku skhozha na ranu." See also Zinchenko, "Yak narodzhuvalys' maky pam'iati."

31. Famous people took part in the popularization of the new May 9 celebration symbol, the poppy, by presenting it and explaining its meaning. On May 7, in the Mystetskyi Arsenal Art Gallery a symbolic poppy was officially presented with the participation of the wife and children of President Petro Poroshenko. On May 1, the Kyiv city administration held a flash mob titled "The Poppies of Memory" at Maidan Nezalezhnosti.

32. Official website National Bank of Ukraine. Commemorative coins of Ukraine and souvenir products, retrieved July 31, 2019, https://bank.gov.ua/control/en/currentmoney/cmcoin/details?coin_id=675. Vypusk poshtovoii marky "Vichna pamiat' heroiam 1941–1945," retrieved July 31, 2019, https://ukrposhta.ua/en/vipusk-poshtovoï-marki-vichna-pamyat-geroyam/. Perhaps the authors did not have time to change the design of the stamp and the traditional dates "1941–1945." The stamp came into circulation on April 30, 2015, one month after the presidential decree of March 24, 2015. But we cannot rule out that the delay could have been motivated by the opinion of the Ukrposhta leadership on the interpretation of Victory Day.

33. On April 23, 2014, at a press conference, the chairman of the Kyiv city administration, Vladimir Bondarenko, said that no traditional Christmas tree would be placed on Maidan Nezalezhnosti anymore. There would also be no entertainment shows, since it is a place where people died ("Na Maidan bil'she ne stavitimut' yalinku," *Gazeta.ua*, April 23, 2015, http://gazeta.ua/articles/kiev-life/_na-majdani-bilshe-ne-stavitimut-yalinku/554219.

34. "Na Khreshhatyku vyklaly' gigantskyi napys iz korobok: 'Pam'iataiemo—1939–1945—Peremahaiemo,'" *Unian*, May 9, 2015, http://www.unian.ua/society/1076269-na-hreschatiku-viklali-gigantskiy-napis-iz-korobok-pamyataemo-1939-1945-peremagaemo-foto.html.

35. Speech of President Petro Poroshenko to the Parliament, May 8, 2015, http://tsn.ua/politika/emociyna-promova-poroshenka-v-radi-do-richnici-peremogi-povniy-tekst-426136.html. On May 9, Russia staged its biggest military parade, marking seventy years since the victory over Nazi Germany in World War II. Ukrainian citizens could watch a fragment of Moscow's parade on the news on television or on the internet (BBC News, "Russia Stages Massive WW2 Parade despite Western Boycott," May 9, 2015, http://www.bbc.com/news/world-europe-32668511).

36. "Pokladannia kvitiv Prezydentom Ukrainy v Parku Slavy," YouTube, May 9, 2015, https://www.youtube.com/watch?v=fOpKseU_rRM.

37. Interview with Yevhen Nishchuk (former minister of culture, an activist in the revolution at Maidan), May 9, 2015, cafés of the War Museum. Private archive of Jochen Hellbeck.

38. "'Opoblok' zibrav mitynh u centri Kyieva," *Ukrains'kyi tyzhden'*, May 9, 2015, http://tyzhden.ua/News/136023.

39. "Ukraintsi vzialy uchast' u Khodi Pamiati 'Bezsmertnyi polk,'" *Polk Inter*, May 10, 2015, http://polk.inter.ua/ru/news/text/2652-ukrayintsi-vzyali-uchast-u-khodi-pamyati-bezsmertniy-polk.
 40. Rolf, *Sowjetische Massenfest*, 346.
 41. Interview, May 9, 2015, female, forty years old, Park of Glory.
 42. Interview, May 9, 2015, female, forty-five years old, Arsenal'na metro square.
 43. Interview, May 9, 2015, man, forty-four years old, Park of Glory.
 44. Interview, May 9, 2015, female, fifty years old, square in front of the War Museum.
 45. Interview, May 9, 2015, man, fifty years old, Lavra street near the Lavra Museum.
 46. Interview, May 9, 2015, man, twenty-five years old, grounds of the War Museum.
 47. Interview, May 9, 2015, female, forty-five years old, grounds of the War Museum.
 48. Brown, "Performativnaia pamiat'."
 49. Interview, May 9, 2015, man, twenty-five years old, grounds of the War Museum.
 50. Interview, May 9, 2015, female, thirty years old, grounds of the War Museum.
 51. Interview, May 9, 2015, female, thirty-five years old, grounds of the War Museum.
 52. In total, four interviews with veterans of the war were recorded.
 53. Interview, May 9, 2015, man, ninety-six years old, Park of Glory.
 54. Interview, May 9, 2015, man, eighty-two years old, Park of Glory.
 55. Interview, May 9, 2015, man, ninety-two years old, grounds of the War Museum.
 56. Interview, May 9, 2015, man, fifty years old, Lavra street near the Lavra Museum.
 57. Interview, May 9, 2015, with Yevhen Nishchuk (former minister of culture, an activist in the revolution at Maidan), cafés of the War Museum. Private archive of Jochen Hellbeck.

Bibliography

Arkhipova, Aleksandra, Dmitry Doronin, Anna Kirzhuk, Daria Radchenko, Anna Sokolova, Alexei Titkov, and Elena Yugai. "Voina kak prazdnik, prazdnik kak voina: performativnaia kommemoratsiia Dnia Pobedy." *Antropologicheskii Forum* no. 33 (2017): 84–122. http://anthropologie.kunstkamera.ru/files/pdf/033/arkhipova_et_al.pdf/.
Brown, Judy. "Performativnaia pamiat': prazdnovanie Dnia Pobedy v Sevastopole." *Neprikosnovennyi Zapas* 3, no. 101 (2015). http://magazines.russ.ru/nz/2015/3/12b.html#_ftnref36.
———. "Walking Memory through City Space in Sevastopol, Crimea." In *Memory and Change in Europe: Eastern Perspectives*, edited by Małgorzata Pakier and Jaonna Wawrzyniak, 212–27. Oxford, UK: Berghahn, 2015.
European Commission for Democracy through Law (Venice Commission). "Law on the Condemnation of the Communist and National Socialist (Nazi) Regimes, and Prohibition of Propaganda of Their Symbols of Ukraine." October 28, 2015. http://www.venice.coe.int/webforms/documents/?pdf=CDL-REF(2015)045-e.
Gabowitsch, Mikhail. "Pamiatnik i prazdnik: etnografiia Dnia Pobedy." *Neprikosnovennyi Zapas* 3, no. 101 (2015). http://magazines.russ.ru/nz/2015/3.
———. "Der Tag des Sieges." *Stuttgarter Zeitung* 106, May 5, 2015, S. V1.
Gabowitsch, Mihhail, Cordula Gdaniec, and Ekaterina Makhotina, eds. *Kriegsgedenken als Event der 9. Mai 2015 im postsozialistischen Europa*. Paderborn, Ger.: Ferdinand Schöningh, 2016.
Hellbeck, Jochen. "Wie der Krieg das Kriegsgedenken überschattet." *Krautreporter*, May 11, 2015. https://krautreporter.de/669--wie-der-krieg-das-kriegsgedenken-uberschattet.
———. "Das zerklüftete Gedenken." *Frankfurter Allgemeine Zeitung*, May 5, 2015. http://www.faz.net/aktuell/politik/die-gegenwart/70-jahre-nach-dem-zweiten-weltkrieg-zerklueftetes-gedenken-13572281.html.
Hrynevič, Vladislav. "Gespaltene Erinnerung/Der zweite Weltkrieg in ukrainischen Gedenken." *Jahrbücher für Geschichte Osteuropa* 4–5, no. 55 (2005): 88–102.
———. "Viina za viinu." *Krytyka* 6, no. 176 (June 2012): 30–32. http://krytyka.com/ua/articles/viyna-za-viynu.
Jilge, Wilfried. "The Politics of History and the Second World War in Post-communist Ukraine (1986/1991–2004/2005)." *Jahrbücher für Geschichte Osteuropas* 1, no. 54 (2006): 50–81.
Makhotina, Ekaterina. "Der 9. Mai in Berlin: Gedenkfeier als Protest und Selbstvergewisserung." May 13, 2015. *Erinnerungskulturen: Erinnerung und Geschichtspolitik im östlichen und südöstlichen Europa*. http://erinnerung.hypotheses.org/144.

Marples, David R. "Open Letter from Scholars and Experts on Ukraine Re. the So-Called 'Anti-Communist Law.'" *Krytyka*, April 2015. http://krytyka.com/en/articles/open-letter-scholars-and-experts-ukraine-re-so-called-anti-communist-law#sthash.Fswc7Tot.dpuf.

Mishakin, Serhii. "Kvitka maku skhozha na ranu, chipliaty 'jiji na komirets'—ce iak prymiriaty' na sebe postril." *Ukrains'ka Pravda*, zhyttia, May 15, 2014. http://life.pravda.com.ua/person/2014/05/15/168426/.Motyl, Alexander J. "Kiev's Purge: Behind the New Legislation to Decommunize Ukraine." *Foreign Affairs*, April 28, 2015. https://www.foreignaffairs.com/articles/ukraine/2015-04-28/kievs-purge.

"Natsional'nyi bank vvodyt' v obih pamiatni monety '70 rokiv peremohy.'" *Ukr.media*, May 6, 2015. https://ukr.media/politics/235878/.

Oushakine, Serguei A. "Remembering in Public: On the Affective Management of History." *Ab Imperio* 1, no. 13 (2013): 269–302.

Pastushenko, Tetiana. "Der 9. Mai in Kiew: Krieg der Erinnerung in 'Friedenszeiten.'" *Erinnerungskulturen Erinnerung und Geschichtspolitik im östlichen und südöstlichen Europa*, July 2, 2015. http://erinnerung.hypotheses.org/297.

Pastushenko, Tetiana, Dmitro Titarenko, and Olena Cheban. "9 travnia 2014–2015 v Ukrayini: stari trady'ciyi—novi ceremoniyi vidznachennia." *Ukrayins'ky'i istorychnyi zhurnal* 3, no. 528 (2016): 106–24.

Poroshenko, Petro. "About the Celebration of the 70th Anniversary of the Victory over Nazism in Europe and the 70th Anniversary of the End of the Second World War in 2015." Presidential Decree 169, March 24, 2015. http://www.president.gov.ua/documents/1692015-18657.

Rolf, Malte. *Das sowjetische Massenfest*. Hamburg: Hamburger Edition, 2006.

Scherrer, Jutta. "Konkurrierende Erinnerungen." In *Mythen der Nationen: 1945—Arena der Erinnerungen*, edited by Monika Flacke, 719–36. Mainz, Ger.: Philipp von Zabern, 2004.

———. "Siegesmythos versus Vergangenheitsaufarbeitung." In *Mythen der Nationen: 1945—Arena der Erinnerungen*, edited by M. Flacke, 619–70. Mainz, Ger.: Philipp von Zabern, 2004.

Sklokina, Iryna. "Oficiina radians'ka polityka pam'iati pro natsysts'ku okupatsiiu Ukrayny (za materialamy' Kharkivs'koi oblasti [1943–1985 rr.])." PhD diss., Institute of History of Ukraine, 2014.

Solod'ko, Pavel. "Liudy', iaki stvoryly' styl' revoliutsii." *Ukrains'ka Pravda*, November 22, 2005. http://www.pravda.com.ua/articles/2005/11/22/3020805/.

Svet, Ala "Staging the Transnistrian Identity within the Heritage of Soviet Holidays." *History and Anthropology* 1, no. 24 (2013): 98–116.

Tumarkin, Nina. *The Living and the Dead: The Rise and Fall of the Cult of WWII in Russia*. New York: Harper Collins, 1994.

Weiner, Amir. *Making Sense of War: The Second World War and the Fate of the Bolshevik Revolution*. Princeton, NJ: Princeton University Press, 2001.

Wylegała, Anna. "Podzielona czy zróżnicowana? Jeszcze raz o pamięci społecznej na Ukrainie (z tożsamością w tle)." *Kultura i Społeczeństwo* 2, no. 59 (2015): 99–116.

Yekelchyk, Serhy. "The Leader, the Victory, and the Nation: Public Celebrations in Soviet Ukraine under Stalin (Kiev, 1943–1953)." *Jahrbücher für Geschichte Osteuropas* 1, no. 54 (2006): 3–19.

Zhurzhenko, Tatiana. "'Chuzha viina' chy 'spil'na peremoha'"? Natsionalizatsiia pam'iati pro druhu svitovu viinu na ukraino-rosiis'komu prykordonni." *Ukraina Moderna* no. 18 (2011): 100–126.

Zhurzhenko, Tatiana., Simon Lewis, and Julie Fedor. "War and Memory in Russia, Ukraine and Belarus." *Ukraina Moderna*, February 2, 2018. http://uamoderna.com/demontazh-pamyati/memory-wars.

Zinchenko, Alexander. "Yak narodzhuvalys' maky pamiati." *Istorychna Pravda*, May 8, 2017. http://www.istpravda.com.ua/columns/2017/05/8/149774/.

TETIANA PASTUSHENKO is Research Associate at the Institute of History of Ukraine, National Academy of Sciences of Ukraine.

4

(IN)DIFFERENT MEMORY

*World War II in the Memory of the
Last War's Generation in Ukraine*

Mykola Borovyk

THE ISSUES OF HISTORICAL MEMORY, PUBLIC REPRESENTATIONS, AND the social role of history have been at the center of attention of historiographical discourse at least for the past two decades. From the very beginning, this problem gained a loud political voice in Ukraine. It was distinctly visible during the Revolution of Euromaidan and later, in the course of Russian aggression against Ukraine. At that moment, historical topics and appeals toward the memory not only became the leading subjects of propaganda but were also predominant among the interpretations suggested by researchers.[1]

Such interpretations traditionally present Ukraine as a divided country inhabited by two confronting communities whose identities are based, at least partly, on different perceptions and evaluations of history. The memory of World War II has allegedly exerted a grave effect on the very formation of such communities.[2] At the same time, the predominance of the divided memory concept in historiography, as regards the Ukrainian memory of World War II, was never complete. Such researchers as Catherine Wanner, Wilfried Jilge, Andrii Portnov have stated the importance of problematizing a two-pole scheme of that kind.[3]

In the present chapter, we intend to address a specific aspect of this issue, namely, the memory of war witnesses in its relation to their self-identification. This group is a subject of special interest for several reasons. First, having a personal experience of living through the war and overcoming all its difficulties, these people are most likely supposed to build their identities on the basis of such an important experience.

In addition, witnesses usually have a special authority in the communities that they belong to as a source of information about the past.[4] Accordingly, the image of the war that the people belonging to the last war generation share and the ways they choose to recollect it are essential for the understanding of the general situation in Ukrainian society.

Finally, the representatives of the last war's generation are not only the bearers of an autobiographical memory of the war. They also have lived under the influence of official discourse of a certain type for decades and then experienced the dramatic change of the political regime and the transformation of memorial landscape. Consequently, by studying the memory of this generation, we can learn more about the functioning of the mechanisms of historical indoctrination.

Sources and Method

There are few points in the theory of memory studies on which a consensus among researchers exists. The identifying function of memory and the strong political implications of its identity potential undoubtedly belong to such points.[5] Collective memory matters politically, since it can be and is being used by political elites to legitimize their power and justify their policies.[6] Therefore, the attention of researchers in the field of memory studies is usually focused on what is called the policy of memory, historical politics, or memory wars.[7] And, when it comes to the politics of memory in Ukraine in the last two decades, at least until the beginning of the military conflict with Russia, it may well be described by the concept of divided memory. The political use of memory by various political players has had apparent expressive poles—nationalistic and post-Soviet, each of which focuses on the history of World War II as a central resource of the symbolic struggle.[8]

But do the politically charged representations of history and memory reflect accurately the perception and understanding of the past to those outside the politically active groups and, if so, to what extent? Tara Zahra, in her study of national identity, rightly noted that such phenomena as nation, gender, and race became ubiquitous in our historical imagination thanks in part to historians' greater focus on textual and cultural sources. Analyzing the contested content of nationalist ideologies and cultures without questioning the extent to which those ideologies resonate with their audiences, "historians risk remaining imprisoned within nationalists' own discursive universe."[9] This point seems relevant for memory studies as well.

I would argue that when it comes to collective identities in their relations with memory, what truly matters are not the politically sustained narratives of identity as such, but their internalization. Cultural representations of the past become an effective social factor only when used and attached to a meaning by individuals and groups.[10] How do individuals adapt common frames for a perception of the past? What occurs with such narratives and meanings that they communicate in the process of such adaptation? Which aspects of their personal and group experiences do individuals choose as the basis for self-identification? Are the events of the world war really decisive in such a role? We hope this chapter will help to move forward in answering these questions.

Evidently, the penetration of the world of the "silent majority's" memory and taking the research out of the framework of elite activities both require expansion of the source base. We consider to be incomplete and sometimes plainly questionable the use of indirect data (including the results of political campaigns) as well as the results provided by quantitative sociology. Only recently has the research on selected aspects of the issue based on the methods of qualitative interviewing been published.[11]

The sources of this chapter are the materials of the oral history project "Ukraine during World War II: The Everyday Experience of Survival." This project was implemented in 2010–15 under my supervision at Taras Shevchenko University of Kyiv. A total of 304 oral autobiographical memories were recorded using the method of semistructured biographical interview. The overwhelming majority of the interviews were conducted by master's candidates of the Department of History, who received appropriate training in the framework of the Oral History course.

Although an interview guide was prepared, we instructed interviewers to avoid rigidly following it and to use prepared questions only if necessary, after completing the biographical part of the interview. Nevertheless, for various reasons, not all interviews contain a broad biographical section. Some of them are recorded mainly on the basis of the guide.

The research objectives of the project, and thereby the content of the guide, was subjected to adjustment in the course of the work. Initially, we wanted to find new sources for the reconstruction of the life circumstances of the civilian population in Ukraine during the war. Accordingly, the guide was structured as four thematic blocks—ways of organizing and implementing power, the material conditions of life, cultural and religious life, and community relations. Later, we decided to reorient research into the field of historical memory studies. Accordingly, a section on the commemoration of war in the postwar period was added.

For the sample, we were not looking for interviewees with specific war experiences. Project participants selected respondents only on the basis of age—born in or before 1938—and the place of residence during the war—the modern territory of Ukraine (in both cases there are certain exceptions—five and six interviews, respectively). Although at the final stage of the project we tried to diversify the sample as much as possible according to regional characteristics, the vast majority of the interviews (219) were conducted with the people who lived during the war in central Ukraine; 14 lived in southern Ukraine, 23 – in eastern Ukraine, and 42 people were from the western regions. As regards other features, the sample roughly reflects the current demographic characteristics of the population of this age group: 204 interviews with women and 100 with men; in 238 cases the language of the interview was Ukrainian; in 65, Russian; in 1, Bulgarian. During the war, 245 of the respondents lived in the countryside, 59 in the city.

When we deal with oral sources, one of the most difficult methodological problems is the issue of classification. Every narration of the autobiographical story is unique. It always is an arbitrary imposition of meaning on the flow of memory. The problem with the meaning imposed is that it can hardly be measured.[12] As Frederick Whitling rightly noted, "The myriad of individual memory narratives might be organized in groups according to themes or clusters of individual memories. However, the problem then arises of distinguishing and identifying certain essential, unifying features."[13] Often such stories are intrinsically controversial. Therefore, it is very difficult to find reliable criteria for dividing sources into groups that would reflect, for example, identities of some kind.

Having the issue of politically relevant divisions of memory in mind, we primarily focused on each author's discursive strategies seeking the author's apparent intention to use his or her recollections about the war to justify or defend a certain political position. Contrary to our expectations, we were able to determine with clarity a very small quantity of interviews of that kind. Within the overall sample, we have identified eleven interviews defending clear pro-Soviet position and only three interviews justifying consistently the nationalists' interpretation of the war.[14] Interviews of the fourteen in these groups were analyzed separately.

The discursive strategies of the other interviews are difficult to identify with clarity in terms of politics or ideology. Even having demonstrated the obvious sympathy toward certain political values, the authors of such stories do not want or are not able to use their memories of the war as an argument in favor of their political preferences. For analysis, we chose a sample of ten interviews. For the selection, interviews with an extensive and free biographical component and more spacious, spontaneous answers were preferred. Since the present chapter, among other things, aimed to examine the hypothesis of the existence of a deep regional split of war memory in Ukraine, we also tried to diversify as much as possible the sampling on the basis of regional features.

In our analysis, the foremost attention will be focused on structural specifics of the texts in search of some common frames of memory representation and traces of competitive narrative forms dominating public discourses. By doing so, we expect to find out to what extent those discourses can influence the meaning of historical events for the bearers of personal memory about them and, consequently, their identities. We also will be attentive to what Michael Billig called "deixis," namely, the "forms of rhetorical pointing" as manifested in the use of the personal pronouns *we* and *they*, *us* and *them*, as well as to other linguistic means of reproducing the boundaries of belonging and exclusion.[15]

The Discourse of Heroes 1—"Soviet People"

The main features of what we call the official Soviet narrative, or the myth of the Great Patriotic War, was formed as early as in the course of the war. The myth changed substantially over time, but even after undergoing significant transformations it has never lost its main semantic core, which is the story of the war as a struggle, sacrifice, and victory, with the Soviet people as the main character thereof.[16]

From the very beginning, the narrative had distinct local peculiarities. In particular, with respect to the occupied regions, the emphasis was placed on the cruelty of the occupation regime and on resistance to invaders. The moments of occupation and, in particular, of the liberation were in the focus of attention almost as much as the dates of the beginning and end of the war. During the war, Soviet politics of history also created a specific Soviet Ukrainian historical image derived from the myth of the Great Patriotic War, which was intended to bolster the legitimacy of the Ukrainian Soviet Republic as a part of the union as a whole.[17]

Contrary to many predictions, this narrative survived the collapse of the Soviet empire. Having lost its socialist component but kept its meaning and form, the myth of the Great Patriotic War remained the only Soviet ideological construct that survived the fall of the communism. In independent Ukraine, however, it did not play the role of a governing myth anymore, although it had not been completely rejected by the postcommunist elites.[18]

In Ukraine's state policy of memory, the myth of the Great Patriotic War had been used variously as an attempt at moderate "nationalization" during the presidency of Leonid Kuchma and Victor Yushchenko or as the mild "resovietization" during Victor Yanukovych's office (when all our interviews were recorded). At the same time, some aspects of the history of World War II have always been at the center of fierce political debates. Such debates also had an important international dimension. Russia was one of the most active players in these processes.[19] Symbols associated with the war were widely used to mark political opponents.

Equating pro-European parties and nationalists with fascists became a common element of political discourse since the 2004 presidential election campaign.

In such a situation, for those who remained committed to Soviet values, the choice in favor of the Soviet narrative was not only the easiest, most familiar way to build their own memories, but also a demonstration of a political position. At the same time, those interviewees could not completely ignore changes in the political situation and new information that appeared in the public sphere.

The main feature that unites the pro-Soviet stories is the similarity of plot, which closely reflects the canonical Soviet way of picturing the war. For the most part, in this case, we come across a story about a struggle, about overcoming difficulties and victory, which is told from the standpoint of an active subject. The subject may be the interviewee him or herself, or, more often, their group, in other words, the Soviet people.

In an attempt to build a heroic plot of this kind, the interviewees try to bring up as many facts as possible about standing up against the enemy, even if they were only children at the time. The facts in an individual biography may be replaced by the stories about partisans or underground movement activities, or some symbolical events. Vira H. from Kyiv, for instance, remembered "the match of death" in Kyiv, the myth cultivated by Soviet and now Russian propaganda.[20]

The storyline of "the proper Soviet stories" also usually follows the established Soviet narrative framework: a deceitful attack, occupation, liberation, victory, and reconstruction. In full conformity with the above-mentioned local peculiarities of the Soviet narrative for Ukraine, the main component of the stories of this group deals with the occupation. Pro-Soviet stories seem very standardized in this component and contain some mandatory elements. Thus, the interviewees try to emphasize the contrast with the Soviet realia, without sparing any emotions. Some interviewees paid much attention to descriptions of the prewar state, trying to remember as many pleasant details as they could. Even if an interviewee did not have personal memories of that time, he or she tried to bring up the stories of third parties to add more contrast in the gap between a happy Soviet life and the occupation.

Besides that, the interviewees of this group make relatively stronger emphasis on the invaders' atrocities than the majority of other oral authors. Stories about Nazi repressions are often filled with graphic symbolism. Some of them carry an ideological subtext: "There was a Lenin monument in the square. The Germans took Lenin's head off, but the raised hand was turned into a gallows. Every morning we were peeking through a fence to see who was hanging there. There were girls and boys with signs on their necks that read 'partisan'; they changed quite often": this is the way Nadiya A. from the Sumy region remembers the first days of the occupation.[21] She also describes with cinematic persistence a scene in which Soviet prisoners of war were burned alive at a sugar plant.

These tragic episodes are very important in the informant's memory about the war. They have shadowed other memories. When she was asked to remember something other than the episodes of the occupants' killings and cruelty, to merely describe a regular day under the occupation, she was puzzled: "Well, I can't just do that. These moments that I told you about, they remain very vivid in my memory all of my life." But then she talks about the difficult everyday life, a half-hungry existence, and she remembers a song called *Natasha* that she memorized back then. We shall note that the song was not written until as late as 1947.

Prominently, the "pro-Soviet" interviewees, unlike the vast majority of our narrators, are not eager to accentuate the Jewish people among the victims of repressions. The above-mentioned story of Vira H. from Kyiv is very telling in this regard. She returns three times to the executions in Babi Yar but not once does she mention the Jews. Such a strategy is completely borrowed from the official Soviet narrative, which did not welcome "the over-accentuation" of Jewish victims.[22]

The occupation is the phase of the story where the main conflict unfolds. Accordingly, it is a time to describe the antagonists and to determine the enemies and allies. The pro-Soviet interviewees are usually clear when describing the Germans as cruel and merciless killers, but sometimes with exceptions. If a humane act on behalf of any occupant occurs in the story, it always demands a special explanation.

A more difficult problem for the Soviet historic consciousness was the phenomenon of collaboration. Neither the scale of this phenomenon nor its origins were ever in the center of the Soviet historical narratives since it could question the postulate of the moral and political unity of the Soviet people. Our respondents mostly tried to omit this topic.[23]

A special place among the Soviet others in the pro-Soviet stories analyzed here belongs to the *banderivtsi*. This term comes from the name of the leader of one of the wings of the Organization of Ukrainian Nationalists (OUN), Stepan Bandera, killed by a KGB agent in 1959. The common noun *banderivtsi* ("banderites") emerged as early as during the war. As a self-description, the term was already used actively in the second half of the 1940s and is present both in printed propaganda and in insurgent folklore.[24] In the Soviet documents and, thus, in propaganda, the term (in Russian *banderovtsy, benderovtsy*) was in use from late 1942.[25] After the liquidation of the nationalist's armed resistance the notion of "banderites" was used in the Soviet discourse as a pejorative for the designation of Ukrainian nationalists, more broadly, for all western Ukrainians. Nowadays in Russian discourse and discourse of pro-Russian groups in Ukraine, the notion is used to refer to all Ukrainians who support the idea of Ukraine's independence from Russia.

It the pro-Soviet interviews, banderites have the most negative character. Stories about the banderites always contain descriptions of inhumanely cruel scenes, tortures, and mass murders of innocent victims that took place during or after the war. According to the traditional Soviet line of critique, collaboration of the nationalists with the Nazis is always emphasized.

Obviously, such an emphasis is a result of the ongoing propagandist war in Ukraine at the time the interviews were recorded. However, the role and meaning of the character of such stories seems to be more complicated. Having no appropriate notion for positive self-description, our interviewees had to determine their identity against the other: "The 'banderites' are a sort of special people, they don't belong to the Ukrainians at all, they are not Ukrainians. The Ukrainians were normal people, just like all of us. Look at me, I'm Ukrainian. I am Ukrainian! The Ukrainians and the Russians are the same thing, but the 'banderites,' they're like fascists."[26] The term "Soviet people" in the current political situation sounded anachronistic; meanwhile, the ethnic terms cannot describe the community of people united by the Great Victory. Thus the banderites, the nearest actual enemy striving to destroy such a community, turns out to be the most likely "other" for negative identification.

Besides that, the lack of a positive self-identification also possibly explains at least partly the most surprising feature of the interviews analyzed here, the noticeable fuzziness of the culmination and resolution, which were always presented as liberation and victory, according to the Soviet war narrative. Despite expectations, in the "pro-Soviet" interviews, we come across very laconic and constricted depictions of Soviet power's return and the end of the war. The state that won the war did not exist anymore, but its enemies—Ukrainian nationalists, who seemed to have been defeated once—were getting the upper hand and compromising the fullness of the victory.

The appearance of such novelties indicates great pressure experienced by the carriers of the Soviet memory. The pressure occurs not only at the level of symbolic events but also through the distribution of information, which obviously contradicts the Soviet war narrative. To protect their position, this group of interviewees chooses a strategy that varies from an offensive mode (e.g., the role of the Ukrainian nationalists) to balancing between keeping silent and attempting to concoct a convincing excuse. Herewith the greatest deal of attention is focused on the most problematic and endangered aspects of the memory.

The beginnings of the war, when the Soviet regime crumbled in Ukraine, and the role of the prewar repressions in the catastrophe of 1941 were traditionally among the biggest silences of the Soviet war narrative.[27] Later, during Perestroika, these subjects became the most salient targets of the historical revelations focusing on the figure of Stalin.[28] Our respondents tried not to touch on these topics willingly. Upon receiving a question about the relations between the government and the population in prewar times, however, when they obviously felt an implicit threat of discrediting the Soviet system, they usually became actively defensive.

Perhaps the most coherent and consistent line of defense was presented in the story of Zinaiida Z. (Zhytomyr region): "It was strict before the war and after [*meaning the government*]. The discipline was strict." She admits that some people were arrested and some displaced, but she tries to downplay the scale of repression. The subject of her special concern is the issue of famine-genocide, the very idea of which she believes was "brought from America" at the time of the Yushchenko presidency. "All through the thirties, I'd never once seen anyone dying of hunger."[29]

The interviewee realizes that she cannot absolutely deny the existence of objective reasons for personal criticism of Stalin. The excuses that she offers obviously have origins in post-Soviet historical discussions: "He was cruel to everyone, including himself." She mentions the popular images of his single pair of boots and his single overcoat as symbols of selflessness, and the story about Stalin's son's captivity as an almost apocryphal example of his largest sacrifice to save the nation.

The explanations of defeat at the beginning of the war also look quite standard: "The war was a surprise for our army everywhere. Stalin didn't believe that. . . . He thought there was an agreement." The narrator also finds it necessary to deny particularly the existence of the German-Soviet plot of splitting Poland. Since Perestroika in the Soviet Union, and then in independent Ukraine, the theme of the Molotov-Ribbentrop Pact has been one of the central issues in historical discussions. For the Ukrainian national narrative, the very fact of the secret agreement between Hitler and Stalin was one of the key facts in its struggle against the Soviet model of memory. It undermined the moral position of the Soviet Union and allowed, as Tatiana Zhurzhenko noted, coping with the main accusations against the OUN of cooperation with the Nazis.[30] For the advocates of the Soviet position, justification of this agreement is one of the most difficult intellectual tasks. But Zinaiida Zh. considers it better to simply deny the very possibility of a conspiracy between the Soviet Union and the Nazis.

Finally, one of the most valuable elements of the Soviet narrative that needs defending for the narrators of this group is the concept of the "friendship of the peoples." In almost all the Russian-language interviews, we come across the display of emphasized affection and respect for the Ukrainian language and culture. Valentyna Z. (born 1925, Sumy region), a teacher of Russian literature, starts her story about studying in school with a mention of the envy toward Ukrainians who were producing plays in Ukrainian.[31] Such episodes must demonstrate the absence of any discrimination against the Ukrainian language and culture in the Soviet Union, contrary to the accusations that are a part of the historical policy in independent Ukraine.

The authors of the pro-Soviet stories often emphasize the unimportance of any ethnic divisions in the Soviet Union, presenting it as one of the biggest advantages of the Soviet society. At the same time, some interviews give the impression that the Jews were outside the natural community of "us," despite the declared insignificance of ethnicity. Thus, Zinaiida Zh. apparently speaks of the Jews rather as of "others": "People, you know, weren't happy about the Jews. Why? You see, the Jews never operated tractors; they were not members of a collective farm, never. They only did their thing, which is commerce, that's it." But with this she quickly mentions a positive example of a Jewish shoemaker and her friendship with the Jewish students at school; she noted that the Jews were never "separated."

Who are these narrators and why is this kind of memory about the war so important for them? The biographies of the interviewees whom we identified as pro-Soviet, while differing in many important aspects, have some similar features. The average age in this group is significantly lower than the average age of all the participants in the project. Most of them had been children during the war. Nevertheless, their stories are much more textured, seem more coherent but at the same time less spontaneous than most of the other stories we have recorded.

A possible explanation for the common aspects could be the much higher educational level of the interviewees in this group than in the others, which should then enhance their narrative capabilities and skills. More than a half the interviewees in this group hold a degree in higher education, twice as many as the average number in the project overall. Another—and obviously the most important—coincidence is that almost all of them after the war had successful careers and held administrative positions. We must also note that there are no inhabitants of western Ukraine in this group, although we were not able to reveal any other regional particularities or language preferences.

The Soviet myth of the Great Patriotic War has definitely preserved some influence in Ukraine. At the same time, nowadays the myth itself and the community of people united by the memory of the Soviet's Great Victory is undergoing significant transformations. Contrary to the functions performed by historical myths in society in general, this narrative strain does not seem to be connected to some clear project of the future, but rather looks like a rudiment of an epoch that is fading away.

The Discourse of Heroes 2—"The Banderites"

The composition of the group of the interviewees whose stories we were able to identify more or less confidently as ones that defended the nationalist interpretation of World War II is very illustrative. Each of them was an active participant in the nationalist underground movement or armed resistance and each of them had experienced imprisonment in the gulag system. It was unexpected for us that among the forty-two interviewees originating from western regions, which are considered to be a stronghold of nationalism in the Ukraine of today and where the OUN was the most active during the war, nobody, except the participants of these structures, has fully adopted the nationalistic heroic discourse of the war history.

The nationalist metanarrative of the war was formed in the Ukrainian diaspora in North America and Western Europe.[32] In the most schematic form, it depicts World War II in Ukraine as a history of two occupations and Ukraine as a victim of two totalitarian regimes, against which the Ukrainian people, led by the nationalists, fought. The ultimate goal of such a struggle was to establish a sovereign Ukrainian state.

This narrative was cut off from the public distribution in Ukraine right up to the moment of the collapse of the Soviet system. In Soviet Ukraine, some version of a counter-memory of the war could be preserved only at the family level. But in the postcommunist period, the situation has changed substantially. Many veterans of the nationalistic underground became active participants in local politics. For them, the attaining of independence became an ultimate historical justification of their struggle and sacrifices made. The participation in the struggle became a sort of political and social capital.

In the public sphere, the nationalistic narrative of "national liberation struggle" had become a significant part of the discourse about the past.[33] The symbolic environment in western regions was changed in favor of the new dominant narrative. Although Soviet war memorials remained mostly intact, new monuments of new heroes symbolizing the struggle for independence were erected.[34] Educational system, at least on the level of textbook content, adopted a heroic interpretation of the OUN's and Ukrainian Insurgent Army's (UPA's) activities.[35] Tania Robertson and Karina Korostelina's researches demonstrate that, since the gaining of independence, the content of the teaching of history in Ukraine has depended not so much on the textbooks as on the personal position of teachers.[36] The teachers in western regions mostly adopted the new national narrative.

Consequently, it is quite possible—even though the problem obviously requires additional scrutiny—that the generation that was being socialized during the independence period has accepted this interpretation as their own "memory" of the war.[37] At the same time, for the majority of our interviewees, even enthusiastic support of national sovereignty turned out to be insufficient for overcoming the complexity of their personal memory about living during the bloodstained partisan war. For some of them, such a support now created a need to explain their own passivity or even "collaboration" with the Soviet regime.

The situation of his own uneasy choice is told by a L'viv region resident, Volodymyr K. In 1944, having been drafted into the Soviet army, he considered the possibility of operating in the interests of the nationalist insurgency ("our Ukrainian national partisans") instead. His father advised against it, however, contending that they did not have any chance of winning and they would all die. Volodymyr K. recollects that his friends joined the underground, "the Ukrainian national army" in his own words, but he went into the Red Army.[38]

It seems as if this choice from the past still remains (or maybe has become now) a painful memory. Volodymyr K. revisits it several times, mentioning the lack of chances for gaining independence at the time. These musings that the chances for the nationalists to win was lacking and that their struggle caused only unnecessary sacrifices can be encountered in many other interviews.

An example of a completely different heroic discourse is the story of Antin M., almost a contemporary of Volodymyr K. and also a resident of Rohatyn.[39] He went through all the stages of a successful career of a politically active nationalist. In 1940, he joined an OUN youth organization and later he was accepted into the main structure. For a long time, he served as a communication agent, and in 1944 he was appointed the leader of the OUN Security Service in his rural district.

The plot of his story generally resembles that of his Soviet counterparts. It is a story of struggle, of overcoming difficulties and of self-sacrifices for a greater goal—all being told from the standpoint of an active subject. The subject here is rather a group, not an individual. But while in the Soviet version such a group is represented by the Soviet people, in the nationalist version it is represented by the Ukrainians, or rather by the "Organization" and the Ukrainians.

Antin M. describes, in an obviously calm manner, the beginning of his political career. He does not provide any motives for his actions. The school where he was a grade-A student, participation in the Prosvita Society, and his admission into the Organization, the narrator regards these as completely normal for a boy of his generation.[40] The pronoun *we*, in Antin M.'s narrative, mostly describes the active members of the national movement. The widest group of interest for the carriers of nationalist discourse is the Ukrainians. To describe this group, alongside the Ukrainians, Antin M. also uses the term *people* (*narid*). All the interviewees in this group were born and raised in a society of prewar Poland where ethnic divisions were the central markers of social identification, and in which they felt discriminated. The war amplified the ethnicization of society even more, but it was hardly a crucial factor in this case.

The nationalists from Galicia and Volyn also unconditionally include Ukrainians from the Soviet Union in their group. But they do not display any connection between their war experience and their self-identification as members of a great Ukrainian nation. Antin M. says that in 1939 they were waiting for "the Ukrainian brothers" to liberate them from Polish captivity. In his description of the welcoming of the Soviet army in his own village in 1944, he offers as a reasonable explanation for the behavior of his fellow villagers that most of the Soviet troops were "our guys" from Vinnytsia and Khmelnytskyi regions who were "just sent to die."

Later, the interviewee revisits the problem of the national unity of Ukrainians several times and even expresses his doubts about the resurrection of the Greek Catholic Church that is so traditional for Galicia and that was "allowed by Gorbachev," since "it was made to prevent people from uniting, to drive them apart."

The standard structure of the nationalist story is a description of the rotation of invasive regimes and the tale of an all-national struggle against these regimes. Herewith, while describing the change of regimes from the standpoint of a Ukrainian nationalist, Antin M.—along with his fellows—often resorts to Soviet vocabulary: "In 1939, we were liberated by the Soviet occupants" or "On 17 September of 1939, the Red army liberated us again."[41] After noticing his slip of tongue, Mykola Y. specifies: "'Liberators' is how they were called, I can only call them 'liberators' in quotation marks." At a different point in the interview, when talking emotionally, his eyes brimming with tears, about the fate of his older brother, who died as a member of the UPA, the narrator called the war the Great Patriotic War. Later he corrected it to World War II.

Such speech errors are hardly accidental. For decades, the authors of the stories lived in a society in which Soviet language was the only possible way to describe the war. Language habits, as well as a lack of alternatives, force them to use the enemy's words and invest them with another meaning. Here, taking part in the fierce war for memory, nationalists, much like their pro-Soviet counterparts, often take a defensive stance. They draw their attention to the most problematic, most endangered aspects of their memory framework.

Traditionally, Soviet propaganda attempted to represent Ukrainian nationalists as a criminal gang of outcasts who enjoyed no support on the part of Ukrainian people and owed their existence to Nazi support. The OUN and UPA were accused of mass murders and plundering of Soviet people. The nationalists' opponents, in the ideological struggle of the past two decades, also revitalized the leading line of accusations that originated from the Soviet era.

On the contrary, the interviewees try to primarily emphasize the nationwide scale of the movement. In the interviews conducted by Oleksandr Pahiria, there was a special question on the sources of support for the insurgent army. The response of Vasyl' P. represents the general enthusiasm of other memories: "We were organizing meetings in villages and spoke about our goal, about our struggle, we were asking the people to donate some clothes or food if they could. Just like that. And so the people responded and donated."[42] Most of the interviewees had the urge to specifically emphasize that they never allowed any violent actions or plundering.

Nationalist discourse bearers also paid much attention to the question of collaboration with the Germans. Antin M.'s memories contain only two detailed descriptions of armed conflicts. Both were between the UPA and Wehrmacht units. Similarly, almost all the battles mentioned by Stepan B., who joined the UPA from its very formation, were fought against the Germans. And only one episode is related to the Red Army. It was a story about nationalist partisans aiding an injured Soviet officer.[43] Antin M. does not hide the reasons for his attention to this question: "I can tell about this event, what I will start with is that those Moscow troubadours state that our insurgent army and our Galician division were helping the Germans, that the Germans were arming them. Those are lies of the Moscow intelligence, made up to demonize them, but it didn't actually happen."

A comparison of the regimes against which nationalists fought during the war is another common tendency of nationalist interviews. "The liberators fled, other liberators came in, same as the previous ones, exactly the same."[44] Obviously, this way of describing them is used to disprove accusations of cooperation with the Nazis. The accusations toward the two regimes are almost identical: the deception of the Ukrainians who wanted independence, repressions, and plundering.

It is interesting that this strategy mostly covers the Nazi and Soviet regimes, but Poland is almost left out despite the fact that the Ukrainian nationalist movement was initially formed as an anti-Polish one, and during the war the Ukrainian-Polish conflict was strongly pronounced. Of course, at the time the recollections were recorded, Poland had ceased to seem a menace to Ukrainian independence. It is very likely, however, that the silence is linked to the most noticeable omission in the nationalist's recollection—the Volhynian massacre.

In the spring of 1943, a Ukrainian-Polish conflict erupted in Volhynia, in which tens of thousands of innocent people were killed. The vast majority of Polish victims were killed during the ethnic cleansing committed by UPA units. In the 2000s, this tragedy became an important part of the discourse on the war in Ukraine. Political opponents of nationalists have actively used the topic to discredit their opponents.[45] But in no interview with the nationalists is there a word about the killing of the Poles.

Thus, in the memoirs of Stepan B., who participated between late 1942 and late 1944 in a large detachment of the UPA operating in Volhynia, the summer of 1943, the period of the highest escalation of ethnic cleansing, is almost completely omitted. But in answering the question about the attitude toward the Poles in the prewar period, he noted that the relations were tense, but no one killed the Poles. We suppose that this phrase referred not so much to the interethnic relations before the war, but as a vague allusion to the "toxic memory" of the 1943 massacre.

Another obvious omission is the tragedy of the Holocaust. Since the beginning of the 1990s, accusations of OUN involvement in the Holocaust have begun to appear in the public sphere, which was obviously a new development in contrast with Soviet times.[46] Soviet propaganda aimed at the Soviet population talked more about the anti-Soviet Union activities of the Ukrainian nationalists and the Zionists. At the time of the interviews, historical research has already revealed a lot of evidence of the nationalists' involvement in many Holocaust actions, in particular, in the wave of pogroms in the summer of 1941.[47] At the same time, the tragedy of the Holocaust has not yet become the focus in discussions about the memory of the war in Ukraine then. At least, it does not seem that any of nationalist narrators considers such accusation to pose a serious hazard.

Antin M. recalled the destruction of the Jewish ghetto in Rohatyn near the end of the interview when answering a question about a comparison of the German and Soviet regimes: "You know what, it was like seeing two thousand Jews being led to execution. It wasn't pleasant." Upon the interviewer's request to tell more about the executions of the Jews, the interviewee very explicitly described how the Jews of Rohatyn were killed. During the conversation, he even briefly mentioned the participation of the Ukrainian police but noticed that they never shot anyone. Unlike the case of the slaughter of the Poles, it does not seem that the nationalists view the Holocaust as "their" crime.

When recalling World War II, the adherents of the nationalist narrative had the most substantial grounds to consider themselves to be winners. From among all the parties to the conflict, they turned out to have come closest to achieving their goals in the long run. Each of these stories, however, carries the strain of the heavy burdens of the past, which one can keep silent about, but which can hardly be forgotten.

Collected Memory

An attempt to define common features in the interviews of the last group has demonstrated that the most obvious aspect is the absence of what is commonly called a collective memory. Most of the people we interviewed had not been encouraged to share their memories during Soviet rule outside the circle of their closest local environment. For most of them, their life under the occupation was a problem rather than an experience that could be considered proper for sharing. "This label was on my forehead for a very long time," states Valentyna Y. (Kerch, Crimea) by the end of her interview.[48]

This does not mean that inside the local communities there was no sharing of information, but the participants of the process realized that they could not move beyond the frames that had been installed by the official discourse. "Everyone was carrying inside their souls that. . . . if living is that difficult, then who would praise him (Stalin)? But in the old times, how could one say anything? God forbid! Everyone was only praising everything."[49]

A personal story, based on one's own experience, coexists in these interviews not with similar stories from witnesses but mostly with an external narrative. Most often, interviewees call this narrative history. The respondents always clearly distinguish the realm of their own memory and the realm of "history." With this, they consider the memory to be most credible because it is based on their own or on their relatives' experience: "We know it all because we've been through it."[50]

The "history" is present—if it is present at all—in most of the interviews as a background to events rather than a plot guide or a storyline, as we can see from the ideologically motivated interviews. Astonishing, in this regard, is the incapability of the Soviet historical narrative to direct and formalize the memories of the representatives of the last war's generation, who were under the pressure of a Soviet ideological machine for most of their lives.

As Catherine Wanner has pointed out, the major problem of Soviet historical mythology was its coexistence with the personal memories of participants and witnesses, which did not fit the official framework. Later, the shock from the discovery of another history during Perestroika seriously damaged Soviet war mythology. The disclosure of the state's manipulations of history legitimized "the people's truth" about the war,[51] while the credibility of any official historiography was seriously compromised.[52] Valentyna Y., a certified teacher of history and Russian, not once during her interview referred to textbooks as a source of historical knowledge. Under such circumstances, it has proved to be very difficult for any viable mythology, including the nationalist one, to replace the Soviet historical narrative.

The crisis of confidence in official history does not mean that viable narratives have lost all influence. The sources of "authentic" historical information referred to by our narrators are, however, quite miscellaneous. The Soviet historical pop culture (fiction literature, historical tours, but never movies), periodicals, and the television programs of the post-Soviet period are often mentioned. We may observe a pressure of history in the descriptions of some events and situations, but this influence now appears to be very fragmented and selective.

How limited the impact of the competitive war narratives upon the personal stories of witnesses and participants is one can see in the organization of time and space of such memories. The chronology in these stories is built hierarchically. Inside the story, three layers of time coexist: the time of personal history and personal biography, sometimes the time of community that the interviewee considers himself or herself a part of, and also the general—"historical" chronology—based on events that have been recognized socially as important and pivotal.[53] It is worth noting that, among our stories, the layer of the family history more commonly appears as a defining one, that it actualizes the priorities in the selection of external reliance on chronological points. When informed that the subject of the project is the war, the narrators nevertheless often start his or her story with the collectivization and famine of 1932–33, which were the most important turning points in the history of the majority of peasants' families in Ukraine.[54]

Another important chronological point in the stories is the beginning of the war. Most respondents consider the beginning of the war to be June 22, 1941. But connections with a personal and family history are also distinctive in many descriptions of the war's beginning. In cases where the everyday life of a family did not significantly shift in June 1941—if no one was drafted, for example—the beginning of the war is not described as a radical change, as was common for the Soviet historical narrative. "How did the war begin? Well, not a war, we only heard there was a war. . . . For two months we only knew there was a war, the plant was evacuated, but there was no fighting, nothing."[55]

The stories about the return of Soviet authorities and the ensuing end of the war, for the most part, contain neither hatred nor alienation, which the carriers of the nationalist point of view would have been likely to express, nor the triumphant enthusiasm supported by Soviet propaganda. The entrance of the Soviet troops is often described rather ordinarily. It is important that, in this case, the respondents also emphasize the return of the Red Army rather than May 9, 1945, which for decades after the war became and remains a crucial culmination point in the war history, according to both Soviet and post-Soviet historical narratives.

In reality, the Victory Day did not change much in the everyday lives of the majority of the population. The period between the return of Soviet authorities and Stalin's death was a time of hardship, poverty, famine, and unbearable taxes, but the hated Nazi regime was finally gone. A distinctive feature is that most of the informants use Soviet vocabulary to describe the end of the war. The Ukrainian-speaking interviewees even use Russian words for "liberation" and "victory" (similar to the way the Russian-speaking Crimean resident uses a Ukrainian word to describe the declaration of independence of Ukraine). Nevertheless, they do not treat these events according to the Soviet narrative. They rather speak of peace, the end of war, hope for the return of their relatives but not of defeating the enemy; they mostly concentrate on the fate of the family, not the country.

The description of the main conflict plots of war stories also looks very problematic from the standpoint of both the Soviet and the nationalist narratives. Perhaps it can most vividly be illustrated by the example of OUN and UPA activities. Unlike pro-Soviet interviews, the banderites are mentioned only by those interviewees for whom the factor of a nationalist movement belongs to their personal experience (three interviews out of ten). In all cases, when the interview touches on the nationalist movement, we see neither distinct condemnation nor glorification. The opinions of Teodozii K. and Volodymyr K. from Galicia and Mariia U. from central Ukraine, do not distinctly differ. "They were against the Germans, and when the Germans left and the Ruskis came, they were against the Ruskis. They were for Ukraine, and it was stupid at the time. Because it was a time when they failed to create anything and brought only damage instead."[56]

Mariia U., a teacher, was appointed to work in Volhynia upon her graduation. She tells about the killings of NKVD members, militiamen, Soviet officials, and the heads of collective farms by the banderites. At the same time, she does not deny the very idea of the struggle for independence, even though during the interview a feeling persisted that she was hardly able to combine this idea with personal experience: "Bandera, Bandera. I don't even know. The fight for independent Ukraine shouldn't be held in such a manner. They had to fight the oppressors, but not those who were sent to help them. This is my view."

They, Ours, We

The interviewees from this group were usually very reluctant to consciously affiliate themselves with any group that went beyond the local. But through their stories we can reconstruct a system of inclusion and exclusion that allows us to grasp the idea of this generation's social world. The picture, just as one concerning any other aspect, is very desultory and fragmented, although certain features can be discerned in the analyzed interviews.

The only apparent and obvious "other" in almost every reminiscence that we documented were the Germans and their allies, the Romanians, Hungarians, and Slovaks. The reason for the distinction is primarily ethnic and cultural, but not political. The Vlasovites and polizei are usually categorized as "ours," even though they could be crucially criticized.

The method of presenting contacts with the Germans is quite diverse. Respondents often stumble upon an inconsistency between personal experience and their general knowledge about the war. In such cases, some are willing to evaluate their own experience as limited and incomplete: "They say that over there [Germans] were committing atrocities. I believe that, but as I see it, they didn't do that here."[57] From their own experience, the respondents latently argue the Soviet narrative—they are trying to differentiate, to humanize the enemy: "There were good Germans, too, there were those who shared their meals. . . . Because he remembers his own children over there."[58]

At the same time, completely anti-Soviet interpretations also occur. Often in the interviews (only one out of ten, in this selection, but only two of them were recorded with residents where the Soviet partisans had been active), accusations of repression are transferred onto the Soviet partisans, who are presented as provocateurs.[59]

There are also narrative models in which the Germans are described as the carriers of European culture and order. For Galicia, such descriptions are more common, but this also often occurs in the stories of residents from other regions of Ukraine. A Soviet veteran, a resident of Luhansk region, Ivan K., speaks about the Romanians and the Germans who occupied his village with neutral emotion, even respectfully. He laughs while telling a story about the way the German administration handled the problem of collective farm property theft by installing a gallows next to a melon patch. The story sounds like the most effective instrument of managing the inhabitants of his village. "Our people are horrible," he says later when he mentions the locals stealing things off the bodies of the killed Soviet soldiers.[60] It is difficult to determine the accuracy of such a story in this case. But it seems as if this plot became a part of the local folklore as a symbol of authoritative power.[61]

The origin, meaning, and limits of the concept of "ours," which is most commonly voiced in the interviews as a marker of positive self-identification for our respondents, are difficult to determine precisely; for instance, it is very difficult to understand whether the concept in its political dimension—when it is applied to Soviet authorities and their representatives or to the Soviet army—belonged to respondents' everyday vocabulary during the war or whether it was introduced later by Soviet art propaganda.[62]

The most obvious example of the discrepancy between the customary concept and the one acquired at the time of the event can be observed in the interview with Olena K. She was born in Slovakia into a Hungarian-Slovak family; in 1944, she was a citizen of Hungary and lived in Uzhhorod. When the Red Army was entering the city, she was not a Soviet citizen and she spoke neither Ukrainian nor Russian. She nevertheless describes the Red Army entering Uzhhorod as "ours came in."[63]

The words that are used in the analyzed interviews for the description of the Soviet army as synonyms, substitutes, or supplements for the marker of "ours" are various. Those can be ethnic terms: mostly *Ruskis*, sometimes *katsaps* (a pejorative for Russians), or more politically driven ones like *Soviets* (almost exclusively in the Russian-speaking interviews) and "the Reds." And all these terms were preserved most likely from the time of acquiring the relevant experience, since none of them, except for *Soviets*, was a part of either Soviet or nationalist (in this case, such terms as *Bolsheviks*, *Soviets*, and *Muscovites* had to be used) competitive discourses in the postwar time.

The method of using ethnic markers for self-description constitutes the most conspicuous difference between the interviews on a regional scale. For the people of Galicia, it is a normal way of self-identification, and the nationality is exclusive; it does not provide the possibility to enter any other wider group. They never identify themselves as Ruskis, but always do so with the Ukrainians outside Galicia. But the formation of such an idea happened long before the war, and judging from our interviews, the war did not bring any significant changes to this order: "We knew there was a famine in 1933. I also remember, I was in school then, I was old enough to go to school . . . they said we have to help our Ukrainians, because there is a famine in the east."[64]

The respondents from eastern and central Ukraine use ethnic categories in a much more complicated and even blurred way. On the one hand, the ethnic background is typically considered to be the most constant identification marker. Our interviews contain surprising concepts that sound like race categories: "I'm Mestizo! My mother is Russian from the Orel region, my father is Ukrainian."[65] On the other hand, nationality is almost never emphasized and is mostly considered to be insignificant. Identification of the Ruskis as "ours" does not prevent the interviewees from identifying themselves as Ukrainians also. In those cases where cultural differences and behavioral patterns cross ethnic unity, the old imperial borders appear dominant. Unable to explain the behavior of the western Ukrainian population, Mariya U. solves the problem for herself by taking them out of the limits of her community: "Since they were under Poland, they're Poles. For the Jews they're scary. It is Poland for them."

The position of the Jews in the them-ours frame of reference is mostly ambiguous. The interviewees analyzed here, more often than the carriers of ideological discourses, voluntarily mention the killings of the Jews. There are three such in the present set of ten. And, while the interviewees have a clear idea of how the Jews were treated by the occupiers, most of them are not inclined to consider the Holocaust as a crime that deserves priority attention. Some of the explanations and interpretations voiced during the interviews display a considerable level of detachment between the Jewish and non-Jewish population. The most accurate description for the Jews on the scale of our non-Jewish respondents' self-identification would be a concept like "the other ours."

Alongside the term *ours* (*nashi*), the respondents also use *we* (*svoji*). In some cases, they sound like complete synonyms, but the term *we* is used as a marker for members of a closely knit community, whereas *ours* is attributed to wider political connotations. That being said, the term *we* is usually more emotionally neutral. The attitude almost always depends on the behavior of the described person. The local members of the occupational administration and the polizei are more commonly described as *we* rather than *ours*. It also can be used for agents of the Soviet authorities, especially those described in a negative light.

By evoking their own experience, most of our interviewees seem to be inclined to show alienation from any government and place themselves in a position of those managed and exploited: "I was fine [with the Soviet government] because people have to fit in, whatever the government, you have to fit in. The Germans were here for four years, we worked for them. . . . When the Reds came in, we worked for them. . . . We did the same under any government."[66]

None of the interviews contains anything that could be regarded as attention to or sympathy with communist ideology. It is worth mentioning that four interviewees out of ten were from families whose members belonged to local communist administrative elites. But in postwar times, they did not have successful administrative careers. It seems to be obvious that for the formation of an ideologically motivated position about the past, the further trajectory of one's life, and one's life interests associated with it were more important.

At the same time, this lack of attention to ideological issues and criticism of certain periods or activities of the Soviet government does not prove any anti-Soviet position of the respondents. Most of them even share the Soviet nostalgia, but their motives for that are not connected to some symbolic events and sound rather pragmatic. Improvement in living conditions in the late Soviet time, a stable social order, and a predictable future seem to be much more persuasive than the heroic narratives of Soviet propaganda and the pride of military success.

Tara Zahra uses the terms "national indifference" and "imagined noncommunity" to denote behavior or people who simply do not organize their lives or political allegiances according to nationalist priorities.[67] Could we describe the memory of people who refused or were not able to bind their memories of war to political positions as "indifferent memory"? Following Zahra, we are far from the idea of either romanticizing or pathologizing such indifference. We also do not have sufficient grounds to claim that indifference was universal. But due attention to the phenomenon makes it possible to raise important questions not only about capabilities but also about the limitations of collective memory.

Conclusions

Thus, if there is a split in the Ukrainian war memory, then we have to locate it outside the world war generation. In the general body of materials that we collected, ideologically or politically motivated methods of World War II memory representation are presented as a rare exception rather than a rule. Stories constructed on the basis of an ideologically motivated narrative strategy make up barely 5 percent of all the interviews we recorded. It is understood that the representativeness of a sample in qualitative research is very relative, but the correlation certainly says something.

Considering the fact that our respondents were under the influence of official mechanisms of historical indoctrination for almost seven decades, in which World War II always was and remains one of the fundamental—if not *the* fundamental—objects of interest, our result challenges the effectiveness of such a mechanism. People can do some things with memory but not everything they want to. We can confirm that personal memories, which are based on a person's own experience, set limits for manipulation that are very difficult to overcome. As James Wertsch rightly pointed out, cultural tools do not act mechanically.[68] Only a combination of the shifting influence of public discourse and at least a minimal level of individual agency and horizontal communication may make those limits more likely to change.

The present study does not resolve the issue of which events or processes are determinative in the formation of group identities, whether as catastrophic shifts or routine processes. Yet our material points rather to the latter. The contents of our interviews confirm the heterogeneity of Ukrainian society. Our respondents often consider themselves to be a part of different communities, which partially appear outside the modern Ukrainian state's context and partially they second old imperial borders. But in the case of the analyzed generation, we were not able to determine any obvious connection between the formation—and even transformation—of such communities and the memory of World War II.

Notes

1. A special issue of *Kritika* is among the prominent examples of such an approach; the very concept of the issue came from "the central position of history in the Ukrainian crisis" (Frede, Jenks, and Werth, "Ukrainian Crisis"); the significance of history and memory in the emergence and deployment of this conflict is also emphasized by the editors of *War and Memory in Russia, Ukraine and Belarus* (Fedor, Lewis, and Zhurzhenko, "War and Memory").

2. One of the writers in that issue of *Kritika*, John-Paul Himka, claims that the biggest memory divide relevant to the Euromaidan events and the separatist movement in eastern and southern Ukraine is the memory of World War II. He thinks that, for the cohort of twenty- and thirty-year-olds—obviously the main human resource for reinforcement of the Donbas insurgents—the fact of "what their grandparents did during the war" is of great importance (Himka, "History behind the Regional Conflict." See also Himka, "Basic Historical Identity"; Hrynevych, "Gespaltene Erinnerung").

3. Jilge, "Politics of History," 75. See also Jilge and Troebst, "Divided Historical Cultures?"; Wanner, *Burden of Dreams*; Portnov, "Pluralität der Erinnerung."

4. Rosenzweig and Thelen, *Presence of the Past*.

5. Mori, "Reflexive Past"; Olick, *Politics of Regret*, 86.

6. Siddi, "Ukraine Crisis," 467.

7. For the definitions of the terms, see Lebow, Kansteiner, and Fogu, *Politics of Memory*; Georgii Kasianov, "K probleme definitsyi"; Miller, "Historical Politics."
8. See Portnov, "Memory Wars"; Kravchenko, "Ukraine Faces Its Soviet Past."
9. Zahra, "Imagined Noncommunities," 111.
10. Bjerg and Lenz, "Time-out?," 44–45.
11. Hrinchenko, *Usna istoriia*; Bodnar, "Tam bulo dobre"; Anna Wylegała, "Absent 'Others'"; Penter and Titarenko, "Local Memory."
12. Bruner, "Experience," 7.
13. Whitling, "Damnatio Memoriae," 93.
14. Considering the small number of such interviews in the project's archive, nine interviews with OUN and UPA members were used for the analysis as a basis for comparison; these interviews were recorded by Oleksandr Pahiria from 2002 to 2008.
15. Billig, *Banal Nationalism*, 11, 93–127; Karner and Bram, "Introduction," 7–8.
16. On the formation of the Soviet narrative of the war, see Tumarkin, *Living and Dead*; Weiner, *Making Sense*; Shcherbakova, "Pobeda vmesto voiny?"
17. Jilge and Troebst, "Divided Historical Cultures?," 1–2.
18. See Tumarkin, *Living and Dead*, 189; Fitzpatrick, "Introduction," 9. On the term "governing myth," see Bell, "Mythscapes."
19. On Russia's involvement in Ukrainian memory battles, see Yurchuk, *Reordering*, 121–24.
20. Vira H., born in 1934, interview by Valeria Vatulina (in Russian), December 15, 2010, Archive of the Center for Oral History of Taras Shevchenko National University of Kyiv [hereafter, Archive of the Center for Oral History], Collection 1, Interview 29. On the formation of the myth of the "match of death," see Hinda, *Ukrains'kyi sport*, 243–337.
21. Nadiya A., born 1935, interview by Veronika Korobets'ka (in Russian), December 1, 2014, Solone (Ternopil region), Archive of the Center for Oral History, Col. 1, Int. 301.
22. On the official Soviet memory politics toward the Holocaust, see Gitelman, "Politics." On post-Soviet Ukrainian memory politics, see Jilge, "Competing Victimhoods," 115–19; Rohdewald, "Post-Soviet Remembrance"; Himka, "Reception of the Holocaust."
23. For a broader discussion on this issue, see Borovyk, "Collaboration," 285–308.
24. See Poltava, *Khto taki banderivtsi*.
25. For example, see Serhiichuk, *OUN-UPA*, 15, 30, 33, 50.
26. Nadiya A. interview.
27. The only exception was a short period of time during and shortly after the Khrushchev Thaw; see Jones, *Myth*, 173–257.
28. On history discussions during Perestroika and their influence on the formation of identities, see Wanner, *Burden of Dreams*, 30–45; Sherlock, *Historical Narratives*.
29. Zinaiida Zh., born 1926, interview by Natalia Murashko (in Ukrainian), December 5, 2010, Ovruch (Zhytomyr region), Archive of the Center for Oral History, Col. 1, Int. 27.
30. Tatiana Zhurzhenko, "From the 'Reunification.'"
31. Valentyna Z., born 1925, interview by Olexandr Zakharchenko (in Russian), November 20, 2012, Ilanovo (Sumy region), Archive of the Center for Oral History, Col. 1, Int. 207.
32. For the role of the diaspora, see Himka, "Central European Diaspora."
33. See Marples, *Heroes and Villains*; Jilge, "Nationalukrainischer Befreiungskampf."
34. For a broader discussion of these issues, see Yurchuk, *Reordering*.
35. The UPA, a paramilitary and later partisan army led by the Organization of Ukrainian Nationalists–Bandera faction. On the use of a scholastic historical education in forming a nationalistic identity in Ukraine, see Popson, "Ukrainian History"; Richardson, "Disciplining the Past."
36. Korostelina, "Reproduction of Conflict."
37. Research that analyzes a "post-memory" of OUN and UPA activities at the level of mass consciousness reveals that perception of the Ukrainian nationalism legacy is very ambiguous; see Yurchuk, *Reordering*.
38. Volodymyr K., born 1927, interview by Lesia Pryshliak (in Ukrainian), November 27, 2011, Rohatyn (Ivano-Frankivs'k region), Archive of the Center for Oral History, Col. 1, Int. 121.
39. Antin M., born 1922, interview by Lesia Pryshliak (in Ukrainian), November 27, 2011, Rohatyn (Ivano-Frankivs'k region), Archive of the Center for Oral History, Col. 1, Int. 122.

40. *Prosvita* societies (enlightenment societies) were Ukrainian community organizations active in Ukraine from the late 1860s to the 1940s and in other countries from the early 20th century. Having had a general educational purpose, *Prosvita* played a significant role in Ukrainian identity formation and political indoctrination; see *Internet Encyclopedia of Ukraine* (Edmonton, AB, Can.: Canadian Institute of Ukrainian Studies), s.v. Prosvita, accessed May 29, 2019, http://www.encyclopediaofukraine.com/display.asp?linkpath=pages%5CP%5CR%5CProsvita.htm.

41. Mykola Y., born 1930, interview by Andrii Dechtiar (in Ukrainian), December 11, 2010, Beresne (Rivne region), Archive of the Center for Oral History, Col. 1, Int. 10.

42. Vasyl' P., born 1921, interview by Olexandr Pahiria (in Ukrainian), October 4, 2008, Archive of the Center for Oral History, Col. 3, Int. 20.

43. Stepan B., born 1925, interview by Yulia Yuskovets' (in Ukrainian), February 5, 2014, Kurash (Rivne region), Archive of the Center for Oral History, Col. 1, Int. 303.

44. Antin M. interview.

45. For a broader discussion of this issue, see Yurchuk, *Reordering*, 113–21, 182–85; Osipian, "Etnicheskiie chistki i chistka pamiati."

46. See Yurchuk, *Reordering*, 99–102.

47. See Struve, *Deutsche Herrschaft*.

48. Valentyna Y., born 1927, interview by Yulia Vasilieva (in Russian), January 5, 2014, Kerch (Crimea), Archive of the Center for Oral History, Col. 1, Int. 278. On similar evaluations in interviews recorded in Donbas, see Penter and Titarenko, "Local Memory," 481.

49. Mariia B., born 1929, interview by Maryna Marchenko (in Ukrainian), January 4, 2014, Ochin'ky (Chernihiv region), Archive of the Center for Oral History, Col. 1, Int. 263.

50. Mariia B. interview.

51. Wanner, *Burden of Dreams*, 37.

52. Wanner, *Burden of Dreams*, xxvi.

53. This sort of layered chronology is typical of the composition of oral autobiographical stories; see Portelli, *Death of Luigi Trastulli*, 20–26.

54. At the time of the interviews, the practice of mentioning the famine was already established in Ukraine, and thousands of testimonies about the Holodomor were recorded. The result could be a formalization that links the mention of the famine as part of the very format of recording the memories of an "ordinary people."

55. Vladyslav S., born 1932, interview by Alina Smyshliak (in Russian), December 2, 2012, Svesa (Sumy region), Archive of the Center for Oral History, Col. 1, Int. 237.

56. Teodozii K., born 1936, interview by Svitlana Strebkiva (in Ukrainian), December 17, 2012, Buchach (Ternopil region), Archive of the Center for Oral History, Col. 1, Int. 182; Mariia U., born 1929, interview by Serhii Hvozdkov (in Ukrainian), December 4, 2011, Usyn (Kyiv region), Archive of the Center for Oral History, Col. 1, Int. 127.

57. Vladyslav S. interview.

58. Mariia T., born 1928, interview by Yulia Tyshchenko (in Ukrainian), December 11, 2010, Korzhivka (Kyiv region), Archive of the Center for Oral History, Col. 1, Int. 100. This ambivalent depiction of the invaders and the occupation, the appearance of stories about "good Germans," contradicting any of the existing dominant narratives about the war, is more or less a general tendency characteristic of all regions of Ukraine; for the interviews recorded in Donbas, see Penter and Titarenko, "Local Memory," 488–91; the same occurs in Belarus: Bartosik, *Byu u pana verabeika havarushchy*, 186–92.

59. On very similar depictions of the partisan war in witnesses' interviews recorded in Belarus, see Bartosik, *Byu u pana verabeika havarushchy*, 134–47.

60. Ivan Kh., born 1926, interview by Maria Klyukalo (in Russian), November 28, 2014, Rubizhne (Luhansk region), Archive of the Center for Oral History, Col. 1, Int. 299.

61. Particularly, a famous Ukrainian historian and publicist, Olena Stiazhkina, during her talk at the TED conference in Kyiv told a similar story, but as a part of the Donetsk region war tales; see Stiazhkina, "See You in Donetsk."

62. Even in prewar times, the concept of "ours" as an antithesis of "the others," the bad ones or the enemies, was a significant part of the Soviet discourse. On this concept as used in Soviet magazines for children of the 1920s–40s, see Litovs'ka, "Radians'ki periodychni."

63. Olena K., born 1924, interview by Andrii Pohasii (in Ukrainian), January 5, 2012, Uzhhorod, Archive of the Center for Oral History, Col. 1, Int. 118.
64. Volodymyr K. interview.
65. Ivan Kh. interview.
66. Mariia T. interview.
67. Zahra, "Imagined Noncommunities," 93–119.
68. Wertsch, "Narrative Tools," 16.

Bibliography

Bell, Duncan. "Mythscapes: Memory, Mythology, and National Identity." *British Journal of Sociology* 54, no. 1 (2003): 63–81.

Billig, Michael. *Banal Nationalism*. London: Sage, 1995.

Bjerg, Helle, and Claudia Lenz. "Time-out for National Heroes? Gender as an Analytical Category in the Study of Memory Cultures." In *Contemporary Europe*, edited by Eric Langenbacher, Bill Niven, and Ruth Wittlinger, 39–54. New York: Berghahn, 2012.

Bodnar, Halyna. "Tam bulo dobre i tut ie nepohano zhyty: osoblyvosti istorychnoii pam'iati pereselentsiv z Pol'shchi." In *Ukraiina–Pol'shcha: istorychna spadshchyna i suspil'na svidomist'*, vol. 2, edited by Mykola Lytvyn, Jaroslav Isaievych, 20–36. L'viv: Instytut ukrainoznavstva im. Kryp'iakevycha NAN Ukrainy, 2007.

Borovyk, Mykola. "Collaboration and Collaborators in Ukraine during World War II: Between Myth and Memory." In *Formulas of Betrayal: Traitors, Collaborators and Deserters in Contemporary European Politics of Memory*, edited by Gelinada Grinchenko and Eleonora Narvselius, 285–308. New York: Palgrave Macmillan, 2018.

Bruner, Edward. "Experience and Its Expressions." In *The Anthropology of Experience*, edited by Victor W. Turner and Edward M. Bruner, 139–55. Urbana: University of Illinois Press, 1986.

Fedor, Julie, Simon Lewis, and Tatiana Zhurzhenko. "Introduction: War and Memory in Russia, Ukraine, and Belarus." In *War and Memory in Russia, Ukraine, and Belarus*, edited by Julie Fedor, Markku Kangaspuro, Jussi Lassila, and Tatiana Zhurzhenko, 1–40. New York: Palgrave Macmillan, 2017.

Fitzpatrick, Sheila. "Introduction: Soviet Union in Retrospect—Ten Years After." In *The Legacy of the Soviet Union*, edited by Wendy Slater and Andrew Wilson, 1–14. Basingstoke, UK: Palgrave Macmillan, 2004.

Frede, Victoria, Andrew Jenks, and Paul W. Werth, "The Ukrainian Crisis and History." *Kritika* 16, no. 1 (Winter 2015): 1–5.

Gitelman, Zvi. "Politics and the Historiography of the Holocaust in the Soviet Union." In *Bitter Legacy: Confronting the Holocaust in the USSR*, edited by Zvi Gitelman, 14–42. Indianapolis: Indiana University Press, 1997.

Himka, John-Paul. "The Basic Historical Identity Formations in Ukraine. A Typology." *Harvard Ukrainian Studies* 28, no. 1–4 (2006): 483–500.

———. "A Central European Diaspora under the Shadow of World War II: The Galician Ukrainians in North America." *Austrian History Yearbook* 37 (2006): 17–31.

———. "The History behind the Regional Conflict in Ukraine." *Kritika* 16, no. 1 (Winter 2015): 129–36.

———. "The Reception of the Holocaust in Postcommunist Ukraine." In *Bringing the Dark Past to Light: The Reception of the Holocaust in Postcommunist Europe*, edited by John-Paul Himka and Joanna Beata Michlic, 616–61. Lincoln: University of Nebraska Press, 2013.

Hinda, Volodymyr. *Ukrains'kyi sport pid natsystskoiu svastykoiu (1941–1944 rr.)*. Kyiv: Ruta, 2012.

Hrinchenko, Helinada. *Usna istoriia prymusu do pratsi: metod, konteksty, teksty*. Kharkiv, Ukraine: HTMT, 2012.

Hrynevych, Vladyslav. "Gespaltene Erinnerung: Der Zweite Weltkrieg im ukrainischen Gedenken." *Osteuropa*, nos. 4–5 (2005): 88–102.

Jilge, Wilfried. "Competing Victimhoods—post-Soviet Ukrainian Narratives on World War II." In *Shared History—Divided Memory: Jews and Others in Soviet-Occupied Poland, 1939–1941*, edited by Elazar Barkan, Elizabeth A. Cole, and Kai Struve, 103–33. Leipzig: Leipziger Universitätsverlag, 2007.

———. "Nationalukrainischer Befreiungskampf: Die Umwertung des zweiten Weltkriegs in der Ukraine." *Osteuropa* 58, no. 6 (2008): 167–86.

———. "The Politics of History and the Second World War in post-Communist Ukraine (1986/1991–2004/2005)." *Jahrbücher für Geschichte Osteuropas* 54, no. 1 (2006): 50–81.

Jilge, Wilfried, and Stefan Troebst. "Divided Historical Cultures? World War II and Historical Memory in Soviet and post-Soviet Ukraine." *Jahrbücher für Geschichte Osteuropas* 54, no. 1 (2006): 1–3.

Jones, Polly. *Myth, Memory, Trauma: Rethinking the Stalinist Past in the Soviet Union, 1953–70*. New Haven, CT: Yale University Press, 2013.

Karner, Christian, and Mertens Bram. "Introduction: Memories and Analogies of World War II." In *The Use of and Abuse of Memory: Interpreting World War II in Contemporary European Politics*, edited by Christian Karner and Mertens Bram, 1–22. New Brunswick, NJ: Transaction, 2013.

Kasianov, Georgii. "K probleme definitsyi: istoricheskaia pamiat, istoricheskaya politika." In *Istoria, Pamiat, Polityka. Zbirnyk statei*, edited by Georgii Kasianov and Oleksandra Haidai, 112–35. Kyiv: Instytut istorii Ukrainy NAN, 2016.

Korostelina, Karina. "Reproduction of Conflict in History Teaching in Ukraine: A Social Identity Theory Analysis." *Identity* 15, no. 3 (2015): 221–40.

Kravchenko, Volodymyr. "Ukraine Faces Its Soviet Past: History versus Policy versus Memory." In *Mass Dictatorship and Memory as Ever Present Past*, edited by Jie-Hyum Lim, Barbara Walker, and Perer Lambert, 87–119. Basingstoke: Palgrave Macmillan, 2014.

Langenbacher, Eric, Bill Niven, and Ruth Wittlinger. "Dynamics of Memory and Identity in Contemporary Europe: Introduction." In *Dynamics of Memory and Identity in Contemporary Europe*, edited by Eric Langenbacher, Bill Niven, and Ruth Wittlinger, 1–13. New York: Berghahn, 2012.

Lebow, Richard Ned, Wulf Kansteiner, and Claudio Fogu, eds. *The Politics of Memory in Postwar Europe*. Durham, NC: Duke University Press, 2006.

Litovs'ka, Mariia. "Radianski periodychni vydanina dlia ditei 1920–1940-h i problema transformatsii ideolohichnykh priorytetiv." *Ukraina Moderna*, February 16, 2015. http://uamoderna.com/md/litovska-soviet-journals-for-children.

Marples, David R. *Heroes and Villains: Creating National History in Contemporary Ukraine*. Budapest: Central European University Press, 2007.

Miller, Alexei. "Historical Politics: Eastern European Convolutions in the 21st Century." In *The Convolutions of Historical Politics*, edited by Alexei Miller and Maria Lipman, 1–20. Budapest: Central European University Press, 2012.

Mori, Luca. "Reflexive Past: Cultural Pragmatics, Identity Formation and the Roles of Social and Collective Memory." In *Italian Sociological Review* 1, no. 3 (2011): 1–11.

Müller, Jan-Werner. "On 'European Memory': Some Conceptual and Normative Remarks." In *A European Memory? Contested Histories and Politics of Remembrance*, edited by Małgorzata Pakier and Bo Stråth, 25–37. New York: Berghahn, 2010.

Olick, Jeffrey K. *The Politics of Regret: On Collective Memory and Historical Responsibility*. New York: Routledge, 2007.

Osipian, Aleksandr. "Etnicheskie chistki i chistka pamiati: ukrainsko-polskoie pogranichie 1939–1947 v sovremennoi politike i istoriographii." *Ab Imperio* 2, no. 2 (2004): 238–97.

Penter, Tanja, and Dmitrii Titarenko. "Local Memory on War, German Occupation and Postwar Years: An Oral History Project in the Donbass." *Cahiers du Monde Russe* 52, nos. 2–3 (2011): 475–97.

Poltava, Petro. *Khto taki banderivtsi i choho vony khochut*. L'viv, 1950.

Popson, Nancy. "The Ukrainian History Textbook: Introducing Children to the 'Ukrainian Nation.'" *Nationalities Papers* 29, no. 2 (2001): 325–50.

Portelli, Alessandro. *The Death of Luigi Trastulli and Other Stories: Form and Meaning in Oral History*. Albany, NY: SUNY Press, 1991.

Portnov, Andrii. "Bandera Mythologies and Their Traps for Ukraine." *Open Democracy*, June 22, 2016. https://www.opendemocracy.net/od-russia/andrii-portnov/bandera-mythologies-and-their-traps-for-ukraine.

———. "Memory Wars in Post-Soviet Ukraine (1991–2010)." In *Memory and Theory in Eastern Europe*, edited by Uilleam Blacker, Alexander Etkind, and Julie Fedor, 233–54. New York: Palgrave Macmillan, 2013.

———. "Pluralität der Erinnerung: Denkmäler und Geschichtspolitik in der Ukraine." *Osteuropa* 58, no. 6 (2008): 197–210.

Richardson, Tanya. "Disciplining the Past in post-Soviet Ukraine: Memory and History in Schools and Families." In *Memory, Politics and Religion: The Past Meets the Present in Europe*, edited by Frances Pine, Deema Kaneff, and Haldis Haukanes, 109–35. Munster, Ger.: Lit, 2004.

Rohdewald, Stefan. "Post-Soviet Remembrance of the Holocaust and National Memories of the Second World War in Russia, Ukraine and Lithuania." *Forum for Modern Language Studies* 44, no. 2 (2008): 173–84.

Rosenzweig, Roy, and David Thelen. *The Presence of the Past: Popular Uses of History in American Life*. New York: Columbia University Press, 1998.

Serhiichuk, Volodymyr. *OUN-UPA v roky viiny, Novi dokumenty i materialy*. Kyiv: Dnipro, 1996.

Shcherbakova, Irina. "Pobeda vmesto voiny? Kak skladyvalas' pamiat' o voinie v Rossii (1945–2010)." *Uroki istorii XX vek*. 21 June, 2012. https://urokiistorii.ru/article/3222.

Sherlock, Thomas. *Historical Narratives in the Soviet Union and post-Soviet Russia: Distorting the Settled Past, Creating an Uncertain Future*. New York: Palgrave Macmillan, 2007.

Siddi, Marco. "The Ukraine Crisis and European Memory Politics of the Second World War." *European Politics and Society* 18, no. 4 (2017): 465–79.

Stiazhkina, Olena, "See You in Donetsk." https://www.youtube.com/watch?v=T5B5UvESc1g.

Struve, Kai. *Deutsche Herrschaft, ukrainischer Nationalismus, antijüdische Gewalt: Der Sommer 1941 in der Westukraine*. Munich: De Gruyter Oldenbourg, 2015.

Tumarkin, Nina. *The Living and the Dead: The Rise and Fall of the Cult of World War II in Russia*. New York: Basic, 1994.

Wanner, Catherine. *Burden of Dreams: History and Identity in post-Soviet Ukraine*. University Park: Pennsylvania University Press, 1998.

Weiner, Amir. *Making Sense of War: The Second World War and the Fate of the Bolshevik Revolution*. Princeton, NJ: Princeton University Press, 2001.

Wertsch, James. "Narrative Tools of History and Identity." *Culture and Psychology* 3, no. 1 (1997): 5–20.

Whitling, Frederick. "Damnatio Memoriae and the Power of Remembrance: Reflections on Memory and History." In *A European Memory? Contested Histories and Politics of Remembrance*, edited by Małgorzata Pakier and Bo Strath, 87–97. New York: Berghahn, 2010.

Wylegała, Anna. "The Absent 'Others': A Comparative Study of Memories of Displacement in Poland and Ukraine." *Memory Studies* 8, no. 4 (2015): 470–86.

Yurchuk, Yuliya. *Reordering of Meaningful Worlds: Memory of the Organization of Ukrainian Nationalists and the Ukrainian Insurgent Army in post-Soviet Ukraine*. Stockholm: Stockholm University, 2014. http://sh.diva-portal.org/smash/get/diva2:770941/FULLTEXT01.pdf.

Zahra, Tara. "Imagined Noncommunities: National Indifference as a Category of Analysis." *Slavic Review* 69, no. 1 (Spring 2010): 93–119.

Zhurzhenko, Tatiana. "From the 'Reunification of the Ukrainian Lands' to 'Soviet Occupation': The Molotov-Ribbentrop Pact in the Ukrainian Political Memory." In *The Use of and Abuse of Memory: Interpreting World War II in Contemporary European Politics*, edited by Christian Karner and Mertens Bram, 229–47. New Brunswick, NJ: Transaction, 2013.

Bartosik, Z'mitser. *Byu u pana verabeika havarushchy*. Radyto Svabodnaia Europa/Radyio Svaboda, 2016.

MYKOLA BOROVYK is Associate Professor of History at the Taras Shevchenko National University of Kyiv.

PART III

HEROES OR TRAITORS: CREATING A HEROIC CANON

5

SYMON PETLIURA, THE UKRAINIAN PEOPLE'S REPUBLIC, AND NATIONAL COMMEMORATION IN CONTEMPORARY UKRAINE

Matthew D. Pauly

IN THE MIDST OF THE CURRENT CRISIS IN Ukraine, the figure of Symon Petliura, a prominent Ukrainian military figure and the effective political leader of the Ukrainian People's Republic (UNR) from 1919 to 1921, has reemerged as a motivating force. A May 2015 article in *Holos Ukrainy* (Voice of Ukraine) reminded readers that Petliura was one of the few in revolutionary Ukraine who understood the need to fight against the Bolsheviks.[1] Although the Bolsheviks enjoyed support in Ukraine's urban and industrial centers, Petliura saw Bolshevism as a foreign import whose political base was in Russia; he understood the UNR Directory's fight against the Red Army to be a war against foreign aggression. The 2015 article conflated Bolshevism with Russia as well. Petliura's struggle, it insists, was the same as the war of today "against Russia" in Ukraine's southeast. According to its interpretation, the historical memory of Petliura's defiance of Bolshevism called for a clear-eyed recognition of the nature of forces opposed to Ukrainian independence in the present and demanded resistance.

This invocation of the memory of Petliura was the result of a concerted public campaign of veneration that began in 2005 under the administration of President Viktor Yushchenko. Yushchenko, the champion of Ukraine's Orange Revolution, sought to counter the legacy of Soviet narratives of Ukraine's past, famously granting the status of "Hero of Ukraine" in 2010 to Stepan Bandera—a highly controversial leader of the Organization of Ukrainian Nationalists (OUN) during World War II.[2] Yushchenko's effort to valorize Petliura was meant to unify Ukrainian citizens, but it was also very fraught. Every post-Soviet government of Ukraine has claimed precedence for Ukrainian sovereignty in the UNR and, as a former UNR head of state, Petliura would appear to invite commemoration. Critics of Petliura have long accused him, however, of two principal crimes: responsibility for anti-Jewish pogroms committed by UNR-affiliated soldiers and the forfeiture of Galicia to Poland. These charges have been levied against Petliura anew, but they partly arise from a larger legacy of the Soviet association of Petliura with an aggressive Ukrainian nationalism.

It is this broad censure of Petliura that complicates his rescue, at least within Ukraine. While historians continue to debate Petliura's complicity in the pogroms of 1919 and the content and wisdom of the Polish-Ukrainian Treaty of Warsaw in 1920, but the conclusions of scholars matter less than public perception for the future of the campaign to honor Petliura. He was the bête-noire of Soviet historiography and his image became a stand-in for contemporary political battles in Ukraine in 2005–13. The ousting of President Viktor Yanukovych and the disintegration of the Party of Regions, whose supporters often led the charge against the commemoration of Petliura, would seem to offer an opportunity for his rehabilitation. Still, acceptance of the infamy of Petliura is so deep-seated that any attempt to promote him as the founder of the Ukrainian state remains problematic.

This chapter's primary focus is on the dispute about politically adapting Petliura's legacy. The Yushchenko-led effort inspired the publication of a wealth of new scholarship on Petliura, in which the emerging consensus among Ukrainian historians was that he deserved major credit for Ukrainian independence, even if the manner in which he pursued this goal was flawed. His primary failure, they argued, was his inability to assert control over the forces and territory that the UNR claimed in spite of his assumption of broad political powers. A reading of historical studies on Petliura requires recognizing nuance; participants in the public debate over the leader's commemoration in 2005 and after were often more interested in assigning definitive blame or accolade. The construction of national myths demands the absence of complexity, and this effort in Ukraine raises the questions Why does Ukraine need heroes? Must these heroes be anti-Russian?

Positioning Petliura in Historical Events

Who was Symon Petliura? As the following discussion of the public controversy over his legacy should make clear, the answer is not simple. Symon Petliura was born in 1879 in the city of Poltava to a family with Cossack roots. He attended the Poltava Theological Seminary but was expelled in 1901 during his last year of study for membership in a secret Ukrainian student society. He was also active in the Poltava cell of the Revolutionary Ukrainian Party (RUP), a clandestine party that espoused socialism as well as territorial autonomy for Ukraine.[3] He subsequently worked as a teacher in the Kuban and was arrested in 1903 for his political activism. Upon his release, he fled to L'viv in the Habsburg Empire, returning to Kyiv after the Russian government declared a general amnesty in 1905 and renewing his employment as a publicist for Ukrainian national interests and the RUP's successor organization, the Ukrainian Social Democratic Workers' Party.[4] During World War I, Petliura aided soldiers on Russia's western front as a representative of the Union of Zemstva, an association of local government institutions.[5] After the ousting of Tsar Nicholas II in early 1917, Ukrainian soldiers and officers who sought to separate from the former imperial armed forces elected Petliura to represent their interests as chairman of a new revolutionary body, the Ukrainian General Military Committee. He then assumed authority as minister of war for the self-declared governing authority in Ukraine, the General Secretariat of the Central Rada (Council).

The history of the revolution in Ukraine then became decidedly complex.[6] Petliura resigned from the secretariat but continued to serve as a key military strategist and organizer for the Ukrainian People's Republic (UNR), a state that first declared its federation with and then independence from Russia. War broke out between the UNR and the Soviet government in Petrograd in December 1917 and forces under the command of Petliura were instrumental in the ultimately unsuccessful effort to defend the UNR's proclaimed capital, Kyiv. After the signing of a peace treaty with the UNR, the German army ejected Soviet forces from the territory but then supported the installation of a conservative government in Ukraine under Hetman Pavlo Skoropadsky in April 1918. The new government placed Petliura under arrest but released him in November 1918. Petliura led an uprising against Skoropadsky after the Germans withdrew their support, joined the resurrected UNR's executive organ (the Directory), and was appointed supreme commander or *otaman* of the reconstituted army. The UNR Directory signed a formal unification agreement with the West Ukrainian People's Republic (ZUNR)—a state constituted from former Habsburg lands, then at war with newly independent Poland for control of this same territory—in January 1919, but quickly lost its control of Kyiv to the Soviet Red Army and was forced into a protracted retreat.

Symon Petliura assumed leadership over the Directory in February 1919 after his political competitor, the more leftist Volodymyr Vynnychenko resigned his position as chairman and went into exile abroad. The UNR Directory exercised minimal control over the territory it claimed. It could not fully realize the social programs it had promulgated under Vynnychenko (including land reform and the nationalization of industry) and was hampered by internal political division, peasant distrust, some popular pro-Soviet sympathy, and military opposition from the monarchist Whites and lack of support from the Entente. The more professional ZUNR Ukrainian Galician Army often disregarded Petliura's command and pursued its own agenda, until typhus decimated its ranks. In the midst of the violence of 1919, the Red Army, Whites, and forces under the Directory's command, including regular troops as well as those of local warlords, participated in the massacre of Jews. Directory soldiers were responsible for 40 percent of the documented pogroms, despite official condemnations and inquiries by Petliura's government.[7]

In December 1919, after the Ukrainian Galicians reached a separate agreement with the Whites, Petliura fled to Poland, ordering his army to continue a guerilla war against its enemies. In April he negotiated a military agreement, known as the Treaty of Warsaw, with the Polish leader, Józef Piłsudski. Partly in return for his recognition of Polish rule over former Habsburg Galicia, Petliura gained Polish backing for a renewed campaign against their common foe, Soviet Russia. The combined UNR and Polish armies captured Kyiv in May 1920, but the Red Army pushed back and Poland concluded its own peace with the Soviet government after facing near disaster. The Poles temporarily permitted Petliura to oversee a government-in-exile in Tarnów, but they interned retreating UNR soldiers and eventually forced the Directory leader to leave the country. Petliura took up residency in Paris in 1924, where he continued to advocate for Ukrainian independence and the return of the UNR. On May 25, 1926, Shalom Schwartzbard, a Jew from Izmail (now in southwest Ukraine) shot and killed him on the Rue Racine, reportedly proclaiming, "This is for the pogroms!"[8] Schwartzbard's attorney, Henri Torrés, constructed his defense around an indictment of Petliura, whom he accused of responsibility for the violence against Ukrainian Jews. A French jury accepted Torrés's argument that Schwartzbard's act was a justifiable crime of passion and acquitted him.

The historiography of Petliura is far too extensive to discuss in full, but the two main issues of dispute are the question of Petliura's forfeiture of western Ukraine in the Treaty of Warsaw and his culpability for the 1919 pogroms. On the Treaty of Warsaw, the best English source is Michael Palij's *Ukrainian-Polish Defensive Alliance*. Palij argues that at the beginning of 1920, Petliura "was in an impossible position, and the treaty with Poland was simply an act of desperation."[9] According to this interpretation, while Petliura recognized that Poland would not permit Ukrainian control over Galicia, he believed that Soviet Russia was opposed to the independence of all Ukraine and was therefore the primary enemy. Serhii Lytvyn, author of one of the definitive Ukrainian biographies of Petliura, concedes that Galician political leaders immediately condemned the Warsaw agreement. A negative popular memory of the conduct of Polish troops in Right Bank Ukraine worked against an acceptance of the treaty outside Galicia, and Soviet interpretations reinforced the image of a national betrayal. But Lytvyn also concludes that, despite the controversy, the agreement was "the only possible step for the continuation of the armed struggle of the Ukrainian people against Bolshevik enslavement (*ponevolennia*) and for the formation of Ukrainian statehood."[10]

The question of Petliura's role in the 1919 pogroms against Jews is even more divisive.[11] Reflections on the relationship between Ukrainian Jews and the Directory began contemporaneously with the latter's fall, but research specifically on the pogroms accelerated in the aftermath of the Schwartzbard trial. A 1927 analysis and collection of documents issued in English and French by a team of Jewish scholars, the Committee of Jewish Delegations, identified Petliura as culpable. Henry Abramson, author of the most authoritative work in English on the subject of Ukrainian-Jewish affairs under the UNR, *A Prayer for the Government*, offers a detailed synopsis of the publications that followed. He maintains that, in addition to the verdict of the Schwartzbard trial, the argument of the Committee of Jewish Delegations "has colored decades of Jewish scholarship and even the popular view of Jews and Ukrainians during the revolution" and that Ukrainian researchers outside the Soviet Union were slow to respond. His own view is that Petliura was absolutely not the organizer of the pogroms, but "as head of state he must be held *accountable* for the actions of his army, despite his relative lack of control over them."[12]

Scholars in post-Soviet Ukraine have generally denied any role for Petliura in the planning or sanctioning of the pogroms and emphasized Petliura's "philosemitism," establishment of a ministry of Jewish affairs, and commitment to the rights of Jews in the UNR. Volodymyr Serhiichuk, the author of the most specialized text published in Ukraine, is categorical in his defense: "In 1919 S. V. Petliura did not succeed in preventing the pogroms, but his sincere advocacy of Jewry is not forgotten. His fame increased immensely and there is no higher authority for the Ukrainian public than Petliura."[13] The views of other writers, such as Lytvyn and Valerii Soldatenko, whose biography of Petliura and Vynnychenko will be discussed later herein, align more readily with Harvard historian Serhii Plokhy's recent conclusion: "In Petliura's mind, attacking Jews was equivalent to betraying Ukraine. The problem was that while he issued decrees, he only rarely or belatedly punished perpetrators."[14] Although Petliura may have viewed Jews as "natural allies in the struggle against national and social oppression" and denounced those who instigated the pogroms, he did not have effective command over his soldiers, some of whom already held antisemitic attitudes that took on a murderous expression in the context of war. As Soldatenko suggests, Petliura's words meant little to the families of the victims if they did not end the violence.[15]

A Requiem Realized

Contemporary work on the rehabilitation of Petliura in Ukraine began before Yushchenko's electoral victory. An all-Ukrainian committee was organized to prepare for the 125th anniversary of the birth of Petliura on May 23, 2004. Along with Ukrainian historians and librarians, the last president of the UNR in exile, Mykola Plaviuk, and a representative of the Petliura Foundation in Great Britain, Roland Franko, held a press conference where they announced the creation of an internet-based virtual museum of Symon Petliura.[16] A major objective of the committee was the establishment of a monument to Petliura in Kyiv. The committee detailed several options for its location, including European Square, in the very center of Kyiv, as well as on Khmelnytsky Street, near the building that housed Petliura's military administration. The committee claimed to have had good discussions with municipal authorities for this endeavor and to have provisionally contracted a sculptor. A 2004 article, however, in the official newspaper of the Ukrainian military, *Narodna Armiia* (People's Army) claimed that no state funds would be released for the establishment of the monument. The project relied especially on funds from the British Symon Petliura Foundation; its organizers could not even open a bank account in Ukraine because governmental authorization was lacking. (A decree sanctioning official recognition of the anniversary had stalled in the Verkhovna Rada, the Ukrainian parliament, because the Ukrainian Communist Party opposed it politically.)[17] Nevertheless, the committee had independently proceeded with plans for honoring Petliura. The National Historical Museum opened an exhibition, "Symon Petliura: Knight of the Ukrainian Revolution," and the Kyiv City Building of Teachers, the site of the proclamation of the UNR, and the Local Studies Museum in Poltava, the city of Petliura's birth, held a meeting on commemoration. The committee planned a formal laying of flowers at Independent Square and a memorial service for Petliura at Saint Volodymyr's Cathedral on May 22.

The withholding of state funds and official authorization was critical. The Ukrainian government had already formally rehabilitated the first UNR president, Mykhailo Hrushevsky, and Volodymyr Vynnychenko. In 2003 the government had quietly celebrated the 130th anniversary of the birth of Pavlo Skoropadsky, who with German aid had overthrown the UNR governing authority, the Central Rada, in 1918. A former lieutenant general in the tsarist army, he proclaimed himself hetman of Ukraine, ruling for some six months with the support of landowners, former tsarist officials, and the occupying Central Powers. If the government of a former Soviet technocrat, Leonid Kuchma, had honored the monarchist Skoropadsky, how could it continue to overlook Petliura? Toleration of an unofficial campaign, funded and partly led by Ukrainians abroad, allowed the Kuchma government to placate some while withholding formal approval of the UNR leader. Such was Petliura's notoriety that Skoropadsky could be venerated before him. Collective memory politics propelled the pro-Petliura cause as well as resistance to him. The government chose to partially satisfy constituencies on both sides of the issue. No statue to Petliura was erected in Kyiv, but the unofficial campaign created precedence for future action.

Viktor Yushchenko gained the presidency on January 23, 2005, after his supporters took to the streets to protest what they viewed as vote rigging by Viktor Yanukovych, his opponent and Kuchma's handpicked successor. Already by May 2005, he had announced a new turn for Petliura, publishing a decree that called for a series of official measures to honor the leaders of the UNR.[18] In accordance with the decree, an organizing committee was established to achieve the goal of honoring UNR leaders by installing monuments (including one to Petliura) in cities throughout Ukraine, the publication of scholarship, museum exhibitions, and the release of commemorative coins. A series of scholarly and commemorative events were held in May 2006 specifically to honor Petliura, including a ceremony at the National Opera in Kyiv. The acting minister of culture, Ihor Likhovy, noted that "We are observers of a simultaneously sad and joyous event. Sad, because soon it will be the eightieth anniversary of the death of Simon Petliura in Paris from terrorist bullets. Joyful, because we know that we have finally reached the age where we can talk about Petliura as a hero."[19] On May 25, on the anniversary of the assassination of Petliura, a requiem was held at St. Volodymyr's, presided over by Patriarch Filaret, the head of the Ukrainian Orthodox Church (Kyivan Patriarchate). Talk of installing a monument to Petliura in central Kyiv by the end of the year was renewed, but it was never accomplished.

This requiem (and the 2004 memorial service) was of particular importance. First, and quite obviously, Ukrainian state, cultural, and religious leaders were completing an interrupted event. They were honoring a former leader of a Ukrainian state in the capital of a successor Ukrainian state and lending his commemoration official sanction in 2006. Second, the Ukrainian Orthodox Church (Kyivan Patriarchate) was seeing itself partly as a descendant of the Ukrainian Autocephalous Orthodox Church (UAOC) that Petliura and the UNR Directory supported. A requiem held in its main cathedral and under its auspices strengthened the Kyivan Patriarchate's claim to historicity and echoed past services held to honor the Ukrainian national movement, such as the participation by Orthodox clergy in a rally held in St. Sophia's Square in June 1917 to celebrate the Central Rada's proclamation of autonomy. Last, intentionally or not, it subverted and co-opted a Soviet accusation against former UNR adherents who were arrested in 1929 on the charge of participating in an anti-Soviet conspiracy, the Union for the Liberation of Ukraine (SVU—*Spilka vyzvolennia Ukrainy*). Organization of this group was fabricated by the Soviet State Political Directorate, the GPU, as a pretext for controlling Ukrainian national expression. The GPU alleged that after the UNR leader's assassination in May 1926 several of those arrested had held a requiem in secret for Petliura in the 11th-century St. Sophia's Cathedral in Kyiv, where they attempted to raise funds for a memorial.[20] The 2006 requiem re-created an event that probably never took place (because of the likely reluctance of those accused to break a clear taboo) but nevertheless should have been performed in the view of some Ukrainians looking back. As such, it was act of defiance against the legacy of Soviet rule.

Paris's Judgment

In the years after the Yushchenko presidential victory, some Ukrainian commentators believed Petliura could be more openly discussed and the Soviet narrative of Petliura contested. This did not mean, however, that the commemoration of Petliura was stripped of its political meaning. At a roundtable held in the Ukrainian Institute of History in Kyiv in May 2006, former UNR president-in-exile Plaviuk insisted that Petliura's legacy could now be calmly analyzed. He maintained that the commemoration of Petliura was possible because "scientific and public representatives found the strength to fight for the reconstruction of historical truth."[21] A more honest account of Petliura, in his opinion, still required struggle and a purposeful revision of thought. In spite of all that was written on Petliura, historian Vladislav Verstiuk noted that much of the work was dated and controversial; a rethinking of Petliura and use of newly available documents had only just begun. Others at the roundtable articulated the same thought.

Thus, although new works on Petliura were being published (some by speakers at the roundtable), the historians at the roundtable contended that considerable work remained to be done. According to Ruslan Pyrih, there remained the matter of correcting an established myth: "We well understand that Bolshevik propaganda created out of S. Petliura an image of the archenemy of the Ukrainian people." He conceded that some of Petliura's contemporaries were responsible for the caricature as well. An unvarnished image of Petliura remained elusive. In the charged partisan context after 2005, Ukraine research had political import; the desovietization of Ukrainian history threatened to unsettle those committed to long-standing Soviet interpretations. Yurii Shapoval observed that Ukrainians generally accepted the defense of Petliura's assassin, Sholom Schwartzbard, at the 1927 Paris trial against him: the killing was justified because of Petliura's leadership of anti-Jewish pogroms in 1919. Regarding the trial, Shapoval commented, "Neither researchers, nor the Ukrainian government dare to give it a public, clear and thorough assessment."[22] The Soviet government capitalized on evidence presented at trial and used it as a basis for constructing an image of Petliura as a pogromist and antisemite. Shapoval suggested a dedicated investigation was needed in order to address the broad influence of this image and its effects on perceptions of Ukrainians at home and beyond.

As discussed, the role of Petliura in the 1919 pogroms has been the subject of considerable research, but it is true that the trial against Schwartzbard (and its specific mechanics) has not featured as prominently. Schwartzbard's defense proved compelling to the French court. He was acquitted and has enjoyed hero status for some in contemporary Israel as an avenger for the suffering of Jews in revolutionary Ukraine. An examination of the trial and indeed further research on the 1919 pogroms is commendable, but the ability of any such work of scholarship to fundamentally alter popular perspectives on either side is doubtful. As we shall see, in Ukraine the issue of Petliura's culpability for the pogroms continues to be a fundamental point of disagreement, and past scholarship has not moved positions greatly. Justice is a relative concept for those involved in the public debate, and others would prefer not to draw attention to an event that is shameful, regardless of Petliura's explicit role. The Soviet government purposefully constructed Petliura's image, and historians are engaged in the process of exposing the layers of this composition but acknowledge this does not mean a universally accepted truth can be readily achieved.

Sabotage?

A key issue for the Petliura debate has been the construction of a monument not in Kyiv, but in Petliura's birthplace of Poltava. Already in 2006, local attempts to honor Petliura in a demonstrable way laid bare the challenges of commemoration on a national scale. Poltava is a particularly interesting place to examine this question because of its association not only with Petliura, but also with Ivan Mazepa, the Ukrainian Cossack leader who famously rebelled against the authority of the Russian tsar Peter the Great. Russian troops defeated Mazepa's followers, together with their Swedish allies, at a decisive battle at Poltava, and Mazepa was subsequently vilified in official histories as a traitor to the Russian Empire. For Soviet-era historians, Petliura offered a convenient substitute for Mazepa, whose name lacked immediate currency and ideological relevance. A 2006 article in *Molod' Ukrainy* (Youth of Ukraine) by Hanna Denysko acknowledged the legacy of this linkage in noting that the administrators of the seminary that Petliura attended in Poltava from 1895 to 1901 saw him as an "unrepentant Mazepist" and not as a socialist, even though his membership in the leftist Ukrainian Revolutionary Party would be the grounds for his expulsion. Pressure from the Ukrainian cultural society Prosvita (Enlightenment) and the political party Narodnyi rukh Ukrainy (People's movement of Ukraine) led the *oblast* state administration to agree to release 5,000 UAH toward installation of a memorial plaque of Petliura. Valerii Asadchev, the governor of the Poltava Oblast appointed by Yushchenko, noted at the unveiling of the plaque there was no street named after Petliura in the city, and a lot of streets carried the names of those "foreign or hostile to Ukraine."[23] He condemned the trepidation of some to confront the past out of fear of potential instability.

For those who supported the further commemoration of Petliura, acceptance of the importance of Petliura to the Ukrainian national movement was a test of patriotism. Mykola Kulchynsky, the head of Prosvita, noted that the installation of a plaque was the culmination of the efforts of many Poltavans, such as those "who in the 1970s raised the Ukrainian flag on the bridge tower near the Kiev Train Station [in Poltava]."[24] Writer Petro Rotach noted that others endured interrogation by the KGB for the sudden appearance of the Ukrainian flag in the Poltava Local Studies Museum at the same time. Both constructed a history of dissent in the Soviet period around a linkage to Petliura. Two lessons might be drawn from the articulation of these memories: not all Poltavans accepted the Soviet narrative of Petliura (and "his" flag) and, paradoxically, resistance to commemoration of Petliura could be construed as a soviet practice. Citing a letter from Petliura to one of his generals, Kulchynsky insisted that the challenge confronting Ukraine had been the same in Petliura's time: "Should Ukraine as an independent state in its foreign policy rely on Europe or Moscow-Asia?"[25] Petliura feared that Ukrainian politicians of the time were reluctant to break the bonds with Russia; for Kulchynsky, such a parting was an imperative in 2006.

The dispute in Poltava raised the essential question, Who was and is a supporter of Ukraine? Who is, in effect, Ukrainian? Speakers at the commemoration of Petliura's plaque suggested all citizens of Ukraine, regardless of ethnicity, needed to honor the struggle for independence. The deputy head of the Poltava Oblast Council, Petro Vorona, criticized the failure of the body to adopt a resolution on the commemoration of Poltavans who had participated in the struggle for a Ukrainian state in the past. The secretary of the Ukrainian Orthodox Church (Kyivan Patriarchate) called for a return of the building where the plaque was installed (the site of Petliura's former seminary, now the Poltava State Agrarian Academy) to the Ukrainian church. Progressive deputies in the Poltava City Council demanded the renaming of Artem Street to Petliura Street.[26] Hanna Denysko, the author of the article in *Molod' Ukrainy* detailing these events, cited the memoirs of the Ukrainian communist leader Volodymyr Zatonsky to argue that that Fyodor Artem was a "Ukrainophobe," who saw the creation of even a Soviet Ukraine as a "reactionary affair" and believed the Donbas was fundamentally Russian. She wrote that Poltava sent thousands of its sons to fight with "bandits" like Artem, and any honoring of Artem had no place in contemporary Ukraine, especially in Poltava, "which calls itself the spiritual capital of Ukraine."[27] In short, invocation of the memory of Petliura called for a partial erasure of the history of Soviet power and a reclaiming of Poltava for those who insisted it was the quintessential Ukrainian region. The fact that so many took pains to make this argument suggested, of course, that not all saw Poltava in the same way.

A fight over the future installation of a larger monument to Petliura in Poltava laid bare the fault lines between imaginations of the Ukrainian past and political present. On May 23, 2007, Asadchev had overseen the placement of a memorial stone in central Poltava, which indicated the site of a future monument to Petliura.[28] A demonstration organized by the Communist Party of Ukraine and Viktor Yanukovych's Party of Regions had protested against this action. On the evening of October 3, 2007, the memorial stone was demolished by municipal authorities, who considered it an "illegally established structure" that would impede the operation of the city's sewers during winter. Asadchev protested, claiming that the *oblast* administration had filed an appeal against a decision by the Poltava Economic Court authorizing the demolition. The city government said it received no notice of an appeal and went ahead with the removal of the stone because of procedural irregularities with its installation, insisting "there was no political subtext concerning the monument to our countryman, the well-known military and political figure of the period of the UNR."[29] Nevertheless, it pointedly refrained from supporting the commemoration of Petliura, and its explanation for its actions appeared a defense against what patrons of the future memorial undoubtedly thought: the city government sought to sabotage plans for the memorial. Both sides had their own constituencies, but in the end the struggle was between Poltavan provincial (*oblast*) and municipal powers that had resorted to unilateral action.

Contesting Commemoration

The Yushchenko government's promotion of Petliura invited response on a national scale as well. The leftist newspaper *Robitnycha hazeta* (in Russian, *Rabochaia gazeta*, Workers' newspaper) led the charge against any honoring of Petliura. Volodymyr Bohun reported in a February 2007 article in the newspaper, "Petliura: Myth and the Bitter Truth," that plans to construct a monument to Petliura in the center of Kyiv had gone awry, ironically suggesting that the cause was Yushchenko's shift in attention to the construction of a new residence on the outskirts of Kyiv. Still, Bohun argued, citing the comments of Vice Premier Viacheslav Kyrylenko, the government intended to pursue its plan to tell the "whole truth" about Petliura, whose name still "frightened children" who knew no better.[30]

In contrast to Kyrylenko, Bohun explained why the Petliura should *still* induce fear. He argued the UNR Directory formed special detachments for killing Jews and that Petliura entrusted a future leader of the OUN, Yevhen Konovalets, with the formation of these groups. Even if the connection between Petliura and individual pogrom organizers was "not absolute and permanent," Bohun insisted that all considered Petliura "to be their unconditional leader, all were part of the armed forces of the UNR, whose supreme commander was Petliura."[31] The article offered evidence of the culpability of UNR troops in the pogroms, citing sources from the Red Cross, the European press, and Entente observers. Bohun claimed he explicitly chose to not cite Soviet sources in constructing his argument in order to avoid the charge "by 'national-patriots' of 'pro-Moscow' propaganda." But he refrained from any examination of the perspective or context of these sources, about which specialists on the 1919 pogroms have written a great deal and offered no new evidence of Petliura's final responsibility. In Bohun's estimation it was enough that witnesses to the pogroms believed it rested with the UNR leader.

Unintentionally offering justification to Shapoval's call for a close examination of the trial of Schwartzbard, Bohun rested his case against Petliura with the court's judgment of acquittal. According to Bohun, Petliura's defenders, who claim Schwartzbard was an assassin in the employment of the Soviet security services, ignored the fact that by 1926, a "demoralized and crushed Petliura was no danger to the Soviet state." The Ukrainian émigré community was largely made up of Galicians who held Petliura responsible for the UNR's military defeats and could not forgive him for the "agreement to give Galicia to the Poles." Schwartzbard acted on his own, according to Bohun, with right on his side. It was not Petliura's critics who ignored history, but his defenders. This indictment had political meaning in the present. The Yushchenko government, which claimed to seek integration with Europe, was "hypocritically" denying European values by refusing to acknowledge "as genocide, the mass murders of Jews by Petliura's followers."[32]

Bohun sought to accomplish a number of objectives in writing his piece. Quite obviously, he defamed Petliura by exposing what he believed was his culpability in the pogroms. But he extended his argument beyond this to explicitly link Petliura to an anti-Soviet group better known to some of the newspapers' readers, the OUN, which had waged a guerrilla war through its military wing, the Ukrainian Insurgent Army (UPA—Ukrains'ka Povstans'ka Armiia), against the Red Army at the end of World War II and was viewed by the newspapers' editors as "fascist," collaborationist, and antisemitic.[33] Bohun also connected Petliura to an event even further in the past, condemning what he called an Orangist ambition to rename January Revolution Street after Ivan Mazepa, "another historical figure rejected by his own people." Bohun added to the list of Petliura's crimes by accusing him of overseeing the UNR's repression of the Bolshevik attempt to seize power in Kyiv in January 1918 through the execution of innocent workers. Any attempt to rename the street would vindicate Petliura's offense. Readers were to internalize the article's logic: Petliura was as abhorrent as the worst traitors to the Russian Empire (Mazepa) and the Soviet Union (the OUN-UPA). If they did not fully know Petliura, he was guilty by association with these antiheroes lauded by the Yushchenko government. Furthermore, nationally conscious Ukrainians in Galicia and elsewhere should have had no reason to support Petliura's commemoration because he was willing to gamble the region away. From this perspective, Schwartzbard's act was justice rendered, even if the Soviet government did not seek it.

The preceding reasoning is strained at several points. First and foremost, Petliura was the bugbear of Soviet power in interwar Ukraine. Soviet security services and the party had an interest in his death: they monitored and arrested former UNR adherents and consistently labeled as Petliurists those they suspected of opposing Soviet power because of their past devotion to (or flirtation with) the Ukrainian national cause. The Soviets defeated Petliura's forces with superior and dedicated arms, and with some popular support as well, and Petliura could not affect a reversal in 1926. But this did not mean that the Soviet authorities did not fear the potential attraction of Ukrainian nationalism and ability of Petliura's name to rally anti-Soviet sentiment. Soviet anxieties fixated on Petliura and arguably bolstered the Petliura myth. Whether Schwartzbard was a Soviet agent is less important; the Soviet government celebrated Petliura's assassination and augmented a narrative of his ignominy to avert hypothetical detractors. Bohun returned to this narrative to disarm those seeking to honor Petliura in the post-Soviet present and to remind his readers of Petliura's sins.

Second, Bohun ironically sought to defame Petliura by painting him as too national and not national enough: his activities led to the eventual formation of the OUN and he forfeited Ukrainian territory (Galicia) to the Poles. But Ukrainians who might be upset about the latter event could also applaud the former. Bohun's criticism was likely not addressed to this audience but intended to demonstrate Petliura's duplicity to a readership already inclined to agree. Still, his comments demonstrated the scattershot nature of the anti-Petliura criticism and the tensions inherent in attacking one of the founders, however flawed, of a Ukrainian state that found itself at war with Soviet power. Could one support Ukrainian independence and skewer the UNR? The making of anti-Soviet Ukrainian heroes invited such a conflict because this construction required disavowal of the Soviet good. Readers of *Robitnycha Ukraina* could not do this, and those in favor of commemoration overlooked at least some of the compromises made in the pursuit of independence, including an alliance with Poland for the defense of Ukraine from the Red Army.

Reckoning with the Soviet Past

The remaining years of the Yushchenko presidency saw the publication of several serious scholarly works in Ukraine about Petliura that further sought to deconstruct the Soviet version of his life, even if they remained critical about his decision making. A series of journal articles on Petliura appeared in a special 2009 issue of *Ukrains'kyi istorychnyi zhurnal* (Ukrainian historical journal) and Valerii Soldatenko wrote a major new biography of Petliura and Vynnychenko in 2008. In a review of Soldatenko's book, Volodymyr Shevchenko praised the book's originality and objectivity, its integration of a range of newly available sources, and its aversion to iconostasis. According to Shevchenko, one of its major contributions was to demonstrate that in spite of the significant political differences between Petliura and Vynnychenko, they both selflessly dedicated themselves to the national struggle, openly and honestly worked with their colleagues, even during disagreements, and shunned personal enrichment. The Ukrainian government under their leadership "managed, in spite of all of its mistakes, to do many useful things for the people that no one had accomplished before in such a short time in history." The review was not unduly celebratory. It argued that the book does not fully address the "problems of the suffering of the innocent population during a time of war," including the anti-Jewish pogroms. Shevchenko noted that "the need is pressing to cover such barbaric events in detail on the basis of documentary data and without politicization."³⁴ He did not accuse Soldatenko of this sort of politicization, but rather gestured to the larger environment in which the book would be read and called for careful research to continue. The review, of course, appeared in Ukraine's main journal for professional historians and it is unlikely that many outside the discipline read it. Yet it also demonstrated awareness that political biographies, however dispassionate, might provide fodder for the public debate. At the same time, the review concluded, "the book gives the opportunity to visually imagine the personality of its heroes . . . [and] is a significant contribution to the national historiography."³⁵ Heroes might be understood here to be the central characters of the work, but observers in the press persisted in their fashioning of conventional champions and used scholarship in broad strokes to advance their claims.

A repeated theme of publications in favor of honoring Petliura was that his memory had suffered a historical injustice. The public release of eleven previously unknown letters by Petliura in May 2009 served as an occasion for a new appeal for historical research.³⁶ The letters were transferred from the archive of the Foreign Intelligence Service of Ukraine (SZR) to the Institute of National Memory. Dated from May to September 1922, they were used in a GPU case against the UNR general Yurii Tiutiunyk, who was lured back to Soviet Ukraine in 1923 by former comrades working for the Soviet security police and then arrested. The letters were addressed to the prime minister of the UNR government-in-exile, Andrii Livytsky; the UNR minister of war Lieutenant General Mykola Yunakiv, and the UNR ambassador to France, Oleksandr Shulhyn. Although the intention was for the letters to be studied by scholars, the SZR also placed copies on its website and gave one to a newly established museum of the UNR in the Kyiv Municipal Building of Teachers, the former home of the UNR Central Rada. In announcing the transfer, SZR head Mykola Malomuzh noted that, in the letters, "the political situation in Europe and Ukraine at that time is evaluated and tasks of the leaders of the Ukrainian emigration determined." What is immediately apparent from a reading of the letters was just how hopeless the UNR cause was once its forces had been ejected from Ukrainian territory. According to Rudnytskyi, Petliura expressed his frustration to Livytsky in a letter dated August 3, 1922: "There were interpellations in the Italian and British parliaments on the Galician question and we were dead asleep. Even if a dog somewhere barked about our affair."³⁷

Publicity about these letters suggested most obviously to Ukrainians that Petliura had not ceased his opposition to Soviet rule of Ukraine even after his military defeat. His anger over the failure of the UNR representatives in exile to press the issue of Polish-ruled Galicia also offered a retort to those who evoked his betrayal of Galicia. They also conceivably taught readers that Ukrainian independence faltered for lack of European support. The point could work both ways. It could suggest that contemporary ties to Europe needed to be further strengthened or it could warn against an undue reliance on a Europe that had failed Petliura in the past. Either way, trust in a historical Russia was misplaced if Petliura's story was held as an example. Any act of commemoration of Petliura meant confronting the history of Soviet antagonism toward the UNR and repression of UNR followers such as Tiutiunyk.³⁸ The fact that Petliura's letters were preserved as part of a GPU case against Tiutiunyk prompted a recalling of the coercive apparatus of the Soviet state.

If researchers scrutinized the letters for greater detail on the relationships between UNR officials and their waning negotiations with European powers, it is this latter point on repression that was repeated in more lyrical public homages to Petliura. As a contributor to a descriptive calendar of historical events, bibliographer Valentyna Patoka noted about Petliura: "the enemies of Ukraine not only destroyed him physically, they did everything possible to erase the memory, to blacken the name Petliura, the state servant of the Ukrainian people." Patoka clearly saw the Soviet government as the chief enemy; she held it responsible for the assassination of Petliura, as well as the distortion of the memory of Petliura through the silencing of those who would defend him and the falsification of history. The extended biographical sketch that she provided of Petliura in her introduction sought to turn the Soviet-inflected narrative of the Petliura on its head. Terms that had been used by imperial and Soviet authorities to slander perceived opponents as a pretext for their arrest are presented as noble: "The name of the chieftain [otaman] became derivative for the concept of 'petliurivshchyna,' just as the word 'mazepivshchyna' was firmly imprinted in the consciousness of many generations of Ukrainians who were seeking freedom."[39] Again Petliura and Mazepa were linked, but affirmatively. Many accused Petliurists were innocent of any conspiracy against Soviet power, but no matter. The allegation was to be worn as a badge of honor.

Petliura, in this sense, was the true representative of the will of the Ukrainian people. Patoka maintained that, regarding Petliura's family, "it is easy to understand that Cossack and Orthodox traditions, which formed the basis of Ukrainian folk culture, were closely intertwined and intermarried in it. The life of the family was permeated by this culture. Ukrainian language, story, song, food, holidays, and customs formed the spiritual, everyday atmosphere in which children grew." This was a particular view of Ukrainian-ness that was intended to reclaim Petliura because of his struggle as well as his origins; Soviet rule of Ukraine was by contrast foreign. In a dramatic flourish, Patoka cited a 1919 poem by the poet Oleksandr Oles (the pseudonym of Oleksandr Kandyba) titled "Petliura," which waxed lyrical about the UNR leader: "And the poor people will run out, To meet their Father, They will fall to the knight's feet, Washing him with tears."[40] It is understandable that at the height of Petliura's popularity for some that such verses would be written. But their republication in 2009 circumvented the complexity of his biography and the present controversy over his commemoration.

Also in 2009, the journal *Literaturna hazeta* (Literary newspaper) republished an excerpt from *Strynozheni koni* (Fettered horses), the first book of an imagined ten-book historical epic on Petliura by the contemporary writer Vasyl Fol'varochnyi.[41] Its multilayered interpretation of Petliura in part resumes a reprise of earlier panegyrics for an audience unfamiliar with the hope that a portion of Ukraine's population invested in him. The distance created by time allowed 21st-century Ukrainians an opportunity to accept a portrait of Petliura shorn of a sense of the immediacy of revolutionary chaos. If those who chose to read the excerpt believed the Soviet narrative was a fabrication, they might be more inclined to permit a distilled literary variant.

Petliura in Stasis

After Yushchenko's remarkable political fall and the election of his former rival, Viktor Yanukovych, to the presidency in 2010, official support for the commemoration of Petliura ceased.

Opponents to his honoring sought to revisit decisions made during the fading years of the Yushchenko era. Volodymyr Bohun wrote another piece in *Robitnycha hazeta*, reporting on a March 2012 demonstration held in Kyiv against a 2009 decision by the Kyiv City Council to rename the centrally located Comintern Street after Petliura. The Anti-Fascist Committee of Ukraine, a public organization formed with the support of the Communist Party of Ukraine largely to oppose Yushchenko's attempts to rehabilitate leaders of the OUN-UPA, led the protest. In his explanation for the protest, Heorhii Buiko, the head of the committee and a former parliamentary deputy for the Communist Party, asserted that Kyiv residents rejected the honoring of a "killer of innocent Ukrainian citizens and seller of national territory to a foreign state."[42] In so doing, he repeated the by now formulaic charges against Petliura, again paradoxically maintaining the charge the Petliura was a contemptible, murdering nationalist and simultaneously a traitor to his nation. Bohun further claimed that the city council's decision to rename the street was undemocratic; according to a decree of the council, commemorative action by the council could be taken only after a survey of the city's population. An appeal made by the committee languished without a response in the Higher Administrative Court of Ukraine.

Clearly, reversal of the city council's decision was difficult and the question of democratic procedure was far from settled. The initial court of judgment, the Shevchenko District Court, had denied the committee's suit and a lower-level appellate court refused adjudication and passed it to the higher court. Bohun closed his article with an anecdote that illustrated the full dilemma of the politics of history in Ukraine: "It is symbolic that the campaign started from the monument to the red commander [Nikolai/Mykola] Shchors on Shevchenko Boulevard, which now adjoins the Petliura Street. By the way, about this, in February 1919 the shattered remnants of Petliurists fled from Kyiv under pressure from the Bogunsky regiment under the command of Shchors."[43] Petliura was ejected from Kyiv by force, the Soviet government installed a monument to the conqueror, and in post-Soviet Ukraine Shchors was consigned to stare out over a street named after his defeated rival. It is difficult to know precisely what the democratic choice for the street should be, but in 2012 municipal (and undoubtedly national) authorities maintained an uneasy balance in hopes of keeping the peace.

Petliura's Future?

There were various local initiatives to honor Petliura during the last years of the Yushchenko presidency and under Yanukovych, but nothing came of the major campaigns in Kyiv and Poltava discussed here.[44] Yanukovych's ousting in February 2014 (as a result of antigovernment demonstrations known as Euromaidan) and the election of a new center-right president and parliament would seem to offer occasion for Petliura's commemoration. Certainly, as has already been noted, the memory of Petliura has been invoked for the war against Russian-supplied rebels in southeastern Ukraine: "Because today, as in the beginning of the 20th century, Ukraine was invaded by the Russian army in order to trample on our independence."[45] Those who draw this parallel admire Petliura for his refusal to submit and claim Bolshevik talk of class solidarity was a ruse for the reimposition of imperial rule. In Poltava, the dramatic shift in political winds has occasioned a confrontation with the former ruling authorities and the issue of commemorating Petliura has become a sort of litmus test for loyalty to a Ukrainian state facing its most serious crisis since independence.

The monument at the heart of the dispute that began in 2006 was never built, but the memorial plaque installed on the wall of Petliura's former seminary remained.[46] After Yanukovych's presidential election victory in 2010, the Orangist Asadchev was removed from the position of governor and deputies from or in coalition with Yanukovych's Party of Regions dominated the new Oblast State Council. They largely ignored the plaque, choosing instead to lay flowers at a memorial plaque to Borys Martos, another native of Poltava who was an associate of Petliura's, served as chairman of people's ministers during the time of the UNR Directory, and in 1920 emigrated to Czechoslovakia. Martos's plaque offered a way for local authorities to honor the UNR precedence of statehood without dealing with the legacy of Petliura or, for that matter, with the Soviet settling of scores against his followers who remained in Ukraine. Those who wished to place flowers at the monument laid them on the ground because there was no shelf. Furthermore, the monument was a regular object of defacement, "under cover of darkness unknown vandals fired at this memorial sign, as evidenced by the dent in the image, just opposite the heart."[47]

In May 2014, shortly before the election of Petro Poroshenko as president, *oblast* leaders reversed course and held a rally to honor the 135th anniversary of Petliura's birth. Led by Viktor Buhaichuk, the Yanukovych-appointed governor who was to be dismissed by Poroshenko in November, as well as several pro-Euromaidan politicians, the meeting demanded the installation of monument to Petliura, because he was "one of the few leaders of the UNR who called for the defense of the independence of our state, primarily from armed Russian aggressors. . . . [Today] this testament is of particular importance." Vasyl Naimazh, the author of the article in *Holos Ukrainy* reporting on the demonstration, noted that the former mayor of Poltava, Andrii Matkovsky, was an "open Ukrainophobe" and disputed the city council's 2007 explanation for the destruction on the platform on which the monument to Petliura was to be built. Naimazh maintained that Matkovsky directly ordered its destruction and in its place installed a bust of Mikhail Naimy, another student of the Poltava Theological Seminary and a Lebanese poet who spent the majority of his life in the United States and Beirut. Naimazh implied Petliura was much worthier of this honor.[48]

Even in a post-Euromaidan era, however, there is no universal consensus on Petliura. The pendulum has shifted in favor of his commemoration, but calls for it seem loudest in May, the month of Petliura's birth as well as his death. Petliura seems stuck in limbo, not fully forgotten or fully resurrected yet. One measure of a contentious package of laws on decommunization passed by the Ukrainian parliament in April 2015 and signed into law in May calls explicitly for "honoring the memory of fighters for Ukrainian independence in the 20th century," including members of the UNR Directory such as Petliura.[49] Much of the attention on these laws has been on memorializing OUN-UPA leaders and, by implication, Ukraine's failure to adequately deal with the difficult issues of wartime collaboration and ethnic cleansing.[50] Public debate in Ukraine also seems centered here as well.

Full public veneration of Petliura does not appear urgent, in spite of a January 2016 decree by former President Poroshenko calling for commemoration of the centennial of the UNR.[51] In October 2017, a sculpture of Petliura was erected in the small city of Vinnytsia, the temporary capital of the UNR after the Red Army expelled its government from Kyiv.[52]

Planning for large-scale monuments in Poltava and Kyiv has continued, but no statue had been installed by the end of 2018, although in January 2019 the Kyiv city administration oversaw the installation of a bas-relief sculpture of Petliura on a building at the beginning of the street that bears his name.[53] These projects represent the fulfilment of the old commitments made during the Yushchenko era, not new initiatives. In May 2018, the Ukrainian minister of culture, Yevhen Nyshchuk, and the director of the Ukrainian Institute of National Memory, Volodymyr Viatrovych, criticized the Kyiv city administration for a year-long delay in a recent decision to dismantle the mounted figure of Petliura's Bolshevik adversary, Mykola Shchors (as a part of the state's "decommunization" campaign). Municipal authorities constructed a high covered barricade around the monument, allegedly to prevent its destruction by activists who had grown frustrated with bureaucratic postponement.[54] In March of that year, unknown vandals sawed off the legs of Schors's horse.[55]

Two recent films have portrayed Petliura. He appears briefly in *Kruty-1918,* a film about the fatal UNR defense of Kyiv against a large Bolshevik army advancing from the northeast in January 1918. The movie, which focuses on the role of student-cadets who made up the bulk of the Ukrainian forces at the battle, was released in February 2019. Petliura is central, however, to the film *Taiemnyi shchodennyk Symona Petliura* (Symon Petliura's secret diary). Released in September 2018, the film's production enjoyed generous support. The Ukrainian state provided half of its nearly 48 billion UAH (1.7 million USD) budget and the Ukrainian Congressional Committee of America also contributed substantial funds.[56] The director of the film, Oles Yanchuk, serves simultaneously as director of the state Oleksandr Dovzhenko Film Studio—where much of the film was shot—and head of the Ukrainian Association of Cinematographers. Two Ukrainian politicians, who are actors by profession, also participated in the film. Minister of Culture Yevhen Nyshchuk plays UNR Prime Minister (and subsequent First Chairman of the Directory) Volodymyr Vynnychenko and People's Deputy Bohdan Beniuk—UNR President Mykhailo Hrushevsky.

The published reviews of *Taiemnyi shchodennyk* in Ukraine were mixed. Historian Andrii Rukkas published a lengthy, detailed review in the online historical journal *Istorychna pravda* (Historical truth). In it, he suggests: "In the socio-political realities of modern Ukraine the relevance of such a film undeniable. It was needed for a long time, and is needed now, because through its accessible language, the movie tells the audience about one of the milestones of the Ukrainian revolution."[57] Knowledge of Petliura is, in short, essential to contemporary Ukrainian citizenship and state-building. Similarly, Valentyna Samchenko, a critic for the one of the main national dailies, *Ukraina moloda* (Young Ukraine), writes that Petliura "again appeals to his countrymen to reflect on Ukraine's independence, Ukraine's friends and enemies, and everyone's responsibility for the kind of country we live in." She reminds readers of the parallels between Mazepa and Petliura, arguing that, although the Soviet government could not excommunicate Petliura as the Russian Orthodox Church did Mazepa, "the 'secular,' or more precisely, the denigration and consignment of labels by the *spetsluzhby* [special forces, e.g. the Cheka/GPU] have proven equally effective for decades."[58] Samchenko underscores the importance of commemorating Petliura, but also acknowledges why such an act is problematic. Such is the legacy of the Soviet Union's slander of Petliura, she argues, that perception of the film by contemporary Ukrainian viewers is contingent on their understanding of history.

Fig. 5.1 Grave of Symon Petliura, Montparnasse Cemetery, Paris (2018). *Source*: Photo by the author.

Some of those who objected to the content of the film outright chose to voice their opposition to its opening in Zaporizhia by marring promotional posters with red paint.[59] However, categorically negative reviews of the film largely avoided repeating the tropes of past polemics. In fact, two reviews took the opposite tact. Anton Filatov, writing for the influential political forum *112.ua* maintains that "the paradox of Yanchuk's films is that he struggles against Soviet myths, making movies in the Soviet tradition. If, in his films, Ukrainian flags take the place of red ones, and our soldiers change places with the Communists, then the films of this director will become typical socialist propaganda."[60] In a scathing review for *LB.ua*, an internet publication founded by a Kyiv sociological research consortium, the Gorshenin Institute, Dariia Badior, laments: "Yanchuk's film is fully consistent with his current stock-list biography—it is the same hackneyed-Soviet [biography], with stale air and loud cries about how to love the Motherland."[61] Instead of lambasting the film for its fixation on an anti-Soviet "nationalist," both writers maintain the director presents an oversimplified narrative that mimics Soviet caricatures of political struggle. As a result, it lacks resonance and emotive power.

For these writers and others, *Taiemnyi shchodennyk* was simply a bad film. They criticize inaccuracies in the film, object to its ploy of a "secret diary" (Petliura did not keep one, although his published articles and correspondence form the basis for the fictional diary's content), and lambast what they view as the one-dimensionality of the films characters and the density of historical detail. Nikolai Milinevskii, a critic for the Russian-language national *Vesti* (The News), puts it succinctly. The audience that saw the film with him apparently laughed repeatedly at "fiery speeches" that sounded "so artificial and naïve"; the film's depiction of the trial of Petliura's killer, Schwarzbard, was so protracted that, "the viewer may not last for the director's argument in defense of Petliura, but rather go for a beer and not return to the [theater] hall."[62] It is difficult to discern a political intent to these reviews. In effect, they propose that contemporary Ukrainian moviegoers are too sophisticated to accept the director's view of Petliura. Petliura, whatever his positive attributes and shortcomings were, cannot be "raised up by popular acclaim to a pedestal"—as Milinevskii puts it.[63] The age of national mythologizing has passed. And yet, there is still a political implication to such a claim. It suggests that Ukraine, because of its "late" achievement of lasting independence, needs no heroes, or at least ones not already valorized and shorn of complication. Positive reviewers share some of the criticisms of their more negative counterparts. For Rukkas, who likes the film generally, the film's chief failing was not its elevation of Petliura, but rather its presentation of a fatalistic character who does not conform to the real historical personage and record: "A desperate and dreary Petliura, who gave up the cause, presented no danger to the Kremlin. But here's a Petliura who did not lay down his weapons.... It is this Petliura—a fighter, not a grumbler—that was killed in Paris in May 1926. This is the Petliura that we need today."[64] In short, the film's Petliura is arguably still burdened by the Soviet construction of the hopeless of the UNR cause.

Literary studies scholar Aleida Assmann famously made a distinction between functional and storage memory, in which she suggests the two types of memory work together: "Just as storage memory can verify, support, or correct functional memory, so functional memory can orient and motivate storage memory."[65] This is partly what is happening with the image of Petliura in contemporary Ukraine. The Soviet government attempted to create a particular functional memory of Petliura to meet a specific ideological need, the destruction of the specter of Ukrainian separatism. But a storage memory preserved in the reminiscences and writings of UNR émigrés, as well as in the Soviet archives themselves, forced a reworking of functional memory after independence. Political authorities have contested the particular contours of this functional memory and attempted to position the historical record according to their respective visions. But not all aspects of this repository can be neatly reined in; for advocates of commemoration, an afterlife of the Soviet narrative lurks, awaiting animation. It is entirely understandable that any independent Ukrainian state should seek to honor the UNR and its promise, but the image of Petliura as a national hero will continue have detractors regardless of what scholars determine. Acknowledging this does not mean that Ukraine need be forever tied to Soviet historiography. Rather, the past public memory of Petliura has a dynamic existence beyond the Soviet state, capable of being contested and altered but not fully effaced.

Notes

1. Neïzhmak, "Zhadaly Petliuru," 18.
2. For a reliable and detailed study on the Ukrainian historiography of the OUN and the public debate that preceded this decision by Yushchenko, see Marples, *Heroes*, 79–313.
3. Smolii, *Entsyklopediia istorii*, 8:176. As Serhii Yekelchyk writes, RUPists such as Petliura maintained a national orientation for the party in spite of a fracturing of its ranks before 1905 because "they felt that only a national Ukrainian party could protect Ukrainian interests in a future socialist federation of Russia's peoples" (Yekelchyk, *Ukraine*, 8).
4. Kubijovyč, *Encyclopedia of Ukraine*, 3:865.
5. The *zemstva* were institutions of self-government that the crown established at the district and provincial levels in 1864. During the war, zemstva representatives joined with the empire's municipal leaders in the United Committee of the Union of Zemstva and the Union of Towns to support Russia's war effort. For more on the zemstva, see Emmons, *Zemstvo*.
6. For more on the Ukrainian Revolution, see Reshetar, *Ukrainian Revolution*; Hunczak, *Ukraine*; Soldatenko, *Ukraina v revoliutsiinu dobu*; Dornik, *Ukraine*; Miller, "Role of the First World War"; Chernev, "Ukrainization."
7. Yekelchyk, *Ukraine*, 81.
8. Abramson, *Prayer for the Government*, 169.
9. Palij, *Ukrainian-Polish Defensive Alliance*, 76.
10. Lytvyn, *Sud istorii*, 343, 400.
11. The debate and scholarship on this question is deep and ongoing. Abramson (*Prayer for the Government*) provides a helpful guide to multilingual sources published in Europe, North America, and Israel. In addition to the sources discussed here, texts in English include Hunczak, "Reappraisal"; Szajkowski, "Reappraisal: A Rebuttal"; Veidlinger, *In the Shadow*, 32–38.
12. Abramson, *Prayer for the Government*, 139, 176 (emphasis in the original).
13. Serhiichuk, *Symon Petliura*, 62. See also his commentary in his collection of archival documents on the pogroms: Serhiichuk, *Pohromy v Ukraiini*.
14. Plokhy, *Gates of Europe*, 223. See also Soldatenko, *Vynnychenko i Petliura*, 330–66; Lytvyn, *Sud istoriii*, 493–530.
15. Soldatenko, *Vynnychenko i Petliura*, 365.
16. Rosliak, "Symon Petliura," 6. There are too many works published on Petliura in Ukraine to cite here, but Rosliak believes Lytyvn's popular 2001 monograph on the UNR leader was the beginning of a fundamental readjustment of Petliura's image in the country.

17. Verstiuk, "Vazhke povernennia."
18. Malyk, "Simonu Petliure ustanoviat pamiatnik," 2.
19. Malyk, "Simonu Petliure ustanoviat pamiatnik."
20. "Kryminal'ni spravy." For a greater discussion of the SVU interrogation files that document the accused members confessing to this charge, see Pauly, *Breaking the Tongue*, 266–72.
21. Rosliak, "Symon Petliura (prodovzh.)," 6.
22. Rosliak, "Symon Petliura (prodovzh.)."
23. Denysko, "Chy postavliat' pam'iatnyk," 11.
24. Denysko, "Chy postavliat' pam'iatnyk."
25. Denysko, "Chy postavliat' pam'iatnyk."
26. Denysko, "Chy postavliat' pam'iatnyk."
27. Denysko, "Chy postavliat' pam'iatnyk."
28. "V Poltave snesli pamiatnik Petliure," 2.
29. "V Poltave snesli pamiatnik Petliure."
30. Bohun, "Petliura," 7.
31. Bohun, "Petliura."
32. Bohun, "Petliura."
33. In addition to Marples, there is a growing body of scholarship on the OUN-UPA and its place in the politics of history in Ukraine. It is far too immense to cite here, but particularly on the question of the organization's role in the Holocaust, see Amir, Balyns'kyi, and Hrytsak, *Strasti za Banderoiu*; Rudling, "OUN, UPA and the Holocaust"; Rossolinski, *Stepan Bandera*. For a broader discussion of the role of public memory in Eastern Europe and the post-Soviet space, including Ukraine, see Miller, *Convolutions*.
34. Soldatenko, *Ukraina v revoliutsiinu dobu*. Shevchenko, "Soldatenko V. F. Vynnychenko i Petliura," 215. Soldatenko's monograph is a highly detailed, lengthy study (over six hundred pages) and includes a section on the pogroms. Among the articles on Petliura in the special issue no. 3 of *Ukrains'kyi istorychnyi zhurnal* is an article dedicated entirely to his murder: Hrynenko, "Materialy zhurnaly 'Tryzub.'"
35. Shevchenko, "Soldatenko V. F. Vynnychenko i Petliura," 215.
36. "Opryliudneno 11 lystiv Petliury," 2.
37. Rudnyts'kyi, "Rozsekrechenyi Petliura," 3.
38. Tiutiunyk's biography further demonstrates the complexity of the Ukrainian Revolution. He was a key leader of the Free Cossacks and an active participant in the military affairs of the Central Rada. He played a critical role in the uprising against Hetman Pavlo Skoropadsky, then allied briefly with Red Army detachments in southern Ukraine, before rebelling, then joining the regular UNR army in May 1919, where he was given a commanding role. After the final expulsion of UNR forces from Ukraine by the Soviets, he was placed in charge of leading partisan operations in occupied Ukraine. After his capture and arrest, he turned on his former compatriots and served as a Soviet propagandist against the UNR cause. From 1923 to 1929 he lived in Kharkiv, teaching at the School for Red Commanders and acting in the 1926 film, *PKP* (*Piłudski Bought Petliura*). He was rearrested in 1929 and executed (Smolii, *Entsyklopediia istoriï*, 8:194–95).
39. Patoka, "23 travnia," 66, 71.
40. Patoka, "23 travnia," 65–66.
41. Fol'varochnyi, "Symon Petliura."
42. Bohun, "Sterty im'ia Petliury," 1.
43. Bohun, "Sterty im'ia Petliury."
44. See Shpyl'ova, "Symona Petliuru khochut' uvichnyty," 6; Tsymbaliuk, "Na persykh rivnens'skykh markakh XXI stolittiia," 4. In April 2009, the Ukrainian Institute of History sponsored a serious scholarly conference on Petliura, but it relied partly on patronage by municipal authorities in Fastiv, the site of a meeting that led to the merger of the UNR with the ZUNR (Pyrih, *Symon Petliura*). A localization of Petliura's commemoration has continued since Yanukovych's ousting and has sometimes been initiated by the ultranationalist Svoboda (Freedom) Party (Brukhal', "Petliura i Vynnychenko," 7).
45. Neïzhmak, "Zhadaly Petliuru," 18.
46. Siriachenko, "'Poliubite Petliuru nasil'no,'" 1; Shebelist, "Pam'iat' i pam'iatnyky."
47. Neïzhmak, "U Poltavi znovu zhadaly," 9.
48. Neïzhmak, "U Poltavi znovu zhadaly."
49. Verkhovna Rada Ukraïny, "Proekt Zakonu."

50. Hyde, "Ukraine to Rewrite Soviet History."
51. Poroshenko, "Ukaz prezydenta Ukraïny No. 17/2016."
52. "U Vinnytsi vidkryly pam'iatnyk Symon Petliuri."
53. "U Kyievi z'iavyt'sia pam'iatnyk Symonu Petliuri"; "U Kyievi vidkryly barel'ief Petliuri." The Ukrainian Institute of National Memory supported the installation of the sculpture to commemorate fighting between Bolshevik forces and UNR units under Petliura's command at this location.
54. "Nyshchuk i V'iatrovych narikaiut'."
55. "A konyk bez nohy."
56. Samchenko, "'Taiemnyi shchodennyk Symona Petliura' vyishov na ekrany zi skandalom u Zaporizhzhi."
57. Rukkas, "Iakoho Petliuru pokazuie 'Taiemnyi shchodennyk'?"
58. Samchenko, "'Taiemnyi shchodennyk Symona Petliura' vyishov na ekrany zi skandalom u Zaporizhzhi."
59. Samchenko, "'Taiemnyi shchodennyk Symona Petliura' vyishov na ekrany zi skandalom u Zaporizhzhi."
60. Filatov, "'Tainyi dnevnyk Simona Petliury': Skuchnyi urok istorii." *112.ua* receives content from the twenty-four hour television news channel, *112 Ukraina*—owned by People's Deputy Taras Kozak (Opposition Bloc) since the end of 2018.
61. Bad'ior, "Stydnoe kino." *LB.ua* stands for *Levyi bereg* (Rus.)/*Livyi bereh* (Ukr.) or Left Bank.
62. Milinevskii, "Smert' Petliury, kotoroi trudno dozhdat'sia."
63. Milinevskii, "Smert' Petliury, kotoroi trudno dozhdat'sia."
64. Rukkas, "Iakoho Petliuru pokazuie 'Taiemnyi shchodennyk'?"
65. Assmann sees functional memory as active knowledge that groups employ in the present; storage memory is knowledge that has lost "its living relevance to the present" and is stored in cultural archives and selectively disseminated by historians (Assmann, *Cultural Memory*, 123–24, 132).

Bibliography

"A konyk bez nohy: u Kyievi nevidomi poshkodyly pam'iatnyk Shchorsu." *UNIAN*, March 21, 2017. https://www.unian.ua/incidents/1834304-a-konik-bez-nogi-u-kievi-nevidomi-poshkodili-pamyatnik-schorsu-foto.html.
Abramson, Henry. *A Prayer for the Government: Ukrainians and Jews in Revolutionary Times, 1917–1920*. Cambridge, MA: Harvard Ukrainian Research Institute and Center for Jewish Studies, 1999.
Amir, Tarik, Ihor Balyns'kyi, and Yaroslav Hrytsak, eds. *Strasti za Banderoiu: statti ta eseï*. Kyiv: Hrani-T, 2010.
Assmann, Aleida. *Cultural Memory and Western Civilization: Functions, Media, Archives*. New York: Cambridge University Press, 2011.
Bad'ior, Dariia. "Stydnoe kino: chto ne tak s 'Tainym dnevnykom Simona Petliury'." *LB.ua*, September 11, 2018. https://lb.ua/culture/2018/09/11/407259_stidnoe_kino_taynim.html.
Bohun, Volodymyr. "Petliura: mif i zhorstoka pravda." *Robitnycha hazeta*, February 3, 2007.
———. "Sterty im'ia Petliury z karty Kyieva." *Robitnycha hazeta*, March 17, 2012.
Brukhal', Halyna. "Petliura i Vynnychenko kolys' buly nashymy susidamy." *Holos Ukrainy*, November 13, 2013.
Chernev, Borislav. "Ukrainization and Its Contradictions in the Context of the Brest-Litovsk System." In *The Empire and Nationalism at War*, edited by Eric Lohr and others, 73–90. Bloomington, IN: Slavica, 2014.
Denysko, Hanna. "Chy postavliat' pam'iatnyk Symonu Petliura na ioho Bat'kivshchyni." *Molod' Ukrainy*, September 14, 2006.
Dornik, Wolfram., ed. *Die Ukraine: zwischen Selbstbestimmung und Fremdherrschaft, 1917–1922*. Graz, Austria: Leykam, 2011.
Emmons, Terence. *The Zemstvo in Russia: An Experiment in Local Self-Government*. Cambridge: Cambridge University Press, 1982.
Filatov, Anton. "'Tainyi dnevnyk Simona Petliury': Skuchnyi urok istorii." *112.ua*, September 7, 2018. https://112.ua/mnenie/taynyy-dnevnik-simona-petlyury-skuchnyy-urok-istorii-461251.html.
Fol'varochnyi, Vasyl'. "Symon Petliura: urivok z romanu." *Literaturna Ukraina*, May 14, 2009, 5.
Hrynenko, O. O. "Materialy zhurnaly 'Tryzub' pro rozsliduvannia vbystva S. Petliury (1926–28 rr.)." *Ukrains'kyi istorychnyi zhurnal*, no. 3 (2009): 34–43.
Hunczak, Taras. "A Reappraisal of Symon Petliura and Ukrainian-Jewish Relations, 1917–1921." *Jewish Social Studies* 32, no. 3 (1969): 246–53.

———, ed. *The Ukraine, 1917–1921: A Study in Revolution*. Cambridge, MA: Harvard Ukrainian Research Institute, 1977.

Hyde, Lily. "Ukraine to Rewrite Soviet History with Controversial 'Decommunisation' Laws." *The Guardian*, April 20, 2015. http://www.theguardian.com/world/2015/apr/20/ukraine-decommunisation-law-soviet.

"Kryminal'ni spravy na reabilitovanykh osib." Fond 6, spr. 67098 FP, vol. 63, archive 19–23, 32; vol. 83, archive 13; vol. 87, archive 117; vol. 85, archive 21. Sectoral State Archive of the Security Service of Ukraine (Haluzevyi derzhavnyi arkhiv Sluzhby bezpeky *Ukrainy*), Kyiv, Ukraine.

Kubijovyč, Volydymyr., ed. *Encyclopedia of Ukraine*. 5 vols. Toronto: University of Toronto Press, 1984–93.

Lytvyn, Serhii. *Sud istorii: Symon Petliura i petliuriana*. Kyiv: Vyd-vo im. Oleny Telihy, 2001.

Malyk, T. "Simonu Petliure ustanoviat pamiatnik." *Rabochaia gazeta*, May 25, 2006.

Marples, David. *Heroes and Villains: Creating National History in Contemporary Ukraine*. Budapest: Central European University Press, 2007.

Milinevskii, Nikolai. "Smert' Petliury, kotoroi trudno dozhdat'sia—retsenziia na novyi ukrainskii fil'm." *Vesti*, September 7, 2018. https://vesti-ukr.com/kultura/302099-smert-petljury-kotoroj-trudno-dozhdatsja-retsenzija-na-novyj-ukrainskij-film.

Miller, Alexei., ed. *The Convolutions of Historical Politics*. New York: Central European University Press, 2012.

———. "The Role of the First World War in the Competition between Ukrainian and All-Russian Nationalism." In *The Empire and Nationalism at War*, edited by Eric Lohr, Vera Tolz, Alexander Semyonov, and Mark von Hagen, 163–88. Bloomington, IN: Slavica, 2014.

Neïzhmak, Vasyl'. "U Poltavi znovu zhadaly pro Petliuru." *Holos Ukrainy*, May 27, 2014.

———. "Zhadaly Petliuru." *Holos Ukrainy*, May 13, 2015, 18.

"Nyshchuk i V'iatrovych narikaiut' na kyïvs'ku vladu cherez obstavyny demontazhu pam'iatynyka Shchors." *Interfaks-Ukraina*, May 8, 2018. https://ua.interfax.com.ua/news/general/503930.html.

"Opryliudneno 11 lystiv Petliury." *Narodna armiia*, May 22, 2009.

Palij, Michael. *The Ukrainian-Polish Defensive Alliance, 1919–1921: An Aspect of the Ukrainian Revolution*. Edmonton, ON, Canada: Canadian Institute of Ukrainian Studies Press, 1995.

Patoka, Valentyna V. "23 travnia: Budivnychyi samostiinoï Ukrainy. Do 130-richchia vid dnia narodzhennia S. V. Petliury (1879–1926)." *Kalendar znamennykh i pam'iatnykh dat*, no. 2 (2009): 65–78.

Pauly, Matthew D. *Breaking the Tongue: Language, Education, and Power in Soviet Ukraine, 1923–1934*. Toronto: University of Toronto Press, 2014.

Plokhy, Serhii. *The Gates of Europe: A History of Ukraine*. New York: Basic Books, 2015.

Poroshenko, Petro. Ofitsiine internet-predstavnytstvo. "Ukaz prezydenta Ukrainy No. 17/2016: Pro zakhody z vidznachennia 100-richchia podii Ukrains'koi revoliutsii 1917–1921 rokiv," January 22, 2016. http://www.president.gov.ua/documents/172016-19736.

Pyrih, Ruslan, ed. *Symon Petliura: mify i real'nist: Materialy naukovykh chytan', prysviachenykh 130-richchiu vid dnia narodzhennia Symona Vasyl'ovycha Petliury (28 kvitnia 2009 r.)*. Fastiv, Ukraine: Fastivs'kyi derzhavnyi kraieznavchyi muzei, 2011.

Reshetar, John. *The Ukrainian Revolution, 1917–1920: A Study in Nationalism*. New York: Arno, 1972.

Rosliak, Roman. "Symon Petliura: povernennia istorychnoi pam'iati." *Narodna armiia*, May 22, 2004.

———. "Symon Petliura: povernennia istorychnoi pam'iati (prodovzh.)." *Narodna armiia*, May 30, 2006.

Rossolinski, Grzegorz. *Stepan Bandera: The Life and Afterlife of a Ukrainian Nationalist: Fascism, Genocide, and Cult*. Stuttgart: ibidem, 2014.

Rudling, Per Anders. "The OUN, the UPA and the Holocaust: A Study in the Manufacturing of Historical Myths." *Carl Beck Papers in Russian and East European Studies*, no. 2107 (2011).

Rudnyts'kyi, Iurii. "Rozsekrechenyi Petliura." *Vechirnyi Kiev*, May 22, 2009.

Rukkas, Andrii. "Iakoho Petliuru pokazuie 'Taiemnyi shchodennyk'? Vrazhennia istoryka." *Istorychna pravda*, September 11, 2018. http://www.istpravda.com.ua/articles/2018/09/11/152907/.

Samchenko, Valentyna. "'Taiemnyi shchodennyk Symona Petliura' vyishov na ekrany zi skandalom u Zaporizhzhi." *Ukraina moloda*, September, 11 2018. https://www.umoloda.kiev.ua/number/3358/164/126313/.

Serhiichuk, Volodymyr. *Pohromy v Ukraini, 1914–1920: vid shtuchnykh stereotypiv do hirkoi pravdy, prykhovuvanoï v radians'kykh arkhivakh*. Kyiv: Vyd-vo im. O. Telihy, 1998.

———. *Symon Petliura and the Jewry*. Kiev: Iunivers, 2000.

Shebelist, Serhii. "Pam'iat' i pam'iatnyky: Poltava bez Mazepy i Petliury." *Den'*, February 6, 2012. http://incognita.day.kiev.ua/pamyat-i-pamyatniki-poltava-bez-mazepi-i-petlyuri.html.

Shevchenko, Volodymyr F. "Soldatenko V. F. Vynnychenko i Petliura: politychni portrety revoliutsiinoï doby." *Ukrains'kyi istorychnyi zhurnal*, no. 6 (2008): 212–15.
Shpyl'ova, Vira. "Symona Petliuru khochut' uvichnyty v Kam'iantsi-Podil's'komu: chy zmozhut'?" *Holos Ukrainy*, February 25, 2009.
Siriachenko, Vladimir. "'Poliubite Petliuru nasil''no.'" *Rabochaia gazeta*, March 20, 2008.
Smolii, Valerii, ed. *Entsyklopediia istorii Ukrainy*. 9 vols. Kyiv: Naukova dumka, 2003–12.
Soldatenko, Valerii. *Ukraina v revoliutsiinu dobu: istorychni ese-khroniky*. Kharkiv, Ukraine: Prapor, 2008.
———. *Vynnychenko i Petliura: politychni portrety revoliutsiinoi doby*. Kyiv: Vyd-vo Svitohliad, 2007.
Szajkowski, Zosa. "A Reappraisal of Symon Petliura and Ukrainian-Jewish Relations, 1917–1921: A Rebuttal." *Jewish Social Studies* 31, no. 3 (1969): 184–213.
Tsymbaliuk, Ievhen. "Na persykh rivnens'skykh markakh XXI stolittiia—Taras Shevchenko, Symon Petliura ta Klym Savur." *Holos Ukrainy*, April 13, 2011.
"U Kyievi vidkryly barel'ief Petliuri." *Radio svoboda*, January 21, 2019. https://www.radiosvoboda.org/a/news-barelief-petluri-kyiv/29722017.html.
"U Kyievi z'iavyt'sia pam'iatnyk Symonu Petliuri." *Uriadovyi kur'ier*, January 23, 2016. https://ukurier.gov.ua/uk/news/u-kiyevi-zyavitsya-pamyatnik-simonu-petlyuri/.
"U Vinnytsi vidkryly pam'iatnyk Symon Petliuri." *Tyzhden'*, October 14, 2017. http://tyzhden.ua/News/201917.
Veidlinger, Jeffrey. *In the Shadow of the Shtetl: Small-Town Jewish life in Soviet Ukraine*. Bloomington: Indiana University Press, 2013.
Verkhovna Rada Ukrainy: ofitsiinyi veb-portal. "Proekt Zakonu pro pravovyi status ta vshanuvannia pam'iati bortsiv za nelazhnist' Ukrainy u XX stolitti." April 4, 2015. http://w1.c1.rada.gov.ua/pls/zweb2/webproc4_1?pf3511=54689.
Verstiuk, Vladislav. "Vazhke povernennia holovnoho otamana." *Ukrains'ka pravda*, May 28, 2009. http://www.pravda.com.ua/articles/2009/05/28/3976958/.
"V Poltave snesli pamiatnik Petliure." *Donbass*, May 10, 2007.
Yekelchyk, Serhy. *Ukraine: Birth of a Modern Nation*. New York: Oxford University Press, 2007.

MATTHEW D. PAULY is Associate Professor of History at Michigan State University. He is author of *Breaking the Tongue: Language, Education, and Power in Soviet Ukraine, 1923–34*.

6

GLORY TO THE HEROES?

Gender, Nationalism, and Memory

Olesya Khromeychuk

On October 12, 2015, the National Bank of Ukraine produced a new five-hryvnia commemorative coin, "dedicated to the celebration of bravery (*muzhnosti*) and heroism, indefatigability and the love of freedom of the fighters for the national cause of all generations."[1] The coin is meant to celebrate the Day of the Defender of Ukraine, a holiday introduced by President Petro Poroshenko in 2014. Established and celebrated during the ongoing war in the Donbas region, the holiday became framed in a particular way in order to be meaningful for the current defenders of the Ukrainian territory fighting in eastern Ukraine; it also created a certain historical connection, linking the contemporary Ukrainian army with historical military formations.[2] It is executed in a style full of war connotations: the reverse of the coin features a trident, the official national symbol of Ukraine, and, as the National Bank explains, "the symbol of the principality under the reign of Volodymyr the Great," which is placed against a camouflage background.[3] The central figure on the obverse of the coin is "the Mother of God, with the Cossacks and the current soldier-defenders under her veil."[4] The symbolism follows a tradition going back to 17th–18th century iconography, in which the Virgin Mary is depicted as covering the military and church rulers of the Cossack polity with her veil.[5] The image is supposed to build a connection between the contemporary Ukrainian army and the 17th-century Cossacks and to create a continuum of statehood between Volodymyr the Great's Kyivan Rus, the Ukrainian Cossack proto-state, and the current Ukrainian state.

The reverse of the coin features a line from a famous Ukrainian song "For Ukraine!" (*Za Ukrainu!*): "For Honour! For Glory! For the People!" The song was written in 1917 by Mykola Voronyi, a Ukrainian poet and one of the founding members of the Ukrainian Central Council (Tsentral'na Rada).[6] He was executed by the NKVD in 1938, and his poem "For Ukraine!" became popular, in particular with the Ukrainian military structures contemporary with Voronyi, but also long after his death, among the armed forces of independent Ukraine. The coin thus also commemorates the struggle for independence between 1917 and 1920 and the brief existence of the Ukrainian People's Republic.

The depiction of the Virgin Mary contains further historical connotations. This particular representation refers to what is known in Ukrainian as *Pokrova*: the Virgin Mary protecting the faithful by covering them with her veil. The feast of *Pokrova* is celebrated on October 14, and it was chosen as the new holiday of the Day of the Defender of Ukraine when President Poroshenko decided to break the Soviet tradition of celebrating the Day of the Defender of the Fatherland on February 23. The *Pokrova* holiday has also been adopted by the Ukrainian Insurgent Army (Ukrains'ka Povstans'ka Armiia, UPA) as the symbolic day of the formation of its organization. Therefore, though the commemorative coin does not overtly represent the UPA members, they can be assumed to be commemorated by it, alongside all other military or paramilitary forces that have fought for Ukraine's independence.

Through the *Pokrova* holiday, the Virgin Mary becomes the guardian of the Ukrainian defenders. The female deity exists in an otherwise all-male world: the word defender (*zakhysnyk*) is almost always used in its masculine form in Ukrainian, including in the name of the holiday, thereby excluding not only 25,000 female members of the contemporary Ukrainian Armed Forces who hold military positions—around 7,000 of whom have taken part in the war in the Donbas region—but also the women from all those historical periods layered onto the coin.[7] A woman is able to enter the world of the military only on a symbolic level, as a holy protectress of the nation, while real women are given no place as actors in the context of war. The gender dynamics visible in this one coin can be extended across the entire discourse surrounding the commemoration and celebration of the military in Ukraine.

War discourses are powerfully gendered and have a profound effect on our wider understanding of gender. As a culturally produced activity, wars are remembered through culturally specific terminology. The traditional representation of war anticipates the separation of the war space into "front" and "home front," where the front is a male space, while the "peaceful" space of civilians, the home front, is a female sphere.[8] This division is depicted as natural, and the repeated representation of it as natural distorts the actual division of labor in times of war, which is much less clearly separated into male and female domains.

Wars and their representations are also powerful instruments in nation-building processes. Rada Iveković and Julie Mostov argue that "Gender and nation are social and historic constructions, which intimately participate in the formation of one another: nations are gendered; and the topography of the nation is mapped in gendered terms (feminized soil, landscapes, and boundaries and masculine movement over these spaces)."[9] When women are included in the space of war, they are included as symbols of peace or victimhood, usually representing the nation itself. "National mythologies draw on traditional gender roles and national narrative is filled with images of the nation as mother, wife, and maiden," state Iveković and Mostov.[10] It is thus important to recognize that nation building involves "social constructions of masculinity and femininity that support a division of labour in which women reproduce the nation physically and symbolically and men protect, defend, and avenge the nation."[11] A woman, thus, becomes "the national iconic signifier for the material, the passive, and the corporeal, to be worshipped, protected, and controlled by those with the power to remember and to forget, to guard, to define and redefine."[12]

The inclusion of women outside the symbolic sphere, as definers of the nation more widely, or as direct participants of violent political conflicts specifically, is difficult.

Patriarchal societies maintain the nation-building process—with participation in wars as one of its key elements—as an exclusively male space, if not in reality then at least in discourse. The language used to describe even the partial inclusion of women into the military sphere can prove to be difficult in that it has to cross the binary structures set out by the gendered discourse of war. Hence, a common adjective to describe a woman in Ukrainian as courageous is *muzhnia*, which literally means "manly" (*muzh* is a man or a husband). The noun *muzhnist* (rather than *vidvaha*, which is gender-neutral) is used by the National Bank of Ukraine when describing the courage of the (male) defenders of Ukraine to whom its commemorative coin is dedicated.[13] This kind of language, therefore, implies either a total exclusion of women from the ranks of the courageous or an assumption that such women must become manly if they are to be included. The construction of the memory about manly women can thus be a complicated task, filled with the obstacles presented by gendered language and discourse.

Miriam Cooke and Angela Woollacott argue that "language transforms experience into consciousness," but "society censors those who write outside of what is considered to be their gender-specific experience: women should not write about the front as a lived experience; men should not describe threatened masculinity."[14] Or as Cooke puts it, "is a soldier a soldier if he is afraid, weak, and vulnerable? Is a mother a mother if she is fearless, strong and politically effective?"[15] Gender-sensitive analysis of mnemonic narratives, which have a direct impact on the formation of the civic or national identity of Ukrainians, is essential both for a deeper understanding of historical events and for a better awareness of the processes that shape contemporary identities. Judith Butler argues that it is "impossible to separate out 'gender' from the political and cultural intersections in which it is invariably produced and maintained."[16] Gender analysis, therefore, can tell us much about these political and cultural intersections.

This chapter will focus on the gendered aspects of the commemoration of the nationalist movement of the 1930s–50s, represented by the Organization of Ukrainian Nationalists (Orhanizatsiia Ukrains'kykh Natsionalistiv, OUN) and the UPA, which has gained great prominence in official discourse in recent years.[17] The chapter discusses how Ukrainian nationalist women are represented, remembered, or forgotten. Analyzing gender dynamics in the nationalist underground, and how they are reflected in later representations, tells us much about the ideology of nationalism, the discrepancy between the theoretical ideals and practical involvement of women and men in the movement, and the impact that political conflicts have on the way that gender is perceived by society. The chapter argues that war itself allows negotiations of gender distinctions, yet the process of remembering and commemorating war produces the type of cultural encoding of experience that reinforces traditional gender roles.

Remembering World War II in Ukraine

The history of World War II for the residents of the region that constitutes contemporary Ukraine is the history of several wars, two occupations, nationalist struggles, ethnic cleansings, and mass killings. Presenting World War II as one single event, especially in the territories so fittingly labeled by Timothy Snyder as bloodlands, leads to an inevitable simplification of its complex history.[18] Considering each conflict separately, however, deprives them of their larger context, for none of these events happened in isolation; many were possible only because of the demoralization of the population, the increasing mundaneness of violence, the collapse of state institutions, the imposition of multiple occupation regimes and other consequences of a conflict as atrocious as World War II. The memory of these events is usually created along two trajectories: private memories that are frequently connected to specific events, such as deportations of relatives or the destruction of a native village, and that are often removed from the wider contextual setting; and a collective memory, devised by state-sponsored institutions or political organizations that produce a single national narrative, seemingly shared by the whole country—accessible, and often in tones of black and white.

Like many other states, Ukraine has put much effort into creating a shared narrative and collective memory of the war, yet the creation of a single national memory is particularly problematic for the region. Although the whole of the population suffered or witnessed unspeakable violence—in particular mass killings of Jews—the key events in private memories will differ regionally because of the difference in the way the war was experienced in particular by the residents of Reichskommissariat Ukraine and Generalgouvernement, both of which constitute what is now Ukraine.[19] Forcing a certain idea of universal memory onto the population of Ukraine as a whole is likely to cause more friction than unity.

The Soviet memory narrative of World War II was constructed for the whole of the Soviet Union and, for many residents of Ukraine, their experience of the war could not be spoken about.[20] As Julie Fedor, Simon Lewis, and Tatiana Zhurzhenko argue, in the Soviet Union, the myth of the Great Patriotic War and the common victory "corresponded to the basic historical paradigm of East Slavic unity and 'brotherhood'" and in Ukraine it "helped to silence the counter-memory of the anti-Soviet nationalist resistance."[21] The collapse of the Soviet Union enabled Ukrainians to uncover their forgotten past and to begin a process of reconstructing the forbidden memories. Although the absence of an agreed nationwide consensus created a certain "situational pluralism" of memories, the regional imagination of the past remained monologic.[22] The desire of each governing elite to rewrite the history and, subsequently, the memory of World War II in Ukraine encouraged neither neutral academic research nor unpoliticized grassroots initiatives. The outcome of the dictation of shared memory from the center resulted in conflicting narratives being propagated by the peripheries. As Tatiana Zhurzhenko argues, "in Ukraine the divided collective memory contributes to regional pluralism and fuels ongoing political conflict." She states that "the memory of the Second World War has been instrumentalized by national as well as regional political actors for legitimizing competing geopolitical projects."[23]

While the regions that composed Reichskommissariat Ukraine commemorate the victims of the Nazi occupation and cherish the narratives of the liberation of the territory by the Red Army, for much of western Ukraine, one of the key memories of World War II and the immediate postwar period is connected with the nationalist struggle for independence. The eastern borderland provinces of Poland, comprising an ethnic Ukrainian majority and Polish and Jewish minorities, were first annexed by the Soviet Union in 1939 as a result of the Treaty of Nonaggression between Germany and the Soviet Union; they were then occupied by the Nazis in 1941 and then, depending on one's choice of terminology, reoccupied or liberated by the Soviet Union in 1944.[24] Thus, during World War II in this region, state institutions were destroyed three times. For most of the population, the collapse of the rule of law meant devastation, but it also offered an opportunity for nationalists to attempt the formation of an independent Ukrainian state on behalf of (although not always supported by) the Ukrainian population of the region. The key players here were the Organization of Ukrainian Nationalists and the UPA, organizations with a complex history of not only fighting for Ukrainian independence but also of collaborating with Nazi Germany and participating in war crimes.[25] After Ukraine's independence, many initiatives to celebrate the nationalists emerged throughout Ukraine, in particular in the regions where they had been most active.

Gender Dynamics in the OUN and UPA

The OUN was formed in 1929 and acted in the territory where Ukrainians constituted a majority.[26] The radical political thinker Dmytro Dontsov had a major influence on the ideology of the OUN. According to Oleksandr Zaitsev, "Dontsov was not an original thinker . . . but by combining ideas borrowed from various sources and giving them brilliant journalistic expression he created an influential doctrine of 'active nationalism.'"[27] The OUN's idea of "organized nationalism" was inspired by Dontsov's writing and became the Ukrainian variation of the integral nationalism that was popular across Europe in the interwar period.[28] Like other right-wing ideologies of the time, the OUN's philosophy placed the nation above all else. This position determined the nationalists' view on gender roles. In a publication on the social role of women, Daria Rebet—a prominent OUN member and the only woman in the leadership (*provid*) of the organization—emphasized the value of the nation and criticized feminism. She stated that "by viewing the individual [*odynytsiu*] as an absolute value and aim in itself" feminism neglects "the basic laws of human existence" because an individual is "only a small cog that cannot exist independently and separately, and naturally must be subordinated to its organically superior society—the nation."[29]

According to the OUN, the main task of women was "the upbringing of the new generation, a physically, spiritually and morally healthy generation." The nationalists argued that "throughout Europe today there is a dominant call: the woman is the educator of children."[30] This limiting ideological perception of the role of women did not, however, prevent the national leadership from recruiting a large number of female members.[31] Martha Bohachevsky-Chomiak argues that there were discrepancies in the attitude that the OUN's leadership took toward women. She states that "in one of its many theses, the nationalists were ordered to treat all women honourably as comrades and potential mothers. But because the nationalists opposed liberalism and perceived radicals as crypto-communists, they viewed as anathema feminism, socialist ideals of equality of women and women's liberation."[32] As a clandestine organization, the OUN valued the ability of women to perform traditional feminine roles and maintain a civilian appearance, highly useful for underground activity.[33]

The UPA, which was created in the early 1940s, needed its female members even more than the OUN did.[34] Being an underground army, the UPA had to rely heavily on the support of people who, in their view, attracted less attention to themselves. Unlike the male insurgents who were often in the forests, many women maintained legal or semilegal status, secured by often fabricated identification documents.[35] The women played a great many roles: the majority were involved in tasks that are traditionally seen as supportive, such as cleaning, mending clothes, nursing the wounded, and cooking; many worked as stenographers; a large number were engaged in reconnaissance work, mostly as liaisons (*zviazkovi*); others served as personal bodyguards of the top nationalists. Finally, there were women who took part in direct combat, although the nationalists did not encourage women to engage in combat tasks.[36] Women who were part of the nationalist movement could deviate from traditional gender norms or adopt conventional masculine roles only if such behavior benefited the nationalist cause.[37]

The Pantheon of Nationalist Ukrainian Heroes

The contemporary representation of the nationalist organizations is highly ambiguous. On the one hand, they are celebrated as heroes, especially in the western regions of Ukraine; on the other hand, they are known to have perpetrated ethnic cleansings, and some of them took part in implementating the Holocaust in Ukraine.[38] Many in Poland regard both the OUN and the UPA as criminal organizations because of their perpetration of violence against the civilian Polish population.[39] In Russia, especially in the light of the Maidan protests and the war in the Donbas region, the nationalists are portrayed as nothing but Nazi collaborators. For much of the population of Ukraine, personal memories or postmemories of World War II merge with the cultural memory prevalent in each region.[40] Thus, the views of the Ukrainian population are polarized on the matter.

Regime after regime tried to swing public opinion of the nationalists one way or the other. President Viktor Yushchenko decided to make Stepan Bandera a hero of Ukraine in January 2010. In January 2011, President Yanukovych annulled the award. In 2013, the minister of education, Dmytro Tabachnyk, removed the names of Bandera and Roman Shukevych, the UPA commander and formerly the *Nachtigall* and *Schutzmannschaft* 201 battalion officer, from the list of political figures with whom students needed to be familiar in order to pass their independent university assessment on the history of Ukraine. They were replaced with Mykola Shchors, a Red Army commander, renowned for his participation in the Russian civil wars, and Yuri Piatakov, a Bolshevik revolutionary leader who headed the Kyiv Committee of the Russian Social Democratic Labour Party.[41] A number of alternative textbooks on history emerged as a result of the policies of Tabachnyk.[42] Thus, since Ukraine became independent, one set of "heroes" has been raised to the official pedestal and another set has been simultaneously elevated by the opposition, in order to cater for the wishes of their potential and existing electorate.[43]

Poroshenko's approach to national memory writing has not been original. Being himself engaged in an actual war, Ukraine's new president left the memory of World War II to the Ukrainian Institute of National Memory (Ukrains'kyi Instytut Natsional'noi Pam'iati, UINP), appointing Volodymyr Viatrovych as its head. A historian known for his pronationalist stance, Viatrovych had headed the State Security Services Archives under Yushchenko but was removed from power under Yanukovych.[44] As soon as he was brought back to power by Poroshenko, together with his team at the UINP, he immediately began to rewrite historical memory by literally erasing many symbols, names, and images of the communist past from public sphere. He achieved this by introducing the controversial decommunization laws.[45]

One of these laws, "On the Legal Status and Honoring the Memory of Fighters for Ukraine's Independence in the Twentieth Century," dedicates a prominent place to the OUN and the UPA, among a number of military organizations with controversial histories.[46] These actions have given a large boost to the already widespread regional commemorations of the two organizations, since they are now officially recognized as fighters for Ukraine's independence. There can be little doubt that the objectives of both of the OUN and UPA were indeed to fight for the sovereignty of Ukraine, their recognition by the decommunization laws serves as a de facto proclamation of them as state-endorsed heroes of Ukraine. In her assessment of the decommunization laws, Yuliya Yurchuk argues that "Those aspects of the new legislation which politicize history, reduce its complexity by establishing 'correct' heroes, and forbid alternative opinions pose a danger of hindering independent historical research and free public debate."[47] She states that "at the level of national memory, the legacy of the OUN and UPA will surely continue to present ground for disputes and discontent."[48] Georgiy Kasianov points out that although the laws insist that "the goal of the authors is to achieve mutual understanding in society, . . . the methods in which these laws were drafted and passed, the terminology, and means of implementation are very reminiscent of the cultural patterns against which these laws are directed."[49]

The most recent developments in Ukrainian memory politics are highly influenced not only by the change of the regime—since the Maidan protests of 2013–14—but also by the ongoing war in the eastern parts of the country. The new team of the UINP is now directly coordinated by the minister of culture of Ukraine and is thus fully in tune with the governing regime's view of memory politics.[50] It is eager to revive the memory of key historical events of the past century, especially of World War II, and to present them in a way that is relevant to the contemporary political situation. Launching the exhibition "The Ukrainian World War II," the head of the UINP argued that "in this war, which Ukraine is fighting against Russia, myths, stereotypes and all kinds of lies connected with World War II are actively used. The absence among Ukrainians of knowledge of what that war was actually like allows the Russian propaganda an opportunity for manipulations."[51] But while fighting against pro-Kremlin propaganda and debunking old Soviet stereotypes, Viatrovych engages in creating new myths, heroes, and memory narratives.[52]

Nationalist Women in Historiography

The historical figures that feature in the discussion of the pantheon of nationalist heroes are almost exclusively male. Women, who were "a very important resource of the OUN-UPA, . . . [and who] to a large extent ensured the longevity of the existence and reinforced the effectiveness of the activity of the insurgents," are largely missing from not only critical but even celebratory public discussions of the nationalist movement.[53] The controversy surrounding the OUN's and UPA's activities and the lack of any consolidated history of the movement makes a critical assessment of the existing polarized—yet mostly male-biased—narratives about the nationalist movement a challenging task. Such a critical assessment can be achieved through gender-sensitive analysis: in most cases, gender analysis is less preoccupied with identifying the nationalists along the hero-traitor trajectory and is much more interested in bringing the study of the movement closer to the reality of the experiences of its participants, thus preventing further distortion and politicization of the memory of the period.

Many studies, while trying to piece together the scarce information on the female nationalists, rarely go outside the established, and often heroicized, portrayal of female insurgents. Collected volumes that present interviews with women who took part in the Ukrainian nationalist resistance or list brief biographical data on the known female participants are mostly constructed to serve the nationalist cause: they justify the aims of the nationalist movement and contain few critical remarks of its gender dynamics.[54] The same is true about memoirs written by participants in the nationalist movement. For instance, an autobiography of Maria Savchyn, an OUN member, which is unique in the detailed description of the underground movement it provides, and which reveals much about the gender-specific experience of being a female insurgent, does not critically assess the ideas of gender as prescribed by nationalism, because her work is written precisely to justify the nationalist struggle.[55] Thus, even the women who might have challenged gender stereotypes through their direct participation in political violence did not challenge the idea that a man has the right to establish what role a woman should play, nor the right of men to represent those roles discursively.[56] In the words of Olena Teliha, a Ukrainian poet, activist and a member of the OUN, "in every nation a woman is that which a man wants her to be."[57] Commenting on precisely this type of problem, Miriam Cooke stresses that "activism and its interpretation . . . function independently," and that "it is not enough for women to have been there; they have to write and interpret what it means to have been there."[58]

Approaches to studying women's involvement in the Ukrainian nationalist movement are varied. In the Ukrainian nationalist historiography, women's stories are at best used as propaganda material for the glorification of the nationalist struggle, and at worst untold. The nationalists who are remembered and celebrated are usually those who have held leading roles, while the rank-and-file get a mention simply as "the boys" or "the girls." The patriarchal ideology of the nationalists kept the women mostly in roles traditionally perceived as supportive, and only a few women held positions of leadership, which diminished the chance that women would be remembered. Jeffrey Burds cites a two-volume edition of the history of the UPA, which tells stories of 338 insurgents, only seventeen of whom are women: "these 17 women heroes were deemed heroic either because they were murdered, because they served prison sentences, or—most often—because of their contributions to ancillary branches of the movement: to culture, child care, or education."[59] Women, thus, are usually represented as supporters of the male partisans, as mothers who nurtured their sons to be good nationalists, or as loyal wives, daughters, sisters, and lovers, who will follow their men anywhere, even to the underground bunker. An equally common depiction of nationalist women is as victims of the enemy regime, symbolically representing Ukraine itself. Sometimes they are portrayed as traitors, who put the (male) nationalists in potential or actual danger.[60]

The interest in female nationalists is growing, and a number of scholars have focused on the participation of women in the movement. Oksana Kis, Lesia Onyshko, Maria Mandryk, and other researchers have analysed the various roles played by the female nationalists.[61] Studies that examine women's active roles in the movement demonstrate their ability to fight for Ukraine's independence on a par with men. Such works discuss the gender-specific experience of women and criticize their being overlooked by historiography and popular representations of the movement. This approach, however, often tries to do justice to women by introducing them into the pantheon of nationalist heroes, thereby endorsing the existence of the pantheon.[62] Borys Savchuk, for instance, portrays the women who fought for Ukraine's independence as those who continued "traditions of the ancient Amazons," and "performed their civic and patriotic duty in their fight for the protection of the statehood, freedom and independence of the nation with great courage [*muzhnio*] and self-sacrifice."[63] Works of this kind lack critical assessment of the nationalist ideology and do not examine critically women's agency (or lack thereof) as perpetrators of violence. Other works tend to tell the story of women's involvement as active members of the movement but portray them as exceptions, thus supporting the conventional idea of a woman's place being at home, or at least the "home front."[64] Two stories of such "exceptional" women are included in Volodymyr Viatrovych's *Istoriia z hryfom "Sekretno"* (Classified history: the secrets of the Ukrainian past in the KGB archives). They tell about Artemiziia Halyts'ka and Liudmyla Foia. Both stories happen to be about the betrayal of the nationalists by these women. Incidentally, Viatrovych explains that, in each case, the women betrayed the movement only on the surface, remaining loyal to the nationalist cause in their hearts.[65]

Some studies approach the subject in a gender-sensitive way and are critical of the movement itself. Olena Petrenko has written the first comprehensive study of women nationalists, and has looked at various aspects of women's participation in the nationalist movement, including the instrumentalization of women as secret agents in the fight against nationalism and the various literary representations of nationalist women.[66] Marta Havryshko has critically examined intimate romantic and sexual relations into which women entered, and the impact that doing so had on their experience of the underground.[67] Most of the studies of Ukrainian nationalism, however, continue to pay little or no attention to the role of women at all.[68] The Ukrainian case is not unique. Nira Yuval-Davis states that "when discussing issues of national 'production' or 'reproduction,' the literature on nationalism does not usually relate to women," even though "it is women . . . who reproduce nations, biologically, culturally and symbolically."[69] She explains that the reason is the social contract, according to which civil society is divided into public and private domains, where "women (and the family) are located in the private domain, which is not seen as politically relevant."[70] She thus argues that "as nationalism and nations have usually been discussed as part of the public political sphere, the exclusion of women from that arena has affected their exclusion from that discourse as well."[71]

The OUN, and later the UPA, greatly benefited from their female members. Oksana Kis argues that the nationalist movement used "the full potential of the local Ukrainian women, including their intellectual and organisational skills, psychological and behavioural specificities, gender stereotypes, as well as particular gender expertise (developed through traditional gender roles and socialisation)."[72] The memory of the women's experiences and perceptions of the nationalist movement are, however, either excluded from the contemporary discourse or included as an addition, which does not challenge the official narrative of nationalism, and does not discuss the instrumentalized use of women by the movement.[73]

Representation of the Past as Construction of the Future

In contemporary memory conflicts in Ukraine, where Stepan Bandera sometimes features in the news as often as current political figures, the women of the nationalist movement seem to be fading into oblivion. Although many of them survived longer than their male leaders, because they were often given lengthy sentences rather than dying in action or taking their own lives as men often did, their voices are quiet and their stories almost unknown. Perhaps it is the actual absence of the heroic death that deprives them of the visibility that men have had. Burds argues that "male suffering is somehow more 'courageous' and 'heroic' than female suffering. . . . In contrast, female victims of gender violence are less likely to be viewed as heroes and more likely to be construed as reminders of defeat. This is especially so in patriarchal societies."[74]

This glorification of male death and the attribution of shame to female death or suffering is not unique to the Ukrainian nationalist movement. In her *Kieszonkowy atlas kobiet* (Pocket atlas of women), Sylwia Chutnik explores Warsaw's commemoration landscape:

> You can try to take a close look at your city. At every step there is a commemoration plaque, flowers, a candle. Shot, fell, murdered, killed. Only "raped" is missing, but such things are not remembered. It is something physiological, unclean. It is like relieving yourself. Rape is not associated with shooting, war, bang-bang-bang, falling, crawling to the trenches.
> Rape is a rolled-up dress, torn underpants, violent movements. And the victim often has a chance of surviving. So it does not count on a scale of war. . . . This is not a heroic death as a result of injuries sustained in battle.[75]

The stories of women who participated in the nationalist movement, which often involved experiences of violence—including sexual violence perpetrated both by the enemy and by fellow nationalists—do not fit the heroic picture of the underground that is being constructed in contemporary Ukraine.

Popular memory formed in present-day Ukraine relies heavily on the references to the heroes of the nationalist movement, drawing parallels with the current resistance to Russian aggression.[76] The construction of the contemporary heroes, as well as the ideals of patriotism, nationalism, and the duty to protect Ukrainian sovereignty, is thus also strongly linked to popularized narratives of World War II. Therefore, the implied message of popular memory that refers to the nationalist movement of the 1930s–50s is that a good citizen of contemporary Ukraine should see the wartime nationalists as role models. This kind of popularization of nationalism was particularly visible among the protesters on the Maidan, who adopted the symbolism of the OUN and UPA, and slogans such as "Glory to Ukraine! Glory to the Heroes!" without delving into their historical origin in any depth.[77] This tendency is being consolidated in the context of the current war in the Donbas region. In October 2018, the Ukrainian Parliament adopted a law amending the salute used by the Ukrainian Armed Forces and the police to "Glory to Ukraine! Glory to the Heroes!"[78] Exploiting the situation in which it is not only the state borders that are being threatened but also, in the perception of many, the national identity of Ukrainians, many politicians choose to flirt with nationalism in one form or another. This uncritical attitude toward nationalism, coupled with the militarization of society, in which traditional masculinity is almost worshipped, have serious repercussions for the perception of gender in Ukraine.[79]

Recent official representations of World War II in general and the activities of the UPA and OUN in particular do not wholly exclude women, but the inclusion of individual female nationalists seems tokenistic and does not reveal much about the larger gender dynamism in these organizations. In its recommendations for the commemoration of the Day of Remembrance and Reconciliation and Victory Day (May 8–9), the UINP openly recognizes the contemporary significance of the way the past is represented. In its recommendations on the discussion of women's experiences of war in schools, the UINP states that "reflections on the phenomenon of women in war, awareness and study of it during events in educational institutions, will enable students to uncover the criminal nature of war. . . . The theme of the tragic and heroic women's fates will also help to make connections with the participation of our female compatriots—the military, physicians, and volunteers—in the contemporary confrontation with Russia's armed aggression against Ukraine."[80]

The UINP suggests that the focus on "the fate of women in war" can help shift the tone of events from celebrations—as was the case in the Soviet Union—to sombre commemorations. The UINP argues that in the Soviet Union "the truth about this theme [women's experiences of war] was forbidden" and recognizes that "even today the question of the role and place of the womenfolk in World War II is underresearched by historians and not yet fully reevaluated by society." The text of the recommendations then proceeds to list the various capacities in which women experienced the war—"wife, mother, nurse-rescuer, fighter, insurgent, prisoner-of-war, ostarbeiter, witness of the Holocaust, the keeper of memory"—but nevertheless refers to women as "the weaker sex."[81]

In 2015 the UINP devised a poster to commemorate the seventy-third anniversary of the founding of the UPA that contains some selected facts about what is presented as "the Ukrainian Liberation Movement in the 1940s–1960s."[82] Among the eight personalities selected to represent the movement, one is female: Kateryna Zaryts'ka ("Moneta"), who was the leader of the Women's Network and the organizer and coordinator of the Ukrainian Red Cross organization. She was a prolific writer and was Roman Shukhevych's liaison (*zviazkova*); her propaganda and educational materials were among the most widely circulated in the underground. Zaryts'ka joined the OUN as a teenager.[83] Twenty-one years old, she was arrested and tried as one of two women among the twelve members of the OUN at the Warsaw Process, in which the nationalists were accused of participating in the assassination of the Polish minister of internal affairs, Bronisław Pieracki. After a number of arrests, she was eventually sentenced to twenty-five years and released only in 1972.[84] The UINP poster mentions a number of key facts about each of the personalities showcased on it, but the only information next to Zaryts'ka's name relates to her coordination of the Ukrainian Red Cross and the fact that she was Shukhevych's liaison.[85] Among her duties, those selected for her portrait on this poster are those traditionally associated with women.

Continuing the theme of war and Ukrainian military tradition, in 2016 the UINP presented a project called "Warriors: History of the Ukrainian Military." Among the twenty-five warriors on display, who were supposed to represent the "history of the military formations on the territory of Ukraine from the times of Rus' until the present," there were two women: one a member of the UPA and the other a veteran of the current war.[86] The poster depicting a female insurgent (*povstanka*) is one of the three posters that focus on the activity of the UPA. This one specifically discusses the roles of women in the organization:

> Ukrainian women were the first to support the warriors of the UPA, providing food, clothes, and shelter for them. However, the participation of womenfolk was not restricted to the external support of the liberation movement: a number of them were active members. Certain parts of insurgent activity relied predominantly on women: they were excellent couriers and liaisons, they made up the majority of the medical personnel who looked after the wounded, were irreplaceable workers on the underground printing press, and successfully performed the functions of reconnaissance workers and informers for the OUN's Security Service.[87]

While the poster gives a brief description of women's duties, it also endorses the narrative of the auxiliary role of women in the nationalist movement. The poster that depicts Iryna Tsvila, a woman who took part in the war in the Donbas region, describes her using the masculine grammatical form as a "warrior [*voiak*] of a volunteer battalion 2014–2016" and proceeds to explain the role of the volunteer battalions in the armed conflict but does not explain the complex reality of women's participation in these battalions, which included the military authorities' refusal to officially register women in the roles they performed at the front line.[88] Thus, the image of a woman is used as a symbol of the "patriotically inclined citizens who felt the need to react urgently to the hybrid war started by the leadership of the Russian Federation against Ukraine," but does not give any detail about the complexity of women's actual part in the war.[89]

The UINP also prepared a project focusing specifically on women and war. "War makes no exceptions. Female history of World War II" presented twelve stories of military and civilian women (four of whom were members of the nationalist movement). The intention of the project, as described on UINP's website, was to attempt to "reveal the criminal nature of war."[90] But rather than challenge the very tradition of glorifying war through its heroes and serving as an example of an inclusive approach to history, the exhibition simply celebrates the women as an addition to the male pantheon of heroes. It separates the female experience of war into a "special project" and does not comment on the specificity of gender norms within which these women functioned and the masculinist values prevalent in the context of political violence.

What unites most contemporary popular representations of the nationalist underground is their largely uncritical portrayal of the movement. The idea that the nation, holding the highest value, comes before the rights and freedoms of individuals has reappeared in Ukraine, in particular at the time of its threatened sovereignty. The lack of knowledge of the reality of women's experience in nationalist structures of the 1930s–50s creates a vacuum of critical analysis of the gender roles proposed by the nationalists not only historically, but also in their contemporary incarnations. In present-day Ukraine, just as during World War II, young women join the cause of the nationalists in their attempt to protect Ukraine's independence; but, once again, they do so at the expense of their rights as women.

During the Maidan protests, female protesters were relegated to the category of "women, children, and the elderly," who allegedly required protection and were prevented from participating in the protests as equal members of civil society.[91] In the war in the Donbas region, positions for which women could be officially recruited were severely restricted. Those serving on the frontline as snipers, combat fighters, or even unit leaders have been registered as performing administrative duties. The semilegal presence of these women at the front line has deprived them not only of the status of a frontline fighter but also of adequate remuneration, subsidies, the use of certain medical facilities, and so on.[92] It is no coincidence that historical figures such as Kateryna Zaryts'ka are glorified by the state institutions as supporters of the heroes who fought for Ukraine's independence and that contemporary women who fight for Ukraine's sovereignty are recorded as part of an auxiliary force to the male fighters, despite the quite different reality of their actual involvement.[93]

The attempts of the Ukrainian state to mobilize the population to support the military efforts resisting the Russian-backed separatists are executed in a highly gendered way. Another initiative dedicated to the celebration of the Day of the Defender in 2015 was a public debate organized by the UINP that invited historians. They set themselves the task of refuting "the thesis of the defenseless 'buckwheat sowers' (*hrechkosii*)," which creates an emasculated image of the Ukrainian people and aims to present the nation as "army-nation" (*narod-viis'ko*).[94] One of the invited historians was Viatrovych, who made an unambiguous, if questionable, connection between the Cossacks, the participants of the Ukrainian Revolution of 1917–20, the UPA, and the current army:

> In the sixteenth-seventeenth centuries the Cossack army was formed before the state, and the state emerged out of it. This was repeated in the twentieth century. Both in 1917–1920 and later, when our land was occupied by the Nazis, people themselves took up arms. The Ukrainian Insurgent Army began to form spontaneously, then the initiative was supported by the Organization of Ukrainian Nationalists. The UPA was formed by ordinary people along the lines of regular armies and became a unique phenomenon in world history. . . . [Contemporary] professional soldiers, volunteer fighters, physicians, volunteers, every male and female citizen who helps the army are themselves the people, capable of forming an efficient army against the enemy virtually with no help of the state. We are the army-nation.[95]

Viatrovych emphasizes the contribution of male and female citizens of Ukraine while addressing both men and women and encouraging the whole population to aid the military effort, yet the state reserves the right to decide in which capacity the female half of the Ukrainian population can contribute to the effort. The notion of the army-nation is presented in a glorified way, suggesting that even when Ukraine had no state, its people were ready to engage in political violence in their fight for independence. The armies selected here by Viatrovych as exemplary have been built on patriarchal principles: the Cossacks banned women from their ranks altogether, while the OUN and the UPA used them instrumentally.[96]

Conclusions

Writing about the participation of women in political violence, Miranda Alison stresses that "women and men are not homogeneous entities in any context, yet the construction of men as warriors and women as linked to peace has been naturalized across social divisions."[97] Thus "women who participate in political violence, war or state repression present a challenge to essentialist conceptions of 'womanhood' and shatter the illusion of feminine peacefulness."[98] Alison adds that "for many women . . . national identity and national*ism* are extremely important. However nationalist movements do not automatically come with principles of women's autonomy and liberation attached. It is often quite the opposite."[99] Iveković and Mostov warn against the dangers of the ethno-national story as a closed narrative: "It is a story in which the contents of the identity in question are given through the official version of a unique and absolute truth/event. . . . The hope for a democratic alternative to this story remains in recognizing our histories, that is, our origins in alterity. Opening the past to multiplicity offers a chance for women to break the old patterns and create emancipatory practices and institutions for both women and men."[100]

This democratic alternative in the Ukrainian case is threatened by the uncritical memory of the nationalist movement that is currently being popularized. There is no denial that, especially at volatile times of political conflict, women seek protection and social security for themselves and their families, and many in Ukraine happily embrace the myth of the *berehynia*—a female goddess whose function is to protect the home and with it the role of a housewife.[101] Having little information or a distorted version about the values of feminist ideology, they see the idea of engaging in the struggle for their rights as irrelevant. The state, in turn, sees gender equality as untimely, especially in times of war. A regularly threatened national identity thus creates perfect conditions for the growth of nationalism, an ideology that issues fixed definitions of masculinity and femininity.

In her essay on retelling the war myth, Miriam Cooke asks an important question: "war is an activity and an event of such cataclysmic, existential significance that it has always been 'above' questions of gender identity. Can gender be relevant when life and death is in the balance?"[102] Cooke's answer is decidedly positive: "gender analysis reveals that the prosecution of mass, legitimized, psychotic violence depends on a particular way of constructing and maintaining gender identities."[103] The employment of gender analysis when studying political violence, especially one as conflictual as the nationalist movement, has implications not only for the accuracy of the historical knowledge of the movement, but also for our understanding of women's experiences of violent conflicts and political resistance.

"Experience, as well as its recollection and transmission, is subject to gendered paradigms," argue Marianne Hirsch and Valerie Smith.[104] Using gender as a lens through which history is assessed is vital not only for the prevention of further distortion of the past, but also to address the problems of contemporary Ukrainian society. It is not only the fact that women participated in the nationalist movement that requires further investigation, it is the nature of their multilayered discrimination and their reaction to it that need additional conceptualization. The examination of women as agents and victims of political violence and the recognition of their experiences under nationalist ideology can also be a key to recognizing more widely women's experiences of patriarchal ideologies, thus leading to the recognition of similar dynamics in contemporary society.

Women have participated in all the violent conflicts that unfolded on the territory of contemporary Ukraine and on all sides. Their participation was varied and not restricted to the roles traditionally defined as feminine. The nationalist movement was not an exception. Popular memory of nationalist women, however, is reduced to a set of symbolic roles of victims or traitors. When women's active involvement is discussed, it is portrayed as exceptional and as evidence that *even* women took up arms to defend their motherland. With the exception of a few recent academic works, texts that discuss the involvement of women even in critical forms still lack a critical assessment of the nationalist ideology and the way it views gender relations.

Writing about the heated debates around the OUN and UPA, John-Paul Himka aptly pointed out that such debates are not simply about the history of these organizations but "about who Ukrainians imagine they are, how they evaluate their past, and who they want to be in the future."[105] Thus, the question of the representation of nationalist women has a direct relevance to the shaping of contemporary Ukrainian society. As long as the state and society have a limited understanding of gender equality, much of society will be excluded not only from the memory of the past but also from the discourse of the present and the perception of the future.

Notes

The research for this chapter was made possible by the Leverhulme Early Career Fellowship. I am grateful to Uilleam Blacker, Marta Havryshko, and the editors for their comments on earlier versions of this chapter. Unless otherwise stated, all translations are mine.

1. "Natsbank uviv monetu."
2. The military hostilities in the Donbas, which started in April 2014 and are ongoing at the time of writing, are referred to in everyday speech in Ukraine as a war. The official term used by the Ukrainian authorities and much of the media was Anti-Terrorist Operation (ATO). In April 2018, the ATO was proclaimed completed by the Ukrainian state and the Joint Forces Operation (JFO) was launched. For further discussion see Ponomarenko, "As ATO Ends."
3. National Bank of Ukraine, "Postage Stamp." The coin was designed by an all-male team of artists.
4. National Bank of Ukraine, "Postage Stamp," para. 4.
5. See the 18th-century icon "Pokrov Bohorodytsi," which depicts hetman Bohdan Khmel'nyts'kyi and Archbishop Lazar Baranovych; at the National Art Museum of Ukraine, Kyiv.
6. The Ukrainian *Tsentral'na Rada* was a revolutionary parliament in 1917 and 1918.
7. As of March 2019, over 55,000 women were employed by the Ukrainian Armed Forces. Although many of them hold civilian posts, almost 25,000 (over 10 percent of all military personnel) hold military positions. On October 12, 2018, two days before the Day of the Defender of Ukraine, a woman was awarded the military title of Major General for the first time in Ukraine. "U Zbroinykh Sylakh Ukrainy prokhodiat' viis'kovu sluzhbu i pratsiuiut' 55629 zhinok," *Ukrainian Military Pages*, November 22, 2017, http://www.ukrmilitary.com/2017/11/female-soldiers.html; "Chysel'nist' ukrains'koi armii nablyzhaiet'sia do 'zakonodavchoho limitu,'" *Ukrinform*, October 3, 2017, https://www.ukrinform.ua/rubric-society/2317217-ciselnist-ukrainskoi-armii-nablizaetsa-do-zakonodavcogo-limitu.html; "V armii maie sluzhyty stil'ky zhinok, skil'ky bazhaie,—ministr oborony Ukrainy," *Povaha: Kampaniia proty seksyzmu*, November 24, 2017, http://povaha.org.ua/v-armiji maje-sluzhyty-stilky-zhinok-skilky-bazhaje-ministr-oborony-ukrajiny/; "V ZSU pochaly rozrobku bilyzny dlia viis'kovykh-zhinok," *Televiziina Sluzhba Novyn (TSN)*, September 28, 2017, https://tsn.ua/ukrayina/u-zsu-pochali-rozrobku-bilizni-dlya-viyskovih-zhinok-999855.html; Hennadii Karpiuk, "Hender, rivnoprav'ia i perevahy. Skil'ky v ZSU zhinok ta chomu im lehshe," *Ministerstvo Oborony Ukrainy*, February 15, 2019, http://www.mil.gov.ua/ministry/zmi-pro-nas/2019/02/15/gender-rivnopravya-j-perevagi-skilki-v-zsu-zhinok-ta-chomu-im-legshe/; "Skil'ky zhinok sluzhyt' v ZSU", *24 Kanal*, March 2, 2919, https://24tv.ua/skilki_zhinok_sluzhit_u_zsu_n1120593; Krasnikov, "Ukraine Appoints Its First Female Military General." See also Berlins'ka et al., *Nevydymyi batal'ion*." According to the Ministry of Defense of Ukraine, as of March 2018, around 7,000 women had received the "status of participants of combat operations." See "About 7,000 Ukrainian Women," *Kyiv Post*.
8. Cooke and Woollacott, *Gendering*, x–xi.

9. Iveković and Mostov, Introduction, 10.
10. Iveković and Mostov, Introduction, 10.
11. Iveković and Mostov, Introduction, 10.
12. Kaplan, Alarcón, and Moallem, "Introduction." 10.
13. See National Bank of Ukraine, "Den' zakhysnyka Ukrainy," para. 1.
14. Cooke and Woollacott, *Gendering*, xii.
15. Cooke, "WO-man," 177.
16. Butler, *Gender Trouble*, 4.
17. Other nationalist groups operated in the period and in the region discussed in this chapter, but the OUN and UPA were the most numerous and influential. Although an analysis of gender dynamics in other Ukrainian nationalist organizations would be interesting, in this chapter I will limit my discussion to the OUN and UPA. In 1940 the OUN split into two factions: one—the OUN-M—was led by the more conservative leader, Andrii Mel'nyk, who was winning support among the older generation; the other—the OUN-B—was led by a more radical nationalist, Stepan Bandera, whose branch of the organization was supported by the younger members. Internal changes of these organizations and the evolution of their politics throughout their existence had an impact on their activity, but their gender politics did not differ in any significant way. Therefore, in relation to gender dynamics, a combined discussion of these groups is justified. For a variety of views on Stepan Bandera, see Shkandrij, *Ukrainian Nationalism*; Rossoliński-Liebe, *Stepan Bandera*; Zaitsev, *Ukrains'kyi integral'nyi natsionalizm*; Himka, "Christianity and Radical Nationalism."
18. Snyder, *Bloodlands*.
19. The German occupation regime split Ukraine into several districts: the region of Galicia became part of the Generalgouvernement of occupied Poland and the territories of most of the Ukrainian SSR were divided into several administrative units, all together known as Reichskommissariat Ukraine, with the exception of the easternmost region of Ukraine, including the city of Kharkiv, which remained under German military administration. In addition, Romania claimed Bukovyna and the port of Odesa, and Hungary was in control of Transcarpathia.
20. The Soviet narrative of history in general, and World War II in particular, constructed a certain image of Ukrainian manhood as emasculated because it belonged to a subordinate nation. For the discussion of a similar issue relating to Belarusian manhood, see Gapova, "Reinventing Men and Women."
21. Fedor, Lewis, and Zhurzhenko, Introduction, 8–9. See also Kas'ianov, "How a War for the Past."
22. Portnov, "Memory," 233.
23. Zhurzhenko, "Shared Memory?," 190.
24. For a detailed and nuanced discussion of this period, see Snyder, *Bloodlands*.
25. One of the most controversial aspects of the nationalist movement is OUN's cooperation with the Nazis. The nationalists presented their collaboration with the German authorities as an opportunity to establish the Ukrainian state, an initiative that the Nazis never endorsed. Shkandrij explains that "The OUN's association with the Germans caused irreparable damage to the organization's image" (Shkandrij, *Ukrainian Nationalism*, 61). OUN members are known to have taken part in the implementation of the Holocaust. John-Paul Himka states that "Not all policemen were in OUN, but OUN was deeply embedded in the police." He also argues that "thousands of these policemen defected to the Volhynian woods with their weapons and formed the leadership of the OUN-led UPA" (Himka, "Collaboration," 8). Besides engaging the military and paramilitary formations of its enemies, the UPA is known to have attacked civilians. Its most notorious activity is the perpetration of the Volhynian massacre in 1943, in which thousands of Polish civilians were killed by the nationalists (Motyka, *Od rzezi wołyńskiej*). See also Kudelia, "Choosing Violence," 155–57; Statiev, *Soviet Counterinsurgency*; Berkhoff, *Harvest of Despair*; Brandon and Lower, *Shoah*.
26. Shkandrij, *Ukrainian Nationalism*; Patryliak, *Peremoha abo smert'*; Yekelchyk, *Ukraine*, 127.
27. Zaitsev, "Ukrainian Integral Nationalism," 15. See also Dontsov, *Natsionalizm*. For more information on Dmytro Dontsov, see Zaitsev, *Ukrains'kyi integral'nyi natsionlalizm*; Shkandrij, *Ukrainian Nationalism*, 79–100.
28. Zaitsev, "Ukrainian Integral Nationalism," 15.
29. Rebet, "Suspil'na rolia zhinky": a publication of the OUN-B, produced by the Women's Section of the Department of Culture of the Ukrainian Central Committee, it is undated, but the likelihood is that it was written in the mid-1940s. Haluzevyi Derzhavnyi Arkhiv Sluzhby Bezpeky Ukrainy (HAD SBU), F. 13, Spr. 376, T. 48, Ark. 15(zv).
30. Women's Division of the OUN-M, "Na probii," undated, Arkhiv Tsentru doslidzhen' vyzvol'noho rukhu (ATsDVR), F. 17, T. 7, Ark. 7.

31. There is no consensus on the number of members in the OUN or UPA. The number of women who participated in the nationalist movement is also not known. Oksana Kis refers to an email exchange with the head of the Ukrainian Institute of National Memory, Volodymyr V'iatrovych, in which he "estimates that the Ukrainian nationalist underground may have number [sic] up to 500,000—including about 100,000 military. He also estimates that women constituted about 1/3 of those who participated in non-military activities" (Kis, "National Femininity," 69n). These estimates are likely to be exaggerated. Grzegorz Motyka argues that, by the end of 1944, the UPA consisted of up to thirty thousand insurgents and around one hundred thousand potential recruits (Motyka, *Ukraińska partyzantka,* 424).

32. Bohachevsky-Chomiak, *Feminists,* 220.

33. The instrumentalization of women's femininity and sexuality in the work of the nationalist movement is described in a reconnaissance manual of the OUN's security service issued in 1940: "A woman is often treated as a confidante, starting with a prostitute and ending with women of high standing. A shrewd woman can be used as a confidante in situations to which a man has no access. For instance, when there is a need to make friendly connections in the officers' circles, which a woman achieves very well. A woman can be used as a courier to the areas inaccessible to men. In a word, a woman through her beauty, her pleasant facial expressions, cunning, and great skillfulness can sometimes perform miracles" ("Rozvidka," HDA SBU, F. 13, Spr. 376, T. 49, Ark. 56).

34. In his assessment of the various versions of the creation of the UPA, David Marples concludes that although the "formation of the UPA, according to its participants and supporters, dates from October 1942," the UPA emerged "in the spring and summer of 1943" (Marples, *Heroes,* 129–30.

35. See Havryshko, "Zhinky"; Petrenko, "Anatomy," 254–55.

36. Havryshko, "Zaboronene kokhannia," para. 4. For the roles women played in the OUN and UPA, see Petrenko, *Unter Männern*; Kis, "Zinochyi dosvid"; Kis, "National Femininity"; Mandryk, "Zhinochi oblychchia"; Petrenko, "Anatomy"; Onyshko, "Rol' zhinky"; Onyshko, *"Nam sontse."*

37. For further discussion of the militarization of women by the nationalists and how the nationalists constructed femininity and used it to their advantage, see Khromeychuk, "Militarizing Women."

38. For a variety of views on the nationalists' activities during World War II, see Zaitsev, *Ukrains'kyi integral'nyi natsionlalizm*; Motyka, *Od rzezi wołyńskiej*; Kentii, "Dokumenty OUN"; Himka, "Lviv Pogrom"; Golczewski, "Nationalsozialisten"; Golczewski, "Shades of Grey"; Honcharenko, "Do pytannia pro uchast'"; Marples, *Heroes*; Motyka, *Ukraińska partyzantka*; Podol's'kyi, "Problema kolaboratsii"; Dean, *Collaboration*.

39. "Poland's Parliament." In July 2016, the Polish parliament adopted a resolution declaring July 11 the National Day of Remembrance of the Victims of the Genocide Perpetrated by Ukrainian Nationalists against Citizens of the Second Polish Republic (*Narodowy Dzień Pamięci Ofiar Ludobójstwa dokonanego przez ukraińskich nacjonalistów na obywatelach II Rzeczypospolitej Polskiej*) ("Polish MPs").

40. Personal memories in each region also depend on age, cultural background, and other factors. See Anna Wylegała's analysis of the memory of the UPA in the town of Zhovkva in western Ukraine, "Bohaterowie." See also Wylegała, "Podzielona."

41. See "Banderu i Shukhevycha."

42. An alternative history textbook has been written by Andrii Zakaliuk, a history teacher in a L'viv school. His book is an introduction to Ukrainian history and has been used by some schools in L'viv as supplementary material for the study of Ukrainian history. See "L'viv vydav." Alternative textbooks, like the one by Zakaliuk, were then banned by the minister of education, Tabachnyk. See "Tabachnyk vymahaie."

43. For further discussion, see Yurchuk, "Reclaiming the Past." See also Kas'ianov, "Istoryky."

44. See Kasianov, "Istoryky," 256.

45. See Ukrainian Institute of National Memory, "On the Legal Status," "On Perpetuation," "On the Condemnation." This set of laws has come to be referred to popularly as decommunization laws. See "Normatyvno-pravovi akty," and Kasianov, "Istoricheskaia politika."

46. See Ukrainian Institute of National Memory, "On the Legal Status."

47. Yurchuk, "Reclaiming the Past," 129.

48. Yurchuk, "Reclaiming the Past," 131.

49. Kasianov, "Istoricheskaia politika," 48.

50. See "Polozhennia pro Ukrains'kyi instytut natsional'noi pam"iati." See also Kas'ianov, "K desiatiletiiu."

51. "Vystavku 'Ukrains'ka druha svitova.'"

52. See Kas'ianov, "K desiatiletiiu."

53. Kis, "Zinochyi dosvid," 121.

54. See, for example, Pan'kiv, *Vira, nadiia, liubov*; Il'kiv, "Providnyk Roman Shukhevych"; Kokhans'ka, *Z Ukrainoiu u sertsi*; Mashchak, *Dorohamy mynuloho*; Poliuha, *Vse zh ne daremno!* See also Vynnyts'ka, *Nezvychaini doli*; Mudra, *Ukrains'ka zhinka*. For a discussion of literature that focuses on the participation of women in the nationalist movement, see Khromeychuk "Militarizing Women."

55. See Savchyn, *Tysiacha dorih*. For a detailed discussion of Maria Savchyn's difficulties with writing a memoir about her life in the underground, see Kis, "Misiia (ne)zdiisnenna."

56. The marginalization of women's experience is reflected in the language and discourse available to describe it. Those women who spoke of their experiences did so often through a male voice. Liudmyla Foia, a double agent recruited by the OUN and the NKVD, told of women's experiences of participation in the nationalist movement in her short stories, but she adopted a male pseudonym, "Marko Perelesnyk." See Ivanchenko, *Kvitka*. Another underground writer, Halyna Holoiad ("Marta Hai"), chose to portray heroic fighting males and naive civilian girls in her poetry, short stories, and political essays, despite having a different experience of active resistance herself. See Ishchuk and Ivanchenko, *Zhyttievyi shliakh Halyny Holoiad*.

57. Teliha, "Iakymy nas prahnete?" See also Aheieva, *Zhinochyi Prostir*, 298; Shkandrij, *Ukrainian Nationalism*, 175–90.

58. Cooke, "WO-man," 177.

59. Burds, "Gender and Policing," 285.

60. In Soviet literature, they were often portrayed as traitors, misguided by the nationalist men. For further details on the representation of Ukrainian nationalist women in Soviet literature, see Petrenko, "Literaturni insynuatsii."

61. See Kis, "Zinochyi dosvid"; Kis, "National Femininity"; Onyshko, "Zhyttia posviachene borot'bi"; Onyshko, *Kateryna Zaryts'ka*; Mandryk, "Zhinochi oblychchia"; Pustomitenko, "Zhinky"; Zariczniak, "Violence and the UPA Woman."

62. For further discussion, see Khromeychuk, "Militarizing Women."

63. Savchuk, *Zhinotstvo v suspil'nomu zhytti*, 97.

64. See Ishchuk and Ivanchenko, *Zhyttievyi shliakh Halyny Holoiad*; Ivanchenko, *Kvitka*.

65. See Viatrovych, *Istoriia z hryfom "Sekretno,"* 91–97 and 146–56.

66. See Petrenko, *Unter Männern*; Petrenko, "Anatomy"; Petrenko, "Instrumentalizatsiia strakhu; Petrenko, "Literaturni obrAzy." See also Petrenko, "Geschlecht, Gewalt, Nation."

67. See Havryshko, "Zaboronene kokhannia"; Havryshko, "Illegitimate Sexual Practices"; Havryshko, "Love and Sex."

68. In his detailed study of the UPA, Ivan Patryliak offers a collective portrait of a Ukrainian insurgent based on recently discovered documents, presenting a great variety of data on ethnicity, occupation, age, place of origin, experience of serving in the army, and many other categories. Patryliak does not, however, include any information on the male-female ratio of the organization or any data relating specifically to women. Patryliak uses exclusively masculine forms when categorizing the data on insurgents' ethnicity, social status, and occupation (e.g., *ukrainets'*, *selianyn*, *robitnyk*). See Patryliak, *Peremoha abo smert'*, 217 and 188–226.

69. Yuval-Davis, *Nation and Gender*, 1 and 2.

70. Yuval-Davis, *Nation and Gender*, 2.

71. Yuval-Davis, *Nation and Gender*, 2.

72. Kis, "Zhinochyi dosvid," 121.

73. For further discussion, see Khromeychuk, "What Place for Women?" See also Khromeychuk, "Militarizing Women."

74. Burds, "Gender and Policing," 314.

75. Chutnik, *Kieszonkowy atlas kobiet*, 94–95.

76. For further discussion of instrumentalisation of history in the context of the war in the Donbas see Khromeychuk, "Militarised Society."

77. Nationalist symbols and slogans, such as "Glory to Ukraine! Glory to the Heroes!," which are associated with the nationalists of the 1930s–50s, were omnipresent on the Maidan and continue to be widely used in Ukraine. Many of those chanting the slogans, however, might not be aware of their origins and might apply to them a meaning that is more relevant to Ukraine's contemporary events. The word *heroes*, incidentally, is almost always used in its masculine form. See Khromeychuk, "Gender and Nationalism." See also Kas'ianov, "How a War for the Past," 154–55.

78. "Rada Approves Salute," *Kyiv Post*.

79. See Khromeychuk, "Militarised Society."
80. Ukrainian Institute of National Memory, "Metodychni rekomendatsii," para. 6.
81. Ukrainian Institute of National Memory, "Metodychni rekomendatsii," paras. 4–5.
82. See Ukrainian Institute of National Memory, "Pam''iati armii neskorenykh prysviachuiet'sia."
83. Roman Shukhevych was commander in chief of the UPA. He had previously served as captain of *Nachtigall* battalion and *Schutzmannschaft* battalion 201, which were formed within the German Armed Forces. See Marples, *Heroes*; Khromeychuk, "Ukrainians in the German Armed Forces."
84. See Onyshko, *Kateryna Zaryts'ka*; Onyshko, "*Nam sontse vsmikhalos'*."
85. See Ukrainian Institute of National Memory, "Pam''iati armii neskorenykh prysviachuiet'sia." The Ukrainian and the Russian versions of these posters refer to her role as the coordinator and leader in a masculine form, *orhanizator i kerivnyk* (Ukr.) or *organizator i rukovoditel'* (Russ.), and the role of the liaison, *zviazkova* (Ukr.) or *sviaznaia* (Russ.), in a feminine form.
86. "Voiny: istoriia Ukrains'koho viis'ka; postery," *Ukrains'kyi instytut natsional'noi pam''iati*, 2016, http://www.memory.gov.ua/page/voini-istoriya-ukrainskogo-viiska-posteri.
87. Ukrainian Institute of National Memory, "Voiny."
88. See Berlins'ka et al., "*Nevydymyi batal'ion*"; Khromeychuk, "From the Maidan"; see also Khromeychuk, "Negotiating Protest Spaces."
89. Ukrainian Institute of National Memory, "Voiny."
90. Ukrainian Institute of National Memory, "Viina ne robyt' vyniatkiv." For further discussion of the role of women in the discourse on Ukrainian defenders, see Khromeychuk, "What Place for Women?"
91. See Khromeychuk, "Gender and Nationalism"; Khromeychuk, "Negotiating Protest Spaces"; Bureichak and Petrenko, "Kanapky."
92. Slavinska's interview with Maria Berlins'ka, "Nevydymyi batal'ion," on *Hromads'ke Radio*. See also Berlins'ka et al., "*Nevydymyi batal'ion*." Under the pressure of the activists who have served in the Ukrainian armed forces in the Donbas region, the law has been altered somewhat. But there are still many positions that women cannot formally occupy in the army. See "Zhinky u ZSU." See also Khromeychuk, "From the Maidan."
93. See Khromeychuk, "From the Maidan." There are a few women in contemporary Ukraine who are presented in nonauxiliary roles in the context of war. Nadiya Savchenko, an officer of the Ukrainian armed forces, a member of the Ukrainian parliament, and a former political prisoner in Russia, has been presented as a symbol of Ukrainian defiance in the war in eastern Ukraine. The perception of her as a modern-day Joan of Arc, however, lasted only for the duration of her captivity. Once Savchenko was released from prison, the attention of the media was drawn to her lack of traditional femininity, which was no longer presented as a sign of defiance but as a weakness in her political career. For more information about Nadiya Savchenko, including her struggle to become a pilot, see Miller, "Many Faces." See also Martsenyuk, "Povernennia publichnoho."
94. Ukrainian Institute of National Memory, "Vitaiemo zakhysnykiv," para. 1.
95. Ukrainian Institute of National Memory, "Vitaiemo zakhysnykiv," paras. 3–4.
96. See O'Rourke, *Cossacks*, 160.
97. Alison, *Women and Political Violence*, 91.
98. Alison, *Women and Political Violence*, 91.
99. Alison, *Women and Political Violence*, 107. Emphasis in the original.
100. Iveković and Mostov, Introduction, 19.
101. See Kis, "Koho oberihaie Berehynia."
102. Cooke, "~~WO~~-man," 177.
103. Cooke, "~~WO~~-man," 177.
104. Hirsch and Smith, "Feminism and Cultural Memory," 7.
105. Himka, "Organization of Ukrainian Nationalists."

Bibliography

"About 7,000 Ukrainian Women Have Status of Participants in Hostilities," *Kyiv Post*, March 7, 2018. https://www.kyivpost.com/ukraine-politics/7000-ukrainian-women-status-participants-hostilities.html.

Aheieva, Vira. *Zhinochyi prostir: feministychnyi dyskurs ukrains'koho modernizmu*. Kyiv: Fact, 2008.

Alison, Miranda. *Women and Political Violence: Female Combatants in Ethno-national Conflict*. London: Routledge, 2009.
"Banderu i Shukhevycha vyluchyly z testiv z istorii Ukrainy?" *Istorychna Pravda*, January 23, 2013. http://www.istpravda.com.ua/short/2013/01/23/109632/.
Berkhoff, Karel C. *Harvest of Despair: Life and Death in Ukraine under Nazi Rule*. Cambridge, MA: Belknap, 2004.
Berlins'ka, Maria. "Nevydymyi batal'ion: zhinky na viini." Interview on *Hromads'ke Radio*, August 29, 2015. https://hromadske.radio/podcasts/antena/nevydymyy-batalyon-zhinky-na-viyni.
Berlins'ka, Maria, Tamara Martsenyuk, Anna Kvit, and Ganna Grytsenko. *"Nevydymyi batal'ion": Uchast' zhinok u viis'kovykh diiakh v ATO* (Ukr.), *"Invisible Battalion": Women's Participation in ATO Military Operations* (Eng.). Kyiv: Ukrainian Women's Fund, 2016.
Bohachevsky-Chomiak, Martha. *Feminists despite Themselves: Women in Ukrainian Community Life, 1884–1939*. Edmonton, ON, Canada: Canadian Institute of Ukrainian Studies, 1988.
Brandon, Ray, and Wendy Lower, eds. *The Shoah in Ukraine: History, Testimony, Memorialization*. Bloomington: Indiana University Press, 2008.
Burds, Jeffrey. "Gender and Policing in Soviet West Ukraine, 1944–1948." *Cahiers du Monde Russe* 2-3-4, no. 42 (2001): 279–320.
Bureichak, Tetiana, and Olena Petrenko. "Kanapky, Sich ta 'banderivky'." *Zaxid.net*, January 8, 2014. http://zaxid.net/news/showNews.do?kanapki_sich_ta_banderivki&objectId=1300428.
Butler, Judith. *Gender Trouble*. New York: Routledge, 2008.
Chutnik, Sylwia. *Kieszonkowy atlas kobiet*. Kraków: Korporacja Ha!art, 2008.
Cooke, Miriam "WO-man, Retelling the War Myth." In *Gendering War Talk*, edited by Miriam G. Cooke and Angela Woollacott, 177–204. Princeton, NJ: Princeton University Press, 1993.
Cooke, Miriam G., and Angela Woollacott, eds. *Gendering War Talk*. Princeton, NJ: Princeton University Press, 1993.
Dean, Martin. *Collaboration during the Holocaust: Crimes of the Local Police in Belorussia and Ukraine, 1941–44*. New York: St. Martin's Press, 2000.
Dontsov, Dmytro. *Natsionalizm*. Lviv, 1926.
Fedor, Julie, Simon Lewis, and Tatiana Zhurzhenko. Introduction to *War and Memory in Russia, Ukraine, and Belarus*, edited by Julie Fedor, M. Kangaspuro, J. Lassila, and Tatiana Zhurzhenko, 1–40. New York: Palgrave Macmillan, 2017.
Gapova, Elena. "Reinventing Men and Women within the Belarusian Nationalist Project." In *From Gender to Nation*, edited by Rada Iveković and Julie Mostov, 81–98. Ravenna, It.: Longo, 2002.
Golczewski, Frank. "Nationalsozialisten und Nationalisten." In *Deutsche und Ukrainer, 1914–1936*, 547–667. Paderborn, Ger.: Ferdinand Schöningh, 2010.
———. "Shades of Grey: Reflections on Jewish-Ukrainian and German-Ukrainian Relations in Galicia." In *The Shoah in Ukraine: History, Testimony, Memorialization*, edited by Ray Brandon and Wendy Lower, 114–55. Bloomington: Indiana University Press, 2008.
Havryshko, Marta. "Illegitimate Sexual Practices in the OUN Underground and UPA in Western Ukraine in the 1940s and 1950s." *Journal of Power Institutions in Post-Soviet Societies* 17 (2016). https://journals.openedition.org/pipss/4214#text.
———. "Love and Sex in Wartime: Controlling Women's Sexuality in the Ukrainian Nationalist Underground." *Aspasia* 12 (2018): 35–67.
———. "Zaboronene kokhannia: faktychni druzhyny uchasnykiv ukrains'koho natsionalistychnoho pidpillia 1940–1950-kh rokiv." In *Zhinky tsentral'noi ta skhidnoi Evropy u druhii svitovii viini: henderna spetsyfika dosvidu v chasy ekstremal'noho nasyl'stva*, edited by Gelinada. Grinchenko, Kateryna. Kobchenko, and Oksana Kis, 123–41. Kyiv: TOV Art Knyha, 2015.
———. "Zaboronene kokhannia: faktychni druzhyny uchasnykiv ukrains'koho natsionalistychnoho pidpillia 1940–1950-kh rokiv." *Ukraina Moderna*, April 20, 2015. http://uamoderna.com/md/havryshko-de-facto-marriages-upa.
———. "Zhinky u natsional'nomu pidpilli: vnesky i vtraty." In *Ukrains'ki zhinky u hornyli modernizatsii*, edited by Oksana Kis, 204–31. Kharkiv, Ukraine: Klub simeinoho dozvillia, 2017.
Himka, John-Paul. "Christianity and Radical Nationalism: Metropolitan Andrei Sheptytsky and the Bandera Movement." In *State Secularism and Lived Religion in Soviet Russia and Ukraine*, edited by Catherine Wanner, 93–116. New York: Oxford University Press, 2012.

———. "Collaboration and or Resistance: The OUN and UPA during the War." Paper presented at the Ukrainian Jewish Encounter Shared Narrative Series: Conference on Issues Relating to World War II. Potsdam, Germany, June 27–30, 2011. https://www.academia.edu/577915/Collaboration_and_or_Resistance_The_OUN_and_UPA_during_the_War.

———. "The Lviv Pogrom of 1941: The Germans, Ukrainian Nationalists, and the Carnival Crowd." *Canadian Slavonic Papers* 2–4, no. 53 (2011): 209–43.

———. "The Organization of Ukrainian Nationalists and the Ukrainian Insurgent Army: Unwelcome Elements of an Identity Project." *Ab Imperio* 4 (2010): 83–101.

Hirsch, Marianne, and Valerie Smith. "Feminism and Cultural Memory: An Introduction." Special issue, *Gender and Cultural Memory, Signs* 1, no. 28 (2002): 1–19.

Honcharenko, Oleksii. M. "Do pytannia pro uchast' mistsevoho naselennia u poriatunku ievreiv na terytorii raikhkomisariatu Ukraina (1941–1944)." *Ukrains'kyi istorychnyi zhurnal* (2010): 128–41.

Il'kiv, Ol'ha. "Providnyk Roman Shukhevych i zhinky." In *Roman Shukhevych: Postat' na tli doby voiuiuchoi Ukrainy*, edited by Vasyl' Shtokalo, 247–50. Ternopil', Ukraine: Ideia i chyn, 2005.

Ishchuk, Oleksandr, and Volodymyr Ivanchenko. *Zhyttievyi shliakh Halyny Holoiad—"Marty Hai."* Toronto: Litopys UPA, 2010.

Ivanchenko, Volodymyr. *Kvitka u chervonomu pekli: zhyttievyi shliakh Liudmyly Foi*. Toronto: Litopys UPA, 2009.

Iveković, Rada, and Julie Mostov. Introduction to *From Gender to Nation*, edited by Rada Iveković and Julie Mostov, 9–25. Ravenna, It.: Longo, 2002.

Kaplan, Caren, Norma Alarcón, and Minoo Moallem. "Introduction: Between Woman and Nation." In *Nationalisms, Transnational Feminisms, and the State*, edited by Caren Kaplan, Norma Alarcón, and Minoo Moallem, 1–16. Durham, NC: Duke University Press, 1999.

Karpiuk, Hennadii. "Hender, rivnoprav'ia i perevahy. Skil'ky v ZSU zhinok ta chomu im lehshe," *Ministerstvo Oborony Ukrainy*, February 15, 2019. http://www.mil.gov.ua/ministry/zmi-pro-nas/2019/02/15/gender-rivnopravya-j-perevagi-skilki-v-zsu-zhinok-ta-chomu-im-legshe/.

Kasianov, Georgiy. "How a War for the Past Becomes a War in the Present." *Kritika* 16, no. 1 (2015): 149–55.

———. "Istoricheskaia politika i 'memorial'nyie' zakony v Ukraine: nachalo XXI v." *Istoricheskaia ekspertiza* 2 (2016): 28–55.

———. "Istoryky ta istorychna polityka." *Istoriohrafichni ta dzereloznavchi problemy istorii Ukrainy* (2017): 243–61.

———. "K desiatiletiiu ukrainskogo instituta natsional'noi pamiati (2006–2016)." *Historians.in.ua*, January 14, 2016. http://www.historians.in.ua/index.php/en/dyskusiya/1755-georgij-kas-yanov-k-desyatiletiyu-ukrainskogo-instituta-natsional-noj-pamyati-2006-2016.

Kentii, Anatolii V. "Dokumenty OUN ta UPA u fondakh TsDAHO Ukrainy." *Ukrains'kyi istorychnyi zhurnal* (2011): 202–22.

Khromeychuk, Olesya. "From the Maidan to the Donbas: The Limitations on Choice for Women in Ukraine." In *Gender and Choice in the Post-Soviet Context*, edited by Lynne Attwood, Marina Yusupova, and Elisabeth Schimpfoessl. Basingstoke, UK: Palgrave Macmillan, 2018.

———. "Gender and Nationalism on the Maidan." In *Ukraine's Euromaidan: Analyses of a Civil Revolution*, edited by D. R. Marples and F. V. Mills, 123–46. Stuttgart: ibidem, 2015.

———. "Militarizing Women in the Ukrainian Nationalist Movement from the 1930s to the 1950s." *Aspasia* 12 (2018): 1–34.

———. "Militarised Society: Memory Politics, History and Gender in Ukraine," *Open Democracy*, October 12, 2018. https://www.opendemocracy.net/en/odr/memory-politics-history-and-gender-in-ukraine/.

———. "Negotiating Protest Spaces on the Maidan: A Gender Perspective." *Journal of Soviet and Post-Soviet Politics and Society* 2, no. 1 (2016): 9–47.

———. "Ukrainians in the German Armed Forces during the Second World War." *History* 100, no. 343 (2016): 704–24.

———. "What Place for Women in Ukraine's Memory Politics?" *Open Democracy*, October 10, 2016. https://www.opendemocracy.net/od-russia/olesya-khromeychuk/what-place-for-women-in-ukraine-s-memory-politics.

Kis, Oksana. "Koho oberihaie Berehynia, abo matriarkhat iak cholovichyi vynakhid." *Ia* 4, no. 16 (2006): 11–16.

———. "Misiia (ne)zdiisnenna: spohady Marii Savchyn iak idea i chyn." In *"I slova staly chynom zhyvym . . .": borot'ba OUN ta UPA kriz' pryzmu liuds'kykh dol' ta stosunkiv; zbirnyk biohrafichnykh narysiv*, edited by O. Stasiuk, 79–116. L'viv: NAN Ukrainy, Instytut ukrainoznavstva im. I. Kryp'iakevycha, 2014.

———. "National Femininity Used and Contested: Women's Participation in the Nationalist Underground in Western Ukraine during the 1940s–50s." *East/West* 2, no. 2 (2015): 53–82.

———. "Zinochyi dosvid uchasti u natsional'no-vyzvol'nykh zmahanniakh na zakhidnoukrains'kykh zemliakh u 1940–50-kh rr." *Skhid–Zakhid: Istoryko-kul'torolohichnyi zbirnyk* 13–14 (2009): 101–25.

Kokhans'ka, Halyna. *Z Ukrainoiu u sertsi*. Toronto: Litopys UPA, 2008.

Krasnikov, Denys. "Ukraine Appoints Its First Female Military General," *Kyiv Post*, October 14, 2018. https://www.kyivpost.com/ukraine-politics/ukraine-appoints-its-first-female-general.html?cn-reloaded=1.

Kudelia, Serhiy. "Choosing Violence in Irregular Wars: The Case of Anti-Soviet Insurgency in Western Ukraine." *East European Politics and Societies* 27, no. 1 (2013): 149–81.

Kul'chyts'kyi, Stanislav, ed. *Orhanizatsiia ukrains'kykh natsionalistiv i Ukrains'ka povstans'ka armiia*. Kyiv: Naukova Dumka, 2005.

Lebid', Natalia. "Vzhe ne ATO, ale shche ne viina." *Ukraina moloda*, October 6, 2017. http://www.umoloda.kiev.ua/number/3221/180/116472/.

"L'viv vydav svii posibnyk z istorii Ukrainy z rozdilom pro UPA." *Zaxid.net*, August 8, 2012. https://zaxid.net/lviv_vidav_sviy_posibnik_z_istoriyi_ukrayini_z_rozdilom_pro_upa_n1261993.

Mandryk, Maria. "Zhinochi oblychchia ukrains'koho pidpillia—hendernyi pryntsyp chy 'cholovicha' istoria borot'by istoriohrafichne osmyslennia." *Kul'tura narodov prichernomoria* 162 (2009): 129–34.

Marples, David R. *Heroes and Villains: Creating National History in Contemporary Ukraine*. Budapest: Central European University Press, 2007.

Martsenyuk, Tamara. "Povernennia publichnoho seksyzmu abo iak 'ubyty' slovamy." *Povaha*, August 18, 2016. http://povaha.org.ua/povernennya-publichnoho-seksyzmu-abo-yak-ubyty-slovamy/.

Mashchak, Ivanna. *Dorohamy mynuloho*. Kyiv: Kupola, 2010.

Miller, Christopher. "The Many Faces of Nadia Savchenko." *Radio Free Europe*, July 2016. http://www.rferl.org/a/the-many-faces-of-nadia-savchenko/27869488.html.

Motyka, Grzegorz *Od rzezi wołyńskiej do akcji "Wisła": konflikt polsko-ukraiński 1943–1947*. Kraków: Literackie, 2011.

———. *Ukraińska partyzantka 1942–1960: działalność organizacji Ukraińskich Nacjonalistów i Ukraińskiej Powstańczej Armii*. Warsaw: Rytm, 2006.

Mudra, Nadiia, ed. *Ukrains'ka zhinka u vyzvol'nii borot'bi 1949–1950*. L'viv: Svit, 2004.

National Bank of Ukraine. "Den' zakhysnyka Ukrainy." *Pam'iatni Monety Ukrainy: Natsional'nyi Bank Ukrainy*, October 12, 2015. http://www.bank.gov.ua/control/uk/currentmoney/cmcoin/details?coin_id=686.

———. "A Postage Stamp and a Commemorative Coin Were Presented on the Occasion of the Defender of Ukraine Day." Press release, October 12, 2015. http://www.bank.gov.ua/control/en/publish/article?art_id=22693965&cat_id=76291.

"Natsbank uviv monetu do Dnia zakhysnyka Ukrainy." *Ukrains'ka Pravda*, October 13, 2015. http://www.pravda.com.ua/news/2015/10/12/7084536/?attempt=2.

Onyshko, Lesia. *Kateryna Zaryts'ka: Molytva do syna*. L'viv: Svit, 2002.

———. *"Nam sontse vsmikhalos' kriz' rzhavii graty": Kateryna Zaryts'ka v ukraiins'komu natsional'no-vyzvol'nomu rusi*. Toronto: Litopys UPA, 2007.

———. "Rol' zhinky v ukrains'komu national'no-vyzvol'nomu rusi seredyny XX stolittia." *Ukrains'kyi vyzvol'nyi rukh* 3 (2004): 30–38.

———. "Zhyttia posviachene borot'bi: suspil'no-politychnyi portret Halyny Dydyk." *Ukraina: Kul'turna spadshchyna, natsional'na svidomist', derzhavnist'* 22 (2012): 388–97.

O'Rourke, Shane. *The Cossacks*. Manchester, UK: Manchester University Press, 2007.

Pan'kiv, Maria, ed. *Vira, nadiia, liubov: spohady zhinok*, vols. 1 and 2. Warsaw: Ukrains'kyi Arkhiv, 2001, 2005.

Patryliak, Ivan. *Peremoha abo smert': Ukrains'kyi vyzvol'nyi rukh u 1939–1960 rr*. L'viv: Chasopys, 2012.

Petrenko, Olena. "Anatomy of the Unsaid: Along the Taboo Lines of Female Participation in the Ukrainian Nationalistic Underground." In *Dynamization of Gender Roles in Wartime*, edited by R. Leiserowitz and M. Röger, 241–61. Warsaw: German Historical Institute, 2012.

———. "Geschlecht, Gewalt, Nation: Die Organization Ukrainischer Nationalisten und die Frau." *Osteuropa* 4 (2016): 83–93.

———. "Instrumentalizatsiia strakhu. Vykorystannia radians'kymy ta pol'skymy orhanamy bezpeky zhinok-ahentiv u borot'bi proty ukrains'koho natsionalistychnoho pidpillia." *Ukraina Moderna* 18 (2011): 139–63.

———. "Literaturni insynuatsii: radians'ka proza pro banderivok ta ikh pobornyts'." *Ukraina Moderna*, September 2, 2014. http://www.uamoderna.com/blog/274-274.

———. "Literaturni obrazy 'banderivok' u konteksti ideolohichnykh voien." In *Zhinky tsentral'noi ta skhidnoi Ievropy u druhii svitovii viini: henderna spetsyfika dosvidu v chasy ekstremal'noho nasyl'stva*, edited by G. Grinchenko, K. Kobchenko, and Oksana Kis, 142–54. Kyiv: TOV Art Knyha, 2015.

———. *Unter Männern: Frauen im ukrainischen nationalistischen Untergrund, 1929–1954*. Paderborn, Ger.: Ferdinand Schöningh, 2018.

Podol's'kyi, Anatolii. "Problema kolaboratsii v dobu Holokostu na terenakh Ukrainy ta Latvii: sproba komparatyvnoho pidkhodu." *Holokost i suchasnist'* 5, no. 11 (2003): 2–4.

"Polish MPs Adopt Resolution Calling 1940s Massacre Genocide." *Poland Radio*, July 22, 2016. http://www.thenews.pl/1/10/Artykul/263005,Polish-MPs-adopt-resolution-calling-1940s-massacre-genocide.

Poliuha, Daria. *Vse zh ne daremno!* L'viv: self-published, 2014.

"Polozhennia pro Ukrains'kyi instytut natsional'noi pam"iati." *Kabinet ministriv Ukrainy*, November 12, 2014. http://www.memory.gov.ua/page/polozhennya-pro-ukrainskii-institut-natsionalnoi-pamyati.

Ponomarenko, Illia. "As ATO Ends, Joint Forces Operation Launched in Donbas," *Kyiv Post*, April 30, 2018. https://www.kyivpost.com/ukraine-politics/ato-ends-joint-forces-operation-launched-donbas.html.

Portnov, Andriy. "Memory in Post-Soviet Ukraine (1991–2010)." In *Memory and Theory in Eastern Europe*, edited by Alexander Etkind, Julie Fedor, and Uilleam Blacker, 233–54. New York: Palgrave Macmillan, 2013.

Pustomitenko, Olena. "Zhinky u pidpilli OUN(B) u roky nimets'ko-radians'koi viiny ta u povoiennyi chas." *Acta Studiosa Historica* 4 (2014): 77–83.

"Rada Approves Salute 'Glory to Ukraine' in Ukrainian Army." *Kyiv Post*, October 4, 2018. https://www.kyivpost.com/ukraine-politics/rada-approves-salute-glory-to-ukraine-in-ukrainian-army.html.

Rebet, Daria. "Suspil'na rolia zhinky," undated. Haluzevyi Derzhavnyi Arkhiv Sluzhby Bezpeky Ukrainy (HDA SBU), F. 13, Spr. 376, T. 48, Ark. 15(zv).

Rossoliński-Liebe, Grzegorz. *Stepan Bandera: The Life and Afterlife of a Ukrainian Nationalist; Fascism, Genocide, and Cult*. Stuttgart: ibidem, 2015.

"Rozvidka: orhanizatsiia, rozvytok, metody," March 1940. Instructions of the Security Service of the OUN, HDA SBU, F. 13, Spr. 376, T. 49, Ark. 56.

Savchuk, Borys. *Zhinotstvo v suspil'nomu zhytti zakhidnoi Ukrainy (ostannia tretyna xix stolittia-1939 r.)*. Ivano-Frankivs'k, Ukraine: Lileia, 1998.

Savchyn, Maria. *Tysiacha dorih: spohady zhinky-uchasnytsi pidpil'no-vyzvol'noi borot'by pid chas i pislia druhoi svitovoi viiny*. Kyiv: Smoloskyp, 2003.

Shkandrij, Myroslav. *Ukrainian Nationalism: Politics, Ideology and Literature, 1929–1956*. New Haven, CT: Yale University Press, 2015.

Snyder, Timothy. *Bloodlands: Europe between Hitler and Stalin*. London: Bodley Head, 2010.

"Skil'ky zhinok sluzhyt' v ZSU," *24 Kanal*, March 2, 2919. https://24tv.ua/skilki_zhinok_sluzhit_u_zsu_n1120593.

"Tabachnyk vymahaie vid L'vova vidmovytysia vid al'ternatyvnoho pidruchnyka istorii." *Ukranews*, October 10, 2015. http://ukranews.com/uk/news/ukraine/2012/10/10/80714.

Teliha, Olena. "Iakymy nas prahnete?" *Visnyk*. Warsaw, October 1935. http://sites.utoronto.ca/elul/lit-crit/Feminism/Teliha-Iakymy.html.

Ukrainian Institute of National Memory. "Metodychni rekomendatsii do vidznachennia dnia pam'iati ta prymyrennia i dnia peremohy nad natsyzmom (8–9 travnia)." Accessed May 22, 2019. http://memory.gov.ua/methodicmaterial/metodichni-rekomendatsii-do-vidznachennya-dnya-pam-yati-ta-primirennya-i-dnya-perem.

———. "Normatyvno-pravovi akty," April 13, 2017. http:/memory.gov.ua/laws.

———. "On the Legal Status and Honouring the Memory of Fighters for Ukraine's Independence in the Twentieth Century." April 9, 2015. http://memory.gov.ua/laws/law-ukraine-legal-status-and-honoring-memory-fighters-ukraines-independence-twentieth-century.

———. "Pam'iati armii neskorenykh prysviachuiet'sia: infohrafika (ukrains'koiu, rosiis'koiu, anhliis'koiu movamy)." Accessed May 22, 2019. http://memory.gov.ua/news/pam-yati-armii-neskorenikh-prisvyachuetsya-infografika-ukrainskoyu-rosiiskoyu-angliiskoyu-movam.

———. "Viina ne robyt' vyniatkiv: zhinochi istroii druhoi svitovoi'; informatsiini materialy dlia ZMI do vshanuvann' 8–9 travnia 2016 roku." http://www.memory.gov.ua/news/viina-ne-robit-vinyatkiv-zhinochi-istorii-drugoi-svitovoi-informatsiini-materiali-dlya-zmi-do-v.

———. "Vitaiemo zakhysnykiv i zakhysnyts' zi sviatom! Ukraintsi—narod-viis'ko." 2015. http://memory.gov.ua/news/vitaemo-zakhisnikiv-i-zakhisnits-zi-svyatom-ukraintsi-narod-viisko.
———. "Voiny: istoriia Ukrains'koho viis'ka; postery." Accessed May 22, 2019. http://memory.gov.ua/page/voini-istoriya-ukrainskogo-viiska-posteri.
———. "Vystavku 'Ukrains'ka druha svitova' mozhna ohlianuty na Khreshchatyku." Accessed May 22, 2019. http://memory.gov.ua/news/vistavku-ukrainska-druga-svitova-mozhna-oglyanuti-na-khreshchatiku.
Viatrovych, Volodymyr. *Istoriia z hryfom "Sekretno": taiemnytsi ukrains'koho mynuloho z arkhiviv KHB*. L'viv: Tsentr doslidzhen' vyzvol'noho rukhu, 2012.
Vynnyts'ka, Iroida, ed. *Nezvychaini doli zvychainykh zhinok: Usna istoriia XX stolittia*. L'viv: L'viv Polytechnic Press, 2013.
Women's Division of the OUN-M. "Na probii," undated. F. 17, T. 7, Ark. 7, Arkhiv Tsentru doslidzhen' vyzvol'noho rukhu (ATsDVR) Ukraine.
Wylegała, Anna. "Bohaterowie czy kolaboranci? Pamięć o UPA na Ukrainie Zachodniej." In *20 lat rzeczywistości poradzieckiej*. Edited by M. Głowacka-Grajper and R. Wyszyński, 134–54. Warsaw: Warsaw Universsity Press, 2012.
———. "Podzielona czy zróżnicowana? Jeszcze raz o pamięci społecznej na Ukrainie (z tożsamością w tle)." *Kultura i Społeczeństwo* 2 (2015): 99–116.
Yekelchyk, Serhy. *Ukraine: Birth of a Modern Nation*. Oxford: Oxford University Press, 2007.
Yurchuk, Yuliya. "Reclaiming the Past, Confronting the Past: OUN-UPA Memory Politics and Nation-Building in Ukraine (1991–2016)." In *War and Memory in Russia, Ukraine, and Belarus*. Edited by Julie Fedor, M. Kangaspuro, J. Lassila, and T. Zhurzhenko 107–40. New York: Palgrave Macmillan, 2017.
Yuval-Davis, Nira. *Nation and Gender*. London: Sage, 1997.
Zaitsev, Oleksandr. "Ukrainian Integral Nationalism in Quest of a 'Special Path' (1920s–1930s)." *Russian Politics and Law* 5, no. 51 (2013): 11–32.
———. *Ukrains'kyi integral'nyi natsionlalizm (1920–1930 roky): narysy intelektual'noi istorii*. Kyiv: Krytyka, 2013.
Zariczniak, Larysa. "Violence and the UPA Woman: Experiences and Influences." *Evropeis'ki istorychni studii* 2 (2015): 243–67.
"Zhinky u ZSU zmozhut' sluzhyty snaiperkamy, rozvidnytsiamy ta komandyramy BMP." *Hromads'ke Radio*, June 24, 2016. https://hromadskeradio.org/programs/rankova-hvylya/zhinky-u-zsu-zmozhut-sluzhyty-snaypеrkamy-rozvidnycyamy-ta-komandyramy-bmp.
Zhurzhenko, Tatiana. "Shared Memory Culture? Nationalizing the 'Great Patriotic War' in the Ukrainian-Russian Borderlands." In *Memory and Change in Europe: Eastern Perspectives*, edited by M. Pakier and J. Wawrzyniak, 169–92. Oxford, UK: Berghahn, 015.

OLESYA KHROMEYCHUK is a Teaching Fellow in Modern European History at King's College London. She is author of *"Undetermined" Ukrainians: Post-war Narratives of the Waffen SS "Galicia" Division* (Oxford: Peter Lang, 2013).

PART IV

TRACES OF THE LOST MULTIETHNICITY
AND MEMORY OF THE ETHNIC CLEANSING

7

MEMORY, MONUMENTS, AND THE PROJECT OF NATIONALIZATION IN UKRAINE

The Case of Chernivtsi

Karolina Koziura

WHEN I ARRIVED IN CHERNIVTSI, A WESTERN UKRAINIAN city and the site of my fieldwork, in June 2014, I noticed that a new memorial site had been established in the city square. It was a small platform with a large cross standing three meters tall and surrounded by flowers. A poster in front of the memorial explained that this place would serve as a memorial to commemorate the victims of the Euromaidan revolution, otherwise known as the "Heavenly Hundred" (*Nebesna Sotnia*).

The creation of the memorial reflected the recent antigovernment and pro-European atmosphere witnessed in many Ukrainian cities. During the period of the so-called Euromaidan revolution (the winter of 2013–14) in Ukraine, I witnessed many antigovernment protests in Chernivtsi. Yet I was surprised that the creators of the Heavenly Hundred monument connected it to the Pietà, a statue that stood in the very same place when the city was under the jurisdiction of the Austro-Hungarian Empire (1775–1918). The site of the former Pietà has been deeply controversial both in its historical dimension and in the post-1991 memory work in Chernivtsi. Since independence, at least three attempts to rebuild the monument after 1991 were undermined. At the core of the debates about the monument were questions about interethnic relations and the identity of Chernivtsi's cityscape. Thus, the idea to recreate the Pietà sculpture and establish the Heavenly Hundred memorial site have revealed multiple, and often contradictory, narratives of the past and shown their importance in the present struggle to redefine the urban identity of this border city.

For a group of local professionals—namely, architects, historians, and artists—the recreation of the Pietà monument is a step toward strengthening the Habsburg identity of Chernivtsi's cityscape. Currently, one of the most significant goals of local urban planners is to preserve the historical city center, and in doing so, transform Chernivtsi into an attractive, and implicitly European, tourist destination. According to local professionals, the importance of the Pietà monument is described in terms of its aesthetic, historical, and commemorative values. The reconstruction of the Pietà would at once attract tourists to the city and strongly encourage the association of the cityscape with Habsburg and, more important, European identity. The creation of Heavenly Hundred's memorial site, at the same time, would reflect the contemporary revolutionary and patriotic spirit felt in the country.

But monuments cannot be perceived only as works of art. They are created for the specific purpose of keeping people or events alive in the consciousness of contemporary and future generations.[1] For the creators of the Heavenly Hundred's monument, future generations are a particularly important audience. The various commemorations of the victims of the previous regime supported by the decommunization wave, which have recently cropped up in many major Ukrainian cities, can be understood as a new wave of Ukrainization. In this context, the Heavenly Hundred should be understood as some of the most important national figures in post-Soviet Ukraine.

In order to understand the various meanings associated with the recreation of the Pietà monument, one needs to examine its complicated history. Chernivtsi occupies an important place in the separate national myths of several groups, such as Ukrainians, Romanians, and Jews, and therefore the past of the city can be told quite differently. The history of the Pietà monument, as described by the contemporary initiators, represents a specifically Ukrainian nationalist history of the city and its spatial development.

In this chapter, I follow the idea that monuments play an integral role in creating, sustaining, and representing memory of a particular place.[2] They are material sites through which states create and distribute a sense of symbolic attachment and belonging. Monuments are also contested sites of remembrance in which the relationship between memory, forgetting, continuity, and change intermingle. Creators must decide who within a particular society should be commemorated and who can be excluded, often causing controversies that reveal different interpretations of the past and ideological divisions between people.[3] Monuments, among them the aforementioned Pietà, are inseparable elements in the collective memory of any city, at once connected to the past and to contemporary politics. Thus, any monuments referencing Chernivtsi's past also touch sensitive aspects of present-day diversity, power relations, and politics.

In this chapter, I ask: What narratives of the past does the Pietà monument reveal and whose history is transmitted through the monument? Who is included and who is excluded in these representations? In answering these questions, I argue that the attempts to recreate the Pietà and memorialize the Heavenly Hundred are inextricably tied to the struggle to change the identity of the cityscape and transform Chernivtsi from a Soviet borderland into a Ukrainian and European heartland. This post-Soviet urban transformation of Chernivtsi is neither easy nor straightforward: it requires the local national ideology, which serves the initiators of the Pietà monument, to go beyond the traditional nationalist narratives of the past and incorporate new narratives, such as those of desovietization and westernization.

In order to show the various meanings attached to the recreation of the Pietà in Chernivtsi, I first discuss the complex history of this monument dating back to the 19th century. Recounting the history of Chernivtsi is complicated by prevalent nostalgic discourse on the peaceful coexistence of various ethnic groups during the reign of the Austro-Hungarian Empire; this image can be deconstructed through analyzing the historical context of the Pietà monument. Second, I draw in the theoretical framework of this work, which is based on the relationship between memory and place-making practices. Finally, I discuss the contemporary significance of the recreation of Pietà monument, particularly with regard to aforementioned struggles to nationalize the cityscape.

It should be mentioned that the city of Chernivtsi is not unique among post-1991 Ukrainian cities. In many Ukrainian cities, various power struggles and tensions can be observed in how cities have been reshaped after the communist period.[4] The contemporary multinational character of the city, however, as well as its status as a historical borderland of Central European empires and states, make Chernivtsi's memory politics an interesting case study that could lay the groundwork for comparative work in the future.

The investigation of memory traces and heritage production in the cityscape requires the application of many research methods.[5] The following study is part of my broader research project on the urban transformation of post-Soviet Chernivtsi. In the course of two years of ethnographic fieldwork conducted between 2010 and 2015, I collected twenty-five semistructured interviews with city officials, architects, and activists. This work was supported by a number of informal and repeated conversations with city dwellers. In addition, I conducted historical and archival research, and through the participant observation method, I merged into the institutional life of various national and religious communities (most important among them local Polish, Ukrainian, and Jewish communities). In the later phase of my research, I was especially interested in the transformation of the built environment in the history of Chernivtsi and the present attempts to recreate the historical, multinational, and European image of Chernivtsi. Although I draw from the entire body of research I have accumulated throughout my fieldwork, in this chapter I use especially the local media discourse on the recreation of the Pietà and interviews with local officials and urban dwellers supported by the detailed analysis of changing visual representations of the built environment of Chernivtsi.

The Pietà Monument and the Multiple Pasts of Chernivtsi

During the last two hundred years, Chernivtsi has had four names. Under the Austro-Hungarian Empire, it was known as Czernowitz (1775–1918); during the Kingdom of Romania, it was renamed Cernăuți (1918–40 and 1941–45); under the Ukrainian Soviet Socialist Republic it was widely known as Chernovtsy (1945–91); and with the emergence of independent Ukraine in 1991, it was renamed Chernivtsi.

In each case, the name of the city was highly symbolic, representing the power dynamics of society and calling for a revolution in the collective psyche of the people occupying the space. Every time Chernivtsi changed its ruler, the city's space changed as well: new buildings constructed, monuments erected, and streets renamed. For each new state, Chernivtsi's streets, squares, buildings, and monuments were important resources through which political power could be transmitted and new forms of attachments created.

Despite the political changes, Chernivtsi managed to sustain its ethno-national diversity. Although different national groups seized power, traditionally Chernivtsi was a space in which Ukrainian, Romanian, Jewish, German, and Polish communities coexisted. It is important to note that Chernivtsi's multinational character is not just a memory of the past—it is a reality of the city's present. Chernivtsi is currently inhabited by around two hundred twenty thousand citizens of sixty-five nationalities with Romanians and Moldovans as the largest minority groups.[6] Thus, every proposed change to Chernivtsi's cityscape intended to represent its historical and political character (by the construction of monuments) becomes a point of contention among the local communities.[7]

The Pietà was erected in 1827 during the rule of the Austro-Hungarian Empire. In the original construction, the Virgin Mary with two angels by her side knelt in front of a cross, holding Jesus in her arms. The figures were situated on an obelisk three meters tall that was placed in the middle of the Ringplatz, the city center in the 19th century. The monument was funded by Lazar Mykhailovych's family, a local Greek Catholic family, and endorsed by the Austrian governor.[8]

In 1875 a group of citizens filed a petition proposing to remove the Pietà monument and replace it with a monument commemorating the hundred-year anniversary of the annexation of Bukovina by Austria.[9] According to petitioners, this new monument would better represent the diverse national character of Chernivtsi. The petition was met with protests organized by local Catholic families, who successfully blocked the petition. The Pietà monument consequently remained in the square for the next fifty years.

Now that the history of the Pietà's construction has been briefly covered, we must turn to the many narratives of Chernivtsi's history that lurk in the background of the present-day restoration of the Pietà. Chernivtsi is not just a physical space: it is also a literary topos filled with nostalgia and traces of various ethnic groups' memories. The literary representations of the city have influenced the contemporary visions of Chernivtsi's history and have defined the city as a certain kind of space. Each national group in the city created their own representation of the cityscape.[10] One in particular—closely related to the time of creation of the Pietà monument—predominated, propounding that 19th-century Chernivtsi was a tolerant multicultural city with a vibrant urban culture.[11] This narrative was certainly grounded in history: during this period, Chernivtsi developed from a peripheral rural settlement into a significant center of eastern crown land while maintaining its image as a typical Habsburg town—eclectic architecture, cobblestone streets, coffeehouses, civic associations, and arts.

Chernivtsi's reputation as a cosmopolitan borderland was noticed and discussed by Bukovinian Jewish writers at the time, such as Rose Ausländer and Paul Celan.[12] In 1876, Karl Emil Franzos concluded that Bukovina was a "Half-Asia," a place where one could encounter European culture alongside Asian barbarism, Western progress next to Eastern indolence, where existed "neither bright day or dark night but rather an eerie twilight."[13] During this period, Chernivtsi started to be perceived as "the Jerusalem on Prut river," mostly because of the predominantly Jewish character of the city; it was described as "a small universe, urban culture, the fascination of café," meaning that it sustained high culture and urban life.[14] The literary topos continued during the Soviet time and was reinforced mostly by foreign writers, publicists, and politicians. For example, Zbigniew Herbert, a Polish poet who had never been in Chernivtsi, stated in an interview that Chernivtsi was the last European city. Hans Prelitsch described it as a multinational, multireligious symbiosis, "a model for a united Europe."[15] Oskar Beck called it "the Switzerland of the East."[16]

Many contemporary scholars challenge this idealized vision of the city's past.[17] For them, it is surprising that the general character of the 19th-century ethnic, religious, and economic mosaic of Chernivtsi was rather balanced. The elites of 19th-century Chernivtsi tried to create and sustain this imperial image. But the city was one of the most peripheral in the empire and hardly anyone in Vienna knew about it. Furthermore, the land of Bukovina was one of the poorest and most economically dysfunctional in the whole empire.

But what is interesting about Chernivtsi at that time was not its economic status, but rather the dynamics between the ethnic groups in the city. Was it in fact the golden age expressed in collective memory? Was 19th-century Chernivtsi a true model of multiculturalism? And most important, was ethnicity the primary means of identification? Or did people define themselves on linguistic or religious terms? How does the Pietà monument elucidate identity politics in Chernivtsi during the 19th century?

The Austrian census is helpful in answering these questions and reveals information on how people under the Habsburg empire's rule identified themselves. For example, the census contained no direct question on nationality. Instead, people were asked to identify their language and religious affiliation. Thus, all present estimates about the national composition of 19th-century Chernivtsi are based on linguistic and religious identity. According to the Austrian census conducted in 1910, Chernivtsi was inhabited by 85,458 citizens: 41,360 (48%) spoke German, 15,254 (18%) spoke Ruthenian, 14,893 (17%) spoke Polish, and 13,440 (15%) spoke Romanian. According to the religious affiliation, 32.8% were Jewish, 27% Roman Catholic, 23.7% Greek Orthodox, 11% Greek Catholic, and 4.9% Protestant.

Nevertheless, while the census provides insight into how citizens under the Habsburg Empire may have identified themselves, it is also a rudimentary analytical tool. For example, each part of the empire constructed census questions differently. In the Austrian part to which Chernivtsi belonged, people were asked to identify the language they used every day, whereas in the Hungarian part, citizens were asked to record their mother tongue. Besides, the "Ruthenian" language category was likely intended to determine who identified with Ruthenian nationality; but those who checked this option may have been struggling for some form of Ukrainian identity, or perhaps identified more with Orthodox and pro-Russian identities. Furthermore, the census showed that a large number of people spoke German, suggesting at first glance that a plurality of citizens were Germans, or German-speaking Jews. Because the census inquired about the language of everyday use, however, the apparent predominance of German language is merely a sign that German was the main language of imperial administration and culture. Thus, while German was widely used by most of the city's citizens (opposed only to some degree by Romanians, Ruthenians, Poles, and Yiddish-speaking Jews), other sources suggest that the citizens of Chernivtsi were multilingual, communicating daily in at least five languages.[18] It seems that religion was a stronger qualifier that we might have expected.

In this context, it can be assumed that those who filed the petition to remove the Pietà monument were predominantly members of the Orthodox community (among them possibly Orthodox Ruthenians and Romanians) and those who preferred a political rather than a religious monument. Although officially the regime promoted migration and repopulation of Bukovinian lands by various groups, it favored the local Greek Catholic population who could counterbalance local Romanian population.[19] Thus, petitioners opposed the Pietà monument not only for religious reasons (sculptures are antipathetic to Orthodox theological sensibilities), but also as a protest against the Austrian government's bias toward local Catholics.

The Pietà monument stood in Chernivtsi until 1923, when the new Romanian governor decided to remove the sculpture from the main square (at that point renamed as Piata Unirii) and placed it next to a local Roman Catholic church. The statue was replaced by the Monument of the Unification, which commemorated the joining of Bukovina to Romania. The monument consisted of a young girl dressed in Romanian national dress who welcomed a young boy. The girl was supposed to represent Bukovinian territory, and the boy Romanian lands.[20]

The creation of this site was connected with the wider process of the Romanianization of Chernivtsi's cityscape. Although authorities did not transform the cityscape significantly during the twenty-year Romanian rule of the city, they embarked on a successful campaign to change many of its identity symbols. Streets were renamed, Romanian flags were raised on public buildings, and Romanian language became the public language, appearing on storefronts, information boards, in everyday conversation, and official dealings.[21] These linguistic and ethnic policies importantly figured into a larger project in Chernivtsi and Bukovina lands—the Romanian nation-state's master project of unification.[22] The destruction of the Monument of Unification was one of the first actions Soviet troops undertook when they entered Chernivtsi in 1944. Shortly thereafter, the monument was replaced by a statue of Lenin, which stood in the square until Ukraine's independence in 1991. Soviet authorities also destroyed the Pietà monument completely, making its reconstruction impossible.

The destruction of both monuments marked a new era for Chernivtsi. In 1944, Chernivtsi was incorporated into the Ukrainian Soviet Socialist Republic; accordingly, a new process of mapping the cityscape began. The life of the citizens was moved from the city center to microdistricts (*mikroraiony*), which were newly established, self-contained communities of residential quarters located on the outskirts of city. The microdistricts depended on built industry and were designed according to the Soviet idea of functional modernism, housing workplaces, apartments, hospitals, cultural centers, and so on.[23] Consequently, the old city center of Chernivtsi began to decline in significance for ordinary citizens.[24] Nevertheless, the city center was never totally neglected. The Soviet authorities marked their territory, changing street names to commemorate Soviet heroes, erected monuments to Soviet leaders, and rewrote the history of public buildings.[25]

When Chernivtsi became a part of independent Ukraine, the city was once again transformed physically and symbolically. The first few years were marked by a steady desovietization and a local Romanian-Ukrainian conflict. The city's authorities removed the most visible markers of the Soviet past, among them the statue of Lenin. As Narvselius and Bernsand noted, however, changes in street names and other signage occurred much slower in Chernivtsi than in other parts of Western Ukraine.[26] The beginning of Ukrainian-Romanian conflict began in the early 1990s when local nationalist elites boycotted the referendum on Ukraine's independence. From this period two policies—and to some extent contradictory ones—were introduced by both Romanian and Ukrainian states. On the surface, Ukrainian and Romanian policies seemed to be completely at odds. Romania established a new citizenship policy, which granted Romanian (and European Union) citizenship to individuals whose ancestors lived in the Kingdom of Romania. Consequently, it was possible for many Chernivtsi citizens to apply for a Romanian passport, which was considered to be much more useful for traveling and working abroad than the Ukrainian one.[27] At the same time, there were several attempts to improve Ukrainian-Romanian relations during this period. In 2000 the "Upper Prut" Euroregion was established and gestures were made toward establishing a multicultural university in Chernivtsi. Although the university was never established, the linguistic and cultural needs of the local Romanian minority were secured through the establishment of various associations.

Since the collapse of the Soviet Union, Chernivtsi's cityscape has entered a new phase. The aforementioned Romanian-Ukrainian conflict, at least officially, seems to be resolved, and the city's authorities are focused on both promoting the multicultural image of the past and present of Chernivtsi and opening the city for Western tourists and investors. The city, especially in the context of the Euromaidan revolution, has also entered a new phase of the desovietization. But even as authorities hope to generate a sense of common territoriality, shared history, and shared politics, different narratives of the past deeply affect Chernivtsi and are revealed in its urban landscape. As in every city, changing relations between different representations of the past and attachments to particular identifications are in the center of the place-making process and the production of locality.[28] Thus, the present transformation of Chernivtsi's cityscape is not just a matter of contemporary politics: rather, the place-making process illustrates the complex relationship between different layers of the city's collective memory of its past interacting with its contemporary context.

The Role of Memory in Place-Making Process

Monuments and memorial sites dedicated to figures of special significance have been an important element of the cityscape of almost every city since the end of the 19th century.[29] City dwellers began to use monuments to shape their collective image and construct a "web of commemorative references."[30] Monuments, in particular, always remember and honor particular figures recognized as important in local, regional, and national history. They can construct a significant public space and in doing so leave traces on the local collective memory and identity. In this sense, monuments share many characteristics with historiography.[31] Both are collectively shared, publicly expressed, and ideologically driven artifacts, and as such, can be leveraged to serve contemporary interests.[32] Subgroups, however, may hold their own narrative of the past that conflicts with the dominant group's narrative of history. "Debatability" is an intrinsic aspect of history that allows each group to confront its understanding of the past.[33] Thus, memory and the past are not simple or unitive narratives but rather contested and central phenomena for present and future social conflicts.

Memory is a crucial concept for the formation and sustainability of national identities.[34] Common and shared memories lie at the core of national historical narratives and provide a sense of longevity and continuity. In particular, beliefs that one's own nation is at the center of the universe and that one's own nation is the first one on a given land play a particularly important role in building and strengthening national myths.[35] These myths serve the nation's claim to be the most important in their land and to have the right to one's own state—they are narratives that stress one's own significance and uniqueness.[36] Nationalist narratives are transmitted through public commemorations, practices, and what Pierre Nora calls *lieux de mémoire*, or fixed sites of memory, which are recognized as linked to national heritage.[37] The analysis of these locations can highlight changes in the landscape and expose layers of identity and memory embodied in a place. Thus, monuments make history and dominant national narratives visible in the cityscape.[38]

At the core of the debatability of the past lies the assumption that a common vision of the past is a necessary element in the formation of a cohesive identity.[39] Thus, the question "who are we?" refers to the question "who were we as a group in the past; who were our ancestors?"[40] Such identifications depend on concrete relationships between space and time that are sustained by an individual's or group's memory.

Another important element for identification is the relationship between memory and space. On the one hand, space accumulates historical experiences—past events, which were very powerful, that are still present in the landscape. In this sense, space is a kind of *model of* representation of the remembered past.[41] On the other hand, space can be consciously created by those people who have the power to shape it and thus show only the elements of the past that somehow serve their needs. In this sense, space is the *model for* a kind of instruction for our memories, in which some of them are more visible and powerful.

This dual character of space is especially visible in cities, which are full of significant places that mirror features of their past. The concretization of history, according to which history is not an objective fact but an intellectual construct, is reflected especially in monuments, street names, and memorial plaques that reveal a given group's memory of the past as they commemorate some and forget others.[42] Citizens' emotional attachments to place are largely dictated by heritage production and management.[43] To classify something as a heritage, an object needs to have a specific cultural-historical significance and represent an identity of a given group.[44] Spatiality is a projection of the human imagination, beliefs, and practices onto the physical environment.[45] Heritage capitalizes on the various projections of spatiality.

The city should be understood as a complicated and multifaceted phenomenon in which various communities and social groups integrate their activity into one system with its own mechanism of social persistence, change, and subordination.[46] Monuments represent changes in the sociocultural space of every city and the analysis of particular heritage demonstrates the general tendencies of society and reveal its power dynamics. Thus, as the city transforms physically and socially, so do its heritage sites.[47]

The Pietà Monument and Multiple Presence of Chernivtsi

In Chernivtsi, the erection of a new monument in April 2014 was an acknowledged event discussed by the major local media. Most of the articles' headlines were very persuasive and expressions, such as "Cross replaced Lenin," "Let's return the Mother of God," and "The history that cannot be returned" easily got readers' attentions. For many citizens of Chernivtsi, the fact itself that the cross was raised at the same place where the monument of Lenin once stood was one of the most important aspects of the inauguration.

The struggle to restore the Pietà dated back to the late 1990s. The first initiative to reestablish the Pietà in Chernivtsi was in 1999, when the Ukrainian government passed a bill supporting the revitalization of the monuments to history and culture in Ukraine. From Chernivtsi's district, only the Pietà appeared on the list. Although members of the local Greek Catholic and Roman Catholic communities tried to force the municipality to recreate

Fig. 7.1 The Pietà Monument during reconstruction. *Source*: Photo by the author.

the monument, no actions were taken. The same happened in the mid-2000s, when a group of activists wanted to restore the Pietà as part of the celebration of the city's six hundredth anniversary and revitalization projects (undertaken in 2008).

The restoration was only recently approved when the Greek Catholic group Caritas proposed that the Pietà be reinstalled to commemorate the Heavenly Hundred. According to the initiators of the Pietà monument, the local government had previously ignored every attempt, claiming that funds were too low to justify such an undertaking. My informal conversations with locals, however, revealed that it was not only the government opposing the restoration—members of local Orthodox churches, and especially Romanians, also opposed the restoration because of the anti-Romanian rhetoric in the local newspapers that supported the restoration. In the historical account of the Pietà provided by local nationally driven newspapers, 1923, the year that the former Romanian governor (or the "Romanian aggressor" as he was called in the article) removed the Pietà, was featured as one of the most important dates in the history of the sculpture. The article further stated that the monument was replaced by an "offensive" Romanian monument of unification, which was described as a sculpture of a young couple.[48]

The tense Ukrainian-Romanian relations on the state and elite levels strongly influenced the way ordinary people perceived ethnic differences in Chernivtsi. The majority of my Ukrainian interlocutors expressed the notion that being Romanian in Chernivtsi is "something people do not talk about," suggesting that Romanians inhabited the lower local strata. Furthermore, although many friends of my interlocutors held Romanian citizenship in order to travel or work abroad, they did not like to talk about it in public. Ukrainians also claimed that Romanians and Moldovans (very often these groups are perceived as one) did not make any effort to learn Ukrainian, instead speaking in Russian, or even worse, *surzhyk*.[49] Although on the level of elite production, Romanian is perceived as one of the fundamental languages in the development of Chernivtsi's literary culture, on the basic of everyday life many think that Romanians, by not knowing Ukrainian or using only Russian, destroy the beauty of the Ukrainian character of the Bukovina region.

The suppressed but ever-present fear of Romanians surfaced again when the war in Eastern Ukraine broke out. People discussed the presence of Russian soldiers in the region and expressed their concerns at the prospects of Romanian troops invading Chernivtsi. What would happen, they asked, if the Romanian army invaded Chernivtsi? Conversations like these revealed both the insecurity of the present situation in Ukraine torn by war and that the rival local nationalizing policies of the two states cleaved Ukrainians and Romanians increasingly further apart, bolstering ordinary Chernivtsi Ukrainians' fears of Romanianization of the region. Still, with the exception of some blatantly anti-Romanian statements, the majority of local Ukrainians had rather neutral position toward Romanians and expressed rather the religious character of monument which is "returning" to Chernivtsi.

Despite the friction between Ukrainians and Romanians, one of Chernivtsi's most distinguishing features, at least in Western Ukraine, is its contemporary diversity. While for other parts of Eastern Europe—for example, L'viv—the multinational character of its cities belong rather to the past; in Chernivtsi it is very much a part of the present. Members of many national communities still live here, and their political stances need to be taken into consideration in every attempt to change the character of the city. Also, the recent revitalization of the Jewish culture led by members of the Jewish diaspora and supported by local activists contributed to the growing debates about the multinational character of Chernivtsi and its associations with European culture.

The anti-Romanian discourse in the Ukrainian nationalist narratives underlying the descriptions of the history of the Pietà in Chernivtsi were accompanied by equally significant anticommunist rhetoric. Communism still has a presence in Chernivtsi, both among its inhabitants and in its cityscape. Nostalgia for communism can be found among a significant number of Russians, Byelorussians, and former soldiers from the former Soviet Union residing in Chernivtsi. In addition, Ukrainian markers coexist alongside Soviet signage in Russian, setting Chernivtsi apart from other West Ukrainian cities.[50] Some of the street names and a number of plaques and monuments are dedicated to the Great Patriotic War, the Afghan War, and the Soviet liberation of Chernivtsi—for example, the largest street in Chernivtsi was named Red Army Street until recently. Only in 2008 with the revitalization of the city center was some of the Soviet signage removed and replaced with signage that highlighted the Habsburg character of the old town. Nevertheless, spaces of previous microdistricts, exemplary models of socialist urban planning, remained or were converted into Western-style shopping centers.

The counter to Soviet imaginary of Chernivtsi is provided by the old literary topos of cosmopolitan Chernivtsi, a myth that several groups relate themselves to in contemporary discourse. For example, Chernivtsi Jews living in diaspora perceive themselves very often as heirs of the Austrian Jewish tradition, which they conflate with the culture of the city.[51] Yet the local Jewish population that originates from post–World War II migrations to the city is largely excluded from this narrative.[52]

Ukrainians also utilize Chernivtsi's cosmopolitan myth. This narrative is different from the one Ukrainians traditionally put forth, which emphasized their historical presence and importance in Bukovina's lands. The traditional narrative often appears in local history books about Bukovina, focusing on the presence of Kyivan Rus in medieval times in Bukovina and, later, the activity of Ukrainian national leaders during Austrian rule.[53] But while the traditional narrative was popular during the early 1990s, today the vision of a distinct, ethnic Ukrainian history of Bukovina is perceived as rather old-fashioned and radical. Thus, the Ukrainian national narrative has been merged with the cosmopolitan myth of the city, which represents the city as part of the Western sphere and associates it with Western European intellectual life and high urban culture. Part of this new trend is also linked to the activity of the Greek Catholic Church and to various ideas to incorporate the distinct religious aspect into the Ukrainian national identity.

The city's administration and Ukrainian elites utilize the new hybrid narrative to promote a multinational image of past and present Chernivtsi. This strategy is shared by local professionals who aim to preserve the historical and, in their sense, European character of the city represented in the narrative. Indeed, most local funds for urban development projects are put toward the dual goal of transforming the city to a tourist-friendly place and emphasizing the Habsburg character of the city of the hybrid narrative.

The restoration of the Pietà is part of this story. On the state level, the replication is fully supported, guaranteeing a reinstitution of one of the most important pieces of regional cultural heritage. The replication itself is a more contentious matter. Some artists and historians hope to replicate the monument with strict adherence to the aesthetic values of the old monument—directly linking the city to its Habsburg past. In 2014, the Chernivtsi City Council organized a special commission to work in the archives in order to reconstruct the shape of the old sculpture. As no detailed sketches of the Habsburg monument have been preserved, however, no consensus has arisen about whether the new Pietà should (or even can) resemble the old one or just loosely refer to it.

Nonetheless, the present initiator, the Greek Catholic Caritas, hopes that the restoration of the Pietà monument in Chernivtsi will clearly represent the Ukrainian national vision of Chernivtsi's past. To this end, local newspapers and the information board placed in front of the cross issued a distinctly Ukrainian story of the Habsburg Pietà, presenting the 19th-century monument as a proof of the Ukrainian community in the city and their resistance to authorities. According to this vision, the Pietà is a monument erected by Ukrainians, even though other sources suggest that it was supported by other Catholic communities, such as those of the Poles and Germans. Furthermore, the text available on the restoration identifies historic regimes in Bukovina as foreign and oppressive to the local Catholic (implicitly Greek Catholic) community. Thus, the Ukrainian national identity is defined according to religion (Greek Catholic) and special traits of character (resistance to foreign authorities). This vision of Ukrainian national character is associated with the commemoration of the modern heroes—the Heavenly Hundred.

In recent years, the commemoration of the victims of the Euromaidan revolution became the vehicle for another wave of Ukrainization and desovietization wave across the country. During the Euromaidan events, which started as protests against Viktor Yanukovych and ended in the overthrow of his government, resulted in the death of nearly 130 civilians. The majority of victims were killed between January 25 and February 13 by snipers in the Independence Square (Maidan Nezalezhnosti) in Kyiv. During the commemorative ceremony held in the square, protestors named the victims as the Heavenly Hundred (*Nebesna Sotnia*). The term "Heavenly Hundred" has a dual meaning. Historically, the term *Sotnia* (hundreds) refers to military units organized by Cossacks, the communities of warriors who inhabited the lands of Ukraine and Russia and are known as central figures of the Ukrainian nationalist myth. More contemporarily, the term was used to describe the self-defense forces formed by volunteers in order to barricade against police and military during the revolutionary events held on the Maidan square. The term *nebesna* (heavenly) links either of the meanings to Heaven or God. Thus, the Heavenly Hundred can be understood as "the legion of those who went to heaven" or "the legion of those who went to God."

The victims of the Euromaidan have become the most important national martyrs in the history of the modern Ukrainian state. The city of Kyiv decided to rename one of its streets Heavenly Hundred Heroes Avenue, and there is a plan to open a memorial complex "to the Heroes of Heavenly Hundred."[54] The Ukrainian parliament established the medal "Order of the Heroes of the Heavenly Hundred" and declared February 20 "the Day of the Heavenly Hundred."[55] In the week leading up to the Day of the Heavenly Hundred, the majority of West Ukrainian cities are decorated with spontaneous memory boards created by citizens. In most cases, posters have pictures of the victims with their names, Ukrainian emblems, candles, and flowers. These memorial sites function like cemeteries established in the middle of cities.

Chernivtsi citizens made their own efforts to commemorate the dramatic events held in the capital. Last year, two streets were renamed: for example, Stasiuk Street became Heavenly Hundred Street and Red Army Street became Maidan Heroes Street. Thus, the commemoration of Maidan heroes overwrote the Soviet past visibly in Chernivtsi's cityscape. Integral to the desovietization process is the growing importance of the religious elements in Chernivtsi's landscape. They are an important part of the decommunization project: in the past, the exposure of religious elements was forbidden in the cityscape, but also they are attached to the modern Ukrainian national idea. For example, the idea to restore the Pietà was first articulated by the establishment of a huge cross in the main city square, which will act as a placeholder until the Pietà is finished in the near future. Moreover, the initiators of the monument made a direct connection between the Pietà and the Maidan heroes. As one initiator remarked, the simultaneous recreation of the Pietà and commemoration of Maidan heroes projects the powerful image of "contemporary Ukraine as a Mother of God and Jesus in her arms represents the victims of the previous regime after which Ukraine (like the Mother of God) will cry for a long time."[56] Thus, the victims of Euromaidan revolution will not only be commemorated but also remind Chernivtsi's citizens of the price of freedom.

Conclusion

Since the dismemberment of the Soviet bloc, many cities in Central and Eastern Europe have faced rapid changes and transformations. On the symbolic level, one of the biggest challenges was the handling of Soviet signage, which needed to be replaced by a new system of meanings connected with the newly established nation-states. In their search for a new urban identity, societies in Western Ukraine turned to both anticommunist and precommunist narratives. The latter functioned as proof of the longevity and continuity of national traditions and the connections to Western culture in new hybrid nationalist narratives.

In this chapter, I used the example of the reconstruction of the Pietà monument in Chernivtsi to discuss how the narrative of the cosmopolitan post-Habsburg glory figures into the Ukrainian state's nationalization project. In times of present instability, this narrative simultaneously creates attachments to patriotic values but also strengthens the position of local Ukrainians and their presence in the history of Chernivtsi. Integral to this discussion was the analysis of monuments as political and ideological projects connected with the visualization of the memory of particular groups. The various meanings attached to the reconstruction of the Pietà monument reflect shadows of regional interethnic relations and the politics of memory. The history of the monument itself shows the power struggles present in the history of this borderland city but also presents the contemporary cityscape as a multilayered symbolic resource that might be activated for various purposes.

The present initiators of the Pietà monument presented their national vision straightforwardly, highlighting the distinct presence and religiosity of Ukrainians in the history of the city. The local government and activists stress instead the aesthetic, commemorative, and finally anticommunist values behind the restoration of the Pietà. It is important to note that the recreation of the Pietà in the form of the Heavenly Hundred commemorative space serves as a symbol of patriotism in a country torn by its ongoing war. In times of insecurity, the new monument should remind people about common values and sacrifice made in the name of the independent state regardless of ethnic origin. Perhaps, the only element that links all these narratives together is a strong pro-European sentiment. No matter whether members of Greek Catholic Church, local Ukrainian nationalists, city officials, civic activists, historians, or artists—they all see Chernivtsi as a city returning to Europe.

Notes

This chapter is based on my research conducted in the framework of grant no 2012/07/N/HS3/04169 provided by the Polish National Science Center.

1. Riegl, "Modern Cult," 83.
2. Rihtman-Auguštin, "Monument."
3. Levinson, *Written in Stone*.
4. Males, *Sotsiolohiia mista*.
5. See, for example, Herzfeld, *Place in History*; Richardson, *Kaleidoscopic Odessa*.
6. Based on the All-Ukrainian Population Census from 2001, accessed September 15, 2011, http://city.cv.ua/portal/8/801-801.html.
7. Narvselius and Bernsand, "Lviv and Chernivtsi," 1.

8. Nykyrsa, *Chernivtsi*.
9. Nykyrsa, *Chernivtsi*, 150.
10. Koziura, "Everyday Ethnicity," 1.
11. Scherzer, *While the Gods Were Salient*; Hirsch and Spitzer, *Ghost of Home*.
12. Czernowitz became popularized by the poetry of Paul Celan and Rosa Ausländer—two Jewish authors who were forced to emigrate during World War II. See, for example, Rykhlo, *Shibbolem*.
13. Pollack, "Nach Czernowitz."
14. Shevchenko, *Chernovetskaia Atlantida*.
15. Hans Prelitsch, "Homo bucovinensis," *Brücke zum Westen* 4–5 (1954): 12–14.
16. Czyżewski, *Linia powrotu*.
17. Horel, "Jewish Associations"; Rechter, "Jewish El Dorado?"
18. Horel, "Jewish Associations."
19. Krughlaschov, "Chernivtsi."
20. Nykyrsa, *Chernivtsi*, 150.
21. Scherzer, *While the Gods Were Salient*.
22. Livezeanu, *Cultural Politics*.
23. French and Hamilton, *Socialist City*, 11; Abitz, *Post-socialist City*, 223.
24. Moreover, since 1944, Chernivtsi witnessed two kinds if immigration. The first was related to rural-urban migrations and the second to the migration within the Soviet Union proper. In this way, the prewar character of the city as well as its ethnic balance was broken.
25. The Soviet culture was also transmitted through the Russian language, which in this period actually came to dominate not only in official media but also in everyday communication.
26. Narvselius and Bernsand, "Lviv and Chernivtsi," 1.
27. It should be noted that many Ukrainian citizens continue to apply for Romanian citizenship, although Ukrainian law forbids dual citizenship. Still, the practice is widespread in Chernivtsi and, during my research, several local Romanian organizations pointed to the problems in distinguishing between real Romanians and those who use the passport for utilitarian reasons.
28. See, for example, Appadurai, "Past as Scarce Resource"; Herzfeld, *Place in History*; Richardson, *Kaleidoscopic Odessa*.
29. Riegl, "Modern Cult," 69.
30. Vukov, "Cities, Memorial Sites, Memory," 129.
31. Nora, "Between Memory and History."
32. Appadurai, "Past as Scarce Resource."
33. Appadurai, "Past as Scarce Resource."
34. Nora, "Between Memory and History," 26.
35. Schöpflin, "Function of Myth"; Smith, "'Golden Age'"; Wilson, "Myths of National History."
36. Malkki, *Purity and Exile*.
37. Nora, "Between Memory and History," 7.
38. Abu El-Haj, *Fact on the Ground*, 17.
39. Lowenthal, *Past*.
40. Lowenthal, *Past*, 42.
41. Geertz, *Interpretation of Cultures*, 90.
42. Edensor, *National Identity*, 65; Rihtman-Auguštin, "Monument," 180; Levinson, *Written in Stone*.
43. Herzfeld, *Place in History*.
44. Abu El-Haj, *Fact on the Ground*, 67.
45. Navaro-Yashin, *Make-Believe Space*.
46. Males, *Sotsiolohiia mista*.
47. Boyer, *City of Collective Memory*, 31.
48. RISU May 12, 2014, https://risu.org.ua/ua/index/exclusive/kaleidoscope/56384/, accessed June 22, 2015.
49. The term *surzhyk* refers to the range of spontaneous mixture of the Ukrainian and Russian languages that is the consequence of unawareness of the rules of the standard languages.
50. Narvselius and Bernsand, "Lviv and Chernivtsi."
51. The members of the local Austrian Jewish community who migrated from the city during and after World War II formed a kind of diaspora mailing list known as Czernowitz-L. Its members were not alone in creating an

online discussion platform through which they shared their memories of living in the city, but also they met each other and visited Chernivtsi. Also recently, they started to influence local politics of heritigization by stressing the importance and need to restore the Jewish heritage sites in the city.

52. Most of the Jews who migrated to the city after 1945 were Russian speakers and industrial workers. Thus, nowadays they do not see connections with local Austrian Jewish heritage.

53. Kostyshyn, *Bukovyna*.

54. Interfax-Ukraine, "Kyiv Council Renames Part of Instytutska Street into Heavenly Hundred Heroes Avenue," November 20, 2014, http://en.interfax.com.ua/news/general/235483.html; Interfax-Ukraine, "Memorial to Heroes of Heavenly Hundred Might Be Opened by Anniversary of Tragic Events on Maidan," *Kyiv Post*, April 24, 2014, http://www.kyivpost.com/content/ukraine/memorial-to-heroes-of-heavenly-hundred-might-be-opened-by-anniversary-of-tragic-events-on-maidan-344928.html.

55. "Rada stvoryla orden Heroiv Nebesnoi Sotni," *Ukraïns'ka Pravda*, July 1, 2014, http://www.pravda.com.ua/news/2014/07/1/7030598/.

56. RISU May 12, 2014, https://risu.org.ua/ua/index/exclusive/kaleidoscope/56384/, accessed June 22, 2015.

Bibliography

Abitz, Julie. "Post-socialist City Development in Tirana." PhD diss., Roskilde University, Denmark, 2006.
Abu El-Haj, Nadia. *Fact on the Ground: Archeological Practice and Territorial Self-Fashioning in Israeli Society*. Chicago: University of Chicago Press, 2001.
Appadurai, Arjun. "The Past as a Scarce Resource." *Man* 16, no. 2 (1981): 201–19.
Boyer, Christine M. *The City of Collective Memory: Its Historical Imagery and Architectural Entertainments*. Cambridge, MA: MIT Press, 1996.
Czyżewski, Krzysztof. *Linia powrotu: zapiski z pogranicza*. Sejny, Poland: Pogranicze, 2008.
Edensor, Tim. *National Identity, Popular Culture and Everyday Life*. New York: Berg, 2002.
French, Richard A., and F. E. Ian Hamilton, eds. *The Socialist City: Spatial Structure and Urban Policy*. New York: John Wiley and Sons, 1979.
Geertz, Clifford. *The Interpretation of Cultures*. New York: Basic Books, 1973.
Herzfeld, Michael. *A Place in History: Social and Monumental Time in a Cretan Town*. Princeton, NJ: Princeton University Press, 1991.
Hirsch, Marianne., and Leo Spitzer. *Ghosts of Home: The Afterlife of Czernowitz in Jewish Memory*. Los Angeles: University of California Press, 2011.
Horel, Catherine. "Jewish Associations in the Multicultural Cities of the Austro-Hungarian Monarchy around 1900." *Colloquia. Journal of Central European History* 18, no. 1 (2011): 81–97.
Kostyshyn, Stepan. *Bukovyna: istorychnyi narys*. Chernivtsi, Ukraine: Zelena Bukovina, 1998.
Koziura, Karolina. "Everyday Ethnicity in Chernivtsi, Western Ukraine." *Anthropology of East Europe Review* 32, no. 1 (2014): 1–21.
Kruglashov, Anatoliy. "Chernivtsi: (Ne)porozuminnia mizh spadshchynoiu ta spadkoiemtsiamy." In *Chernivtsi v konteksti urbanistychnykh protsesiv tsentralnoi ta skhidnoi Evropy XVIII–XX st*, edited by Michael Dippeltreiter and Serhij Osatschuk, 1–21. Chernivtsi, Ukraine: Zelena Bukovina, 2008.
Levinson, Sanford. *Written in Stone: Public Monuments in Changing Societies*. Durham, NC: Duke University Press, 1998.
Livezeanu, Irina. *Cultural Politics in Greater Romania: Regionalism, Nation Building and Ethnic Struggle, 1918–1930*. Ithaca, NY: Cornell University Press, 2000.
Lowenthal, David. *The Past Is a Foreign Country*. Cambridge: Cambridge University Press, 1985.
Males, Ludmila., ed. *Sotsiolohia mista: navchalnyi posibnyk*. Donetsk, Ukraine: Znannia, 2010.
Malkki, Liisa H. *Purity and Exile: Violence, Memory, and National Cosmology among Hutu Refugees in Tanzania*. Chicago: University of Chicago Press, 1995.
Narvselius, Eleonora., and Niklas Bernsand. "Lviv and Chernivtsi: Two Memory Cultures at the Western Ukrainian Borderland." *East/West* 1 (2014): 1, 59–83.
Navaro-Yashin, Yael. *The Make-Believe Space: Affective Geography in a Postwar Polity*. Durham, NC: Duke University Press, 2012.

Nora, Pierre. "Between Memory and History: Les Lieux de Mémoire." *Representations* 26 (1989): 7–24.
Nykyrsa, Marija. Chernivtsi: Dokumentalni narysy z istorii vulyts' i ploshch [Chernivtsi: the history of streets and squares]. *Chernivtsi, Ukraine: Zolotye Litavry, 2008.*
Pollack, Martin. "Nach Czernowitz." In *Mythos Czernowitz: Eine Stadt im Spiegel ihrer Nationalitäten*, edited by Helmut Kusdat, 1–13. Potsdam, Ger.: Deutsches Kulturforum östliches Europa, 2008.
Prelitsch, Hans. "Homo bucovinensis." *Brücke zum Westen* 4–5 (1954): 12–19.
Rechter, David. "A Jewish El Dorado? Myth and Politics in Habsburg Czernowitz." In *Insiders and Outsiders: Dilemmas of East European Jewry*, edited by Richard I. Cohen, Jonathan Frankel, and Stefani Hoffman, 207–20. London: Littman Library, 2010.
Richardson, Tanya. *Kaleidoscopic Odessa: History and Place in Contemporary Ukraine.* Toronto: University of Toronto Press, 2008.
Riegl, Alois. "The Modern Cult of Monuments: Its Essence and Its Development." *Historical and Philosophical Issues in the Conservation of Cultural Heritage*, edited by Nicholas Stanley-Price, M. Kirby Talley Jr, and Alessandra Melucco Vaccaro, 69–83. Los Angeles: Getty Conservation Institute, 1996.
Rihtman-Auguštin, Dunja. "The Monument in the Main City Square: Constructing and Erasing Memory in Contemporary Croatia." In *Balkan Identities: Nation and Memory*, edited by Maria Todorova, 180–96. New York: New York University Press, 2004.
Rykhlo, Petro. *Shibbolem: poshuky ievreiskoi identychnosti v nimetskomovnii poezii Bukovyny.* Chernivtsi, Ukraine: Zelena Bukovina, 2008.
Scherzer, Julius. *While the Gods Were Salient: Growing Up under Fascists and Communists.* Baltimore, MD: Publish America, 2005.
Schöpflin, George. "The Function of Myth and a Taxonomy of Myths." In *Myths and Nationhood*, edited by Geoffrey Hosking and George Schöpflin, 19–35. London: Co&Ho, 1997.
Shevchenko, Natalya. *Chernovetskaia Atlantida.* Chernivtsi, Ukraine: Zolotye Litavry, 2004.
Smith, Anthony D. "The 'Golden Age' and National Renewal." In *Myths and Nationhood*, edited by Geoffrey Hosking and George Schöpflin, 36–59. London: Co&Ho, 1997.
Vukov, Nikolai. "Cities, Memorial Sites, Memory: The Case of Plovdiv." *Our Europe: Ethnography-Ethnology-Anthropology of Culture* 2.1 (2013): 129–44.
Wilson, Andrew. "Myths of National History in Belarus and Ukraine." In *Myths and Nationhood*, edited by Geoffrey Hosking and George Schöpflin, 182–97. London: Co&Ho, 1997.

KAROLINA KOZIURA is PhD Candidate in Sociology and Historical Studies at The New School for Social Research, New York.

8

COLLECTIVE MEMORY OF THE HOLOCAUST IN POST-SOVIET UKRAINE

Anna Chebotarova

During World War II, the territory of modern Ukraine became one of the largest killing fields in Europe and resulted in millions of civilian victims, among whom from 1 to 2 million were Jews.[1] Although the mechanisms of extermination varied from one region to another, it was the Ukrainian case that triggered the development of the "Holocaust by bullets" concept in genocide studies to describe the mass killing of Jews in situ by members of the *Einsatzgruppen* and their collaborators. The genocide mostly took place before the very eyes of neighbors and sometimes with their direct participation—either voluntary or forced. The role of the local population, the auxiliary police, and members of the Ukrainian nationalist movement in the killing of Jews remains one of the most sensitive and problematic topics in discussions about the Holocaust in Ukraine.[2] Diverse historical experiences under different administrations have resulted in regionalized variations of the historical memory of World War II. The Soviet narrative of the "Great Patriotic War" versus glorification of the Organization of Ukrainian Nationalists (OUN) and the Ukrainian Insurgent Army (UPA) represent two extremes of this divided memory. As many scholars argue, neither of these narratives includes a memory of the Holocaust in Ukraine.[3] The fragmented, eclectic, and often contested historical policy of the independent Ukrainian state has become the subject of many academic studies; some of them have taken into account the level and context of the inclusion (or rather exclusion) of the Holocaust in Ukraine's official historical discourse and politics of memory.[4] Particular attention was paid to studying the representations of the Holocaust in school textbooks, which are considered to be a tool for developing the values and loyalties of young people and are one of the main instruments of state politics on history.[5] The perception of the Holocaust by various "communities of memory" in Ukrainian society, however, has very rarely been addressed. With the exception of several interesting case studies, the historical (un)consciousness of the Holocaust among average Ukrainians remains a rather understudied topic.[6]

In this chapter, I will consider the question of the place that the Holocaust occupies in the popular imagination of Ukrainian history at the all-national and local levels. The former is derived from Benedict Anderson's concept of a nation as an imagined community, in which an understanding of the past is constructed by power institutions of memory management through discourse, rituals, and symbols in order to provide legitimacy and to mobilize the population for political purposes.[7] At the same time, the internalization of dominant memory narratives is a very complex process that can be contested and resisted by various countermemory groups. The perception of a constructed, national macrohistory can vary greatly according to personal biographical experiences and the socialization of communities of memory. Therefore, apart from the results of all-Ukrainian statistical surveys, I will also regard Holocaust memory on the level of local mnemonic communities by examining cases of several Ukrainian towns that had, before the war, a significant Jewish population that was annihilated during the Holocaust.

Studying collective memory of the Holocaust—a tragic event that happened more than seventy years ago—we understand that only for the oldest generations can it be a part of the individual biographical memory. To analyze the memory of the past not experienced directly and personally Marianne Hirsch introduced the influential concept of postmemory, which "describes the relationship of the second generation to the powerful, often traumatic, experiences that preceded their births but that were nevertheless transmitted to them so deeply as to seem to constitute memories in their own right."[8] Hirsch applies this concept to family frameworks of memory by considering the case of Holocaust survivors' children. Studying the memory of the "vanished others" in the urban spaces of Eastern Europe, Uilleam Blacker suggests using the concept of postmemory to describe the experiences of the present inhabitants of post-Holocaust localities in East Central Europe. As Blacker argues, these people often may have no direct familial or community connections to the pasts of the places they inhabit, but they do have access to these pasts through a variety of media—from the urban environment itself to poetry, memorials, and touristic attractions.[9] In our opinion, however, it is important to distinguish between family-transmitted (as postmemory is in Hirsch's definition) and culturally mediated memories. Alison Landsberg's concept of prosthetic memory seems more appropriate in this case. By studying US society in the age of mass culture, Landsberg argues that "prosthetic memory emerges at the interface between a person and a historical narrative about the past, at an experiential site such as a movie theater or museum. In this moment of contact, an experience occurs through which the person structures himself or herself into a larger history."[10] According to Landsberg, prosthetic memory appears where kinship and community ties were broken and alternative methods for the transmission and dissemination of memories were required. In our opinion, the concept is particularly useful for studying post-Holocaust communities with an interrupted continuity in Eastern Europe. The borderline between two types of remembering a nonexperienced past, postmemory and prosthetic memory, is very thin, as a person internalizes collective memories in different groups and through various media: family stories, the urban environment, books, the internet, museums, and other contacts. In my research, I aim to analyze the social construction of Holocaust memory in post-Soviet Ukraine at the national and local levels and to trace the influence of transborder communities of memory on the process. I argue that although Holocaust memory in contemporary Ukraine is very eclectic and fragmented, we can speak about the phenomenon of *shield memory*. In this case, the voids in awareness about Jewish history as well as uncomfortable topics are overlaid or "shielded" with the projection of people's own biographical experiences and a more comfortable versions of the past that do not threaten the positive image of a we-group from which Jews are still largely excluded.

The Holocaust in Soviet and Post-Soviet Memory Politics in Ukraine

In order to provide a general introduction, it is important to briefly analyze memory politics on the Holocaust in the postwar years—both under Soviet rule and after the Soviet Union's collapse. The period of the 1940s and early 1950s was particularly drastic in terms of population changes in Ukraine, and generally in Eastern Europe. As John Paul Himka emphasizes, one of the outcomes of the war was the unification of Ukraine and its national homogenization, as the Holocaust had sharply diminished the Jewish population while nationalist ethnic cleansing, Stalinist repressions, and deportations removed most of its German and Polish minority groups.[11] The "Great Patriotic War" (1941–45) was constructed as the new main Soviet founding-myth and communist memory politics refused to single out the Jewish Holocaust from the general sufferings of Soviet citizens. Selected places of mass murder were commemorated under societal pressure (for example, Babi Yar), but the only recognized victim group were the "peaceful Soviet citizens," without any specification of their national identity.[12] Many scholars agree that, with rare exceptions, Soviet audiences were not familiar with the Holocaust; Yaroslav Hrytsak, for example, draws attention to the fact that neither Jews nor the Holocaust were mentioned even once in the official history of Soviet Ukraine that was published in 1982.[13] Tarik Cyril Amar warns against describing Soviet memory politics on the Holocaust simply as communicative silence, organized forgetfulness, or amnesia. Such a description, according to Amar, "credits the Soviet system with an efficiency it never possessed—thus we believe that it could create or maintain an information space isolated enough to prevent alternative stories from leaving, entering, or being created inside it."[14]

On the other part of the globe, Ukrainian diaspora communities, particularly in the United States and Canada, developed their own discourse on World War II—in many ways as a counternarrative to the Soviet model. Per Rudling argues that in the narrative that dominated postwar Ukrainian émigré circles, the OUN was presented as a leading force in the struggle against both the Nazis and the Soviets. According to Rudling, the Holocaust was not only omitted from this discourse but was, in fact, excluded and obfuscated by presenting the OUN as a leading force in the struggle against the Nazis and the Soviets and denying its pro-German orientation, antisemitism, and totalitarianism as well as its involvement in the pogroms.[15] One of the reasons for the whitewashing is that many activists in the Ukrainian diaspora were themselves members of the OUN or UPA who fled the Soviet Union in fear of repressions or their descendants. By excluding the Holocaust, nationalist intellectuals strove to preserve an unambiguously positive image of the OUN and UPA, thus of their function as state-legitimizing symbols, and of the Ukraine as a victim nation.[16] John-Paul Himka describes this process as "deflective negationism," which implies not denying the Holocaust itself but denying the participation of one's own group in it. Another important tragic event, which was often emphasized in diaspora circles, was the man-made famine, or Holodomor, of 1932–33 as the central element of Ukrainian history.[17] Before the term *Holodomor* appeared in the 1980s, it was often referred to as "the Famine Holocaust" or "the Ukrainian Holocaust." As Wilfried Jilge argues, not only was the national discourse about the Great Famine of 1932–33 symbolically linked to the Holocaust, but through such nationalization, the memory of the Jewish Holocaust was eclipsed and the two tragedies were presented as competitive.[18]

After the proclamation of independence, the view of Ukrainian history that had developed in diaspora circles was partially re-exported to the new independent state and gained particular support in Western Ukraine. One of the first general textbooks on the country's history, published after the fall of communism, was a translation of diaspora historian Orest Subtelny's book *Ukraine: A History* (1988 in North America, 1991 in Ukraine).[19] The book was reedited several times and received rather positive reviews. Subtelny mentions the history of the Jews and the Holocaust in Ukraine only superficially. As Jilge argues, since Perestroika a part of the Ukrainian North American diaspora had a key impact on the establishment of an ethnically centered view of Ukrainian history, and especially of World War II. Therefore, a nationalist reevaluation of the history of World War II became a central element in constructing an anti-Soviet Ukrainian national narrative.[20]

The ethnically centered approach also found its vivid reflection in new textbooks. As several authors argue, most of the history textbooks published in the mid-1990s follow a monolithic narrative perspective presenting the Ukrainians as an almost homogeneous nation with special emphasis on its victimization.[21] In most schoolbooks, the fact that Ukraine had become a major killing field during the Holocaust is marginalized. In Jilge's opinion, the ethnically centered narrative is an improvement on Soviet schoolbooks, where any special mention of the murder of Jews was completely suppressed. At the same time, in new Ukrainian school textbooks, the Holocaust was not connected to the national history in any way. The histories of this time usually presented the events of the Shoah in other European countries, but not for Ukraine. Thus, Jilge concludes, this limited information about the Ukrainian context of the Holocaust in Ukrainian history textbooks leads to paradoxical consequences: the result of silence is not only an exclusion of the dark sides from the national narrative but also an exclusion of the Ukrainian "Righteous among Nations" who risked their lives to save their Jewish neighbors.[22] Analyzing the representations of the Holocaust in the textbooks on Ukrainian and world history, Johan Dietsch comes to similar conclusions, accentuating the structural reasons behind the exclusion. Thus, Dietsch argues, in the post-Soviet period, Ukrainian history has been constructed as nation-centered rather than state-centered and Ukrainians were put at the core of a historical narrative, leaving little space for the story of other people in Ukraine.[23]

Jilge's essay on the image of the "other" in the Ukrainian narratives of World War II was titled "Competing Victimhoods." Many other scholars also tend to describe postcommunist sentiments in East European memory cultures precisely in terms of a rivalry of sufferings.[24] Alexander Etkind and Uilleam Blacker argue for a more nuanced approach to memory cultures in Eastern Europe. Competitive victimhood is indeed a strong tendency in postcommunist memory debates, but one needs to be careful when mechanically applying Western memory study paradigms to local contexts. As Etkind and Blacker argue, reflections on the Holocaust in postwar Europe undoubtedly shaped the current conception of human rights, which, in turn, became an important framework for discussing communist crimes after the collapse of the Soviet Union. And memories of the Gulag, the famines, and other socialist atrocities have also contributed to the formation of Western ideas of human rights.[25]

As a possible alternative to competitive memory—a zero-sum struggle over the scarce resources of memory—Michael Rothberg suggests the concept of *multidirectional memory*: a subject of ongoing negotiation and cross-referencing. Bridging Holocaust and postcolonial studies, Rothberg considers "a series of interventions through which social actors bring multiple traumatic pasts into a heterogeneous and changing post-World War II present."[26] In our opinion, the models of Eastern European Holocaust memory should be understood in the dynamics of both competition and multidirectionality. In the Ukrainian case, this tendency can be vividly illustrated by the memory activity of Viktor Yushchenko, the third president of Ukraine, who was notorious for his priority-driven historical politics. On the one hand, he was quite active in challenging the policy of state nonintervention in Shoah commemoration, by mentioning the Holocaust in his inauguration speech, for example, and emphasizing the necessity of fighting antisemitism and xenophobia in his politics, or by initiating and collaborating in organizing the Second World Forum of Holocaust Memory during the 65th Anniversary Remembrance of the Babi Yar Tragedy.[27] But in Yushchenko's speeches, commemorative activities, and legislative initiatives, the Shoah usually appeared along with the Holodomor, which became the core of a new official historical narrative.[28] In the internal policy such a juxtaposition was meant to "evoke empathy between two suffering peoples" and to approximate the catastrophe of the Jews to that of average Ukrainians, while at the international level this framework was often used to promote the recognition of the Holodomor as genocide.[29] At the same time, Yushchenko's politics featured attempts to "surpass" the number of Shoah victims (by promoting the debatable number of 7–10 million Holodomor victims).[30] Moreover, his approach to Holocaust commemoration fell short of recognizing the role of Ukrainians in the Shoah, particularly members of the OUN and UPA, who were now promoted as new national heroes.[31]

Transnational communities of memory—such as members of the European Union—often play the role of catalyst in the rethinking of national historical paradigms. As many scholars argue, the Holocaust became one of the negative founding myths of united Europe. The genocide of European Jewry was invented and started in Nazi Germany and carried, to various degrees, in almost all European states.[32] Therefore, various forms of official recognition and commemoration of the Holocaust as well as recognition of local participation in it have become a kind of precondition for entry into the European Union.

Even though Ukraine has not yet become an official candidate for admission to the European Union, new European and global strategies of coming to terms with a difficult past have also had an influence on the politics of memory as well as on popular attitudes. In 2000, Ukraine was one of the participants of the Stockholm International Forum on the Holocaust, but so far the country has not become a member of the International Holocaust Remembrance Alliance (IHRA)—an international organization aimed at advancing and promoting Holocaust education, research, and remembrance worldwide. Yet the democratization of the public sphere as well as closer contacts between Ukrainian and Western intellectuals fostered discussions on the "white spots" of Ukrainian history, including the Holocaust and the nationalists' role in it. While most such debates have been limited to professional circles, there were several important public discussions—namely in the *Krytyka* and *Ukraina Moderna* academic journals and on the *Istorychna Pravda* (Historical truth) internet portal.[33] Several Ukrainian universities have offered regular or guest courses on the history of the Holocaust in their curricula—namely Ivan Franko Lviv National University, Taras Shevchenko Kyiv National University, Ukrainian Catholic University, and Kyiv-Mohyla Academy. Two major all-Ukrainian nongovernmental organizations are directly involved in improving Holocaust research and education: the Ukrainian Center for Holocaust Studies (Kyiv, since 2002) and the Tkuma Center for Holocaust Studies (Dnipropetrovsk, since 1999). The latter has also initiated and cofounded a museum, "The Memory of the Jewish People and the Holocaust in Ukraine" in Dnipro (opened in 2012). Both centers lack state support and rely mostly on international funding. As Tomasz Stryjek rightly points out, the civic factor has superseded the state in Holocaust commemorations in Ukraine, and in some cases even assumed its role.[34]

Such tendencies in Ukrainian discussions on Holocaust memory are diverse, dynamic, and fluid. There is no doubt that the events of the Euromaidan, the annexation of Crimea, and the war in Donbas became turning points in Ukraine's history, which also strongly influenced the field of memory politics. For now, it is difficult to state what impact recent events will have on the perception of Ukrainian history in general and the Holocaust in particular. New tendencies—such as the declared European vector of Ukrainian foreign policy, the growing role of the governmental Ukrainian Institute of National Memory, and the adoption of the controversial decommunization laws, as well as the information war against Russian propaganda and the use of history as a weapon in it are very important in this context and require further analysis.[35]

The Holocaust in Popular Memory: Regional and Sociodemographic Aspects

The Jewish Anti-Fascist Committee started documentation of Nazi crimes against Jews and of Holocaust testimonies while World War II was still going on. But the subsequent persecution of its members as well as the prohibition of the *The Black Book* in the Soviet Union made these findings unavailable for a wider Soviet audience until the times of Perestroika.[36] Several large-scale international projects, designed to collect the oral testimonies of the survivors and eyewitnesses of the Holocaust in Ukraine, were launched after 1991.[37] These efforts have an inestimable meaning after decades of silence about the tragedy. As Patrick Desbois, a French priest who traveled across Ukraine and Belarus in the early 2000s to locate the sites of Jewish mass graves, recalls in his interview for the Ukrainian television channel 5TV, "We went from one village to another talking to ordinary poor people, who 70 years ago were forced to dig graves for their Jewish neighbors. When we asked them why they did not tell about this horror earlier, their answer was that nobody had asked."[38] This quote neatly points to the lack of interest in the memory of the Shoah in Ukrainian society, not only during Soviet rule but also after its collapse.

Speaking of academic scholarship, the collective (non)memory of the Shoah in Ukraine remains a largely understudied topic. Most research studies have addressed the question in the context of related issues—such as the oral history and collective memory of World

War II (Gelinada Grinchenko, Iryna Sklokina), commemoration in urban spaces and place memory (Uilleam Blacker, Maria Lewicka, Viktoriia Sereda), studies on antisemitism and xenophobia in Ukrainian society (Volodymyr Paniotto, Ireneusz Krzeminski), or studies on trauma in postmodern Ukrainian literature (Iryna Starovoyt).[39] A number of authors considered the level and context of the inclusion (or, rather, exclusion) of the Holocaust in Ukraine's official historical discourse and politics of memory[40]. Despite the fact that these studies focused on representation of the Holocaust in specific political, spatial, and media contexts, little attention was paid to the perception of the Shoah on a vernacular level in Ukrainian society. Among the exceptions we can name several interesting case studies—thus Anna Wylegała analyzed the collective memory and forgetting about the Holocaust in the Western Ukrainian town of Zhovkva, and Olena Ivanova compared awareness and memory of the Holocaust among university students in L'viv and Kharkiv.[41] In her dissertation, historian Anna Medvedovska has thoroughly addressed the reception of the Holocaust in official politics, cultural memory (literature, movies, museums), and academic discussions of both the Soviet and the post-Soviet period in Ukraine.[42]

The results of a research project called "Region, Nation, and Beyond: Interdisciplinary and Intercultural Reconceptualization of Ukraine" (2012–15) give us the opportunity to address the question of Holocaust memory in Ukraine in a complex way.[43] The overarching objective of the project was to challenge the dominance of the nation-state paradigm in analyses of Ukraine by illustrating the interrelationship between national and regional dynamics of change. Among the five focus areas (economy, religion, language, literature, and history), historical memory was studied as one of the identity-building factors. The project included both a quantitative (an all-Ukrainian statistical surveys, February 2013, N = 6,000 and February–March 2015, N = 6,000) and a qualitative (in-depth interviews and focus group discussions in twelve Ukrainian regions) component.

A statistical questionnaire has its pros and cons as a tool for studying the phenomenon of collective memory. It allows us to speak about general tendencies in collective memory while the personal dimension and the motivations behind certain choices remain beyond its scope. Several questions on the perception of most positive and negative events in Ukrainian history were asked in 2013 and 2015 "Region, Nation and Beyond" statistical surveys. To avoid giving any hints to respondents or imposing a certain frame of answers to them, a set of open questions about positive and negative events and personalities in Ukrainian history was purposely placed prior to another set, which included close-ended questions measuring the respondents' attitudes toward previously given events and personalities. As a result, the survey provides us with interesting information about the patterns of the respondents' perceptions of Ukrainian history. In the following section I will analyze the question of Holocaust memory in this context.

As we can see in table 8.1, the Great Famine (the Holodomor), occupies a central place in the narrative of collective suffering. A quarter of the respondents recalled it as the most negative event in the history of Ukraine (open question[44]). All in all, this result can be understood as evidence of a significant influence of official memory politics on public opinion. As the results of another survey, conducted by the sociological group "Rating" show, since Yushchenko's presidency, the support for recognizing Holodomor as genocide has been steadily growing in Ukrainian society: from 61 percent in 2010 to 80 percent in 2015.[45]

Table 8.1. The most negative events in the history of Ukraine, 2013.

Event	Percentage
Holodomor	24.4%
World War II	20.7%
Collapse of the Soviet Union	14.1%
Soviet period, repressions	8.8%
Chornobyl	7.7%
Political and economic problems of the 1990s	7.1%
Orange Revolution	6.6%
Holocaust	0.9%
Don't know/Not applicable	15.6%

Source: "Region, Nation and Beyond" survey (2013).

Table 8.1 vividly reflects the diverse and sometimes contradictory nature of Ukrainians' collective vision of the past: while for 8.8 percent the Soviet regime and its political repressions signified the most negative historical experience, more than 14 percent mourned the collapse of the Soviet Union. The Holocaust was named only by 53 respondents (less than 1%). Although this result is indeed very low, the Holocaust appeared to be the only tragedy of a group other than Ukrainians that has appeared in the list of the most negative events. And even though the year 2013 marked the seventieth anniversary of the Volyn massacre, which was accompanied by heated debates in the media, the respondents did not mention it at all. Another example is the deportation of the Crimean Tatars (May 1944), which was recalled by only 5 respondents—all of whom identified themselves as representatives of this ethnic minority.

In addition, the respondents were asked to evaluate the importance of fifteen prelisted events or periods in the history of Ukraine on a 5-point scale (where 1 = not important, 2 = rather not important, 3 = neutral, 4 = rather important, and 5 = very important). Table 8.2 shows mean values on this scale by *oblast'*. World War II was evaluated as one of the most important events, which can be explained not only by its centrality in Soviet and Ukrainian memory politics but also by its deep-rootedness in family histories and biographical memories. The other three events with very high importance were the state-founding pillars of Ukraine's official historical narrative: the Kyiv Rus period, the Cossack state, and the proclamation of Ukrainian independence in 1991. The Holocaust was estimated as a rather significant event (mean of 3.8) but, most important, only 1.5 percent of respondents in 2013 and 1.73 percent in 2015 were not able to answer the question about the Holocaust. To compare, in 2013 more than 13 percent refused to answer the question about the Austrian-Hungarian period in the history of Ukraine, and 9.6 percent gave no answer about the Polish-Lithuanian Commonwealth. A nonresponse in this case is the indicator of general unfamiliarity with the particular historical event or period.

The question on the importance of events in the history of Ukraine also revealed regional divisions in their perception. In the case of the Holocaust, these differences were quite noticeable (see table 8.3). Thus, in the Ternopil and Khmelnytsky regions, where the

Table 8.2. Estimated importance of selected events and periods in the history of Ukraine (average on the scale between 1 = not important at all and 5 = very important).

Event	2013 Mean	2015 Mean
World War II	4.49	4.39
Kyiv Rus	4.43	4.43
Ukrainian Cossacks	4.43	4.41
Independence in 1991	4.34	4.48
Soviet Union	4.16	3.99
Pereiaslav Treaty	4.1	3.88
Holodomor	4.09	4.07
Ukrainian Renaissance in 20th century	4.08	4.16
Ukrainian People's Republic	4.04	4.16
Holocaust	3.9	3.82
Russian Empire	3.73	3.38
Mazepa Uprising	3.65	3.8
Polish-Lithuanian Commonwealth	3.43	3.52
OUN/UPA	3.35	3.78
Austro-Hungarian Empire	3.15	3.28
Euromaidan	0	4.22
Crimea and Donbas conflict	0	4.1

Source: "Region, Nation and Beyond" surveys (2013 and 2015).

scale of the Shoah was significant, the mean importance assigned was relatively low (4.2 and 3.9 respectively), while in northwestern parts Kherson and Kirovohrad Oblast, as well as in the most multicultural regions of Ukraine (Zakarpattia, Crimea, and Chernivtsi regions), it was predominantly seen as a rather important or very important event (see table 8.3). Various factors—such as the activism of the local Jewish communities, the nongovernmental organizations, and educational initiatives—could have influenced such differentiation, and further research is needed to answer the question of the reasons behind it. For now, we can infer that ethnic and cultural diversity of the local population contribute to a more open attitude toward the history of other communities, including traumatic memories. As we can see from table 8.3, how the Holocaust is perceived does not simply fit into the "east-west divided memory" model, which has become somewhat cliché in Ukrainian studies. Moreover, sociodemographic factors (such as education, gender, age, and size of settlement) turned out not to have a significant influence on the estimated importance of the Holocaust in Ukrainian history.

As for the issue of competitive victimhood, respondents were asked about effects of the tragedy of World War II on various groups (see fig. 8.1). The respondents were to estimate the level of suffering of different nations during the war on a scale between 1 (they did not suffer at all) and 7 (they were victims of genocide). The pregiven list included only ethnic groups, and therefore, some groups of victims of Nazi atrocities were not mentioned (for example, homosexuals, prisoners of war, or Jehovah witnesses).

It is not surprising that the respondents perceived their own group (Ukrainians) as the main victims of World War II, but Jews appeared to be the second group in this "rating."

Table 8.3. Regional distribution of the estimated importance of the Holocaust in Ukrainian history (mean value per *oblast*).

Oblast	2013	2015
Cherkasy	3.8	3.8
Chernihiv	3.7	4.1
Chernivtsi	4.3	3.8
Crimea	4.3	—
Dnipropetrovsk	3.9	3.9
Donetsk	3.8	3.8
Ivano-Frankivsk	3.8	3.3
Kharkiv	3.8	3.9
Kherson	4.2	3.5
Khmelnytskyi	2.9	4.1
Kyiv	4.2	4.1
Kirovohrad	4.6	4
Kyiv City	4.3	4.4
Lugansk	3.9	3.6
L'viv	3.7	3.8
Mykolayiv	4	4
Odesa	3.6	3.8
Poltava	4	3.6
Rivne	3.9	4
Sumy	3.9	4
Ternopil	3.2	3.9
Vinnytsia	3.6	3.5
Volyn	4.1	4.5
Zakarpattia	4.1	3.6
Zaporizhzhya	4	4.1
Zhytomyr	4.1	2.9

Source: "Region, Nation and Beyond" surveys (2013 and 2015).

Thus, 68 percent of respondents agreed that Jewish people were victims of genocide; the nonresponse rate was very low (2%). We can therefore conclude that general awareness of the Jewish Holocaust is relatively high, whereas, for example, the fate of the Roma people during World War II remains a blank page (only 24.8 percent of respondents believe the Roma were victims of genocide, whereas 20 percent stated they knew nothing on this topic). We also see a significant impact of the Soviet narrative of the war: the deethnicized and generalized category of the "Soviet people" is perceived as the major victim group along with Russians and Belarusians, while, for example, the Polish people are seen as having been much less aggrieved by the war. Even though a question about the role of various ethnic groups as the perpetrators in World War II was not posed, we can assume that this lower estimation of Polish suffering might be the result of the respondents' unwillingness to tackle the uncomfortable issue of the Volyn tragedy and the Ukrainians' role in it. Sociodemographic factors were influential here, as older people tend to estimate the level of the suffering of Jews, Soviet

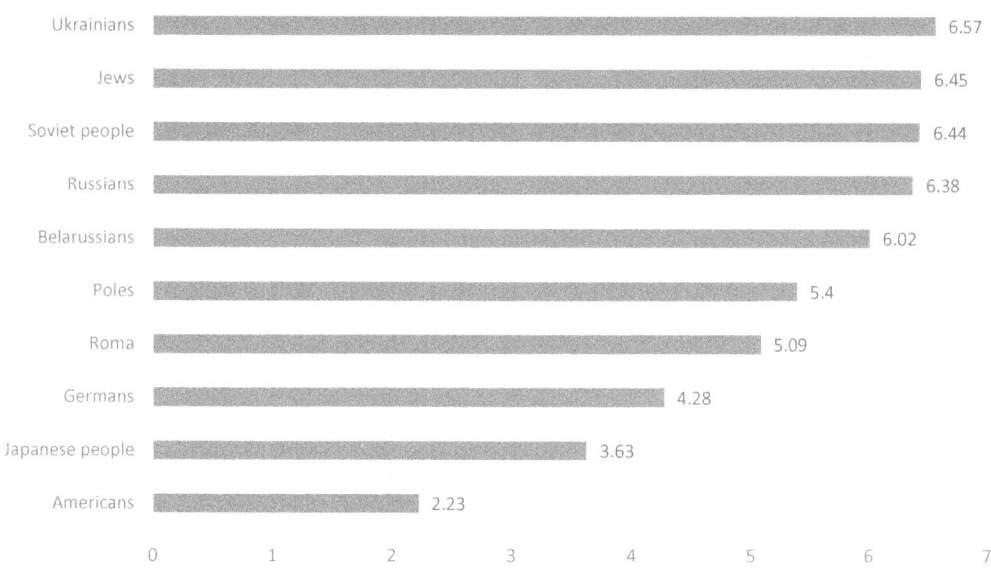

Fig. 8.1 Estimated suffering of various groups during World War II (mean). *Source*: "Region, Nation and Beyond" project survey (2013). Prepared by the author.

people, Russians, and the Roma people higher than do the younger generations. The level of education correlated positively with the estimation of suffering of both the German and the Roma people. One of the most interesting outcomes was the impact of the native language factor—bilingual people tend to express a more empathic attitude, estimating the suffering of groups higher than do those who speak only Ukrainian or Russian.

As we can see from the statistical data, both the Soviet and national Ukrainian models of the historical past influenced the respondents' perceptions and attitudes toward the Shoah in Ukrainian history. It would be wrong to assert that average Ukrainians know nothing about the Holocaust: only 1.5 percent of respondents gave no response to the question about its importance and 68 percent believe Jews became the victims of genocide during the war (see fig. 8.1). At the same time, one can assume that the general knowledge has been internalized not so much from education or official memory politics but from a globalized mass culture—such as in fiction, films, the internet, and so on. Therefore, it is crucial to address the memory of the Holocaust on a micro level in order to investigate the peculiarities of local memory cultures.

Local Dimension: Memory and Oblivion of the Holocaust in Postwar Shtetls (Case Studies)

Because of the Holocaust, most of the generations in postwar Ukraine had little to no direct contact with representatives of the Jewish community. Therefore, attitudes toward Jewish heritage were derived from secondary sources, such as from literature, schoolbooks, mass media, family stories, museums, and preserved traces of Jewish history in urban landscapes.

Forced population movements, however, and several decades of Soviet ideology heavily affected transmission of the local memory. More often than not, the only sources of knowledge for the inhabitants of former shtetls, who grew up in the shadow of ruined synagogues and dilapidated cemeteries, were vanishing material traces of the Jewish community. At the same time, the Ukrainians' fragmented perception of Jewish history in their towns and cities cannot be reduced to either philosemitism or antisemitism. Between these two extremes one can find a whole spectrum of emotions and attitudes—such as fear, curiosity, envy, shame, admiration, suspicion, or simply indifference.

In this section, I consider the local dimension of Holocaust memory by examining cases of several Ukrainian towns that had, before the war, been homes to large Jewish communities and became mass-killing sites during the Shoah (namely Zolochiv, Vyzhnytsia, and Balta). In the interwar period, these towns belonged to different states (Poland, Romania, and the Soviet Union, respectively), and therefore comparisons can be made between regions—both administrative and historical (such as Galicia, Podillia, and Bukovina). Although these case studies cannot be called fully representative as reflecting the all-Ukrainian situation, an analysis allows us to show the diversity of the local cultures of memory. Forty in-depth interviews with the current inhabitants of these localities (primarily ordinary dwellers, but also "memory actors"—history teachers, museum workers, etc., and representatives of existing Jewish communities) were conducted in May–August of 2013 in the framework of the "Region, Nation and Beyond" qualitative research project. The methodology of a semistructured interview was applied. In the first part of the interview, the respondents were asked to freely narrate their biographies; in the second part, more specific questions were posed about their perception of the local and national history as well as of the symbolic urban landscape and its changes. These questions were formulated in an unimposing way in order to diminish any influence of the interviewer on the topics that the respondent chose to emphasize. Therefore, contextual (e.g., "Who lived here in the past?") rather than direct (e.g., "Do you know anything about the history of Jews in your town?") questions were asked. In this case, the lack of a response was an equally important research finding because it would show not only how certain topics and communities are remembered but also how they are forgotten. The interviews will let us look at the processes by which the national, local, and international narratives of the historical past, as manifested in cultural landscapes, become a part of personal, individual narratives. In particular, I investigated how the dominant postwar narratives in memory politics (Soviet and later Ukrainian) have shaped and continue to shape personal attitudes and memory of the Holocaust and what place the Shoah occupies in biographical narratives.

On the basis of the preliminary interview analysis, I will generally reflect on whether and how the history and annihilation of the Jewish community as a whole is remembered. For now, I will concentrate on the main tendencies and shared narratives. Before coming to any conclusions, it is important to briefly introduce the general background and history of local Jewish communities.

Balta is situated in the Odesa region, but historically it belongs to Podillia and was a borderland town on the frontier between the Polish-Lithuanian Commonwealth and the Ottoman Empire. Jewish life flourished there from the 16th century—the town became one of the main trade centers of the Pale of Settlement in the Russian Empire and later in the Soviet Union, with the share of the Jewish population varying from 56 percent (1897) to 39.5 percent (1926). Prior to the Holocaust, the local community had suffered from anti-Jewish violence several times—during the Koliivshchyna uprising (1768), the pogroms of 1882 and 1905, and during the Civil War of 1919. During World War II, Balta became a part of Transnistria district under the Romanian administration. A Jewish ghetto was created in the town in which many people died from hunger and diseases, and around 1,500 were deported to labor camps. Around 2,000 Jews survived the Holocaust (approximately 40 percent of the prewar population), and so Jewish life continued in Balta also after the war. Even though today the community consists of only about 100 members, it is very vibrant. The head of the community is actively engaged in local political and cultural life. The old Jewish cemetery has partly been preserved in the town, but at the time of the fieldwork no synagogue was functioning and the community gathered at the local café Ivushka to conduct religious and civic celebrations.

The history of the Jewish community in Zolochiv (L'viv region) is typical for a Galician shtetl. Jews and Armenians settled here in the 16th–17th centuries under the privileges of the royal Sobieski family, who owned the town. From the end of the 19th century till the eve of World War II, Jews constituted about half of the town's population. In the first days of the Nazi occupation, a wave of extreme anti-Jewish violence, similar to the infamous L'viv pogrom, erupted in Zolochiv.[46] After the bodies of political prisoners were found in the Soviet People's Commissariat for Internal Affairs (NKVD) prison (situated in the former 17th-century Zolochiv castle), the Jews, accused of having cooperated with the Soviets, were brutally beaten and murdered—mostly by their non-Jewish neighbors and the Ukrainian auxiliary police. The pogrom began on July 4, 1941, lasted for three days, and resulted in three to four thousand Jewish victims. Subsequently, the local Jewish community was almost entirely annihilated in the ghetto in mass shootings and in deportations to the Bełżec death camp. Only a small group of Jews survived the Shoah, and today there is basically no Jewish community in the town. The Zolochiv castle is now considered one of the symbols of the town and has become a very popular tourist attraction. The dark side of its history has not been completely forgotten (there is an exhibition about the victims of the NKVD prison), but the story of the pogrom and the murder of the Jews, which partly took place in the castle's courtyard, is hardly ever mentioned. A debate was sparked in Ukrainian academic circles by Sofia Hrachova's article "Did They Live among Us?" (2005) followed by Marko Tsarynnyk's "Zolochiv Is Silent."[47] The authors criticized the local authorities for tabooing the subject of Ukrainians' role in the Holocaust and neglecting the disturbing matter. The topic did not attract wider public attention beyond the scholarly debates.

Vyzhnytsia (Chernivtsi region)—a town with a particularly rich Jewish history—is situated in yet another borderland region—Bukovina. This mountainous town was home to a famous Hasidic community. Baal Shem Tov (or Besht, the founder of Hasidism) is believed to have visited Vyzhnytsia. His disciple, Menachem Mendel Hager, settled in the town in 1854 and quickly gathered many followers around him. His successor, Rav Yisrael, founded a yeshiva in the town, which attracted students from all over Bukovina. According to the census of 1880, the town's Jewish population was 3,795 (91%), while on the eve of World War II, there were 5,000 Jews in Vyzhnytsia. In the interwar period, and during the Nazi occupation, the town was under Romanian authority. The majority of the local Jews perished in the camps of Mohyliv and Dzhuryn, and the town's population changed completely after the war. Today, Vyzhnytsia's Jewish heritage attracts numerous Hasidic pilgrimages, particularly to places connected with Baal Shem Tov and Menachem Mendel Hager. Most of the prewar synagogues and Jewish heritage sites survived the war but are currently used for different purposes; for example, the tzaddik's palace was used as a butter factory in Soviet times and is currently abandoned and neglected, and the central synagogue has been used as a House of Culture since the 1950s.

The local inhabitants' awareness of Jewish history in their towns remains rather ambiguous. On the one hand, Jews were almost never mentioned in the freely narrated biographical part of the interviews. This can primarily be explained by the fact that most of the respondents were born or came to these towns after the war, and so their direct contact with any representatives of the Jewish community was very limited. On the other hand, the interviewees tended to acknowledge the significant historical presence of Jews in the prewar period by commonly calling their localities "Jewish towns." Most often, the respondents first mentioned the Jews in the context of describing the composition of the city's population (the local "imagined community") and then the changes in its structure. The Jewish history of the towns was commonly juxtaposed with their contemporary Ukrainian identity:

> There are Jews, not so many already, but there are, and in the past we had a lot of them. (Balta, female, 64, nurse)[48]

> There were seven synagogues. Hasidism spread its teaching here. These were one people, one history, and now there is another and only one man remained from all of this Jewish community. (Vyzhnytsia, male, 58, local administration member)

A major source of knowledge about the Jewish past turned out to be stories transmitted in families. Institutions of cultural memory—such as museums or schools—were almost never mentioned in this context. Typical narratives of Jewish life were depersonalized and concerned mainly the economic sphere. Apart from ethnic boundaries, class divisions were emphasized quite often. Two stereotypical images appeared in a number of interviews—that of the Jewish merchant and that of the Jewish doctor:

> People say there were many Jews, even my grandmother told me that all the shops here belonged to the Jews. There were also Poles, Ukrainians, some Germans, and maybe also some Tatars. (Zolochiv, male, 54, worker)

> Respondent (R): Well, Vyzhnytsia was a Jewish town. I remember my dad telling me about that.
> Interviewer (I): Your father was born here? What exactly did he tell you?
> R: He told me that Jews were everywhere, Vyzhnytsia was a Jewish town and ordinary people, peasants—they lived on the outskirts. (Vyzhnytsia, female, 20, student)

> We were under Polish rule, and my mother told me there used to be a lot of Poles and Jews and whenever someone was sick and could not go to the city, they took a horse carriage and looked for the Jewish doctor, because he was very smart—that is what I remember from my mother's stories. (Zolochiv, female, 43, social worker)

Other sources of knowledge had local peculiarities. For example, in Balta, people mentioned having actual contact with the Jewish community, and in Vyzhnytsia encounters with Hasidic pilgrims played an important role:

> Before the war, . . . My grandma told me there were wealthy *pany* (landowners). She was born in 1932 and remembers that Germans, Romanians, and Hungarians were here. However, it was not that bad here because we have mountains, a very large area that is protected—people in Eastern Ukraine suffered much more. Of course, the Jews were also here—we have a synagogue that later became a butter factory. . . . Every year these people come and visit our places—it is a kind of pilgrimage. The town has Jewish roots, but eventually the Hutsuls settled here and Vyzhnytsia became "the gate to the Carpathian mountains." (Vyzhnytsia, male, 28, worker)

> R: I know there was a war.
> I: What do you know about the war in your town?
> R: That there was a Jewish ghetto.
> I: Where did you find out about the ghetto? What exactly do you know?
> R: Not much. We've got a Jewish community—they recall it. They always celebrate their holidays together. (Balta, female, 50, seamstress)

Because of the lack of pieces of knowledge, the contemporary inhabitants tend to replenish the voids in their imagination of Jewish life in the frames of their own biographical experiences and cultural backgrounds. This is a phenomenon that I would call *shield memory*. It results in the linguistic and cultural domestication of local Jewish spaces and cultural practices. This way, an ohel becomes a *ievreiska kaplychka* (Jewish chapel), a rabbi becomes a "Jewish priest," or a mikva becomes *vodokhreshcha* (baptism). This is very well reflected in the quote below from an interview with an inhabitant of Vyzhnytsia, who described the Vyzhenka River where local zaddikim used to take a ritual bath:

> And at one time there lived here their famous high priest. . . . The holy man who worked miracles, like Jesus Christ, though it is a tricky question, because each author writes differently. Well, he was an outstanding person, that is why all these people came to honor the place where he lived, where he studied, and the river where he was baptized. (Vyzhnytsia, male, 48, electrician)

This seemingly harmless tendency leads to the emergence of historical myths and silencing dissonant past. Thus, a shared narrative, encountered in many interviews in all three localities, is the idea that Jews disappeared from Ukrainian towns and cities because they "all left for Israel" or "just died because of old age."

> I: Who lived here in the past? And what do you know about it?
> R: My father told me before the war there where Jews, Gypsies, Moldovans, and Russians. But now it is different.
> I: How is it different and what has changed?
> R: Almost all of the Jews went to Israel. And the older ones died. (Balta, female, 50, seamstress)

> Typical inhabitants? You understand that until the 1940s it was a real Jewish town. Synagogues were everywhere. Today almost all the people here are newcomers. It is almost impossible to find Jews today, they've all left. (Vyzhnytsia, male, 63, teacher)

As can be seen, poor awareness of the local context and of the scale of the Holocaust is often replaced by one's own biographical experience of postwar Jewish neighbors migrating in the 1990s. One of the most obvious reasons behind such a distortion is the lack of knowledge on this topic, which became the result of an interrupted continuity in the towns' demographic structures as well as oblivious local memory politics about the Holocaust. Another influential factor is the tacit tabooing of violence—"a mechanism of memory aimed at excluding drastic events that might put blame on the speaker's own group."[49] When analyzing the local memory of the postwar deportation of Poles among Ukrainians in the town of Zhovkva (L'viv Oblast), Anna Wylegała describes a similar case of the interviewees choosing not to remember the connection between the mass killings of Poles in neighboring villages during the war and of them leaving the town.

Another example of such memory substitution is the belief that the Jews were actually annihilated by the Soviets (or "the Russians"), not by the Nazis. This narrative was most often encountered in the Zolochiv interviews—the town in Western Ukraine where many of the locals themselves suffered from the Soviets, the Ukrainian nationalistic underground was very active and the memory about it has strongly been cultivated since 1991, as in other localities in Galicia.[50] By blaming the Soviets, the history of one's own group's victimization is expanded to explain the disappearance of the "others" in order to emphasize the cruelty of the perpetrators. Moreover, the mechanism of defensive externalization of guilt is applied here: by putting all the blame on the Soviets, the question of one's own group's responsibility is avoided.[51] Thus, none of the respondents from Zolochiv mentioned anything about the pogrom of 1941. Such externalization is manifested even more strongly in wording patterns: by calling the perpetrators "the Russians" the respondents tend to separate the we-group from the Soviet system that Ukraine was a part of.

> Who lived in Zolochiv? Well, apart from the Ukrainians, there were Poles and Jews. Well, then, of course, the Russians came and turned everything upside down and harmed people's lives—all those killings, resettlements, deportations—it is a nightmare. This is a bleeding wound and there are still many people who suffered from them. . . . And the impact, I think that the Russians had the greatest negative impact. (Zolochiv, male, 45, artist)

> Vyzhnytsia was a Jewish town. . . . Then the Russians came and were killing them all and deporting them and everything changed since then. At least, that is what I know, what my father told me. (Vyzhnytsia, female, 20, student)

While the traumatic memories of World War II constituted a significant share of family-transmitted memories, the Holocaust occupies a marginal place in them. Both the eyewitnesses of war events and their children tended to avoid the topic, or described it as "undesirable":

> I: Are there any historical subjects you try to avoid?
> R: Well, I cannot judge the other generations but the past hides its own dark sides. If we take the history of these places, there were people of different nationalities—some were tolerant towards each other, and others had a different attitude. If Ispas did not allow the local Jews to be killed, the situation in Milievo was different and the Germans destroyed them all.[52] (Vyzhnytsia, male, 48, electrician)

I did not notice any national divisions. There were lots of Jews and then they started moving to Israel. However, my mom taught me that people should treat each person favorably, no matter the nationality. Moreover, during the war when the train was going to Uman and the Germans bombed it, our mother took me and my little brother and tried to escape through the rye to the river. She then fell down and a man helped her. She looked at him and she realized he was a Jew. And since then she was telling me: "They saved my life and yours, so no matter what, we have to treat them well, just like the Ukrainians." (Vyzhnytsia, female, 79, teacher)

The motif of tolerating a person "no matter" his or her Jewish origin is a recurrent pattern in a number of interviews. Here the respondent felt the need to justify her good attitude toward Jews by telling the story of her family's rescue. All in all, the oblivion about and distortion of the Holocaust can be considered as a part of the wider process of "forgetting, which is constitutive in the formation of a new identity."[53] As Paul Connerton argues, in this case forgetting becomes a process by which newly shared memories are constructed because a new set of memories is frequently accompanied by a set of tacitly shared silences. In that the Holocaust may cast a shadow on the positive image of the ingroup, it becomes an undesirable topic. It is easy to notice that in the narrations of the local Jewish history, the "us-them" dichotomy is very strongly manifested. This particularly concerns attitudes toward Jewish heritage and attempts to shift responsibility of caring about it solely to the absent Jewish community. Such a tendency is often referred to as *pillarization of memory*, the belief that each population's group is the custodian of its own heritage.[54] Sometimes this belief also has strong antisemitic roots, for example, by emphasizing the idea of the omnipotence, conspiracy, or illimitable wealth of the Jews. The durability of antisemitic stereotypes in post-Holocaust societies has often been addressed—particularly in East Central Europe.[55] Antisemitism may become a strategy of "blaming in order not to be blamed" and of avoiding questions about one's own group's responsibility—both for the disappearance of the Jews and for the dilapidated state of their heritage.[56]

At the same time, the transnational memory of the Holocaust, mediated through museums, films, literature, or the internet, has also been shaping individual imaginations. For example, a retired teacher from Vyzhnytsia (female, 79) remembered visiting the Auschwitz museum in detail and was very empathic about the fate of the Jewish people there. At the same time, she did not mention anything about the annihilation of the Jewish population in her own town. Therefore, general knowledge about the Shoah does not imply awareness of its local dimension. We can also observe the influence of the age factor: among the respondents of the younger generations (below thirty) in all three towns, recollections of the history of the local Jewish communities or the Holocaust were much rarer than among respondents age forty and above.

Another important external factor that shapes attitudes toward local Jewish heritage and Holocaust sites is tourism. As we have discussed before, in some cases the very presence of Jewish tourists or pilgrims became a trigger of the local people's own interest in the Jewish history of their towns. Demand in this case, however, preceded supply and a very observable tendency is the orientation toward commercialized representations of the

Jewish past, mostly for the visitors and not the local inhabitants. This was a part of my experience as a researcher—while interviewing "memory entrepreneurs" in former shtetls, that is, local guides, historians, or museum workers, I had to be very careful not to hint to them that I was particularly interested in Jewish heritage, because doing so might have completely changed their narrative of the local history. Ashworth, Graham and Tunbridge describe this phenomenon as the *bipolar* or *double heritage approach*, that is, the presentation of two different public heritages in parallel, one for external and the other for internal consumption.[57]

Conclusions

Population movements and deportations, erasing memory politics of the Soviet era, and the indifferent approach of the Ukrainian state are the most significant factors that have shaped the current state of Holocaust memory in Ukrainian society. Official Ukrainian historical politics since 1991 is actively engaged in the processes of nation (re)building, and the place that the Shoah occupies in it should be understood through the dynamics of both memory and oblivion, of competition and multidirectionality. The Holocaust remains a dissonant topic for the formation of a common Ukrainian identity in that it may question the positive image of the "we-group," from which Jews are still largely excluded. The attitudes toward the Shoah are strongly influenced by the dominant tendency of understanding Ukrainianness in ethnic rather than civic terms. These tendencies and challenges find reflection in the popular memory. On the one hand, the Holocaust as a European tragedy is not unknown to average Ukrainians, and the majority recognize that the Jews were victims of genocide during the war. At the same time, general knowledge about the Shoah does not imply awareness of its local dimension. As the case study of three post-shtetl towns reveals, the transmission of memory about anti-Jewish atrocities as a part of the local history is very fragmented. With little to no presence of Jewish communities and a general lack of attention on the topic from the institutions of cultural memory, this transmission is often limited to family frameworks, where it might become distorted. A number of factors shape local memory culture and the inclusion or exclusion of Jewish history in it: such as the visibility of the urban traces of the Jewish past, the presence or absence of a Jewish community today, Jewish heritage tourism and religious pilgrimages, the activity of local "memory entrepreneurs." Although each of the discussed case studies has its own peculiarities that deserve separate research, we can distinguish common tendencies in Holocaust memory formation—such as the phenomena of shield memory, the tabooing of violence, defensive externalization of guilt, and ingroup bias that results in "othering," stereotyping, and pillarization of Jewish history.

Notes

1. Dawidowicz, *War against Jews*, 403.
2. Desbois, *Holocaust*.

3. See Podol's'kyi, "Ukrain'ske suspil'stvo"; Dietsch, *Making Sense*; Himka, *Ukrainians, Jews and the Holocaust*; Portnov. "The Holocaust in the Public Discourse."

4. For example, Portnov, "The Holocaust in the Public Discourse"; Amar, "Disturbed Silence"; Rudling, "Memories of 'Holodomor'"; Hrytsak, *Strasti*; Himka and Michlic, *Bringing the Dark Past to Light*; Bartov, *Erased*; Fainberg, "Memory at the Margins."

5. Ivanova, "Ukrainian High School Students"; Jilge, "Competing Victimhoods"; Dietsch, *Making Sense*.

6. Wylegała, "(Nie)pamięć na gruzach"; Ivanova, "Ukrainian High School Students."

7. Anderson, *Imagined Communities*.

8. Hirsch, "Generation," 103.

9. Blacker, "Living."

10. Landsberg, *Prosthetic Memory*, 3.

11. Himka, "Reception of the Holocaust," 626.

12. See more on Soviet cultural-political perspective on the Holocaust in Medvedovska, "Holokost v Ukraini."

13. See Gitelman, "Soviet Reactions"; Hrytsak, *Strasti*, 51–61.

14. Amar, "Disturbed Silence," 160.

15. Rudling, "Memories of Holodomor," 233.

16. Jilge, "Competing Victimhoods," 122.

17. Himka, "Reception of the Holocaust," 651.

18. Jilge, "Competing Victimhoods," 121.

19. Subtelny, *Ukraine*.

20. Jilge, "Competing Victimhoods," 104.

21. See Jilge, "Competing Victimhoods"; Dietsch, *Making Sense*.

22. Jilge, "Competing Victimhoods."

23. Dietsch, *Making Sense*.

24. Rudling, "Memories of Holodomor"; Himka, "Reception of the Holocaust"; Dietsch, *Making Sense*.

25. Etkind and Blacker, "Introduction," *Memory and Theory*, 1–22.

26. Rothberg, *Multidirectional Memory*, 4.

27. It is interesting that Yushchenko inscribed Holocaust victims in a "glorious" narrative by urging commemoration of "the heroes who fought for the victory: the martyrs of Auschwitz and Gulag, the victims of Holodomors, deportations, and the Holocaust." The full text of the inauguration speech from January 23, 2005, is at http://www.pravda.com.ua/articles/2005/01/23/3006391/.

28. In 2008 Yushchenko submitted to the Supreme Council a draft of a new article 4421 for the Criminal Code of Ukraine prohibiting "Public denial of the Holodomor of 1932–1933 as genocide of the Ukrainian people and of the Holocaust as genocide of the Jewish people." More on the issue at "Za publichne zaperechennia Holodomoru ta Holokostu Yushchenko proponuiezaporvadyty administratyvnu ta kryminal'nu vidpovidal'nist'," Zaxid.net, January 17, 2008, http://zaxid.net/news/showNews.do?za_publichne_zaperechennya_golodomoru_ta_golokostu_yushchenko_proponuye_zaprovaditi_administrativnu_ta_kriminalnu_vidpovidalnist&objectId=1048328.

29. For example, in his speech at the Knesset on November 14, 2007, Yushchenko stressed the importance of Israel's recognizing the Holodomor as genocide, thus emphasizing the equivalency of the historical fate of the two nations. See more at "Yushchenko zaklykav Izrail do vyzannnia Holodomoru," BBC Ukrainian, November 14, 2007, http://www.bbc.com/ukrainian/indepth/story/2007/11/071114_yuschenko_israel_oh.shtml.

30. According to the latest report by the Institute for Demography of the Ukrainian Academy of Sciences (press release, November 26, 2015), the total loss of human life caused by the Holodomor in 1932–33 was around 4.5 million people. The numbers, however, are a still subject of debate. The press release is available at: http://www.idss.org.ua/arhiv/2015_26_11_press_release.pdf.

31. For a more detailed analysis of Yushchenko's political stance on the Holocaust, see Stryjek, *Nevlovni Katehorii*; Hrytsak, *Strasti*, 219–61.

32. Etkind and Blacker, "Introduction," *Memory and Theory*, 20.

33. See Hrachova, "Vony zhyly sered nas?," 90, and the subsequent discussion; "Ievreis'ka spadshchyna v Ukraini." The Ukrainian translation of Himka, "Lviv Pogrom," evoked a wave of comments and discussions, including a forty-page response from the lawyer Serhii Ryabenko attempting to prove the OUN's innocence,

"Slidamy 'L'vivs'koho pogromu' Dzhona-Polia Khymky," *Istorychna Pravda*, February 20, 2013, http://www.istpravda.com.ua/articles/2013/02/20/112766/.

34. Stryjek, *Nevlovni Katehorii*, 246–53.

35. On April 9, 2015, the Ukrainian Parliament adopted a package of four decommunization laws, introducing "Remembrance and Reconciliation Day" on May 8 for victims of World War II (to counterbalance the Soviet tradition of May 9 as Victory Day), opening access to former Soviet archives, and banning Communist and Nazi symbols and names (particularly in toponymy). One of the most controversial initiatives was a bill on the legal status and commemoration of the memory of the fighters for Ukrainian independence in the 20th century, which established a pantheon of military and political organizations—as diverse as the OUN, UPA, and, even, Ukrainian dissidents. Public denial of the legitimacy of their struggle was proclaimed unlawful. The bill raised significant concerns among many Holocaust scholars, who are very critical of the role of the Ukrainian nationalist movement during World War II. In general, the ambiguity of the formulations, the attempt to consolidate a single version of the historical past, and the methods and timing of such legislative initiatives have been a subject of concern and debates in Ukraine and abroad (for one example, an open letter calling on President Poroshenko to veto these laws was signed by prominent Western and Ukrainian scholars and experts; retrieved December 1, 2015, http://krytyka.com/en/articles/open-letter-scholars-and-experts-ukraine-re-so-called-anti-communist-law). See more at Shevel, "No Way Out?"

36. *The Black Book* was originally compiled during World War II (1943–44) by Soviet Jewish writers Ilya Ehrenburg and Vasily Grossman about the crimes committed by the Nazis in the Soviet Union. A Russian-language edition of *The Black Book* was not published until 1980 (Jerusalem), and finally in Kyiv, Ukraine, in 1991.

37. Examples are the USC Shoah Foundation testimonies project, Centropa, USHMM interviews, Judaica Institute in Kyiv interview collection, and Yahad in Unum eyewitness interviews project—to name but a few.

38. See "Pro Holokost slovamy svidkiv rozpovist' ukraintsiam frantsuz'kyi sviashchennyk," a stenogram of a television program from September 8, 2011, http://www.5.ua/suspilstvo/pro-holokost-slovamy-svidkiv-rozpovist-ukraintsiam-frantsuzkyi-sviashchenyk-38659.html.

39. See Grinchenko, "Babyn Yar"; Sklokina, "Radians'ka polityka"; Lewicka, *Psychologia Miejsca*; Sereda, "The Changing Symbolic Landscape"; Blacker, "Living Among"; Krzemiński, *Antysemityzm*; Paniotto, "Dinamika ksenofobii"; and Starovoyt, "Holodomor, Amnesia and Memory," among others.

40. Portnov, "The Holocaust in the Public Discourse"; Podol's'kyi, "Ukrain'ske suspil'stvo"; Jilge, "Competing Victimhoods"; Dietsch, *Making Sense*; Hrytsak, *Strasti*; Himka, "Reception of the Holocaust"; among others.

41. See Wylegała, "(Nie)pamięć na gruzach"; Ivanova, "Ukrainian High School Students."

42. Medvedovska, "Holokost v Ukraini."

43. The project was launched jointly by St. Gallen University (Switzerland) and the Center for Urban History (L'viv). The project is sponsored by SNF Grant CR11I1L_135348, "Region, Nation, and Beyond: A Transcultural and Interdisciplinary Reconceptualization of Ukraine." More information on the project and its outcomes are provided at the Ukrainian Regionalism website, uaregio.org.

44. The question was: "Please name the 1–2 most negative events in the history of our country."

45. See the report by the Rating Group, "Dynamika stavlennia do Holodomoru: Lystopad 2015," November 24, 2015, http://ratinggroup.ua/research/ukraine/dinamika_otnosheniya_k_golodomoru_noyabr_2015.html.

46. On the mechanisms and actors behind the L'viv pogrom, see Himka, "Lviv Pogrom."

47. See Hrachova, "Vony zhyly sered nas?"; Tsarynnyk, "Zolochiv movchyt."

48. Each quotation notes the respondent's town, gender, age, and occupation. The archive of the original audio records and transcripts of the interviews are kept at the Center for Urban History in East-Central Europe in L'viv.

49. Wylegała, "Absent 'Others,'" 477.

50. See Bartov, "Erased."

51. Wylegała, "Absent 'Others,'" 481; Assmann, "Pięć strategii."

52. Ispas and Milievo are two villages near Vyzhnytsia. In July 1941, members of the Kuzi antisemitic organization started a pogrom in Milievo and Banyliv, killing the local Jews. The same would have happened

in Ispas, but the locals prevented the massacre and saved all fifteen of the village's Jewish families (about one hundred people). A monument commemorating the event was unveiled in Ispas in 2012. See more at http://www.day.kiev.ua/uk/291151.

53. Connerton, "Seven Types," 62.
54. Narvselius and Bernsand, "Lviv and Chernivtsi," 75.
55. Karlsson and Zander, *Holocaust*.
56. Chebotarova, "How Mikveh Became Vodokhreshcha."
57. Ashworth, Graham, and Tunbridge, *Pluralising Pasts*, 75.

Bibliography

Amar, Tarik Cyril "A Disturbed Silence: Discourse on the Holocaust in the Soviet West as an Anti-site of Memory." In *The Holocaust in the East: Local Perpetrators and Soviet Responses*, edited by Michael David-Fox, Peter Holquist, and Alexander M. Martin, 158–83. Pittsburgh, PA: University of Pittsburgh Press, 2014.

Anderson, Benedict. *Imagined Communities: Reflections on the Origin and Spread of Nationalism.* London: Verso, 1991.

Ashworth, Gregory, Brian Graham, and John Tunbridge. *Pluralising Pasts: Heritage, Identity and Place in Multicultural Societies.* London: Pluto Press, 2007.

Assmann, Aleida. "Pięć strategii wypierania ze świadomości." In *Pamięć zbiorowa: współczesna perspektywa niemiecka*, edited by Magdalena Saryusz-Wolska, 333–51. Kraków: Universitas, 2009.

Bartov, Omer. *Erased: Vanishing Traces of Jewish Galicia in Present-Day Ukraine.* Princeton, NJ: Princeton University Press, 2007.

Blacker, Uilleam. "Living among the Ghosts of Others: Urban Postmemory in Eastern Europe." In *Memory and Theory in Eastern Europe*, edited by AlexanderEtkind, Julie Fedor, and Uilleam Blacker, 173–93. New York: Palgrave Macmillan, 2013.

Chebotarova, Anna. "How Mikveh Became Vodokhreshcha." *New Eastern Europe*, no. 3-4 (2015): 63–73.

Connerton, Paul. "Seven Types of Forgetting." *Memory Studies* 1, no. 1 (2008): 59–71.

Dawidowicz, Lucy. *The War against the Jews, 1933-1945.* New York: Bantam, 1986.

Desbois, Patrick. *The Holocaust by Bullets.* New York: Palgrave Macmillan, 2008.

Dietsch, Johan. *Making Sense of Suffering: Holocaust and Holodomor in Ukrainian Historical Culture.* Lund, Sweden: Lund University Press, 2006.

Etkind, Aleksander and Uilleam Blacker. "Introduction." In *Memory and Theory in Eastern Europe*, edited by Aleksander Etkind, Julie Fedor, and Uilleam Blacker, 1–22. New York: Palgrave Macmillan, 2013.

Fainberg, Sarah. "Memory at the Margins: The Shoah in Ukraine." In *History, Memory and Politics in Central and Eastern Europe: Memory Games*, edited by George Mink and Laure Neumayer, 86–102. Houndmills, Basingstoke, UK: Palgrave Macmillan, 2013.

Gitelman, Zvi. "Soviet Reactions to the Holocaust, 1945–1991." In *The Holocaust in the Soviet Union: Studies and Sources on the Destruction of the Jews in the Nazi-Occupied Territories of the USSR, 1941–1945*, edited by Lucjan Dobroszycki and Jeffrey Gurock. New York: Routledge, 1994: 3–28.

Grinchenko, Gelinada. "Babyn Iar v usnii istorii." In *Babyn Iar: Istoriia i Pamyat*, edited by Vladyslav Hrynevych and Paul-Robert Magocsi, 191–217. Kyiv: Dukh I Litera, 2016.

Grossman, Vasily, and Ilya Ehrenburg. *The Complete Black Book of Russian Jewry.* Translated and edited by David Patterson. New Brunswick, NJ: Transaction, 2003.

Himka, John-Paul. "The Lviv Pogrom of 1941: The Germans, Ukrainian Nationalists, and the Carnival Crowd." *Canadian Slavonic Papers* 53, nos. 2–4 (2011): 209–43.

———. "The Reception of the Holocaust in Postcommunist Ukraine." In *Bringing the Dark Past to Light: The Reception of the Holocaust in Postcommunist Europe*, edited by John-Paul Himka and Joanna Beata Michlic, 626–61. Lincoln: University of Nebraska Press, 2013.

———. *Ukrainians, Jews and the Holocaust: Divergent Memories*. Saskatoon, Can.: Heritage, 2009.
Himka, John-Paul, and Michlic, Joanna Beata. *Bringing the Dark Past to Light: The Reception of the Holocaust in Postcommunist Europe*. Lincoln: University of Nebraska Press, 2013.
Hirsch, Marianne. "The Generation of Post-memory." *Poetics Today* 29, no. 1 (2008): 103–28.
Hrachova, Sofia. "Vony zhyly sered nas?" *Krytyka* 4, no. 90 (2005): 22-26.
Hrytsak, Yaroslav. *Strasti za natsionalizmom*. Kyiv: Krytyka, 2011.
"Ievreis'ka spadshchyna v Ukraini ta reprezentatsii Holokostu: obhovorennia knyzhky Omera Bartova 'Zabuti.'" *Ukraina Moderna* 15, no. 4, 2009.
Ivanova, Olena. "Ukrainian High School Students' Understanding of the Holocaust." *Holocaust and Genocide Studies* 18 (2004): 402–20.
Jilge, Wilfried. "Competing Victimhoods—Post-Soviet Ukrainian Narratives on World War II." In *Shared History–Divided Memory: Jews and Others in Soviet-Occupied Poland, 1939-1941*, edited by Elazar Barkan, Elizabeth A. Cole, and Kai Struve, 103–35. Leipzig: Leipziger Universitätsverlag, 2008.
Karlsson, Klas-Göran, and Ulf Zander, eds. *The Holocaust on Post-war Battlefields: Genocide as Historical Culture*. Malmö, Sweden: Sekel, 2006.
Krzeminski, Ireneusz ed., *Antysemityzm w Polsce i na Ukrainie*. Warsaw: Scholar, 2004.
Landsberg, Alison. *Prosthetic Memory: The Transformation of American Remembrance in the Age of Mass Culture*. New York: Columbia University Press, 2004.
Lewicka, Maria. *Psychologia Miejsca*, Warszawa: Scholar, 2012.
Medvedovska, Anna. "Holokost v Ukraini v suspil'nii dumtsi kintsia XX–pochatku XXI st." PhD diss., Oles Honchar National University, Dnipro, Ukraine, 2016. http://www.dnu.dp.ua/docs/ndc/dissertations/D08.051.14/dissertation_58459fad28388.pdf.
Narvselius, Eleonora, and Niklas Bernsand. "Lviv and Chernivtsi: Two Memory Cultures at the Western Ukrainian Borderland." *East/West* 1 (2014): 59–84.
Paniotto, Volodymyr. "Dinamika ksenofobii i antisemitizma v Ukrainie (1994–2007)." *Sociologia: teoriya, metody, marketing* no. 1 (2008): 197–214.
Podol's'kyi, Anatoliy. "Ukrain'ske suspil'stvo i pamiat' pro Holokost." *Holokost i Suchasnist'* 1, no. 5 (2009): 47–59.
Portnov, Andrii. "The Holocaust in the Public Discourse of Post-Soviet Ukraine." In *War and Memory in Russia, Ukraine and Belarus*, edited by Julie Fedor, Markku Kangaspuro, Jussi Lassila, and Tatiana Zhurzhenko, 347–70. New York: Palgrave Macmillan, 2017.
Rothberg, Michael. *Multidirectional Memory: Remembering the Holocaust in the Age of Decolonization*. Stanford, CA: Stanford University Press, 2007.
Rudling, Per A. "Memories of Holodomor and National Socialism in Ukrainian Political Culture." In *Rekonstruktion des Nationalmythos? Frankreich, Deutschland und die Ukraine im Vergleich*, edited by Yves Bizeul, 227–58. Göttingen, Ger.: Vandenhoeck and Ruprecht, 2013.
Sereda, Viktoriia, "The Changing Symbolic Landscape of Lviv" In *Politics, History and Collective Memory in East Central Europe*, edited by Zdzislaw Krasnodebski, Stefan Garsztecki, and Rüdiger Ritter, 359–86. Hamburg: Krämer, 2012.
Shevel, Oksana. "No Way Out? Post-Soviet Ukraine's Memory Wars in Comparative Perspective." In *Beyond the Euromaidan: Comparative Perspectives on Advancing Reforms in Ukraine*, edited by Henry E. Hale and Robert W. Ortung, 21–40. Stanford, CA: Stanford University Press, 2016.
Sklokina, Iryna. "Radians'ka polityka pam'iati pro kolaboraciju periodu nacystskoji okupaciyi yak instrument natsionalnoyi polityky." *Natsional'na ta istorychna pam'iat': zbirnyk naukovykh prats* 3 (2013): 118–41.
Starovoyt, Iryna. "Holodomor, Amnesia and Memory-(re)making in Postwar Ukrainian Literature and Film." *Journal of Soviet and Post-Soviet Politics and Society* 2 (2015): 341–66.
Stryjek, Tomasz. *Nevlovni katehorii: narysy pro humanitarystyku, istoriiu i polityku v suchasnyh Ukraiini, Polschi i Rosii*. Kyiv: Nika-Centr, 2015.
Subtelny, Orest. *Ukraine: A History*. Toronto: University of Toronto Press, 1988.
Tsarynnyk, Marko. "Zolochiv movchyt." *Krytyka* 10, no. 96 (2005).

Wylegała, Anna. "The Absent 'Others': A Comparative Study of Memories of Displacement in Poland and Ukraine." *Memory Studies* 8 (2015): 470–86.

———. "(Nie)pamięć na gruzach: Zagłada Żydów żółkiewskich w świadomości nowych mieszkańców miasta." *Zagłada Żydów* 7 (2011): 144–69.

ANNA CHEBOTAROVA (NÉE SUSAK) is Research Associate and Project Coordinator at St. Gallen University (Switzerland) and Researcher at the Center for Urban History in East-Central Europe (Lviv, Ukraine).

9

EXTERMINATION OF THE ROMA IN TRANSNISTRIA DURING WORLD WAR II

Construction of the Roma Collective Memory

Anna Abakunova

THE ROMANIAN OCCUPATION AUTHORITY CREATED AN ADMINISTRATIVE UNIT that was officially called the Governance of Transnistria Province and widely known as Transnistria, where the Jews and Roma from Ukrainian, Moldovan, and Romanian territories were concentrated and annihilated. The administrative center of Transnistria was the city of Odesa (before Odesa fell on October 17, 1941, the administrative center was the city of Tiraspol). The borders of Transnistria were demarcated in accordance with the German-Romanian treaty of 1941 and included the entire eastern part of contemporary Moldova (which is situated beyond the Dniester River) and the southern part of Ukraine (in its contemporary borders): the western and southwestern parts of Mykolaiv Oblast (region), the entire Odesa Oblast, and the major part of Vinnytsia Oblast, excluding its northern part and the main city of Vinnytsia. The terms of the treaty granted control of Transnistria to the Nazi Germany–allied Romania.

The main discussion in historiography on the annihilation of the Roma is centered on one conceptual question: whether the Roma were annihilated because of racial ideology or because they were considered "asocial elements."[1] This chapter does not discuss the reasons for the extermination of the Roma. Instead, first, it examines the historical facts that remain in the personal recollections of the Roma about their deportations to Transnistria and their murder and survival there; second, it reconstructs the deportation of the Roma to Transnistria in the Roma collective memory inside and outside the Roma community.

This research is based on interviews collected by the author personally both from the Roma who were deported to Transnistria during World War II and survived there and from the Roma who were born during the wartime and could not remember the deportations but received the memory about the wartime suffering from the older generation. An analysis of both categories of interviews allows us to reveal connections between the individual and collective memory of the Roma. In addition, this chapter includes interviews with Roma activists who worked with the Roma communities and discussed the topic of extermination of the Roma. All interviews were conducted in the territories of contemporary Ukraine and Moldova in 2010 and 2013.[2] The main part of the interviews was collected with the Roma survivors who were in Transnistria and were seven to fourteen years old at the beginning of the occupation of Ukraine in June 1941. Another part consists of interviews with Roma survivors who were in Transnistria and were between two and six years old in June 1941 but did not remember their own experience there or survived in another occupied territory of Ukraine and in both cases received information from their close relatives (usually parents). The last group of interviews was conducted with Roma who were born during the occupation (in 1941–43) and those born soon after the liberation of Ukraine (1944–1951) and can represent the second generation of survivors. Two interviews were recorded with those Roma who were born in 1970s and since late 1990s worked at Roma nongovernmental organizations. Gender was not considered in the selection of the respondents, but as a matter of record, 34 percent of the recorded interviews were taken from male respondents and 66 percent from female. The languages used by the interviewees were Russian, Ukrainian, or the mixture of Ukrainian and Russian so-called *surzhyk*.

During the first session of fieldwork in 2010, recorded interviews were limited to the Odesa and Vinnytsia *oblasts* in former Transnistria, with some information taken in Tiraspol, a Moldovan territory. During the second session in 2013, the interviews were recorded in Odesa Oblast in Ukraine and in the city of Soroca in Moldova. Also, as a primary source, I use recorded interviews with the Roma survivors from Transnistria from the documentary *Prigoana*, directed by Sergiu Ene and produced in 2012.[3] The survival experiences of the respondents covered the territories of Odesa, Vinnytsia, and Mykolaiv *oblasts* (in the contemporary borders of Ukraine), the routes of the deportation of the Roma to Transnistria from Bessarabia and inside Transnistria, and the methods that were employed for the organization of the deportations.

The methodology of the research includes the oral history method used both to record the narrations and to examine the data. All interviews are used as primary sources and described specific survivor experiences in specific locations that relates this research to the multiple (collective) case study method. First, data was examined for systematization and classification of narrations on the deportation to Transnistria and the survival experience there. Then data was classified in terms of the facts about the deportations and survival that the respondents remembered and the way they remembered; that is, the Roma survivors' perceptions and interpretations of what had happened. The analyzed data was divided into two categories: individual memory about historical events experienced by the Roma during wartime and collective memory of the Roma as constructed narrative over time after the events.

One of the complicated methodological questions is the question of terminology related to the Roma annihilation during World War II. The scholars and activists argue how to name the persecution of the Roma and how to name Roma themselves. This terminological discussion is not directly related to this research, though the terms used remain important, and therefore it should be briefly mentioned.[4] To point out, in Ukraine, Russia, and other post-Soviet countries, the common term for the Roma remained *Gypsies* until today and did not convey any pejorative sense except in some particular cases. Along with this, Roma call one another *Rom* for a man and *Romka* for a woman inside Roma communities in Moldova and Ukraine. The term *Roma* is used by scholars as a politically correct one to denote "Gypsies" or if scholars are talking about the main group of the Gypsies called the Roma. The Roma informants, in most cases, call themselves Gypsies. In such cases, the term *Gypsies* appeared in the text in the way the respondent used it. Because of the foregoing, and following Western historiography practices, the term *Roma*, when referring to the Roma in the plural, is used for this research.

The following analysis and presumptions, built only on the examination of sources just described, is limited to a certain group of the Roma of particular geographical locations. Consequently, this research does not pretend that its results extrapolate to other Roma communities or groups.

Specificity of Roma Collective Memory

To analyze Roma memory, one must consider its uniqueness and complexity. Moreover, to examine collective memory of the Roma, it should be emphasized that the division of memory into individual and collective is merely conditional. Moreover, the definition of "collective memory" is disputed among the scholars. Noa Gedi and Yigal Elam stated that "All 'collective' terms are problematic—and 'collective memory' is no exception—because they are conceived of as having capacities that are in fact actualized only on an individual level, that is, they can only be performed by individuals."[5] Indeed, it is complicated to make a distinction between individual and collective memory because both memories supplement each other.

Following Maurice Halbwachs, the originator of the term *collective memory*, an argument is developed around the collective memory rather than the individual one for this research.[6] The analyzed data showed that very fragmentary episodes from wartime have remained in the recollections of the Roma; often there was no connection between either time and the events, or the events and their aftermath in the Roma narrations. In most cases, the Roma do not remember (do not want to remember or just do not want to retell) the details of their deportations and survival in Transnistria. One can presume that such a situation with memory partially reflects the illiteracy of Roma who are older than fifty (at the time of the interviews); in most cases they did not and still do not know the names of the places through where they passed and they cannot collect historical events in one image or rely on any chronology of World War II. Therefore, to identify historical facts based on the memories of the Roma is extremely difficult. One can, however, research the attitudes of the Roma to different historical events, such as Roma perception and comprehension of certain historical facts of the wartime. It may be presumed that the Roma have a clean memory that has been relatively less affected by mass education and extra-community narratives of the past. Nevertheless, the narrations of the interviewees were sometimes interlaced with many other episodes told by others, mainly Roma, survivors. This phenomenon has been defined by Jan Assmann as a "communicative memory." This type of memory includes those "varieties of collective memory that are based exclusively on everyday communications,"[7] because "on the *social level*, memory is a matter of communication and social interaction."[8] Individuals provide interpretations for other individuals, which are dealt with as information to be assimilated, remembered, or archived to create the multiple pasts.[9] From this perspective, to analyze the Roma collective memory is feasible.

Telling their life stories by recalling events from their memory, the Roma appealed more to feelings than to facts. Therefore, one can suppose that the Roma revive their memories through emotions rather than through rational analysis of the past. In most cases, to recall their past, the Roma in these interviews have told their stories hastily and without details, demonstrating that details did not seem so important to them. Conceivably, the details were truly not important to them or, perhaps, the Roma were just trying to avoid telling the details because of their traumatic experiences. Often the Roma emphasized that they had nothing to remember.[10] Analyzing the interviews, however, one can find two main reasons the Roma may have avoided telling the details: first, they did not trust the interviewer or their recollections were too personal, deep, and tragic. Thus, the Roma simply did not want to make their memory public. Ostensibly, it is not always relevant to talk about traumatic issues in the Roma case: often the Roma did not want to share even very happy but very personal things with strangers. Sometimes they were simply testing the interviewer to see whether she was truly interested in their life experiences. Then, after many questions and waiting for a while, the details began to emerge, and the narration was not confusing anymore because of fragmentation but became more consistent.

It should be emphasized that the settled Roma talked about the war with more details as well as feelings and emotions than the Roma from nomadic or seminomadic backgrounds. One might assume that the settled Roma remember the war better than other Roma, or, probably, they were not hesitant to reveal their experience. This could be the case for either of two reasons. The first would be that settled life is less complicated and exhausting than nomadic life. The settled Roma could have a job; they did not need to think about where to live and how to get there. The second would be that settled Roma usually were treated as equals by the other locals—the Roma were indeed the locals. These reasons could lead to the conclusion that settled Roma had less fear in front of strangers than other Roma and, therefore, the settled Roma had more communications with the outer world that led to better and more knowledge (and probably, understanding) about what happened during wartime.

To reconstruct historical details from the narrations of the nomadic Roma is also possible, as the following example from an interview with a nomadic Roma who was deported to Transnistria from Moldovan territory shows:

> Well, I remember it all. . . . We lived in Tiraspol, when the war broke out we were sent there, and then to somewhere else, to Ukraine before the Buh.[11] . . . There was a lot of water. . . . That water was called the Buh, and before that there was another water. . . . They [guards] were drowning people, little children, grownups, they drowned them all. . . . First, we had the Germans, and then the Romanians came there on the way to Ukraine. At first, they were set up there in Moldavia. But then they went on to Ukraine. They sent us to the camp. We walked for two or three days to the camp from Tiraspol. In the camp where we lived, there were Romanians [guards].[12]

One can understand from this narration that the Roma were deported from Moldovan territory to Ukrainian territory. The informant said that "There was a lot of water. . . . That water was called the Buh, and before that there was another water," which describes Transnistria, which lay between the Dniester and Southern Buh Rivers. Another indicator that the location of origin was Transnistria is the reference to the Romanian-guarded camp in the narration, for it is known that Transnistria was under the rule of Romania. Analyzing this interview further, the route of deportation and location of the camp can be identified.

In consideration of the fact that most of the respondents were five, six, or seven years old when the extermination and deportations started, their narratives can be analyzed within framework of collective memory. According to psychological research, children of this age can remember some events of critical importance in their life experiences, but to reconstruct the social context or to comprehend events in detail might be possible only in older years. At some point, a lot of internal and external factors influence memory: stories of relatives about the same event, television programs, including documentaries, books, and articles that a person reads, participation (or not) in commemorations, worldview formed over time, and so on. Even considering Roma's often enclosed style of life with little impact from the exterior, one cannot reduce the impact of internal factors such as family conversation about particular events. Also, the lack of communication Roma have with other people (non-Roma as well as Roma living in other communities) allows the Roma to save episodic memory of events they lived through. All these factors construct collective memory.

Following the definition of Pierre Nora after Maurice Halbwachs, "Collective memory is what remains of the past in the lived experience of the groups, or what these groups make of the past."[13] To be more precise, collective memory is the "collective construction of the past made by a present community."[14] When considering the Roma of Ukraine and Moldova as a community or society, a researcher deals with many levels of the past's construction on the basis of the following complications:

- The division of the Roma into several groups: the largest groups the Sinti (just a few families) and the Roma group. Within the Roma group there are many subgroups: the Servitka Roma (Servy, who often call themselves "Ukrainian Gypsies" or "Ukrainian Roma"), the Vlaxičkos or Vlaxija, the Lovari, the Kelderari (Kalderash, Kalderaš, Căldărari; in Ukraine they are often called Kotliary), the Kišinjovcurja or Kishinyovtsy, and the Krymurja or the Kyrymlytika Roma (Tatarika Roma, Crymy, or Krymy)[15]
- Religion: most of the Roma in Ukraine and Moldova are Orthodox, with exception of the Kyrymlytika Roma (Krymy), who are Muslims
- The place where the occupation regime existed: the entire Ukraine, including Crimea, and Moldova
- Roma communities in towns and cities
- Roma families who lived separately from the Roma community

The Roma in Central and Eastern European countries have a complicated internal structure that also must be taken into consideration when researching Roma collective memory: "Gypsies are a specific ethnic community, an 'intergroup ethnic community' which has no analogue in the other nations of Europe. The Gypsy community is divided into a number of separate (and sometimes even opposed to one another) groups, subgroups, and metagroups with their own ethnic and cultural features, and often their problems are completely different in nature and thus not susceptible to generalizations."[16] In many cases, the Roma of one community are distanced from the Roma of another community even though they live in the same town or city. The attitude of the Roma to "others," that is, non-Roma, is very adversarial and, in most cases, is negative: the Roma generally do not like to talk about themselves to strangers, even if the person was brought inside the community by other Roma and introduced to the rest of the Roma family or community as "one of us." Even if the person truly has Roma roots but does not live the Roma lifestyle, the other Roma will not recognize such a person as "one of us." The same attitude can be observed toward a Roma person who does not live in a certain Roma community for a long time: he or she will always be considered by the

Roma as *gadje* (stranger, non-Roma) even if the person speaks the Romanes (Romani, Roma language) dialect of the region. It means that an outsider in Ukraine and Moldova is unlikely to be able to rely on a sincere conversation with the Roma, and it is unlikely Roma can talk about personal things that happened to them during wartime. What the Roma remember and what they "want to recall" during the interview is different, which means that they control their narrations. The pattern was clearly observable while interviewing the Roma. According to the theory of Halbwachs, collective memory "evolves according to its own laws, and even if individual recollections sometimes also penetrate it, they [recollections] change their appearance when they are replaced in the unit that is not a personal conscience anymore."[17] In the case of the Roma, the opposite is true: very rarely do the Roma recall something without controlling it. The Roma tell what they want to tell at that given moment. It means that their recollections appeal to their individual and personal memory rather than collective memory. This confirms Nancy Wood's point of view that the "emanation of individual memory is primarily subject to the laws of the unconscious,"[18] whereas "collective representations of the past represent the conscious purpose of social groups"; that is, the Roma family or community.[19] Thus, the collective memory of Roma can be correlated with their public memory as the Roma recall what should be told and what is permitted to be told to non-Roma or Roma from another communities. The qualification "should be told" means certain narrative patterns that were constructed by non-Roma society for the Roma communities and often correspond to the stereotypes created around Roma lifestyle. Among such narratives one can find mention of poverty of the Roma (even if they have a large, wealthy house), the suffering of the Roma in history, and the will to gain some benefit from telling their story to non-Roma. The qualification "permitted to be told" refers to the control of a senior Roma over the stories being told: it is unofficially forbidden to complain about the Roma head of the community, to tell internal negative stories about the community, and to relate any shameful recollections even though they touched the narrator personally (for example, the rape of Roma women). If the Roma wanted to tell something forbidden during an interview, a safe place would be sought (for example, a distant room in the house) and the story told in a whisper.

Halbwachs's argument about different kinds of spaces such as the religious, economic, urban, and so on, can be applied to the case of Roma more than to any other groups: "there are as many ways of representing space as there are groups."[20] Every group has its own rules and its own permission for what they can tell to strangers on an individual, informal level, which "is determined not by personal feelings but by rules and customs independent of [them] that existed before."[21] Usually, the Roma gathered together as a family, or even as an entire community in the case of tabor or village life (which always has family ties) when telling something about themselves. Thus, the narrative is constructed around the family, because the other relatives must hear what is being told. The reasons for this might be that it is easier for the older Roma to control the words of every person in this way, or that every older member of the family or community can add some details from his or her own recollections to make the picture more complete, or yet again that the younger generation can listen to the recollections too. The participants can support the main narrator and—what is very important—can confirm that everything being told by the narrators is true. Some of the children and grandchildren always sit and listen to the stories. As a rule of thumb, the older generation of the Roma in the communities of Moldova and Ukraine is uneducated and uses such oral narratives for the transmission of their experience and their memory to subsequent generations. Many Roma narrators, when telling their stories, use the pronoun *we* instead of *I* to emphasize that the narrator is speaking not for or from himself or herself but for or on behalf of his or her family, or on behalf of the Roma in general.[22] In such a way, the collective reality of historical events is (re)constructed. Overall, all these are indirect reasons that the Roma narratives about World War II can be exemplified as a collective memory rather than as individual experience.

Deportations and Annihilation of the Roma in Transnistria: Traces of Memory

In the analysis of the destruction of the Roma in Transnistria, three categories of survivors should be taken into consideration. First is the Roma who were deported to the territory of Transnistria from Romania and Moldova (within the present-day borders of these countries), mainly from Bessarabia and Bukovina, and who after the deportations stayed in Transnistria in the concentration or labor camps and survived there. The second category is the Roma who resided in Transnistria's territories before the war started; then they were deported to the concentration or labor camps in the same territory. The final category is the Roma who lived in the Transnistria region before World War II and continued to live there when the war started; they were not deported to the camps. Some of the Roma of this last group tried to mix in with the rest of the local population (in general, Ukrainians), to hide or to reject their Roma identity. Each category of the Roma survived the war in different ways, especially the last group. On the one hand, the memories of these people are also different: they described different experiences of survival and emphasized different issues and problems in their narratives. Some of the issues that were very important to the people in one category were irrelevant to others. On the other hand, the Roma of all categories had certain similar experiences, for example, all of them tried to survive under extreme war circumstances and, therefore, the narrations of Roma survivors of that regions overlap.

The purpose of this research was not an analysis of the historical facts about the deportations and murders in Transnistria that remained in Roma memory. Still, it seems important to draw attention to the main subjects emphasized by the Roma in their recollections. The common question raised by the Roma, regardless of whether they were deported, is "why they went through the persecutions." In most cases, the Roma's comprehension of the reasons has nothing to do with the historical facts. The question why appears in a literal sense in the Roma narrations simply because they are not involved in the common consumerism of history, such as popular writings and mass-produced videos on the history of World War II. The Roma tried to understand why they were persecuted by the German Nazis and their Romanian allies. The Roma constructed several explanations, and one of which was that Germans "did not like Jews and Gypsies, simply they did not like these nations, but for what [reason]? I do not know."[23] This informant assumed that all people feel sympathy and antipathy toward certain people, and in the same way the German Nazis could also feel negative emotions toward the Roma. Other respondents offered more a deliberated explanation of the persecution of the Roma. Iona Matrache, born in 1936 in the village of Manici in the Nisporeni district, said that "We owned a house, cows, oxen, horses, and were deported because of our wealth."[24] L.P. from Soroca also stated that Nazis "gathered rich Gypsies, Kelderari especially; they were many and the Germans started to gather them and to punish them."[25] L.P. was born in 1942 and cannot remember that time, but she heard this from her mother's recollections. The conclusion is that the Roma were rich, and the German and Romanian Nazis wanted to expropriate their property and money. It should be mentioned that not only the Roma who were deported raised the question why it happened to them, but also the Roma who were not deported and did not suffer the persecution. P.F., a settled Roma whose family stayed in the village of Zaria near the border between contemporary Moldova and Ukraine, stated that "nobody deported our Gypsies, we were few in number and we worked, we did not live as tramps, maybe because of this."[26] The narration of Z.D., a younger and educated Roma woman from the Kirimlitika Roma, corroborates P.F.'s theory that the working Roma were left in the localities and were not deported:[27] "My grandma told me that . . . the Germans lived in our house. Our Gypsies were absolutely different Gypsies and [German] treatment of us was absolutely different from [the treatment] of other Gypsies. This was an urban group of Gypsies, such Gypsies were only in Odessa and Nikolaev [regions].[28] During the Soviet times the men got up early in the morning and went to work. The women were housewives in general. . . . That is why the attitude toward them [this group of Gypsies] was also different."[29] Having a job during wartime is one of the major explanations of the Roma for why they were not persecuted as other Roma communities were. Further examination of how these theories correspond to the historical evidence is a subject for other research. It should be emphasized, however, that all interviewed Roma who survived in Transnistria or were descendants of survivors, regardless of age, not only "recalled" the deportations but tried to understand why they happened. This finding shows that at the family level the topic of the destruction of the Roma in Transnistria was discussed largely with attempts to comprehend what happened and to draw conclusions. Thus, the persecution of the Roma in Transnistria is inscribed in the Roma collective memory.

One of the most important issues in the discussion on Roma recollections is the confiscation of Roma's property or the abandoning of their needs. Every recollection contained a narration about the property that the Roma lost during the war. During the interviews, Roma talked about the subject in a way that the property issue was the most dramatic among all that happened to them in wartime. The Roma discussed the murdering less often than confiscation of their property. They often mentioned loss of their horses, which draws attention to Roma's close relationship with and dependence on their horses.[30] Some of the Roma remembered how many horses, cows, pigs, and chickens were taken from them by the German or Romanian occupiers: Germans "came and took from my father all the piglets, we had thirteen piglets. They took all of them."[31] There might be two reasons why the property issue remained in the recollections of the Roma. The first is the Roma's attitude to their wealth: when one enters a Roma house, one can see that the Roma try to showcase all the expensive things, decorated with gold, and carpets in a fashion to show others the wealth of the owners. In most cases, before the war the Roma did not have luxury goods, and whatever remained in their hands after the war became more valuable. The loss of property—be it a chicken or a house—was a huge tragedy for the Roma in their recollections.[32] The second reason for the Roma to emphasize the property issue is the survival of the Roma during the famine after the war in 1946–47. Many Roma recollections started exactly with the descriptions of their starvation in 1946–47. Roma respondents continued to talk about their survival experience during the period of famine even after direct questions were addressed to them about the wartime experiences and persecutions. Every narration contained recollections about the famine, which shows a deep trace engraved in the Roma memory by this traumatic event, which affected Roma memory even more than World War II and the destructions and murdering of the Roma in the labor and concentration camps.

The deportations themselves did not occupy a significant place in the Roma recollections. Certainly, the Roma mentioned the difficulties they encountered on their way to Transnistria, the destitution and suffering: hunger, thirst, death of relatives, and more. Nazis "sent us [Gypsies] to Transnistria, they beat and killed us, left us with no food. We lived on hills, in stables. They [Nazis] came during the night and forced us and many others to climb into carts. We were walking on the hills and woods with our nomadic families; we were working in villages where we often arrived. There were thousands of other Roma deported alongside ourselves. We were dying from hunger and cold."[33] Nonetheless, the descriptions of killings of the Roma by drowning them in the river during their deportation takes a special place in the collective memory of the Roma from various regions:

> They [Nazis] were drowning many of them—the [deported] Gypsies. Over the Dniester we passed [when this was happening]. They [Nazis] stood us on a boat, they cut down trees, made sticks, and made boats [rafts]. The Germans did this, the landlords.[34]
>
> The Germans took one half of the Gypsies there [to the Buh] and the Jews also, and the other half stayed here, [these were] local Gypsies who were here [before]. And the Buh [was] there, it was a river, maybe you have heard, and they [Germans or Romanians] drove them [Gypsies] to the Buh—to shoot and drown them.... They [Germans or Romanians] took them [Gypsies] to the Buh, and the children too.... The Buh was far away. They [Gypsies] walked on foot, sometimes they fell down. If the Romanians did not like something they shot them [the Gypsies].... My grandma told me and so did my mother-in-law; they were there, they cried when they told [this story].[35]

The drowning of the Roma during their deportation to Transnistria has strongly remained in the Roma collective memory: even Roma who were not deported and survived the war without much trouble heard about the drowning of the other Roma in the Dniester River. For example, V.V. spent the wartime in a village in the Mykolaiv Oblast and recalled that "[I] did not see where they [Gypsies] were driven, but how I was told after the war, [the Gypsies were driven] on a barge and then were drowned. People told [me so] in Odessa."[36]

The younger the Roma narrators were, the more tragic the presentation of the deportations and especially the part about drowning the people. Apparently, the drowning was the most terrifying episode during the entire period of the persecutions of the Roma. Despite the impact that the drowning had on Roma memory, narrators mixed up the German Nazis and the Romanians in their recollections. This confusion shows that the Roma recollections were focused on victims more than perpetrators.

The Roma who went through deportations recalled their everyday life in the camps of Transnistria as a continuation of their routine despite the inhuman conditions. (The Roma lived with scarce food supplies and survived the winters in barracks without heating.)

> There were Romanians in the camp where we lived. I still remember that camp. It was a building of some sort, some kind of a barn, stables, where they [Romanians] used to keep horses and

cows. That is where they [Romanians] put us, to live how we could. The barn was locked, and we were stuck there. We were fed occasionally. . . . People mostly died of starvation there. My whole family was there. My eldest brother died because of hunger. There was nowhere to go. Next to the building was a vegetable patch, and there were posted the guards so that no one could run away. If not for this [the guards], we could run and hide somewhere. How could we [do it], if those guards were there, with their guns, machine guns? They would just shoot us from far away and that would be it. What else was there? How can I remember? . . . What do children know? We were hungry, crying. . . . They [Romanians] forced us to work.[37]

These terrible facts were told by the respondent in a very unemotional tone, as if it had been a routine in her life. It should be mentioned that the respondent kept a nomadic style of life before the war. Ostensibly, the Roma who led a nomadic lifestyle perceived the deportations and life in the camps as everyday difficulties, or something of the sort, with which they were faced in their usual nomadic everyday life. Hunger, cold, poverty, attempts to survive while experiencing hostilities of non-Roma (in many cases), the death of relatives from sicknesses and starvation—all the foregoing was the routine of the day for many of the nomadic and seminomadic Roma. To compare, the settled Roma had a different perception of everyday life under the German Nazi and Romanian occupation that reflected in their recollections. The settled Roma were scared; they tried to hide and escape.[38] On this basis, it might be concluded that both nomadic or seminomadic and settled Roma could have had different perceptions about their experiences of everyday life in Transnistria.

The interethnic relations are another dimension in the Roma recollections. To draw a parallel with the Jewish recollections, the Jewish survivors mentioned in their testimonies two aspects: non-Jewish rescuers and collaborators with the Nazis and their allies. The Roma recollections are different in nature: in the Roma recollections, collaborators or rescuers were almost not mentioned. When the question of rescuers was raised, the Roma mentioned only their own efforts in fighting for their lives; that is, self-rescue. To the question about non-Roma neighbors (particularly Ukrainians, Russians, and Moldovans), the Roma did not say anything about their collaboration with the occupiers except for the recurring phrase in multiple interviews: "What could they do? They also suffered."[39] Three nationalities usually appeared in the Roma narrations about Transnistria: Germans, Romanians, and Jews. The Germans were always characterized by the Roma as the very cruel people who were in power: "The Germans were very bad, without a soul," said P.F., who was not persecuted during the war.[40] Regarding the Romanians, the recollections of the Roma are diverse. On the one hand, the Roma respondents said that the Romanian administration and soldiers were much better than the German: the Roma could negotiate with the Romanian authority and redeem themselves, recalled T.T., who had survived in the village of Ivanovka (Odesa Oblast): "When the Germans went away, the Romanians came. The Romanians were under the German power, but with them [Romanians], the people could negotiate. . . . We could pay off the Romanians, but from the Germans we could not,"[41] and the same was confirmed by her younger sister, Y.W.: "When they [Romanians] took away our relatives to the camp, we could give money to the Romanians and escape from the camp, my mother told [us]. . . . With the Romanians one could negotiate, everybody said this."[42]

The nomadic Roma Z.P., who survived the war in the camp in Transnistria, also recalled that "the Romanians were not like us but at least we could talk to them; they were also bad, but that was still endurable. The Germans tortured us very much. . . . If you did something bad, the Romanians also punished you. But they did not touch you in general. With them we could at least talk. The Germans and Romanians gathered us, but the Romanians did not torture us very much. The Romanians did not kill many [of us]."[43]

Other Roma who experienced the attitudes of both the German and the Romanian authorities considered the Romanians the same as the German Nazis: "The Germans and Romanians had the same blood. When the Germans were here, they [the Romanians] were with the Germans, when the Russians [came]—[the Romanians] walked with the Russians hand in hand. They were not good. . . . The Romanians treated us badly. Whatever the Germans did, the same [did] the Romanians."[44]

Some of the Roma highlighted the conformism of the Romanians occupiers: "The Romanians and the Germans beat people, they were similar in this. The Romanians were like this: if you win the war they will be with you, if you do not win they will be against you, they are such people."[45]

These recollections about the Romanian authorities show that their attitude toward the Roma depended on the location: in some places, Romanian and German Nazi administrations' treatment of the Roma were similar, in other places, the Romanian authorities treated the Roma better than Germans did.

In their recollections, the Roma always mentioned the Jews as the people who were persecuted on a par with the Roma and even more. Z.C. said that the "Germans hated the Gypsies, [they hated] Jews and Gypsies."[46] Z.P. also recalled that

> I remember the Germans [and] the Romanians, they sent us to the camp to the Buh, they gathered the Gypsies and the Jews and sent them to the camp to the Buh. . . . The Germans tortured us very much. It was very, very bad. The Romanians were not like [the Germans], that was still endurable, but the Germans tortured the Gypsies and the Jews. The Germans did with them what they wanted: tortured them, closed [them] up in the camp. . . . They [the Germans] did not like the Jews and the Gypsies, simply they did not like these nations, but for what? I do not know.[47]

Information about the torturing of the Jews was transmitted to other generations. The Roma who were born during or after the war and did not experience the persecution still mention the Jews along with the Roma: "When the Germans came, they gathered the Gypsies and the Jews together; they wanted to annihilate the Gypsies and the Jewish as one mass," said L.P., who was born in 1942 and apparently used the words of her mother or grandmother.[48]

This section discussed the main issues of the Roma recollections about their persecution in Transnistria: the deportations, theft and confiscation of Roma property, everyday life in Transnistria camps, and interethnic relations. The wartime experience connected with deportations and survival of the Roma in Transnistria during World War II exist in the Roma memory. The Roma discuss these issues at the family level, trying to understand their past and transmit this knowledge to other generations. Thus, the experience of World War II and, particularly, of survival in Transnistria did not vanish from the Roma collective memory. In their recollection, the Roma touch on all significant issues such as the German Nazi policies toward them, the role of the Romanian allies, the Holocaust, and the rest, and provide their own comprehension of these matters. In this way, the Roma preserve their experience of World War II in their collective memory.

(Re)Construction of the Roma Collective Memory on Roma Destruction in Transnistria

This section discusses the construction of the Roma collective memory about the Roma destruction in Transnistria on three levels: everyday life, sociopolitical, and historic. It should be emphasized that analyzing the (re)formation of the Roma collective memory of wartime everyday life level is extremely difficult for researchers. The anthropological approach—living with the community and observing it as an insider—probably is the most reliable way to conduct such research. Michael Stewart, who lived in one Hungarian Roma community with the purpose of researching the Roma life and memory, noted that "talk about the war was rare and moreover popped up in fleeting, fragmentary images."[49] With memories of such a quality, anthropological research is a good approach to penetrate Roma life and to analyze the reality that existed in the Roma community, including the attitude to the war and the memory of it. A person who lives inside a Roma community with time becomes not a stranger but an "own stranger" to this community. People start to be more open and began to tell things, as they usually would do, without paying attention to the "strangerness" of the person. Other types of research on the Roma are always done with a purpose of getting from the Roma information about the war. The Roma understand this rather unnatural context of communications and either tell what the researcher wants to hear without much detail or, what is common, give the impression that the Roma really do not care what happened to them during World War II. Elena Marushiakova and Veselin Popov explain why the Roma do not talk much about the war in their everyday life: "one of the specific features of Gypsy ethnic culture is that their communities don't preserve in their collective memory tragic historical events. Thus, in general in Gypsy families as a whole and in families of Holocaust survivors in particular, the Gypsies prefer not to remember and not to speak about past sufferings and past hardships and past events are being forgotten very quickly. Our experience in this regard is that even when the Roma are provoked to speak about it, they don't like to mention the hardships."[50]

The author also observed that the Roma have a tendency not to talk about their suffering. Some of the Roma respondents talked about their deportations and extermination in Transnistria in their interviews as a bad episode that is not so important to remember because it has already passed, and there are many other problems in the present everyday life that the Roma must resolve every day. Another tendency observed in the Roma way of talking about Transnistria is the telling of their life stories from the position of outsiders without becoming involved emotionally in the event. The purpose of such behavior might be to show an observer that in the telling the Roma has switched attention to extraneous things.

The Roma reveal their attitude toward tragic moments through optimism: "It was horrible, but we survived. We are lucky."[51] This attitude one can find mostly in the recollections of former nomadic or seminomadic Roma rather than among settled Roma. On the contrary, settled Roma perceive their deportations as a tragedy in which they lost everything: their families, and their property: "My grandma told me and my mother-in-law, both were there [in Transnistria], they cried when they told it; if they told something I always saw tears in their eyes."[52] Folksongs about Roma deportations over the Dniester River exist in some

Roma communities. The deportation of the Roma appears as a dramatic episode of Roma history in these songs.[53]

The perception of deportations of the Roma to Transnistria is diverse in Roma society and depends on how the family lived through it. Therefore, understanding of the deportation and accumulating memory about it on an everyday level also varies among the different strata of the Roma communities. In addition, the Roma, on an individual level, have different motives for telling stories about their deportation. One is gaining material benefits from the interviewers, the sort of benefit does not matter: products, money, or various gifts, the Roma just want to know whether they would get something in return for their story. Another motive is a demonstration of the connection between a certain person from the Roma family or community and the history of the entire Roma population. For instance, in several interviews, one can find narrations about the Roma being an ancient people who were expelled from many countries throughout history; they were humiliated and killed, but despite all, they still exist. During the occupation, the Roma were again persecuted and destroyed, but still they managed to survive.[54]

The second level of (re)construction of the Roma collective memory is the sociopolitical level. On this level, the tendency to create a common collective memory based on the Roma persecution during World War II can be observed. This tendency relates to the building of national identity, which requires a common national idea(s). Marushiakova and Popov explain it as "development within global Roma nationalism":

> This is the relatively latest trend of development of the Roma community, born in our century. Since the birth and the first steps of the organized Romani movement, the representatives of the community from Central and Eastern Europe (or immigrants from this region) have been its main moving and leading force. This trend in community development gradually constructs its new national ideology with a strong emphasis on certain ideas—such as the use of the general name of Roma for all Gypsy subdivisions, . . . a new view of Roma history and a powerful emphasis on the Holocaust; the standardization of Romanes (the Gypsy language), and others. A very thin layer of the so-called "international Roma" or "professional Roma" has come in existence. Some of these people are now in the process of rediscovering their forgotten Romani ancestors (who in some cases could even be imaginary ones). They are not bound to a specific country, but to an international institution or non-governmental organization and have carried their work to a global level (often without the support of the Romanies in their own country).[55]

Recently in the public space there has appeared a tendency to "canonize" the deportations as a "national trauma."[56] Nonetheless, the question is whether the "Roma nation" or "Roma community" exists as an entire group from the Roma's point of view. No doubt, the Roma elite want to present the Roma as a close-knit, united people, as an entire community, but researchers emphasize that the Roma can be described as an "intergroup ethnic community" rather than as a "nation" by reason of their split into numerous subgroups that are distant, distinct, and sometimes opposed to one another.[57] Thus, the public or sociopolitical level of the collective memory of the Roma can be considered through either the public discourse of representatives of the Roma elite, or through certain statements of diverse Roma subgroups and unions.

Some Roma activists, however, try to extrapolate the suffering of certain Roma groups to the entire Roma population and to present the Roma as an eternal victim of persecution and anti-Tsyganism. Leaders of the Roma whose relatives experienced the deportations and extermination during World War II try to share this experience with other Roma groups and communities, including Ukrainian Roma communities, and to transform this already shared experience into the collective memory of "all Roma." Thereby, Roma activists try to build a new national identity through a shared common collective memory based on a past that would unite all Roma into one nation. In fact, the result, the author can observe, is that through these attempts, Roma leaders are gradually gaining the right to make a statement on behalf of all Roma groups and communities. Eventually, it is very difficult to create a shared collective memory because not all Roma went through deportations during World War II. For example, one can observe that the experience of the Roma in Transnistria differed with the oblast where they lived during the persecutions. For the Roma who lived in the Odesa Oblast, wartime was hard: the Roma had to hide from the occupiers (both the German Nazis and their Romanian allies). T.T., a seminomadic Roma who survived World War II in the Odesa Oblast, recalled that

> We were in Ivanovka when the war began. There were a lot of Gypsies in Ivanovka, and they were all taken away.[58] . . . The Gypsies were treated terribly. . . . Seventy-five of our relatives were killed by the Germans, two hundred kilometers from Odessa. They roamed with their carriages, so the Germans said they were partisans and threw them into the pit alive. There was a basement there, they [Gypsies] removed the roof and tried to escape on the roof where everyone who was shot fell into the hole, and some fell into it alive. I guess they thought if they fell down they would survive. No one did. Who could survive there? Whom would the Germans leave alive? No one [survived]. Small children were thrown in [the pit] there. The ground rose there for three days. [This was] in 1941. They [the Germans] did that when they were leaving, and then the Romanians came. They [the Gypsies] were under German rule. . . . When the Germans came, we ran away. [We] stopped at a remote village. My father rented a house from the Russians, and we told them that we were refugees. We spent the rest of the war there, nobody knew we were there, and then we went back to Ivanovka. . . . My aunt and [my] relatives were taken to the camp in Nikolaev.[59]

T.T.'s younger sister Y.W. was born in 1941 and in fact retold everything through the recollections of her mother and older sister, confirming that "Somebody [from the Gypsies] was driven, somebody was shot. . . . No one left."[60] Some of the Roma of the Odesa region were not deported or killed because they hid their Roma identity. T.T. recalled: that "We stayed under Romanian rule and we asked the neighbors not to tell anyone that we were Gypsies."[61] K.S. told a story of how her family hid their Roma identity:

> We were German Gypsies. . . . [But] I did not look like a Gypsy girl. . . . We lived in Berezovka, in the center.[62] As soon as the Germans saw a black-haired girl, they asked her in German: "Gypsy?" And then they shot her: she would go out somewhere and then just not return. . . . We did not go to the other Gypsies. Mother would not let us. They lived nearby, but we did not associate with them because we were afraid that we would be killed. The Germans did not know that we were Gypsies since we were white.[63]

At the same time, just about ten kilometers from Odesa, in the city of Izmail (the Moldovan side), the Roma lived a normal life without any disturbance or deportations. P.F., a settled Roma whose family lived in the village of Zaria near the border between contemporary Moldova and Ukraine, recalled that throughout the entire wartime period her family worked as they worked in times of peace, and nobody deported them.[64] Other Roma who survived the war in the same area (Izmail district) and in another area (Mykolaiv Oblast) also confirmed that they had fairly usual life conditions much as they had before the war:

> When the Romanians came, everything was all right. . . . Nothing to remember about the war, everything was as usual: we danced, sang. They [the Romanians] only took away the horses. . . .

When everybody was gone, and the Soviet Union was coming in, it got worse than during the war because it was forbidden to nomadize, they forced us to work.... In wartime we lived better than now.... No violence.... Nobody touched us... we worked. Nobody drove us anywhere.[65]

We lived normally, nobody touched us. Nobody persecuted us. Robbery and rapes did not take place there, they [the Romanians] respected us.[66]

Thus, even in the small territory of Transnistria, memory of the war experience varies and depended on the location where the Roma lived at the time. The persecution of the Roma during World War II as a common Roma collective memory is not relevant to all Roma groups and communities in the world, or moreover, to all those in Europe.

The third level of (re)construction of the Roma collective memory is the historical level. The writing of the history of the Roma annihilation under the Nazi occupational regimes was late in comparison with the writing of the history of the Jewish Holocaust. Knowledge about the fate of the Roma, in Transnistria for instance, was not available at large. Romania as a state tried to maintain silence. The documents about the persecution of the Roma were found in Romanian archives much later than documents about the Jews. The Roma did not have a written tradition and did not put on paper any events of their history. The Nazis did not keep exact records of Roma victims, contrary to those for the Jews. The Soviet archives were closed, and after the collapse of the Soviet Union, materials about the Roma were dispersed from the archives of many post-Soviet countries. On the individual level, the Roma respondents did not tell their life stories to non-Roma. Perhaps a similar situation took place in other Roma communities in Ukraine and Moldova. There were no court cases for the persecutors of the Roma and the Roma did not claim compensation for their persecution.

For more than forty years, there was no public event that would encourage society to think about what the Roma had endured. For the Jews, such an event happened in 1961 in Israel: the Eichmann trial forced the world to comprehend what had truly happened to the Jews during World War II. No similar event focused world attention on the persecution of the Roma, and the persecution remained hidden until young, educated Roma leaders appeared and started to recover and reconstruct the historical events. Certainly, "public debates about the meaning of negative pasts have more to do with political interest and opportunities than the persistence of trauma or with any 'leakage' in the collective unconscious,"[67] but public debate helps to construct new memory and identity for the Roma and contributes to the understanding of the rest of the world more than Roma history and culture, which remain obscure topics. The world and particularly Europe have created the tragedy of the Roma Holocaust as a historical memory for the Roma, regularly reminding the Roma about their deportations and extermination by commemorations that have already acquired a sacral character. Michael Stewart made a point that "the Roma do not need commemorations to remember—the rest of the world does it for them on a daily basis."[68]

Regarding current research, academia is developing curricula on Roma studies. Scholars pay special attention to the deportations of the Roma to Transnistria. A final report, published in 2004, was conducted by the International Commission of Historians on the Holocaust in Romania and chaired by Elie Wiesel; it is one of the most significant research projects on the persecution of the Roma in Romania and their deportation to Transnistria.[69] Now Roma outside academia are also involved in the process of writing their history; many of them have agreed to give interviews and to write down the recollections of their relatives who survived the war. The fieldwork for collecting interviews with the Roma who lived through deportations and persecutions in Transnistria has been conducted by several organizations in the last few years.[70] After the appearance of scholarly publications on the extermination of the Roma in Transnistria, new methodology and approaches were established, more questions were raised, and new perspectives for further research of the Roma history were proposed. Further historiography will consider these developments. Using the published researches, the Roma also might be included in writing their history and thereby to (re)construct their collective memory.

Constructing the Collective Memory of the Roma: Application of the Jewish Experience

Some of the Roma activists want to use memory "as a mechanism that unites groups and cements identity,"[71] much as the way it is usually used by political elites of sovereign states. The Roma have good examples how to construct, transform, and use collective memory about World War II. For instance, the memory of World War II or, to be more precise, of the Great Patriotic War in Russia, is an integral part of society on any level—individual or collective.[72] The Jews are another example of a group who has the history of the Holocaust as an inherent part of their collective memory—not only in Israel but wherever they live. Being distinct from the Russians who represent their memory as a memory of victors, the Roma decided to take the perspective of the Jews, for whom the Holocaust is a crucial tragic apogee of all the persecution of the Jewish people through their history. As was mentioned by Stauber and Vago: "It seems to outside observers as if Romani activists are trying to condense a process that took the Jews years to digest and evaluate. Admiration as well as pragmatism dictates their readiness to utilize the Jewish experience."[73]

To incorporate the Jewish experience is complicated for the Roma because, besides the Roma elite, many Roma do not even consider the question whether to accept such ideas. They live their own lives, sometimes in isolated groups or communities in their own micro locations, and they do not engage in the wider social life outside their communal life. Analyzing the recollections of the Roma from Ukraine and Moldova, one can find a significant difference between information obtained from the Roma and that obtained from other Nazi-victimized groups. The memories of the Roma almost never overlap with other sources such as books, newspapers, films, exhibitions, and internet sites. This is largely because the literacy level is low among the Roma and because they rarely attempt to learn about the period of the occupation from printed sources. In addition, the written tradition on World War II, such as diaries, recordings of the recollections of older generation, and so on, is underdeveloped among the Roma particularly in Moldova and Ukraine. Therefore, many of them, particularly among the youngest generations, who did not live through the deportations, feel the insignificance and remoteness of these events. As a result of all the foregoing, the Roma do not communicate about World War II with other victims and survivors and do not incorporate the symbols, which are constantly being created by other groups of society, into the Roma collective memory. According to Kansteiner and other researchers, however, "Collective memories originate from shared communications about the meaning of the past that are anchored in the life-worlds of individuals who partake in the communal life of the respective collective. As such, collective memories are based in a society and its inventory of signs and symbols."[74] Monuments and commemorations are the main symbols that remind people of their past. The Roma hardly have one or the other. Only recently in some countries were monuments erected in honor of the Roma who survived World War II. Those who erected the monuments and organized Roma Holocaust commemoration events are Roma and non-Roma governmental organizations that often do not reflect the ideas and wishes of the ordinary Roma. Various scholars have analyzed the issue of commemoration and how it relates to the Roma collective memory many times.[75] All this sort of attention raises the question of the relevancy of speaking about the collective memory of all Roma. It must be reiterated that the Roma have a divided memory and Roma groups, communities, and societies are spread out across the world. In fact, Roma society itself is divided in many aspects: the social life, languages and dialects, cultural and educational differences, and, all in all, their perception of Roma history. The tool that Roma activists use to unite the Roma is the call to the individual (not collective) memory of the survivors, including those who survived in Transnistria. Certainly, the individual memory is not fully isolated or completely closed. As Maurice Halbwachs noted,

> A person, to evoke his own past clearly, needs to appeal to the recollections of others. It turns back to reference points that exist outside that person and are already fixed by the society. Moreover, the functioning of the individual memory is not possible without such tools as the words and ideas that the individual did not invent but borrowed from his or her milieu. . . . Therefore, indeed there is a ground to distinguish between two memories, one of which we would call the inner or internal, and the other external; or one is the personal memory and the other is the social memory.[76]

In fact, it is irrelevant to talk about the Roma collective memory of World War II in the sense of common memory for the entire Roma society. For the construction of Roma collective memory based on the Roma persecution during World War II, the Roma elite has tried to use the same component that the Jews used to construct their own collective memory about the Holocaust immediately after the war: about antisemitism (in the case of the Roma, it is anti-Tsyganism) and victimization, using the individual memory of eyewitnesses to reconstruct the past, because "all memories, even the memories of eyewitnesses, only assume collective relevance when they are structured, represented, and used in a social setting."[77]

Professional scholars (of both Roma and non-Roma origin), be it intentionally or not, help Roma activists to construct a common memory for different Roma groups and communities without the consent of these groups and communities. Scholars transform individual memories of certain Roma groups and transfer them onto the collective memory of all Roma. The desire of the researchers to write a "truthful history" in which nobody will be forgotten requires significant effort. At the same time, the art of forgetting is a feature inherent in European society rather than in Roma communities.[78] The forgotten holocaust of the Roma (which is not actually forgotten at least in the last ten to fifteen years) is being imposed on ordinary Roma as their traumatic, hidden, or suppressed memory.[79]

Conclusions

In analyzing individual recollections about deportations of the Roma to Transnistria, one can observe common statements and draw conclusions about questions such as why the

Roma were deported or explore the property issue. Some such observations have formed as a result of a common discussion within the Roma family or community, especially if the story was told by those who were not eyewitnesses. These life stories are likely the product of common thinking and communication inside the Roma community. Therefore, the present research made reference to the collective memory of the Roma. On the one hand, the collective memory absorbs certain practices and symbols, such as commemoration and the erection of monuments, which the Roma did not have until recently. It means that this research was concerned more with the transferred individual memories than with collective memory. On the other hand, as Halbwachs stated, "each individual memory is a point of view of collective memory, which is the reflection of changes that depend on the place occupied by [a person]. This place changes depending on the relations which the [person] maintains with other milieus."[80] This more or less explains the process going on in Roma society: the transformation of individual memory of a given Roma stratum into a social or collective memory serves as a foundation for the formation of a common Roma identity and thereby for the integration of the diverse Roma society into one unit.[81]

The recollections of the Roma can be construed in different ways. The result can be a reconstruction of the past in the light of present interests or it can be a recovering of traces "of what has been lost, forgotten, covered over or censored."[82] For some Roma groups and communities, or rather the Roma representatives of their communities, a reconstruction of the past is undoubtedly the main way to unite the Roma through the common past in light of present interests. The persecution of the Roma during World War II has served as a tool to energize Roma leaders, who can lobby their own interests internationally. From another point of view, reporting on all public levels the murders of the Roma under the Nazi regime is a retribution for the many years of silence about the fate of the Roma. From the research perspective, the discovery and use of Roma recollections about their annihilation in Transnistria is "recovering of traces of what has been lost, forgotten, covered over" rather than construction of the common Roma past.

The academic community is helping Roma leaders to create this common multiple past and to inscribe it in the European collective memory. This places the persecution of the Roma during World War II on an equal basis with the other mass murders and thereby helps to construct a new reality for Roma society. In this new reality, the Roma will have more opportunities to develop as a people: to obtain an education and medical help, to struggle for their human rights, and, probably, to take a step on the way to form a nation. Researchers should realize, however, that not all Roma lived through extreme persecution during World War II and not all Roma share the memory about the war in general—and the memory of the persecution particularly. Even the Roma who lived during the war in Transnistria described their life as being routine in some cases, as if the war had not happened at all. For these Roma, other postwar events have much more importance and meaning because they brought greater disasters in their experience (for instance, the famine of 1946–47).

The case of the deportations of the Roma to Transnistria occupies a special place in the process of forming Roma collective memory for several reasons. One is that the deportations were very cruel and are engraved in the memory of the survivors. Another reason is that mass persecution of the Roma happened relatively recently (as the flow of history measures time) and memory about it can still be transmitted to other generations through oral tradition, because, according to Assmann, the time allotted to communicative memory is limited and "reaches no farther back than eighty years, the time span of three interacting generations."[83] The Roma preserved in their memory what happened to them in various ways of the sort Assmann refers to (stories, songs) and transmitted it (and continue to transmit it) to younger generations.

Besides, the documents from the Soviet archives that contain information about the Roma life and persecution in World War II have become available to scholars rather recently. The fieldwork on collecting Roma testimonies about their survival the wartime are conducted by various organizations. Young, educated Roma are maturing and starting to recover their own roots and their own family histories (in the large understanding of the word *family*). All these factors influence the construction of the Roma collective memory through the sharing of individual narrations in the social space and form diverse, more complicated comprehension of the role of Roma in World War II, and not only as the victims.

Notes

1. See the contrasting points of view in Hancock, *Pariah*; Achim, *Roma*; Ioanid, *Holocaust*; Holler, *Nationalsozialistische Völkermord*; Solonari, "Etnicheskaia chistka."

2. Fieldwork was conducted in 2010 for the research project "Routes of Disappearance. Jewish and Roma Memory of Transnistria." The project was implemented within the program Paths of Remembrance, undertaken by Geschichtwerkstatt Europa and realized by the Institute for Applied History in cooperation with the European University Viadrina, Frankfurt am Oder, under financial support from the Remembrance, Responsibility, Future foundation (EVZ). Fieldwork in 2013 was conducted for the research project Holocaust and Porrajmos in the Transnistria Region during the Second World War: History and Memory during the Black Sea Link Fellowship at the New Europe College (Bucharest, Romania).

3. I am grateful to Ion Duminica for providing me with this resource.

4. Many scholars who work on this topic have mainly borrowed approaches from the Holocaust studies and consider the Roma extermination to be a part of the Holocaust, using the term *Holocaust* in relation to any group of victims under Nazi rule. Other scholars argue that they are studying a specific phenomenon inside the Holocaust. These academics use the term *Roma Holocaust* to underline the similar fate of the Jews and the Roma under the Nazi regime, on the one hand, and to specify the annihilation of the Roma as a separate group of victims, on the other hand. The term *Roma Holocaust* has become widespread in recent decades in referring to the fate of the Roma in World War II. In Roma historiography, one can find three other terms: *Porrajmos* (*Porajmos, Pharrajimos, Parajmos*), *Samudaripen*, and *Kali Trash* (*Kali Traš*). The term *Porraymos* was proposed by historian Ian Hancock and has become the most widely used term at present in scholarly circles. The word *Porrajmos*, however, is derived from one of the many Roma dialects and is synonymous with *poravipe*, which can be translated as "violation," "abuse," or "rape." Some Roma communities consider this term offensive. Balkan Roma activists prefer the term *Samudaripen*, which is translated as "mass killing" or "murder of all." The term *Kali Trash* (*Kali Traš*), proposed by Russian Roma activists, is translated as "Black Fear." But the last one is a less well known term among the other Roma and is not used by scholars. On the terminology debates, see, for example, Hancock, "Uniqueness"; Hancock, "Responses"; Hancock, "Downplaying"; Fraser, *Gypsies*; Bessonov, "Ob ispolzovanii terminov 'Poraimos' i 'Kholokost'"; Marushiakova and Popov, "Holocaust" (Polish version).

Because of all the above complications, a common term such as *extermination* (or *annihilation*) of the Roma during World War II is used in this chapter.

Naming of the Roma is another methodological problem. As Elena Marushiakova and Veselin Popov ("Historical and Ethnographic Background," 52) have argued, "Before the changes in 1989–1990, the name 'Roma' was used as an endonym . . . in the countries of Central and Eastern Europe (except for former Yugoslavia) when the Gypsies spoke *Romanes* (the Gypsy language). This name was not widely popular and did not have an official status." In their research, Marushiakova and Popov used the word *Roma* only for the period after 1989. In all other cases, they used the term *Gypsies* because, according to them, the name *Gypsies* is wider in scope than *Roma* and "include the Gypsy communities that are not Roma or that are considered to be 'Gypsies' by the surrounding population."

    5. Gedi and Elam, "Collective Memory," 34.

    6. Maurice Halbwachs tried to explain this phenomenon: "there are two ways of organizing recollection: they sometimes can be organized and formed around one particular person who can consider recollections from his or her point of view, and sometimes recollections can be spread within a large or small society as partial images. Hence, there we have individual memory . . . and collective memory. In other words, an individual has two types of memories. . . . On the one hand, those [memories] are situated in the frame of a personality or his or her personal life where these recollections take place: even those recollections that are common with others will be considered by the person as distinct. On the other hand, at certain moments, a person is capable of behaving simply as a member of a group who participates in evoking and supporting impersonal recollections to a certain extent of group interest. Often these two memories penetrate one another. . . . The collective memory . . . covers individual memories but does not mix with them" (Halbwachs, *Mémoire collective*, 25–26). Translation by the author.

    7. Assmann, "Kollektives Gedächtnis," 10.

    8. Assmann, "Communicative and Cultural Memory," 109.

    9. Crane, "Writing," 1381–82.

    10. Z.P., interview by Anna Abakunova and Józef Markiewicz, Odesa region, June 20, 2010, in the author's personal archive; P.D., interview by Anna Abakunova, Izmail, June 4, 2013, in the author's personal archive; Z.C., interview by Anna Abakunova, Izmail, June 4, 2013, in the authour's personal archive.

    11. Yuzhnyi (southern) Bug (in Russian) or Pivdennyi Buh (in Ukrainian).

    12. Z.P. interview.

    13. Nora, "Mémoire collective," 398.

    14. Gildea, *Past*, 10.

    15. I am grateful to Elena Marushiakova and Veselin Popov for their help on this matter.

    16. Marushiakova and Popov, "Historical and Ethnographic Background."

    17. Halbwachs, *Mémoire collective*, 26.

    18. Wood, *Vectors*, 2.

    19. Green, "Society," 37.

    20. Halbwachs, "Space," 14.

    21. Halbwachs, *On Collective Memory*, 55.

    22. T.T., interview by Anna Abakunova and Józef Markiewicz, Odesa region, June 21, 2010, in the author's personal archive; Z.C. interview by Anna Abakunova in the author's personal archive; L.P., interview by Anna Abakunova, Soroca, June 16, 2013, in the author's personal archive.

    23. Z.P. interview.

    24. Iona Matrache interview on Ene, *Prigoana*.

    25. The Kalderash (Kalderaš) is a subgroup of the Roma that was widely spread in Romania, and also in Ukraine several families lived on the border with Romania and Bessarabia. Traditionally, members of this group were blacksmiths, coppersmiths, and tinsmiths, producing iron and copper kitchenware (pots, buckets, and so on) (L.P. interview).

    26. P.F., interview by Anna Abakunova, Bilhorod-Dnistrovskyi, June 6, 2013, in the author's personal archive.

    27. This group of the Roma traditionally dwells in Crimea and in the southern regions of Ukraine. The group formed during the time of the Crimean Khanate. The Crymy migrated from the Balkans to Crimea and settled among the Crimean Tatars. Their language and culture were strongly influenced by the Crimean Tatars and Russians. In 1944 Crimean Roma and Crimean Tatars were deported to Central Asia. Some of the Crymy were registered as Tatars on Soviet passports. Most Crymy Roma are Sunni Muslims. Their traditional occupations are retail trade, musical performances, primitive trade, blacksmith, jewel art, fortune-telling, and begging.

    28. She mentioned previously that this group of the Roma also lived in the Crimea region.

    29. Z.D., interview by Anna Abakunova and Józef Markiewicz, Odesa region, June 21, 2010, in the author's personal archive.

    30. Z.C. interview by Anna Abakunova, Izmail, June 4, 2013, in author's personal archive.

    31. S.P., interview by Anna Abakunova, Soroca, June 16, 2013, in the author's personal archive.

    32. It should be noted that a similar attitude toward property can be observed in many cases in the narrations of other groups of people, regardless of their origin and style of life.

33. Matrache interview.
34. Z.P. interview.
35. L.P. interview.
36. V.V., interview by Anna Abakunova, Izmail, June 4, 2013, in the author's personal archive.
37. Z.P. interview.
38. K.S., interview by Anna Abakunova and Józef Markiewicz, Odesa region, June 21, 2010, in the author's personal archive; T.T. interview.
39. Z.P. interview; L.P. interview; Y.P., interview by Anna Abakunova, Soroca, June 16, 2013, in the author's personal archive.
40. P.F. interview.
41. T.T. interview.
42. Y.W., interview by Anna Abakunova and Józef Markiewicz, Odesa region, June 21, 2010, in the author's personal archive.
43. Z.P. interview.
44. L.P. interview.
45. P.D. interview.
46. Z.C. interview.
47. Z.P. interview.
48. L.P. interview.
49. Stewart, "Remembering," 565.
50. Marushiakova and Popov, "Holocaust" (internet version), 10. Some Roma activists shared the same point of view, including Valery Novoselsky, editor of the Roma Public Diplomacy Network: Novoselsky, interview by Anna Abakunova, Kiryat Shmona, June 1, 2014, in the author's personal archive.
51. Z.P. interview; T.T. interview.
52. L.P. interview.
53. Stewart, "Remembering," 566–67.
54. For instance, T.T. interview; L.P. interview; Z.D. interview.
55. Marushiakova and Popov, "Historical and Ethnographic Background," 49.
56. Felcher, "Memory."
57. Marushiakova and Popov, "Historical and Ethnographic Background," 33. Professor Henriette Asséo emphasizes that "the Roma way of life does not correspond to specific current territorial boundaries or modern complexity of the movement of nationalities" Asséo, "Identité."
58. A village in the Odesa region, Ukraine.
59. T.T. interview.
60. Y.W. interview.
61. T.T. interview.
62. A village in the Odesa region, Ukraine.
63. K.S. interview.
64. P.F. interview.
65. Z.C. interview.
66. V.V. interview.
67. Kansteiner, "Finding Meaning," 187.
68. Stewart, "Remembering," 576.
69. Wiesel et al., *Final Report*. Also see Ancel, *Transnistria*; Achim, *Documente*, among others.
70. See, for instance, reports of the Yahad-in Unum website, which has systematically been collecting interviews with eyewitnesses since 2004, including survivors of the mass murder of Jews and the Roma on the territory of Ukraine https://www.yahadinunum.org/. See also Lenchovska, "Videosvidchennia."
71. Green, "Society," 38.
72. The Great Patriotic War corresponds to the timeframe of the Soviet participation in World War II, that is, from 1941 to 1945.
73. Stauber and Vago, *Roma*, 124.
74. Kansteiner, "Finding Meaning," 188.
75. See the different points of view in Fonseca, *Bury Me*; Hodgkin and Radstone, *Contested Pasts*, 242; Stewart, "Remembering"; Stauber and Vago, *Roma*; Marushiakova and Popov, "Holocaust" (*Romologica* version).

76. Halbwachs, *Mémoire collective*, 26.
77. Kansteiner, "Finding Meaning," 190.
78. Fonseca, *Bury Me*.
79. Katz, *Visszafojtott emlékezet*; Stauber and Vago, *Roma*, 125.
80. Halbwachs, *Mémoire collective*, 24.
81. Some scholars, when examining memories from the psychological point of view, have proposed to consider the "shared individual memory" as the link between the individual and collective memory; see Coman et al., "Collective Memory."
82. Eyal, "Identity," 8.
83. Assmann, "Communicative and Cultural Memory."

Bibliography

Achim, Viorel. *Documente privind deportarea țiganilor în Transnistria*. 2 vols. Bucharest: Enciclopedică, 2004.
———. *The Roma in Romanian History*. Budapest: Central European University Press, 2004.
Ancel, Jan. *Transnistria, 1941–1942: The Romanian Mass Murder Campaigns*. 3 vols. Tel Aviv: Tel Aviv University, Goldstein-Goren Diaspora Research Center, 2003.
Asséo, Henriette. "L'identité tsigane." http://barthes.ens.fr/clio/revues/AHI/articles/preprints/asseo.html.
Assmann, Jan. "Communicative and Cultural Memory." In *Cultural Memory Studies: An International and Interdisciplinary Handbook*, edited by Astrid Erll, Ansgar Nünning, and Sara B. Young. Berlin: Walter de Gruyter, 2008.
———. "Kollektives Gedächtnis und Kulturelle Identität." In *Kultur und Gedächtnis*, edited by Jan Assmann and Tonio Hölscher. Frankfurt am Main: Suhrkamp, 1988: 9–19.
Bessonov, Nikolai. "Ob ispolzovanii terminov 'Poraimos' i 'Kholokost' v znachenii 'genotsyd tsygan.'" *Kholokost i Suchasnist Studii v Ukraini i Sviti* 1, no. 2 (2007): 71–82.
Coman, Alin, Adam D. Brown, Jonathan Koppel, and William Hirst. "Collective Memory from a Psychological Perspective." *International Journal of Politics, Culture and Society* 22 (2009): 125–41.
Crane, Susan A. "Writing the Individual Back into Collective Memory." *American Historical Review* 102, no. 5 (December 1997): 1372–85.
Ene, Sergiu, dir. *Prigoana din Basarabia* [The persecution from Bessarabia]. Filmed in 2012. Chisinau: Centrul National al Romilor din Moldova, Center. Stockholm: E Romani Glinda. Video, 57:00.
Eyal, Gil. "Identity and Trauma: Two Forms of the Will to Memory." *History and Memory* 16, no. 1 (Spring–Summer 2004): 5–36.
Felcher, Anastasia. "The Memory of Vanished Population Groups in Today's East- and Central European Urban Environment: Memory Treatment and Urban Planning in Lviv, Cernivci, Chisinau and Wroclaw." Report for the international conference Lieux de Mémoire: Memory, Forgetting and History: Mapping in the Postcommunist World. Kharkiv, Ukraine, April 17–18, 2014.
Fonseca, Isabel. *Bury Me Standing: The Gypsies and Their Journey*. New York: Vintage, 1995.
Fraser, Angus. *The Gypsies*. Oxford, UK: Blackwell, 1995.
Gedi, Noa, and Yigal Elam. "Collective Memory—What Is It?" *History and Memory* 8, no. 1 (Spring–Summer 1996): 30–50.
Gildea, Robert. *The Past in French History*. New Haven, CT: Yale University Press, 1994.
Green, Anna. "Society Individual Remembering and 'Collective Memory': Theoretical Presuppositions and Contemporary Debates." *Oral History* 32, no. 2, *Memory and Society* (Autumn 2004): 35–44.
Halbwachs, Maurice. *La mémoire collective*. Paris: Presses universitaires de France, 1967.
———. *On Collective Memory*. Edited, translated, and with an introduction by Lewis A. Coser. London: University of Chicago Press, 1992.
———. "Space and the Collective Memory." Chap. 4 in *The Collective Memory*. Translated by Francis J. Ditter Jr. and Vida Yazdi Ditter. New York: Harper and Row, 1980.
Hancock, Ian. "Downplaying the Porrajmos: The Trend to Minimize the Romani Holocaust." *Journal of Genocide Research* 2, no. 3 (2000): 56–63.
———. *The Pariah Syndrome: An Account of Gypsy Slavery and Persecution*. Ann Arbor, MI: Karoma, 1987.

———. "Responses to the Porrajmos: The Romani Holocaust." In *Is the Holocaust Unique: Perspectives on Comparative Genocide*, edited by Alan S. Rosenbaum, 39–64. Oxford, UK: Westview, 1996.

———. "Uniqueness of the Victims: Gypsies, Jews and the Holocaust." *Without Prejudice: The EAFORD International Review of Racial Discrimination* 1, no. 2 (1988): 45–67.

Hodgkin, Katharine, and Susannah Radstone. *Contested Pasts: The Politics of Memory*. New York: Routledge, 2003.

Holler, Martin. *Der nationalsozialistische Völkermord an den Roma in der besetzten Sowjetunion (1941–1944)*. Heidelberg: Dokumentations- und Kulturzentrum Deutscher Sinti und Roma, 2009.

Ioanid, Radu. *The Holocaust in Romania: The Destruction the Jews and Gypsies under Antonescu Regime, 1940–1944*. Chicago: Ivan R. Dee, 2000.

Kansteiner, Wulf. "Finding Meaning in Memory: A Methodological Critique of Collective Memory Studies." *History and Theory* 41, no. 2 (May 2002): 179–97.

Katz, Katalin. Visszafojtott emlékezet. A magyarországi romák holokauszttörténetéhez [*Repressed Memory: Contribution to the Gypsies' Holocaust Story*]. Budapest: Pont Kiado, Serial Interface, 2005.

Lenchovska, Anna. "Videosvidchennia Instytutu Fondu Shoah jak dzherelo do vyvchennia ta vykladannia istorii romiv Ukrainy u period 1941–1944 rr." *Holokost i Suchasnist: Studii v Ukraini i Sviti* 2, no. 6 (2009): 114–23.

Marushiakova, Elena, and Veselin Popov. "Historical and Ethnographic Background: Gypsies, Roma, Sinti." In *Between Past and Future: The Roma of Central and Eastern Europe*, edited by Will Guy, 33–53. Hatfield, UK: University of Hertfordshire Press, 2001.

———. "Holocaust, Porrajmos, Samudaripen: . . . Creation of New National Mythology." https://www.researchgate.net/profile/Vesselin_Popov/publication/235700074_Holocaust_Porrajmos_Samudaripen_Creation_of_New_National_Mythology/links/0912f512b84b1c8ab7000000.pdf?origin=publication_detail.

———. "Holocaust, Porrajmos, Samudaripen . . . Tworzenie nowej mitologii narodowej." *Studia Romologica* 3 (2010): 75–94.

Nora, Pierre. "*Mémoire collective*." In *La nouvelle histoire*, edited by Jacques Le Goff, Roger Chartier, and Jacques Revel, 398–401. Paris: Retz, 1978.

Solonari, Vladimir. "Etnicheskaia chistka ili borba s prestupnostiu? Deportaziia rumynskikh tzygan v Transnistriiu v 1942." *Holokost i Suchasnist: Studii v Ukraini i Sviti* 1, no. 3 (2008): 65–87.

Stauber, Roni, and Raphael Vago. *The Roma: A Minority in Europe; Historical, Political and Social Perspectives*. Budapest: Central European University Press, 2007.

Stewart, Michael. "Remembering without Commemoration: The Mnemonics and Politics of Holocaust Memories among European Roma." *Journal of the Royal Anthropological Institute* 10, no. 3 (September 2004): 561–82.

Wiesel, Elie, Radu Ioanid, Tuvia Friling, and Mihail E. Ionescu, eds. *Final Report: International Commission on the Holocaust in Romania*. Iași: Polirom, 2004.

Wood, Nancy. *Vectors of Memory: Legacies of Trauma in Postwar Europe*. Oxford, UK: Berg, 1999.

Archives and Websites

Author's personal archive. To access the raw data, please contact the author of this article, Anna Abakunova, via email: habakunova1@sheffield.ac.uk.

Yahad in-Unum official website. https://www.yahadinunum.org/.

ANNA (HANNA) ABAKUNOVA is Associate Tutor of History at the University of Sheffield. She is coauthor of *The Genocide and Persecution of Roma and Sinti, Bibliography and Historiographical Review*.

10

POLAND AND POLES IN THE COLLECTIVE MEMORY OF GALICIAN UKRAINIANS

Anna Wylegała

MODERN UKRAINIAN GALICIA (ENCOMPASSING THE PRESENT-DAY L'VIV, IVANO-FRANKIVSK, and Ternopil Oblasts) is one of the most ethnically uniform regions of Ukraine, but several dozen years ago, its inhabitants shared their lands with Jews, Poles, and many other smaller minorities, such as Germans, Armenians, and Czechs. As a result of the Holocaust, wartime ethnic cleansings, and postwar resettlement, Poles, Jews, and other minorities disappeared and Russians arrived. The course of changes in ethnic composition was particularly dramatic in towns and cities, where Poles and Jews were the dominant groups. In this chapter I would like to explore the subject of Poland and Poles in the collective memory of the inhabitants of Galicia. Poles were a particular sort of minority in the region. First, they were a very old minority that had been gradually settling in Galicia ever since the region became a part of Poland in the 14th century, and hence it is hard to classify them as migrants in ethnically Ukrainian territories.[1] Second, although they were far less numerous than Ukrainians, they remained a privileged group in terms of culture, economy, and politics even at times when the Polish state did not exist. They were a classic minority in power.[2] Third, their disappearance from Galicia did not happen without bloodshed. The Polish-Ukrainian conflict over Galicia, which ended with Poland acquiring the region after World War I, escalated during the interwar period and culminated during World War II with ethnic cleansing of the Polish population. This action was met with equally brutal retaliatory strikes orchestrated by Poles.[3] The Poles who did not die during the ethnic cleansing or did not leave immediately afterward abandoned Galicia shortly after the war during the so-called repatriation, a deportation of the Polish population from the Ukrainian SSR organized by the Soviet government in cooperation with Poland's new communist authorities, characterized by various degrees of coercion.[4]

It is only after outlining this historical context that it becomes possible to ask about the place of Poland and Poles in the contemporary collective memory of Galician Ukrainians.[5] Because of Poles' aforementioned particularity as a minority group—a minority in the scale of the region, but also a majority dominant in a Polish national state in the interbellum—this memory will encompass two components: it will be the memory of Poles as a community, of its specific representatives, and of Polish power, statehood, and culture. I will focus on one small town where I conducted field research in the years 2007–10: Zhovkva near L'viv. Zhovkva is a very typical Galician town. Until 1939 it was inhabited by Poles, Jews, and Ukrainians in roughly equal proportions. During the war, the Jewish community perished, the Polish and Ukrainian intelligentsia was almost destroyed by the Soviets, and most of the Poles were "voluntarily" resettled to Poland after the war. In addition, after the Red Army arrived in 1944, a conflict between the new Soviet authorities and the Ukrainian partisans (UPA, Ukrainian Insurgent Army) broke out, resulting in the deportation of hundreds of Ukrainian families who supported the insurgents (or were only accused of doing so) to Siberia. Only a few of the old inhabitants remained in the town. The new settlers in Zhovkva were Ukrainians from neighboring villages who moved to the town in search of better living conditions, Ukrainians from eastern Poland deported to Ukraine in 1944–47, and, finally, people from Russia and Eastern Ukraine, sent to Zhovkva to ensure the Sovietization of the town: teachers, engineers, party officials. After 1945, Zhovkva was forced to become a new, perfectly Soviet town, with an uprooted population and only a few links to its prewar history. The identity of new Zhovkva—soon renamed as Nesterov after a Russian pilot who died in the vicinity of Zhovkva in 1914—was built on the myth of an immemorial Ukrainian character of the town, an underground communist movement in the interwar period, and the martyrdom of Ukrainians oppressed by Polish lords, all of which was legitimized by energetic state propaganda. Memories of certain groups (for example, the few remaining Poles and Jews, but also Ukrainians who returned from Siberia in the late 1950s–60s, and Ukrainian deportees from eastern Poland) were entirely repressed, while memories of others (Red Army veterans, settlers from Eastern Ukraine) were privileged and promoted in official discourse at the local level.

In present-day Zhovkva there is an active Roman Catholic church, attended mostly by older members of a small Polish community, a cloister of Polish nuns who, among other activities, look after children and old people, and a functioning Polish association. Local Poles are, however, neither a numerous nor a significant group—even visiting Polish tourists are more visible. In a town with such a classic Galician history, I and my Ukrainian colleagues recorded more than one hundred biographical interviews with representatives of various groups of citizens from different generations, mostly in family (generational) cycles.[6] The rich material collected in this way allows for analyzing Galician collective memory in miniature, on the scale of a single town. In the present chapter, I will pursue the subject of how the contemporary inhabitants of Zhovkva remember specific "absent others"—Poles who used to be a privileged minority. Is this memory rich and expansive, or fragmentary and poor? Which events or characters dominate it, what kind of emotions accompany it, which judgments of the historical coexistence of Poles and Ukrainians are voiced today? Are there any areas that are taboo, forgotten, or repressed? How does this memory look among people from various groups of citizens (for example, old, prewar inhabitants, Ukrainian deportees from Poland, migrants from the countryside, Russians who settled in the town after 1945) and representatives of different generations? Finally, is the memory of Poles in Zhovkva, or the fact that the town was previously located in Poland, in any way significant for the identity of its present inhabitants?

"A Long Time Ago, in the Days of Poland"

The awareness of the fact that the town used to be a part of a different state is still common in Zhovkva. Only a few interviewees from the youngest age group are unaware that "this used to be Poland." What is interesting is that this ignorance does not depend on origin. Respondents for whom the Polish allegiance of Zhovkva was news had various roots—including Polish ones; one of them (male, born in 1985 in Zhovkva), when asked whether his grandmother told him how life used to be in Poland, answered in the following way: "What—in Poland. . . ? What do you mean, in Poland? (This used to be Poland.) Oooh . . . (Before the war.) Oh, I didn't know that." These were usually the same people who did not know about the existence of a Jewish community in prewar Zhovkva, and hence it is possible to risk the claim that their ignorance not only is the result of prejudice or specific gaps in cultural transmission, but also stems from a general lack of interest in the past. Nevertheless, despite their general awareness of the town's ties with Poland, Zhovkvians often confuse basic facts and do not know what the Polishness of Zhovkva implies: "There was a battle here between Poles and . . . as far as I know, Germans. And they divided the land, as was common back then. And this land went to the Polish side. And when Ukraine regained its independence, then. . . . New borders were drawn and Zhovkva belonged to Ukraine, not Poland. And that's it. And this is the reason for which many people of Polish origins remained here" (female, born in 1988 in Zhovkva).

Confusion about the details is not the exclusive domain of the young; responses of this type came from many representatives of the middle generation. Especially in the latter case, my view is that the cause of their disorientation is to be found in the process of postwar socialization. Soviet propaganda used worn clichés to describe Poles in Ukraine, such as "eternal enemies," "invaders," and "plunderers," focusing on historically remote cases of Polish repression against Ukrainians, such as during the Cossack uprisings. Contemporary history, including the Polish-Ukrainian conflict during World War II and postwar deportations of Poles, was uncomfortable because it did not pair with the official vision of brotherly relations between the simple folk of Poland and Ukraine. The moments in which the simple folk—indifferent to the decrees of official historiography—jumped at each other's throats were consequently ignored or marginalized.[7] Perhaps this is why Zhovkvians from the middle generation find it so difficult to grasp 1939 or 1945 as dates of a change in the town's state allegiance.

The simple statement that Zhovkva used to belong to Poland ends the calm narrative about the Polishness of the town and begins the arguments about its Ukrainian identity. Citizens of Zhovkva "agree to remember" about the Polishness of their city only under the condition that it does not endanger their belief about Zhovkva always being primarily "our" town. This is clearly visible on the example of Zhovkva's old history in connection to Poland and Poles. The interviewees name the famous Poles related to the town, Żółkiewski (the founder, a 17th-century magnate and hetman), sometimes Sobieski (a Polish king from the 17th century), but always add that although a Polish hetman founded Zhovkva, it was created on the site of a Ukrainian village. Those who know more about Zhovkva's history very often emphasize its Ukrainian aspects, at the same time not negating, but ignoring,

Polish ones, thus making it clear that the latter are far less significant to them. A respondent working at the tourist center (male, born in 1980 in Eastern Ukraine) frankly lamented the absence of a town monument dedicated to Żółkiewski because according to him the hetman was really a Ruthenian, not a Pole. When asked about Zhovkva's oldest history, one interviewee named only Ukrainians. There were also very isolated cases—especially among members of the older generation who still had negative views about Poles—of radically diminishing the Polish presence in Zhovkva or even negating it: "And even now they keep bugging us. (Who?) Poles. (But here. . . ?) Yes, here, [they have issues] about Zhovkva. This is where Żółkiewski supposedly lived. Well, Żółkiewski might have lived here. But what they called Zhovkva used to be a village called Vynnyky. And they keep brining up Żółkiewski over and over" (male, born in 1926 in southeast Poland, in Zhovkva since 1944).[8]

In general terms, however, the period of the Commonwealth of Poland is seen positively as a time during which the town prospered and flourished. Although they are remembered unequivocally as Polish lords, Żółkiewski and Sobieski are not evil, foreign invaders but simply a part of Zhovkva's history. Perhaps the familiarity and acceptance of Żółkiewski and Sobieski can be explained by the remoteness of events that can no longer elicit strong emotions. Historical Polishness is treated in a way similar to fairy tales, remote and unreal, almost exotic and, hence, harmless.[9]

Whereas the memory of the Commonwealth of Poland is positive, everything that took place in the 19th and 20th centuries (in a period when Galician Ukrainians had aspirations to independence rivaling those of Poles) is described as occupational government, even if the phrase is not pronounced in so many words. This is illustrated shortly and succinctly by the following quote: "From what my relatives say, they had it best under Austria. It was the most loyal occupation. Because everything that's foreign, not Ukrainian, I will call an occupation, if you don't mind" (female, born in 1951 in Zhovkva). What then does the picture of the "less loyal" occupation, the interbellum, look like in the memories of Zhovkvians? It is dominated by two motifs: on the one hand, the oppression of the Polish authorities; on the other, Polish culture and prosperity. The hardships of life in the Poland of lords are remembered almost exclusively by people who experienced them themselves, while the Second Polish Republic is recalled with fondness mostly by younger people. The memory of negative events focuses on the personal experiences of interviewees, beginning with the earliest periods, associated with school and childhood and marked by unequal treatment. A respondent born in Zhovkva (female, born in 1928 in Zhovkva) remembered a poignant sense of injustice when, as a student in a Polish school, she received a good grade in her mother tongue while her Polish colleagues who did not speak Ukrainian at all got "very good" marks. She also remembers the jeering of her Polish peers: "We talked however we wanted to, but some Poles were tenacious and when they heard someone speaking Ukrainian they immediately responded with 'Oh, look, she's babbling like a swine again!' Yes, these things happened!"

Apart from minor grievances and humiliations from childhood, the interviewees also spoke about the difficulties that adults faced, such as problems with employment or harassment of persons involved in Ukrainian cultural and political life. Sometimes they add with bitterness that it is normal to favor "your own" in a national state, but Poland had an assimilation policy. It is interesting to note that almost no one from the younger generation or the migrants from the East talks about the heavy burden of Polish rule—with one exception.

Polish clout was also strongly and lengthily criticized by a respondent from a Polish family from the region of Zhytomyr, who came to work in Zhovkva in the beginning of the 1950s and married a local Pole:

> For example, I asked my mother-in-law: "Mother, so when you lived in Poland, how was it supposed to be better than it is now? If it was really better, why did you have such a miserable house, and why were there so many of you in it? Grandpa, each child born in a different place. Why—I asked—did you wander around the whole of Western Ukraine like God knows who?" "Well, because there was no work, life was hard." I say: "Well, I don't know, now [in the Soviet Union] there's work for everyone, and you're still not happy." Well, whatever. . . . And now—look, her brother's children all finished university, mother built a house, not minding that her brother spent fifteen years in Vorkuta. And from Vorkuta he brought money and built a very decent home. (female, born in 1933)

Migrants from the East and local Ukrainians in postwar Zhovkva were not only divided by completely different experiences, they also shared a great deal of animosity and prejudice toward each other. Perhaps the locals did not want to openly complain about the Poland of lords because that might in some way put the later, Soviet regime in a higher position—and the locals did not want to voice such opinions when the eastern settlers could hear them.

The second recurrent motif in the interviews are fond recollections of the culture, civilization, and relative prosperity of Poland. Significantly, such opinions are limited to representatives of younger generations with local roots, who have no negative associations with interwar Poland. In their accounts, the leading belief is that their families had a better life in Poland than in the Soviet Union. "They had their own field, they worked, they had their own bread, their own groats, as they say, you understand? Their own cattle. My family had quite a lot of land, they weren't so poor. And then they took it all away and that was that. What's to recollect? We had quite a bit of land, a large house, and then all those horrible things happened, I don't know how we managed to survive all of that, I just don't know" (female, born in 1960 in Zhovkva).

Among people from the older generation, this tone in memories about the interbellum, if it appears at all, is crushed by a poignant sense of injustice suffered from Poles. The only really positive tale about Poland, sentimental and almost idealistic about the period, was found in a narrative of a woman from the oldest generation who came from a mixed Polish-Ukrainian family:

> In Poland this was a wonderful town. . . . The coffeeshops were great, the coffeeshops were wonderful. There was—I just remembered—that there was a great store on this corner—and I always liked to buy myself a *bułka kajzerka* [in Polish, kaiser roll] with ham, sliced with a. . . . And they sliced the ham so evenly! All of it was so fresh, so fragrant, I can't begin to tell you. . . . They say that we have culture now. They call it culture [with irritation]. . . . I have only the best memories from those times. You know, if this was still Poland, we'd have a villa on the main street. We'd be great lords, not bums like we are now, under Soviet regime. (female, born in 1930 in southeast Poland, in Zhovkva since 1939)

Like the younger respondent quoted before, this interviewee spoke about interwar Poland as a country and time in which her family was very well off. In her narrative, the Second Polish Republic becomes the lost country of her childhood, an ideal country in which even ham was sliced more evenly than it is today; the key component seems to be a sense of a lost chance for a better, more fulfilling, and wealthier life.[10] This respondent is the only interviewee who came from a family of intelligentsia and enjoyed wealth and a high social status before the war. The turmoil of war and the postwar Soviet enforcement of uniformity degraded her family on all those levels, which must have been painful for a growing child.

In Times of Terror: Reflection from the Fieldwork

Wartime memories (or lapses of memory) about Poles are centered around the Polish-Ukrainian conflict. As in the case of interwar harassment, it is remembered mostly by representatives of the oldest generation—usually people born in Zhovkva or in the neighborhood, less frequently by migrants from Poland. Among the respondents, there is a common belief that despite the fact that Poles suffered more locally, they only had themselves to blame because they had provoked the Ukrainians with their brutal behavior from before the war ("State terrorism always causes terrorism," female, born in 1960 in L'viv, in Zhovkva since 1992). According to some opinions, only the Poles who really deserved it became victims of violence, because of their attitudes in the interwar period; one of the respondents had this to say about a Polish friend from the time: "There was this R. here, he was a peaceful Pole, they didn't touch him" (male, born in 1929 in southeast Poland, in Zhovkva since 1945). A different argumentation, aimed at reducing the guilt of Ukrainians, points out that the conflict was caused by the Soviets—they disguised themselves as UPA partisans and started killing Poles, who retaliated against the Ukrainians. A woman who witnessed this (but not in Zhovkva) eagerly attempted to convince me that this was the truth: "It wasn't the Ukrainian partisans who murdered Poles, it was done by Russians, Russian partisans, just in time for the holidays they killed the Poles to inspire hatred, here and abroad, well there was no abroad, this was all Galicia. They [killed] the Poles, to provoke them to start killing Ukrainians. I witnessed this" (female, born in 1922 in Bydgoszcz in Poland, since 1944 in L'viv, since 1951 in Zhovkva). Such statements are connected by a desire to remove the odium of murderers from Ukrainians, which my respondents believe Poles view them as. The interview becomes an opportunity to argue that Ukrainians were not guilty of the massacres of Poles in Galicia at the end of World War II, or that they were not the only parties involved. The argumentative strategies of the interviewees take several forms. The first woman claims that Poles began the conflict before the war; the events that took place during the war were a reaction to pacifications, hence Poles are to blame for the results of the conflict. Another respondent portrays the killing of Poles as a simple meting out of justice—in his opinion persons who did no harm to Ukrainians in the interbellum had no reasons to worry. The final interviewee places the blame for starting the conflict on the Soviets, whose aim was to sow discord between Poles and Ukrainians. It is worth noting that these respondents are not attempting to completely acquit Ukrainian insurgents or deny the fact of the mass murders perpetrated by partisans on the Polish population; their argumentation should be described as justification, or rationalization. None denies that Poles were the principal victims of the conflict in Galicia. A tonally similar opinion belongs to another interviewee, who represents the most common view about the Polish-Ukrainian conflict among my respondents (and seemingly also the most widespread view in Ukraine):

> With these Poles it was. . . . It was unpleasant, you know? I for one think that it was done on purpose. For example, we lived together, I have a house in Vynnyky, my parents lived there, and Poles

lived nearby—and we got along well. And then, during the war, they started fighting, someone did this on purpose. Ukrainians started shooting Poles, Poles shot Ukrainians, and a whole lot of people died here. Then most of the Poles left, because it wasn't the same as with those Jewish pogroms, but enough people died. Putting it simply, they turned on each other. (male, born in 1927 in Zhovkva)

While previous interviewees justified the mass murders perpetrated on Poles, this respondent clearly shifts the accents: the killings were not an effect of organized actions directed against the Poles, but a fratricidal conflict, deviously provoked by outside forces. When the issue is presented in this way, all questions of guilt and responsibility are removed, and the only matter left is the experience of a mutually suffered wrong. Whereas such statements among older persons might simply be a reflection of their wartime experiences, similar views among younger people usually evolve toward the effacement of the problem of responsibility; the murders of Poles are lumped into a general lot of wartime woes, horrible, but so remote that it is difficult to judge who fought whom and for what reasons: (Interviewer: Sometimes older people speak about some Polish-Ukrainian conflict here.) "Yes, it happened, it happened. There were some conflicts in the past, my grandmother told me about it. These conflicts took place a long time ago. Well, was it because of the war that these conflicts took place, I don't know. . . . As grandma told it, during the war Poles killed Ukrainians, Ukrainians killed Poles, they shot each other, things happened" (female, born in 1963 in Zhovkva).

On the opposite end of the spectrum is the opinion that the Ukrainians were the main victims of the fratricidal conflict, not Poles. It is interesting that respondents who remember it this way—since they are chiefly older persons—use specific examples in their argumentation, unlike the previous interviewees. Even more interesting is the way they use their examples. Against a backdrop of stories about acts of Polish terror, the subject of the Polish village of Stanyslivka near Zhovkva, whose inhabitants were murdered by Ukrainian insurgents, definitely stands out. In the accounts of my interviewees, Stanyslivka appears as a site of Ukrainian suffering, with a population harassed by troops of the Home Army stationed in the village for a short time. Its subsequent fate is mentioned only in passing, or not at all. Any reference to the later burning down of the village are preceded by arguments somehow sanctioning the deed and transforming its moral status—into an act of necessary self-defence, with the conclusion of the story based on examples of violence against Ukrainians. Thanks to these measures, the mass murder of Poles is lost among a multitude of other details, and the most damning judgment voiced by Ukrainians is the statement that "It was a mutual mass-slaughter" (male, born in 1934 in southeast Poland, in Zhovkva since 1946).

Sharp views about Ukrainian guilt seldom appeared in the accounts of respondents. After the recorder was switched off, an interviewee from the area of Zhytomyr told me with bitterness that her grandson considers the UPA to be heroes, when in fact they were bandits responsible for exterminating many Polish villages in the vicinity. The second person who did not attempt to justify Ukrainian actions in any way while describing the conflict was an older woman from a village near Zhovkva. Perhaps she told her story the way she did because the interviewer was Ukrainian; in any case, it is significant that this woman was visibly afraid that what she said might cause trouble for her even today.

> You see, after the war things were.... That conflict. I still remember, you know, how can one not talk about it, in N.,... there were two or three Polish families. Our distant cousin married a Polish man, and during the conflict, you know, the OUN-UPA, these against others, those against others.... They burned.... I remember when my father woke up and said, "There's a fire in N." I mean, they wanted the Poles to ... [pause] (Leave?) Leave. Maybe you could not record this, no, it won't be necessary, but I'm telling it anyway. (female, born in 1929 in a village near Zhovkva, in Zhovkva since 1951)

An unavoidable question is why the Polish-Ukrainian conflict is remembered only by older people, in other words: Why are the Polish victims remembered in biographical memory but not in collective memory? The majority of the youngest respondents are simply unaware of any wartime wrongdoings between Poles and Ukrainians in Zhovkva. In the middle generation, the vague understanding that "something happened" was common, but the dominant narrative spoke about a brotherly conflict, in which both the Poles and Ukrainians suffered. The only interviewees who claimed that this was a planned operation of the Ukrainian underground aimed at removing Poles from Galicia (and Volhynia)—who mentioned it only in passing while judging the UPA for its political activities—were people who felt nostalgic about the Soviet Union. But even for them, the slaughter of Poles was simply another argument against the UPA, rather than an independently functioning fact.

Remembering the Conflict: The Wider Picture

It seems that the key to explaining the lapses in memory consists of two issues: the direct perception of the conflict, and postwar and contemporary suggestions. In the words of Aleida Assmann (who refers to Freud)—something that was never properly noticed cannot be remembered or forgotten.[11] Assmann's example of an unperceived event of this kind is the Holocaust in Germany, but the perception of the tragedy of Galician Poles by Galician Ukrainians seems to have been similar. Those who lived in towns may never have experienced it directly. The rest did not notice because they did not want to, for many reasons—fear, shame, overwhelming emotions or the desire for national heroes to remain pure.[12] The new arrivals never heard about the slaughter from the locals for obvious reasons, and the Soviet authorities wanted to denigrate the UPA but not at the cost of reminding people about the presence of Poles in Galicia. The Polish-Ukrainian conflict could exist only on a social level in Soviet historiography: the Poles were described using clichés such as Polish lords, bourgeois imperialists, and invaders and uncomfortable subjects were ignored. At the same time, common and local memory in Galicia fostered the myth that it was the Poles who murdered Ukrainians during the war and collaborated with the Germans, while Ukrainians killed Poles only in retaliation.[13] An unnoticed slaughter could not have been described to children and grandchildren—if it was noted, it was probably not a subject pleasantly brought up at family gatherings.[14]

In the case of the youngest generation, who grew up in an independent Ukraine, an additional factor influencing the lack of remembrance of Polish victims is undoubtedly school socialization. There is no place for reflections about the victims (both Polish and Ukrainian) of the UPA in a historical narrative constructed on the myth of a heroic independence underground—and despite the lack of universal Ukrainian acceptance of the heroic perception of the UPA, it is currently the dominant narrative in textbooks and school syllabi. According to L'viv historian Leonid Zashkilniak, although the image of Polish-Ukrainian relationships in Ukrainian textbooks has markedly improved, difficult subjects, especially those in which Ukrainians are guilty, are simply overlooked, while others are analyzed using double standards. (For example, Operation Vistula is presented as a Polish initiative, while the deportation of Poles is blamed on Soviet authorities.)[15] Andrii Portnov bitterly notes that the new Ukrainian textbook on history, published in 2011, makes no mention of the Polish-Ukrainian conflict. (Portnov writes about the ethnic cleansing in Volhynia, but his remarks *de facto* concern the entirety of the Polish-Ukrainian conflict in the war).[16] The previous textbook reduced the mass murders of Poles to a tragedy "of the civilian population on both sides of the conflict." The wartime fate of Poles is perceived in a similar way by the Ukrainian Institute of National Remembrance. In a documentary film recommended by the institute, *Khronika Ukrains'koi Povstans'koi Armii 1941–1954* (A chronicle of the Ukrainian Insurgent Army 1941–1954), two and a half minutes are dedicated to the role of the UPA in the orchestration of the purge of Poles in Volhynia, while the commentary of the narrator (set against a picture of a burning village) stated, "The situation in the region was made more difficult by the conflict between Poles and Ukrainians. . . . The provocative policy [of the Germans] was the reason for the bloody conflict that spread throughout Volhynia and eastern Galicia. Tens of thousands of innocent people died on both sides."[17] From this narrative, it is difficult to understand why these tens of thousands had to die. Also, the dialogue in the spirit of reconciliation at the highest political level came to a halt, although recent events (such as the demolition of the monument of the Polish victims in Huta Pieniacka in L'viv Oblast by unknown perpetrators, subsequently condemned by the Ukrainian Ministry of Foreign Affairs) might activate it again. The strong position of the UINR, headed by Volodymyr Viatrovytch, a historian who has propagated the theory that it was a domestic war between Poles and Ukraine that happened between 1942 and 1947, and not ethnic cleansing, gives no reason to suspect that anything will change in the matter.

Any discussion about the events in Volyn was practically absent from wider public discourse until Polish director Wojciech Smarzowski shot his film *Wołyń* (Volhynia) in 2016. Before that, Ukrainian public intellectuals did talk about Polish heritage in Ukraine, but their reflection concerned cultural heritage, responsibility for historical monuments, the continuity of urban identities, as, for example, in L'viv.[18] Discussions about the Polish-Ukrainian conflict took place in a small circle of professional historians who have had some success in writing balanced opinions, but their voices were rarely heard outside their milieu.[19] Among those who write for a wider audience, the rhetoric of the fratricidal conflict and the search for guilty parties from outside, by blaming the Germans, was dominant. The killings in Volhynia were euphemistically described as "the anti-Polish operation" or even more enigmatically as the "Volhynian tragedy" or "Volhynian massacre," focusing on the victims, and not on the perpetrators. Only a small group of historians (among well-reputed scholars Ihor Iliushyn, Yaroslav Hrytsak, Andrii Zayarniuk, and Andrii Portnov shall be named) used the term *ethnic cleansing*; the events in Galicia, because of their smaller scale, were completely overlooked.[20] Independent associations working for Polish-Ukrainian reconciliation tended toward a compromise, rather than openly (and hence painfully, and with an initial polarizing effect) speak about clear responsibility.[21]

The situation changed slightly after the screening of Smarzowski's movie in Kyiv was widely announced and later canceled. In Poland, *Wołyń* was received rather warmly on the merits of its artistic value, cautiously where it concerned its perspective on improving Polish-Ukrainian dialogue, but nobody criticized its historical correctness and accuracy. In Kyiv, the screening (with the director in attendance) was organized by the Polish Institute but was canceled after the Ukrainian Ministry of Foreign Affairs issued a letter warning that the event could become a threat to public security. Although there was no official possibility of seeing the picture, fervent discussion on the movie started in Ukrainian media. Most of the participants admitted that they had not seen the movie, but nevertheless *Wołyń* was judged and condemned as "anti-Ukrainian," "propagandist," and harmful to mutual Polish-Ukrainian relations. It is interesting that nobody argued with the facts pictured in the film—the general opinion was that it simply should not have been made in the current political situation, when Ukraine needed Poland's support instead of another "war of memory."[22]

Unfortunately, the qualitative data this chapter is based on was gathered before current developments in the Ukrainian debate took place, and it is not possible to clearly estimate how much they might have influenced the local perception of the Polish-Ukrainian conflict. The preliminary results of the first opinion poll on the issue, however, allow one to risk a conjecture that the changes, if any, were probably not that significant.[23] In Western Ukraine, the statistical data show no radical changes in the declared knowledge of and opinions on what happened in Volhynia in 1943. In 2003 41.3 percent of the respondents (from Volhynia) thought that Ukrainians were the main victims in the conflict, 14.4 percent that only Ukrainians were victims, 25.7 percent believed that both sides suffered equally; 38.7 percent claimed that Poles started the conflict, 16.1 percent blamed Ukrainians, and 23.2 percent blamed Germans or Soviets. In 2016, 39.7 percent of the interviewees saw the conflict as fratricidal, 2.1 percent blamed Ukrainians only, 6.4 percent blamed Ukrainians and Poles, but mostly Ukrainians; 13.7 percent Ukrainians and Poles, but mostly Poles; 12.1 percent claimed Poles suffered because of the Polish pacifications in the 1930s; 2.1 percent blamed the Germans, and 16.1 percent blamed the Soviet Union. 42 percent answered with the "difficult to say" option. Of course, it is difficult to compare answers to differently formulated questions, but most of the important judgments seem to correspond well with each other; the new trend in 2016 is to perceive the conflict more as a "common tragedy," and less as a "tragedy of the Ukrainians." Another important finding is that even after the 2016 discussion, only 17.6 percent of Western Ukrainians possessed good knowledge on the subject, 44.5 percent knew "very little," and 37.9 percent knew nothing.

Hence, while Ukrainian reactions to Smarzowski's film show that, in general, Ukrainians are not ready to face the fact that the ethnic cleansing of Poles took place in Western Ukraine during the war, it is also difficult to expect that the inhabitants of Zhovkva, and more generally, Galicia—especially the youngest ones—would remember or commemorate the Polish victims of the UPA and wartime neighborly violence.

Exodus, Deportation, Marginalization

At first glance, it seems puzzling that although the Polish-Ukrainian conflict is absent from the consciousness of the majority of interviewees, these same people broadly speak about the postwar departure of Poles from Zhovkva. The respondents are convinced that the Poles left the town voluntarily and that deportations were rare. A dominant conviction exists that Poles simply did not want to live in the Soviet Union and left for Poland to live in their motherland. According to an interviewee who came to Zhovkva from Eastern Ukraine, the Poles "left themselves. But they were given the. . . . They left of their own will, there was no violence. The people who wanted to left. But most of them went to Poland. . . . They didn't want a Soviet regime" (female, born in 1927, in Zhovkva since 1948). The desire to "return" is quoted as the reason for the Poles' departure by both older and younger respondents. It is interesting that, when speaking about the subject, a large number of them use propagandist clichés, such as "returning to the motherland": "The Poles simply went home, because, as I understand it, back then there was simply a lot of. . . . There was the opportunity, because the Germans were taken from Poland, and there was land, and they simply returned. (But this . . .) See, even the grandparents' house, my grandpa's parents, that's also a Polish house. And they returned as well" (female, born in 1982 in Zhovkva).

The abundance of such formulations in narratives about the Poles' departure to the West, especially among interviewees from the second and third generations, illustrates the power of Soviet propaganda. It also seems to show how easy it is to make an Other into an alien, and to consider a group that lived in a given area for centuries as migrants from abroad, who have settled there because of some historical mistake. Under such circumstances, the postwar activities of the regime are welcomed as an "ordering of a national mess" and allow one to place the responsibility of the deportations on the authorities. There is no shortage of older respondents who not only believe that the Poles were not harmed, but that they in fact benefited from exchanging Galicia for the "reclaimed lands": "Well, and that was great for Poles, because they got the German territories and our lands [the interviewee is referring to the region of Chełm], and now Poland is a bit richer. . . . They had no fertile soil, and now it's all turned out for the better for them, that's why they did this" (female, born in 1928 in southeast Poland, in Zhovkva since 1945).

Claims about the alleged benefits of resettlement are often accompanied by somewhat ironical commentaries that the Poles left because they did not want to live with Ukrainians any more. "They didn't want to live with Ukrainians, oh no. They wanted to go to Poland, to their own lands" (female, born in 1928 in southeast Poland, in Zhovkva since 1944). Only older persons use this tone, however, and it seems that the attitude may be the result of their unpleasant experiences of living with Poles in Zhovkva, or some other town in the case of deportees from Poland. At times, this argumentation is coupled with downplaying the scale of the deportations; the interviewees claim that yes, Poles were resettled, but there was only a handful of them in Zhovkva, so the scale of the process cannot be described as massive. This type of memory is to some degree a continuation of the debate about Zhovkvian identity, signalized in the first part of this chapter: statements about postwar resettlement are used to indirectly convey the argument that Poles were never the majority in the town (as they were in L'viv), and hence there is no point in dwelling upon their disappearance.

In the entire sample of nearly one hundred interviewees, only two people (from the oldest generation) clearly stated that the Poles left because they were afraid of Ukrainians, and that the brutality of the conflict made further coexistence impossible: "(Interviewer: Why didn't the Poles want to stay in Zhovkva?) Well, you see, these were times when an awful lot of them were murdered. (Here, in Zhovkva?) Yes, why not here? When we came here there were very few Poles left. But the slaughter here was massive. Massive. They told us that one was burned here, another was killed there, another one" (male, born in 1934 in southeast Poland, in Zhovkva since 1946).

Rarely does the awareness that the Poles were losing their homeland (often after losing their loved ones) and suffering through an enormous tragedy appear in the interviews from Zhovkva—and it is more prevalent among educated younger respondents.

> In reality they were driven out. . . . But even here I can't see that they were right. . . . Casimir III took Galicia then [in the 14th century], Ukrainian lands, that's a fact, yes. But, on the other hand, entire generations lived here through all these years. So you can't say that this wasn't, that this wasn't their homeland. Take, for example, the Turks or the Tatars, they conquered, invaded, looted, and left. But this was different. (female, born in 1968 in L'viv Oblast, in Zhovkva since 1974)

An important part in the quoted fragment concerns the comparison of Poles with Turks and Tatars, which was intended to emphasize that the former could not be treated as invaders after so many centuries. They were as tied to Galicia as the local Ukrainians. Such beliefs are extremely rare among respondents from Zhovkva. Any signs of sorrow caused by the departure of Poles seem equally rare—among the many people who went to school with them, worked and shared their everyday lives with Poles, only one person said it is sad that they are no longer here. "And then our folks from Poland, even this V., she was brought from Poland, and the man from that house [was taken away]. And there were these great Poles here, these girls, we used to go to school together. (They were told to leave, yes?) You had to do what they said" (female, born in 1924 in Zhovkva).

Why is the memory of the resettlement of Poles from Zhovkva, while so rich in comparison to other "Polish" subjects, at the same time almost devoid of any compassion or empathy? Several causes of this apparent lack of sensitivity toward the suffering of others might be enumerated. Perhaps the most important factor, referring to the earlier biographical experience of the oldest respondents, are the problematic relations between Poles and Ukrainians from the interwar period and their dramatic deterioration during the war. Ukrainians in Zhovkva (including those resettled from Poland) have many negative experiences associated with Polish authorities and Polish neighbors. The Poles were a side in a neighborly, and thus far more painful, conflict with the Ukrainians. The conflict also had a deeply internalized class aspect—although the objective economical differences between Galician Poles and Ukrainians might have been practically nonexistent at the time of the confrontation, many Ukrainians (and Poles) continued to think in class categories of Polish lords and Ukrainian peasants. For the forced migrants from Poland, Poles—Zhovkvians or not—were the people who had dispossessed them of their homes. All these factors contributed to the Zhovkvian Poles becoming an unwelcome group. In such a situation, their disappearance was met with relief or indifference, but not with regret.

Another issue of some significance here is the fact that the majority of the Poles left Zhovkva at the beginning of the repatriation, shortly after the war, while most of the new settlers—from Eastern Ukraine or from Poland—appeared in the town in the following year, already after the largest wave of "repatriates" had departed. Thus, the new arrivals rarely witnessed the deportations directly, and seldom did the people who had just lost their homes live together with those awaiting the same fate. The Ukrainians who came from Poland rarely spoke about settling in Polish homes or contacting the Poles preparing to leave, and when they mentioned these things, they were terse. Perhaps this is why the issue of meeting the departing Poles seldom appears in conversations with younger persons. Whenever anyone actually mentions it, it is usually within the context of moving into Polish homes, although that is very rare as well. For the majority of the younger respondents—in this case, regardless of their origins—it no longer matters whether the house they live in once belonged to a Jew or a Pole. It might be useful to ask whether it was so insignificant that their grandparents never mentioned it, or whether the architecture of the Polish and Jewish houses appeared similar to the style the older generation knew from their hometowns, several dozen kilometers away from Zhovkva. The acquisition of Polish property is far more important to members of the older generation—local Zhovkvians and Polish migrants—and the middle generation of local families. Various groups of citizens blame each other for claiming Polish estates:

> And in Zhovkva, the Polish houses. . . . Some Poles were still here, not all of them had left. And they said: "Wait until they leave, there'll be room, if some place is vacant you can move in." But there were almost no vacant homes because after the Poles had left, their neighbors, Ukrainians, took the houses for themselves. And there was no place to go. (male, born in 1929 in southeast Poland, in Zhovkva since 1945)

> They [the Poles] were resettled. This person died, that person was deported to Siberia, and another person was resettled. But the houses remained, huge tenement houses. So the Muscovites moved in. . . . All those houses are inhabited by easterners now. None of us locals live there. (female, born in 1963 in Zhovkva)

The Poles remembered from the interbellum and the time of the war—suddenly disappear from view after the war ends, they become socially invisible. If anyone mentions Poles in Soviet Zhovkva at all, they recall individual persons, never social Ukrainian-Polish relations or the Polish community as a whole. Stereotypical phrases so common in tales about the interwar period, such as "Poles were nasty" or "Poles were good to live with," are absent. They are replaced with declarations that the nationality of the respondent's neighbors has no meaning to them, and never had. Migrants from the East are particularly adroit at offering statements downplaying the significance of nationality. The Poles are invisible in memory is not only because of their physical disappearance but is also because of the social marginalization of the ones who remained—as a result of Soviet activities aimed at erasing the traces of Polish presence, as well as the fear of manifesting, or even disclosing, their identities among the remaining Zhovkvian Poles themselves: "(Interviewer: When you came here, were there many Poles left?) As in people admitting to being Polish? What are you talking about?! Maybe there were two or three people that I knew were Polish because they spoke the language. . . . This was a place where you hid the fact that you were Polish" (female, born in 1933 in Central Ukraine, in Zhovkva since 1954). Apart from the fear of revealing themselves, the increasing marginalization of Poles was caused by their ongoing assimilation, partly connected to fear of standing out and social ostracism on many levels. It interesting that the marginalization of the Poles was noticed primarily by younger, more educated interviewees, who were perhaps more sensitive to the identity changes taking place before them. As one respondent said, "If you had anything in the family, you had to hide it as best as you could and never tell anyone, because if, God forbid, you played with someone and they went home and said anything—you'd get a visit, there'd be talks, plans for educational work" (female, born in 1972 in Zhovkva).

The postwar situation of Poles in Zhovkva might be summed up briefly in the following words: those who survived left, and those who stayed were forgotten anyway. Only the breakthrough of the 1990s changed the status of the Polish community—both in the new sociopolitical reality of Ukraine and in the consciousness of Zhovkva's citizens.

"Now It's All Over"

After Ukraine regained its independence, Zhovkvian Poles, like other marginalized groups, "went out of hiding": they took back their church, formed an association, started visiting Poland and having Polish guests. But their position in the consciousness of Ukrainian Zhovkvians is rather problematic. Respondents make decisive claims about the presence of a Polish community in modern-day Zhovkva, offering the Catholic congregation as proof, but they fall silent when asked about specific people—neighbors, colleagues at work or school. The older interviewees talk about persons their own age, who are often already dead, sometimes mentioning the mayor (the mayor at the time of recording the interviews did indeed have Polish roots), while younger respondents say that they are unsure whether the Poles they know are "real" Poles. It is striking that asking about Poles in today's Zhovkva immediately elicits reassuring claims that there are no conflicts about the issue, even though the question suggests no such context. This is seen in the quote below: "Poles? You can see that it's better now, maybe back then, in the Soviet Union. . . . I'd say that here in Zhovkva, there's no Ukrainians versus Poles, Zhovkva's just like any other town" (female, born in 1982 in Zhovkva).

The first (and sometimes only) association with the present-day Polish community in Zhovkva is the collegiate church. Poles are perceived as people who go to church and cultivate Catholic religious traditions. Their distinctness in this regard is treated with sympathy, and even a sort of local pride: Zhovkva becomes more colorful and original in the eyes of strangers for possessing a small but ethnographically charming (different creed, different language and customs) minority. Without exception, all respondents emphasize the harmonious coexistence of the Roman and Greek Catholic Churches in Zhovkva, offering examples of the friendship and mutual holiday visits between priests—often as a counterbalance to the tense relations with the Orthodox Church of the Moscow Patriarchate:

> Our churches—we attend them both, we come to worship on Christmas Eve, we sing, everything. There's friendship, and the priest. . . . At first, almost everything was in Polish, few people worshiped here—everything was in Polish. Then it started to be in Ukrainian as well, fifty-fifty. . . . All this, and they see that a lot of folks worship at the church, pure Ukrainians. So that Poles here now. . . . They are well regarded, treated with sympathy by people. (male, born in 1960 in Zhovkva)

Respondents regard today's Polish-Ukrainian relationships as very good, both on the level of the local Polish community in Zhovkva and in contacts with Poles visiting the town (people in the latter group are sometimes called real Poles, in contrast with local Poles, because they live in Poland). This is easily seen in the accounts of two middle-aged siblings from a family of migrants from Poland; notably, both of them emphasize that Poles have nothing to worry about in an independent Ukraine.

> Poles have it good now, isn't that true! Nowadays, no one will say anything bad to them. When our people started going there, my God, they have such contacts there now! The youth has such contacts—they go to visit people, they pack the meat into cars.... A shared business. (So there are contacts?) Yes, and they are extensive! They come here, at every local celebration there's a whole bunch of them. They drink, they talk, there's no hatred, and among young people—there's friendship. They became really well liked. People treat them well, they forgive them everything, they let things be! Well, it is practically their town. We built it, the Poles ran the businesses, it's their town.... (Do they say it's their town when they come here?) They used to say that a lot, but now that's no longer the case. (They don't say that any more?) It used to be: *it's our town, it's our town* [in Polish]. Now it's all over with. (male, born in 1960 in Zhovkva)

> Don't believe it when people tell you that you'll get beaten up or murdered here. Everyone lives in harmony. There are bandits here, and there are bandits in your country. It's just people talking nonsense. (female, born in 1963 in Zhovkva)

Both interviewees argue that there is no more conflict, shared businesses and social contacts flourish among the youth. It seems that Poles have irrevocably—and the younger the respondents, the more permanently—lost their status of significant Others, which they traditionally held among Ukrainian Galicians. Whereas up until World War II, and to some extent also in the early postwar years, Galician Ukrainians defined their national and cultural identity in opposition to Poles, now Poles have lost their significance—both the ones who stayed in Zhovkva, and those who left. According to Yaroslav Hrytsak, this degradation in the hierarchy of enmity was caused by the physical absence of Poles and the loss of their prior status.[24] Absent or harmless, Poles became unimportant; their place in the national imagination was taken by Russians/Soviets.

Despite this, I expected to hear about the symbolic significance of Poles when I asked for opinions about Polish tourists visiting Zhovkva today. But such visits are received with favorable indifference, they conjure no demons from the past, they do not become a pretext for difficult conversations about the past, and especially not a pretext for a new conflict. The majority of Zhovkvians (and particularly the more educated ones) regard the Poles with understanding; the town was founded by a Pole, it is tied with Polish history, hence the Polish tourists. Migrants from the oldest generation also notice an obvious analogy: Poles come to Zhovkva in the same way as they visited their former homes in Poland after 1991. Most often, their views take the form of a simple consent for the presence of Polish tourists, as in the statement of a woman who answered the question of whether Poles come to Zhovkva with "And why wouldn't they? They come, tourists come, and these Poles [former inhabitants] also come.... At first, everyone wanted to go. I also went to see my old home" (female, born in 1928 in southeast Poland, in Zhovkva since 1945). Less frequently, a more elaborate thought appears—and the respondent uses his experience of visiting his former home to comment on the Poles' visits in Zhovkva: "It's the same here. The historical heritage remains and these people, Poles who used to live here, who used to work here, who built and renovated these houses, they are happy about it. They have some feelings for this place. They are happy. When they come, and they come often, they say: 'We lived here, we worked here.'

These aren't even parents, but children and grandchildren" (male, born in 1934 in southeast Poland, in Zhovkva since 1946).

When asked if they find the numerous groups of Poles coming to Zhovkva annoying, the respondents quickly deny, and sometimes were even outraged that their community could be suspected of such a lack of hospitality. They jokingly added to their answers that only an unreasonable person would saw off a branch they were sitting on—the interviewees perceived the Polish tours from a purely economical perspective. It is worth noting that some respondents' lack of understanding of the reasons of a possible animosity toward Polish tourists results from their misapprehension of the feelings that motivate some Poles to visit Zhovkva in the first place. When asked why—in her opinion—Poles come to Zhovkva in such large numbers, one respondent said that she did not know. Her perception of the Poles coming to Zhovkva was entirely positive because she saw them as regular tourists, not associating their presence with any historical context: "(Interviewer: Doesn't it make people unhappy, you know, that Poles and Jews come to visit?) No! Thank God that they have the opportunity to come here and see the town, I'd like it too if someone took me on a visit to Poland, took me on a tour, why not? People are wealthier, they can afford it, so why not? I'm all for it, let them come, let them see our town!" (female, born in 1971 in Zhovkva).

Unfavorable opinions about Polish tourists appeared sporadically and usually in the form of reported speech—interviewees claimed that there were people who disliked the Polish visits, and they pointed clearly at "nationalists," who, broadly speaking, represent here the part of Zhovkvian community characterized by patriotic and radical anti-Russian or anticommunist views: (Interviewer: So then, Poles are treated normally?) "Yes, even.... You know who doesn't treat them normally? Nationalists, those . . . [whispering]. In Ukraine they.... They don't take kindly to, they have something against Russians and, and ... 'Psheki'[25] have come.' I can't even understand what they're trying to say by that, what's hiding in their souls" (female, born in 1954 in Zhovkva). None of my interviewees, however, expressed any open discontent about Polish visits in Zhovkva. It should be questioned whether the situation would have been different if I were not a Pole; but such views did not appear even in interviews recorded by my Ukrainian coworkers.

Instead of Conclusions

The memory of Poles in Zhovkva is substantially varied, primarily because of generational differences, but also because of the origins of the respondents or their family roots. Among older people—both locals and migrants from Poland—memory is dominated by an "account of grudges" that opens with prewar grievances and wartime conflict. Migrants from the East know little about the Polish presence in the town's past—there was a dramatic lack of mutual trust between the newcomers and the locals after the war, which might have affected the transmission of local memory. Easterners, if they know anything about the Poles in general, usually talk about the departure of the group (possibly because they witnessed it at least partially), but not about the wartime conflict. Accounts of persons from the middle generation are somewhat similar: their accounts consist mainly of generalities, a conviction about the voluntariness of the postwar repatriation—with sparse mentions of the interwar period among respondents from local families. With rare exceptions, they do not talk about the conflict. In the youngest generation, many interviewees were ignorant of the fact that Zhovkva was once a town within Polish borders. This historical unawareness of the younger generations often concerned both Poles and Jews; many of the respondents could be described by paraphrasing the saying "after us, the deluge" and changing it into "before us, the deluge." It is interesting that the young are not selective in this regard; their lack of memory is equally ruthless in relation to the wartime conflict and the interwar repressions against Ukrainians. I wrote earlier about why Zhovkvian families did not transmit the memory of the conflict. But why were the periods of Polish-Ukrainian relations in which the Poles were the bad ones also ignored, that is the interbellum and the Polish repressions against the Ukrainian independence movement? It seems that the interests of the local community and the historical policies of the postwar and independent Ukrainian authorities coincided in the case of memories of Poles. The past existence of a significant Polish community in Galicia that dominated culture and politics did not mesh well with the goals of propagandists in the Ukrainian SSR, or with the designs for new Ukraine's historical policy. In turn, family memory (in contrast to the biographical memory of the oldest respondents) was not a good match for recollections about interwar repressions because a logically arising consequence would be the uncomfortable question of what happened to the oppressors.

Apart from the silence at home, the (lack of) memory about Poles has been shaped by official discourse. The changes that occurred in it after 1991 are substantial, but Poles are still represented as a side in the conflict, with far less attention given to Polish-Ukrainian cultural ties and social life.[26] Meanwhile, as Natalia Yakovenko rightly notes, the stereotypes of one's own and neighboring nations, "us-aliens" and "enemy-friend" positioning, are shaped in childhood and adolescence through literature, historical cinema, and the history taught at school.[27] It is hard to expect that the youngest generation of Zhovkvians—which is presented with a broad vision of Poland and Ukraine as hostile, separate cultural entities—would be interested in discovering the history of Zhovkva's Poles. The situation is also made problematic by the fact that Poles are absent from the new image of the town's history, formed after 1991, and appear only when it is comfortable and safe. A glance at the exhibition at the town museum or the locally published guides, albums, and maps with landmarks allow one to conclude that today, Żółkiewski and Sobieski are a part of Zhovkva's history, but social and political activists from the 19th century are not. A mysterious lacuna of several hundred years occurs in the narrative about Polish elements in the town's history after the times of the hetman and the king, and then, deus ex machina, neat and renovated Polish churches suddenly emerge. In calendars with Polish postcards from the interwar period published by the Zhovkvian museum, there is no explanation of what happened to the world these pictures depict.

Today's Zhovkvians associate Poles with modern times—Poland is a rich neighbor, a role model of successful political transformation. An additional factor influencing its positive image is the support Ukraine received from Poles during the Orange Revolution of 2004. The studies on which this chapter is based were conducted before the outbreak of the present

Ukrainian-Russian conflict, but one can imagine that Poland's attitude toward that war can only strengthen the trend of positive perception. These suspicions can be confirmed by quantitative studies that show that opinions about Poles and Poland among Ukrainians are the best they have been in years, distancing representatives of other nations, with Russians very far behind.[28] Apart from the oldest generation, historical associations and stereotypes are rare—and this does not seem to be limited to Western Ukraine.[29] This diagnosis was confirmed by studies conducted in recent years among history students from L'viv. The majority of the students had positive opinions about Poles and Poland because they related them to contemporary times.[30] Similar conclusions stem from studies done in Ukraine in 2013 by Joanna Konieczna and her team: only 9 percent of Ukrainians associated Poland with history.[31]

Thus, for Zhovkvians, Poland and Poles represent European standards—both economical and cultural; it would be difficult for them not to be regarded positively, especially among young people, with pro-Western and pro-European beliefs. Today's attitudes toward Poles in Zhovkva might be described as model, a situation unlikely to be stable because the model character has its roots in the superficiality and incompleteness of collective memory, especially when almost all difficult issues are ignored. It is easy to declare warm feelings toward a person one sees only occasionally; it is equally easy to have good memories about the Other who disappeared from the area along with his baggage of difficult experiences related to his historical presence. It is easy to imagine that when the generation of witnesses for whom the presence of Poles was part of their experience passes away, young Zhovkvians will lose the awareness of an element of their local history, since that memory has never been transmitted to them. Stopping the transmission may result only in ongoing forgetfulness and a mythologizing of the remaining pieces in order to make them fit present needs. In the context of Ukrainian-Polish relations, suppression of the memory carries the threat of an eventual outburst: at some moment, it may turn out that Zhovkvians—Ukrainians, Russians, and maybe even Poles—will be unable to understand Poles from Poland who will want to speak openly about a shared history and reconciliation.

Of course, forgetting is also a part of memory—according to Aleida Assmann, only the combination of remembering and forgetting at an individual and collective level creates the cultural memory of a given group.[32] Assmann believes that forgetting can be active—in which case an element is lost forever—or passive, when something can be brought back to memory, and the act of forgetting occurs through a lack of attention, rather than intentionally; Assmann uses the metaphor of an exhibition and a storage room at a museum (active and passive memory, canon and archive). It seems that the Zhovkvian memory of historical Polishness has not been irreversibly lost yet—one can still reach into the storage room and bring the remembrance out to one of the exhibition rooms, if only one in the back. The painful, antagonizing memory still pierces through the veil of forgetfulness; for example, at times when respondents reflexively say that "everything is fine with the Poles *now*." The future fate of the memory depends primarily on whether the young generation will consider it potentially important for constructing their own identity. This, in turn, both in Zhovkva and Western Ukraine as a whole, relies on the evolution of Ukrainian remembrance policy at the central level.

Notes

1. An exception to this rule were Polish settlers, the so-called colonists, who appeared in Galicia and Volhynia after these regions became a part of the Second Polish Republic. These were primarily military settlers (soldiers from Józef Piłsudski's legions, among others) who received or bought land on favorable conditions for their services in the fight for independence, but also peasants from overpopulated regions of Central Poland and Podkarpacie. See, for example, Stobniak-Smogorzewska, *Kresowe*.

2. For more on the specificity of privileged ethnic minorities in Central-Eastern Europe, see Deak, "How to Construct," 207.

3. For objective studies on the Polish-Ukrainian conflict, see Motyka, *Od rzezi wołyńskiej*; Iliushyn, *UPA i AK*.

4. See Kochanowski, "Gathering Poles."

5. Because of the empirical, rather than theoretical nature of this chapter, I will not delve into terminological disputes over the concept of collective memory. In my understanding of collective memory, I will use the classic definition of Maurice Halbwachs, developed in modern times by such scholars as Aleida and Jan Assmann, Harald Welzer, and Astrid Erll.

6. A methodological inspiration for the generational cycle (family) interviews were the studies of Gabriele Rosenthal and Harald Welzer. See Rosenthal, *Holocaust*; Welzer, Moller, and Tschuggnall, *"Opa war kein Nazi."*

7. See Ruda, "Do dzherel mifolohizatsii."

8. In her research on the relations people have with the places where they live, Maria Lewicka stated that in all the towns with "transferred blood" that she studied (L'viv, Szczecin, Wrocław, Vilnius), citizens overestimated the percentage of their nationality in the prewar population (Lewicka, *Psychologia miejsca*, 466).

9. It is worth noting here that despite the positive memory of the Commonwealth of Poland, it never became a foundation for a myth that would make Ukraine a part of Europe in the eyes of Galician Ukrainians—either in Soviet times or later. Whereas the European character of Ukrainian (or Galician) culture was uncontested in discussions among intellectuals, Polish cultural and civilizational mediation—in contrast to, for example, its Austrian equivalent—was accepted much less enthusiastically. See Hnatiuk, *Pożegnanie*; Yakovenko, *Paralelnyi svit*, 333–65.

10. This type of narrative, filled with nostalgia for the lost country of one's childhood, is characteristic primarily among people who physically lost their countries—deportees and migrants. As we can see here, however, similar narrative patterns also appear in interviews with persons who did not change their home—it is the hometown that changed. See Kaźmierska, *Doświadczenia wojenne Polaków*.

11. See Assmann, "Pięć strategii." An interesting comment on the issue appears in social psychology. According to Martin A. Conway, the failure of facts to match current structures of biographical memory may never be registered by it; in other words, we do not remember things that are uncomfortable for us, or we remember them differently, because the main function of biographical memory is maintaining the consistency of the self. See Conway, "Autobiographical Knowledge."

12. Jacek Nowak writes about the lack of remembrance of Poles murdered in a neighboring village in Ukraine in *Społeczne reguły pamiętania*, 238.

13. See Ruda, "Do dzherel mifolohizatsii."

14. It is possible that some form of the memory existed at a certain point but was later rejected. A similar mechanism was described by Harald Welzer and Karoline Tschuggnall; analyzing the generational transfer of memory of the time of Nazism, they reached the conclusion that children and grandchildren suppress the issues that might threaten the moral integrity of their ancestors' images or familial or social solidarity. See Tschuggnall and Welzer, "Rewriting Memories."

15. See Zashkilniak, "Istoriia 'svoia.'"

16. See Portnov, "Ukraińska (nie)pamięć."

17. *Khronika Ukrains'koi Povstans'koi Armii 1941–1954*, video, part one: https://www.youtube.com/watch?v=c1bX6em5PRs; part two: https://www.youtube.com/watch?v=LxGbJ-RyuTU, accessed February 15, 2017.

18. See Narvselius, "Tragic Past."

19. In the years 1996–2001, a series of cyclical meetings of Polish and Ukrainian historians, initiated by the KARTA Center and the International Association of Soldiers of the Home Army, were held and resulted in

several extremely valuable publications. For a summary of the articles in English, see Rezmer, "Ethnic Changes." In October 2015, a new committee of historians accredited by the Polish and Ukrainian Institute of National Remembrance was created.

20. See Portnov, *Istorii*.

21. A project dedicated to commemorating the "Righteous"—Ukrainians who saved Poles and Poles who saved Ukrainians during World War II, organized by Brama Grodzka and Panorama Kultur in Lublin and the Lesya Ukrainka Eastern European National University in Lutsk, may serve as an example of such activities. See Zińczuk, *Pojednanie: Galicja*; Zińczuk, *Pojednanie: Wołyń*.

22. For a short overview of the discussion that followed in Ukraine, see Konończuk, "Ukraińcy patrzą na 'Wołyń.'"

23. For the quantitative studies from 2003, see Berdychowska, "Ukraińcy wobec Wołynia." For the results of the new opinion poll, see Romanenko, "Kak ukraintsi."

24. Hrytsak, "Historical Memory."

25. A depreciating, vernacular term for Poles in Ukrainian that references Polish phonetics and its large number of sibilant sounds such as "sz."

26. See Zashkilniak, "Istoriia 'svoia'"; Sereda, "Vplyv pol's'kykh."

27. Yakovenko, *Paralelnyi svit*, 366–82.

28. See Rating Group, "IRI Ukraine Poll."

29. The disappearance of past stereotypes on the Ukrainian-Polish border has been described by Yaroslav Hrytsak among others. See Hrytsak, "Stereotypy o stereotypach."

30. See Arkusza, "Pol's'kyi i rosiiskyi."

31. Fomina et al., *Polska-Ukraina*, 49–51.

32. See Assmann, "Canon and Archive."

Bibliography

Arkusza, Olena. "Pol's'kyi i rosiis'kyi chynnyky u formuvanii suchasnoi natsional'noi svidomosti halytskykh ukraintsiv: istorychnyi dosvid i suchasni paraleli." In *Istorychni mify i stereotypy ta mizhnatsional'ni vidnosyny v suchasnii Ukraini*, edited by Leonid Zashkilniak, 144–209. L'viv: Instytut Ukrainoznavstva im. Kryp'iakevycha, 2009.

Assmann, Aleida. "Canon and Archive." In *Cultural Memory Studies: An International and Interdisciplinary Handbook*, edited by Astrid. Erll and Ansgar Niinning, 97–108. Berlin: Walter de Gruyter, 2008.

———. "Pięć strategii wypierania ze świadomości." Translated from German by Artur Pełka. In *Pamięć zbiorowa i kulturowa: współczesna perspektywa niemiecka*, edited by Magdalena Saryusz-Wolska, 333–50. Warszawa: Universitas, 2009.

Berdychowska, Bogumiła. "Ukraińcy wobec Wołynia." *Zeszyty historyczne* 146 (2003): 65–104.

Conway, Martin. A. "Autobiographical Knowledge and Autobiographical Memories." In *Remembering Our Past: Studies in Autobiographical Memory*, edited by David Rubin, 67–93. New York: Cambridge University Press, 1996.

Deák, István. "How to Construct a Productive, Disciplined, Monoethnic Society: The Dilemma of East Central European Governments, 1914–1956." In *Landscaping the Human Garden, Twentieth-Century Population Management in a Comparative Framework*, edited by Amir Weiner, 205–17. Stanford, CA: Stanford University Press, 2003.

Fomina, Joanna, Joanna Konieczna, Jacek Kucharczyk, and Ł. Wenerski. *Polska-Ukraina, Polacy-Ukraińcy: spojrzenie przez granicę*. Warsaw: Instytut Spraw Publicznych, 2013.

Hnatiuk, Ola. *Pożegnanie z imperium: ukraińskie dyskusje o tożsamości*. Lublin: UMCS, 2003.

Hrytsak, Yaroslav. "Stereotypy o stereotypach: pogranicze ukraińsko-polskie i problemy jego prezentacji." In *Akulturacja/asymilacja na pograniczach kulturowych Europy Środkowo-Wschodniej w XIX i XX w.* Vol. 1, *Stereotypy i pamięć*, edited by Robert Traba, 53–77. Warszawa: Instytut Studiów Politycznych PAN, 2009.

———. "Historical Memory and Regional Identity among Galicia's Ukrainians." In *The Roots of Ukrainian Nationalism: Galicia as Ukrainian's Piemont*, edited by Paul Robert Magocsi, 185–209. Toronto: Toronto University Press, 2002.

Iliushyn, Oleh. *UPA i AK: protystoiannia v zakhidnii Ukraini 1939–1945*. Kyiv: Vydavnychyi Dim Kyievo-Mohylians'ka Akademiia, 2009.

Kaźmierska, Kaja. *Doświadczenia wojenne polaków a kształtowanie tożsamości etnicznej: analiza narracji kresowych.* Warszawa: Instytut Filozofii i Socjologii PAN, 1999.

Kochanowski, Jerzy. "Gathering Poles into Poland: Forced Migration from Poland's Former Eastern Territories." In *Redrawing Nations: Ethnic Cleansing in East-Central Europe, 1944–1948,* edited by Philipp. Ther and Ana Siljak, 155–66. Lanham, MD: Rowman and Littlefield, 2001.

Konończuk, Wojciech. "Ukraińcy patrzą na 'Wołyń.'" *Tygodnik Powszechny* 47 (2016).

Lewicka, Maria. *Psychologia miejsca.* Warszawa: Wydawnictwo Naukowe Scholar, 2012.

Motyka, Grzegorz. *Od rzezi wołyńskiej do akcji "Wisła": konflikt polsko-ukraiński 1943–1947.* Kraków: Literackie, 2011.

Narvselius, Eleonora. "Tragic Past, Agreeable Heritage: Post-Soviet Intellectual Discussions on the Polish Legacy in Western Ukraine." *Carl Beck Papers in Russian and East European Papers* No. 2401 (2015): 1–75.

Nowak, Jacek. *Społeczne reguły pamiętania: antropologia pamięci zbiorowej.* Kraków: Nomos, 2011.

Portnov, Andrii. *Istorii dla domashnioho vzhytku: esei pro pol's'ko-rosiis'ko-ukrains'kyi trykutnyk pam'iati.* Kyiv: Krytyka, 2013.

———. "Ukraińska (nie)pamięć o Wołyniu 1943." Accessed February 15, 2017. http://www.pk.org.pl/publikacje/pojednanie_przez_trudna_pamiec_wolyn1943.pdf.

Rating Group. "IRI Ukraine Poll: The Dynamics of Socio-Political Views in Ukraine." *Rating,* August 26, 2015. http://ratinggroup.ua/research/ukraine/dinamika_obschestvenno-politicheskih_vzglyadov_v_ukraine.html.

Rezmer, Waldemar. "Ethnic Changes in Volhynia and Eastern Galicia during the Second World War in the Light of the Work of the 'Poland–Ukraine: Difficult Questions' International Historical Seminar." In *Divided Eastern Europe: Borders and Population Transfer, 1938–1947.* Edited by Aleksandr Dyukov and Olesya Orlenko, 132–46. Newcastle upon Tyne, UK: Cambridge Scholars, 2012.

Romanenko, Iurii. "Kak ukraintsi smotryat na otnosheniya mezhdu Ukrainoy i Pol'shey." *Hvylya.net,* January 29, 2017. http://hvylya.net/analytics/politics/kak-ukraintsyi-smotryat-na-otnosheniya-mezhdu-ukrainoy-i-polshey.html.

Rosenthal, Gabriele, ed. *The Holocaust in Three Generations: Families of Victims and Perpetrators of the Nazi Regime.* Opladen and Farmington Hills: Barbara Budrich Publishers, 2010.

Ruda, Oksana. "Do dzherel mifolohizatsii ukrains'ko-pol's'kykh vidnosyn." In *Istorychni mify i stereotypy ta mizhnatsional'ni vidnosyny vy suchasnii Ukraini,* edited by Leonid Zashkilniak, 289–333. L'viv: Instytut Ukrainoznavstva im. Kryp'iakevycha, 2009.

Sereda, Viktoria. "Vplyv pol's'kykh ta ukraiins'kykh pidruchnykiv z istorii na formuvannia pol's'ko-ukrains'kykh etnichnykh stereotypiv." *Visnyk L'vivs'koho Universytetu: seriia istorychna,* 35–36 (2000): 387–97.

Stobniak-Smogorzewska, Janina *Kresowe osadnictwo wojskowe 1920–1945.* Warszawa: Rytm, 2003.

Tschuggnall, Karoline, and Harald Welzer. "Rewriting Memories: Family Recollections of the National Socialist Past in Germany." *Culture Psychology* 8, no. 1 (2002): 130–45.

Welzer, Harald, Sabine Moller, and Karoline Tschuggnall. *"Opa war kein Nazi": Nationalsozialismus und Holocaust im Familiengedächtnis.* Frankfurt: Fischer, 2002.

Yakovenko, Nataliia. *Paralel'nyi svit: doslidzhennia z istorii uiavlen' ta idei v Ukraiini XVI–XVII st.* Kyiv: Krytyka, 2003.

Zashkilniak, Leonid. "Istoriia 'svoia' i istoriia 'chuzha'." *Krytyka* 9–10, nos. 143–44) (2009): 24–26.

Zińczuk, Aleksandra. *Pojednanie przez trudną pamięć: Galicja Wschodnia.* Wojsławice, Pol.: Panorama Kultur, 2017. http://pk.org.pl/publikacje/Pojednanie_Galicja_PL_A.pdf.

———. *Pojednanie przez trudną pamięć: Wołyń 1943.* Lublin, Pol.: Panorama Kultur, 2014. http://www.pk.org.pl/publikacje/pojednanie_przez_trudna_pamiec_wolyn1943.pdf

ANNA WYLEGAŁA is Assistant Professor at the Institute of Philosophy and Sociology, Polish Academy of Sciences. She is author of *Displaced Memories: Remembering and Forgetting in Post-War Poland and Ukraine* and *Przesiedlenia a pamięć: studium (nie)pamięci społecznej na przykładzie ukraińskiej Galicji i polskich 'ziem odzyskanych'* (Resettlement and memory: study of social memory on the example of Ukrainian Galicia and Polish "recovered lands").

PART V

HISTORY AND POLITICS IN
A POST-SOVIET STATE: UKRAINE,
RUSSIA, AND INDEPENDENCE

11

UKRAINE BETWEEN THE EUROPEAN UNION AND RUSSIA SINCE 1991

Does It Have to Be a Battlefield of Memories?

Tomasz Stryjek

THIS CHAPTER AIMS TO EXPLAIN, FIRST, WHY UKRAINE's transformation after it gained independence in 1991, and especially starting from the Orange Revolution in 2004 to the Revolution of Dignity in 2013–14, has been so exceptionally marked by disputes over the general history of the 20th century, both in domestic policy and in relations with its neighbors.[1] Second, it aims to deliberate what has changed in this regard in the three years since the revolution in Kyiv on November 21, 2013. Do the images of the events of the last century still attract the attention of Ukrainian public opinion so strongly? And do both the supporters and opponents of Ukraine's accession to the European Union (EU), to slightly simplify the issue, represent opposing assessments of Soviet rule and of World War II? Or the opposite—will a revolutionary breakthrough allow Ukraine to free itself from the burden of the past and will any disputes over this country be left to professional researchers and to the narrow circle of some history enthusiasts? In connection with an attempt to answer these questions, I am also going to consider what in the near future might be the possible impact of external players, that is, of the EU and Russia, in the field of Ukraine's collective memory.[2]

After the annexation of Crimea and the outbreak of the war in Donbas, it goes without saying that the Russian authorities attach great importance to Ukraine as a strategic area of confrontation with the West. It remains an open question whether the EU will accept the challenge, but it seems that its policy toward Ukraine will not be more involved than it was for those Central European countries that tried to gain membership until their accession in the years 2004–13. Apart from the financial and military aspect of this engagement (which this chapter does not deal with), it remains to be considered whether the EU should also try to influence the politics of Ukraine's memory of the era from 1917 to 1991. Doing so would entail including in the current conflict between the EU and Russia a dispute over an interpretation of the history of the 20th century.

If the EU did indeed try to exert such an influence, the clash between Russia and the EU in the assessment of the effects of Sovietism and World War II on Eastern Europe would rise from a different axiology, one that underlies historical narratives on both sides. In Russia, the impetus to restore a positive memory of the Russian Empire and of the Soviet Union may be observed and, in the EU, individual member states explicitly critically recognize their historical imperial ambitions conducted both inside Europe and on other continents. In addition, the European Parliament adopted a resolution that classifies the Soviet Union—as well as the Third Reich—as a totalitarian state that is guilty of mass crimes committed against its own citizens and other countries of Central and Eastern Europe.[3] These two historical discourses—on the one hand, a postimperialistic one and on the other an anti-imperialistic and antitotalitarian one, which more or less was also adopted by Central European countries after 1989—have crossed into the public debate in Ukraine with particular force since 2004.

I use three terms in this chapter: *transitional justice*, *politics of memory*, and *identity politics*. The first term can be understood as "the full set of processes and mechanisms associated with a society's attempts to come to terms with a legacy of large-scale past abuse in order to secure accountability, serve justice and achieve reconciliation."[4] I assume that without introducing at least some transitional justice measures that were developed by countries participating in the "third wave of democratization" in the 20th century to address histories of crime and persecution during periods of war and dictatorship, it is impossible to (re)construct a democratic state based on justice and integrity; that is, a political community characterized by such standards, which new members of the EU are expected to fulfill.

The term *politics of memory* means constructing images of the past publicly and using them to form symbols and identity.[5] While *transitional justice* is inherently applied to a transitional period, politics of memory is realized all the time, even when political entities completely turn away from the past. Politics of memory is a term with a much broader application. First, transitional justice can be a part of it. Any measure of justice—beginning with a new historical narrative in school textbooks and ending in punishment of the perpetrators by the court—shapes an image of the past in the public opinion. Second, *politics of memory* refers not only to the last period of large-scale human rights violations but to the whole past. Thus it goes beyond the 20th century, usually reaching past epochs up to the historical moment in the national mythology that is considered to be the community's founding act.

Transitional justice and politics of memory may have the same goals. This convergence, however, does not usually occur in the postcommunist countries of Central and Eastern Europe. While the point of reference of the former is human rights, the aim is first and foremost to serve justice and the latter most often serves as an integration of people in the community united by their conviction of a common history. Therefore, the legal principles are a reference point for those pursuing a politics of memory less than they are for other participants in the politics. Wars of memory in Central and Eastern Europe appear precisely against the background of this discrepancy. Politics of memory, in practice, often remains a part of an even wider issue—identity politics. Instruments used by the state to carry out identity politics largely depend on the dominant type of nation building in the region. In Central and Eastern Europe, nations were often formed around common features of ethnic culture (language, religion, traditional customs) rather than around long-lasting integrating efforts by the state.

Contemporary identity politics to a large extent refer here precisely to ethnic cultures, although now to a lesser extent than in the 19th and first half of the 20th century. Therefore, the characteristics of culture as well as the image of the past in the titular nations are of primary importance in the identity politics of its political authorities. The role of aliens is often imputed to national minorities, or sometimes simply descendants of the occupiers. In Central and Eastern Europe, this is particularly true of nationalities that once had the status of rulers of empires or multinational states and then assumed the role of minorities in the nation states created in the 20th century, among others, the Russians.

Since 1989 in the countries of Central and Eastern Europe, identity politics strongly determined the objectives of politics of memory. The latter, in turn, adapted the implementation (sometimes it was an abandonment of implementation) of transitional justice measures to its assumptions. The fact that many countries were new, as was the case with Ukraine, was an additional complicating factor in the transformation process. Thus, those countries were forced to formulate each of those three politics from scratch.

The EU and the Challenge of Detotalitarianization of Symbolic Space in Ukraine

How the state deals with war periods and totalitarianism in the past does not belong to official negotiations in candidacy for membership in the EU. Requirements in this area are not included in the Copenhagen criteria (1993) for admission. But stipulations to change the narrative in history books or those stigmatizing the perpetrators were (and still informally are) imposed on those countries that participated in the Yugoslav Wars in 1991–2001.[6] Expectations of changes in the politics of memory were also expressed to Poland, Lithuania, Latvia, Estonia, and Romania before their admission to the EU. In all these cases, the expectations concerned the commemoration of victims of crimes committed during World War II by members of those countries out of ideological incentives of native nationalism and antisemitism or out of encouragement from the Third Reich, mainly against Jews.[7] Protection of the memory of the Holocaust by the aforementioned candidate countries was a kind of maturity test for EU membership.[8] At the same time, the EU was not interested in what kind of politics the candidates conducted in relation to the heritage of Sovietism (communism). The representatives of EU institutions, the majority being countries of Western Europe, showed greater understanding in condemning crimes committed by the Third Reich and its satellites and coworkers than by the Soviet Union and governments that were dependent on it. Only after the accession of countries from Central Europe to the EU, and largely on the initiative of those countries, did the European Parliament from 2004 to 2009 adopt a position that also stigmatized communist crimes.

A new situation emerged along with the breakthrough in Ukraine in 2014. The expansion of the EU already extended not only over the borders of the Iron Curtain (which happened in 2004), but also over the western border of the Soviet Union that had existed in 1939–41 and in 1945–91 (along the section of the Baltic states), as well as over the border in 1921–39. The earlier accession of post-Soviet Baltic states still had not made such a significant change. In Lithuania, Latvia, and Estonia, incorporation into the Soviet Union in 1940 started, from the late 1980s onward, to be treated by the communities of memory (including most of the citizens) as an occupation of their countries. They supported the complete removal of Soviet symbols from the public space, providing support for unequivocal politics of memory of the state for the period of 1940–91. The communities largely overlapped with the titular nations (numbering more than half of the population), which provided democratic legitimacy for settling accounts with Sovietism. Desovietization activities had been conducted there before any negotiations for membership had started, and so taking a stand against them by the EU would not matter significantly. After the Baltic states gained their independence in 1991, the EU and other organizations (Organization for Security and Co-operation in Europe, Council of Europe) suggested that the Baltic states apply for membership, which facilitated both the access to citizenship for Russian-speaking inhabitants who settled in the Baltics in 1940–91 and protection of the memory of the Holocaust and the exclusion of anti-Soviet collaboration with the Third Reich in 1941–45 from the official state tradition.

In 2014, Ukraine and Georgia became the first countries aspiring to EU membership that had been occupied by the Red Army not in the years 1939–45 under Stalin but in 1918–20, when the head of the Soviet state was Lenin. What differentiated them from current candidates is the lack of a tradition of statehood not only in 1940–91 but also in the interwar period. A third such country is Moldova (being a part of the kingdom of Romania in the past), which was incorporated into the Soviet Union in 1940. Since 1991 they may use national symbols in their politics of memory only from the premodern era, that is, from the period prior to their gradual integration into the Russian Empire in the 17th–19th centuries. As for the history of the state in the 20th century, they have at their disposal only the symbols of the proclamation of independence in 1918, failed attempts to fight for its maintenance in 1918–21 and, until 1991, the activities of their governments in exile whose actions barely affected the countries they ruled in theory. In this situation, since 1991, the memory of anti-Soviet independence movements gained great political importance. In particular, it appeared very visibly in Ukraine, in the western part of which the insurgency strongly resisted the Soviets in 1944–50.[9] After 1991, and especially after 2004, many symbols of this struggle were established in the western part of the country, mostly with the participation of the local authorities. Moreover, Ukraine was the most affected by Soviet rule until 1939, not only among these three countries but also among all the countries emerging from the collapse of the Soviet Union, because the largest losses were incurred as a result of the Great Famine (Holodomor) of 1932–33.[10]

The participants of the Ukrainian anti-Soviet movement of the 1930s-1940s, however, also committed acts that belong to the category of acts clearly stigmatized by the EU. In the summer of 1941, along with the impact of Germany on the Soviet Union, western Ukraine was the scene of an attempt to create, by the Organization of Ukrainian Nationalists (*Orhanizatsiia Ukrains'kykh Natsionalistiv,* OUN), its own state in the system of the Axis powers' reign in Europe. Local Jews fell victim to the actions of the Germans and of the Ukrainian local population.[11] This happened (as in the whole belt of lands annexed to the Soviet Union after the conclusion of the Ribbentrop-Molotov Pact on August 23, 1939, from Estonia to Moldova) because, on the one hand, antisemitic prejudices existed and Sovietism was commonly identified with Jews, and, on the other, because the Third Reich encouraged antisemitism. In turn, in 1943–50 in the western part of Ukraine, the Ukrainian Insurgent Army (*Ukrains'ka Povstans'ka Armiia,* UPA), established by the OUN, first fought, using its limited resources, against Germany (1943–44), and then, with all its power, it resisted the Soviets

(1944–50). Even during the first of these two occupations, UPA conducted ethnic cleansing in Volyn and eastern Galicia, killing almost one hundred thousand Polish civilians in 1943–44.[12] The Organization of Ukrainian Nationalists (OUN), roughly from the mid-1930s until 1944, was a kind of totalitarian movement that practiced propaganda directed against national minorities and was inspired by, inter alia, the example of Italian fascism. But the UPA since 1944 until its end around 1950, having in its ranks many new volunteers, fought against the Soviet armed forces. For that reason, it may be regarded also as an independence organization.

I believe that detotalitarianization would serve best for the reconstruction of the Ukrainian state after the revolution in 2013–14 in the sphere of politics of memory, removing from the public sphere those symbols that relate to the activities of 1917–91, which are symbols of the representatives of both the extreme left (desovietization) and of the rightmost fractions of that time.[13] Detotalitarianization, first, would essentially consist of a negative assessment in the national historical narrative of all governments and organizations from 1917 to 1991 that represented totalitarian ideologies—for example, fascists, extreme nationalists, and Soviets—in particular those who called for a cleansing of society of enemies, however they were defined. Second, detotalitarianization would consist of commemorating all victims, on condition that the perpetrators are not to be hidden and the motives behind their actions are to be honestly researched and presented. Third, detotalitarianization would also mean deleting from the public sphere the commemoration of those responsible for the crimes that were committed. And not only the direct perpetrators but also those who, although they did not give the orders, remained the creators and ideologists of the organizations that committed the crimes, as well as those who in some periods of their lives became the victims (which, inter alia, is the case of the leader of the OUN, Stepan Bandera, who was murdered by a Soviet agent in 1959). Fourth, detotalitarianization would not mean dismantling the monuments of the Red Army that relate to its victories over the Third Reich's armies and its allies at the front. It would further mean abandoning commemorating the actions of Soviet security forces and internal forces against hiding members of the underground. These actions were done to deport people, to fight political opposition and any freedom of thought, or to persecute those whose only fault was their opposition to the Soviet Union. When it comes to battles between Soviet forces and the Ukrainian Insurgent Army (UPA), the commemoration might be in a form that could help to achieve some internal unity, such as in the form of a common burial of the dead and by presenting the struggle as tragic without heroizing any of the parties. Fifth, and finally, detotalitarianization could not deprive anyone of the right to be buried. This applies to all participants of the armed formations, be it Soviet, Ukrainian, or Polish, the soldiers of the Third Reich or members of its allies.

During the five years after Ukraine's Revolution of Dignity, significant progress of desovietization, thus understood, took place. Until the revolution, Soviet symbolism was the primary point of reference for the identity of the population of both eastern and southern Ukraine. In the country's center, Soviet symbolism was treated with indifference and ambivalence, and in the western part, it had largely been eliminated in the 1990s. In February and March 2014, the so-called Lenin fall took place—when approximately one hundred statues of Lenin were demolished during social actions, mainly in the central part of the country.

Some attempts to defend Soviet symbols were made from time to time only in the eastern and southern districts.

At the same time, neither before the Revolution of Dignity nor after it were there signs in the activities of the Ukrainian state to plan to remove from the public space symbols relating to the extreme right. Moreover, the symbolism of the Ukrainian nationalist movement from the 1930s and 1940s gained wider popularity throughout the country. Until now, the nationalist movement has been popular mainly in the western part of Ukraine as a historical counternarrative in relation to the actions of the central government that supported Soviet symbolism (most during the reign of Viktor Yanukovych in 2010–14). It was expressed mainly in the founding of a series of monuments of Bandera (among other places, in L'viv). Among the supporters of the full desovietization of Ukraine, there was a common tendency to treat members of the OUN and the UPA as mere heroes of the struggle for independence and as victims of the Soviet Union, the Third Reich, and the Second Polish Republic. According to this interpretation, the entire responsibility for the crimes committed in the 1930s and 1940s fell on the NKVD on one side, and, on the other, on the Einsatzgruppen, SS, and Wehrmacht. In the conflict with the Poles, the administration of the Second Polish Republic was blamed, and then the Home Army (*Armia Krajowa,* AK), which through its anti-Ukrainian actions was believed to have provoked the anti-Polish campaigns that were carried out by the UPA in 1943–44.[14] The problem, however, is that some members of the OUN and the UPA were both heroes and victims, and others were perpetrators of what the population of Ukraine endured in the 1940s. Moreover, many of them played each of these three roles at various stages in their lives.

From 1991 to mid-2019, the Ukrainian state did not relate critically to the ideology that the OUN represented in 1933–45, it did not name the UPA's anti-Polish actions in 1943–44 as ethnic cleansing, and it did not initiate investigations into the participation of the members of these formations, nor of the Ukrainian police battalions, nor of the civilian population in the murdering of Jews in 1941–44. At the same time, in 2014 accession to the EU was reported as its main objective in its external policy. EU institutions faced the question of how to respond to the politics of memory about Ukraine's history in the 20th century. Although the EU did not develop a coherent collective memory project and accepted the presence of internal differences in interpretations of the past, it seems that the gap between Ukraine's politics of memory and the EU's general approach to 20th-century history was greater than that between the politics of memory of the countries that had been candidates for EU membership and the EU approach before their accession in 2004–13.

On the one hand, the Baltic strategy of the EU (waiting for the removal of symbols relating to the extreme right and *désintéressement* in desovietization) in relation to Ukraine would not give any of the expected results. In the face of the conflict with Russia, which will probably take many years, a significant portion of Ukrainians would not accept the Baltic strategy with understanding. Most citizens of Ukraine were not familiar with the state's assessment of the OUN ideology and the crimes committed by the UPA through historical education and initiatives implemented in the framework of politics of memory. Ukrainians know them but mostly in the form passed on by the former Soviet and contemporary Russian authorities and the Russian media. And because of the current Ukrainian-Russian conflict, they rightly reject them, since instead of a proper assessment of events and reconciliation of the historical conflicts between the participants, Russian-initiated information serves international discrediting of the pro-European authorities in Ukraine.[15] Russia has credited Ukrainian authorities only with rehabilitating the Nazis (an accusation that was addressed in 2005–10 to President Viktor Yushchenko and his political camp, called "the Oranges"), or even that they took power by a "fascist coup d'état" (an accusation against Arseniy Yatsenyuk cabinet since February 2014).

On the other hand, the strategy of promoting desovietization and *désintéressement* toward symbols of the extreme right would collide with the axiology of the project of European integration and would expose the EU to the Russian accusation of betrayal of the values of the anti-Hitler coalition. It seems that the requirement of full detotalitarianization in Ukraine remains the only action that the EU could, and should, expect to be fulfilled. Such a requirement could also, however, have certain negative effects, especially if it was applied with undue pressure. It could contribute to intensifying disputes about history and to disintegrating Ukrainian society. I will return to the issue of the EU's choice of strategy in the last part of this chapter.

Transitional Justice in Ukraine in 1991–2014

Ukraine implemented only four of eight transitional justice measures postcommunist countries in Europe used in 1991–2014:

a. Rehabilitating victims and paying out compensation
b. Providing citizens access to partly open archives of the former security services
c. Making negative reference to the former regime by its new authorities
d. Formulating a new historical narrative in textbooks

These measures were mainly restorative and were introduced to identify and disseminate the truth about the past and to compensate the victims. They included neither criminal courts trying the perpetrators and their lustration of being security force officers or collaborators (retributive measures) nor the Truth and Reconciliation Commission and restitution of property (other restorative measures).[16] What is more, after 1991, Ukraine carried out neither a verification of former Committee State Security (KGB) employees nor a restructuring of the security, justice, and law enforcement sector. Until the postrevolutionary Supreme Council enacted the Lustration Act in October 2014, there were no legal mechanisms that could prevent the perpetrators of human-rights violations in 1917–91 from holding public offices.

Moreover, the effects of the implemented measures were incomplete. Stigmatizing the old regime was evident, as all the governments were determined to legitimate Ukraine's independence historically, but the Ukrainian SSR's assessment was not formulated in any piece of legislation. The historical narrative in textbooks often used the term *totalitarian system* to describe the nature of Soviet rule, but the guilt was ascribed solely to the successive first secretaries of the All-Union Communist Party (Bolshevik)—which was later renamed the Communist Party of the Soviet Union (KPZR)—the Communist Party of Ukraine (KPU), and the heads of the security apparatus of the Soviet Union and the Ukrainian SSR.

Apart from those persons, the guilt in the historical narrative was presented in an entirely impersonal way. Under those assumptions, ordinary citizens obviously could not share responsibility for the persecutions during seventy years of dictatorship. The debate over the Soviet period was accompanied by a sense of sacrifice, and because the victims were neither precisely counted nor commemorated by name, anyone could have been a victim, even some midlevel civil-servant officers executing orders "from above." Last, there was another aspect of coping with the past. In the light of the dominant discourse on martyrdom, public opinion was not interested in the issue of guilt of representatives of their own nation in their dealings with ethnic minorities.

Until 2014, another factor had hindered the building of a governance in Ukraine that could be based on trust of the state and the law. The historical events that have been the subject of that dispute took place in 1917–53, mostly in the framework of large international conflicts, and the Ukrainian state did not participate in them as a recognized entity. Consequently, every position the authorities took in relation to the past was subject to review from a foreign external entity—mostly Russia, sometimes Poland, and, rarely, from international organizations set up to protect the memory of the Holocaust and of Israel (but not the EU, which did not directly comment about the politics of memory).[17] The representatives of these entities are still largely perceived only as representatives of former exploiters and not as victims of historical conflicts with the Ukrainians. Thus, their observations are often seen as a violation of the sovereignty of the state and, thus, the promoting of them is counterproductive—regardless of their intentions.

Three Levels of Political Disputes in Ukraine of 2004–13

In the first decade of independence, Ukraine developed without any projects. In the second decade, two projects from which the country could choose crystallized and reached its borders. From the Orange Revolution to the Revolution of Dignity, a fierce conflict existed in which three levels of disagreement could be identified. First, there was a dispute over the state model (whether to be democratic or neo-authoritarian), and therefore a dispute over membership in the EU or the Eurasian Union (which was in preparation for a long time and was finally established in 2014). Developing transitional justice in a way that would not depend on the identity politics of the titular nation could have been instrumental in the state's evolution toward the first of these models. Second, the war of memory was then very vividly contested between some apologists of Ukrainian independence in the 20th century, including the OUN and the UPA, and the defenders of a good image of the Soviet Union. On the one hand, this conflict was a result of the politics of memory of two opposing parties; on the other hand, it was a result of supporting a vision of the past of just one of them by the Russian authorities. Both parties of that conflict called for changes in the symbolic space, but the changes were to be unilateral—either desovietization or removing the symbols of the OUN and the UPA. They used the media (which, in turn, from their own motives were involved in maintaining dichotomies in the public debate) for identity consolidation of their own followers. Third, since 1991, there was a conflict over which cultural characteristics to construct the identity of citizens on, that is, as ethnic Ukrainian or united with the Russians and Belarusians, which would imply consistency with the belief that Ukrainity is a regional cultural variation in the frame of a cross-border area of east Slavic-Orthodox civilization. In that dispute, the supporters of identity politics of a civic nation were rather unnoticeable. The development of transitional justice measures could also foster shaping that identity. Any attempts to implement these measures, however, had no effect because they did not consist of serving justice but of integrating the memory of the entire nation. On the one hand, the opponents of coming to terms with Sovietism in the country and the Russian authorities discredited them as a part of an Ukrainization program, that is, as ethnic identity politics. On the other hand, the proponents were confirmed in their grossly simplified opinion that the history of Ukraine from the 17th to the 20th century had been a continuous period of Russian colonialism.

It was not until the repetition of the second round of presidential elections in Ukraine in December 2004 that, for the first time, the formation of an absolute majority of citizens appeared, which included those who were in favor of participation in European integration and supporters of full independence from Russia. In the course of protests against the rule of President Leonid Kuchma in 2001–4, and during the Orange Revolution, an informal alliance was established between Viktor Yushchenko and Yulia Tymoshenko that formed around a broad coalition of pro-European parties and many smaller and organizationally dispersed groups of nationalists, that is, supporters of a simultaneous desovietization and de-Russification of Ukraine, who were against integration with any union of states. The former agreed to the alliance because of the need to consolidate forces opposing a Eurasian orientation, the latter agreed because they would otherwise not have a chance to participate in parliamentary politics. Moreover, as Yushchenko's policy showed in the next five years, the leaders of the Orange camp did not consider the challenge of removing the nationalism symbols from the public space as important for Ukraine's relations with the outside world.

Because of lack of any determination in introducing reforms, the conflict between the leaders of the Orange Revolution, Russian counteractions against the country's pro-European direction, the global economic crisis, and, finally, little involvement from the EU, five years of President Yushchenko's rule ended in failure. His politics of memory, to which I will return later in this chapter, also played a significant role. In the subsequent presidential election in February 2010, in turn, the coalition forces won, that is, those that had failed in 2004. In this coalition, three groups could be identified. First, the realists, who argued that Ukraine should primarily take into account its economic dependence on Russia and its strategic interests. Second, the voters who understood the concept of Ukrainity as an identity subordinate to that of East Slavic-Orthodox civilization. And, third, a group that felt some kind of nostalgia for the Soviet Union (largely communist supporters). The coalition brought to power President Viktor Yanukovych of the Party of Regions. With its neutral or positive attitude to the legacy of the Soviet Union, the coalition was united in a rejection of the nationalist symbols of the 1930s and 1940s. At the same time, it represented an indifferent attitude toward other mainstream struggles for independence and anti-Sovietism: the Ukrainian People's Republic (UNR) from 1918 to 1921, nonnationalist political groups from 1918 to 1939 and their followers in exile since 1945, and, finally, dissidents in the country from the 1960 and 1980s. The ruling coalition did not try to limit the role of the first of these traditions—that the symbols of the Republic of Ukraine, introduced in 1991, derived from and created by a leftist Ukrainian People's Republic.

The paradox of 2010–13 was the fact that the politicians of the EU who were worried about the incompetence of the previous "Orange" authorities and about the growth in popularity of nationalist groups remaining in opposition to Yanukovych displayed more common points in their assessment of the situation in Ukraine with the ruling camp (supporting an oligarchic form of neo-authoritarian government) than with the pro-European camp. Moreover, the Russian politics of memory, which accused Ukraine of a "rehabilitation of fascism," gained at least as much esteem in the eyes of Western observers as the attitude toward the past, expressed by the Ukrainian democratic opposition that objected to the Yanukovych government. Russia, well aware of the similarities between the pro-European and nationalist oppositions, sought to show the world their evidently ideologically and ethically disqualifying image. EU countries had a poor understanding of the entanglements of Ukrainian politics of memory and identity politics. The difference between the EU and Russia, however—two external entities that can affect the politics of memory in Ukraine—lies in the fact that only in the first case do public opinion, government authorities, and political forces (with the exception of the extreme right) agree that the 20th-century history of all nations on the continent consists of episodes of martyrdom and heroism as well as of persecution and crime perpetration. The Russian authorities represent a different position. They treat the past in terms of either-or and insist on a unilaterally heroic interpretation of the historical role of the Soviet Union.

Politics of Memory Implemented by the Presidents of Ukraine, 1991–2014

Today it seems that desovietization without nationalization of the symbolic space could have been carried out most easily at the beginning, during Leonid Kravchuk's administration (1991–94). It was believed more or less across the country that the period of Soviet rule in Ukraine was irretrievable, and the heroic version of the history of the OUN and the UPA was not disseminated. Although today the president's policy appears to be composed mainly of omissions, there were several factors that could explain his actions.

First, the economic crunch and monetary chaos until the introduction of the hryvnia in September 1996 were so overwhelming that they obscured all other issues. Second, at exactly that time the aforementioned rehabilitation was carried out most intensively. Public attention was focused on coping with the scale of atrocities and not on identifying the perpetrators. Although in 1991 the KPU was banned, two years later it was reregistered. Referring to the lawlessness that took place during the chaotic privatization, the party defended a good memory of the Soviet Union, which allowed it to maintain its position as the largest opposition force until the end of the 1990s. Third, the very concept of transitional justice was not yet formulated, not to mention the range of methods for its implementation, adequate to the situation of the postcommunist countries (mainly lustration).[18] Fourth, under the influence of the concept of Ukrainity by former dissidents, building a new state was understood primarily as a completion of the nation-building process that had been initiated by the so-called national revival in the 19th century. Therefore, identity politics was brought to the forefront, emphasizing the ethnic characteristics of Ukrainian culture. Fifth, there was no one who could replace the personnel, especially in the security services and the military. If, therefore, those people were about to carry out desovietization of the symbolic space, they would not have been credible.

Kravchuk's regime was the first period in the history of independent Ukraine in which the lack of national development strategies and the lack of determination to implement reforms were obscured by intense identity politics and symbolic changes. References to the past from that period did not relate to the nationalist movement but mainly to the Cossacks of the 17th and 18th centuries and to the UNR. It was different in the next decade, when Leonid Kuchma was the head of state (1994–2004). Kuchma won the election because public opinion rejected his predecessor's policy of "Ukrainization," which was associated with a reduction in living standards and a glaring decrease in the efficiency of state institutions. His foreign policy was "multivector," which meant balancing between Russia and the EU. The balance he had shaped was destroyed after the decision to transfer power (after two presidential terms) to Viktor Yanukovych in 2004. This meant a shift toward a Eurasian model and resembled the succession from Boris Yeltsin in Russia to Vladimir Putin. In contrast to the latter, however, it could not lead to strengthening state structures in that it did not transfer power to a representative of the security forces and the army but to a leader of one of the oligarchic groups and, at the same time, the governor of the Donetsk Oblast who had broad support only in the east and in the southern part of Ukraine.

By not implementing any bold reforms, Kuchma allowed for the oligarchization of the economy and then of state power. This power structure was unprecedented in the history of the Ukrainian governance system and maintained internal cohesion only as long as Kuchma allowed the competing clans to act as the main regulator of access to a state pension. He undermined it himself by deciding to transfer the office not only to one of the current players but also to a representative of one of the two poles of political culture and collective memory of Ukraine—the Donbas community, which to the greatest extent, out of all the parts of the country, had been formed in Soviet times.

From the point of view of transitional justice, a decade of Kuchma's regime brought no changes. And only slight progress had been made since the implementation of remedial measures initiated by Kravchuk. Kuchma's entire policy, however, including identity politics and memory, served internal integration and strengthened the state while not favoring the development of the rule of law, freedom of speech, or building a civil society. Kuchma did not withdraw guarantees for the usage of the Ukrainian language as the only official language, but he did abandon the rhetoric of continuation of the national-building process that had been interrupted by Soviet governments in favor of the ideology of state-creation (*derzhavotvorennia*). During his rule, the concept of Ukrainity was more and more associated with the state, with an increase in its recognition in the arena of international politics and, also, in the end, with an improvement of its citizens' living standards.[19]

Kuchma also put emphasis on the restoration of the cultural heritage, which had been destroyed during the Soviet era (among other projects, historical Orthodox churches in Kyiv were rebuilt), and on the formation of a textbook narrative showing the individuality of the

Ukrainian historical process, from the formation of Kyivan Rus up to the disintegration of the Russian Empire in 1917. In the model elaborated by the Institute of History of Ukraine of the National Academy of Sciences of Ukraine, the country's history was based on its efforts to build its own state by the local elites, and on the struggle for social justice.[20] In this way, the foundation of the collective memory of history before the beginning of the modern era was developed and disseminated. At the same time, the authorities avoided expressing a clear assessment of the most controversial events from the 1930s and 1940s. They could not carry out desovietization because they felt too attached themselves to the achievements of civilization under the Soviet Union, and they did not want to start a dispute with Russia. On the other hand, the announcement of only removing the nationalist symbols from the public space was rightly considered as the spark of an internal conflict. The most important national holidays, next to the anniversaries of the founding events of the modern state, August 24, 1991 (Independence Day), and June 28, 1996 (Constitution Day), remained those that came from the Soviet Union: May 9, 1945 (Victory Day), and February 23, 1918 (Defender of the Fatherland Day).[21]

Nevertheless, careful initiatives of memory changes were conducted without upsetting the balance between public representations of the symbolism of the two old enemies. On the one hand, they sought to disarm the explosive potential of the main anti-Soviet myth, creating by the decision of the Supreme Council a special committee whose task was to examine the ideology and activities of the OUN and the UPA. The report of this committee from 2004, edited by professional historians under the direction of Professor Stanyslav Kulchytskyi, confirmed the propaganda of the OUN against ethnic minorities and its resemblance to fascist organizations in Europe, but it still avoided any explicit formulations. This was the first official attempt to reflect the true nature of the narratives about the OUN, rejecting both the slanderous Soviet narrative and the contemporary Russian one, as well as any heroic or nationalist ones.[22] On the other hand, on the occasion of the seventieth anniversary of the Holodomor in 2003, the state authorities took steps on the international arena (although, in general, they failed) to achieve recognition of the Holodomor as genocide under the UN Convention of December 9, 1948. The state's application had both the capacity to be a restorative measure of transitional justice (getting the witnesses out of their collective trauma) and to advance the objective of integrating the society's identity, because an event from the period of Soviet rule was chosen that had affected the entire population of the Ukrainian SSR in 1932–33. It should be emphasized that Kuchma deftly sustained the image of the KPU as the main obstacle to modernization of the country and, at the same time, he did not allow an increase in support for the nationalists. His political camp was positioned as left center, and for international opinion he presented himself as the only force able to stop the seizure of power by either of the two extreme groups.[23]

When its creator left this model of governance, he turned out to not have enough support in the community. Not only because in 2001–4 Kuchma strengthened the eastern vector too much, among other moves by appointing as his successor (accepted also by President Putin) the leader of the Donbas clan, but also because he did not foresee the development of a civil society. In the presence of the street demonstrations that were organized by the opposition and because of its acquisition of the project for Ukraine's integration with the

EU, the Kuchma administration tried to limit the freedom of speech in the media (for one thing, by avoiding the topic of extreme positions in disputes about the most difficult issues in the history of the 1940s). The formation of a Ukrainian middle class, the individualization of lifestyles, and the development of social aspirations created the conditions for the emergence of the majority, which opposed Yanukovych's acquisition of presidency.

The project of the Orange camp, when Yushchenko took power in January 2005, accelerated both implementation of reforms to adapt the country to EU requirements and significantly expanded the application of transitional justice. The experience accumulated in this regard by Central European countries found its way in Ukraine just at the moment when their politics of memory took on a stronger tone of identity. This reversal was to some extent a response to Russia's efforts to recover its role as a great power. But the reversal also happened because of the triumphant mood of the public in these countries after their accession to NATO and the EU. The reversal manifested itself in the strengthening of the right-wing groups, in their demands for complete desovietization (decommunization) of the symbolic space, in commemorating the resistance against the Soviet Union in the 1940s, and in the outlawing of left-wing parties of postcommunist descent. In Poland, the project took the form of the Fourth Republic, which the Law and Justice party and President Lech Kaczyński tried to implement in 2005–7. In Lithuania, the fear of Russia increased, which resulted in the dismissal of President Rolandas Paksas in 2004. In Hungary, the discreditation of leftist governments in 2006 was accompanied by sharp clashes in the streets of Budapest, on the occasion of the fiftieth anniversary of the anti-Soviet uprising in 1956. At the same time, the beginning of Yushchenko's presidential term coincided with the involvement of George W. Bush's administration in strengthening the pro-Western orientation in countries of the former Soviet Union. Poland became the main partner in that US policy in Central and Eastern Europe. It was mainly its experience with lustration, in museum projects commemorating the resistance against the Third Reich and the Soviet Union (mainly the Warsaw Rising Museum), and, finally, historical education (mainly the Institute of National Remembrance), which were now tactics to be used by Yushchenko.

At the beginning, Yushchenko's objective was to bring about national reconciliation, so he reached for another restorative measure from the arsenal of transitional justice. The policy of Ukrainization of World War II (most importantly by establishing in 2005 a new tradition to celebrate the anniversary of May 9 by the Red Army together with the partisans of the UPA) was aimed neither toward Russians living in Ukraine nor toward the Russian state. This policy, however, unexpectedly, was not understood by those invited to participate in the celebrations. What was even more important—it was rejected by President Putin. Already during the Orange Revolution, Russian media showed Yushchenko as an ardent nationalist. Russian authorities were alarmed by, on the one hand, the unambiguously pro-European orientation of the Orange camp and, on the other hand, by the acceleration of both Yushchenko's and Kaczyński's reconciliation efforts between Ukrainians and Poles over the conflict between them in 1939–47, an effort that had been initiated by their predecessors, Kuchma and Kwaśniewski If reconciliation had happened, it would have removed the last of the obstacles to full support of Polish public opinion for Ukraine's accession to the EU.

In terms of relationships with Poland, Yushchenko's strategy resembled that which was used in the domestic politics of memory. He assumed a mutual confession and thought that acts of public forgiveness and reconciliation would occur on a large scale in the following years. He did not estimate the changes of public opinion in Poland, however, in relation to the crime of Volhynia. Since 1989, historical research developed in the country indicated that the UPA had started and methodically conducted ethnic cleansing and had murdered the populations of entire villages in Volhynia and East Galicia.[24] This fact put an end to the formula of reconciliation on the basis of recognizing equivalent guilt in the Ukrainian-Polish conflict. Yushchenko did not see either that President Kaczynski persisted in the formula because of the chance of a final separation of Ukraine from the Russian sphere of influence, and not because he shared the view of equal responsibility of the UPA and the AK for the events that had taken place in 1943–44. He also did not seem to appreciate the fact that the Polish president's policies were not understood by a growing portion of Polish public opinion.[25]

Yushchenko's policy with respect to the memory of the Holocaust also proved to be based on erroneous assumptions. The president sought to obtain the support of as many states as possible to qualify the Holodomor as genocide, carried out by the leadership of the Soviet Union on the Ukrainian nation. In particular, he wanted Israel to take a position on the issue, which seemed unattainable. First, because of the statements of the president's entourage, which had overstated the number of victims of the famine by double (7–10 million—thus exceeding the number of victims of the Holocaust). Second, because of his participation in the heroization of the OUN and the UPA, whose members, according to Israeli public opinion, are believed to have cooperated in exterminating Jews in Ukraine. And, third, because Israel did not want to find any reasons to strain its relations with Russia. Nevertheless, Yushchenko made the attempt. Addressing the Knesset in his speech on November 14, 2007, with a request in that case, he encountered only diplomatic silence. It seems that the president did not consider his effort a failure. He did not see a connection between the cold reception he had received and the fact that the only position taken by the Ukrainian state on the participation of Ukrainians in the Holocaust was a vague apology that Kravchuk had made during his visit to Israel in 1993. Moreover, the fact that, two months before his visit, he posthumously awarded Roman Shukhevych the Gold Star Medal of the Hero of Ukraine (Shukhevych was the commander of the *Nachtigall battalion* in 1941, a soldier of the *Schutzmannschaft Battalion* 201 in Belarus in 1942, and, finally, the commander-in-chief of the UPA in 1943–50) also contributed to the cold reception in the Knesset.[26]

In 2005–10 the conflict over the memory of World War II entered its international phase. Countries that had maintained their relationships with Russia on grounds of bilateral relations (Latvia and Estonia attempted to condemn the territorial losses of 1940, Lithuania attempted to compensate for the whole of Soviet rule from 1940 to 1941 and from 1944 to 1991, and the Polish attempted to declassify the Katyn investigation records) changed their policy and began to regard their claims as a common matter. The claims were moved to the international forum (Council of Europe, European Court of Human Rights, European Parliament, Organization for Security and Co-operation in Europe Parliamentary Assembly) and combined with the desovietization of Ukraine. The considerations that caused Yushchenko to switch actions, however—from attempts to reconcile the country by strengthening nationalist symbols and by openly confronting Russia—were as much international as internal ones. The president, not having enough strength to break the oligarchic system, which would weaken the base of the Party of Regions, tried to implement a policy of agreement with individual oligarchs. This did not bring any effect, and the party won the parliamentary elections in 2006 and 2007. The Orange camp could defeat it only if it were united, but the president was arguing more and more acutely with Yulia Tymoshenko, who, among other objections, did not share his preferences for politics of memory. Finally, Yushchenko chose the gamble to consolidate the anti-Soviet electorate, including the nationalist one. This meant that the politics of memory turned toward unilateral martyrologization of the Ukrainian nation without regarding the common experience of the peoples of Soviet nations and the heroization of all struggles for independence, including the nationalist one, which even might have been seen as the most important one. Consequently, transitional justice was now to be extended to retributive measures, but it was aimed primarily not so much at the creators of the totalitarian system but at the enemies of the Ukrainians. For those Ukrainian citizens who did not share anti-Soviet beliefs, it was interpreted as antagonizing identity politics. A similar view prevailed in the Polish public opinion. In Russia, it was even seen as politics of ethnic mobilization.

Yushchenko's reversal after the parliamentary elections of 2007 expressed itself in awarding Roman Shukhevych the aforementioned medal. In 2007–8 the president accelerated works on the documentation of victims of the Soviet famine and on a permanent exhibition of the Holodomor Memorial in Kyiv. The latter was given a very anti-Soviet accent, making Stalinist and Nazi crimes equivalent. At the president's request, the Supreme Council in 2006 recognized the Holodomor as an act of genocide against the Ukrainian nation. But only in the following years did Yushchenko step up efforts (which failed, in the end) to include criminalization of denial or of questioning the legal status of that tragedy into the criminal code. Before Yushchenko's term ended in January 2010, two weighty acts of politics of memory were implemented. First, the Administrative Court in Kyiv, ruling at the request of the subordinate to the President of the Security Service of Ukraine, issued a judgment declaring the Holodomor to be genocide that had been carried out on the Ukrainian nation by the Soviet government under the leadership of Stalin. Second, also Stepan Bandera, by the president's decision, posthumously received the Gold Star Medal of the Hero of Ukraine. Both these acts provoked strong opposition in Russia, and the latter also among Polish public opinion.

During the next four years, Yanukovych's rule did not turn Yushchenko's policy in a completely different direction, but it was a period of regression in every aspect of the state's conduct toward the past. The medals for Bandera and Shukhevych were canceled by court order, but the judgment in the Holodomor case was not revoked—only on the international forum did the president repeatedly emphasize that Ukraine considered the famine in 1932–33 as a collective tragedy for all Soviet Union nations. The change meant that transitional justice in general was found to be negligible, and politics of memory was moved to a remote place on the list of priorities of the state. The historical narrative was slightly changed in the textbooks. On the other hand, Victory Day was strongly accentuated by coordinating the May 9 anniversary celebrations with those in Russia. The importance of identity politics did not diminish, but its direction was changed—to emphasize the membership of Ukraine in the East Slavic-Orthodox cultural community. This was reflected in closer relations of the Ukrainian authorities with the Ukrainian Orthodox Church of the Moscow Patriarchate but, above all, in a change in law on the official language. According to the act of July 2012, for the first time since 1991 minority languages were permitted as the official languages, thus leaving the right decision about their use to the local authorities. The act allowed candidates to hold office in the Russian language in about half the country.

The turn of Ukraine toward Russia was manifested most evidently in concluding the so-called Kharkiv settlements in April 2010. In one of the provisions, Yanukovych agreed to extend the lease of Russia's Black Sea Fleet base in Sevastopol until 2042. The progressive oligarchization of power also indicated that the country was backing away from the disposition toward EU integration. Opposition to this course of action grew, both pro-European and nationalist, from authorities who were only outwardly directed toward Europe. In 2012, the radically nationalist *Svoboda* party received as much as 10.4 percent of the votes in the parliamentary elections. Many citizens with moderate views voted for the party despite their awareness doing so this could stop the process leading to the participation of Ukraine in the Eurasian Union.[27] At the same time, under Yanukovych's rule and as a result of grassroots activities, the unveiling of monuments devoted to the OUN and the UPA in western Ukraine and resovietization of the eastern part of the country progressed. In this situation, the withdrawal of the government from signing onto the EU, that is, the Ukraine Association Agreement, in November 2013, sparked the revolution supported by the followers of Ukraine's European integration as well as the nationalists.

After the Revolution of Dignity: New Attempts to Solve Ukrainian Problems

At first, the revolution in 2013 and later in 2014 were somewhat of a youth protest in the capital against the shift of the government's policy toward Europe. Then it took the form of mass contestation of the corrupt regime in the form of an occupation of the central squares and in marches in many cities of the country. Eventually it turned into clashes between demonstrators and security forces in Kyiv and Western Ukraine.[28] A coalition of pro-European and nationalist forces again led to victory. The degree of support for the nationalists exceeded the level of sympathy for them in a ratio of up to 10:1, but this time the nationalists were much better organized (next to the *Svoboda* party, an important role in the revolution was played by the paramilitary Right Sector). Moreover, they openly used the symbolism of the OUN and the UPA and influenced the attitudes of other participants through their own steadfast determination. In the course of events in Kyiv in January and February 2014, and then in the war with Donbas separatists and the Russian troops supporting them, the symbolism of the nationalists (mainly the red-and-black flag) became more popular outside the western part of Ukraine and the capital.

At the same time, Ukrainian society did not support the nationalist candidates in the May 25 presidential election and in the October 26 parliamentary elections.[29] In both elections, the overwhelming majority voted for pro-European candidates who had emerged from the revolution, and the degree of support for Ukraine's accession to the EU and the Customs Union with Russia, Belarus, and Kazakhstan moved from an equal level of 37–38 percent in February 2013 to a difference of 58 percent and 11 percent, respectively, in December 2016.[30]

This paradox, which is unknown in Western Europe, of the coexistence of broad consent for manifesting under nationalist symbols and, at the same time, not sharing the nationalists' ideas and programs by the vast majority of citizens can be explained by perceiving the revolution as a fight for freedom from Russian dependence. The majority of the public does not recognize the symbols of the OUN and the UPA as a conflict with democratic order and with the European narratives of the history of the 20th century because, on the one hand, those symbols relate to liberation and defense, and, on the other hand, as was already mentioned, the public does not see the events of the 1940s as representing a stain on the honor of Ukraine.

The victory of the Revolution of Dignity in Ukraine opened the way for a breakthrough in three disputes stemming from the Orange Revolution. Within three years after it, however, not all of those disputes went in the same direction. The main outcome—the emergence of an absolute majority that was in favor of a democratic country belonging to the European community—occurred in the May 25 and October 26 elections. Also, in a dispute over identity politics, there were no indications that the authorities would impose ethnic Ukrainian culture on the minorities.

Furthermore, the wide participation of Russian-speaking citizens in the revolution and in defense of the country proved that those speaking Ukrainian also accepted the public use of the Russian language-, as it also expressed ideas of liberation and modernization. Since 1991, Ukraine never had more favorable conditions for social and political consensus on the concept of a civic nation.

In contrast, in the third dispute, a change in the politics of memory, approved by the adoption of four bills by the Supreme Council on April 9, 2015, only partially corresponded with the two mentioned pro-European changes. They were prepared by the new leadership of the Ukrainian Institute of National Remembrance that was appointed in March 2014 and established on the initiative of Yushchenko in 2006. First, all restrictions of public access to Soviet security forces documents were lifted, yet all files from that era, which had previously been spread out across various archives, would be accessible only after they were gathered in one place at the Institute. In this way, conditions were created for one of the main measures of transitional justice to be fully carried out. Second, the attributed meaning of the holiday of victory over the Third Reich in 1945 was changed. So far, according to the Act of 2000, May 9 was celebrated as Victory Day in the Great Patriotic War. From 2015 on, it was to be Victory Day over the Nazis in World War II. Moreover, joining the European countries in their recognition of the date the war ended and referring to their ways of commemorating the anniversary, May 8 became a second holiday, the Day of Remembrance and Reconciliation. This change meant a further step toward the Europeanization of memory in Ukraine. Third, propaganda activities favoring Soviet and Nazi regimes was banned. Laudatory statements and the use of symbolism of these two totalitarian regimes were made illegal—both were considered equally criminal. Although this looked like the introduction of full detotalitarianization of the symbolic space, it was not the intention of its designers.

The ban did not apply to symbols relating to the activities of the OUN and the UPA—the former was not considered to be totalitarian, the latter was not classified as having committed mass war crimes. And, finally, the fourth bill caused the state to take particular care of memory about organizations fighting for the independence of Ukraine in the 20th century, and to honor their members. The document specifically mentioned structures representing all ideological trends, including unarmed ones, such as the Ukrainian Helsinki Group. The OUN and the UPA were among them. Granting by this act the status of "fighters for the independence of Ukraine" to all members of these organizations led to state defense against any accusations against members of these organizations who had committed crimes on national minorities.

The acts of April 9, 2015, gave the basis for a new politics of memory of the Ukrainian state. They meant a symbolic victory of an anti-Soviet narrative over the post-Soviet one, and they did not favor the public functioning of memory of victims killed by members of the nationalist movement. They showed that the majority of the Ukrainian elite after the Revolution of Dignity appreciated the role of the collective memory in the process of nation building. They illustrated at the same time, however, that these elites treated the assumptions of the policies of EU countries toward the memory of Nazism, communism, the integral nationalisms, and World War II in a selective manner. The Ukrainian Institute of National Remembrance and those members of parliament who had voted for the third and fourth of these acts deferred the usage of a European antitotalitarian criterion for their "own" national political and military formations.

Modern Actors in the Field of Memory in Ukraine and the EU Strategy toward Them

At the same time, the polling results showed that there was a far greater number of people in Ukraine than in the countries of Central Europe who did not have a clear view about the controversial events in the history of the 20th century and who appreciated the individual right to choose the image of the past. In a study conducted in December 2007, as many as 16 percent of respondents gave an affirmative response to the question of whether the members of the UPA should be recognized by the state as "participants in the national liberation struggle" (this is what happened as a result of the adoption of one of the acts of April 9, 2015), but on condition that the government would not impose this view and everyone would be able to decide for themselves whether to honor UPA members. In addition, as many as 18 percent of respondents chose the option "I do not know." Although in the western regions 77 percent respondents supported the unconditional granting of this status to the UPA (as compared with just 13 percent in Donbas and Crimea), the distribution of responses in the center was different: against, 38 percent; for, 38 percent (including supporters of conditional granting), and "it is difficult to answer," as many as 24 percent.[31]

I did not find any results of subsequent studies that could give the same choice of answers. We can consider, however, that the intermediate views of the center of the country in disputes in the four years after the Euromaidan in a fairly large part was divided between the two opposite sides. It can be seen in the results in the same central region from January and February 2018 when Ukrainians were asked to assess the struggle of the UPA (1942–50). The average clearly positive responses in the western circuit (Galicia and Volyn) were 62 percent; for the central circuit (Kyiv, Dnieper, and Polissia), 34 percent; for the eastern circuit (Donbas, Kharkiv, Dnipro, Zaporizhzhia), 13 percent, and for the southern circuit (Odesa, Mykolaiv, Kherson), 15 percent. On the other hand, the clearly negative responses amounted to 4 percent in the west, 10 percent in the center, 32 percent in the east, and 40 percent in the south. At the same time, for this question in the center there were still relatively many respondents assessing the activity of the UPA as good and bad at the same time (34%) and answering "It is difficult to say" (22%), which expressed views similar to views deferring to individual judgment whether to grant a special status by the state to UPA members, subject to one's own judgment on that issue, and to the "I do not know" answer in the study from 2007. Comparing the outcome of these two studies suggests that, in the center, the number of Ukrainians relating positively to the OUN and the UPA increased over a period of eleven years and those relating to them negatively decreased. In interpreting the results of 2018, however, it cannot be stated that the first of these responses in the center won decisively, or that it ceased to play an intermediate role between the west and the east.[32]

In her text written at the end of 2013, Oxana Shevel put forward the hypothesis that the memory of Ukrainians (not at the elite level but at the popular one) is not so deeply divided as is often claimed. Using the terms introduced by Michael Bernhard and Jan Kubik, she stated that Ukraine's memory field, understood as "the whole set of official [memory] regimes existing in a given country in a given period,"[33] is "fractured." In turn, a memory regime was defined by those authors as "a set of cultural and institutional practices that are designed to commemorate and/or remember a single event."[34] Shevel showed that Ukraine's memory field includes many fractured memory regimes, including that which applies to the OUN and the UPA.[35]

Using the four-part typology of mnemonic actors by Bernhard and Kubik, we can understand that the fractured memory regimes in relation to many events of the 20th century in Ukrainian history took place because most of the participants in politics represented a confrontational politics of memory warriors), which meant a lack of recognition granted to the public functioning of other interpretations of the past than their own. Only a minority was in favor of leaving the memory beyond the sphere of politics (abnegators), and only individuals (and from the scientific world rather than from politics) represented a third type of memory actors—they were former supporters of the public coexistence of various memories of the same events (pluralists). It should be added that the fourth type, prospectives, was also very poorly represented in the Ukrainian politics until 2013.[36]

Therefore, according to Shevel, mostly the political elite was fractured with regard to memory. In her view, the majority of Ukrainians functioned daily in pluralized memory environments. What is more, many of them distantly observed the ineffective efforts of politicians to impose a public image on the past. Eventually, she thought, Ukraine had a chance of creating "pillarized memory regimes" for many events of the 20th century and, consequently, a pillarized memory field, which Bernhard and Kubik classified as the main alternative model to the fractured field.[37] This may occur, she claimed, when such a majority of actors appears who will be oriented either toward maintaining the coexistence of different memories (mnemonic pluralists) or at an exclusion of the memory from the field of politics (mnemonic abnegators).[38]

In my opinion, this image of Ukrainian society was valid also after the Revolution of 2013–14. Its accuracy was indirectly connected with the interest of public opinion in the effects of the Lustration Act of October 2014, which prevented from holding public offices former KGB officers and their secret collaborators, among others. Public opinion was far more interested in the results of the lustration of officials achieved according to other criteria (provided by the same act), for example, of individuals who have illegal sources of wealth and performed management functions in the security apparatus in 2010–14, as well as of state officers and judges who acted against the revolution in the period from November 2013 to February 2014. Also, desovietization of the symbolic space carried out from above on the base of the mentioned acts of April 9, 2015 did not cause serious social conflicts.

There is a chance, however, that in Ukraine the probability that most political actors transition from the warriors category to the pluralists, abnegators, or even prospectives category would increase. Taking into account the adoption of the Acts of April 9, 2015, by a majority of approximately 60 percent of the *Verkhovna Rada*, one might even conclude that the strategy of the warriors among the political elite strengthened. There are two interpretations of the motives behind such politics of memory. According to the first, which I refer to as Ukrainian right-wing forces, one should take advantage of the atmosphere of the society's fear of Russia to finally shape a homogeneous national memory of events from 1917 to 1991. According to the second, which, I believe, explains the strategy of President Poroshenko and the centrist bloc in parliament that is associated with him, the acts of April 9, 2015, were adopted in response to Russian propaganda and to preserve the unity of the post-Euromaidan reformist camp. In that part of Ukrainian politicians' opinions, in the face of the conflict with Russia, a public debate on the dark side of the history of the OUN and the UPA has to be avoided. Only when the main danger to the state is dismissed (it seems that they argue in that way) will it be possible to present a more balanced assessment of those organizations.

Described state policy of memory was continued until the end of President Poroshenko term in 2019. Soon after there was an earthquake on the Ukrainian political scene. It is likely that overwhelming victory of Volodymyr Zelenski in the presidential election in May 2019 and his party *Sluga Narodu* (Servant of the people) in the parliamentary election in July 2019 is a strong symptom that the domination of the mnemonic abnegators and prospectives is coming. At the same time, it is also too early to state for sure whether the new authorities will definitely not continue the policy of memory of the politicians governing in 2014–19.

Taking it into account, I believe that there is no need to draw conclusions that the EU should infringe on the policy of memory in Ukraine. In the country, the full detotalitarianization of the symbolic space remains the optimal solution. Nevertheless, if it is too strictly imposed by the authorities in Kyiv—assuming that at the same time Russia will not change its policy of defaming Ukraine—it could contribute to a disintegration of the Ukrainian general public, which, with great difficulty and after many sacrifices, succeeded in 2014 to consolidate around a common, future-oriented project. In this difficult situation, the EU could then implement two actions. First, it could carefully observe and collect data on the Ukrainian memory actors and the sphere of their influence. Second, it could support the process of the Ukrainian reforms, with particular preference for the protection of human rights—as part of the basis of transitional justice.

In connection with the decentralization reform in Ukraine, it is likely that the local communities will in the long run be more entitled to their own commemorations of the past. Ultimately, the pluralization of memory, which will occur as a result of the activities of the local authorities and the nongovernmental organizations, should contribute to the development of beliefs in a full detotalitarianization of Ukraine's symbolic space. The factors that should also influence this direction are historical education reforms, the observation by Ukrainians of the politics of memory realized in EU countries (which have more and more visitors from Ukraine), and a gradual takeover of public roles by representatives of the younger generation. I would primarily expect changes to arise from these factors. It will take much time before the last statues not only of Lenin, but also of Bandera, disappear in Ukraine. After the events of 2013–1 and the elections in 2019, in the long run, this is more likely than after events from 1991 or 2004.

Notes

1. Wilson, *Ukraine's Orange Revolution*; Wilson, *Ukraine Crisis*; Marples, *Heroes and Villains*.
2. On the concept of "field of (collective or historical) memory," see Bernhard and Kubik, "Theory," 16.
3. European Parliament, "Resolution of 2 April 2009."
4. The definition from Kofi Annan appears in Sandoval Villalba, *Transitional Justice*.
5. See Wolfrum, *Geschichtspolitik*.
6. Ramet, "Serbia and Montenegro," 299.
7. See Himka and Michlic, *Bringing the Dark Past*; Potel, *Fin de l'innocence*; Budryte, *Timing Nationalism?*; Berg and Ehin, *Identity*.
8. In fact, when the text presents how the candidate countries receive the EU's expectations for their politics of memory, it also considers the positions taken by other organizations representing the public opinion of the West. The EU's observations in this matter addressed to the governments were confidential, but the positions of other entities were presented publicly. About the Romania case, see United States Holocaust Memorial Museum, *Romania*.
9. Motyka, *Ukraińska partyzantka*.
10. Kulchytskyi, *Holodomor*
11. Himka, "Lviv Pogrom."
12. In retaliation, the Polish underground forces (mainly the AK) killed approximately fifteen to twenty thousand civilian Ukrainians. See Motyka, *Od rzezi wołyńskiej*.
13. I do not enter here into a dispute about whether the OUN was an extreme nationalist movement or a fascist one. See Zaitsev, *Ukrainskyi intehralnyi natsionalizm*.
14. Hud', *Ukraintsi—Polaky*; Viatrovych, *Druha*.
15. Snyder, "Putin's Project."
16. On the implementation of transitional justice measures in postcommunist countries in Europe, see Stan, *Transitional Justice*; Pettai, *Transitional and Retrospective Justice*.
17. The exception was European Parliament, "Resolution of 25 February 2010," which enjoined Victor Yushchenko to annul his decision to award Stepan Bandera the Gold Star Medal of the Hero of Ukraine.
18. See Kritz, *Transitional Justice*.
19. On the characteristics of Kravchuk's and Kuchma's rules, see Kasianov, *Ukraina*, 34–208.
20. See the fifteen-volume series *Ukraina kriz' viky*.

21. On August 24, 1991, the Supreme Council of the Soviet Union accepted the Declaration of Independence of Ukraine. On June 28, 1996, the Ukrainian Parliament passed the constitution of the new state, legitimizing a presidential-parliamentary system (preferred by Kuchma) to govern the state. In turn, February 23, 1918, was celebrated in the Soviet Union as the day of the appointment of the Red Army in defense against the intervention of the Central Powers. The latter symbol along with the date of May 9, 1945, were the strongest associations linking independent Ukraine with the fundamental historical traditions of post-Soviet Russia. In October 2014, President Poroshenko abolished the Defender of the Fatherland Day and established the Defender of the Ukraine Day on October 14 referring to the Cossack tradition of the 17th century and presumed date of establishment UPA in 1942.

22. Hrechina and Dubych, *Problema OUN-UPA*.
23. See Shevel, "Politics of Memory."
24. Motyka, *Od rzezi wołyńskiej*, 109–50, 229–55, 446–68.
25. Hrytsak, "Stumbling Block."
26. Kasianov, *Danse macabre*.
27. Shekhovtsov, "From Electoral Success."
28. Wilson, *Ukraine Crisis*.
29. Oleh Tyahnybok from Svoboda and Dmytro Yarosh from Right Sector together gained 1.86 percent of the votes. Both nationalist groups, together, won 6.51 percent of the votes, but none exceeded the 5 percent barrier clause. See *Pozacherhovi vybory prezydenta Ukrainy 25 travnia 2014 roku*.
30. See Ilko Kucheriv Democratic Initiatives Foundation and the Razumkov Center, *2016: Political Results*.
31. A study of the Ilko Kucheriv Democratic Initiatives Foundation in Kyiv from December 2007 from Shevel, "Memories," 162.
32. Konieczna-Sałamatin, Otrishchenko, and Stryjek, *History*, 34. This study did not include Crimea. In Donbas it was carried out only in the area under the authority of the Ukrainian government.
33. Bernhard and Kubik, "Theory," 16.
34. Bernhard and Kubik, "Theory," 14.
35. Shevel, "Memories."
36. Bernhard and Kubik, "Theory," 11–14.
37. Bernhard and Kubik, "Theory."
38. Shevel, "Memories," 163–64.

Bibliography

Berg, Eiki, and Piret Ehin, eds. *Identity and Foreign Policy: Baltic-Russian Relations and European Integration*. Burlington VT: Ashgate, 2009.

Bernhard, Michael, and Jan Kubik, "A Theory of the Politics of Memory." In *Twenty Years after Communism: The Politics of Memory and Commemoration*, edited by Michael Bernhard and Jan Kubik, 7–36. Oxford: Oxford University Press, 2014.

Budryte, Dovile. *Timing Nationalism? Political Community Building in the Post-Soviet Baltic States*. Burlington: Ashgate, 2005.

European Parliament. "Resolution of 2 April 2009 on European Conscience and Totalitarianism." Document R6-0170/2009. http://www.europarl.europa.eu/sides/getDoc.do?pubRef=-//EP//TEXT+TA+P6-TA-2009-0213+0+DOC+XML+V0//EN.

European Parliament. "Resolution of 25 February 2010 on the Situation in Ukraine." Document P7_TA(2010)0035. http://www.europarl.europa.eu/sides/getDoc.do?pubRef=-//EP//TEXT+TA+P7-TA-2010-0035+0+DOC+-XML+V0//EN.

Himka, John-Paul. "The Lviv Pogrom of 1941: The Germans, Ukrainian Nationalists, and the Carnival Crowd." *Canadian Slavonic Papers* 2–3–4, no. 53 (2011): 209–43.

Himka, John-Paul, and Joanna Beata Michlic, eds. *Bringing the Dark Past to the Light: The Reception of the Holocaust in Post-communist Europe*. Lincoln: University of Nebraska Press, 2013.

Hrechina, L. A., and L. W. Dubych, eds. *Problema OUN-UPA: Zvit robochoi hrupy istorykiv*. Kyiv: Instytut Istorii Ukrainy NANU, 2004.

Hrytsak, Yaroslav. "A Stumbling Block of Reconciliation." *New Eastern Europe* 4, no. 9 (2013): 163–68.
Hud', Bohdan. *Ukraintsi-Polaky: khto vynen? U poshuku pershoprychyn ukrains'ko-pol's'kykh konfliktiv pershoi polovyny XX stolittia*. L'viv: Kalvaria, 2000.
Ilko Kucheriv Democratic Initiatives Foundation and the Razumkov Center. *2016: Political Results—A Nationwide Poll*. December 28, 2016. http://dif.org.ua/article/2016-y-politichni-pidsumki-zagalnonatsionalne-opituvannya.
Kasianov, Heorhiy. *Danse macabre: Holod 1932–1933 rokiv u politytsi, masovii svidomosti ta istoriohrafii (1980-ti-pochatok 2000-kh)*. Kyiv: Nash Chas, 2010.
———. *Ukraina 1991–2007: narysy novitnioi istorii*. Kyiv: Nash Chas, 2008.
Konieczna-Sałamatin, Yoanna, Natalia Otrishchenko, and Tomasz Stryjek. *History, People. Events. Research Report on the Memory of Contemporary Poles and Ukrainians*. Collegium Civitas: Warsaw, 2018. http://konieczna-salamatin.eu/pliki/History_People_Events.pdf.
Kritz, Neil J., ed. *Transitional Justice: How Emerging Democracies Reckon with Former Regimes*. Washington, DC: United States Institute of Peace, 1995.
Kulchytskyi, Stanyslav. *Holodomor 1932–1933 rr. iak henotsyd: trudnoshchi usvidomlennia*. Kyiv: Nash Chas, 2008.
Marples, David Roger. *Heroes and Villains: Creating National History in Contemporary Ukraine*. Budapest: Central European University Press, 2007.
Motyka, Grzegorz. *Od rzezi wołyńskiej do akcji "Wisła": konflikt polsko-ukraiński 1943–1947*. Kraków: Literackie, 2011.
———. *Ukraińska partyzantka 1942–1960: działalność Organizacji Ukraińskich Nacjonalistów i Ukraińskiej Powstańczej Armii*. Warsaw: Instytut Studiów Politycznych Polskiej Akademii Nauk–Rytm, 2006.
Pettai, Eva-Clarita. *Transitional and Retrospective Justice in the Baltic States*. Cambridge: Cambridge University Press, 2014.
Potel, Jaen-Yves. *La fin de l`innocence: la Pologne face à son passé juif*. Paris: Autrement, 2009.
Pozacherhovi vybory prezydenta Ukraini 25 travnia 2014 roku. Protokol Tsentralnoi Vyborchoi Komisii. https://www.cvk.gov.ua/info/protokol_cvk_25052014.pdf.
Ramet, Sabrina Petra. "Serbia and Montenegro since 1989." In *Central and Southeast European Politics since 1989*, edited by S. P. Ramet, 286–310. Cambridge: Cambridge University Press, 2010.
Sandoval Villalba, Clara. *Transitional Justice: Key Concepts, Processes and Challenges*. Briefing Paper IDCR-BP-07/11. University of Essex, Institute for Democracy and Conflict Resolution. http://repository.essex.ac.uk/4482/1/07_11.pdf.
Shekhovtsov, Anton. "From Electoral Success to Revolutionary Failure: The Ukrainian Svoboda Party." *Eurozine*, March 5, 2014. https://www.eurozine.com/from-electoral-success-to-revolutionary-failure/.
Shevel, Oxana. "Memories of the Past and Visions of the Future. Remembering the Soviet Era and Its End in Ukraine." In *Twenty Years after Communism: The Politics of Memory and Commemoration*, edited by Michael Bernhard and Jan Kubik, 146–70. Oxford: Oxford University Press, 2014.
———. "The Politics of Memory in a Divided Society: A Comparison of Post-Franco Spain and Post-Soviet Ukraine." *Slavic Review* 1, no. 70 (2011): 137–64.
Snyder, Timothy. "Putin's Project." *Frankfurter Allgemeine Politik*, April 16, 2014. http://www.faz.net/aktuell/politik/ausland/timothy-snyder-about-europe-and-ukraine-putin-s-project-12898389.html?printPagedArticle=true#pageIndex_2.
Stan, Lavinia. *Transitional Justice in Eastern Europe and the Former Soviet Union: Reckoning with the Communist Past*. New York: Routledge, 2009.
Ukraina kriz' viky. 15 vols. ed. Valeriy Smoliy, Kyiv: Alternatyvy, 1999–2001.
United States Holocaust Memorial Museum. "Romania: Facing Its Past—Evaluation of the Romanian State Policy towards the Memory of the Holocaust after 1989." Retrieved March 26, 2015. http://www.ushmm.org/research/scholarly-presentations/symposia/holocaust-in-romania/romania-facing-its-past.
Viatrovych, Volodymyr. *Druha pol's'ko-ukrains'ka viina 1942–1947*. Kyiv: Kyievo-Mohylanska Akademia, 2011.
Wilson, Andrew. *Ukraine Crisis: What It Means for the West*. New Haven, CT: Yale University Press, 2014.
———. *Ukraine's Orange Revolution*. New Haven, CT: Yale University Press, 2005.
Wolfrum, Edgar. *Geschichtspolitik in der Bundesrepublik Deutschland: der Weg zur bundesrepublikanischen Erinnerung 1948–1990*. Darmstadt, Ger.: Wissenschaftliche, 1999.
Zaitsev, Olexandr. *Ukrainskyi intehralnyi natsionalism (1920–1930-ti roky): heneza, evolutsia, porivnialnyi analiz*. Kyiv: Krytyka, 2013.

TOMASZ STRYJEK is Associate Professor at the Institute of Political Studies, Polish Academy of Sciences, and Lecturer at the Collegium Civitas. He is author of *What Kind of Past Does the Future Need? Interpretation of the National History in the Historiography and Public Debate in Ukraine, 1991–2004* (Warsaw 2007) and *Ukraine before the End of the History: Sketches on the State Memory Politics* (Warsaw 2014).

12

A DESIRED BUT UNEXPECTED STATE

The 1990s in the Memory and Perception of Ukrainians in the 21st Century

Joanna Konieczna-Sałamatin

ON AUGUST 24, 1991, THE UKRAINIAN PARLIAMENT ADOPTED the Independence Act, joining the few other Soviet republics that by this time had already declared their independence. The dissolution of the Soviet Union was finished by the end of 1991.[1] Ukraine became a state, in many senses unexpectedly. Andrew Wilson, who named his book *The Ukrainians: Unexpected Nation*, pointed out in the introduction that Ukraine's emergence on the map of Europe surprised many politicians, scholars, and businesspeople.[2] And while the event is, in the Ukrainian discourse, presented sometimes as the crowning success of many generations of activists seeking independence, it seems that it also surprised the Ukrainians themselves. Just to remind the reader: the Ukrainians radically changed their views on independence within just the few months between the beginning and the end of 1991. On March 17, 1991, the governing authorities of the still existing Soviet Union conducted a referendum with a question about supporting the preservation of the state.[3] Not all Soviet republics decided to organize the referendum: Armenia, Moldova, Georgia, Lithuania, Latvia, and Estonia announced a boycott; but the Ukrainian Soviet Socialist Republic did not, and so the referendum in Ukraine was conducted. Of those who took part in the vote (58.6% of all registered voters), 70.2 percent voted in favor of the preservation of the Soviet Union.[4] In fact, this was the lowest "yes" score of all the republics that had organized a referendum (the percentage of those voting "no" was highest in Ukraine), but the substantial public support for preservation of the Soviet Union was not then raising doubts.

A few months later the Ukrainian Parliament passed the Act of Independence (August 24, 1991) and, in the referendum that approved the Act (December 1, 1991), the percentage of votes "for" exceeded 90 percent.[5] Such a result was unexpected even by the Ukrainian authorities; especially as in the opinion poll that had been conducted a month before the December referendum, one out of four Ukrainians were unable to take a firm position on the issue of supporting or rejecting the historical resolution of the *Verkhovna Rada* of Ukraine.[6]

Alexander Motyl points out the historical irony in the fact that the Ukrainian state, in its present form, is to a large extent due to the contributions of its fundamental opponents:

"Lenin created Soviet Ukraine as a republic. Stalin provided it with well-defined territorial boundaries by annexing Volhynia, Galicia, and Transcarpathia. Khrushchev permitted its political elite to survive physically. Brezhnev enabled them to thrive as stable cadres within their own imperial bailiwicks. And Gorbachev destroyed the totalitarian underpinnings of the empire and thus the empire."[7] This, together with the diverse historical experience of the territory and people of Ukraine, left its mark on contemporary Ukrainian society.[8]

Events of the late 1980s and 1990s aroused great expectations in Ukrainian society for new opportunities in all dimensions of life: expectations related to both the sphere of political freedom and material prosperity. At the time, it was considered self-evident that one causes the other. "In the shops nothing could be bought without queuing. There was no freedom nor democracy. . . . Moscow and the Party decided about everything. Holodomor and repression have shown us where it can lead. The nation has matured spiritually and politically to change this situation," said Leonid Kravchuk in an interview for *Gazeta Wyborcza*.[9]

Naturally, the great expectations associated with a regime change were not only the domain of Ukrainians—a similar situation was found in all countries of the former Eastern Bloc. These expectations were sometimes paradoxical: in Poland, at the end of the 1980s, it was expected that the new system would bring strong leadership and at the same time protection of fundamental freedoms.[10] The Central and Eastern European societies had no direct experience of living in a democratic system and they connected all their hopes and aspirations with the upcoming transition. They expected, simply, a comprehensive improvement in living conditions, in both the public and the private sphere. Some researchers are of the opinion that the widespread process of combining the political expectations with the hopes of a higher standard of living has significantly broadened the social base of the independence movements, which has contributed to their success.[11] The same idea appears often in essays by Timothy Garton Ash, who describes the very beginning of the transition in Central Europe.[12]

The transformations, which began in Ukraine with the collapse of the Soviet Union, are often called the "quadruple transition," because they combine four transitions simultaneously: changing the political system from an authoritarian to a democratic one, replacing the centrally controlled economy with a market-based economy, building the state, and building a political nation.[13] The extent to which each component of these transitionals will be successful in Ukraine remains an open question.[14] The elements are interrelated—one supports the other. It is hard to talk about "democracy" if we do not know what the *demos* is; that is, when the people lack a unifying idea. Roeder goes quite far by saying that "In the post-communist world, stable democracy has triumphed only in countries that have solved their nation-ness problem. That is, democratization has been most successful in states that are both older and more homogeneous."[15] This point of view sounds controversial, or is obviously false, when talking about the ethnic homogeneity or heterogeneity of states. But if the nation is understood as a civic, not ethnic, community united by a set of values shared in common by its members, it is hard to disagree that successful nation-building supports the processes of democratic transition and economic reforms. On the other hand, a successful transition could become a part of the national identity, as an element of national pride: in this way, a successful transition could contribute to the nation building. Unfortunately, the Ukrainian transition had many aspects that were not so successful.

This chapter analyzes the Ukrainians' perception of the early transition period from the perspective of ten and more years of independence. It shows how the memory and the evaluation of what had happened in August 1991 and afterward are connected with the views on Ukraine's real and desired role and place in Europe. The analysis of the image of the early 1990s that appears in Ukrainians' memory is preceded by a presentation of some facts about the state of the Ukrainian economy just after the dissolution of the Soviet Union. The economic dimension of the Ukrainian transition is quite important, since the economic crisis was one of the most important elements of Ukrainians' memories about the early years of independence. The core of the empirical base of this chapter is composed of the qualitative and quantitative data from three research projects: a national survey conducted in 2005, a qualitative study from 2006 (life-story interviews on the first fifteen years of Ukrainian independence), and another national survey from 2013.[16] In various places, the chapter will also cite other research data, such as in-depth interviews collected during research visits to Kyiv from 2010 to 2014, as well as survey data published on the websites of various Ukrainian analytical centers and data from international research projects such as the European Values Survey.

The Economic Context of the Ukrainian Transition

Before analyzing attitudes, we should have at least a general view of the economic context of the Ukrainian transition. Doing so helps us to understand the variation in attitudes to the 1990s from today's perspective: attitudes that were greatly affected by the economic situation.

The collapse of the Soviet Union meant the dissolution of economic ties between Ukrainian enterprises and plants and those in other former Soviet republics. Many of the enterprises simply stopped working and stopped paying salaries. The practical absence of small business led to an economic downturn that was deeper than in other transition economies[17]. As Anders Aslund put it, unlike other post-Soviet countries, in the period of 199198 Ukraine "has not had a single year of growth but a significant decline in GDP has continued every single year."[18] The Ukrainian government started implementing some economic reforms in order to build—at least in declarations—the foundations of a market economy. A high level of corruption, however, the reforms have never been finished and were implemented so as to avoid harm to businessmen closely connected with the government. These developments led to the emergence of oligarchs as a strong and influential group rather than to modernization and economic growth. Figure 12.1 shows that in first ten years of Ukrainian independence, its economy shrank by a factor exceeding 2. There was practically no Ukrainian family that was not affected by the shrinking economy. Ukrainian GDP per capita had reached the level it was in 1991 only in 2005. We should keep this in mind when trying to understand Ukrainians' attitudes toward the Soviet period, which are usually a mixture of nostalgia, longing for a predictable world, and satisfaction from the national freedom and independent state they had obtained.

There is another element of the economic context that strongly affected both the evaluation of the new political system and the today's memories of the early transition period.

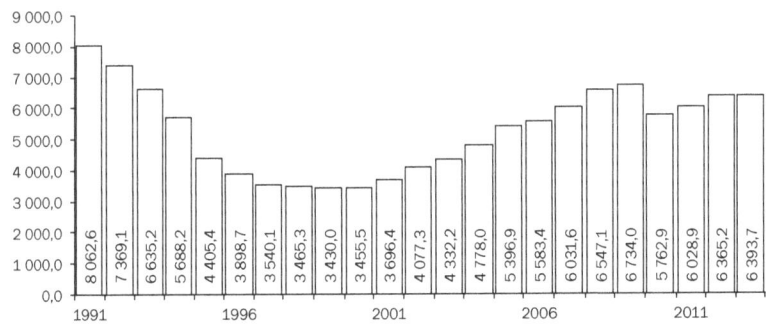

Fig. 12.1 GDP per capita in Ukraine for 1990–2016 (PPP). *Source*: https://data.worldbank.org/country/ukraine (Retrieved January 24, 2018).

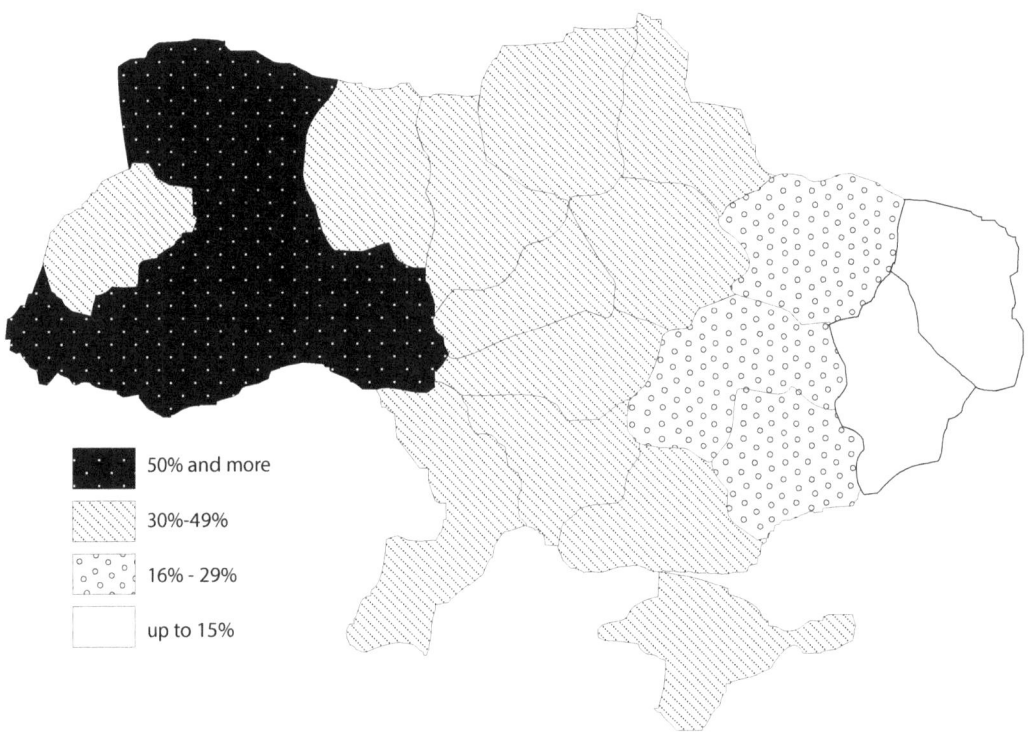

Fig. 12.2 Percentages of rural population in Ukrainian regions in 1989. *Source*: Author's calculations based on data from State Statistical Service (www.ukrstat.gov.ua).

The urban–rural structure of the population is shown in figure 12.2,[19] which determines the potential level of resistance to the crisis.

The dramatic economic collapse just mentioned led to such a change in many families' financial situations that some of them were put on the edge of physical existence: no salaries, no money even to satisfy the most basic needs. Living in a rural settlement is a substantial advantage in times of crisis. The inhabitants of industrialized eastern Ukraine had little chance of changing their primary activity and switching to farming: the soil in the area is not good for farming (in Lugansk region) and there was also simply insufficient know-how. In the central and western parts of the country farming was a widespread activity, which presented a natural way of dealing with the crisis. Central Ukraine is an area with the most fertile soils in Europe, but even disregarding this, there was tradition and know-how that allowed people quickly change their main source of living to farming. In the early 1990s, many of those who had not been farmers previously turned to a self-sufficient way of living and simply grew food for their families, sometimes exchanging it with the neighbors. As a result of this phenomenon, in areas where growing food was possible because of the natural conditions and social structure, the inhabitants learned a lesson about not being so dependent on what was going on at the state level and whether the reforms were successful.

The Beginning of the Ukrainian Transition in Memories

When talking about the early 1990s, most Ukrainians witnessed more or less the same facts: an intense political life with live transmissions of the Supreme Council of the Soviet Union, which was watched with true interest; the attempted Soviet coup d'état; then the Act of Independence of Ukraine, approved by referendum, and then the dissolution of the Soviet Union. These were followed by hyperinflation and a deep economic crisis. Some also remember patriotic enthusiasm and a national renaissance.

In the summer of 2006, a group of researchers, along with the author of this chapter, conducted a series of life-story interviews, trying to find out what independence meant to the people living in Ukrainian small and midsized towns (the areas where interviews were conducted are shown in fig. 12.3).[20] The respondents were asked directly to describe in their own words what had happened in their lives in 1991 and directly afterward, when Ukraine became an independent state. The picture that comes out of these interviews creates the context for the following presentation on the public opinion polls regarding, primarily, the two historical events mentioned; namely, the proclamation of independence by Ukraine and the dissolution of the Soviet Union.

Questions about the beginning years of the transition period almost automatically induced in respondents' memories of what their life had looked like before. They referred mostly to the end of the 1980s. The period after the collapse of the Soviet Union was compared to the last years of the state before the transition, to the period of perestroika. In most cases, the results of the comparison were not positive for the still young Ukrainian independence. This result is not surprising in consideration of the economic data presented in the previous section. Nevertheless, the memory of the early 1990s was not exclusively negative and the memories of the last years of the Soviet Union were also not exclusively positive. The bright side of the 1990s story was mostly connected with a national renaissance as well as a substantial improvement from the point of view of personal freedom and the possibilities of implementing this freedom; for example, the real possibility of traveling abroad. It is probably worth emphasizing that the possibility of travelling abroad was really an important and positive outcome of the system changes, even if the interviewees could not use this freedom because of their economic situation.

282 | *The Burden of the Past*

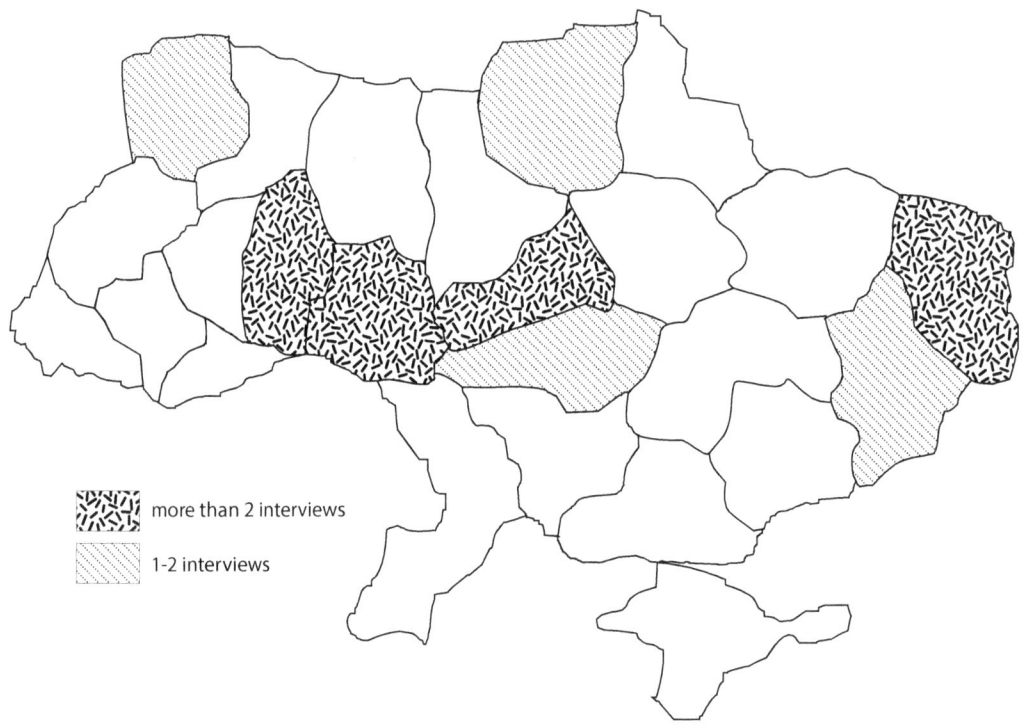

Fig. 12.3 The location of interviews conducted in 2006. *Source*: From the author's own data.

The economic crisis of the 1990s in respondents' memories was usually one of great severity, with a strong and painful personal impact. The second, virtually universal, feature of the interviewees' narratives (though not appearing in the Donbas region) was that surviving these difficult times was attributed to the central role of household plots, farmed either directly for family subsistence or for sale at local markets.

Thus, a school director from a town in Kirovohrad Oblast described the 1990s as "very hard, so hard that God forbid that they will return, and you don't want to remember [them]." She, however, is also one of the very few respondents who also mentioned that the last years of the Soviet Union were not the most prosperous either; and so, she saw the first years of independent Ukraine as a continuation of a crisis that started before the collapse of the Soviet Union. For her, the final years of the Soviet period were already marked by great psychological oppression, but also general instability and insecurity, a "very terrible situation." Her point of view was rather unique, since most of our respondents made a clear distinction between the Soviet period—a time of relative economic stability with a predictable future—and the "period of Ukraine," when hyperinflation ruined the majority of people's savings. Another teacher—from a village in Cherkasy Oblast—remembers a life with five children and neither money nor anything to buy. It was possible to survive, nevertheless, because she had a private plot of land that she used for farming. She states that she was not interested in politics and felt that her family situation was beginning to improve when her oldest child finished high school in 1997 and, in spite of some difficulties, succeeded in entering a university for free: apparently meaning that neither fees nor bribes had to be paid. Referring to her whole village, she deplored the wasted passage of time, in which jobs for young people and, in general, prospects had been lacking. At the same time, it is important to note that she insists that life has become better during the period of independent Ukraine, notwithstanding her family's severe financial problems. She said there was more effort required to survive, but "one also lives more freely."

Nearly all the respondents from the towns visited, especially in central Ukraine, repeated stories about a piece of land that had made the crisis less painful and let their family survive the most difficult times. Even those whose profession was not connected with agriculture and who lived in towns still had strong personal connections with rural areas. In central and western Ukraine (see fig. 12.2), the percentage of rural population was quite high, so almost everyone had somebody who was a close relative living in a village who supplied him or her with necessary (and free) food. The urban–rural connection and this specific way of living, in which farming holds such an important place, is to a great extent practiced up to the present day and must have an effect on people's values and attitudes. This effect could be a subject for further research. The picture of larger and smaller Ukrainian towns becoming almost empty on most weekends and public holidays because everyone is going to help their relatives with the farming is something that still surprises visitors from abroad.

There was also another thread in the respondents' narratives about the 1990s. Some of them remembered their hometowns having "more life" in Soviet times: when local factories worked and the local infrastructure looked better. We found these kinds of memories both in central and eastern Ukraine. In the central part of the country, the interviewees also usually noted recent (in 2005) positive changes: some of the factories started working again and the development of small business helped to slowly overcome the unemployment crisis. Our observation of recent improvements in infrastructure was in line with the interviewees' comments on the topic.

A chief librarian from a town in Vinnytsia Oblast associated the Soviet period with large factories with many employees. When the Soviet Union collapsed, the big industries generally stopped working—as she recalled from her memories. In the Soviet Union, the industrial entities, especially those in small towns, were not only the dominant employers, but also very often the main organizers of the social life in the community.[21] Such was the case in the town in which this interviewee lived.

For her, the situation has improved again over the five years leading up to the interview (2000–2005); and she stressed that a core piece of Soviet industry, the local canned food plant, had started work again. Most respondents who had also noted the decrease of industry in their locality did not make similar statements; it looked like the deindustrialization after the collapse of the Soviet Union was perceived subjectively as a kind of force majeure, and therefore their statements were without any strong emotional interest.

These stories demonstrate that the early transitional period was generally difficult for the respondents; as well as being simply confusing in regard to what to think about, or how to address, the Soviet period. A museum curator from Khmelnytskyi Oblast remembered the Soviet past, above all else, as a time of suppression of national Ukrainian tradition and a time of national inferiority. Complementarily, she thought the achievement of independence as the point where "we [Ukrainians] came out on top." At the same time, she pointed out that under the Soviet regime her town used to be one of the most important in the *raion*;[22] not only in name but in substance, with infrastructure that she clearly saw as far superior to what existed at the time of the interview. In the Soviet period, the town was, in the respondent's eyes, full of life; with cultural events organized from time to time by the local authorities and bazaars. At the time of the interview, the town was clearly on the periphery; the local authorities had no money to maintain the infrastructure or to maintain the numerous historical monuments in the town.

The curator also said that in the exhibitions that had just been planned, when we met in summer 2006, the Soviet period was not to be represented in any manner, since—in the interviewee's words—"it needed to be further rethought." To add a final twist to the complex attitude of this respondent to the Soviet past, she also explained that one of the planned exhibitions would have a section on the local *mishchanstvo* (bourgeois) lifestyle in order to demonstrate that the town, in pre-Soviet times, used to be a major urban center and not a mere village.

The picture in eastern Ukraine was different, even if there was a substantial amount of common experience, such as big Soviet industries that ceased to work and a general lack of money, which affected a great majority of households. In the narratives from this area, the interviewees paid little attention to the issue of national renaissance, and social problems appeared at the top of the list.

A representative of the younger generation who graduated from a high school in 1994 and lived in the Donetsk region remembered little of the Soviet period. He saw some continuation in terms of the concentration of capital, stating that "those who were well off during the Soviet period remained rich after [the Soviet Union's] collapse and new rich people also appeared." For him, the 1990s and 2000s were marked by their perceived sameness and stasis; as being constantly the same with no dynamic or change. At the level of his personal life, he remembered the 1990s as a period of study at an institute in Kharkiv, a stay abroad as an au pair in Germany, a return to his hometown, small salaries for jobs in his area of training (engineering in agricultural machines), and employment at a combination gas station and motel. Looking for a job in the West was (and still is) not common in the eastern regions of Ukraine. If they do decide to leave their community, people usually choose Russia because it is close in both geographical and cultural distance. According to estimations provided by Malynovska, former Soviet countries used to be the destination for about 74 percent of Ukrainian emigrants from all the regions.[23]

Another picture of eastern Ukraine was drawn by a nongovernmental organization activist from a town in Luhansk Oblast. For him the early 1990s were, first of all, a period of experimentation with *ersatz* currencies and temporary food scarcity in shops.[24] *Horilka* (vodka) was becoming a replacement currency, but it was not so easy to get, so that "people were fighting for vodka, even killing each other." Yet an important change was that he also noticed a new general interest in politics in these crisis years. It is interesting that this greater interest in politics was not—in his memories—a reaction to independence. He thought it was rather the experiments with currency that made people more interested in politics than they had been before the collapse of the Soviet Union. "This was the beginning of a new development in society," he said. The first thing that came to his mind about his 1990s was his voluntary military service in 1997. He was trying to escape unemployment and find a position as a military physician, in what he expected to be a reputable hospital, but he was instead sent to a railway unit as a junior medical assistant. His experience there left a lasting impression: "What I got to see was awful. I felt that I had ended up in prison. The quality of dress [was] like in the 1940s, like [in] punishment battalions, [it] resembled the [penitentiary] zone. Food bad, bad attitude, and dirt."

It is clear that in the eastern regions people were coping with the crisis differently from those in other parts of the country. Those most proactive sought unofficial employment in Russia or (rarely) in the West, and tried to earn some money rather than "organize" food by becoming farmers. This choice seemed rational, since the natural conditions in eastern Ukraine are not so good for farming. Generally speaking, a migration strategy was not the most popular one: in 2001, only about 10 percent of all emigration from Ukraine came from the eastern regions.[25] Most of the eastern Ukraine inhabitants were simply forced to reduce their needs. The workers in heavy industry in the east did not have any alternative ways of earning money; they depended much more on industrial activity.

The general picture that appears from the cited interviews and from observation of the social environment of the interviewees correlates quite well with the regional divisions of Ukraine.[26] The differences, or even cleavages, between Ukrainian regions have been the subject of many studies,[27] which mostly point to the differences in political culture between the eastern, central, western, and southern parts of the country, which are outcomes of the history of these geographical regions, a history that goes back to the 17th century.

Even if a greater part of the early transition's experience was common to the whole of society—as was the economic crisis—there were substantial differences in the meanings attached to this experience and in the different strategies for dealing with the crisis. As a result, the lessons that the inhabitants of the eastern and other parts of Ukraine had learned were also different.[28] The majority of Ukrainian citizens, those from the central and western parts of the country, understood that they could live without the state's support and survive as long as the state did not disturb them. They also enjoyed independence as a value in itself, and so being a citizen of the new Ukrainian state might serve as a sort of compensation for the painful crisis. At the same time, those living in eastern Ukraine got a lesson in strong dependence on the state or, to be more precise, on the state–oligarch relationship. For them, the crisis was also more painful because of the dissolution of the Soviet Union, a system with which many of them felt at home: in 1994 the predominant self-identification in Donetsk was "Soviet."[29] The new Ukrainian state failed to provide them with an identity that could replace the lost one.

Paradoxes in the Ukrainian Perception of the History

Interviews conducted fifteen years after the collapse of the Soviet Union suggested that by this time there had already been a noticeable tendency to remember the Soviet era in a somewhat positive light. The national surveys conducted in Ukraine are in line with this

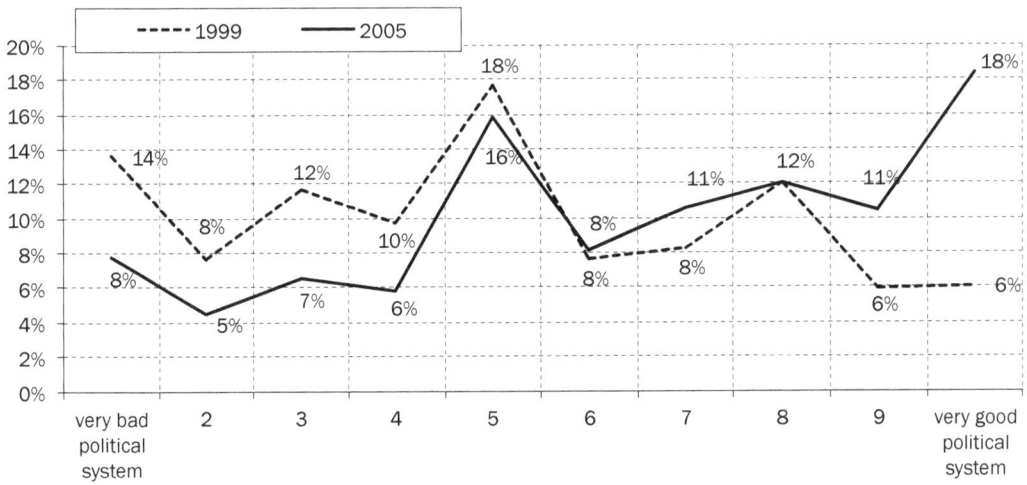

Fig. 12.4 Popular attitudes toward the political system at two points in time: 1999 and 2005. *Source*: Author's calculations based on data from the European Values Survey (1999) and Schumann Foundation Survey (2005).

observation. The likelihood of evaluating the Soviet political system as better than the current one became stronger with time. In 1999, only 12 percent of Ukrainians gave the highest grades (9 or 10 on a 10-point grading scale) to their country's system before the dissolution of the Soviet Union. Six years later, in 2005, the percentage had increased by 17 points to 29 percent. (See fig. 12.4.)

There are at least two interrelated factors that can explain this result: the first is the crystalizing over time of a positive memory of the Soviet period, and the second is huge disappointment in the current (at the time of survey) political system. "Memory reflects [the] present state of the past."[30] The political system that came to replace the Soviet one has not met expectations, and so memory has tended to idealize the past, when there was at least more stability ("salaries were paid on time" was something frequently pointed out in the interviews). In both surveys (the results of which are presented in the graph), there were also questions about the evaluation of the current (in 1999 and 2005) political system. In both measurements, the current system was assessed as much worse than the Soviet one.

The picture can be completed with the results of the Pew Global survey, "Two Decades after the Wall's Fall," and the European Social Survey of 2012.[31] In the first, 65 percent of Ukrainians indicated that, at the time of the survey (2009), the economic situation of the majority of their compatriots was worse than in Soviet times (which looks probable from the GDP data presented in fig. 12.1). The opposite view was expressed by only 13 percent; more or less the same percentage did not report any change in the matter. The European Social Survey (2012 data) measured the level of satisfaction with democracy: the result in Ukraine was the second lowest among twenty-nine countries (just above Bulgaria).[32]

Independently of the fact that the economic indicators shown at the beginning of this chapter confirmed, in general terms, the widespread belief that before 1991, the average Ukrainian lived better than in the last years of 20th century; at the time of the surveys, the results of the comparison were not so obvious. This is especially so when the comparison is not focused purely on economic indicators and also takes political freedom into consideration. Assessing whether now is better or worse than before the dissolution of the Soviet Union is to a great extent a political declaration rather than an objective evaluation of the indicators. The interviews presented in the previous section showed that the respondent's personal values had a great influence on his or her evaluation of life experience. The statistical analysis conducted using the survey data from 2005 and 2009 also indicated that the odds of returning a positive evaluation for the current (at the survey time) political system when the respondent holds a patriotic political orientation was nearly double the odds of a positive evaluation of the previous system.[33] "Patriotic orientation" comprised two indicators: living in the western region of the country and choosing Ukrainian as the language of the interview.[34] The measured effect remains significant even when the income level is controlled for, which additionally supports the argument that the respondent's assessment is not strictly of an economic character.

Readers from Poland and Central Europe may be surprised by the fact that in Ukraine, the Soviet period has been an example of positive rather than negative reference until recent times. As Piotr Pogorzelski writes, "It was the 1st and 9th of May, not Easter or Christmas, when one could feel an atmosphere of true holiday in the streets of Kyiv."[35] Only the events at the end of 2013 made it clear to many Ukrainians that nostalgia for the Soviet Union, and building an independent Ukrainian state, are things that are difficult to combine in one narrative and in one political project. Only twenty-five years after the fall of the Soviet Union, the Soviet symbols started to become associated with the aggressive politics of Russia and not with a kind of golden age of Ukrainian society. A convincing illustration of the change is the so-called *leninopad*: the mass removal of statues of Lenin from Ukrainian towns. The climax of *leninopad* came at the beginning of 2014, when several hundred monuments were removed throughout the country. We should not forget, however, that up until April 2015, when the decommunization laws were passed, there were still towns and villages in Ukraine (usually small entities in the east and south of the country) where statues of Lenin were still in a good shape.

The results of the surveys from 2005 and 2013 are a good illustration of the fact that, within the social consciousness, the emergence of the Ukrainian state in the early 1990s is not generally perceived as a kind of liberation or a break with the Soviet past. The surveys included questions about evaluating various events from Ukraine's history, including the proclamation of independence by Ukraine (only in the 2005 survey) and the collapse of the Soviet Union (in both polls). The question about opinions of the collapse of the Soviet Union asked in 2013 was worded slightly differently from the one eight years before, so the results cannot be directly compared. It is possible, however, to compare the characteristics of the social groups that in 2005 and eight years later in 2013 expressed regret for the dissolution of the Soviet empire.

In 2005, more than half the respondents welcomed the independence the country received in 1991 and evaluated the event positively (51 percent). For many of them, however, it was not strange to simultaneously regret the collapse of the Soviet Union (62 percent regretted the Soviet Union's dissolution) and yet welcome Ukrainian independence; which, along with the independence of the other republics, led to the collapse. Such illogical and inconsistent answers were given by 21 percent of respondents: they recognized the proclamation

Table 12.1. Attitudes toward the dissolution of the Soviet Union versus the proclamation of independence by Ukraine (2005).

Dissolution of the Soviet Union	Proclamation of Independence of Ukraine			
	Positive	Neutral	Negative	Don't Know
positive	19%	1%	0	0
neutral	5%	3%	1%	0
negative	21%	10%	23%	8%
don't know	5%	1%	0%	3%

Source: Author's calculations based on data from the Polish Robert Schuman Foundation, 2005.

of independence to be positive, but the collapse of the Soviet Union that resulted from it was for them negative. It is interesting to note that consistent views—that is, a positive evaluation of both events—occurred less often: in only 19 percent of cases (table 12.1).

As one can see in table 12.1, in 2005 the dominant attitude toward the starting points of the Ukrainian state was a negative assessment of both the collapse of the Soviet Union and the proclamation of independence by Ukraine. The second most popular was a positive attitude toward the independence of Ukraine but negative toward the breakdown of the Soviet Union.

There is an interesting group who did not express an opinion about either of these events. These respondents made up 17 percent of the total and can be described as "average Ukrainian people," since this group reflected quite well the whole population. The structure with regard to age group and region of residence was nearly identical to the structure of the greater population. The only difference was in gender: this "don't-know" group had a slight underrepresentation of people with tertiary educations and had a greater female representation than the population as a whole. Nevertheless, uncertainty about the evaluation of the events discussed seemed to be quite uniformly distributed throughout Ukrainian society. The problem of the "don't-know" group in Ukraine, and its stability over time, has already been discussed with regard to foreign policy issues, but here we can see it is also quite noticeable in opinions about internal Ukrainian politics.[36] Chudowsky and Kuzio explain the phenomenon as being the result of an insufficient level of national integration across Ukraine. Another factor that could lead to this phenomenon is the low level of trust in public institutions (the interviewer comes from a public institution) that is connected with the absence of an official position on both of the historical events. In the latter case, the "don't know" answer is a short version of "I don't know what I should say" or "I don't know, what is worth saying."

Another interesting group consisted of respondents who thought there was nothing contradictory in regretting that the Soviet Union no longer existed and also expressing satisfaction with the independence of Ukraine. Analysis reveals that the demographic structure of this group is practically the same as for the whole population, with only a slight overrepresentation in respondents 50 to 59 years old, but the average age was the same as that for the whole population. There were also no differences when considering education level, the language spoken, or the region of residence; and their evaluation of the current political system was practically the same as for the wider population.

A Desired but Unexpected State | 289

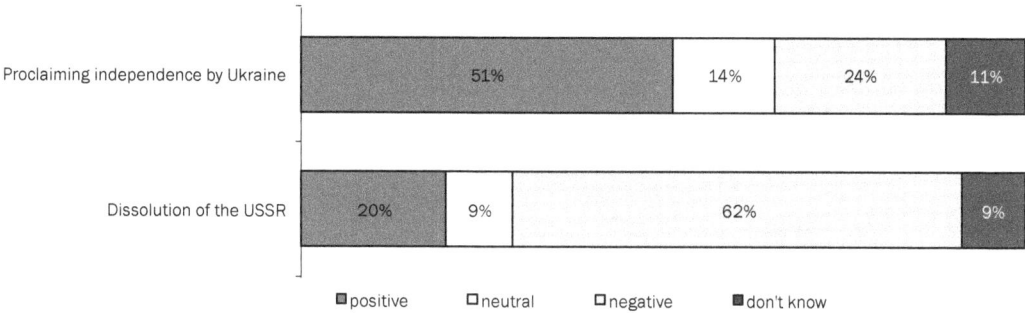

Fig. 12.5 Regional distribution of the attitudes toward Ukrainian independence and the dissolution of the Soviet Union (2005). *Source*: Author's calculations based on data from the Polish Robert Schuman Foundation (2005).

The above described group evaluated the Treaty of Pereiaslav[37] (51 percent in the specific group and 36 percent for the rest of population) and the October Revolution in 1917 (41 percent positive evaluations from this group and 33 percent from the others surveyed) more positively than the other respondents. This meant the respondents from this group not only regretted that the Soviet Union no longer existed, but that they shared the official Soviet view of the past. This was, however, for them not in contradiction with support for creating the independent Ukrainian state.

Two of the attitudes presented in table 12.1 were strongly differentiated regionally and are shown in figure 12.5. There were also substantial differences in the popularity of these attitudes between age groups.

The label "coherent-independence" was assigned to those who evaluated the Ukrainian independence as positive or neutral and also evaluated the dissolution of the Soviet Union as positive or neutral (excluding those who gave a neutral evaluation of both events—they were added to "don't know" group). A "coherent-USSR" attitude meant a negative evaluation of both events, or a neutral evaluation of one and a negative evaluation of the other. "incoherent-independence" meant a positive evaluation of Ukrainian independence with a negative one connected with the collapse of the Soviet Union. The opposite incoherent attitude was expressed by only one respondent.

The western region was the only one where the "coherent-independence" (pro-independence and pro-Soviet breakup) attitude appeared more frequently than any of the other attitudes. Similarly, for the age group 18–29, the same "coherent-independence" attitude was shared by 34 percent of respondents, while the second most popular attitude, "coherent-USSR" received only 23 percent of choices. In all other age groups, the "coherent-USSR" attitude was the dominant one.

Although the level of support for Ukrainian independence became greater over time (as shown in fig. 12.6), the percentage of supporters only in 2014 reached the same level as was attained in December 1991 when the independence referendum was published.

Some researchers question the validity of such methods for measuring attitudes toward independence in a situation where the independence has been a fact for over twenty years and view conducting another referendum about it to be completely hypothetical. Instead, they suggest asking, for example, about the relations that are desired between Ukraine and

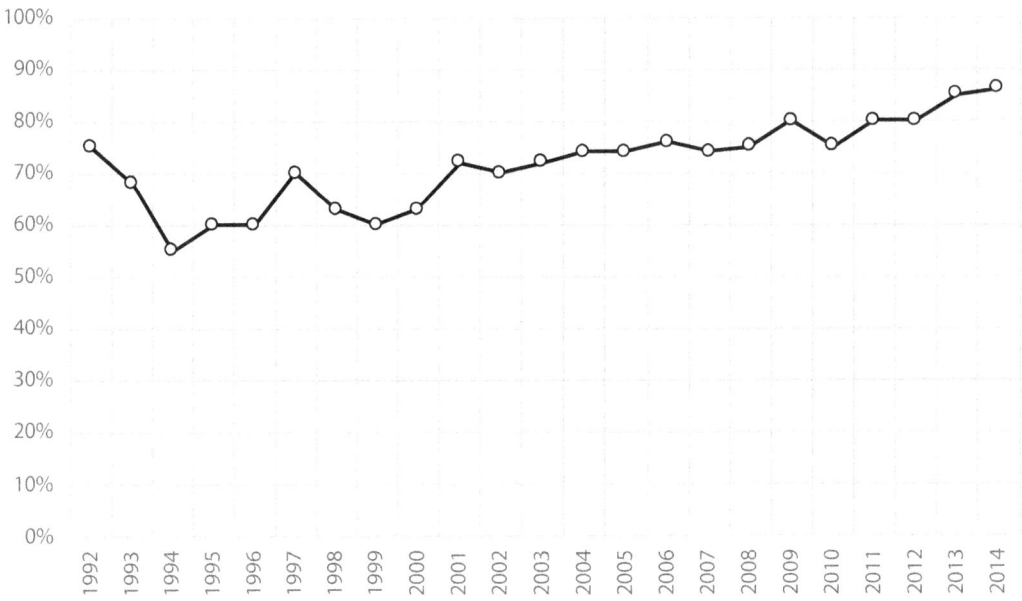

Fig. 12.6 Percentages of Ukrainian independence supporters (1992–2014). *Source*: Kyiv International Institute of Sociology, Khmel'ko, *Dinamika poddderzhki*, http://www.kiis.com.ua/materials/articles_HVE/Support_of_State_Sovereignty_in_Ukraine.pdf, 5.

Russia.[38] It turns out, however, that the conclusions from an analysis of the two formulations are consistent: the proportion of supporters for state independence slowly but steadily increases with time but remains lower than the December referendum (1991) up until the annexation of Crimea by Russia in March 2014. With the annexation, the percentage of those who support Ukrainian independence rose to over 90 percent, as it had done in the time of the referendum.

The growing support for independence still does not preclude the persistence of a relatively high percentage of people who regret that the Soviet Union dissolved, even if this percentage gradually decreases. According to data released by Rating Group, in 2010, 46 percent of respondents regretted the collapse of the Soviet Union; in 2013, the percentage was less and reached only 41 percent, while in 2014 only one in three respondents (33%) shared this attitude.[39] The percentage of those longing for the Soviet Union has recently decreased, but it still remains quite high when there is open conflict with Russia. For many Ukrainians, it is not so easy just to reject the Soviet period as a "foreign project," something that was imported from outside. Their common notion of the past is "rooted in a shared Soviet history, with its hopes, failures, horrors and crimes; where the Ukrainians were not just victims of an imposed external power but also active agents of their own history."[40] The perception of the Soviet period as one in which Ukrainians were as victims of external power is quite widespread in the western part of the country, where Soviet Union came only for a while in 1939 and for a long time in 1945.

Possibly, the negative memories of the period that followed the collapse of the Soviet Union makes it harder to accept the version of history that presents the year 1991 as mainly a time of liberation from the communist regime. It also seems that the negative aspects of the Soviet Union's last years are poorly remembered by Ukrainians, and so these memories are not widely transmitted to younger generations within families. In the interviews in 2006, only a few people recalled that the period before 1991 was not such a rosy time when it came to not only the political but also the economic situation, nor did they seem to realize that in the independent Ukraine there is much more freedom. In the 2005 survey, negative evaluations of the Soviet Union's dissolution also prevailed in the relatively young age group of 30 to 39 years old, but not among the youngest.

The collapse of the Soviet Union meant primarily a loss of confidence in tomorrow, and for many it also meant a loss of social status and relative economic stability, which in particular affected the residents of Eastern Ukraine with its dominant heavy industry. This highly populated region used to supply large areas of the Soviet Union with coal and steel. The concept that "we [Eastern Ukraine, Donbas] are feeding all the country" returns, from time to time, to the public discourse on some Ukrainian media.

Therefore, the Soviet Union is for many Ukrainians still their "paradise lost." The memory of the deep crisis of the 1990s (after the Soviet Union broke down) fixes this version of history, according to which the Soviet period was in a sense a golden age, and neither the discourse in Ukrainian media nor school education prevents the dissemination of this point of view.[41]

In a survey conducted in summer 2013, 38 percent of Ukrainians said that the collapse of the Soviet Union brought more harm than good, and only every fourth respondent expressed the opposite opinion (fig. 12.7).[42] In addition, a very small percentage of the respondents (only 3%, which is one-third as large as in 2005) had no opinion on the issue and chose "do not know." This shows that the issue was, by that time, already well grounded in the public consciousness of Ukraine.

Opinions on the amount of harm or good that resulted from the dissolution of the Soviet Union were differentiated regionally and on this question the country was divided into three (not four) parts: the west, where "more good" (38%) was chosen more frequently than "more harm" (25%); the center, where there was a statistically insignificant difference ($p > 0.1$) between the two percentages (28 percent said "more good" and 31 percent said "more harm"); and the southeast, where nearly half of the inhabitants (48%) thought the Soviet Union's breakdown brought more harm than good while only 16 percent expressed the opposite view.

It is surprising that the distribution of the opinions described was practically independent of age group. Even in the youngest group (15–24), the opinion about "more harm" appeared more often (36%) than "more good" (23%), which is practically the same as for the general population.

A more detailed analysis of the results from the 2013 survey shows yet another paradox in the Ukrainian perception of history. It seems the opinion that the collapse of the Soviet Union brought more harm than good has become a way of expressing an antisystem, rebellious attitude. Let us recall that the survey was conducted in May 2013 when the government of President Yanukovych seemed as if it were going to remain in power for some time. His term of office was to last until 2015. Civil liberties were gradually reduced and corruption had reached unprecedented proportions. No one was then thinking about Maidan.

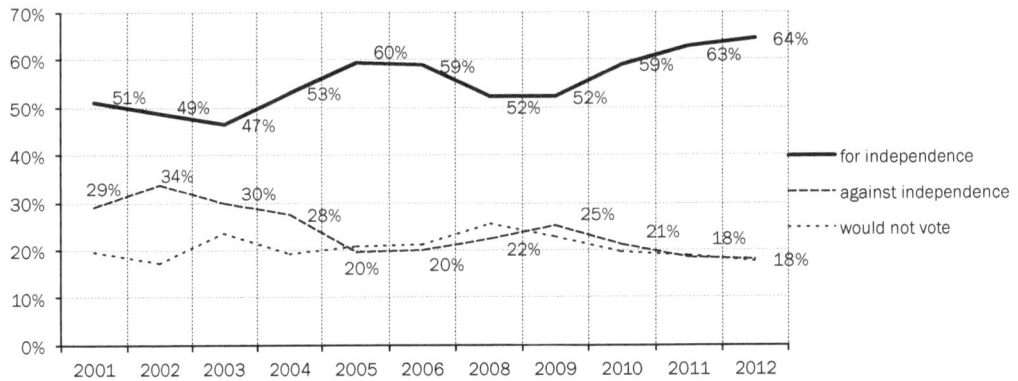

Fig. 12.7 Attitudes toward the dissolution of the Soviet Union (data from 2013). *Source*: Fomina et al., *Polska-Ukraina*, 74.

In mid-2013 many citizens had reason to be frustrated because of the state of public affairs in Ukraine. When we check the regional–generational breakdown of the opinions, we see that the youngest respondents (15–24 years) in the western part of the country argue that the collapse of the Soviet Union brought more harm than good almost as often as their counterparts in the east.[43] This is rather unexpected because, in the western region, the level of Soviet nostalgia was historically the lowest in Ukraine. In 1991, the oldest of these young respondents would have only just been born, and so they could not have had their own positive (or any other) experience of life in the Soviet Union. Obviously, such an unexpected attitude in this young generation in western Ukraine could just be a result of the attitudes of their parents, but an analysis of the available survey results, both from 2005 and from 2013, do not confirm this hypothesis, as older inhabitants of western region indicated "more harm than good" from the Soviet Union with greater frequency than the youngest generation. Other results from the 2013 survey indicate a greater number of pro-Western rather than conservative–Soviet views from residents of Western Ukraine, especially the youth. If it is so, the "protest hypothesis" seems the only logical explanation for this paradoxical distribution of answers about the dissolution of the Soviet Union.

Do You Have to Deny the Soviet Past in Order to Build an Independent Ukraine?

It is clear that Soviet nostalgia was not uniformly distributed across the country and still is not, nor is the importance attached to an independent Ukrainian state. The research of Hrytsak showed how different the perceptions of the Soviet past were in L'viv and Donetsk. In the latter, "Soviet'" self-identification was dominant and chosen by 45 percent of respondents, while in the former only 5 percent thought of themselves as "Soviet" people."[44]

The evaluation of the Soviet era, and the processes that followed it—that is the creation of an independent Ukraine—strongly differentiated Ukrainians across the regions of the country.[45] As Stryjek points out, the conflicts of memory of the Soviet era "everywhere [in all postcommunist countries] divided public opinion, but in no country had they a character

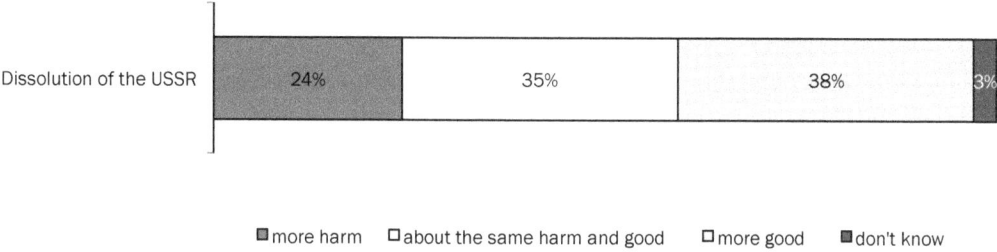

Fig. 12.8 Nostalgia for the Soviet Union in regions (May 2014). *Source*: The Rating Group, http://ratinggroup.ua/research/ukraine/dinamika_patrioticheskih_nastroeniy.html (Retrieved April 27, 2015).
Note: The Rating Group company divides Ukraine into six regions (as if the central region from previous analyses was divided into north and center and the eastern region into east and Donbas).

Table 12.2. Change in support for Ukrainian independence in regions between 2013 and 2014.

	West		North		Center		South		East		Donbas	
	2013	2014	2013	2014	2013	2014	2013	2014	2013	2014	2013	2014
Definitely yes	60%	89%	43%	71%	34%	60%	14%	34%	18%	43%	15%	13%
Rather yes	29%	10%	30%	19%	33%	28%	34%	30%	26%	27%	17%	21%
Do not know	6%	1%	9%	6%	8%	4%	17%	15%	16%	16%	11%	32%
Rather not	3%	0%	9%	2%	16%	6%	16%	12%	20%	8%	21%	12%
Definitely not	2%	0%	9%	2%	9%	2%	19%	9%	20%	6%	36%	22%

Source: Based on data from the Rating Group Company, http://ratinggroup.ua/research/ukraine/dinamika_patrioticheskih_nastroeniy.html (Retrieved April 27, 2015).

so strongly regionalised as in Ukraine, and nowhere were [they] to this extent associated with the opposition between the two identity projects addressed to one nation."[46] Figure 12.8 presents results from one survey.

In 2014, many Ukrainians (33%) still regretted that the Soviet Union had broken up, which, however, did not prevent them from expressing support for the independence of Ukraine: 76 percent would support the eventual independence referendum.[47] It seems clear that the military conflict with Russia made many Ukrainians really appreciate independence. This growth in support for independence took place in all the regions, including Donbas, but in Donbas the changes were less spectacular than in the rest of Ukraine, and the process of changing opinion seems to be the hardest there. Table 12.2 shows the distribution of answers to the question "If there was such a choice, would you support the independence of Ukraine today?" for two points in time: August 2013 (when no Maidan protests were expected) and in August 2014 (after the annexation of Crimea by Russia). Results are displayed by region.

The greatest increase in support was noted in the eastern (by 26 percentage points) and central regions (by 21 percentage points). In Donbas, there was a substantial increase in the percentage of those who chose not to express their opinion; the percentage share of independence supporters remained practically unchanged from 2013.

The analysis of opinions presented in figure 12.8 and table 12.2 shows that, on a regional level, there was an almost perfect negative correlation ($r = -0.98$) between the percentage of those who in 2014 regretted that the Soviet Union had collapsed and those who would "definitely" support the independence of Ukraine if such a choice were presented again. This was not the case in 2005, when the first of the analyzed surveys was conducted.

Conclusions

The results of research conducted in Ukraine at different points in time have shown that there is no common or even dominant narrative for the 1990s, just as there is no single coherent vision of what it means to be Ukrainian. It is clear that, for the majority of Ukrainians, the 1990s were not a time of liberation from the yoke of communism, and in particular, it was not like that for the residents of the small and medium-sized towns whose statements were analyzed as a context for the results of the national surveys. A thread of liberation occurs in their narratives, but it is not dominant or even the most important one.

The memory of the 1990s is dominated by examples of a deep economic degradation that affected people personally. They remembered how they handled day-to-day experiences during these hard times, remembered the energy and vitality of Ukrainians, which allowed them to survive. During this time, they realized they could live independently from the state, which was not even able to pay their salaries and pensions on time. They developed and maintained horizontal cooperation, for example, by exchanging the food products they grew. Possibly, this experience contributed to the extraordinary growth and effectiveness of today's voluntary movement in Ukraine that solves most of the current problems connected with the functioning of the state: from food supplies for refugees from the areas affected by the war to the purchase and delivery of weapons for fighting soldiers.

The topic of the joy of independence felt in 1991 appears in the narratives, but it seems that the circle of people for whom it was a matter of personal importance is rather small—especially if seen from the perspective of small and medium-sized towns—and it did not appear at all in the east of the country. In this sense, Ukraine was really an "unexpected state." Few believed that this state would be created, and almost no one suspected that it was going to happen when it happened.

For all these reasons, the Ukrainian state was perhaps desired, but completely unexpected; and no one imagined how it was going to function. There were expectations that "it would be better," but there was no vision for what this "better" should look like. That is why we still see some contradictions both in the interpretation of the past and in the approach to what should be built in the future. Nevertheless, it seems that now there is less confusion about the perception of the Soviet past and support for Ukrainian independence. The events at the end of 2013 and beginning of 2014, especially the annexation of Crimea by Russia and the attacks on the eastern part of Ukraine, forced many to clarify their attitude. This situation makes Soviet nostalgia less popular, though in Ukrainian society there was no radical rejection of the Soviet heritage. The Soviet Union still preserves warm feelings in the hearts of many Ukrainians, with the possible exclusion of the Western part of the country.

In conclusion, it should be added that, after Russia's actions in relation to Ukraine in 2014, the proportion of people who wanted an independent Ukraine rose to the level of the 1991 result for the first time in twenty-three years. The independent state became desired as much as it had been in the very beginning.

Notes

1. The dissolution of the Soviet Union was formally accomplished by the Supreme Soviet of the Soviet Union on December 26, 1991, by adopting Declaration No. 142-H, which at the same time proclaimed the Commonwealth of Independent States (http://vedomosti.sssr.su/1991/52/#1561).

2. Wilson, *Ukrainians*.

3. The question was formulated as follows: "Do you consider it necessary to preserve the Union of Soviet Socialist Republics as a renewed federation of equal sovereign republics, in which the rights and freedoms of an individual of any nationality will be fully guaranteed?" (For the Russian version of the question, dated March 17, 1991, see http://histrf.ru/ru/lenta-vremeni/event/view/riefieriendum-o-sokhranienii-sssr-6-riespublik-boikotiruiut.) In the Ukrainian SSR there was an additional question: "Do you agree that Ukraine should be part of a Union of Soviet sovereign states on the basis of the Declaration of State Sovereignty of Ukraine?" To which 81.7 percent of voters said "yes." Data and English translation of the questions provided by Kuzio, *Ukraine: Perestroika to Independence*, 167–69.

4. The results are available on the site Direct Democracy, retrieved April 18, 2015, http://www.sudd.ch/event.php?lang=en&id=su011991.

5. D'Anieri, Kuzio, and Kravchuk, *Politics and Society*.

6. Wojciechowski, "Król był już"; Khmelko, "Dinamika."

7. Motyl, "Making Ukraine," 4.

8. Ukraine first became independent in the period 1917–21, during which time several Ukrainian states or several different governments were established in Ukraine. They were merged into the Ukrainian Soviet Socialist Republic, which was one of the building blocks of the Soviet Union. Galicia was added as a result of the Molotov–Ribbentrop Pact in 1939, South Bessarabia and Northern Bukovina in 1940, and Carpathian Ruthenia in 1945. In 1954, the Supreme Soviet of the Soviet Union transferred the Crimean Peninsula from the Russian FSSR to the Ukrainian SSR (see Subtelny, *Ukraine*).

9. Wojciechowski, "Król był już."

10. Rychard, "Centralizm polityczny."

11. Fuchs and Roller, "Cultural Conditions."

12. Ash, *Pomimo i wbrew*.

13. Kuzio, "Transition."

14. Korostelina, "Ukraine Twenty Years After; Wilson, *Ukrainians*.

15. Roeder, "Peoples and States," 860.

16. The 2005 survey was conducted by the Kyiv International Institute of Sociology for the Polish Robert Schumann Foundation. The sample of two thousand respondents was representative of the adult population of Ukraine. The 2006 study was designed and conducted by Tarik Cirill Amar, Sofiya Dyak, and Joanna Konieczna-Sałamatin in August 2006 and consisted of about twenty interviews in twelve small and midsized towns in central and eastern Ukraine. Some of the results have been presented in Konieczna-Sałamatin "Middle Town Ukraine." The coauthors of the study have agreed that the results of the research may be used in this publication. The 2013 study was a national public opinion poll conducted by GfK Ukraine for the Institute of Public Affairs. The sample of one thousand respondents was representative of the adult population of Ukraine.

17. Coupé and Vakhitova, "Costs and Benefits."

18. Aslund, "Problems."

19. Calculations were based on 1989 data, being the period just before the collapse of the Soviet Union.

20. The respondents mostly belonged to the local elite: teachers, the heads or employees of various institutions of culture, librarians, nongovernmental organization activists, local authorities, and one Roman Catholic priest. In order to preserve the anonymity of respondents, we do not indicate the names of the towns where the interviews were conducted.

21. Eaton, *Daily Life*.

22. Administrative unit: second level of administrative division in Ukraine. Currently Ukraine is divided into 490 *raion*s.

23. Malynovska, "Caught." The data refer to the 1991–2004 period and does not say what part of those 74 percent who migrate to former Soviet states accounts for emigration to Russia, but in the MFA estimations cited by Coupe and Vakhitova "Costs and Benefits," 43, about 50 percent of Ukrainian emigrants went to Russia. Russia remains a

popular destination for labor migration also after 2014, especially short-term migration. These are findings of the Ukrainian Office of MOM, *Migratsiia*, http://iom.org.ua/sites/default/files/ff_ukr_21_10_press.pdf, 13.

24. After the proclamation of independence (in August 1991), Ukraine left the ruble zone but did not introduce its own currency: payments were still made in rubles, but with the addition of "single-use coupons." From January 1, 1992, Soviet rubles were fully replaced with multiple-use coupons, which were in use until 1996.

25. Author's calculations made on the basis of data published by CASE: Coupé and Vakhitova, "Costs and Benefits," 49.

26. Katchanovski, "Regional Political Divisions."

27. See, for example, Pirie, "National Identity"; Bugajski, "Ethnic Relations"; Nemyria, "Regionalism."

28. The 2006 qualitative study did not include the southern part of Ukraine (the *oblasts* of Mykolaiv, Odessa, Kherson, and Crimea), which might be slightly different in their main strategies of dealing with the crisis, but other research indicates many similarities between the south and the east of Ukraine.

29. Hrytsak, "National Identities," 266.

30. Lavabre, "Historiography."

31. Pew Research Center, "Two Decades after the Wall's Fall"; European Social Survey, 2012 data, http://www.europeansocialsurvey.org.

32. Author's calculations based on European Social Survey, 2012 data, http://www.europeansocialsurvey.org.

33. These are the results of a logistic regression analysis, where the dependent variable was coded 1 when the respondent thought that "now" is better than before the dissolution of the Soviet Union, and 0 for all other attitudes (including "don't know").

34. Unfortunately, there was insufficient data to construct a subtler measurement of the political attitudes of respondents. "Patriotic orientation" was meant to be the commitment to the idea of building the Ukrainian state, independent of Russia, and led by a sense of its own politico-economic interests.

35. Pogorzelski, *Barszcz ukraiński*, 193. Pogorzelski recalls that the "Day of Workers' Solidarity," the official name of the May 1 holiday, was especially solemnly celebrated in 2013. During this time, nostalgia for the Soviet Union and the pro-European values of the youth coexisted without disturbing each other.

36. Chudowsky and Kuzio, "Does Public Opinion Matter?"; Konieczna-Sałamatin, "Ukraina."

37. The agreement between Cossack hetmanate and Muscovy in 1654. Reportedly the council adopted a decision on the unification of Ukraine with Russia, but no original documents have been preserved.

38. Khmelko, "Dinamika."

39. Data from Rating Group, accessed January 9, 2015, http://ratinggroup.ua/research/ukraine/nostalgiya_po_sssr_i_otnoshenie_k_otdelnym_lichnostyam.html.

40. Zaharchenko, "Polyphonic Dichotomies."

41. Kulyk, *Ukrainian Media*, 297–401.

42. Fomina et al., *Polska-Ukraina*, 74.

43. For the breakdown, see Fomina et al., *Polska-Ukraina*, 77.

44. Hrytsak, "National Identities."

45. Hrytsak, "National Identities."

46. Stryjek, *Ukraina*, 90.

47. A study from August 2014, accessed January 20, 2015, http://ratinggroup.ua/research/ukraine/dinamika_patrioticheskih_nastroeniy.html.

Bibliography

Ash, Timothy. Garton. *Pomimo i wbrew: eseje o Europie Środkowej*. London: Polonia Book Fund, 1990.

Aslund, Anders. "Problems with Economic Transformation in Ukraine." June 23, 1999, https://carnegieendowment.org/1999/06/23/problems-with-economic-transformation-in-ukraine-pub-60.

Bugajski, Janusz. "Ethnic Relations and Regional Problems." In *Ukraine: The Search for a National Identity*, edited by Sharon. L. Wolchik and Volodymyr. Zviglyanich, 165–81. Lanham, MD: Rowman and Littlefield, 2000.

Chudowsky, Victor, and Taras Kuzio. "Does Public Opinion Matter in Ukraine? The Case of Foreign Policy." *Communist and Post-communist Studies* 36, no. 3 (2003): 273–90.

Coupé, Tom, and Hannah Vakhitova. *Costs and Benefits of Labour Mobility between the EU and the Eastern Partner Partnership Countries: Country Report; Ukraine*. CASE Network Studies and Analyses No.

464/2013. Warsaw: Center for Social and Economic Research, 2013. http://www.case-research.eu/sites/default/files/publications/CNSA_2013_464.pdf.
D'Anieri, Paul, Taras Kuzio, and Robert S. Kravchuk. *Politics and Society in Ukraine*. Boulder, CO: Westview, 1999.
Eaton, Katherine B. *Daily Life in the Soviet Union*. Westport, CT: Greenwood, 2004.
Fomina, Joanna, Joanna Konieczna-Sałamatin, Jacek Kucharczyk, and Łukasz. Wenerski. *Polska-Ukraina, polacy-ukraińcy: spojrzenie przez granicę*. Warsaw: Instytut Spraw, 2013.
Fuchs, Dieter, and Edeltraut Roller. "Cultural Conditions of the Transition to Liberal Democracy in Central and Eastern Europe." In *The Postcommunist Citizen*, edited by Samuel. H. Barnes and János. Simon, 35–77. Budapest: Central European University Press, 1998.
Hrytsak, Yaroslav. "National Identities in Post-Soviet Ukraine: The Case of Lviv and Donetsk." *Harvard Ukrainian Studies* 22 (1998): 263–81.
Katchanovski, Ivan. "Regional Political Divisions in Ukraine in 1991–2006." *Nationalities Papers* 34, no. 5 (2006): 507–32.
Khmelko, V. *Dinamika podderzhki naseleniem suvereniteta v pervye desyatiletya ieio gosudarstvennoi nezavisimosti Ukrainy (1991–2014 gody)."* KISS, 2014. http://www.kiis.com.ua/materials/articles_HVE/Support_of_State_Sovereignty_in_Ukraine.pdf.
Konieczna-Sałamatin, Joanna "Middle Town Ukraine: A Life-History Approach to Ukraine's Neglected Hinterland." Paper presented at the Second Danyliw Research Seminar in Ukrainian Studies, Ottawa, Canada, October 12–14, 2006.
———. "Ukraina—ucieczka od wyboru." *Nowa Europa Wschodnia* 3–4 (2011): 205–14.
Korostelina, Karina V. "Ukraine Twenty Years after Independence: Concept Models of the Society." *Communist and Post-communist Studies* 46, no. 1 (2013): 53–64.
Kulyk, Volodymyr. *The Ukrainian Media Discourse: Identities, Ideologies Power Relations*. Kyiv: Krytyka, 2010.
Kuzio, Taras. *Ukraine: Perestroika to Independence*. 2nd ed. London: Palgrave Macmillan, 2000.
———. "Transition in Post-communist States: Triple or Quadruple?" *Politics* 21, no 3 (2001): 168–77.
Lavabre, Marie-Claire. "Historiography and Memory." In *A Companion to the Philosophy of History and Historiography*, edited by Aviezier. Tucker, 362–71. Oxford, UK: Blackwell, 2010.
Malynovska, Olena. "Caught between East and West, Ukraine Struggles with Its Migration Policy." *Migration Policy Institute*, January 1, 2006. https://goo.gl/a4jKp3.
Motyl, Alexander. J. *Making Ukraine, and Remaking It*. Petryshyn Memorial Lecture, Harvard University, April 14, 2003. Cambridge, MA: Harvard Papers in Ukrainian Studies, 2003.
Nemyria, Hryhorii. "Regionalism: An Underestimated Dimension of State-Building." In *Ukraine: The Search for a National Identity*, edited by Sharon Wolchik and Volodymyr Zviglyanich, 183–98. Lanham, MD: Rowman and Littlefield, 2003.
Pew Research Center. "Two Decades after the Wall's Fall: End of Communism Cheered but Now with More Reservations." Pew Global Attitudes Project (2009). Retrieved January 1, 2015. http://www.pewglobal.org.
Pirie, Paul. "National Identity and Politics in Southern and Eastern Ukraine." *Europe Asia Studies* 48, no. 7 (1996): 1079–1104.
Pogorzelski, Piotr. *Barszcz ukraiński*. Warsaw: Helion, 2013.
Rating Group. "Nostalgia for the Soviet Union and the Attitude to Separate Persons." 2014. Retrieved April 27, 2015. http://ratinggroup.com.ua/products/politic/data/entry/14092/.
Rating Group. "The Dynamics of Patriotic Moods." 2014. Retrieved April 27, 2015. http://ratinggroup.com.ua/products/politic/data/entry/14101/.
Roeder, Philip G. "Peoples and States after 1989: The Political Costs of Incomplete National Revolutions" *Slavic Review* 58, no. 4 (1999): 854–82.
Rychard, Andrzej. "Centralizm polityczny: centralizm i pluralizm w opinii Polaków." In *Polacy 88*. Warsaw: Instytut Filozofii i Socjologii PAN, 1989.
Stryjek, Tomasz. *Ukraina przed końcem historii: szkice o polityce państw wobec pamięci*. Warsaw: Naukowe Scholar, 2014.
Subtelny, Orest. *Ukraine: A History*. Toronto: University of Toronto Press, 1988.
Ukrainian Office, International Organisation for Migration. *Migratsiia v Ukraini: Fakty i tsyfry*. Kyiv: International Organisation for Migration, Ukrainian Office, 2016. http://iom.org.ua/sites/default/files/ff_ukr_21_10_press.pdf.

Wilson, Andrew. *The Ukrainians: Unexpected Nation*. New Haven, CT: Yale University Press, 2002.
Wojciechowski, Marcin. "Król był już wtedy nagi." An interview with Leonid Kravchuk. *Gazeta Wyborcza*, August 24, 2001.
Zaharchenko, Tanya. "Polyphonic Dichotomies: Memory and Identity in Today's Ukraine." *Demokratizatsiya* 21, no. 2 (2013): 241–69.

JOANNA KONIECZNA-SAŁAMATIN is Associate Professor at the Institute of Sociology, University of Warsaw.

INDEX

Abakunova, Anna, 9, 11
Abramson, Henry, 120
Alison, Miranda, 152
All-Union Communist Party (Bolshevik), 259, 271
Amar, Tarik Cyril, 185
amnesia: and Great Famine, 53; and Holocaust, 185
Anderson, Benedict, 183
Angelina, Pasha, 27–28
Anti-Fascist Committee of Ukraine, 130
antimemorials, 69
"Arch of Friendship of Nations," Kyiv, 83
army-nation, 152
Artem, Fyodor, 125
Asadchev, Valerii, 124
Ash, Timothy Garton, 278
Assmann, Aleida, 134–35, 208, 224, 232, 246
Auge, Marc, 54
Auschwitz, 199
Ausländer, Rose, 170
Austro-Hungarian Empire, 168, 169, 170, 190
Avanposty (Krylenko), 35–36

Baal Shem Tov, 195–96
Babi Yar executions, 96, 187
Badior, Dariia, 134
Balta mass-killing site, 10, 194–95, 197
Bandera, Stepan, 1, 12n20, 96, 145, 149, 257, 258, 273
banderites (*banderivitsi*): in heroic discourse, 99–105; as term, 1, 96
Ban Ki-moon, 82
Barka, Vasyl', 38, 39
Beniuk, Bohdan, 132
Bernhard, Michael, 11, 270–71
Bernsand, Niklas, 172
Billig, Michael, 94
biographical experience, 10, 11, 91–93, 147, 184, 197, 198, 240
biographical memory: 9, 10, 11; vs. collective memory, 236; of ethnic cleansing of Poles, 236, 240, 245, 247n11; of Holocaust, 184, 194, 197–98; of World War II, 91–94, 110n53
biographical sociology, 5
bipolar or double-heritage approach, 200
Bitter Memory of Childhood statue, 63, *64*
Black Book, The, 188, 202n36
Blacker, Uilleam, 184, 186–87
Blocha, Alexi, 59

Bloodlands (Snyder), 23
Bohachevsky-Chomiak, Martha, 144
Bohun, Volodymyr, 125–27, 130
Bolsheviks: church desecration by, 59; defiance of, 117; described as Jewish, 41; jargon of, 21; Petliura and, 117; portrayal in fiction, 19, 35; as term, 106
Borovyk, Mykola, 9, 10
Borysenko, Valentyna, 23
Brown, Judy, 85
Browning, Christopher, 22
Buhaichuk, Viktor, 131
Buiko, Heorhii, 130
Burden of Dreams (Wanner), 8
Burds, Jeffrey, 147
Bush, George W., 265
bystander role, as shifting, 4, 5

"Candle of Memory" Holodomor Victims Memorial, Kyiv, 50–51, 62–63, *64–66*, 67–68
Celan, Paul, 170
cemeteries: and Holodomor, 53–55, 58, 60–61, 71n30; Jewish, 194, 195; and Petlura, 133
Central Committee of the Communist Party [Bolshevik] of Ukraine (CCCP[b]U), 30, 32, 33, 34, 35
Chebotarova, Anna, 9, 10
Chekists: uniform of, 36; described as Jewish, 40–41
Chernivtsi: cityscape of, 10, 168–79; ethnic groups in, 169, 171–72, 176, 177; memory in, 169, 171, 173; streets renamed, 178
Chorna doshka (Doliak), 40–42
Chornobyl, *190*
Chudowsky, Victor, 288
Chutnik, Sylwia, 149
cityscape, 10, 168–79
collaboration: with Nazis, 101, 126, 131, 155n25, 215; with Soviets, 99
collaborator role: as shifting, 4; Soviets on, 190
collective memory: 2, 3, 8–9; vs. biographical memory, 236; in Chernivtsi, 169, 171, 173; effect of EU and Russia on, 253, 258, 263–54, 264, 267, 270, 273; of Galician Ukrainians, 229–46; of Holodomor, 50, 51, 55, 69; of Holocaust, 10, 183–200; limits of, 103, 107; in memorials, 50–51, 55, 69; in memory studies, 92; and Petliura, 121; Poles in, 229–46; of Roma, 11, 206–24, 225n6, 227n81; as term, 208, 247n5; in Ukraine, 4–8; of World War II, 92–94, 103–108, 143
collectivization, 49

299

commemoration: 4, 8, 10; and EU, 273; of Holocaust, 187, 188, 189, 201n27, 202n35; of Holodomor, 51, 52–69, 71n1; of Heavenly Hundred, 168, 178; of nationalist movement, 141–54; of perpetrators, 257; of Petliura, 117–35, 136n44; in place-making, 173; and Roma, 210, 220, 221, 223; of victims, 255; of World War II, 77–87, 93, 189
Committees of Nonwealthy Peasants (KNS), 25–27
Commonwealth of Poland, 232
communism: nostalgia for, 3, 4, 107, 176, 261, 279, 287, 292, 294; elites under, 107; suppression of memory under, 2–3; symbols prohibited, 80
Communist Party of Ukraine (KPU): and Holodomor, 49, 259–60, 262, 264; and Petliura, 125, 130
community memory, 9, 51, 57, 58, 104, 107, 183–84, 206, 210, 223, 229, 231, 241, 242, 245, 263
"Competing Victimhood" (Jilge), 186
competitive victimhood, 186, 191
Confino, Alon, 51
Connerton, Paul, 199
Cooke, Miriam, 142, 147, 153
Cossacks: gender and, 152; in nationalism, 178, 190, 263; and military tradition, 151, 178; Petliura and, 129; Tiutiunyk and, 136n38; on Ukraine coin, 140
Crimea, annexation by Russia, 1, 7, 10, 77, 79, 80, 87n15, 103, 188, 253, 270, 290, 294

Danse macabre (Kasianov), 49–50
Day of Defender of the Fatherland holiday, 141, 152, 264, 274n21
Day of Defender of Ukraine holiday, 140–41
Day of Victory holiday, 10, 78–79, 86, 150, 264, 267–68, 269–70
Day of Memory and Reconciliation holiday, 83, 86, 150, 202n35, 269–70
decommunization, 80, 131, 132, 202n35
dekulakization, 26, 28
Demchenko, Maria, 27–28
Denysko, Hanna, 124–25
deixis, 94
democracy, 278–89
denazification, 80
desovietization, 6, 11, 123, 168, 173, 178, 256–66, 268, 272
detotalitarianization, 253–73
diaspora, Ukrainian, 19, 33, 38, 40, 42, 49, 55, 58, 68, 70–71n24, 99, 176, 177, 185, 186
Dietsch, Johan, 186
Dimarov, Anatoliy, 36–37
Djebabla, Mourad, 58
Doliak, Natalia, 40–42
Donbas, conflict with Russia in, 1, 10, 77, 79, 83, 85, 86, 87n15, 108n2, 125, 140, 141, 145, 149, 151–52, 154n2, 188, 253, 263, 264, 268, 270, 271

Dontsov, Dmytro, 144
Dubois, Patrick, 188
Dukyn, Mykola, 36
Dun, Olena, 21

Eastern Orthodox Church, 59, 268
economic crisis of 1990s, 279–81
Eichmann, Adolf, 22, 37, 220
Einsatzgruppen, 183, 258
Elam, Yigal, 208
ethnic cleansing: Holocaust as, 2; in Galicia, 7, 229, 234–237; nationalist, 131, 145, 185, 234–37, 257, 258; and Petliura, 102; as term, 237–38; in Volhynia, 102, 237, 266; in World War II, 142–43
ethnic markers for self-description, 106–107
Etkind, Alexander, 186–87
Euromaidan protests: 1, 10; and Heavenly Hundred, 168–69, 178–79; May 9 celebrations and, 77, 82; and Petliura, 131–32; and politics of memory, 270–71; and social role of history, 91; and women, 145, 146, 151, 157n77
European Social Survey, 286
European Union (EU): and detotalitarianism, 253–73, 273n8; and Holocaust, 187; and memory of nationalism, 11, 255, 261, 270; and Ukrainian memory fields, 12
experience: biographical, 10, 11, 91–93, 147, 184, 197, 198, 240; of hard times, 294; of history, 5, 8

family memory, 11, 210, 245
fascism: and historical rhetoric, 7; rehabilitation of, 262; in Soviet propaganda, 56
Fedor, Julie, 143
feminism, 144–45
fiction, Holodomor in, 19, 34–42
Filatov, Anton, 134
films: documentary, 210; Galician Poles in, 236; and Holodomor, 34, 38; on Petliura, 132; and prosthetic memory, 184; UNR in, 132, 134; Volhynian massacre in, 1, 13n31, 238
"First Minute of Peace" action, 83
Fol'varochnyi, Vasyl, 129
Foreign Intelligence Service of Ukraine (SZR), 128
Forever Flowing (Grossman), 37–38
forgetting, 143, 168, 189, 199, 222, 246
"For Ukraine!" song, 140
Fourth Polish Republic, 265
Franko, Roland, 121
functional vs. storage memory, 134–35

Gabowitch, Mischa, 78
Gazeta Wyborcza, journal, 278
Gedi, Noa, 208

gender in memory of nationalist movements, 10, 140–54
Generalgouvernment, 143–44
generational transfer/transmission of memory, 108n2, 210, 245, 247n14
German-Romanian Treaty of 1941, 206
Germans: blamed for Galician ethnic cleansing, 238; as "good," 105, 110n58; as "other," 105–106; Roma views of, 215–16
Glory Obelisk, Kyiv, 78, 82, 83
Gourlan, Eric, 77
Grave of the Unknown Soldier, 82, 83
Great Famine. *See* Holodomor
Great Patriotic War. *See* World War II
Greek Catholic Church, 59, 100, 170, 171, 177–78, 179
Greek Orthodox Church, 6
grief, 84, 87
Gross, Jan T., 7
Grossman, Ekaterina, 38
Grossman, Vasilii, 37–38
guilt, historical, 259–60

Habsburg Empire, 118, 167–68, 171, 177
Hager, Menachem Mendel, 195–96
Halbwachs, Maurice, 208, 210, 211, 222, 225n6, 247n5
Hall, Stuart, 51
Hasidism, 195–96
Havryshko, Marta, 148
Haydamaka, Anatolii, 62
Heavenly Hundred (*Nebesna sotnia*): attempted monuments to, 168–79; and May 9 celebrations, 82
Heavenly Hundred Heroes Avenue, 178
Hellbeck, Jochen, 77–78
Herbert, Zbigniew, 170
heritage tourism, 199–200, 242–44
hero role: new canon of, 9; and Heavenly Hundred, 178; and May 9 celebrations, 77; as shifting, 258; in World War II memory, 99–103
Himka, John Paul, 185
Hirsch, Marianne, 153, 184
history: guilt in, 259–60; and memory, 1–4; role in national identity, 1, 183–200, 281–85; state and, 103, 186; Ukrainian perception of, 183–84, 285–87, 291–95
"History and Dialog in Ukraine: The May 9 Documentary Project" (Hellbeck), 77–78
History of Happiness (Le), 36
Holocaust, the: bystander role and, 5; in collective memory, 10, 106–107, 183–200; East vs. West attitudes on, 3, 187, 255; and Galician Poles, 236–38; and Holodomor, 187, 189–90; Kravchuk apology for, 266; memory of hidden/suppressed, 2, 102, 188–89, 223, 236; Roma in, 206–24, 224–25n4; Ukrainian collaboration in, 7, 102, 183, 185, 187; and World War II commemoration, 86–87
Holod-33, film, 38
Holodomor (Great Famine): burials in, 53–54; as genocide, 264, 267; creation as historic event, 49–51; in fiction, 19, 34–42; and Holocaust, 187, 189–90, 266; *lieux de memoire* of, 10, 50–69; and national identity, 51, 107–108; memorials commemorating, 50–69, 267; as term, 70nn 1, 6, 71n41; visual culture of, 52, 55–62, 68; as unpresentable, 69
Holodomor Victims Memorial, 57, 64, 267
Holos Ukrainy, journal, 131
Home Army (*Armia Krajowa*/AK), 258, 266
Hrachova, Sofia, 195
Hrushevsky, Mykhailo, 121, 132
Hrytsak, Yaroslav, 6, 8, 185, 237, 243
Hungry Thirties, The (Dimarov), 36–37

identity: collective, 10; and forgetting, 189; local, 173; and memory, 1–2, 51, 189; national, 7, 8, 50, 85, 92, 96–98, 124–25, 129, 185, 200, 283–84, 294; politics of, 8, 171, 254, 255, 261, 262–63, 267; urban, 179
Iliushyn, Ihor, 237
imagined community, 183–84, 196
imagined noncommunity, 107
"Immortal Regiment" performance, 83
In Autumn (Dukyn), 36
Independence Square (*Maidan Nezalehezhnosti*), 77, 82
indoctrination, historical, 108
Institute of History of Ukraine, 264
International Commission on the Holocaust in Romania, 220–21
International Holocaust Remembrance Alliance, 187
International Workers Solidarity Day, 79
Istoriia z hryfom "Sekretno" (Viatrovych), 148
Istorychna pravda, journal, 132, 188
Ivanova, Olena, 189
Ivashko, Pavlo, 32–33
Iveković, Rada, 141

Jewish people: absence of, 96; in Chernivtsi, 176, 177; and Galician Poles, 231; Hasidic, 195–96; in Holocaust, 54, 119, 143, 183–200; as "other," 98, 106–107; pogroms against, 102, 117–20, 123, 125–28, 185, 195–200, 202n33, 235; Roma views of, 215–16; and shtetls, 193–94
Jilge, Wilfried, 91, 186
Judt, Tony, 3

Kaczyński, Lech, 265, 266
Kansteiner, Wulf, 3, 221
Karlson, Karl, 34
Kasianov, Georgii, 49–50, 70n6

Katyn massacre, 266
KGB, 124, 259, 272
Khromeychuk, Olesya, 9, 10
Khronika Ukrains'koi Povstans'koi Armii 1941–54, film, 237
Kieszonkowy atlas kobiet (Chutnik), 149
Kis, Oksana, 148–49
knowledge, coded vs. uncoded, 51
Kohut, Zenon, 8
Koliivshchyna uprising, 195
Komsomol, 24, 25, 27–28, 31, 35, 36, 39
Konieczna-Sałamatin, Joanna, 9, 11
Kononovych, Leonid, 41
Konovalets, Yevhen, 125
Kopelev, Lev, 22–23, 29, 35
Korostelina, Karina, 99
Kosior, Stanislav, 34
Kostryha (Liubchenko), 35
Koziura, Karolina, 9, 10
Kravchuk, Leonid, 262–63, 266, 278
Kruty-1918, film, 132
Krylenko, Ivan, 35–36
Krytyka, journal, 188
Kubik, Jan, 11, 270–71
Kuchma, Leonid: administration of, 263–65; and nationalization, 94; and Petliura, 121–22; and state policies of memory, 94; protests against, 261
Kudela-Świątek, Wiktoria, 9, 10
Kulchynsky, Mykola, 124
Kulchytskyi, Stanylav, 264
Kuzio, Taras, 288
Kwaśniewski, Aleksander, 265
Kyivan Rus, 140, 177, 190, 264
Kyiv City Council, 130
Kyiv City Organization of Veterans, 83
Krylenko, Ivan, 35–36
Kyrylenko, Viacheslav, 125

language: Polish, 232; Romanes, 193, 210–11, 218, 222, 224–25n4; Russian, 6, 207, 268; Ruthenian, 171; Ukrainian, 6
Lanzmann, Claude, 54
Law and Justice Party, 265
laws: on decommunization, 80, 131; on independence, 277, 281; on lustration, 259; on naming independence fighters, 1, 146; and politics of memory, 269–70, 272
Le, Ivan, 36
Lenin, V. I.: statue of, Chernivtsi, 172, 174; and Ukraine, 257, 278
leninopad destruction of Soviet monuments, 1, 258, 273, 287
Lewis, Simon, 143

lieu/lieux de mémoire: of Holodomor, 10, 50–53, 70; in place-making, 173
Likhovy, Ihor, 122
Literaturna hazeta, journal, 129
Liubchenko, Arkadii, 35
Livytsky, Andrii, 128
Local Studies Museum, Poltava, 121
lustration, 259, 265, 272
Lytvyn, Serhii, 120

Maidan, the. *See* Euromaidan
Malomuzh, Mykola, 128
Malynovska, Olena, 284
Mandryck, Maria, 148–49
Maria: The Chronicle of One Life (Samchuk), 38
Martos, Borys, 131
Marushiakova, Elena, 217, 218
Matkovsky, Andrii, 131
Matrache, Iona, 212–13
Mattingly, Daria, 9, 10
May 8 celebrations. *See* Day of Memory and Reconciliation holiday
May 9 celebrations, 77–87, 265, 269–70, 274n21
Mazepa, Ivan, 12n16, 124, 126, 129
Memorial against Fascism, War and Violence, Hamburg, 69
"Memorial Complex: National Museum of the Great Patriotic War," 81, 83, 84, 86
memorials to Holodomor: aesthetics of, 57–58, 61; towns located in, 58–59, 60–61; mother figures in, 58, 61, 62; national vs. religious, 67–69; symbols in, 59–62, 67
Memorial to the Soldiers of the Great Patriotic War, 57
memory: 1–5, 8–10; of 1990s, 278–294; biographical, 9, 10, 11, 91–94, 110n53, 184, 194, 197–98, 236, 240, 245, 247n11; collective, 2–11, 49–51, 55, 69, 92–94, 103–108, 121, 143, 183–200; communicative, 208; community of, 57–58, 187, 206–24, 225n6, 227n81, 229–46; cultural, 29–43, 50, 145; "Day of," 10, 78–79, 83, 86, 140–41; field, 12; functional vs. storage, 134–35; and Holocaust, 183–200; individual, 222–23; multidimensional/multidirectional, 187, 200; (non)-, 188–89; oral, 20, 21, 23, 25, 26, 31, 32, 42–43, 223–24; pillarization of, 11, 13n41, 199, 270–71; and place-making, 173–74; places and nonplaces of, 52–55; pluralization of, 3–4; politics of, 8–11, 52, 185–88, 257, 260–63, 265, 267, 269, 272–73; post-, 40, 41, 184; prosthetic, 184; as regime, 11, 271; shield, 184, 197, 200; social, 4–6, 8, 10, 55, 60, 222, 223; socially constructed, 5; state policies of, 94; study of, 3–4, 50–51, 92; transfer/transmission of, 108n2, 210, 245, 247n14; vernacular, 8, 189
"memory entrepreneurs," 200

"memory fever," 1–2
memory of 1990s, 278–294
Memory of Childhood memorial, 59
memory regime, 11, 271
memory studies, 3–4, 50–51
milieux de mémoire, 53–54
Mykhailovych, Lazar, 170
Milinevskii, Nikolai, 134
military parades, 78–79, 87n15
minority in power, 229–30
Mishakin, Serhii, 81
mnemonic actors, four-part typology of, 271–72
Molod' Ukrainy, journal, 124
Molotov-Ribbentrop Pact, 97–98, 256, 295n8
Monument of Unification, Chernivtsi, 172
Mostov, Julie, 141
Motherland Monument, 81
museums: and Galician Poles, 245; and Holocaust, 199, 265; and Petliura, 121; and prosthetic memory, 184; and Soviets, 283–84; and UNR, 128; and World War II, 81, 150–51, 265

Naimazh, Vasyl, 131
Naimy, Mikhail, 131
Narodna Armiia, journal, 121
Narvselius, Eleonora, 172
Natasha, song, 95–96
National Book of the Memory of Holodomor Victims, 23, 25
National Bank of Ukraine, 137, 140–42, 154n3
"National Museum of the History of Ukraine in the Second World War: Memorial Complex," 86, 121
nationalism: and Bandera, 1; and ethnic cleansing, 131, 145, 185, 234–37, 257, 258; and EU, 11, 255, 261, 270; and gender, 140–54; and Petliura, 127; and Roma, 218; and World War II history, 99
nation-building, 7, 11, 200, 262–63
NATO, 265
Nazis: collaboration with, 96, 98, 101, 126, 131, 145, 155n25, 215; Holocaust by, 183–200, 212–16; stories about, 95–96; and Soviets, 99–103, 104; symbols prohibited, 80, 269; victims of, 191–93; victory over, 77, 78
neo-Soviet discourse, 85
New Economic Policy (NEP), 26
Nicholas II, Tsar, 118
Nishchuk, Yevhen, 86–87
(non)memory, 188–89
Nora, Pierre, 51, 52–55, 210
nostalgia: in Chernivtsi, 170; for communism, 4, 107, 176, 261, 279, 287, 292, 294; and homeland, 247n10; and identity, 87; urban, 10
Nyshchuk, Yevhen, 132

October Revolution, 79, 82, 289
Ohiienko, Vitalii, 50, 63
Oleksandr Dovzhenko Film Studio, 132
Olick, Jeffrey, 3
Onyshko, Lesia, 148–49
oral history, 9, 92–95, 188–89, 207–208, 212
oral memory, 20, 21, 23, 25, 26, 31, 32, 42–43, 223–24
Orange Revolution, 80–81, 117, *190*, 245, 253, 260, 261, 265, 269
Organization of Ukrainian Nationalists (OUN): collaboration with Nazis, 98, 155n25; and EU, 260–61, 268, 269–70; and gender, 155n17; heroic view of, 99–103; and Holocaust, 96, 183, 185, 187, 256–59; and Maidan protestors, 149; monuments to, 268; and Petliura, 125, 127; women and, 142, 144–54, 156n31, 157n56; and World War II commemoration, 80, 104–105
Orthodox churches: 63, 171; competing Patriarchates of, 6; Eastern, 59; Greek, 6; rebuilt, 263–64; Ukrainian, 122, 124–25, 242, 268
"other": absent, 230; in fiction, 42–43; Germans as, 105–106; and Holocaust, 186–87; Jews as, 98, 106–107
Oushakine, Serguei, 81

Pahira, Oleksandr, 101
Paksas, Rolandas, 265
Pale of Settlement, 195
Palij, Michael, 120
Party of Regions, 118, 125, 131, 261, 267
Patoka, Valentyna, 129
Patushenko, Tetiana, 9, 10
Pauly, Matthew D., 9, 10
Pechersk Lavra, Kyiv, 57
People's Commissariat for Internal Affairs (NKVD), 105, 140, 157n56, 195
Pereiaslav, Treaty of, 289
Perestroika, 54, 97, 103, 186, 188, 189, 281
perpetrator role: and commemoration, 257; differentiating from victim, 69; and Galician Poles, 237; and Holodomor, 69; as shifting, 4, 258; and violence, 148
Peter the Great, 124
Petliura, Symon: commemoration of, 117–35; early life, 118–19; killing of, 119, 126; letters of, 128–29; monument to, 121–25; and pogroms, 119–21, 123, 125–26; Soviet-sponsored memory of, 10
Petliura Foundation, 121
"Petliura: Myth and Bitter Memory" (Bohun), 125–27
Petrenko, Olena, 148
Petrovskyi, Hryhorii, 35
Piatakov, Yuri, 145
Pieracki, Bronisław, 150
Pieta statue, Chernivtsi, 168–72, 174–79

pillarization of memory, 11, 13n41, 199–200
Piłsudski, Józef, 119
place-making, 173–74
places and nonplaces of memory, 52–55
Plaviuk, Mykola, 121, 123
Plokhy, Serhii, 120
pogroms, 102, 117–20, 123, 125–28, 185, 195–200, 202n33, 235
Pokrova, feast of, 141
Poland: Commonwealth of, 232; and European standards, 246; Fourth Republic, 265; German-Soviet split of, 97–98, 143–44, 155n19; as role model for transformation, 246; Second Republic, 232, 235–36, 247n1, 258; and Ukrainian memory fields, 12; UNR treaty with, 120; Yushchenko and, 265–67
Poles, Galician: collective memory of, 229–46; in contemporary memory, 11, 211, 244–45; deportation of, 229–30; discrimination against, 232; ethnic cleansing of, 7, 198, 229–46; ethnic terms and, 106–107; property of, 241; Soviets on, 231, 236, 241; and UNR, 117, 126–27, 128, 145; and UPA, 230, 234–37, 257, 258, 266; in World War II memories, 100
Polish Institute Kyiv, 238
Polish language, 232
Polish-Lithuanian Commonwealth, 190
politics of memory: 8–11, 52, 185–88, 257, 260–63, 265, 267, 269, 272–73; and detotalitarianization, 257; and EU, 265, 269–73; Holocaust in, 187–88; recent, 272; Soviet, 52; state vs. local, 8–9, 11; and textbooks, 254; in transitional justice, 259
Poltava Local Studies Museum, 124
Pomian, Krzysztof, 54–55
Popov, Veselin, 217, 218
poppy symbol, 57, 81, 88n31
Poroshenko, Petro, 131, 140–41, 145–46, 272, 274n21
Portnov, Andrii, 8, 91, 237
postmemory, 40, 41, 184
Prayer for the Government, (Abramson), 120
Prelitsch, Hans, 170
prosthetic memory, 184
Prosvita Society, 100, 110n40
Putin, Vladimir, 263
Pyrih, Ruslan, 123

Rebet, Daria, 144
Red Army: and Galician Poles, 230; and May 9 celebrations, 77, 81, 83, 104; and OUN, 126; veterans of, 7, 11, 100
regimes of memory, 11
regional differences of memory: on Holocaust, 188–94; on Galician Poles, 237–38, 244–45; on Holodomor, 51; on postcommunist transition, 281–87, 290–92; on World War II, 5–6, 105–107, 142–44; in Ukraine, 188–93, 271
Reichskommissariat Ukraine, 143–44
resovietization, 268
Revolutionary Ukrainian Party (RUP), 118
Revolution of Dignity, 7, 253, 257–58, 268–70
Riabchuk, Mykola, 6
RIA Novosti, 81
Ribbentrop-Molotov Pact. *See* Molotov-Ribbentrop Pact
Ridnyi, Alexandr, 62
"Righteous Among Nations," 186, 248n21
Robertson, Tania, 99
Robitnycha hazeta, journal, 125, 127
Roeder, Phillip, 278
Roma, the: collective memory of, 11, 206–24, 225n6, 227n81; diversity of, 210–13, 219, 225nn25, 27; in Holocaust, 192, 193, 206, 212, 215–16, 219–24, 224–25n4; language, 193, 210–11, 218, 222, 224–25n4; nomadic vs. settled, 209, 215; as term, 207–208
Roman Catholic Church, 171, 172, 174, 230, 242, 296n20
Romanes language, 193, 210–11, 218, 222, 224–25n4
Romania: Kingdom of, 172–73; in Transnistria, 206–224; Ukraine relationships with, 172–73, 175–76
Rotach, Petro, 124
Rothberg, Michael, 187
Rudling, Per, 185
Rukkas, Andrii, 132, 134
Russia: annexation of Crimea, 1, 77, 79; discourse on Ukrainian independence, 96; Donbas conflict with, 1, 10, 77, 79, 83, 85, 86, 87n15, 108n2, 125, 140, 141, 145, 149, 151–52, 154n2, 188, 253, 263, 264, 268, 270, 271; fear of, 272; politics of memory in, 262; in Ukrainian debates on history, 6–7; and Ukrainian memory fields, 12; and Yanukovych, 80, 268
Russian Empire, 124, 126, 256, 264
Russian language, 6, 207, 268
Russian Orthodox Church, 132
Russians: ethnic terms for, 106; in present Ukraine, 84, 85
Ruthenians/Ruthenian language, 171, 232, 295n8

St. George Ribbon, 80–81, 88n28
St. Michael Church, Kyiv, 60
Saint Volodymyr's Cathedral, Kyiv, 121, 122
Samchenko, Valentya, 132
Samchuk, Ulas, 38
Samvydav and *Tamvydav* fiction, 19, 34, 42
Savchenko, Nadiya, 158n93
Savchyn, Maria, 147
Schütze, Fritz, 5
Schwartzbard, Sholom, 119, 120, 123, 126, 127, 134
Second Polish Republic, 232, 235–36

Second World Forum of Holocaust Memory, 187
Semenova, Pelageia, 37
Sendyka, Roma, 54
Serhiichuk, Volodymyr, 120
Shapoval, Yurii, 19, 123, 126
Shchors, Mykola, 132, 145
Shevchenko, Taras, 63, 127–28
Shevel, Oxana, 11, 270–71
shield memory, 184, 197, 200
Shoah. *See* Holocaust
shtetls, 193–200
Shukhevych, Roman, 150, 266, 267
Shulhyn, Oleksandr, 128
Shulika, Nadiia, 26
Sich Riflemen, 83
Sindbæk Andersen, Tea, 4
Skoropadsky, Pavlo, 119, 121
Sluga Narodu party, 272
Smarzowski, Wojciech, 7, 12n21, 237
Smith, Valerie, 153
Snyder, Timothy, 23, 143
Sobieski, John, 231, 245
social memory, 8–9
Society of Assistance to Defense and Aviation-Chemical Construction (OSOAviaKhim), 33, 34, 45n82
Soldatynko, Valerii, 120, 127–28
Sovietization, 230
Soviet Union: architecture of, 58; collaboration with, 99; commemoration of World War II in, 56–57, 77–79, 86, 94–98, 143; dissolution of, 11, 277, 279, 290–91, 295n1; and EU, 255–59; and Holodomor, 49–69; legacy of, 9, 287–94; memory politics of, 185–88; monumental culture of, 68; nostalgia for, 4, 107, 176, 261, 279, 287, 292, 294; politics of memory of, 52; pop culture of, 103; recent perception of, 291–95; symbolic domain of, 56–57; symbols banned, 269; and Ukrainian language, 98
Stalin, Josef, 77, 97, 267, 278
State Political Directorate (GPU): and Holodomor, 22, 23, 34, 35, 39, 41; and Petliura, 122, 128, 132
Stauber, Roni, 221
Stewart, Michael, 217, 220
Stockholm International Forum on the Holocaust, 187
streets renamed, 178
Stryjek, Tomasz, 9, 11, 188
Strynozheni koni (Fol'varochnyi), 129
Subtelny, Orest, 186
suffering: and memorials, 67; remembrance as, 55
survivor role: and Holocaust, 21, 184, 188, 217; and Holodomor, 23–29, 30, 33, 41, 42; and Roma, 207, 212–13, 215
Svoboda party, 268

symbolic domain, 56–57
"Symon Petliura: Knight of the Ukrainian Revolution" exhibition, 121

Tabachnyk, Dmytro, 145
Taiemnyi shchodennyk Symona Petliury (Yanchuk), 132
Taras Shevchenko University, 92
Teliha, Olena, 147
Tema dlia medytatsii (Kononovych), 41
textbooks: alternative, 156n42; Holocaust in, 183, 186; Holodomor in, 267; nationalism in, 99, 103; Poles in, 236–37; and politics of memory, 254; in transitional justice, 259–60, 268
Tiutiunyk, Yurii, 128, 136n38
Tkuma Center for Holocaust Studies, 188
Törnquist-Plewa, Barbara, 4
Torrés, Henri, 119
traitor role, 9, 124, 126, 130, 147, 154, 157n60
transformation, postcommunist, 1–3, 5, 7, 9, 11, 20, 78–94, 246, 255–56, 277–87
transitional justice, 254, 255, 259–70, 273
Transnistria Governorate, 11, 195, 206–224
trauma: collective, 264; and commemoration, 59, 69; and experience, 9, 184; national, 218; study of, 189; of survivors, 21, 23, 59, 70, 220
Treaty of Nonaggression, 144
Treaty of Warsaw, 119–20
Truth and Reconciliation Commission, 259
Tsarynnyk, Marko, 195
Tsyganism, 218–19, 222
"Two Decades After the Wall's Fall" survey, 286
Tymoshenko, Yulia, 261, 267

Ukraina Moderna, journal, 188
Ukraina moloda, journal, 132
Ukraine: in Europe, 2–4; and European Union, 11, 253–73; exceptionalism of, 4–8; and Holocaust, 183–200; and Holodomor, 50–69, 107–108; independence of, 11, 96, 190, 242, 277–87, 289–90, 296n24; national character of, 177–78, 294; perception of history in, 183–84, 285–87, 291–95; and Russia, 267–68, 284; statehood of, 10, 140–54; transformation of, 1–3, 5, 7, 9, 11, 20, 78–94, 246, 255–56, 277–87; as victim nation, 50–51, 69; World War II in, 77–103
Ukraine: A History (Subtelny), 186
Ukraine Association Agreement, 268
"Ukraine During World War II: The Everyday Experience of Survival" project, 92–94
Ukrainian Army, 83, 86
Ukrainian Association of Cinematographers, 132
Ukrainian Autocephalous Orthodox Church (UAOC), 122
Ukrainian Center for Holocaust Studies, 188

Ukrainian Central Council, 118, 140
Ukrainian Congressional Committee of America, 132
Ukrainian General Military Committee, 118
Ukrainian Helsinki Group, 270
Ukrainian Institute of National Memory (UIPN): 1; and Galician Poles, 237; and gender, 10; and Holocaust, 188; and Holodomor, 112; and law, 269; and nationalists, 145–46; and women's experience, 149–52
Ukrainian Insurgent Army (UPA): 5; and EU, 260–61, 268, 269; and Galician Poles, 230, 234–37, 257, 258, 266; heroic view of, 99–103, 150; and Holocaust, 8, 183, 185, 187, 256–59; and Maidan protestors, 149; and May 9 celebrations, 77, 80, 104–105; and memory regimes, 11; monuments to, 268; state recognition of, 270–71; veterans of, 7, 83; and Volhynian killings, 266; and women, 141, 142, 144–54, 155n17, 156n31, 157n68
Ukrainian language, 6, 98, 207, 269
Ukrainian Ministry of Culture, 51
Ukrainian Orthodox Church: Kyivan Patriarchate, 122, 124–25; Moscow Patriarchate, 242, 268
Ukrainian Parliament, 1, 8, 82, 121, 130–31, 149, 154n6, 178, 261, 267, 268, 270, 272, 274n21, 277
Ukrainian People's Republic (UNR): Directory of, 125, 131; and Petliura, 10, 117–35; and pogroms, 117–118, 119–21, 123, 125–26; recent attitudes toward, 261–63; and Soviets, 119
Ukrainian-Polish Defensive Alliance (Palij), 120
Ukrainian Red Cross, 150
Ukrainian Revolutionary Party, 124
Ukrainian Social Democratic Workers' Party, 118
Ukrainian Soviet Socialist Republic, 87n8, 94, 169, 172, 278, 295n8
Ukrainian symbolic domain, emerging, 60–61
"Ukrainian World War II, The" exhibition, 146
Ukrainians, The: Unexpected Nation (Wilson), 277
Ukrainity concept, 262–63
Ukrains'kyi istorychnyi zhurnal, journal, 127
Uniate Church, 59
Union for the Liberation of Ukraine (SVU), 122
Union of Zemstva, 118

Vago, Raphael, 221
Verdery, Katherine, 3
Verstiuk, Vladislav, 123
Viatrovych, Volodymyr, 1, 132, 145–46, 148, 152, 237
victim role: and commemoration, 10, 77, 255; as competitive, 186, 191; and Holocaust, 191–93, 200, 218–19; and Holodomor, 52, 69; as shifting, 4, 258; and Ukraine, 50–51; women in, 147, 149
Victory Day. *See* Day of Victory holiday
"Victory-Liberation-Occupation" project, 78

violence: collective, 20–23, 42, 43; historical, 4–8; and Holodomor, 26, 28, 30, 38, 39, 41; institutionalized, 55, 220; against Jews, 195, 198, 200; as mundane, 143; and nonplaces, 54; against Poles, 234, 235, 238, 239; political, 147; rationalization of, 234–36; against Roma, 208, 212, 220; against women, 149, 151–53
Virgin Mary, 141, 178
"Voice of Heroes" performance, 83
Volhynia, genocide of Poles in, 1, 6; film on, 7, 12n21, 237, 238; silence on, 102, 192; UPN and, 266
Volodymyr the Great, 140
Vorona, Petro, 124
Voronyi, Mykola, 140
Vynnychenko, Volodymyr, 40, 119, 120, 121, 127, 132
Vyzhnytsia mass-killing site, 10, 195–99, 203n52

Wanner, Catherine, 8, 91, 103
"War Makes No Exceptions" project, 151
"Warriors: History of the Ukrainian Military" project, 150–51
Wehrmacht, the, 77, 101, 258
Wertsch, James, 108
West Ukrainian People's Republic (ZUNR), 119
White Movement, 81
Whitling, Frederick, 93
Wiesel, Elie, 220–21
Wilson, Andrew, 277
Wołyń film (Smarzowski), 7, 12n21, 237
women: representations of, 10; nationalist, 140–54; in Ukrainian Armed Forces, 154n7
Wood, Nancy, 211
Woollacott, Angela, 142
Workers' and Peasants' Red Army (RSChA), 32; Workers' Solidarity Day, 79, 296n35
World War I, in Galicia, 230
World War II: and collective identity, 10; conflicted memory of, 266–67; East vs. West attitudes on, 2–3; and Galician Poles, 234–35; generational divide on, 91–92; and Holocaust, 183–200; indoctrination on, 108; May 9 celebrations and, 77–87, 265, 269–70, 274n21; in memory of survivors, 91–108; nationalist narrative of, 99–103, 145–46; regional divide in memories of, 5–6, 94, 99; Roma in, 206–24; Soviet Commemoration of, 56–57, 77–79, 86, 94–98, 104; as term, 79–80, 86
Wylegała, Anna, 9, 11, 189, 198

Yanchuk, Oles, 132
Yanukovych, Viktor: and Bandera, 145, 258; and May 9 celebrations, 79; ouster of, 118, 130; and Petliura, 129–30; and Russia, 80, 267–68; and Soviet legacy, 94, 261; and state policies of memory, 94, 263, 267–68; and vote-rigging, 122

Yellow Prince, The (Barka), 38, 39
Yeltsin, Boris, 263
Yisrael, Rav, 195–96
Yugoslav Wars, 255
Yunakiv, Mykola, 128
Yurchuk, Yuliya, 146
Yushchenko, Victor: and Bandera, 145, 273n17, 267; election of, 122, 265; fall of, 129–30; and Holocaust, 187, 201n27; and Holodomor, 49–50, 59, 62, 97, 267; and Nazis, 259; and Orange Revolution, 81, 261; and Petliura, 124–28, 129; and Poland, 265–66; and state policies of memory, 94, 265–67, 269–70; and UPA, 7, 117, 118
Yuval-Davis, Nira, 148

Zabolotskii, Nikolai, 38
Zahlada, Nadiia, 27–28
Zahra, Tara, 92, 107
Zaitsev, Oleksandr, 144
Zaryts'ka, Kateryna, 150
Zashkilniak, Leonid, 237
Zayarniuk, Andrii, 237
Zelenski, Volodymyr, 272
Zhovkva, removal of Galician Poles from, 230–44
Zhurzhenko, Tatiana, 98, 143
Żółkiewski, Stanisław, 231–32, 245
Zolochiv mass-killing site, 10, 195–99
ZUNR Ukrainian Galician Army, 119

www.ingramcontent.com/pod-product-compliance
Lightning Source LLC
Chambersburg PA
CBHW061124010526
44114CB00029B/2998